Sales Management
Analysis and Decision Making

Fourth Edition

DRYDEN

soon to become

Harcourt College Publishers

A Harcourt Higher Learning Company

Soon you will find The Dryden Press' distinguished innovation, leadership, and support under a different name . . . a new brand that continues our unsurpassed quality, service, and commitment to education.

We are combining the strengths of our college imprints into one worldwide brand: Harcourt Our mission is to make learning accessible to anyone, anywhere, anytime—reinforcing our commitment to lifelong learning.

We'll soon be Harcourt College Publishers. Ask for us by name.

One Company
"Where Learning Comes to Life."

Sales Management
Analysis and Decision Making

Fourth Edition

Thomas N. Ingram
Colorado State University

Raymond W. LaForge
University of Louisville

Ramon A. Avila
Ball State University

Charles H. Schwepker Jr.
Central Missouri State University

Michael R. Williams
Illinois State University

Harcourt College Publishers
Fort Worth   Philadelphia   San Diego   New York   Orlando   Austin   San Antonio
Toronto   Montreal   London   Sydney   Tokyo

Publisher	Mike Roche
Acquisitions Editor	Bill Schoof
Market Strategist	Lisé Johnson
Developmental Editor	Jana Pitts
Project Editor	Jim Patterson
Art Director	April Eubanks
Production Manager	James McDonald

Cover image © Guy Crittenden, www.getphoto.com

ISBN: 0-03-026699-8
Library of Congress Catalog Card Number: 99–69567

Copyright © 2001 by Harcourt, Inc.

All rights reserved. No part of this publication may be reproduced or transmitted in any form or by any means, electronic or mechanical, including photocopy, recording, or any information storage and retrieval system, without permission in writing from the publisher.

Requests for permission to make copies of any part of the work should be mailed to the following address: Permissions Department, Harcourt, Inc., 6277 Sea Harbor Drive, Orlando, FL 32887-6777.

Portions of this work were published in previous editions.

Copyrights and Acknowledgments appear on page 436, which constitutes a continuation of the copyright page.

Address for Domestic Orders:
Harcourt, Inc., 6277 Sea Harbor Drive, Orlando, FL 32887-6777
800-782-4479

Address for International Orders:
International Customer Service
Harcourt, Inc., 6277 Sea Harbor Drive, Orlando, FL 32887-6777
407-345-3800
(fax) 407-345-4060
(e-mail) hbintl@harcourtbrace.com

Address for Editorial Correspondence:
Harcourt College Publishers, 301 Commerce Street, Suite 3700, Fort Worth, TX 76102

Web Site Address:
http://www.harcourtcollege.com

Printed in the United States of America

0 1 2 3 4 5 6 7 8 9   043   9 8 7 6 5 4 3 2 1

To Jacque
    —Thomas N. Ingram

To Susan, Alexandra, Kelly, my Dad, and in memory of my Mom
    —Raymond W. LaForge

To Terry, Sarah, Anne, Ryan, Laura, Kate, and my parents
    —Ramon A. Avila

To Laura, Charlie III, and my parents
    —Charles H. Schwepker Jr.

To Marilyn, Aimee, Kerri, my Mom, and in memory of my Dad
    —Michael R. Williams

The Harcourt Series in Marketing

Assael
Marketing

Avila, Williams, Ingram, and LaForge
The Professional Selling Skills Workbook

Bateson and Hoffman
Managing Services Marketing: Text and Readings
Fourth Edition

Blackwell, Blackwell, and Talarzyk
Contemporary Cases in Consumer Behavior
Fourth Edition

Blackwell, Miniard, and Engel
Consumer Behavior
Ninth Edition

Boone and Kurtz
Contemporary Marketing
Tenth Edition

Boone and Kurtz
Contemporary Marketing 1999

Churchill
Basic Marketing Research
Fourth Edition

Churchill
Marketing Research: Methodological Foundations
Seventh Edition

Czinkota and Ronkainen
Global Marketing

Czinkota and Ronkainen
International Marketing
Sixth Edition

Czinkota and Ronkainen
International Marketing Strategy: Environmental Assessment and Entry Strategies

Dickson
Marketing Management
Second Edition

Dunne and Lusch
Retailing
Third Edition

Ferrell, Hartline, Lucas, and Luck
Marketing Strategy

Futrell
Sales Management: Teamwork, Leadership, and Technology
Sixth Edition

Ghosh
Retail Management
Second Edition

Hoffman
Marketing: Best Practices

Hoffman and Bateson
Essentials of Services Marketing
Second Edition

Hutt and Speh
Business Marketing Management: A Strategic View of Industrial and Organizational Markets
Seventh Edition

Ingram, LaForge, Avila, Schwepker, and Williams
Professional Selling

Ingram, LaForge, Avila, Schwepker, and Williams
Sales Management: Analysis and Decision Making
Fourth Edition

Krugman, Reid, Dunn, and Barban
Advertising: Its Role in Modern Marketing
Eighth Edition

Lindgren and Shimp
Marketing: An Interactive Learning System

Oberhaus, Ratliffe, and Stauble
Professional Selling: A Relationship Process
Second Edition

Parente
Advertising Campaign Strategy: A Guide to Marketing Communication Plans
Second Edition

Reedy
Electronic Marketing

Rosenbloom
Marketing Channels: A Management View
Sixth Edition

Sandburg
Discovering Your Marketing Career CD-ROM

Schaffer
Applying Marketing Principles Software

Schaffer
The Marketing Game

Schellinck and Maddox
Marketing Research: A Computer-Assisted Approach

Schnaars
MICROSIM

Schuster and Copeland
Global Business: Planning for Sales and Negotiations

Sheth, Mittal, and Newman
Customer Behavior: Consumer Behavior and Beyond

Shimp
Advertising and Promotion: Supplemental Aspects of Integrated Marketing Communications
Fifth Edition

Stauble
Marketing Strategy: A Global Perspective

Talarzyk
Cases and Exercises in Marketing

Terpstra and Sarathy
International Marketing
Eighth Edition

Watson
Electronic Commerce

Weitz and Wensley
Readings in Strategic Marketing Analysis, Planning, and Implementation

Zikmund
Exploring Marketing Research
Seventh Edition

Zikmund
Essentials of Marketing Research

Harcourt College Outline Series

Peterson
Principles of Marketing

PREFACE

Our objective in writing the fourth edition of *Sales Management: Analysis and Decision Making* was to continue to present comprehensive and rigorous coverage of contemporary sales management in a readable, interesting, and challenging manner. Findings from recent sales management research are blended with examples of current sales management practice into an effective pedagogical format. Topics are covered from the perspective of a sales management decision maker. This decision-making perspective is accomplished through a modular format that typically consists of discussing basic concepts, identifying critical decision areas, and presenting analytical approaches for improved sales management decision making. Company examples from the contemporary business world are used throughout the text to supplement module discussion.

Changes in This Edition

Several significant changes have been made in the fourth edition of *Sales Management: Analysis and Decision Making*. All of the authors teach the sales management course. We also interact with sales management professors from around the world. We know, and these professors tell us, that sales management texts are too long, cost too much, do not reflect leading sales management practice and do not offer the desired flexibility for teaching the sales management course. Most of the changes in this edition are being made to address these concerns:

- The most significant change is replacing the previous 15 chapters with 11 modules. We accomplished this by combining several previous chapters into a single module. The new modules retain the important content from the previous chapters, but eliminate much of the extraneous material. It is much easier to schedule 11 modules into a semester or quarter sales management course than the previous 15 chapters.
- This edition is offered in a low-cost format, so the price to the student will be much less than previous hardcover editions. One of the reasons we changed to modules is so the text could be easily adapted to custom publishing. Thus, this edition is available as a complete book, or professors can order customized versions with only the modules desired. For example, many professors like the personal selling coverage we have offered in all editions. However, some schools have a personal selling class and professors do not want personal selling coverage in a sales management text. These professors can order a customized version without the personal selling modules.
- Incorporating leading sales management practice and the latest sales management research remains a hallmark of this edition. One of the ways we accomplish this is by assembling a Sales Executive Panel. This panel consists of sales executives from different types of companies and with different management positions. Each sales executive provides two comments for a specific chapter in a box entitled "Sales Management in the 21st Century." These comments typically address "best practices" for sales management in the future.

- The modular approach and customized publishing capability offers tremendous flexibility for sales management professors. This flexibility will be expanded in the future. You will notice that we have added Ramon Avila (Ball State University) and Mike Williams (Illinois State University) to our author team. Our five-author team is also writing a professional selling textbook to be available in summer 2000. *Professional Selling* will also be in a modular, low-cost format. When this book is available, sales professors will be able to use a complete sales management or personal selling book, or can create their own customized text by mixing sales management and personal selling modules in any desired way. We think this approach offers the flexibility requested by many sales professors around the world.

Level and Organization

This text was written for the undergraduate student enrolled in a one-semester or one-quarter sales management class. However, it is sufficiently rigorous to be used at the MBA level.

A sales management model is used to present coverage in a logical sequence. The text is organized into five parts to correspond with the five stages in the sales management model.

Part One, "Describing the Personal Selling Function," is designed to provide students with an understanding of personal selling prior to addressing specific sales management areas. Colleagues across the country have suggested that available sales management texts do not provide enough coverage of personal selling. We decided to devote two modules at the beginning of the text to this topic.

Part Two, "Defining the Strategic Role of the Sales Function," consists of two modules; one discusses important relationships between personal selling and organizational strategies at the corporate, business, marketing, and sales levels. This module focuses on how strategic decisions at different organizational levels affect sales management decisions and personal selling practices.

The second module in this part investigates alternative sales organization structures and examines analytical methods for determining salesforce size, territory design, and the allocation of selling effort.

Part Three, "Developing the Salesforce," changes the focus from organizational topics to people topics. The two modules in this part cover the critical decision areas in the recruitment and selection of salespeople and in training salespeople once they have been hired.

Part Four, "Directing the Salesforce," continues the people orientation by discussing the general supervisory and leadership roles necessary for successful sales management and examining important areas of salesforce motivation and reward systems.

Part Five, "Determining Salesforce Effectiveness and Performance," concludes the sales management process by addressing evaluation and control procedures. Differences in evaluating the effectiveness of the sales organization and the performance of salespeople are highlighted and covered in separate modules.

Pedagogy

The following pedagogical format is used for each module to facilitate the learning process.

LEARNING OBJECTIVES. Specific learning objectives for the module are stated in behavioral terms so that students will know what they should be able to do after the module has been covered.

OPENING VIGNETTES. All modules are introduced by an opening vignette that typically consists of a recent, real-world company example addressing many of the key points to be discussed in the module. These opening vignettes are intended to generate student interest in the topics to be covered and to illustrate the practicality of the module coverage.

KEY WORDS. Key words are highlighted in bold type throughout each module and summarized in list form at the end of the module to alert students to their importance.

BOXED INSERTS. Each module contains two boxed inserts titled "Sales Management in the 21st Century." The comments in these boxes are provided by members of our Sales Executive Panel and were made specifically for our text.

FIGURE CAPTIONS. Every figure in the text includes a summarizing caption designed to make the figure understandable without reference to the module discussion.

MODULE SUMMARIES. A module summary recaps the key points covered in the module by restating and answering questions presented in the learning objectives at the beginning of the module.

DEVELOPING SALES MANAGEMENT KNOWLEDGE. Ten discussion questions are presented at the end of each module to review key concepts covered in the module. Some of the questions require students to summarize what has been covered, while others are designed to be more thought provoking and extend beyond module coverage.

BUILDING SALES MANAGEMENT SKILLS. Three application exercises are supplied for each module, requiring students to apply what has been learned in the module to a specific sales management situation. Many of the application exercises require data analysis. Many modules also have an Internet exercise to get students involved with the latest technology.

MAKING SALES MANAGEMENT DECISIONS. Each module concludes with two short cases. Most of these cases represent realistic and interesting sales management situations. Several require data analysis. Most are designed so that students can role play their solutions.

Cases

The book contains a mixture of short, medium, and long cases. The 20 short cases at the end of modules can be used as a basis for class discussion or short written assignments. The longer cases are more appropriate for detailed analysis and class discussions or presentations by individuals or student groups. The longer cases are located at the end of the book. Additional cases will be available to professors and students from the World Wide Web site for the book.

Supplements

Instructor's Manual, Test Bank. A comprehensive package of supplementary materials is available to make it easy for professors to teach a rigorous and interesting sales management course. The *Instructor's Manual, Test Bank,* prepared by the authors, contains a separate section for each module as well as teaching notes for all of the cases. Each section includes a summary; examples, exercises, and materials not covered in the book that could be incorporated into class discussion; and answers to review questions and application exercises. The manual also contains sample course outlines. The *Test Bank* contains multiple-choice and true-false questions and is available in a computerized version for Windows.

MICROCOMPUTER SOFTWARE. The SPREE (Salesperson Review and Evaluation) software has been very popular with professors and students in the past. The software is designed to be very easy for students to use, and everything necessary to incorporate the microcomputer analysis into a sales management class is provided in the *Instructor's Manual.* The software has been revised and improved by updating to a Windows environment.

VIDEOS. A new video package has been prepared to provide a relevant and interesting visual teaching tool for the classroom. Two distinct selling series headline this video package. *Direct Selling on the Global Frontier* presents an overview of the global sales operation of direct selling companies and has a specific case situation for a particular company. *Inc. Magazine* videos show portrayals of "real" sales people and sales calls with "real" clients in a variety of occupations. Companies represented include: Shearson-Lehman, 3M Health Care, and Ben & Jerry's.

INTERNET SUPPORT. Visit the Harcourt Web site at http://www.harcourtcollege.com for the latest support material for the Harcourt series in marketing. These resources include annotated articles, resource links, and other pedagogical aids which will be constantly updated. Also, included on the Web site is the popular Sales Management Update.

The update will include the latest company examples, new research findings, and other teaching aids geared to each chapter, making it easy for professors to incorporate this current information into their class sessions.

NEW! **POWERPOINT PRESENTATION.** This enables professors to customize their own multimedia instruction. Organized by modules, this presentation includes highlights of important concepts, figures from the text, and footage from the video package to help illustrate the text discussion. Slides for both Sales Management and Professional Selling are included.

Harcourt College Publishers will provide complimentary supplements or supplement packages to those adopters qualified under our adoption policy. Please contact your local sales representative to learn how you may qualify. If as an adopter or potential user you receive supplements you do not need, please return them to your sales representative or send them to:

Attn: Returns Department
Troy Warehouse
465 South Lincoln Drive
Troy, MO 63379

Acknowledgments

The writing of a book is a long and arduous task that requires the dedicated efforts of many individuals. The contributions of these individuals are greatly appreciated and deserve specific recognition. We are especially grateful for the efforts of the 98 instructors who participated in the market survey and to the following reviewers who provided useful suggestions for previous editions of this text.

> Karen Anderson, *Iowa State University*
> Kenneth Anglin, *Mankato State University*
> Steve Castleberry, *University of Minnesota–Duluth*
> Steve Clopton, *Appalachian State University*
> Cathy Cole, *University of Iowa*
> Bob Collins, *University of Nevada, Las Vegas*
> John Coppett, *University of Houston–Clear Lake*
> Kenneth Evans, *University of Missouri, Columbia*
> Sarah Gardial, *University of Tennessee, Knoxville*
> David Good, *Central Missouri State University*
> Harrison Grathwol, *California State University, Chico*
> Jon Hawes, *University of Akron*
> Vince Howe, *University of North Carolina, Wilmington*
> Theodore F. Jula, *Stonehill College*
> Bruce MacNab, *California State University, Hayward*
> Philip Mahin, *West Virginia University*
> Walter Pachuk, *University of Scranton*
> Bruce Pilling, *Georgia State University*
> Alison A. Pittman, *Brevard Community College*
> Michael Swenson, *Brigham Young University*
> Hal Teer, *James Madison University*
> Dan Weilbaker, *Northern Illinois University*
> Frank Zuccaro, *Hofstra University*

We sincerely appreciate the willingness of many individuals to allow us to include their cases in the book. These cases have substantially enhanced the effectiveness and interest of the text.

A great deal of credit for this book should go to all of the wonderful people at Harcourt. Their expertise, support, and constant encouragement turned an extremely difficult task into a very enjoyable one. We would like to recognize specifically the tremendous efforts of the following professionals and friends: Bill Schoof, Lisé Johnson, Jana Pitts, Jim Patterson, James McDonald, April Eubanks, Linda Blundell, Lisa Kelley, and Beverly Dunn. Without their efforts this edition would not have seen the light of day. However, we also want to thank the many individuals with whom we did not have direct contact but who assisted in the development and production of this book. We have been treated superbly by everyone at Harcourt during this project.

We are also very appreciative of the support provided by our colleagues at Colorado State University, the University of Louisville, Central Missouri State University, Ball State University, and Illinois State University.

Thomas N. Ingram
Raymond W. LaForge
Ramon A. Avila
Charles H. Schwepker Jr.
Michael R. Williams

January 2000

ABOUT THE AUTHORS

Thomas N. Ingram (Ph.D., Georgia State University) is department chair and professor of marketing at Colorado State University. Before commencing his academic career, he worked in sales, product management, and sales management with Exxon and Mobil. Tom is a recipient of the Marketing Educator of the Year award given by Sales and Marketing Executives International (SMEI). He was honored as the first recipient of the Mu Kappa Tau National Marketing Honor Society recognition award for Outstanding Scholarly Contributions to the Sales Discipline. On several occasions, he has been recognized at the university level for outstanding teaching. Tom has served as the editor of *Journal of Personal Selling and Sales Management*, chair of the SMEI Accreditation Institute, and as a member of the Board of Directors of SMEI. He is the editor of *Journal of Marketing Theory and Practice*. Tom's primary research is in personal selling and sales management. His work has appeared in the *Journal of Marketing, Journal of Marketing Research, Journal of Personal Selling and Sales Management,* and *Journal of the Academy of Marketing Science,* among others. He is the co-author of *The Professional Selling Skills Workbook* and *Marketing Principles and Perspectives,* and co-editor of *Emerging Trends in Sales Thought and Practice.*

Raymond W. (Buddy) LaForge (DBA, University of Tennessee) is the Brown-Forman Professor of Marketing at the University of Louisville. He founded the *Marketing Education Review,* served as editor for eight years, and is currently executive editor. Buddy has co-authored *Marketing: Principles & Perspectives, Sales Management: Analysis and Decision Making, The Professional Selling Skills Workbook,* and co-edited *Emerging Trends in Sales Thought and Practice.* His research is published in many journals including the *Journal of Marketing, Journal of Marketing Research, Journal of the Academy of Marketing Science,* and *Journal of Personal Selling and Sales Management.* Buddy currently serves on the Direct Selling Education Foundation Board of Directors and Executive Committee, DuPont Corporate Marketing Faculty Advisory Team for the Sales Enhancement Process, Family Business Center Advisory Board, as Vice President of Conferences and Research for the American Marketing Association Academic Council, and as Vice President/Marketing for the Academy of Business Education. He is developing the Sales Program at the University of Louisville and establishing the Sales Professional Network (http://cbpa.louisville.edu.salesnetwork) linking sales faculty, students, and executives to improve sales careers, education, research, and practice. Buddy and his wife, Susan, and daughters, Alexandra and Kelly, enjoy tennis, golf, and thoroughbred racing in Louisville, Kentucky.

Ramon A. Avila (Ph.D., Virginia Tech University) is the George and Frances Ball Distinguished Professor of Marketing at Ball State University. Before coming to Ball State, he worked in sales with the Burroughs Corporation. He has also held two visiting professorships at the University of Hawaii. Ramon was presented the 1999 Mu Kappa Tau's Outstanding Contributor to the Sales Profession. He is only the third recipient of this award. Ramon has also received the University's Outstanding Junior Faculty award, the University's Outstanding Service award, the College of Business Professor of the Year, and the Dean's Teaching award every year since its inception in 1987. Ramon also sits on six editorial review boards. Ramon's primary research is in personal selling and sales management. His work has appeared in the *Journal of Marketing Research, Journal of Personal Selling and Sales Management, Industrial*

Marketing Management, Journal of Marketing Management, and the *Journal of Marketing Theory and Practice,* among others. He is the co-author of *The Professional Selling Skills Workbook.*

Charles H. Schwepker Jr. (Ph.D., University of Memphis) is professor of marketing at Central Missouri State University. He has experience in wholesale and retail sales. His research interests are in sales management, personal selling, marketing ethics and consumer behavior. His articles have appeared in the *Journal of the Academy of Marketing Science, Journal of Public Policy and Marketing, Journal of Personal Selling and Sales Management* and *Journal of Business Ethics,* among other journals, various national and regional proceedings, and books, including *Marketing Communications Classics.* He is on the editorial review boards of the *Journal of Personal Selling and Sales Management, Journal of Marketing Theory and Practice, Journal of Business & Industrial Marketing* and *Southern Business Review.*

Michael R. Williams (Ph.D., Oklahoma State University) is associate professor of marketing at Illinois State University. Coinciding with his successful academic and research career, Mike brings with him a rich experience of more than 20 years' work in industrial sales, sales management, and marketing research. Mike's research has been published in a variety of journals, including the *Journal of Personal Selling and Sales Management, International Journal of Purchasing and Materials Management, Journal of Business and Industrial Marketing, Quality Management Journal, Competitiveness Review, Journal of Industrial Technology, Journal of Marketing Theory and Practice,* and *Simulation and Gaming: An International Journal of Theory, Design, and Research.* His work has also received numerous honors, including Outstanding Article for 1998 in the *Journal of Business and Industrial Marketing,* the AACSB's Leadership in Innovative Business Education Award, and the Marketing Science Institute's Alden G. Clayton Competition. Mike has also been honored with numerous university and college research and teaching awards, and his work in the field of corporate and university education has resulted in his being named to *Who's Who in American Education.* Recognition of his work in the areas of sales and organizational performance, customer orientation, and corporate culture have further resulted in Mike's being honored in *Who's Who in the South and Southwest,* and *Who's Who in America.* Mike is currently national director for the National Conference in Sales Management, faculty advisory board member for the Fisher Institute of Personal Selling at the University of Akron, and co-director of the Market-Driven Quality Group.

BRIEF CONTENTS

Preface	ix	
Module 1	Changing World of Sales Management 1	
PART I	**Describing the Personal Selling Function 15**	
Module 2	Overview of Personal Selling 17	
Module 3	Personal Selling: Approaches and Process 39	
PART II	**Defining the Strategic Role of the Sales Function 65**	
Module 4	Organizational Strategies and the Sales Function 67	
Module 5	Sales Organization Structure and Salesforce Deployment 95	
Appendix 5	Developing Forecasts 131	
PART III	**Developing the Salesforce 143**	
Module 6	Staffing the Salesforce: Recruitment and Selection 145	
Module 7	Continual Development of the Salesforce: Sales Training 171	
PART IV	**Directing the Salesforce 195**	
Module 8	Sales Management Leadership and Supervision 197	
Module 9	Motivation and Reward System Management 223	
PART V	**Determining Salesforce Effectiveness and Performance 247**	
Module 10	Evaluating the Effectiveness of the Organization 249	
Module 11	Evaluating the Performance of Salespeople 275	
Cases	306	
Notes	424	
Credits	436	
Company Index	441	
Name Index	443	
Subject Index	447	

CONTENTS

Preface ix

Module 1 **Changing World of Sales Management** 1
Sales Management Process 2
Sales Management Trends 5
Module Format 12
Concluding Statement 13
Sales Executive Panel 14

PART I **Describing the Personal Selling Function** 15

Module 2 **Overview of Personal Selling** 17
Sales Team Drives Auto Dealer's Profits 17
Evolution of Personal Selling 18
Contributions of Personal Selling 20
Classification of Personal Selling 24
Characteristics of Sales Careers 26
Qualifications and Skills Required for Success by Salespersons 30
Summary 32
Case 2.1: Concourse Catering Company 36
Case 2.2: Justin Webb's Career Dilemma 37

Module 3 **Personal Selling: Approaches and Process** 39
Bryan Hollingsworth: Trustworthy Sales Professional 39
Classification of Personal Selling Approaches 40
Sales Process 45
Summary 58
Case 3.1: Biomod, Inc. 62
Case 3.2: Plastico, Inc. 63

PART II **Defining the Strategic Role of the Sales Function** 65

Module 4 **Organizational Strategies and the Sales Function** 67
Strategic Change and the Sales Function: America Online 67
Organizational Strategy Levels 68
Corporate Strategy and the Sales Function 69
Business Strategy and the Sales Function 71
Marketing Strategy and the Sales Function 72
Sales Strategy Framework 77
Organizational Buyer Behavior 78
Sales Strategy 81
Summary 90
Case 4.1: Pronto Retail Centers 93
Case 4.2: National Communications Manufacturing 94

Module 5 Sales Organization Structure and Salesforce Deployment 95
Reorganizing the Salesforce: Pinacor 95
Sales Organization Concepts 96
Selling Situation Contingencies 100
Sales Organization Structures 102
Comparing Sales Organization Structures 108
Salesforce Deployment 109
"People" Considerations 122
Summary 124
Case 5.1: Protek Packaging, Inc. 127
Case 5.2: Opti-Tax Consulting 128

Appendix 5 Developing Forecasts 131

PART III Developing the Salesforce 143

Module 6 Staffing the Salesforce: Recruitment and Selection 145
Finding Successful Salespeople at Edward Jones 145
Importance of Recruitment and Selection 146
Introduction to Salesforce Socialization 147
Recruitment and Selection Process 148
Legal and Ethical Considerations in Recruitment and Selection 163
Summary 166
Case 6.1: Sweet-Treats, Inc. 168
Case 6.2: Titan Industries 169

Module 7 Continual Development of the Salesforce: Sales Training 171
Training Wheels: How Raleigh USA Bicycle Company Peddled Its Way to Success 171
Role of Sales Training in Salesforce Socialization 172
Sales Training as a Crucial Investment 173
Managing the Sales Training Process 174
Ethical and Legal Issues 188
Summary 190
Case 7.1: Solutions Software, Inc. 192
Case 7.2: Computersystems, Inc. 192

PART IV Directing the Salesforce 195

Module 8 Sales Management Leadership and Supervision 197
Hands-on Leadership at SAS Brings Great Success 197
Salesforce Socialization Revisited 198
Contemporary Views of Sales Leadership 199
A Leadership Model for Sales Management 200
Selected Leadership Functions 209
Problems in Leadership 215
Summary 219
Case 8.1: Tasti-Fresh Bakery Products 221
Case 8.2: Global Enterprise 221

Module 9 Motivation and Reward System Management 223

Motivation and Rewarding: A Tale of Large and Small 223
Motivation and Reward Systems 224
Optimal Salesforce Reward System 225
Types of Salesforce Rewards 226
Financial Compensation 226
Nonfinancial Compensation 232
Sales Expenses 234
Additional Issues in Managing Salesforce Reward Systems 237
Guidelines for Motivating and Rewarding Salespeople 241
Summary 242
Case 9.1: Stalwart Industrial Products 245
Case 9.2: Floor-Shine Cleaning Products 245

PART V Determining Salesforce Effectiveness and Performance 247

Module 10 Evaluating the Effectiveness of the Organization 249

Focus on Productivity at Dealer Truck Accessory Warehouse 249
Sales Organization Audit 251
Benchmarking 253
Sales Organization Effectiveness Evaluations 255
Ethical Issues 268
Concluding Comments 269
Summary 269
Case 10.1: Beauty Glow Cosmetics Company 273
Case 10.2: Induplicate Copiers, Inc. 273

Module 11 Evaluating the Performance of Salespeople 275

Changing Environment Prompts Changes in Salesperson Evaluation 275
Purposes of Salesperson Performance Evaluations 276
Salesperson Performance Evaluation Approaches 277
Key Issues in Evaluating and Controlling Salesperson Performance 279
Salesperson Job Satisfaction 299
Summary 301
Case 11.1: Labels Express 304
Case 11.2: Oakmaster Furniture Inc. 304

Cases 306
Notes 424
Credits 436
Company Index 441
Name Index 443
Subject Index 447

Sales Management
Analysis and Decision Making

Fourth Edition

MODULE 1

Changing World of Sales Management

Von Oliver is district sales manager for Boise Cascade Office Products. The company sells office products to customers in almost every industry from financial services companies to heavy equipment manufacturers. Although each day is different and challenging, Von describes a "typical day" in his sales management position:

> 7:30 a.m.—Arrive at the office. My first hour is usually spent getting organized for the day. I grab some coffee and check voice-mail and e-mail messages. Usually there are 10 or more messages requiring some immediate response or future action. I then prioritize the activities for the day.
>
> 8:30 a.m.—Visit with the sales representatives to get the day off to a positive start. I like to talk informally with each rep to see what they have going and how I might help them.
>
> 9:00 a.m.—I normally spend some time reviewing various reports and making plans for the future. Some of my time is spent on district activities such as making sales forecasts, developing budgets, and planning recruiting efforts. The rest of my time is spent on individual salespeople. I continuously monitor the performance and professional development of each salesperson and make plans to help them improve.
>
> 10:00 a.m.—I try to spend some time each week in the field with my sales reps. We start in the office developing target account strategies and reviewing progress. As we ride together making sales calls, we talk about the objectives and strategy for each upcoming sales call. A typical sales call involves many questions to explore account needs. Once we meet with the account, the salesperson takes the lead in asking questions and discussing current issues, objectives, and opportunities. When completed, we evaluate the sales call to identify areas for improvement and to plan follow-up steps with the account.
>
> 12:00 p.m.—Lunch with a client and sales representative. Several times a week, we will take clients to lunch. The purpose of these lunches is to strengthen our relationship with the client. The lunch setting provides the opportunity for us to get to know each other outside the office boundaries. We normally gain a better understanding of the client's situation and use this insight to serve the client better in the future.
>
> 1:30 p.m.—More sales calls. I spend time coaching and counseling sales representatives in the field. I focus on general topics, such as the salesperson's selling skills, as well as specific issues with individual accounts, such as additional people to contact, and anticipating obstacles and how to handle them.
>
> 3:30 p.m.—Back in the office. A host of phone calls to return and issues to discuss with salespeople about things that happened during the day. Typically, I'm contacting manufacturing or support personnel on delivery issues, pricing concerns, or other things needed to serve our customers.
>
> 5:00 p.m.—Review the day and plan for tomorrow. I examine operational reports concerning performance relative to sales and profit objectives. I also try to talk with each salesperson to see how the day went and to discuss plans for tomorrow. My sales administrative assistant and I meet to take care of correspondence and other important issues. I review the day and devise my schedule for tomorrow.
>
> 6:30 p.m.—Head home.

What an interesting day! Von Oliver was involved in a variety of different activities. He spent much of his time interacting with individuals, especially salespeople and customers. But he also had to plan strategies and continuously monitor performance. Thus, he performed all the major sales management functions.

Our objective in this module is to introduce the exciting world of sales management. We begin by presenting a general sales management model and discussing each stage in the sales management process. Then we examine some of the emerging trends in sales management and describe the basic format of each module. The goal is to "set the stage" for your journey into the dynamic and challenging world of sales management.

Sales Management Process

The marketing communications tools available to any firm are typically classified as personal selling, advertising, sales promotion, and publicity. *Personal selling* is defined as personal communication with an audience through paid personnel of an organization or its agents in such a way that the audience perceives the communicator's organization as being the source of the message. This definition differentiates personal selling as personal communication, whereas advertising and sales promotion are nonpersonal. Second, in personal selling the audience perceives the message as being delivered by the organization, whereas in publicity, even when it is in the form of personal communication, the audience typically perceives the medium, not the organization, as being the source of the message.

Sales management is simply management of an organization's personal selling function. Sales managers are involved in both the strategy (planning) and people (implementation) aspects of personal selling, as well as in evaluating and controlling all personal selling activities. They must be able to deal effectively with people in the personal selling function, with people in other functional areas in the organization, and with people outside the organization, especially customers. The sales management model presented in Figure 1.1 illustrates the major stages in the sales management process.

FIGURE 1.1 **Sales Management Model**

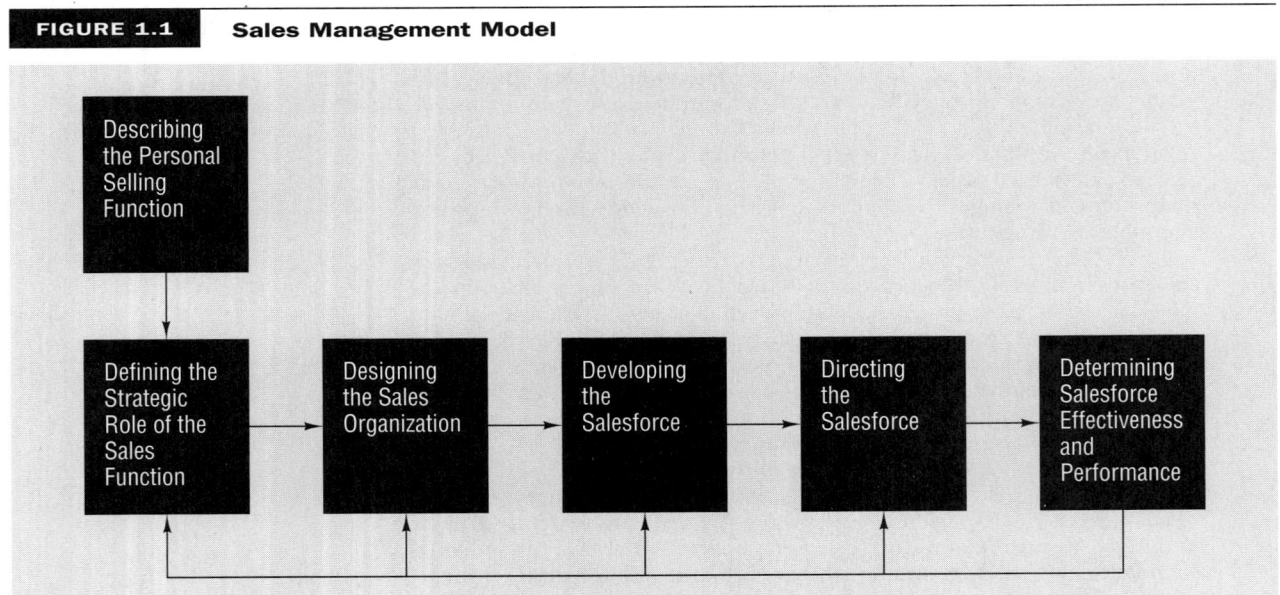

The five major stages of sales management as presented in this model correspond to the five major parts of this textbook.

Describing the Personal Selling Function

Because sales managers are responsible for managing the personal selling function, they must thoroughly understand it. This text therefore devotes two modules to that subject before discussing sales management activities. Module 2 (Overview of Personal Selling) presents the historical evolution of selling, along with a contemporary look at the contributions of personal selling to our economic and social systems. The module also discusses different types of sales jobs and sales career paths. Module 3 (Personal Selling: Approaches and Process) examines various personal selling approaches and presents a comprehensive review of the sales process.

Defining the Strategic Role of the Sales Function

Many firms in the contemporary business world consist of collections of relatively autonomous business units that market multiple products to diverse customer groups. These multiple-business, multiple-product firms must develop and integrate strategic decisions at different organizational levels. Module 4 (Organizational Strategies and the Sales Function) discusses the key strategic decisions at the corporate, business, marketing, and sales levels and the basic relationships between these decisions and the personal selling and sales management functions. Corporate- and business-level strategic decisions typically provide guidelines within which sales managers and salespeople must operate. By contrast, personal selling is an important component of marketing strategies in specific product market situations. The role of personal selling in a given marketing strategy has direct and important implications for sales managers.

Strategic decisions at the corporate, business, and marketing levels must be translated into strategies for individual accounts. We discuss the major elements of a sales strategy: account targeting strategy, relationship strategy, selling strategy, and sales channel strategy. Because personal selling is typically important in organizational marketing situations, we provide an explanation of organizational buyer behavior as a foundation for the development of sales strategies.

Sales strategies are designed for individual accounts or groups of similar accounts. Therefore, an account targeting strategy is needed to identify and classify accounts into useful categories. Then, the type of relationship, the desired selling approach, and the most productive mix of sales channels are determined for each account category. These decisions result in an integrated sales strategy for each targeted account and account group.

The development and integration of corporate, business, marketing, and sales strategies establishes the basic strategic direction for personal selling and sales management activities. However, an effective sales organization is necessary to implement these strategies successfully. Module 5 (Sales Organization Structure and Salesforce Deployment) presents the basic concepts in designing an effective sales organization structure: specialization, centralization, span of control versus management levels, and line versus staff positions. Different decisions in any of these areas produce different sales organization structures. The appropriate structure for a firm depends on the specific characteristics of a given selling situation. If major account selling programs are used, specific attention must be directed toward determining the best organizational structure for serving these major accounts.

Closely related to sales organization decisions are decisions on the amount and allocation of selling effort. We present specific methods for making salesforce deployment decisions. Because the decisions on selling effort allocation, salesforce size, and territory design are interrelated, they should be addressed in an integrative manner. A number of different analytical approaches can assist in this endeavor, but "people" issues must also be considered.

Developing the Salesforce

The sales strategy, sales organization, and salesforce deployment decisions produce the basic structure for personal selling efforts and can be considered similar to the "machine" decisions in a production operation. Sales managers must also make a number of "people" decisions to ensure that the right types of salespeople are available and have the skills to operate the "machine" structure effectively and efficiently.

Module 6 (Staffing the Salesforce: Recruitment and Selection) discusses the key activities involved in planning and carrying out salesforce recruitment and selection programs. These activities include determining the type of salespeople desired, identifying prospective salesperson candidates, and evaluating candidates to ensure that the best are hired. Legal and ethical issues are important considerations in the recruitment and selection process. The ramifications of this process for salespeople's subsequent adjustment to a new job (socialization) are also examined.

Module 7 (Continual Development of the Salesforce: Sales Training) emphasizes the need for continuous training of salespeople and the important role that sales managers play in this activity. The sales training process consists of access training needs, developing objectives, evaluating alternatives, designing the training program, carrying it out, and evaluating it. Sales managers face difficult decisions at each stage of the sales training process, because it is not only extremely important but also expensive, and there are many sales training alternatives available.

Directing the Salesforce

Hiring the best salespeople and providing them with the skills required for success is one thing; directing their efforts to meet sales organization goals and objectives is another. Sales managers spend a great deal of their time in motivating, supervising, and leading members of the salesforce.

Module 8 (Sales Management Leadership and Supervision) distinguishes between the leadership and supervisory activities of a sales manager. *Leadership activities* focus on influencing salespeople through communication processes to attain specific goals and objectives. By contrast, *supervisory activities* are concerned with day-to-day control of the salesforce under routine operating conditions. The use of power and influence strategies is discussed in the context of an overall sales leadership model. Different styles of sales management are illustrated, and key issues and problems in sales management leadership and supervision are discussed.

Module 9 (Motivation and Reward System Management) presents several content and process theories of motivation that attempt to explain how individuals decide to spend effort on specific activities over extended periods of time. Sales managers can use these theories as a foundation for determining the best ways to get salespeople to spend the appropriate amount of time on the right activities over a period of time. These theories provide the basis for specific salesforce reward systems. Both the compensation type of rewards and the noncompensation types are examined. The advantages and disadvantages of different compensation programs are investigated, as well as different methods for sales expense reimbursement. Specific guidelines for developing and managing a salesforce reward system are suggested.

Determining Salesforce Effectiveness and Performance

Sales managers must continually monitor the progress of the salesforce to determine current effectiveness and performance. This is a difficult task, because these evaluations should address both the effectiveness of different units within the sales organization and the performance of individual salespeople.

Module 10 (Evaluating the Effectiveness of the Organization) focuses on evaluating the effectiveness of sales organization units, such as territories, districts, regions, and zones. The *sales organization audit* is the most comprehensive approach for evaluating the effectiveness of the sales organization as a whole. Specific methods are presented for assessing the effectiveness of different sales organization units with regard to sales, costs, profitability, and productivity. Skill in using these different analyses helps a sales manager to diagnose specific problems and develop solutions to them.

Module 11 (Evaluating the Performance of People) changes the focus to evaluating the performance of people, both as individuals and in groups. These performance evaluations are used for a variety of purposes by sales managers. Specific criteria to be evaluated and different methods for providing the evaluative information are examined, and the use of this information in a diagnostic and problem-solving manner is described. A method for measuring salesperson job satisfaction, which is closely related to salesperson performance, is presented as well.

Sales Management Trends

The turbulent business environment presents a variety of challenges. Many sales organizations face fierce global competition in both home and international markets. The purchasing function is increasingly viewed as an important way for organizations to lower costs and increase profits. Therefore, buyers are more demanding, better prepared, and highly skilled. The costs of maintaining salespeople in the field are escalating at the same time that sales organizations are being pressured to increase sales but decrease the costs of doing business. Thus, sales organizations are being challenged by competitors, customers, and even their own firms.

Many sales organizations are responding to these challenges by making dramatic changes in sales operations. Consider what some of *Sales and Marketing Management*'s 1999 Best Sales Forces are doing.[1]

- GE Capital Services is a financial services company that has generated double-digit net income growth for more than 10 years. The company is connecting all business units to a standardized automation system. This allows salespeople to share databases of common customers and to cross-sell better across business units. GE Capital Services is also expanding globally. It is developing a salesforce in Japan, the world's second largest financial market.

- Pfizer Pharmaceuticals has increased sales for 49 straight years. The company has been introducing many new pharmaceutical products and has doubled the size of its U.S. salesforce to approximately 5,400. Pfizer wants to be known as the "premier employer" in the pharmaceutical industry. One program consistent with this objective is Vista Rx, an in-house, part-time field salesforce. Vista Rx consists of 70 experienced sales reps that desired to work part time. These reps work hard but only during 60 percent of the workweek. This allows Pfizer to keep successful sales reps, and the reps are able to achieve a better work/life balance.

- Ernst & Young has 20,000 client services employees in its consulting operations. The company has created a sales culture and a team-based selling approach. Each consultant team is led by a salesperson. The company uses a very selective recruiting process to hire salespeople from outside the firm. The salespeople must be effective in a team environment and be able to help the sales team grow business with existing clients.

- Marriott salespeople represent different hotel brands, such as Ritz-Carlton, Courtyard, and Fairfield Inns. Because customers differ in purchasing preferences, Marriott employs several sales channels. Customers who already know what they want can make bookings directly through the Internet or by calling one of Marriott's 50 event-booking centers staffed by inside salespeople. Customers who need help in determining what is needed are serviced by the field salesforce.
- Salespeople at Johnson Control's Automotive Systems Group (ASG) try to create long-term relationships with customers. This requires that the sales and marketing departments work closely together, even going on joint sales calls. The marketing department does extensive consumer research. Salespeople use this research to add value to their relationship with automobile manufacturers. Sometimes, salespeople set up offices at customer sites to service these customers more quickly.

These situations illustrate some of the ways sales organizations are responding to the challenges facing them. Some of the changes are relatively minor, whereas others represent radical departures from past operating methods. Even though many firms are making significant changes in sales management, the framework presented in Figure 1.1 is still relevant. All sales organizations must somehow address each stage of the sales management process. What is changing, however, are the types of decisions made at each stage and how these decisions affect other stages in the sales management process.

We think that the challenges facing sales organizations will continue to increase. Therefore, successful sales organizations will be those that are willing to change and meet these challenges. Several of the most important sales management trends are presented in Figure 1.2. Although we discuss each trend separately,

FIGURE 1.2 Sales Management Trends

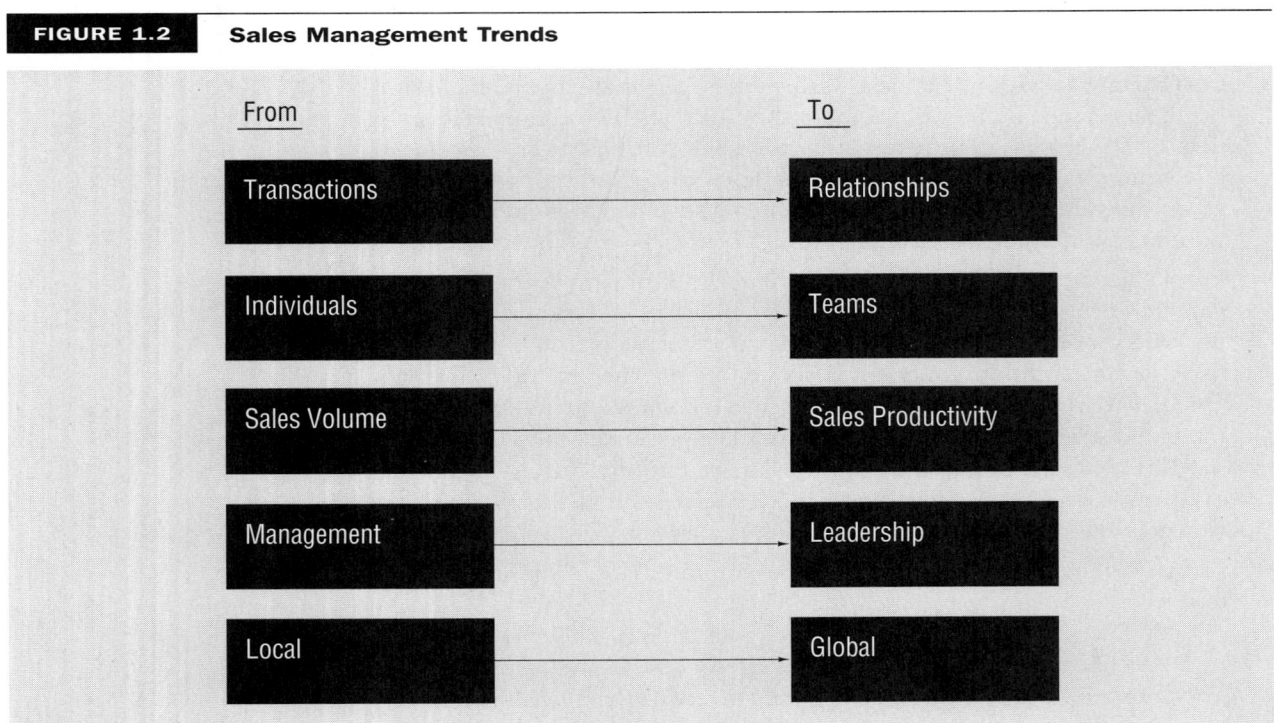

Many sales organizations are responding to the challenges facing them by making changes in their sales operations.

the trends are interrelated and many sales organizations are using new technologies to implement the trends.

From Transactions to Relationships

The traditional transaction selling model is increasingly being replaced by more relationship-oriented selling approaches. Instead of an emphasis on selling products in the short run, salespeople are being required to develop long-term relationships by solving customer problems, providing opportunities, and adding value to customer businesses over an extended period of time. Sometimes, the shift to a relationship approach is demanded by specific customers. For example, companies such as Ford, Xerox, Whirlpool, and General Electric have drastically reduced the number of their suppliers. Instead of working with many suppliers for a particular product or service, these firms want to deal with only one supplier or a few suppliers. Because these buyers desire long-term relationships with fewer suppliers, suppliers have no choice but to adopt a relationship approach if they want to sell to them.

In other cases, sales organizations have been more proactive in establishing a relationship strategy. These sellers realize that their long-term success depends on having long-term customers. Helping customers improve their business operations is the best way to develop the long-term customer relationships that will lead to long-term success.

The key sales management task is determining the appropriate type of relationship to pursue with specific customers. Some customers want and can best be served with a transaction approach. Others require some type of relationship strategy. There are, however, different types of relationships that might be established between buyers and sellers. These are difficult but critical decisions for sales organizations, because the type of relationship affects all other aspects of sales management.

The relationship selling trend is exhibited in the following examples:

- Texas Nameplate Company (TNC), with $4 million in annual sales, is the smallest company to win the Malcolm Baldridge National Quality Award. TNC focuses on retaining customers by being viewed as a trusted and valuable supplier. The company uses customer visits and response cards to generate feedback from customers and to take corrective action when problems are identified. Twice a year salespeople get a printout of customers who have not made a purchase during the past 12 months. The salespeople visit these customers, and last year they recovered 78 inactive accounts. This relationship orientation is working, as more than 62% of customers have been doing business with TNC for more than 10 years.[2]
- DXI sells software and services to companies that use ocean transportation. The company's online database with ocean transportation rates can help customers solve a variety of problems, but many customers viewed the company as just another vendor. Ed Ryan, vice president of sales and marketing, decided to change this. He initiated a sales training program to help salespeople develop different types of relationships with different customers. Strategic resource relationships were established with the best customers. In these relationships, DXI is regarded as a consultant helping the customer improve its business by reducing transportation and other costs. DXI benefits from these relationships by generating higher margins and having more control over the sales process.[3]
- Salespeople from General Motors Service Parts Operation (GMSPO) used to focus entirely on selling car parts to dealers. Now, the emphasis is on helping the dealers improve business operations. The salespeople present

detailed, easy-to-read reports on a dealer's business in the form of a Dealer Business Profile and Dealer Dashboard. The salesperson and dealer discuss this information to identify problem areas and to devise solutions to these problems. This consultative service is valued by the dealer and helps to strengthen the relationship with GMSPO.[4]

We examine the move from transactions to relationships throughout the remainder of the text. However, particular attention to relationship selling approaches is provided in the personal selling modules (Modules 2 and 3). In addition, an important element of a sales strategy is determining the type of relationship desired with each account. This strategic decision is examined in detail in Module 4.

From Individuals to Teams

The importance of the "lone-wolf, superstar" salesperson is diminishing in many sales organizations, especially when the focus changes from just selling products to solving customer problems. In many situations, no one person possesses the knowledge and skills needed to identify and solve customer problems. Typically, some type of teamwork is required. This teamwork may be among different individuals in the sales organization, between the sales and marketing departments, or among the different functions within the business. Although there are many different teamwork approaches, the trend from individuals to teams is becoming increasingly prevalent.

One way to view the different teamwork approaches is presented in Exhibit 1.1.[5] At one extreme is a core selling team—a formal sales team assigned to a specific customer. Team members can come from all business functional areas. Normally, a core selling team is headed by a sales manager. An example of the use of core selling teams is the national account program employed by Nalco. When Nalco wins a national account, employees from both companies form an account team. The team includes a Nalco senior executive who is paired with a senior executive from the customer company. The remainder of the team consists of people from sales and other functions at Nalco matched by the customer's counterparts.

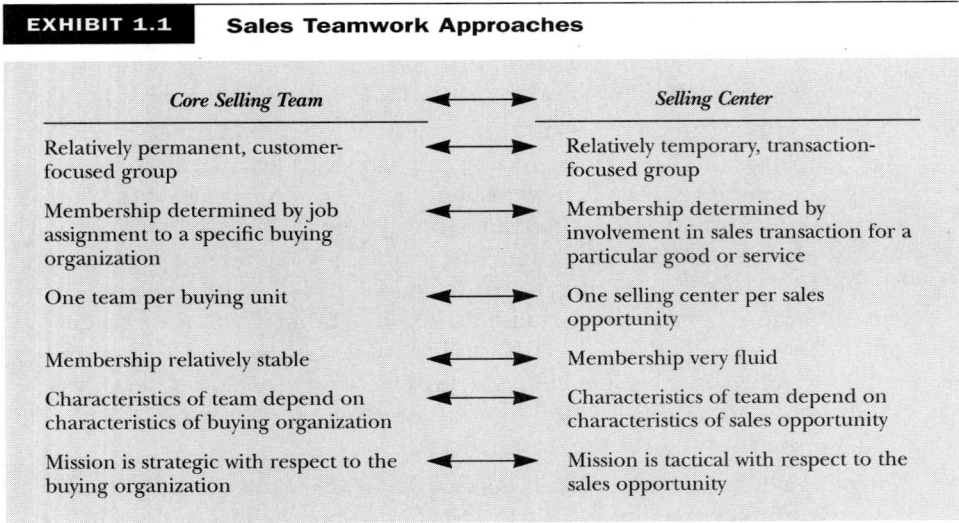

EXHIBIT 1.1   Sales Teamwork Approaches

Core Selling Team	⟷	*Selling Center*
Relatively permanent, customer-focused group	⟷	Relatively temporary, transaction-focused group
Membership determined by job assignment to a specific buying organization	⟷	Membership determined by involvement in sales transaction for a particular good or service
One team per buying unit	⟷	One selling center per sales opportunity
Membership relatively stable	⟷	Membership very fluid
Characteristics of team depend on characteristics of buying organization	⟷	Characteristics of team depend on characteristics of sales opportunity
Mission is strategic with respect to the buying organization	⟷	Mission is tactical with respect to the sales opportunity

Different teamwork approaches that sales organizations can use are represented by this continuum.

As expressed by Jim Scott, Nalco's vice president of corporate sales: "To be successful, you have to have people matched up from both the customer and supplier sides, from the executive level on down."[6]

At the other extreme is a selling center where different individuals are involved in a particular sales transaction. This is an informal teamwork approach. Team members can come from any business function and can participate at any stage of the sales process. Often, it is the responsibility of the salesperson to orchestrate the resources of the selling organization to meet the needs of the buying organization. The Holophane Corporation implemented a sales automation system to facilitate teamwork among the different business functions. All orders are entered directly into a database that is accessible to all departments involved in manufacturing and executing the order. As engineering and manufacturing work on the order, its status is continuously updated. Customer service personnel can easily respond to customer inquiries about the order or make changes in the order requested by customers. The sales automation system provides the information needed for the different business functions to work as a team to meet customer needs.[7]

Between these two extremes is a variety of approaches that differ in degree of formality, composition of team members, number of teams, and other characteristics. The important point is that the need for teamwork and the development of various types of selling teams is likely to increase in the future. And, as sales organizations move from a focus on individuals to an emphasis on teamwork, many aspects of sales management must change. Therefore, we examine the teamwork trend throughout the text.

From Sales Volume to Sales Productivity

The basic role of a sales organization has been to sell. Salespeople and sales mangers are normally evaluated and rewarded according to total sales volume generated over some time period. Although sales volume is important, many companies are finding that all sales are not equal. Some sales are more profitable than others. Therefore, more sales organizations are focusing not just on "sales for the sake of sales," but on the profitability of sales. This changes the focus from sales volume only to sales productivity. Sales productivity includes the costs associated with generating sales and serving customers. A sales productivity orientation emphasizes producing more sales for a given level of costs by doing things more effectively or more efficiently.

Increasing sales productivity usually requires a sales organization to do some things differently. Consider the following examples:

- AT&T's Middle Markets Division consists of about 5,000 salespeople serving 250,000 business customers who spend between $10,000 and $1 million a year on telecommunications services. One problem facing the division was the difficulty and high cost of communicating with these salespeople. Middle Markets Village, an Intranet site, was developed to address this problem. The text-only site provides information in three categories: news and information, reference documents, and interactive communication. Salespeople find the site easy to use and valuable to them in their work. The Intranet has virtually eliminated the cost of printed communication materials.[8]
- Intel's Business Conferencing Group uses what it makes to increase sales productivity. The company used a multipoint videoconference to communicate the launch of its new Team-Station 4.0 videoconferencing system to about 40 sales reps in North America and Europe. The full-day program

linked 20 sales offices and some reps in their homes. The videoconference was interactive as all participants could ask questions at any time. The participants rated the program as very effective, and the cost savings in relation to bringing everyone to the same location were substantial.[9]

- Fisher Scientific International's salespeople often show up for training programs in their pajamas. That is because the training programs are on the Web. The salespeople can receive training programs in their homes, cars, hotel rooms, or wherever they bring their laptop computers. Using a Web-based product called Performance Learning System, salespeople receive product training, take an exam, or post messages to product experts wherever and whenever they want. The company saves money on travel costs and the salespeople save valuable selling time.[10]

The common element in all these situations is that some changes were made to increase sales productivity. Some things were done differently to get "more bang for the sales buck." This pressure to increase sales productivity is likely to intensify in the future for most sales organizations.

In one sense, all sales management decisions can be viewed from a sales productivity perspective. Sales managers should continuously be trying to "do more with less." Therefore, we address sales productivity throughout the sales management process. However, sales productivity is especially relevant when developing sales strategies (Module 4), organizing selling activities and deploying selling effort (Module 5), and evaluating sales organization effectiveness (Module 10).

From Management to Leadership

Many sales organizations use a hierarchical, bureaucratic structure. Sales managers operate at different levels with direct supervisory responsibility for the level below and direct accountability to the management level above. Thus, field sales managers operate as the "boss" for the salespeople who report to them. They are responsible for the performance of these salespeople and exercise various types of control to get salespeople to produce desired results.

Although this approach might work well in very stable environments, many sales organizations realize that this approach makes it difficult for them to be responsive in a rapidly changing environment. These sales organizations are "flattening" the hierarchy and empowering salespeople to make more decisions in the field. This changes the role of sales managers and their relationship with salespeople. The basic trend is for a sales manager to lead more and manage less. One study found that sales managers are playing more of a leadership role by emphasizing:

- collaboration rather than control
- coaching instead of criticism
- salesperson empowerment rather than domination
- sharing information rather than withholding it
- adapting to individual salespeople rather than treating everyone the same.[11]

This emphasis on leadership means that a sales manager's job is more to help salespeople perform better and less to control and evaluate salespeople. This change in orientation is illustrated in Exhibit 1.2.

Several studies reinforce the importance of leadership skills for sales managers. One study of 900 salespeople found that the skills salespeople most desired from their sales managers were good communication skills, the ability to motivate, and

EXHIBIT 1.2	Leadership Trends
Yesterday	*Today*
Natural resources defined power.	Knowledge is power.
Leaders commanded and controlled.	Leaders empower and coach.
Leaders were warriors.	Leaders are facilitators.
Managers directed.	Managers delegate.

Several important changes in effective leadership have occurred over the years.

listening skills.[12] Another study indicated that the major reason salespeople leave their firms is because of dissatisfaction with their sales manager.[13] Similar results were found in another study in which salespeople suggested less loyalty to their firm because of concerns about their sales manager's ability to lead them.[14] Finally, a study of 130 global firms reported that leadership was the most important quality of sales executives.[15]

Debbie Smith, North American sales manager for Extended Systems, agrees with the results of these studies:

> Salespeople want to know that you're there for them. Managers need to show their reps that they're prepared to listen and work with them. Managers who just hand out leads, sit in their office doing budgets, and talk to salespeople only when necessary are going to be hated by their people.[16]

The trend toward a leadership orientation by sales managers is examined throughout the text. However, Module 8 (Sales Management Leadership and Supervision) is devoted entirely to discussing the important leadership versus management issues.

From Local to Global

The marketplace is now global. Products and services are produced and marketed throughout the world. Most companies are involved in the international marketplace in some way now and are likely to be more involved internationally in the future. This trend toward a global orientation includes operating in international markets but goes well beyond just this geographic dimension. Even companies that do business only in the United States, or only in a region of the United States, might compete against firms from other countries, use international suppliers, work with international partners, be affected by international events, serve customers from different countries regardless of where the customers are currently located, and/or have employees from different countries and cultures. Any of these situations requires a sales organization to expand from a local to a more global focus.

The most obvious need for a global orientation occurs when a company moves into different international markets. More and more companies are having to do this to achieve growth objectives, because many local markets are not growing. Operating in international markets presents difficult challenges for sales managers. Take the situation faced by Doug Loewe, director of sales/Europe for MCI WorldCom Advanced Networks. Doug oversees nine sales offices in nine countries. He is based in London, has a second home in Spain, regularly travels to Germany and the United States on MCI business, and often visits three countries in the same week. His approach is to hire individuals he can trust and then empower them. He does, however, communicate often with his sales team through e-mail but also tries to have personal phone conversations and meetings whenever possible.[17]

Less obvious, but of increasing importance, are the many situations in which a global orientation is needed to be effective in a sales organization's domestic market. Competing against international competitors, serving customers from different countries and cultures, and managing a diverse salesforce are of particular relevance to sales managers. Few markets or sales organizations are homogeneous. Most are becoming more and more heterogeneous and diverse.

Take the situation in the United States. One study projected that 75 percent of the future population growth in the United States will come from Asian, Hispanic, and African-American groups.[18] Thus, in the years to come, an increasing proportion of the labor pool for sales organizations and customers for consumer marketers in the United States will come from different cultural groups. Jerry DiMonti, Century 21 People Services Realty, has taken advantage of this situation. His company operates in an area outside New York City with 89 different nationalities. To sell effectively in this type of marketplace, his 33 sales agents include individuals with Italian, French, African-American, Guatemalan, Puerto Rican, Jamaican, Nigerian, Jewish, Indian, and South African backgrounds. This diverse sales organization selling to diverse customers has increased company sales dramatically in the past 2 years.[19]

Module Format

Sales Management: Analysis and Decision Making was written for students. Therefore, its aim is to provide comprehensive coverage of sales management in a manner that students will find interesting and readable. Each module blends recent research results with current sales management practice in a format designed to facilitate learning.

At the beginning of each module, "Learning Objectives" highlight the basic material that the student should expect to learn. These learning objectives are helpful in reviewing modules for future study. An opening vignette then illustrates many of the important ideas to be covered in the module, using examples of companies in various industries to illustrate the diversity and complexity of sales management. Most of the companies described in the vignettes are well known, and most of the situations represent recent actions by these firms.

Key words in the body of each module are printed in bold letters, and figures and exhibits are used liberally to illustrate and amplify the discussion in the text. Every figure contains an explanation so that it can be understood without reference to the text.

Each module contains two boxed inserts entitled **Sales Management in the 21st Century.** The examples in both boxes have been provided specifically for this textbook by sales executives from various companies whom we recruited to serve as a **Sales Executive Panel.** To ensure that the textbook includes the latest practices from leading sales organizations, each executive was asked to provide specific examples of "best practices" in their company. Backgrounds of each executive are provided at the end of this module.

Sales managers are confronted with various ethical issues when performing their job activities. Many of these ethical issues are addressed in the **Ethical Dilemma** boxes that appear in the remaining modules. You will be presented with realistic ethical situations faced by sales managers and asked to recommend appropriate courses of action.

A module summary is geared to the learning objectives presented at the beginning of the module. **Understanding Sales Management Terms** lists the key words that appear in bold throughout the module. **Developing Sales Management Knowledge** presents 10 questions to help you develop an understanding of important sales management issues and relationships. **Building Sales Management Skills** consists of three exercises in which you can apply the sales management knowledge learned in the module. **Making Sales Management Decisions** includes two interesting case situations that allow you to make important sales management decisions. If you understand sales management terms, develop sales management knowledge, and build sales management skills, you will be prepared to make successful sales management decisions.

Concluding Statement

This brief overview of contemporary sales management and summary of the contents and format of *Sales Management: Analysis and Decision Making* set the stage for your journey into the dynamic and exciting world of sales management. This should be a valuable learning experience as well as an interesting journey. All the information contained in this textbook should prove very relevant to those of you who begin your career in personal selling and progress through the ranks of sales management.

Sales Executive Panel

Sandy Apple is sales manager for Automatic Data Processing (ADP) Emerging Business Services Division. She manages nine associates who sell payroll, tax filing, time and attendance, and human resource–related services to business customers. Sandy has a B.S.B.A. in finance from the University of Louisville.

John Carey is district manager for Harcourt College Publishing. He supervises nine sales representatives in the southeast and midwest. John has a B.S. from State University of New York and an M.B.A. from Eastern Kentucky University.

Jane Hrehocik Clampitt is marketing process manager for DuPont Consulting Solutions. Jane has spent most of her time at DuPont in sales and marketing roles with her current position aimed at raising the competency of sales and marketing professionals at DuPont. She has a B.S. in chemical engineering from Pennsylvania State University.

Doug Clopton is district sales manager for Hershey Chocolate. His duties include managing a 14-member sales team selling more than $40 million of confectionery items in a three-state area. Doug has a B.S.B.A. in marketing and an M.B.A. from Central Missouri State University.

Jerry Heffel started with The Southwestern Company as a college student salesperson in 1965, and has been president of the company since 1980. He is responsible for current profitability and setting the future direction for the company. Jerry has a B.A. in history from Oklahoma State University, and an M.B.A. from the University of Oklahoma.

Charlie Kowalczyk is vice-president, regional sales manager for State National Companies. Charlie was branch sales manager for Pitney Bowes Office Systems when he made the comments for this book. He has a B.S. in business administration from Towson University and an M.B.A. from Loyola College in Maryland.

Anthony Lockhart is director of central region sales for FirstEnergy. He is responsible for planning and implementing sales activities and policies in his region. Anthony earned a B.S. in industrial technology from Miami University (Ohio), a master's degree in economics from Case Western Reserve University, and a law degree from Cleveland State University.

L.A. Mitchell is sales planner, business management, for Lucent Technologies. She works with the sales team as a strategic financial partner with the sales directors which involves financial analysis, forecasting, and the identification of sales opportunities. L.A. has B.S.B.A. in marketing and an M.S. in marketing from Colorado State University.

Von Oliver is district sales manager for Boise Cascade Office Products. He supervises salespeople who sell various office products to business and organizational customers. Von has a B.S. in marketing from Western Kentucky University.

Steve Randazzo is regional sales manager for Schein Pharmaceutical, Inc. His primary customer base includes drug wholesalers, retail chains, managed care facilities, and hospitals in the central and southeastern United States. Steve has a B.S. in advertising from Southeast Missouri State University.

Andre Wickham is corporate regional sales manager southeast region and corporate national accounts sales manager for Hormel Foods' Foodservice Group. He provides sales leadership in the southeast region and directly manages sales activities with many national foodservice chains throughout the United States. Andre has a B.S. in business administration from Morgan State University in Baltimore.

PART I

Describing the Personal Selling Function

The two modules in Part One describe the personal selling function. A clear understanding of personal selling is essential to gain a proper perspective on the issues facing sales managers. Module 2 presents the historical evolution of selling, along with a contemporary look at the contributions of personal selling to our economic and social systems. In addition, classifications of the various approaches to personal selling and types of personal selling jobs are discussed.

Module 3 reviews the key job activities of salespeople. In addition to selling, salespeople are involved in time and territory management, assisting sales managers, and providing support for other organizational activities. This module also reviews the sales process.

MODULE 2

Overview of Personal Selling

Sales Team Drives Auto Dealer's Profits

A well-coordinated sales team from Reynolds & Reynolds Automotive Products Group has a simple message for auto dealer's such as American Ford in Bloomington, Minnesota: we can help you make more money. The Reynolds & Reynolds sales team has two key strengths that allow them to make such a claim. First, they have expertise in database marketing for automotive clients. Second, they have sufficient time to implement direct marketing incentive programs. These strengths match up well with American Ford's needs, as busy dealer personnel lack expertise in database analysis and in the implementation of direct marketing incentive programs.

Working from American Ford's database, Reynolds & Reynolds determined which customers were returning for service work. The Reynolds team then recommended marketing programs designed to increase the frequency of return visits and to encourage visits from new car buyers who had not returned to the dealership for service work. American Ford expects to gain approximately $30,000 per month in additional service department revenue by adopting the recommendations of the Reynolds team.

To gain the American Ford account, Reynolds deployed a three-person sales team comprising a regional sales manager, a sales associate, and a marketing specialist. Sales associate Bob Sherman made initial contact with American Ford. After two sales calls, Sherman brought in his sales manager, Tim O'Neil, an expert in service reminder programs. Sherman and O'Neil succeeded in getting approval from American Ford's Carol Bemis, new parts and service director, to analyze the American database. This analysis served as the basis for Reynolds' proposal to American. The proposal was made by Sherman, O'Neil, and marketing specialist Chuck Wiltgen, each of whom played specific roles in developing and delivering the proposal. Sherman provided findings from Reynolds' analysis of the American Ford database analysis, pointing out several opportunities for improving the profit picture for American through the service department. Wiltgen handled the details of implementing direct marketing programs to take advantage of these opportunities. O'Neil provided support at each step in the sales process and took the lead in gaining a commitment from the American management team.

After the sale was made, Carol Bemis noted the professionalism of the Reynolds team and described the meeting as very productive. She observed that Reynolds had developed a customized solution for American, rather than "having to squeeze into something prefabricated." She added, "I also didn't feel pressured . . . I didn't feel they were selling something just for the sake of selling something. I left the meeting with the confidence that no matter what we ended up with it would be the best decision made with the most accurate information."

Source: Malcolm Fleschner, "Anatomy of a Sale," *Selling Power* (January/February 1999): 78.

Learning Objectives

After completing this module, you should be able to

1 Describe the evolution of personal selling from ancient times to the modern era.

2 Explain the contributions of personal selling to society, business firms, and customers.

3 Describe different types of personal selling jobs.

4 Discuss the characteristics of sales careers.

5 Describe the skills and characteristics required for success in most sales positions.

Evolution of Personal Selling

The successful professional salesperson of today and the future is likely a better listener than a talker, is more oriented toward developing long-term relationships with customers than placing an emphasis on high-pressure, short-term sales techniques, and has the skills and patience to endure lengthy, complex sales processes. In earning the American Ford account, the Reynolds & Reynolds sales team displayed these qualities of sales professionals.

Personal selling has evolved into a different activity than it was just a decade ago. Throughout this course, you learn about new technologies and techniques that have contributed to this evolution. This module provides an overview of personal selling, affording insight into the operating rationale of today's salespeople and sales managers. In the highly competitive, complex environment of the world business community, personal selling and sales management have never played more critical roles.

Origins of Personal Selling

Ancient Greek history documents selling as an exchange activity, and the term *salesman* appears in the writings of Plato.[1] However, true salespeople, those who earned a living only by selling, did not exist in any sizable number until the Industrial Revolution in England, from the mid-eighteenth century to the mid-nineteenth century. Prior to this time, traders, merchants, and artisans filled the selling function. These predecessors of contemporary marketers were generally viewed with contempt because deception was often used in the sale of goods.[2]

In the latter phase of the Middle Ages, the first door-to-door salesperson appeared in the form of the peddler. Peddlers collected produce from local farmers, sold it to townspeople, and, in turn, bought manufactured goods in town for subsequent sale in rural areas.[3] Like many other early salespeople, they performed other important marketing functions—in this case, purchase, assembly, sorting, and redistribution of goods.

Industrial Revolution Era

As the Industrial Revolution began to blossom in the middle of the eighteenth century, the economic justification for salespeople gained momentum. Local economies were no longer self-sufficient, and as intercity and international trade began to flourish, economies of scale in production spurred the growth of mass markets in geographically dispersed areas. The continual need to reach new customers in these dispersed markets called for an increasing number of salespeople.

It is interesting to note the job activities of the first wave of salespeople in the era of the Industrial Revolution. The following quotation describes a salesperson who served the customer in conjunction with a producer:

> Thus, a salesman representing the producing firm, armed with samples of the firm's products, could bring the latter to the attention of a large number of potential customers—whether buying for sale to others or for their own production requirements—who might not, without the salesman's visit, have learnt of the product's existence, and give them the opportunity of examining and discussing it without having to go out of their way to do so. . . . Even if the salesman did not succeed in obtaining an order, he frequently picked up valuable information on the state of the market, sometimes the very reasons for refusal. . . . This information could be very useful to the producer.[4]

Post–Industrial Revolution Era

By the early 1800s, personal selling was well established in England but just beginning to develop in the United States.[5] This situation changed noticeably after 1850, and by the latter part of the century, salespeople were a well-established part of business practice in the United States. For example, one wholesaler in the Detroit area reported sending out 400 traveling salespeople in the 1880s.[6]

At the dawning of the twentieth century, an exciting time in the economic history of the United States, it became apparent that marketing, especially advertising and personal selling, would play a crucial role in the rapid transition of the economy from an agrarian base to one of mass production and efficient transportation.

Glimpses of the lives of salespeople in the early 1900s gained from literature of that period reveal an adventuresome, aggressive, and valuable group of employees often working on the frontier of new markets. Already, however, the independent maverick salespeople who had blazed the early trails to new markets were beginning to disappear. One clear indication that selling was becoming a more structured activity was the development of a **canned sales presentation** by John H. Patterson of the National Cash Register Company (NCR). This presentation, a virtual script to guide NCR salespeople on how to sell cash registers, was based on the premise that salespeople are not "born, but rather they are made."[7]

Sales historians noted the changes occurring in personal selling in the early twentieth century. Charles W. Hoyt, author of one of the first textbooks on sales management, chronicled this transition in 1912, noting two types of salespeople:

> The old kind of salesman is the "big me" species. . . . He works for himself and, so far as possible, according to his own ideas. . . There is another type of salesman. He is the new kind. At present he is in the minority, but he works for the fastest growing and most successful houses of the day. He works for the house and the house works for him. He welcomes and uses every bit of help the house sends to him.[8]

Hoyt's observations about the "old" and the "new" salesperson summed up the changing role of personal selling. The managements of firms in the United States were beginning to understand the tremendous potential of personal selling and, simultaneously, the need to shape the growth of the sales function. In particular, a widespread interest arose in how to reduce the cost of sales. According to Hoyt, this did not mean hiring lower-cost salespeople, but instead called for "distributing much larger quantities of goods with less motion."[9]

War and Depression Era

The 30-year span from 1915 to 1945 was marked by three overwhelming events—two World Wars and the Great Depression in the United States. Because economic activity concentrated on the war efforts, new sales methods did not develop quickly during those periods. During the Great Depression, however, business firms, starved for sales volume, often employed aggressive salespeople to produce badly needed revenue. Then, with renewed prosperity in the post–World War II era, salespeople emerged as important employees for an increasing number of firms that were beginning to realize the benefits of research-based integrated marketing programs.

Professionalism: The Modern Era

In the middle 1940s personal selling became more professional. Not only did buyers begin to demand more from salespeople, but they also grew intolerant of high-pressure, fast-talking salespeople, preferring instead a well-informed, customer-oriented salesperson. In 1947, the *Harvard Business Review* published "Low-Pressure Selling,"[10] a classic article followed by many others that called for salespeople to increase the effectiveness of their sales efforts by improving their professional demeanor.

An emphasis on **sales professionalism** is the keynote of the current era. The term has varied meanings, but in this context we use it to mean a customer-oriented approach that uses truthful, nonmanipulative tactics to satisfy the long-term needs

EXHIBIT 2.1 Continued Evolution of Personal Selling

Change	Salesforce Response
Intensified competition	More emphasis on developing and maintaining trust-based, long-term customer relationships
More emphasis on improving sales productivity	Increased use of technology (e.g., laptop computers, electronic mail, fax machines)
	Increased use of lower-cost-per-contact methods (e.g., telemarketing for some customers)
	More emphasis on profitability (e.g., gross margin) objectives
Fragmentation of traditional customer bases	Sales specialists for specific customer types
	Multiple sales channels (e.g., major accounts programs, telemarketing, electronic networks)
	Globalization of sales efforts
Customers dictating quality standards ad inventory/shipping procedures to be met by vendors	Team selling
	Salesforce compensation sometimes based on customer satisfaction and team performance
Demand for in-depth, specialized knowledge as an input to purchase decisions	Team selling
	More emphasis on customer-oriented sales training

of both the customer and the selling firm. The effective salesperson of today is no longer a mere presenter of information but now must stand equipped to respond to a variety of customer needs before, during, and after the sale. In addition, salespeople must be able to work effectively with others in their organizations to meet or exceed customer expectations.

The current stage in the evolution of the sales professional is aptly illustrated in a *Selling* magazine interview with Stephen E. Heiman, a leading sales consultant and trainer:

> The future will call increasingly for non-manipulative sales skills. Twisting a customer's need to fit our product or service is "yesterday's way of selling," says Heiman. The new way requires an ability to "ask, listen, and understand the issues behind the product need," he says. Forget the notion that your job is to tell the customer why your product is better than all the rest. "The major job you have is understanding the customer's concept," Heiman maintains. "Unless you're perceived to be making a contribution to your customer's success," Heiman says, "you're not ready for selling in the 21st century."[11]

Future evolution is inevitable as tomorrow's salesperson responds to a more complex, dynamic environment. Also, increased sophistication of buyers and of new technologies will demand more from the next generation of salespeople. Exhibit 2.1 summarizes some of the likely events of the future.[12]

Contributions of Personal Selling

Although advertising has traditionally captured most of the attention of students and researchers, personal selling is actually the most important part of marketing communications for most business firms. This is particularly true in firms that engage in business-to-business marketing. More money is spent on personal selling than on any other form of marketing communications, whether it be advertising, sales promotion, publicity, or public relations.

The sizable investment in personal selling is reflected in the estimated costs of employing a salesperson. A common denominator of this investment is the **cost per sales call index** as calculated by various organizations. For example, *Sales and Marketing Management* magazine, a well-known source, estimates an approximate cost range of $80–242 for a single sales call.[13] Multiply this estimate by multiple sales calls per day for each salesperson, and extend the mathematics for an entire year, and the conclusion is clear—personal selling is expensive. A sales manager's response is to ask, how can we make such an investment pay off? Indeed, this may be the most crucial question a sales manager deals with, at both strategic and tactical levels. We now take a look at how this investment is justified by reviewing the contributions of personal selling to society in general, to the employing firm, and to customers.

Salespeople and Society

Salespeople contribute to their nations' economic growth in two basic ways. They act as stimuli for economic transactions, and they further the diffusion of innovation.

SALESPEOPLE AS ECONOMIC STIMULI Salespeople are expected to stimulate action in the business world—hence the term **economic stimuli.** In a fluctuating economy, salespeople make invaluable contributions by assisting in recovery cycles and by helping to sustain periods of relative prosperity. As the world economic system deals with issues such as increased globalization of business, more emphasis on customer satisfaction, and building competitiveness through quality improvement programs, it is expected that salespeople will be recognized as a key force in executing the appropriate strategies and tactics necessary for survival and growth.

SALESPEOPLE AND DIFFUSION OF INNOVATION Salespeople play a critical role in the **diffusion of innovation,** the process whereby new products, services, and ideas are distributed to the members of society. Consumers who are likely to be early adopters of an innovation often rely on salespeople as a primary source of information. Frequently, well-informed, specialized salespeople provide useful information to potential consumers who then purchase from a lower-cost outlet. The role of salespeople in the diffusion of industrial products and services is particularly crucial. Imagine trying to purchase a companywide computer system without the assistance of a competent salesperson or sales team!

While acting as an agent of innovation, the salesperson invariably encounters a strong resistance to change in the latter stages of the diffusion process. The status quo seems to be extremely satisfactory to many parties, even though, in the long run, change is necessary for continued progress or survival. By encouraging the adoption of innovative products and services, salespeople may indeed be making a positive contribution to society.

Salespeople and the Employing Firm

Because salespeople are in direct contact with the all-important customer, they can make valuable contributions to their employers. Salespeople contribute to their firms as revenue producers, as sources of market research and feedback, and as candidates for management positions.

SALESPEOPLE AS REVENUE PRODUCERS Salespeople occupy the somewhat unique role of **revenue producers** in their firms. Consequently, they usually feel the brunt of that pressure along with the management of the firm. Although accountants and financial staff are concerned with profitability in bottom-line terms, salespeople are constantly reminded of their responsibility to achieve a healthy "top line" on the profit and loss statement. This should not suggest that salespeople are concerned only with sales revenue and not with overall profitability. Indeed, salespeople are increasingly responsible for improving profitability, not only by producing sales revenues but also by improving the productivity of their actions.

MARKET RESEARCH AND FEEDBACK Because salespeople spend so much time in direct contact with their customers, it is only logical that they would play an important role in market research and in providing feedback to their firms. For example, on a weekly basis, regional sales managers from the Discovery Channel discuss details of the past week's activity with each of their sales representatives. On an ongoing basis, Discovery Channel sales managers encourage new ideas from the salesforce, and actively seek input while working with salespeople in the field. This regular solicitation of ideas helps to improve sales performance, formulate future strategies, and build a sales culture based on communication and cooperation.[14]

Some would argue that salespeople are not trained as market researchers, or that salespeople's time could be better used than in research and feedback activities. Many firms, however, refute this argument by finding numerous ways to capitalize on the salesforce as a reservoir of ideas. It is not an exaggeration to say that many firms have concluded that they cannot afford to operate in the absence of salesforce feedback and research.

SALESPEOPLE AS FUTURE MANAGERS In recent years, marketing and sales personnel have been in strong demand for upper management positions. Recognizing the need for a top management trained in sales, many firms use the sales job as an entry-level position that provides a foundation for future assignments. As progressive firms continue to emphasize customer orientation as a basic operating concept, it is only natural that salespeople who have learned how to meet customer needs will be good candidates for management jobs. For more on salespeople as future managers, see "Professional Selling in the 21st Century: The Value of Sales Experience."

Salespeople and the Customer

Extensive research by Learning International, a large training and consulting firm, reveals the expectations that buyers have of salespeople. According to respondents of a Learning International survey, buyers like to deal with salespeople who

- are honest

PROFESSIONAL SELLING IN THE 21ST CENTURY

The Value of Sales Experience

Jerry Heffel, president of The Southwestern Company, comments on the importance of sales experience as preparation for upper management positions:

Peter Drucker wrote many years ago that the purpose of business can be stated succinctly: The purpose of business is to create a customer. In well-managed businesses, every level of management—from the CEO to the first-line supervisor—should be oriented toward creating and retaining customers. Salespeople are the crucial spark that ignites a prospect into a customer, and having that first-hand experience is enormously important at higher levels of management. Here at Southwestern, every single person in sales and marketing management started as a direct salesperson, making between 4 and 10 thousand one-on-one presentations before moving into their present positions. For more than 130 years, our effectiveness in helping college students in our summer program has been directly related to the emotional intelligence that each of us gained from those first-hand experiences in selling.

- understand general business and economic trends, as well as the buyer's business
- provide guidance throughout the sales process
- help the buyer to solve problems
- have a pleasant personality and a good professional appearance
- coordinate all aspects of the product and service to provide a total package[15]

The overall conclusion is that buyers expect salespeople to contribute to the success of the buyer's firm. Buyers value the information furnished by salespeople, and more than ever before, they value the problem-solving skills of salespeople. See "An Ethical Dilemma" for a scenario in which the salesperson must think about where to draw the line in sharing information with customers.

An Ethical Dilemma

Terry Kelly, sales representative for EFAX, a computer software company, has just concluded a sales call with Landnet, one of his distributors. During the call, purchasing agent Linda Meyer mentioned that Ron Hawkins, Landnet's top salesperson, had suddenly resigned and moved out of the state. Ms. Meyer said that this unexpected resignation could not have come at a worse time, as several key customer contracts were pending renewal, and Landnet had no candidates to replace Hawkins. On his way to his next sales call with Netserve, his largest distributor, Terry debated whether or not he should share the news of Hawkins' resignation. After all, the buyer at Netserve viewed Terry as a great source of market information, and Terry figured that the Netserve buyer would hear the news anyway before the day was over. What should Terry do?

As salespeople serve their customers, they simultaneously serve their employers and society. When the interests of these parties conflict, the salesperson can be caught in the middle. By learning to resolve these conflicts as a routine part of their jobs, salespeople further contribute to developing a business system based on progress through problem solving. An important part of resolving potential conflict between customers and salespeople is to have a customer-oriented code of ethics for salespeople. An example of such a code is shown in Exhibit 2.2.

EXHIBIT 2.2   Code of Ethics for Professional Salespeople

As a Certified Professional Salesperson, I pledge to the following people and organizations:

The Customer. In all customer relationships, I pledge to	The Company. In relationships with my employer, coworkers, and other parties whom I represent, I will	The Competition. Regarding those with whom I compete in the marketplace, I promise to
Maintain honesty and integrity in my relationships with customers and prospective customers.	Use their resources that are at my disposal for legitimate business purposes only	Obtain competitive information only through legal and ethical methods.
Accurately represent my product or service to place the customer or prospective customer in a position to make a decision consistent with the principle of mutuality of benefit and profit to the buyer and seller.	Respect and protect proprietary and confidential information entrusted to me by my company.	Portray my competitors and their products and services only in a manner that is honest and truthful and that reflects accurate information that can or has been substantiated.
Keep abreast of all pertinent information that would assist my customers in achieving their goals as they relate to my product(s) or service(s).		

Classification of Personal Selling Jobs

Because there are so many unique sales jobs, the term *salesperson* is not by itself very descriptive. A salesperson could be a flower vendor at a busy downtown intersection or the sales executive negotiating the sale of Boeing aircraft to the People's Republic of China.

We briefly discuss six types of personal selling jobs:

- sales support
- new business
- existing business
- inside sales (nonretail)
- direct-to-consumer sales
- combination sales jobs

Sales Support

Sales support personnel are not usually involved in the direct solicitation of purchase orders. Rather, their primary responsibility is dissemination of information and performance of other activities designed to stimulate sales. They might concentrate at the end-user level or another level in the channel of distribution to support the overall sales effort. They may report to another salesperson, who is responsible for direct handling of purchase orders, or to the sales manager. There are two well-known categories of support salespeople: missionary or detail salespeople and technical support salespeople.

Missionary salespeople usually work for a manufacturer but may also be found working for brokers and manufacturing representatives, especially in the grocery industry. There are strong similarities between sales missionaries and religious missionaries. Like their counterparts, sales missionaries are expected to "spread the word" with the purpose of conversion—to customer status. Once converted, the customer receives reinforcing messages, new information, and the benefit of the missionary's activities to strengthen the relationship between buyer and seller.

In the pharmaceutical industry, the **detailer** is a fixture. Detailers working at the physician level furnish valuable information regarding the capabilities and limitations of medications in an attempt to get the physician to prescribe their product. Another sales representative from the same pharmaceutical company will sell the medication to the wholesaler or pharmacist, but it is the detailer's job to support the direct sales effort by calling on physicians.

Technical specialists are sometimes considered to be sales support personnel. These **technical support salespeople** may assist in design and specification processes, installation of equipment, training of the customer's employees, and follow-up service of a technical nature. They are sometimes part of a sales team that includes another salesperson who specializes in identifying and satisfying customer needs by recommending the appropriate product or service.

New Business

New business is generated for the selling firm by adding new customers or introducing new products to the marketplace. Two types of new-business salespeople are pioneers and order-getters.

Pioneers, as the term suggests, are constantly involved with either new products, new customers, or both. Their task requires creative selling and the ability to counter the resistance to change that will likely be present in prospective customers. Pioneers are well represented in the sale of business franchises, in which the sales representatives travel from city to city seeking new franchisees.

Order-getters are salespeople who actively seek orders, usually in a highly competitive environment. Although all pioneers are also order-getters, the reverse is not true. An order-getter may serve existing customers on an ongoing basis, whereas the pioneer moves on to new customers as soon as possible. Order-getters may seek new business by selling an existing customer additional items from the product line. A well-known tactic is to establish a relationship with a customer by selling a single product from the line, then to follow up with subsequent sales calls for other items from the product line.

Most corporations emphasize sales growth, and salespeople operating as pioneers and order-getters are at the heart of sales growth objectives. The pressure to perform in these roles is fairly intense; the results are highly visible. For these reasons, the new-business salesperson is often among the elite in any company's salesforce.

Existing Business

In direct contrast to new-business salespeople, other salespeople's primary responsibility is to maintain relationships with existing customers. Salespeople who specialize in maintaining existing business include **order-takers.** These salespeople frequently work for wholesalers, and as the term *order-taker* implies, they are not too involved in creative selling. Route salespeople who work an established customer base, taking routine reorders of stock items, are order-takers. They sometimes follow a pioneer salesperson and take over the account after the pioneer has made the initial sale.

These salespeople are no less valuable to their firms than the new-business salespeople, but creative selling skills are less important to this category of sales personnel. Their strengths tend to be reliability and competence in assuring customer convenience. Customers grow to depend on the services provided by this type of salesperson. As most markets are becoming more competitive, the role of existing-business salespeople is sometimes critical to prevent erosion of the customer base.

Many firms, believing that it is easier to protect and maintain profitable customers than it is to find replacement customers, are reinforcing sales efforts to existing customers. For example, Frito-Lay uses 18,000 route service salespeople to call on retail customers at least three times weekly. Larger customers see their Frito-Lay representative on a daily basis. These salespeople spend a lot of their time educating customers about the profitability of Frito-Lay's snack foods, which leads to increased sales for both the retailer and for Frito-Lay.[16]

Inside Sales

In this text, **inside sales** refers to nonretail salespeople who remain in their employer's place of business while dealing with customers. The inside-sales operation has received considerable attention in recent years, not only as a supplementary sales tactic but also as an alternative to field selling.

Inside sales can be conducted on an active or passive sales basis. Active inside sales include the solicitation of entire orders, either as part of a telemarketing operation or when customers walk into the seller's facilities. Passive inside sales imply the acceptance, rather than solicitation, of customer orders, although it is common practice for these transactions to include add-on sales attempts. We should note that customer service personnel sometimes function as inside-sales personnel as an ongoing part of their jobs.

Direct-to-Consumer Sales

Direct-to-consumer salespeople are the most numerous type. There are more than 4.5 million retail salespeople in this country and perhaps another million selling real estate, insurance, and securities. Add to this figure another several million selling direct to the consumer for such companies as Tupperware, Mary Kay, and Avon.

This diverse category of salespeople ranges from the part-time, often temporary salesperson in a retail store to the highly educated, professionally trained stockbroker on Wall Street. As a general statement, the more challenging direct-to-consumer sales positions are those involving the sale of intangible services such as insurance and financial services.

Combination Sales Jobs

Now that we have reviewed some of the basic types of sales jobs, let us consider the salesperson who performs multiple types of sales jobs within the framework of a single position. We use the case of the territory manager's position with Beecham Products, U.S.A., to illustrate the **combination sales job** concept. Beecham, whose products include Aqua-Fresh toothpaste, markets a wide range of consumer goods to food, drug, variety, and mass merchandisers. The territory manager's job blends responsibilities for developing new business, maintaining and stimulating existing business, and performing sales support activities.

During a typical day in the field, the Beecham territory manager is involved in sales support activities such as merchandising and in-store promotion at the individual retail store level. Maintaining contact and goodwill with store personnel is another routine sales support activity. The territory manager also makes sales calls on chain headquarters personnel to handle existing business and to seek new business. And it is the territory manager who introduces new Beecham products in the marketplace.

Characteristics of Sales Careers

Although individual opinions will vary, the ideal career for most individuals offers a bright future, including good opportunities for financial rewards and job advancement. As you read the following sections on the characteristics of sales careers, you might think about what you expect from a career and whether your expectations could be met in a sales career. The characteristics to be discussed are

- job security
- advancement opportunities
- immediate feedback
- prestige
- job variety
- independence
- compensation
- boundary-role effects

Job Security

Salespeople are revenue producers and thus enjoy relatively good job security compared with other occupational groups. Certainly, individual job security depends on individual performance, but in general, salespeople are usually the last group to be negatively affected by personnel cutbacks.

Competent salespeople also have some degree of job security based on the universality of their basic sales skills. In many cases, salespeople are able to successfully move to another employer, maybe even change industries, because sales skills are largely transferable. For salespeople working in declining or stagnant industries, this is heartening news.

Furthermore, projections by the U.S Department of Labor indicate strong demand for salespeople in all categories in the future (see Exhibit 2.3). And growth in the number of salespeople should bring a corresponding growth in the numbers of sales management positions. According to Exhibit 2.3, there are particularly good opportunities in service industries, including financial services.

Advancement Opportunities

As the business world continues to become more competitive, the advancement opportunities for salespeople will continue to be an attractive dimension of sales careers. In highly competitive markets, individuals and companies that are successful in determining and meeting customer needs will be rewarded. A case in point is Carly Fiorina, CEO of Hewlett-Packard, who began her career as a sales representative for AT&T. She later led the spinoff of Lucent Technologies from AT&T and used her sales skills to raise $3 billion on Wall Street to fund the largest public offering in U.S. history. According to Jo Weiss of Catalyst, Inc., a company that tracks women in business, a sales background was key to Ms. Fiorina's ascent to the top at Hewlett-Packard. Joel Ronning, CEO of Digital River, an e-commerce company in Minneapolis, adds, "Any good CEO has to understand sales. You're constantly selling in all aspects of your life. In my early sales experience, I learned persistence and not to take rejection personally, which made all the difference in the world."[17]

Immediate Feedback

Salespeople receive constant, immediate feedback on their job performance. Usually, the results of their efforts can be plainly observed by both salespeople and their sales mangers—a source of motivation and job satisfaction. On a daily basis, salespeople receive direct feedback from their customers, and this can be stimulating, challenging, and productive. According to a survey conducted by *Purchasing* magazine, business buyers want suppliers to work closely with them to raise performance levels, contain costs, and develop the latest technologies. The same survey indicates a need for salespeople to overcome obstacles and solve problems that inhibit the accomplishment of mutually agreed-on goals. With such buyer expectations, it is readily apparent that seeking and using feedback is an important part of salespeople's careers.[18]

Prestige

Traditionally, sales has not been a prestigious occupation in the eyes of the general public. There is some evidence that as the general public learns more about the activities and qualifications of professional salespeople, the image of salespeople, and

EXHIBIT 2.3 Occupational Outlook for Salespeople

Job Type	1996 Employment	Projected Growth 1996–2006 Percentage
Manufacturers and Wholesale	1,557,000	10–20
Services Sales Representative	694,000	36 or more
Real Estate	408,000	0–9
Securities/Financial Services	263,000	36 or more
Insurance Agents	409,000	0–9
Retail	4,522,000	10–20

thus the prestige of selling, is improving. An analysis of the popular press (excluding business publications) reveals that there are more positive than negative mentions of news-making salespeople. In a positive light, salespeople are frequently seen as knowledgeable, well trained, educated, and capable of solving customer problems. The negative aspects of salespeople's image often center on deception and high-pressure techniques.[19]

The struggling, down-and-out huckster as depicted by Willy Loman in Arthur Miller's 1949 classic *Death of a Salesman* is hardly typical of the professional salesperson of today and the future. Professional salespeople destroy such unfavorable stereotypes, and they would not jeopardize customer relationships by using high-pressure sales techniques to force a premature sale.[20] These perceptions are especially true in the business world, where encounters with professional salespeople are commonplace.

Job Variety

Salespeople rarely vegetate due to boredom. Their jobs are multifaceted and dynamic. For a person seeking the comfort of a well-established routine, sales might not be a good career choice. In sales, day-to-day variation on the job is the norm. Customers change, new products and services are developed, and competition introduces new elements at a rapid pace.

The opportunity to become immersed in the job and bring creativity to bear is demonstrated by General Mills, whose salesforce has been named one of the best in America. According to John Maschuzik, vice president of sales in the western United States, salespeople's customization of promotional efforts for their customers is crucial to the company's success. Mr. Maschuzik says that General Mills gives their salespeople a lot of latitude and the opportunity to be creative in spending retail promotion money.[21]

Independence

Sales jobs often allow independence of action. This independence is frequently a by-product of decentralized sales operations in which salespeople live and work away from headquarters, therefore working from their homes and making their own plans for extensive travel.

Independence of action and freedom to make decisions are usually presented as advantages that sales positions have over tightly supervised jobs. College students who prefer sales careers rate freedom to make decisions second only to salary as an important job consideration.[22] Despite its appeal, however, independence does present some problems. New recruits working from their homes may find the lack of a company office somewhat disorienting. They may need an office environment to relate to, especially if their past work experience provided regular contact in an office environment.

The independence of action traditionally enjoyed by salespeople is being scrutinized by sales managers more heavily now than in the past. The emphasis on sales productivity, accomplished in part through cost containment, is encouraging sales managers to take a more active role in dictating travel plans and sales-call schedules.

Compensation

Salesforce compensation is discussed in detail in a later module, but a few generalizations are in order now. Compensation is generally thought to be a strong advantage of sales careers. Pay is closely tied to performance, especially if commissions and bonuses are part of the pay package.

Starting salaries for inexperienced salespersons with a college degree typically average $40,000. Between the extremes of the highly experienced salesperson and the inexperienced recruit, an average salesperson earns approximately $45,000–60,000 per year. More experienced salespersons, including those who deal with large customers, often earn in the $85,000–135,000 range.[23]

Boundary-Role Effects

Salespersons are **boundary-role performers.** That is, they occupy boundary-spanning positions between their employers and their customers. Their loyalties are sometimes torn between customer demand and the expectations of their company or their sales manager. For example, the company may want to sell at list price, whereas the customer demands a discount. The salesperson is caught between the two parties and somehow must resolve the situation. This is but one example of the **role conflict** routinely experienced by salespeople.

Another dimension of boundary-spanning jobs such as sales jobs is **role ambiguity.** It occurs when the salesperson is unsure about what to do in a situation in which no policy or procedure applies. This is not an uncommon event, given the variable nature of sales situations, which sometimes require innovative problem solving.

The uncertainty arising from a lack of direction can contribute to **role stress.** Role conflict may also contribute to role stress, which salespeople, sales managers, organizational psychologist, and sales researchers all agree is strongly associated with sales careers. There is no escaping the conclusion that sales is a high-visibility, "spotlight" position. The revenue-production responsibilities of salespeople create considerable pressure to perform. When customer expectations are at odds with the employer's expectations, the pressure rises. See "An Ethical Dilemma" for a scenario in which the salesperson must think about where to draw the line in sharing information with customers.

An Ethical Dilemma

Charles Lambert, sales manager for YourWay, a manufacturer of customized furniture, believed in putting his salespeople under pressure to perform. During his 20 years in sales management, Mr. Lambert had always pushed his salespeople to maximize short-run sales volume. Simply put, Lambert advocated that his salespeople sell as much product as possible, as soon as possible, and at the highest possible price. Recently, the retail buyers of YourWay furniture had begun requesting, even demanding, lower prices and more flexible buying arrangements that would reduce their inventory carrying costs. YourWay salespeople were also asking Mr. Lambert to reconsider his stance on pricing and the maximization of short-term volume. Charles Lambert is unfazed by these developments, even though YourWay recently lost a key retail chain customer. His reaction was to fire the sales representative who, in Lambert's judgment, "lost the account." The remaining salespeople were then urged to increase their sales levels to compensate for the lost volume. Is there anything unethical about Mr. Lambert's approach to sales management? If you were Mr. Lambert's supervisor, would you have any concerns about his management style?

For most salespeople, stress is simply part of the job. It can add an element of excitement to the workday and provide motivation. However, if it becomes excessive, it may produce detrimental results. Successful salespeople are usually driven by a sense of purpose and believe that the opportunities provided by their jobs are worth the efforts required to deal with stress.

Qualifications and Skills Required for Success by Salespersons

Because there are so many different types of jobs in sales, it is rather difficult to generalize about the qualifications and skills needed for success. This list would have to vary according to the details of a given job. Even then, it is reasonable to believe that for any given job, different persons with different skills could be successful. These conclusions have been reached after decades of research that has tried to correlate sales performance with physical traits, mental abilities, personality characteristics, and the experience and background of the salesperson.[24]

Many of the skills and characteristics leading to success in sales would do the same in practically any professional business occupation. For example, the *Occupational Outlook Handbook* published by the U.S. Department of Labor points out the importance of various personal attributes for success in sales, including the following: initiative, tact, patience, good communications skills, motivation, honesty, and maturity.[25] Who could dispute the value of such traits for any occupation?

Success in sales is increasingly being thought of in terms of a strategic team effort, rather than the characteristics of individual salespersons. For example, three studies of more than 200 companies that employ 25,000 salespersons in the United States and Australia found that being customer oriented and cooperating as a team player were critical to salespersons' success.[26] For more on teamwork, see "Professional Selling in the 21st Century: The Importance of Teamwork in Sales."

Being careful not to suggest that sales success is solely a function of individual traits, let us consider some of the skills and qualifications that are thought to be especially critical for success in most sales jobs. Five factors that seem to be particularly important for success in sales are empathy, ego drive, ego strength, verbal communication skills, and enthusiasm. These factors have been selected after reviewing three primary sources of information:

- a study of more than 750,000 salespeople in 15,000 companies (Greenberg and Greenberg)[27]
- two reviews of four decades of research on factors related to sales success (Comer and Dubinsky; and Brown, Leigh, and Haygood)[28]
- surveys of sales executives[29]

PROFESSIONAL SELLING IN THE 21ST CENTURY

The Importance of Teamwork in Sales
Jerry Heffel, president of The Southwestern Company, offers his perspective on teamwork:

Sometimes the salesperson is referred to as the lead car in the business train. But just having a lead car doesn't make a train. For this reason, a salesperson who is effective long-term is also an effective team player—he or she realizes they need coordinated involvement from many different parts of the organization in order to serve the customer. At the same time, whenever they see themselves as part of the customer's team, and that they are both striving for the same outcome, they become an indispensable part of the value chain for that customer. Southwestern's sales training philosophy stresses this team aspect: we tell our salespeople that they are the gas and oil of the free enterprise system, but they also need the tires, the car body, the drive train, and what's in the trunk to get anywhere significant.

Such a situation is described in "An Ethical Dilemma" on page 29.

Empathy

In a sales context, **empathy** (the ability to see things as others would see them) includes being able to read cues furnished by the customer to better determine the customer's viewpoint. According to Spiro and Weitz, empathy is crucial for successful interaction between a buyer and a seller.[30] An empathetic salesperson is presumably in a better position to tailor the sales presentation to the customer during the planning stages. More important, empathetic salespeople can adjust to feedback during the presentation.

The research of Greenberg and Greenberg found empathy to be a significant predictor of sales success. This finding was partially supported in the review by Comer and Dubinsky, who found empathy to be an important factor in consumer and insurance sales but not in retail or industrial sales. However, Pilling and Eroglu found that retail buyers were more likely to listen to future sales presentations and make purchases from salespeople who displayed empathy.[31] Even though some studies do not find direct links between salesperson empathy and success, empathy is generally accepted as an important trait for successful salespeople.[32] As relationship selling grows in importance, empathy logically will become even more important for sales success.

Ego Drive

In a sales context, **ego drive** (an indication of the degree of determination a person has to achieve goals and overcome obstacles in striving for success) is manifested as an inner need to persuade others in order to achieve personal gratification. Greenberg and Greenberg point out the complementary relationship between empathy and ego drive that is necessary for sales success. The salesperson who is extremely empathetic but lacks ego drive may have problems in taking active steps to confirm a sale. However, a salesperson with more ego drive than empathy may ignore the customer's viewpoint in an ill-advised, overly anxious attempt to gain commitment from the customer.

Ego Strength

The degree to which a person is able to achieve an approximation of inner drives is **ego strength.** Salespeople with high levels of ego strength are likely to be self-assured and self-accepting. Salespeople with healthy egos are better equipped to deal with the possibility of rejection throughout the sales process. They are probably less likely to experience sales call reluctance and are resilient enough to overcome the disappointment of inevitable lost sales.

Salespeople with strong ego drives who are well equipped to do their job will likely be high in **self-efficacy;** that is, they will strongly believe that they can be successful on the job. In situations in which their initial efforts meet resistance, rejection, or failure, salespeople high in self-efficacy are likely to persist in pursuing their goals. For example, Gene Benassi, a sales representative with office furniture supplier Herman Miller, persevered with the Pentagon for more than 10 years, occasionally receiving small contracts. Finally, he landed a large, 15-year contract. As noted by a Herman Miller executive, Mr. Benassi "never gave up on getting a big deal. With teamwork and perseverance and the ability to build a long-term relationship, he finally got the customer to sign."[33]

Interpersonal Communication Skills

Interpersonal communication skills, including listening and questioning, are essential for sales success. An in-depth study of 300 sales executives, salespeople, and customers of 24 major sales companies in North America, Europe, and Japan found that effective salespeople are constantly seeking ways to improve communications skills that enable them to develop, explain, and implement customer solutions. The companies in the study are some of the best in the world at professional selling: Sony, Xerox, American Airlines, Fuji, and Scott paper.[34]

To meet customer needs, salespeople must be able to solicit opinions, listen effectively, and confirm customer needs and concerns. They must be capable of probing customer expectations with open- and closed-ended questions and responding in a flexible manner to individual personalities and different business cultures in ways that demonstrate respect for differences.[35] This requires adaptable, socially intelligent salespeople, especially when dealing with multicultural customers.[36]

The importance of communications skills has been recognized by sales managers, recruiters, and sales researchers. These skills can be continually refined throughout a sales career, a positive factor from both a personal and a career development perspective.

Enthusiasm

When sales executives and recruiters discuss qualifications for sales positions, they invariably include **enthusiasm.** They are usually referring to dual dimensions of enthusiasm—an enthusiastic attitude in a general sense and a special enthusiasm for selling. On-campus recruiters have told us that they seek students who are well beyond "interested in sales" to the point of truly being enthusiastic about career opportunities in sales. Recruiters are somewhat weary of "selling sales" as a viable career, and they welcome the job applicant who displays genuine enthusiasm for the field.

Comments on Qualifications and Skills

The qualifications and skills needed for sales success are different today from those required for success two decades ago. As the popularity of relationship selling grows, the skills necessary for sales success will evolve to meet the needs of the marketplace. For example, Greenberg and Greenberg's research has identified what they call an "emerging factor" for sales success, a strong motivation to provide service to the customer. They contrast this **service motivation** with ego drive by noting that, although ego drive relates to persuading others, service motivation comes from desiring the approval of others. For example, a salesperson may be extremely gratified to please a customer through superior postsale service. Greenberg and Greenberg conclude that most salespeople will need both service motivation and ego drive to succeed, although they note that extremely high levels of both attributes are not likely to exist in the same individual. A survey of 28,000 people in 59 major companies by the Forum Corporation reports that a service motivation, along with understanding and respect for customers, is far more effective than aggressive selling tactics in terms of generating sales.[37]

Our discussion of factors related to sales success is necessarily brief, as a fully descriptive treatment of the topic must be tied to a given sales position. Veteran sales managers and recruiters can often specify with amazing precision what qualifications and skills are needed to succeed in a given sales job. These assessments are usually based on a mixture of objective and subjective judgments that is discussed in the module on recruitment and selection later in the book.

Summary

1. **Describe the evolution of personal selling from ancient times to the modern era.** The history of personal selling can be traced as far back as ancient Greece. The Industrial Revolution enhanced the importance of salespeople, and personal selling as we know it

today had its roots in the early twentieth century. The current era of sales professionalism represents a further evolution.
2. **Explain the contributions of personal selling to society, business firms, and customers.** Salespeople contribute to society by acting as stimuli in the economic process and by assisting in the diffusion of innovation. They contribute to their employers by producing revenue, performing research and feedback activities, and comprising a pool of future managers. They contribute to customers by providing timely knowledge to assist in solving problems.
3. **Describe different types of personal selling jobs.** Among the countless number of different personal selling jobs are the following six types: sales support, new business, existing business, inside sales (nonretail), direct-to-consumer sales, and combination jobs. Sales support positions include missionary or detail salespeople and technical support salespeople. Two types of new-business salespeople are pioneers and order-getters. The primary responsibility of existing-business salespeople is to maintain relationships with present customers through routine sales calls and follow-up. Inside sales in nonretail settings is typified in telemarketing operations and is also used to handle walk-in sales transactions. Direct-to-consumer sales include retail selling, as well as the sale of insurance, securities, and real estate. Combination sales jobs are commonplace and may combine new-business selling with sales support and existing-business responsibilities, as shown in the Beecham Products example. Other combinations are also frequently encountered.
4. **Discuss the characteristics of sales careers.** Sales careers are characterized by relatively good job security and reasonable opportunities for advancement. Salespeople get immediate feedback on the job, and this may explain why job satisfaction for salespeople is higher than in many other occupational groups. The prestige of selling seems to be improving gradually. An advantage of sales careers is that they offer the salesperson the chance to become totally involved in a creative, dynamic occupation in which boredom is rare. Sales careers have long been associated with independence of action, although sales managers lately are monitoring sales activities more closely to improve sales productivity. Salespeople are paid fairly well, with those receiving incentive pay such as commissions being paid better than those on a straight salary. Salespeople occupy boundary roles between their customers and their employers. These roles often produce conflict and stress due to pressure to perform well for multiple parties.
5. **Describe the skills and characteristics required for success in most sales positions.** Although no universal profile of the successful salesperson exists, research indicates certain characteristics may be associated with sales success, namely, empathy, ego drive, ego strength, interpersonal communication skills, and enthusiasm.

Understanding Sales Management Terms

- Canned sales presentation
- Sales professionalism
- Cost per sales call index
- Economic stimuli
- Diffusion of innovation
- Revenue producers
- Sales support personnel
- Missionary salespeople
- Detail salespeople
- Technical support salespeople
- Pioneers
- Order-getters
- Order-takers
- Inside sales
- Combination sales job
- Boundary-role performers
- Role conflict
- Role ambiguity
- Role stress
- Empathy
- Ego drive
- Ego strength
- Self-efficacy
- Interpersonal communication skills
- Enthusiasm
- Service motivation

Developing Sales Management Knowledge

1. What factors will influence the continued evolution of personal selling?

2. How do salespeople contribute to our society? Are there negative aspects of personal selling from a societal perspective?
3. What are the primary contributions made by salespeople to their employers?
4. Most businesses would have a difficult time surviving without the benefits of the salespeople who call on them. Do you agree?
5. What are the differences in key responsibilities of missionary salespeople and pioneer salespersons? What recurring problems would you expect each type to encounter as they call on their customers?
6. How would you assess sales in terms of the criteria for an ideal career presented in this chapter?
7. How do sales jobs prepare individuals for career advancement?
8. Salespeople enjoy relatively good job security and opportunities for advancement into management. Why is this so, and will these conditions hold true in the future?
9. Explain what is meant by the statement that "salespeople are boundary-role performers."
10. What factors contributed to job stress for salespeople?

Building Sales Management Skills

1. a. An important part of being a sales professional is to practice ethical selling. For the situations that follow, rate each one as A, B, or C, in which
   A = Unethical/unprofessional
   B = Justifiable in some circumstances
   C = No problem, just a good business practice
   Be prepared to defend your responses.
   1. The salesperson exaggerates how quickly orders will be delivered to get a sale.
   2. The salesperson stresses only positive aspects of the product, omitting possible problems the purchasing firm might have with it.
   3. In a shortage situation, the salesperson allocates product shipments to purchasing agents the seller personally likes.
   4. The salesperson attempts to use the economic power of his or her company to obtain concessions from the buyer.
   5. The salesperson gives a purchaser who was one of the best customers a gift worth $50 or more at Christmas or other occasions.
   6. The salesperson gives a potential customer a gift worth $50 or more at Christmas or other occasions.

   b. As a sales manager, how would you encourage your salespeople to sell ethically? (*Source:* Adapted from Ramon A. Avila, Thomas N. Ingram, Raymond W. Laforge, and Michael R. Williams, *The Professional Selling Skills Workbook* (Fort Worth, TX: The Dryden Press, 1996), 31–34.)

2. Assume you are a salesperson for a packaging manufacturing company that supplies retail stores with custom-imprinted shopping bags. The company has manufacturing facilities in Texas, Georgia, New York, and California. There are five functional areas in the company: marketing (includes sales), production, finance and accounting, customer service and shipping, and human resources. You work out of the California plant, which serves the United States west of the Rocky Mountains. Within the marketing department, your key contact is the product manager who routinely interacts with individuals from production, customer service, and shipping to coordinate production runs with promised delivery dates. The product manager has no direct authority over any of the personnel in production or customer service and shipping. For the following situations, explain how you would try to gain the cooperation of the right people to meet customer needs.

   Scenario A: A large customer unexpectedly runs out of shopping bags and is requesting a shipment within 72 hours. Normal lead time for existing customers is 10 working days. Production is fully booked, that is, there is no idle capacity in the California plant.

   Scenario B: A long-time customer buys three different sizes of shopping bags, all shipped in identical corrugated boxes. The smallest size bags are packed 500 to a box, the medium-size bags 250 to a box, and the largest 100 to a box. Black and white labels on one end of the corrugated boxes denote bag sizes. The customer wants brightly colored labels of three different colors to denote bag size. According to the customer, store employees could then tell at a glance if stock for a particular size was running low and thus place prompt requests for reorders. Currently, the black and white labels are applied by a machine as part of the manufacturing process. The colored labels would have to be custom produced and hand-fed into the labeling machine, whereas existing labels are printed inexpensively in large quantities and fed automatically into the labeling machine.

3. Your knowledge of selling can help you get started in a sales career. Landing a job is like making a major sale in that your knowledge, skills, and attitudes must meet the needs of the employer. One way to match up with employer needs is to use the feature-advantage-benefit (FAB) approach to assess yourself relative to employer needs. In selling, a feature is a factual statement about the product or service, for example, "at 10 pounds, it is the lightest electrical motor in its performance category." An advantage describes how the product can be used or help the customer, for example, "it is light enough to be used in portable applications." The benefit is the favorable outcome the customer will experience from the advantage, for example, "your customers no longer will have to come to the repair center for assistance, as service reps will be able to use portable repair kits in the field." To translate this method to the job search, think of yourself as the "product." Select an appropriate company and discover what they are looking for in sales job applicants. You can use classified ads, the college placement center, personal contacts, or other sources to find a sales position that you are interested in. Using the following example as a starting point, complete a FAB worksheet that shows how you are qualified for the job. In a real job search, this information could be translated to your résumé or cover letter requesting an interview.

The FAB Job-Search Matrix (Example)

A Need	B Feature	C Advantage	D Benefit
Employer or Problem	Student		Employer
"This job requires . . ."	"I have . . ."	"This means . . ."	"You will . . ."
frequent sales presentations to individuals and groups	taken 10 classes that required presentations	I require limited or no training in making presentations	save on the cost of training; you have ability and confidence to be productive early

(List additional needs, features, advantages, and benefits.)

Making Sales Management Decisions

CASE 2.1 Concourse Catering Company

Background

Concourse Catering Company is a leading food supplier to major airports in the United States. Founded in 1968, the company has maintained its leading position in the market by providing high-quality, yet reasonably priced prepackaged meals to the airlines. In recent years, Concourse has branched into the employee cafeteria market for businesses located adjacent to airports in Atlanta, Chicago, Los Angeles, and New York.

The company has a salesforce of 100 that sells directly to the airlines and to the cafeteria customers. Salespersons are paid on a salary-plus-commission basis, which encourages the growth of annual sales volume in each sales territory. Both the airline and cafeteria markets are extremely competitive, and both markets are experiencing slow but fairly steady growth. In such a market environment, Concourse logically emphasizes customer retention as a major focus of its sales strategy.

Current Situation

Courtney Quinn was recently hired to replace retiring veteran Ken Clark as one of the eight Concourse sales representatives in the Los Angeles market. Having graduated from college just 3 months ago, Courtney had joined Concourse as an eager sales trainee. With her sales and sales management courses from college serving as a strong foundation, she had truly enjoyed her initial training. Courtney came out of the training program excited about her first "real" job and anxious to become a top performer.

Following initial sales training, Courtney began a 2-week swing through her future sales territory with Ken Clark. Clark introduced Courtney to the key contacts in each account and provided her with account profiles that detailed their buying history and future sales opportunities. Normally, the district sales manager, Bill Pennick, would accompany the outgoing and incoming salespersons when a territory personnel change was made. However, Pennick was busy preparing for the upcoming annual national sales meeting and left it up to Clark to familiarize Courtney with her new territory.

On their second day of sales calls together, Courtney and Ken were planning to visit Intermodal Container and Shipping, a large freight forwarding company near Los Angeles International Airport. Concourse has been supplying the large Intermodal employee cafeteria for the past year. They would meet with Nelson Gadlage, the cafeteria manager. On the way to visit Intermodal, the following conversation ensued:

Ken: Before we go to Intermodal, I need to stop by Best Buy and pick up a couple of cell phones for Gadlage.

Courtney: [jokingly] . . . Wow! What service! I wish I had someone to run errands for me during the day!

Ken: Well, I'm not exactly running an errand. The phones are not for Gadlage, it's just that I am doing him a favor . . . one of those things you do to keep the customer happy.

Courtney: Sure, I understand. So you are just picking up some phones that Intermodal has in for repair?

Ken: No. These are new phones that I am donating to a good cause. Hey, look, you might as well know the score. Gadlage has been leaning on me to make a contribution to his brother-in-law's campaign for state senator. This goes back several months, and I have been dropping a little cash on him from time to time. Now he wants more, and I agreed to furnish cell phones for two of his brother's staffers during the campaign.

Courtney: But I thought our company policy prohibits us from making contributions to political campaigns through our customers.

Ken: True, but Courtney, you will quickly learn in this business that sometimes you have to grease the wheels. We do a little favor for Gadlage, and he throws the majority of his cafeteria business our way. It's as simple as that.

Courtney: Well, I see it as a political contribution, and I'm not planning on continuing this practice once the territory is mine.

Ken: Fine, do what you've got to do. As for me, I see it as gesture of goodwill. You will find that very few customers expect such gestures, but with Gadlage, I am afraid that we wouldn't do nearly the volume we are without taking care of this request. Besides, nobody really gets hurt. I am paying for the phones out of my own pocket. I win, Concourse Catering wins, and Gadlage wins. One more thing, some of our veteran salespeople who have succeeded in a tough market for many years have told me they do similar things now and then.

After picking up the phones, Courtney and Ken proceeded to meet with Gadlage. During their visit, Courtney got the distinct feeling that Gadlage expected business as usual once she took over the territory. He mentioned several times that he was an avid supporter of his brother-in-law's campaign and thanked both Ken and Courtney for providing the phones. As Courtney and Ken were leaving, Gadlage made it a point to tell Courtney that he "looked forward to working with her to their mutual benefit."

Later that evening on her way home, Courtney began to wonder if she had made the right choice to join Concourse Catering in a sales position. Ken mentioned that some of the company's top performers were doing unethical things to keep their customers happy. Was this true? She explicitly remembered spending the better part of one morning in training discussing ethics and the company's policy on gift-giving, including political contributions. Maybe Ken was just saying that he was not alone in doing customers unauthorized favors. Or if the practice was common, maybe the company's managers were just ignoring it. Courtney recalled that her college had an honor system, yet some students routinely cheated on exams. She thought that maybe she was making a big deal out of the contribution of cell phones and that maybe she should continue the practice. After all, Ken had been successful for many years, and maybe his customers would expect her to follow in his footsteps. Courtney thought, what happens if I don't continue Ken's special favors? Will I make my sales quota and earn what I expected? Then again, she thought that maybe she should report Ken to Bill Pennick. She didn't really want to continue Ken's unauthorized methods, but she hated to ruin his reputation just as he was retiring. Ken was popular with his colleagues, and Courtney didn't want to alienate his friends, her future colleagues.

Questions

1. How would you handle this situation if you were Courtney?
2. What can be done to ensure that this type of situation does not happen again?

CASE 2.2 *Justin Webb's Career Dilemma*

Background

Justin Webb will graduate from the University of Arizona in 4 weeks, and he has been seeking an entry-level sales position. Justin appears to be a prime job candidate. He is an outstanding student. He has been on the Dean's List every semester and will graduate with honors. Justin will receive his bachelor's degree in business with majors in marketing and finance. He is also very active in school. He is a member of the student council, president of the university's American Marketing Association chapter, and a long jumper for the university's track team.

Justin is well liked by both teachers and friends. He has a strong zest for life that seems to permeate those with whom he comes in contact. One of Justin's professors describes him as follows:

Justin is a strong student and exhibits tremendous leadership potential. In class, he's always attentive and asks insightful questions. He is dependable, and other students look to him for advice and support. When working in group projects, his enthusiasm for learning is contagious, and other group members often elect him as the group leader or spokesperson. He has a confident, but not arrogant, attitude. He relates well to his peers but also to the faculty. On many occasions, I have observed his behavior in business settings such as our annual career fair, and I am certain that he is well prepared for the business world. He is mature and knows the value of hard work. He supplemented his track scholarship with part-time jobs to pay for 100 percent of his college education. He has my highest possible recommendation.

Justin's first choice for an employer is Dell Computer Company. He interviewed with a Dell representative who came to campus seeking entry-level sales candidates. Prior to his interview, Justin researched the company and carefully read the information that was available in the campus placement center. Desiring to learn more, he surfed the Web and went to the library to find additional sources of information on Dell. He discovered what he had expected—Dell's training was rated highly and their employee benefits package was generous. After thoroughly researching the company, he was convinced he wanted to work for Dell. His initial interview with Dell went so well he was granted additional interviews. These, too, went well, but Dell has informed Justin that hiring has been suspended for 60 days. Dell management is telling Justin that it is likely he will receive an offer, but there are no guarantees.

Meanwhile, Justin has a firm offer from Coca-Cola to begin work immediately on graduation. Coca-Cola has given Justin a week to decide on its offer, which would involve a relocation to its Atlanta headquarters. Coca-Cola is an attractive company to David, but he believes he would be happiest at Dell. At this point, Justin is considering accepting the Coca-Cola offer but switching to Dell if an offer materializes. A week has passed, and Justin is on the phone with the recruiter from Coca-Cola.

Questions

1. What qualifications and skills does Justin possess that would enable him to be a successful salesperson?
2. What would you do if you were Justin Webb?

MODULE 3

Personal Selling: Approaches and Process

Bryan Hollingsworth: Trustworthy Sales Professional

George F. Cram Company, a globe and map supplier, is fortunate to have Bryan Hollingsworth on its sales team. Hollingsworth knows that earning the customer's trust is the key to successful selling. Asked to define trust, he says, "To me, trust is an unwritten agreement between two parties for one party to perform a set of agreed-on activities and the other party to perform an agreed-on set of activities, and here's the key part of it—without fear of change from the other party. You trust me to do what I said I would, and I trust you to do the same. That's my definition."

According to Hollingsworth, salespeople must make an extra effort to show their trustworthiness. He believes that honest salespeople have nothing to hide and that they will be forthright with the buyer on all matters. For Hollingsworth, this begins when he first contacts a prospective customer. Rather than being evasive about why he wishes to see the prospect, Hollingsworth gets right to the point and refuses to be pushy if the prospect is not interested in buying globes or maps. Hollingsworth notes, "I'm not here to waste my time or theirs."

To gain the respect of the prospect, Hollingsworth does his homework and customizes his presentations to the buyer's situation and personal style: "Based on the response to the benefit, I can usually tell what kind of personality I'm dealing with. Some individuals want the bottom line right away, and if they say they need to know their potential gross profit margin when they sell my products in their stores, I'll tell them. That builds trust because they see that I get right up to speed and play the game the way they play it."

Seemingly minor details can make a difference in building trust with customers. Hollingsworth cautions salespeople not to use the phrase *to be honest with you,* because it implies that up to that point perhaps the salesperson has been less than honest. He also advises salespeople never to fake a response to a buyer question. He would answer a tough question about delivery by saying, "Okay, you want to buy this many globes to ship on this date. I don't know. It depends on these factors. If I find out by this time today and get back to you, is that soon enough?"

Finally, Hollingsworth knows that consistently doing what you say you will do over time is essential for gaining customer trust: "I'll do what you ask, and I'll do it in a timely fashion, so you can expect that from me when and if the day comes that we can conduct business together."

Source: Dana Ray. "Bank on Trust," *Selling Power* (March, 1999): 23–25.

Learning Objectives

After completing this module, you should be able to

1 Distinguish between transaction-focused traditional selling and trust-based relationship selling.

2 Discuss five alternative approaches to personal selling.

3 Describe the three primary roles fulfilled by consultative salespeople.

4 Identify five salesperson attributes that are essential for building customer trust.

5 Discuss the sales process as a series of interrelated steps.

Bryan Hollingsworth is a fine example of successful salespeople in today's demanding business world. He views sales as a long-term process of gaining buyer trust and generating beneficial results for both buyer and seller. In this module, we take a closer look at alternative approaches to personal selling that professionals such as Hollingsworth may choose from to best interact with their customers. Some of these approaches are simple. Others approaches are more sophisticated and require that the salesperson play a strategic role to use them successfully. We also devote considerable discussion to the sales process, whereby salespeople initiate, develop, and enhance customer relationships.

Classification of Personal Selling Approaches

More than three decades ago, four basic approaches to personal selling were identified: stimulus response, mental states, need satisfaction, and problem solving.[1] Since that time, another approach to personal selling, termed *consultative selling*, has gained popularity. All five approaches to selling are practiced today. Furthermore, many salespeople use elements of more than one approach in their own hybrids of personal selling.

As a prelude to our discussion of different approaches to personal selling, an expansion of two key points from Module 1 is in order. Recall that personal selling differs from other forms of marketing communications because it is a personal communication delivered by employees or agents of the sales organization. Because the personal element is present, salespeople have the opportunity to alter their sales messages and behaviors during a sales presentation or as they encounter different sales situations and different customers. This is referred to as **adaptive selling.** Because salespeople often deal with multicultural buyers in domestic and international markets, adaptive selling is an important concept.

A second point made in Module 1 is that personal selling is moving from transaction-based methods to relationship-based methods (refer to Figure 1.2). Rather than trying to maximize sales in the short run, relationship-based selling approaches focus on solving customer problems, providing opportunities, and adding value to the customer's business over an extended period. Exhibit 3.1 illustrates how transaction-based selling differs from relationship-based selling. We now explore one element of Exhibit 3.1 in detail—personal selling approaches.

Stimulus Response Selling

Of the five views of personal selling, **stimulus response selling** is the simplest. The theoretical background for this approach originated in early experiments with animal behavior. The key idea is that various stimuli can elicit predictable responses. Salespeople furnish the stimuli from a repertoire of words and actions designed to produce the desired response. This approach to selling is illustrated in Figure 3.1 on page 42.

An example of the stimulus response view of selling would be **continued affirmation,** a method in which a series of questions or statements furnished by the salesperson is designed to condition the prospective buyer to answering "yes" time after time, until, it is hoped, he or she will be inclined to say "yes" to the entire sales proposition. This method is often used by telemarketing personnel, who rely on comprehensive sales scripts read or delivered from memory.

Stimulus response sales strategies, particularly when implemented with a canned sales presentation, have some advantages for the seller. The sales message can be structured in a logical order. Questions and objections from the buyer can usually be anticipated and addressed before they are magnified during buyer–seller

EXHIBIT 3.1 Comparison of Transaction-Focused Traditional Selling with Trust-Based Relationship Selling

	Transaction-Focused Traditional Selling	Trust-Based Relationship Selling
Primary perspective	The salesperson and the selling firm	The customer and the customer's customers
Personal selling approaches	Stimulus response, mental states	Need satisfaction, problem solving, consultative
Desired outcome	Closed sales, order volume	Trust, joint planning, mutual benefits, enhance profits
Role of salesperson	Make calls and close sales	Business consultant and long-term ally Key player in the customer's business
Nature of communication	One-way, from salesperson to customer	Two-way and collaborative
Degree of salesperson's involvement in customer's decision-making process	Isolated from customer's decision-making process	Actively involved in customer's decision-making process
Knowledge required	Own company's products Competition Applications Account strategies Costs Opportunities	Own company's products and resources Competition Applications Account strategies Costs Opportunities General business and industry knowledge and insight Customer's products, competition, and customers
Typical skills required	Selling skills	Selling skills Information gathering Listening and questioning Strategic problem solving Creating and demonstrating unique, value-added solutions Teambuilding and teamwork

Postsale follow-up	Little or none: move on to conquer next customer	Continued follow-through to
		  Ensure customer satisfaction
		  Keep customer informed
		  Add customer value
		  Manage opportunities

interaction. Inexperienced salespeople can rely on stimulus response sales methods in some settings, and this may eventually contribute to sales expertise.

The limitations of stimulus response methods, however, can be severe, especially if the salesperson is dealing with a professional buyer. Most buyers like to take an active role in sales dialogue, and the stimulus response approach calls for the salesperson to dominate the flow of conversation. The lack of flexibility in this approach is also a disadvantage, as buyer responses and unforeseen interruptions may neutralize or damage the effectiveness of the stimuli.

Considering the net effects of this method's advantages and disadvantages, it appears most suitable for relatively unimportant purchase decisions, when time is severely constrained and when professional buyers are not the prospects. As consumers in general become more sophisticated, this approach will become more problematic.

Mental States Selling

Mental states selling, or the *formula approach* to personal selling, assumes that the buying process for most buyers is essentially identical and that buyers can be led through certain mental states, or steps, in the buying process. These mental states

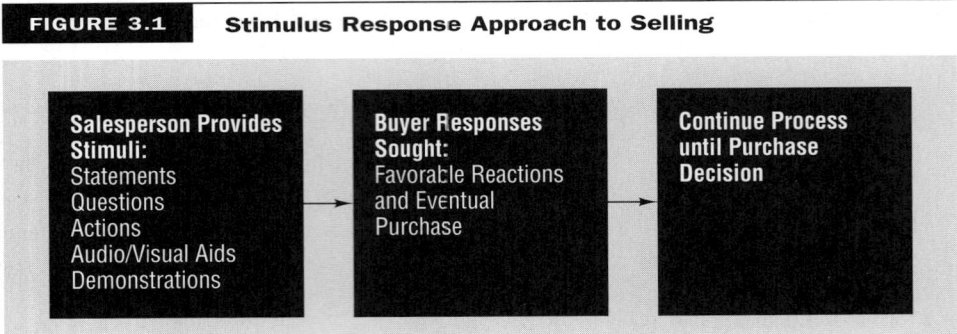

FIGURE 3.1 Stimulus Response Approach to Selling

The salesperson attempts to gain favorable responses from the customer by providing stimuli, or cues, to influence the buyer. After the customer has been properly conditioned, the salesperson tries to secure a positive purchase decision.

are typically referred to as **AIDA,** (attention, interest, desire, and action). Appropriate sales messages provide a transition from one mental state to the next.

Like stimulus response selling, the mental states approach relies on a highly structured sales presentation. The salesperson does most of the talking, as feedback from the prospect could be disruptive to the flow of the presentation.

A positive feature of this method is that it forces the salesperson to plan the sales presentation prior to calling on the customer. It also helps the salesperson recognize that timing is an important element in the purchase decision process and that careful listening is necessary to determine which stage the buyer is in at any given point.

A problem with the mental states method is that it is difficult to determine which state a prospect is in. Sometimes a prospect is spanning two mental states or moving back and forth between two states during the sales presentation. Consequently, the heavy guidance structure the salesperson implements may be inappropriate, confusing, and even counterproductive to sales effectiveness. We should also note that this method is not customer oriented. Although the salesperson tailors the presentation to each customer somewhat, this is done by noting customer mental states rather than needs. See "An Ethical Dilemma" for a situation in which the salesperson is contemplating the movement of the prospect into the "action" stage.

The mental states method is illustrated in Exhibit 3.2. Note that this version includes "conviction" as an intermediate stage between interest and desire. Such minor variations are commonplace in different renditions of this approach to selling.

An Ethical Dilemma

Rachel Duke sells advertising for her college newspaper. One of her potential clients is contemplating buying an ad for an upcoming special issue featuring bars and restaurants. Over the past two weeks, Rachel has tried unsuccessfully to get a commitment from the restaurant owner to place an ad. Her sales manager has suggested that Rachel call the prospect and tell him that there is only one remaining ad space in the special issue, and that she must have an immediate answer to ensure that the prospect's ad will appear in the special issue. The sales manager said, "Rachel, this guy is stalling. You've got to move him to action, and this technique will do the trick." Rachel was troubled by her manager's advice, since the special issue had plenty of ad space remaining. If you were Rachel, would you follow her sales manager's advice? Why or why not?

EXHIBIT 3.2 Mental States View of Selling

Mental State	Sales Step	Critical Sales Task
Curiosity	Attention	Get prospects excited, then get them to like you
Interest	Interest	Interview: needs and wants
Conviction	Conviction	"What's in it for me?" Product—"Will it do what I want it to do?" Price—"Is it worth it?" "The hassle of change?" "Cheaper elsewhere?" Peers—"What will others think of it?" Priority—"Do I need it now?" (sense of urgency)
Desire	Desire	Overcome their stall
Action	Close	Alternate choice close: which, not if!

Need Satisfaction Selling

Need satisfaction selling is based on the notion that the customer is buying to satisfy a particular need or set of needs. This approach is shown in Figure 3.2. It is the salesperson's task to identify the need to be met, then to help the buyer meet the need. Unlike the mental states and stimulus response methods, this method focuses on the customer rather than on the salesperson. The salesperson uses a questioning, probing tactic to uncover important buyer needs. Customer responses dominate the early portion of the sales interaction, and only after relevant needs have been established does the salesperson begin to relate how his or her offering can satisfy these needs.

Customers seem to appreciate this selling method and are often willing to spend considerable time in preliminary meetings to define needs prior to a sales presentation or written sales proposal. Also, this method avoids the defensiveness that arises in some prospects when a salesperson rushes to the persuasive part of the sales message without adequate attention to the buyer's needs.

Problem-Solving Selling

Problem-solving selling is an extension of need satisfaction selling. It goes beyond identifying needs to developing alternative solutions for satisfying these needs. The problem-solving approach to selling is depicted in Figure 3.3. Sometimes even competitors' offerings are included as alternatives in the purchase decision.

FIGURE 3.2 Need Satisfaction Approach to Selling

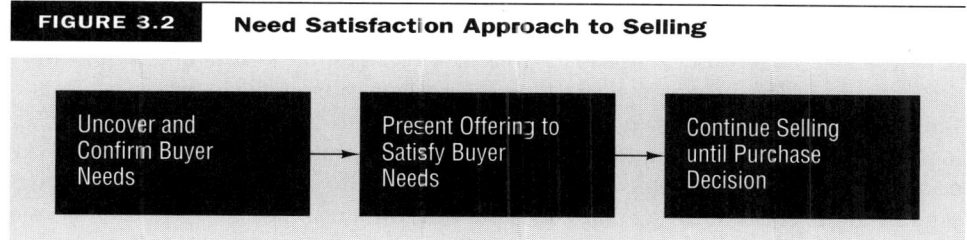

The salesperson attempts to uncover customer needs that are related to the salesperson's product or service offering. This may require extensive questioning in the early stages of the sales process. After confirming the buyer's needs, the salesperson proceeds with a presentation based on how the offering can meet those needs.

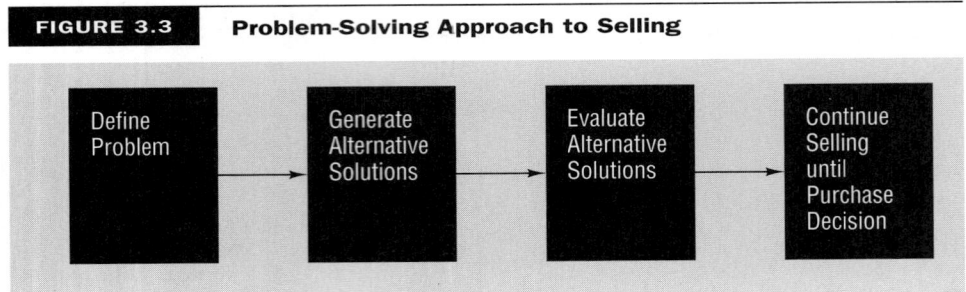

FIGURE 3.3 Problem-Solving Approach to Selling

The salesperson defines a customer problem that may be solved by various alternatives. Then an offering is made that represents at least one of these alternatives. All alternatives are carefully evaluated before a purchase decision is made.

The problem-solving approach to selling is practiced by Square D sales representative Randy Scott in Altamonte Springs, Florida. Scott sells electronic products to industrial distributors. According to Scott,

> Certainly the product has to solve a problem for the customer. With our customers, that means either reducing or removing costs. Distributors want to keep their inventory at a low cost. When we come out with something new, they're hesitant to put it out without any proven wins for them. So first, it has to be a problem solver—it has to address a concern they have about the existing product. Second, we demo it for them, show them how it will work. Third, we have to leave samples with them. Fourth, and this actually takes place before the other three, we have to plant the seed of enthusiasm for the product in the customer's mind ahead of time.[2]

As the Square D example points out, the problem-solving approach to selling can take a lot of time. In some cases, the selling company cannot afford this much time with each prospective customer. In other cases, the customers may be unwilling to spend the time. Insurance salespeople, for example, report this to be so in their field. The problem-solving approach appears to be most successful in technical industrial sales situations, in which the parties involved are usually oriented toward scientific reasoning and processes and thus find this approach to sales amenable.

Consultative Selling

Consultative selling is the process of helping customers reach their strategic goals by using the products, services, and expertise of the sales organization.[3] Notice that this method focuses on achieving strategic goals of customers, not just meeting needs or solving problems. Salespeople confirm their customers' strategic goals, then work collaboratively with customers to achieve those goals.

In consultative selling, salespeople fulfill three primary roles: strategic orchestrator, business consultant, and long-term ally. As a **strategic orchestrator,** the salesperson arranges the use of the sales organization's resources in an effort to satisfy the customer. This usually calls for involving other individuals in the sales organization. For example, the salesperson may need expert advice from production or logistics personnel to fully address a customer problem or opportunity. In the **business consultant** role, the salesperson uses internal and external (outside the sales organization) sources to become an expert on the customer's business. This role also includes an educational element—that is, salespeople educate their customers on products they offer and how these products compare with competitive offerings. As a **long-term ally,** the salesperson supports the customer, even when an immediate sale is not expected.

Among the successful consultative selling organizations is Airgas, a large industrial gas company with 950 salespeople in North America. In selling oxygen, nitrogen, and argon for various applications, Airgas becomes the long-term ally of its customers by fulfilling the two additional roles of the consultative seller. According to Pat Visintainer, Airgas sales and marketing vice president, sales personnel serve as strategic orchestrators in that they recognize that they "can no longer do it all alone. Good salespeople recognize the resources at their disposal and tap into those resources." According to Mr. Visintainer, Airgas salespeople fulfill the business consultant role by focusing on vendor reduction and process cost reduction for their customers rather than simply selling at a lower price. By identifying customer cost savings, Airgas salespeople become value-added long-term consultants rather than one-shot low-price sellers.[4] For more on consultative selling, see "Professional Selling in the 21st Century: Consultative Selling."

Sales Process

The nonselling activities on which most salespeople spend a majority of their time are essential for the successful execution of the most important part of the salesperson's job, the **sales process.** The sales process has traditionally been described as a series of interrelated steps beginning with locating qualified prospective customers. From there, the salesperson plans the sales presentation, makes an appointment to see the customer, completes the sale, and performs postsale activities.

As you should recall from the discussion of the continued evolution of personal selling in Module 2 (refer to Exhibit 2.1), the sales process is increasingly being viewed as a relationship management process, as depicted in Figure 3.4. In this conceptualization of the sales process, salespeople strive to attain lasting relationships with their customers. The basis for such relationships may vary (see Module 4 for discussion of different types of relationships), but the element of trust between the customer and the salesperson is an essential part of enduring relationships. To earn the trust of customers, salespeople should be customer oriented, honest, dependable, competent, and likable.[5] These attributes are reflected by Blake Conrad, who sells medical supplies for Centurion Specialty Care. Conrad, based in Denver, says:

PROFESSIONAL SELLING IN THE 21ST CENTURY

Consultative Selling

L.A. Mitchell, sales planner for Lucent Technologies, comments on the increasing use of consultative selling.

Professional selling is becoming much more of a consultative process than in years past. The pace of business has accelerated, and it is hard for individual buyers to be experts on everything they buy. That's where consultative selling comes in. When buyers know they have a problem, but don't know how to solve it, our salespeople can offer a tailored solution. The solution must fit within the buyer's allotted budget, and it must be consistent with the goals and strategies within the buying organization. Consultative salespeople must also be on the scene after the sale to be sure that any necessary training and service issues are handled to the client's satisfaction. With consultative selling, making the sale is important, but the real focus is on providing expertise which enables clients to improve company operations and productivity.

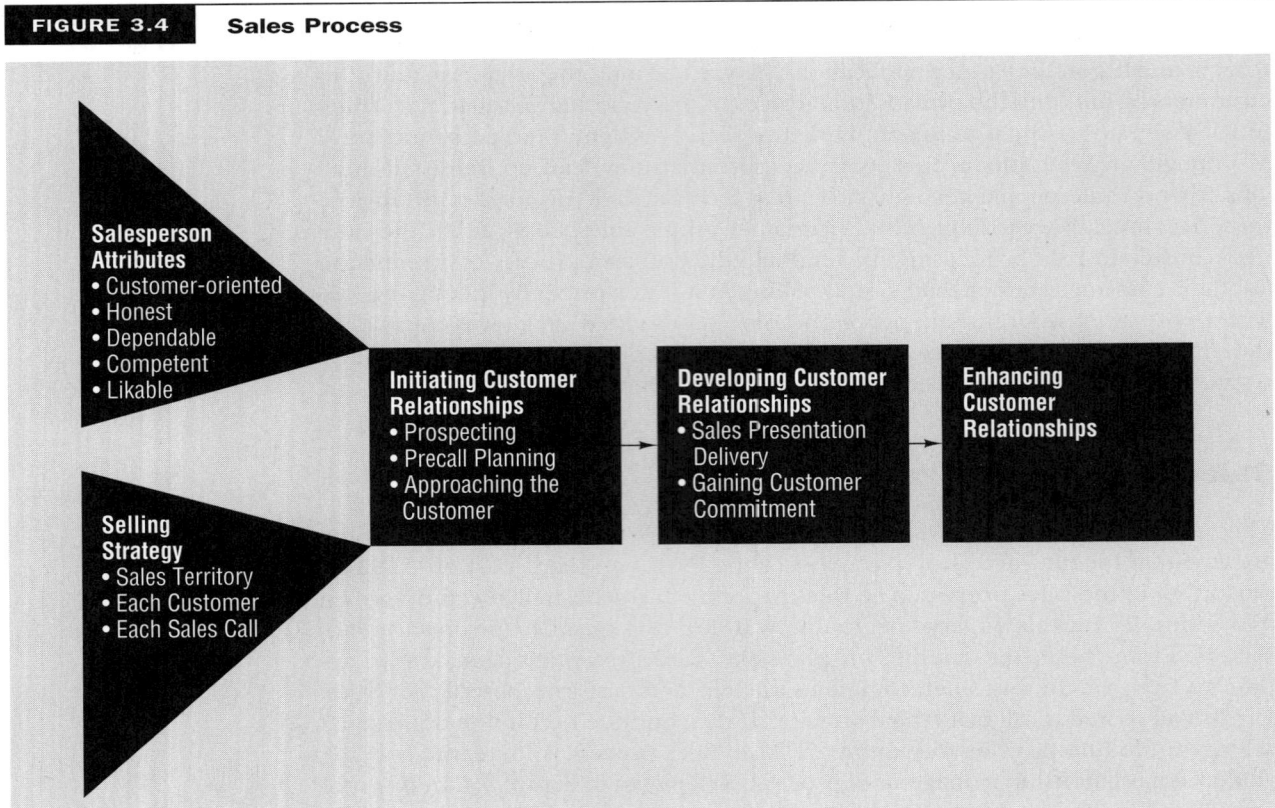

FIGURE 3.4 Sales Process

Salespeople must possess certain attributes to inspire trust in their customers and to be able to adapt their selling strategy to different situations. One or more selling approaches are used in the sales process. The three major phases of the sales process are initiating, developing, and enhancing customer relationships.

You simply cannot have productive relationships with your customers unless they trust you. I work really hard to show customers that I care about their bottom line, and I would never sell them something they don't really need. If I don't have an answer for them on the spot, I make every effort to get the answer and get back to them the same day. Customers appreciate the fact that I do what I say and follow up on all the details. To me, being customer oriented and dependable is just part of my job. It makes selling a lot more fun when your customers trust you, and—guess what—I sell more to customers who trust me.[6]

Another important element of achieving sound relationships with customers is to recognize that individual customers and their particular needs must be addressed with appropriate selling strategies and tactics. In Module 4, we discuss strategy at four levels: corporate, business unit, marketing department, and the overall sales function. An individual salesperson is strongly guided by strategy at these higher levels in the organization but must also develop selling strategies and tactics to fit the sales territory, each customer, and ultimately, each sales call.

When studying the sales process, we should note that there are countless versions of the process in terms of number of steps and the names of the steps. If, however, you were to examine popular trade books on selling and training manuals used by different corporations, you would find that the various depictions of the sales process are actually more alike than truly unique. The sales process shown in Figure 3.4 is comparable with most versions of the sales process, with the exception of those versions that advocate high-pressure methods centering on how to get the customer to "say yes" rather than focusing on meeting the customer's true needs. This version of the sales process suggests that salespeople must have certain attributes to inspire trust in their customers and that salespeople should adapt their selling strategy to fit the situation. The three phases of the sales process are initiating, developing, and enhancing customer relationships. For discussion purposes, the first two phases have been subdivided into a total of five steps. The sixth and final step in the sales process is that of enhancing customer relationships, which, in many cases, extends over a prolonged time period.

Another point that should be stressed is that the sales process is broken into steps to facilitate discussion and sales training, not to suggest discrete lines between the steps. The steps are actually highly interrelated and, in some instances, may overlap. Further, the stepwise flow of Figure 3.4 does not imply a strict sequence of events. Salespeople may move back and forth in the process with a given customer, sometimes shifting from step to step several times in the same sales encounter. Finally, completion of the sales process typically will require multiple sales calls.

As we proceed to discuss the steps in the sales process, we present an overview of each step. The overviews describe the objectives of each step and identify key issues to be dealt with in each step. Selected techniques and activities that are usually associated with each step are presented as well.

Initiating Customer Relationships

PROSPECTING   The term *prospecting* as used in the sales context is analogous to the prospecting process for gold as practiced in the 1800s. The prospector for gold would work a stream, separating the sludge and mud in a search for strains of the precious metal. The contemporary salesperson locates a pool of potential customers and then screens them to determine which ones are qualified prospects. In some situations, such as in most retail operations, salespeople are only slightly involved in prospecting; usually, however, they play an important role.

Locating Prospects   The initial part of the prospecting process is the generation of a pool, or list, of potential customers. Various methods are used to locate potential prospects. As Exhibit 3.3 indicates, a salesperson may use sources outside the organization along with internal company sources. Exhibit 3.3 includes some methods in which the salesperson plays a fairly passive role in this part of prospecting and others in which the salesperson is directly responsible for locating the potential customer.

Screening Prospects   After potential prospects are located, they must be evaluated in terms of **screening criteria** to determine whether they merit further sales attention. These criteria vary from one sales organization to the next, but some that are commonly used follow:

- compatibility—between the seller's product and the needs or wants of the prospect
- accessibility—to the prospect
- eligibility—in terms of geographic location and type of business the prospect is engaged in
- authority—to make the purchase decision
- profitability—as estimated based on the prospect's willingness and ability to pay and on predicted sales expenses

EXHIBIT 3.3 Prospecting Methods

Category	Prospecting Techniques
1. External sources	Referral approach: Ask each prospect for the name of another potential prospect. Community contact: Ask friends and acquaintances for the names of potential prospects. Introduction approach: Obtain introduction by one prospect to others via phone, by letter, or in person. Contact organizations: Seek sales leads from service clubs and chambers of commerce. Noncompeting salespeople: Seek leads from noncompeting salespeople. Cultivate visible accounts: Cultivate visible and influential accounts that will influence other buyers.
2. Internal sources	Examine records: Examine company databases, directories, telephone books, membership lists, and other written documents. Inquiries to advertising: Respond to customer inquiries generated from company advertising. Phone/mail inquiries: Respond to phone or mail inquiries from potential prospects.
3. Personal contact	Personal observation: Look and listen for evidence of good prospects. Cold canvassing: make cold calls on potential prospects (by phone or in person).
4. Miscellaneous	Surf the Web: Identify prospects by name and location. Hold/attend trade shows: Organize or participate in a trade show directed toward potential prospects. Bird dogs: Have junior salespeople locate prospects that senior salespersons will contact. Sales seminar: Prospects attend as a group to learn about a topic in which the salesperson's product is involved.

Questions involving these criteria may be hard to answer fully in the prospecting stage. As a case in point, consider the profitability element. A salesperson may not be able to estimate whether a prospect will prove profitable at some future point in time. It is certainly possible for a prospect to become an unprofitable customer in the future and subsequently lose customer and prospect status with the selling firm. However, the prospecting stage does not require irrevocable decisions regarding the suitability of a prospect, only sufficient indications that the prospect is worthy of sales pursuit.

Prospecting Issues Three managerial issues of extreme interest occur in the prospecting stage. One is the persistent question of which method or methods work best for locating qualified prospects. The second is the problem of **cold-call reluctance** in many salespeople. The third is the issue of using technology to complete the basic tasks of prospecting.

Which method or methods work best? There is no answer to this question without some experimentation by the selling firm. For one firm, a trade show may be a bonanza, whereas another will find it more profitable to rely exclusively on cold canvassing. With the costs of personal sales calls continuing to rise, sales managers and salespeople must experiment with new prospecting methods in an effort to reduce selling expenses and optimize personal contact activities.

The subject of cold-call reluctance is especially important, because this method of locating prospects is crucial in many sales situations. Call reluctance experienced later in the sales process is generally not as acute as in the prospecting stage, in which the salespeople are encountering strangers on their (the strangers') turf and may feel as if they are intruding. Many have a hard time dealing with the face-to-face rejection that often accompanies this prospecting method.

Salespeople may also be reluctant to make cold calls because they know that many customers do not particularly like the tactic. Buyers are busy individuals, and a cold call can be an unwelcome interruption. Recognizing that many customers are annoyed by cold calls, American Express Financial Advisors (Amex) have banned the practice for its 8,000 Amex financial advisors.[7] Amex financial planners now rely more heavily on referrals from satisfied clients o find additional prospects.

Noting that the origins of call reluctance are multiple and complex, experts in this phenomenon have reported that approximately 40 percent of all salespeople will experience at least one serious encounter with cold-call reluctance during their careers.[8] The problem is of sufficient magnitude that sales managers and sales trainers frequently address it in training and development programs. For advice on how to deal with cold-call reluctance, see "Professional Selling in the 21st Century: Overcoming Call Reluctance."

Another prospecting topic that is generating considerable discussion among sales managers is the use of technology to perform some or all prospecting. In recent years, automated systems combining computers with communications equipment have become widely available. Some systems extend beyond prospecting to include other sales functions such as account tracking and postsale follow-up. An example of such a system is shown in Exhibit 3.4. The system uses the computer to screen prospects against initial qualifying criteria. Potential prospects are further qualified by phone, with some receiving sales contact and eventually becoming customers. As the quest for improving sales productivity continues, the use of the latest technology to perform certain prospecting activities has become commonplace.

Precall Planning

PREAPPROACH In the **preapproach,** the salesperson gathers information about the prospect that will be used to formulate the sales presentation. During this step, the salesperson may determine buyer needs, buyer motives, and details of the buyer's situation that are relevant to the upcoming sales presentation.

Various information sources may be consulted in this undertaking. Published materials such as industry newsletters, magazine articles, and newspaper accounts may be useful. The Internet is a valuable source of information, as are online services, such as DIALOG, Dow Jones News/Retrieval, and LEXIS-NEXIS. Another alternative is to call on the prospect for information-gathering purposes.

In addition to gathering information to be used in the sales presentation, the preapproach offers other benefits. Because of the information it provides, the

---

PROFESSIONAL SELLING IN THE 21ST CENTURY

Overcoming Call Reluctance

L.A. Mitchell, sales planner for Lucent Technologies, offers this advice on overcoming call reluctance:

Most salespeople will tell you that there are times when they just don't feel like making cold calls. But cold calls can be an important step in building future sales, and there are some things salespeople can do to overcome call reluctance. Most importantly, salespeople have to be absolutely convinced that their product or service delivers value to the customer. When you know you have a great product, you feel good about telling any and all potential customers about it. Putting yourself in the buyer's shoes can be helpful in overcoming call reluctance. Just ask yourself, "if I were the customer, would I want to know about this opportunity?" Salespeople should also de-personalize rejection if it occurs. Just because a buyer is too busy to see you at the moment doesn't mean he or she dislikes you or that you won't eventually do business together.

EXHIBIT 3.4   Prospect Screening and Tracking System

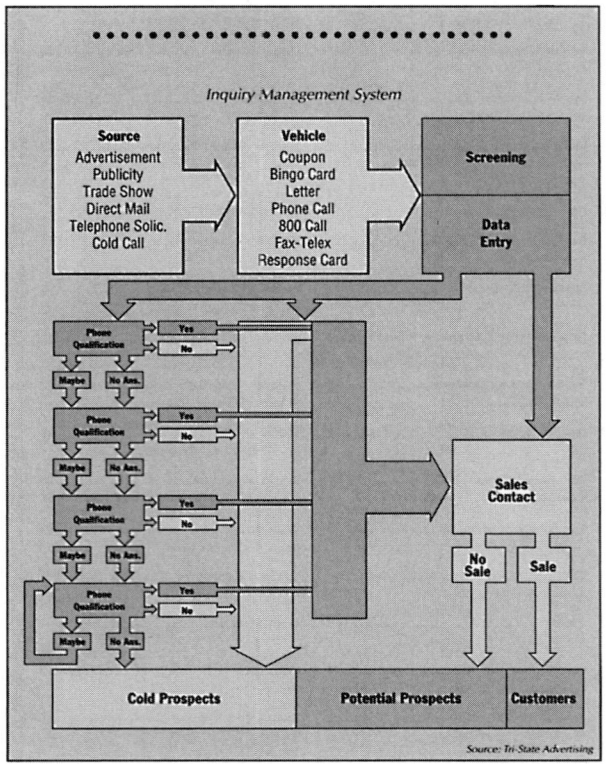

This exhibit illustrates a system for screening prospects by computer and telephone. Appropriate follow-up is conducted by the salesforce, with some of the prospects becoming active customers.

salesperson may avoid serious blunders based on false assumptions. Also, the self-confidence of the salesperson is increased by the acquisition of knowledge, and the salesperson's credibility with the prospect is enhanced.

The preapproach raises two issues worthy of management attention. First is the question of how extensive the preapproach should be. Second is the issue of invasion of privacy.

The extensiveness of the preapproach depends on the nature of the sales situation. For example, if the salesperson is in the consultative selling mode, the preapproach will be extensive to clarify the customer's strategic goals and how the sales organization can help the customer achieve those goals. The preapproach will be more extensive in high-stakes situations—those that are very important to the salesperson and the sales organization. The preapproach also tends to be more extensive when the solution to the buyer's problem is not obvious. In other situations, such as when selling a simple, low-cost product with obvious benefits, the preapproach may be less extensive.

Sales managers and salespeople should also be sensitive to the issue of invasion of privacy when conducting the preapproach. There have been instances in which surreptitious methods were used to learn personal details about prospects. Such tactics are unethical, and they often backfire if the prospect becomes aware of the practice. A related tactic is the use of so-called market research that purports to be "selling nothing" when, in reality, selling is precisely the purpose. As was indicated in the previous module, straightforward sales techniques have proved more effective over the long run.

SALES PRESENTATION PLANNING This step has become more important in recent years, as evidenced by increased coverage on the topic in sales training programs. The requirements of professional selling today make **sales presentation planning** imperative, and it is often extensive, because it is increasingly viewed as a critical link in the sales process.

As with other planning processes, the salesperson must begin with a specifically stated objective, or perhaps multiple objectives, for each sales presentation. Typical objectives might be stated as order quantities or dollar values, or even in communications terms, such as reaching an agreement in principle with the prospect. Once a clearly stated objective has been formulated, the salesperson can focus on how the benefits of his or her offering can best serve the needs of the prospect.

Taken to the ultimate, sales presentation planning might actually result in a script to guide sales encounters. Not to be confused with a scripted sales message to be delivered over the telephone, this script would be a guide to expected sales activities given a particular buying situation. Research has been conducted that suggests that scripts could help salespeople learn how to adapt to the customer and the selling situation, while developing their own personal style and sales tactics.[9]

Sales Presentation Format To plan the sales presentation, salespeople must decide on a basic **presentation format.** Alternatives include a canned sales presentation, an organized presentation, and the written sales proposal. A salesperson might use one or more of these formats with a particular customer. Each format has unique advantages and disadvantages.

The highly structured, inflexible, **canned sales presentation** does not vary from customer to customer. When properly formulated, it is logical and complete and minimizes sales resistance by anticipating the prospect's objections. It can be used by relatively inexperienced salespeople and perhaps is a confidence builder for some salespeople.

The major limitation of the canned sales presentation is that it fails to capitalize on the strength of personal selling—the ability to tailor the message to the prospect. Further, it does not handle interruptions well, may be awkward to use with a broad product line, and may alienate buyers who want to participate in the interaction.

Despite its limitations, the canned sales presentation can be effective in some situations. If the product line is narrow and the salesforce is relatively inexperienced, the canned presentation may be suitable. Also, many salespeople may find it effective to use canned portions in a sales presentation to introduce their company, to demonstrate the product,, or for some other limited purpose.

Sales presentations that are tailored to each prospect are far more popular with salespeople than are canned sales presentations. In the **organized sales presentation,** the salesperson organizes the key points into a planned sequence that allows for adaptive behavior by the salesperson as the presentation progresses. Feedback from the prospect is encouraged, and therefore this format is less likely to offend a participation-prone buyer.

One reality of this presentation format is that it requires a knowledgeable salesperson who can react to questions and objections from the prospect Further, this format may extend the time horizon before a purchase decision is reached, and it is vulnerable to diversionary delay tactics by the prospect. Presumably, those who make these arguments think that a canned presentation forces a purchase decision in a more expedient fashion.

Overall, however, most agree that the organized presentation is ideal for most sales situations. Its flexibility allows a full exploration of customer needs and appropriate adaptive behavior by the salesperson.

A written sales presentation, the **sales proposal,** may be developed after careful investigation of the prospect's needs; or, alternatively, a generic proposal may be presented. With the increasing prevalence of word processing, computer graphics, and desktop publishing, the written sales proposal is being used in a growing number of situations. These technologies have minimized the traditional disadvantage of the written proposal—the time it takes to prepare it.

The sales proposal has long been associated with important, high-dollar-volume sales transactions. It is frequently used in competitive bidding situations and in situations involving the selection of a new supplier by the prospect. One advantage of the proposal is that the written word is usually viewed as being more credible than the spoken word. Written proposals are subject to careful scrutiny with few time constraints, and specialists in the buying firm often analyze various sections of the proposal.

Sales proposals are often combined with face-to-face presentations and question-and-answer periods. Their content is similar to other sales presentations, focusing on customer needs and related benefits offered by the seller. In addition, technical information, pricing data, and perhaps a timetable are included. Most proposals provide a triggering mechanism such as a proposed contract to confirm the sale, and some specify follow-up action to be taken if the proposal is satisfactory.

Sales Mix Model To this point, our discussion of the sales presentation planning process should have clearly suggested a need for a specific objective for each presentation and a need to determine the basic format of the presentation. In general terms, we have spoken of blending information into a palatable sales message. This is best done within the context of the **sales mix model** shown in Figure 3.5. The model includes five variables that require planning effort: presentation pace, presentation scope, depth of inquiry, degree of two-way communication, and use of visual aids.

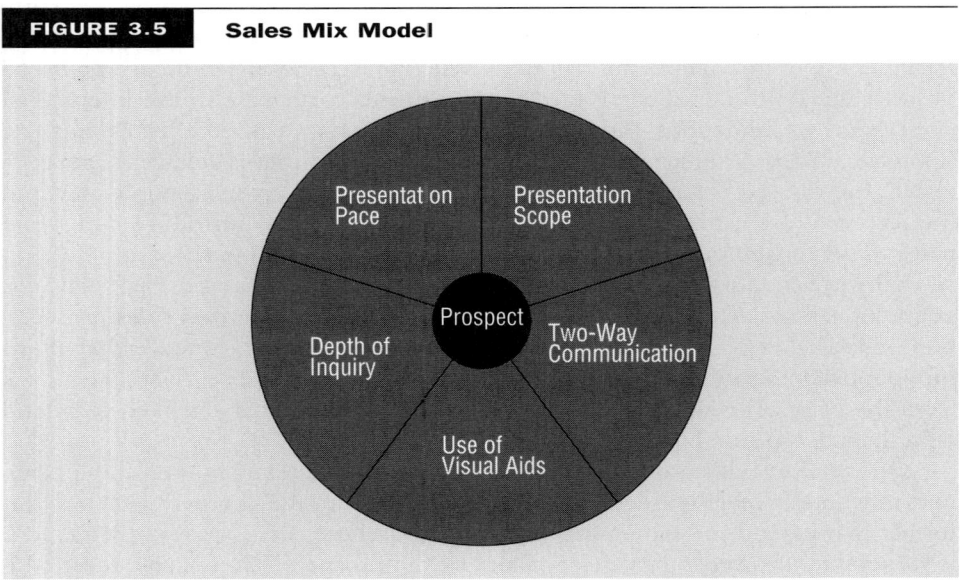

FIGURE 3.5   Sales Mix Model

Five variables require planning effort after the salesperson has set objectives for the presentation and selected a basic presentation format.

Presentation pace refers to the speed with which the salesperson intends to move through the presentation. The appropriate pace will be determined largely by the preference of the prospect and may be affected by such variables as complexity of the product or the number of products to be presented. Another determinant of pace would be past experiences with a particular customer, as a quicker pace may be possible with a familiar customer.

Presentation scope involves the selection of benefits and terms of sale to be included in the presentation. This narrowing-down process can be a challenge for the knowledge-laden salesperson, who may know more about the product than will be of interest to the prospect. Time and again, we see reports of jargon-spouting salespeople who have talked themselves out of a sale through indiscriminate use of their extensive product knowledge. An illustration of this problem comes from Charles O'Meara, an expert who advises customers on how to buy stereo equipment. O'Meara says that if a salesperson "tries to, say, inundate your aural sensibility with a plethora of polysyllabic terminology—watch out! Either the salesperson is trying to confuse you or he is a techie who can't relate to other human beings. The salesperson should talk technical only if the customer wants to talk technical."[10]

Depth of inquiry refers to the extent to which the salesperson goes to ascertain the prospect's needs and decision process. Some of this information may have been gained in the preapproach, and some probing is usually necessary during the presentation. The planning task is simply to identify gaps in needed information and plan the presentation accordingly.

The issue of **two-way communication** is partially addressed when the sales person selects a basic format for the presentation. By definition, the canned presentation does not allow for significant two-way communication. The organized presentation allows for, and usually encourages, a two-way flow. The degree of interactive flow is often dictated by buyer expertise, with more allowance for two-way flow planned with expert buyers.

Visual aids to supplement the spoken word have become an important element in sales presentations, and their use must be carefully planned. Unless sales aids are used with caution, they may actually detract from rather than enhance the sales presentation. When properly orchestrated, visual aids ranging from flip charts to video demonstrations can be valuable tools during the sales presentation. The computer is increasingly being used as the basic tool for enhancing presentations. Multimedia packages are plentiful and inexpensive, and packages such as Power Point are routinely used to construct and integrate photographs, graphics, statistical data, sound effects, and video into a complete presentation.

After the sales presentation is planned, the salesperson is ready to shift to an active selling mode. Although the customer may have been contacted earlier in the sales process, the emphasis has been on information gathering and planning. Now, the actual selling begins as the salesperson seeks an interview with the prospect.

Approaching the Customer

Approaching the customer involves two phases. The first phase is securing an appointment for the sales interview. The second phase covers the first few minutes of the sales call. Each step in the sales process is critical, and the approach is no exception. In today's competitive environment, a good first impression is essential to lay the groundwork for subsequent steps in the sales process. A bad first impression on the customer can be difficult or impossible to overcome.

GETTING AN APPOINTMENT Most initial sales calls on new prospects require an appointment. Requesting an appointment accomplishes several desirable outcomes.

First, the salesperson is letting the prospect know that the salesperson thinks the prospect's time is important. Second, there is a better chance that the salesperson will receive the undivided attention of the prospect during the sales call. Third, setting appointments is a good tool to assist the salesperson in effective time and territory management. The importance of setting appointments is clearly proclaimed in a survey of secretaries, administrative assistants, and other "gatekeepers" responsible for scheduling appointments. A majority of respondents thought that arriving unannounced to make a sales call is a violation of business etiquette.[11] Given this rather strong feeling of those who represent buyers, it is a good idea to request an appointment if there is any doubt about whether one is required.

Appointments may be requested by phone, mail, or personal contact. By far, setting appointments by telephone is the most popular method. Combining mail and telephone communications to seek appointments is also commonplace. Regardless of the communications vehicle used, salespeople can improve their chances of getting an appointment by following three simple directives: give the prospect a reason why an appointment should be granted; request a specific amount of time; suggest a specific time for the appointment. These tactics recognize that prospects are busy individuals who do not spend time idly.

In giving a reason why the appointment should be granted, a well-informed salesperson can appeal to the prospect's primary buying motive as related to one of the benefits of the salesperson's offering. Being specific is recommended. For example, it is better to say that "you can realize gross margins averaging 35 percent on our product line" than "our margins are really quite attractive."

Specifying the amount of time needed to make the sales presentation alleviates some of the anxiety felt by a busy prospect at the idea of spending some of his or her already scarce time. It also helps the prospect if the salesperson suggests a time and date for the sales call. It is very difficult for busy individuals to respond to a question such as, "What would be a good time for you next week?" In effect, the prospect is being asked to scan his or her entire calendar for an opening. If a suggested time and date are not convenient, the interested prospect will typically suggest another.

STARTING THE SALES CALL Having secured an appointment with a qualified, presumably interested prospect, the salesperson should plan to accomplish some important tasks during the first few minutes of the call. First in importance is to establish a harmonious atmosphere for discussion. Common rules of etiquette and courtesy apply here. Some preliminary small talk is usually part of the ritual, then the discussion should turn to business. Adaptive salespeople can learn how to interpret the prospect's signals and move into the sales message reasonably soon.

Another important aspect in starting a sales call is to ascertain the customer's needs as related to the benefits of the salesperson's offering. In many cases, salespeople will ask questions pertaining to the prospect's situation and then, at the appropriate time, show the prospect how the salesperson's product or service can benefit the customer. It is well known that successful salespeople ask more questions that do those who are less successful. Further, successful salespeople focus on the benefits of their offering, rather than the features of the offering. For example, Frito-Lay salespeople can offer their customers next-day delivery, a feature of their offering. The benefits of next-day delivery include reduction of inventory cost, avoidance of out-of-stock situations, and fresher product for the consumer.

Developing Customer Relationships

SALES PRESENTATION DELIVERY During the **sales presentation,** the salesperson expands on the basic theme established in the first few minutes of the sales call or during previous sales calls. Specifically, more details are furnished regarding how offered benefits will meet customer needs. If the prior steps in the sales process have been properly implemented, the salesperson is now interacting with a qualified interested prospect at a convenient time. Given these circumstances, three major goals remain: building credibility, achieving clarity, and coping with questions and objections raised by the prospect.

BUILDING CREDIBILITY   With any major purchase, prospects perceive a considerable amount of risk. To be able to reduce that perception of risk in the prospect, the salesperson must appear a credible source of information. In a classic study, Harvard professor Theodore Levitt found *source credibility* for salespeople to be a function of three factors: the individual salesperson, the company image, and the product being sold.[12] In our discussion of source credibility, we concentrate on factors that can, to a significant degree, be controlled by the salesperson. These factors can be divided into two categories—personal behavior and sales techniques.

Personal Behavior   The basics of personal behavior that build credibility are dressing appropriately, showing common courtesy for all personnel in the prospect's organization, and being customer oriented. As previously mentioned, all words and actions should be consistent with the traits of honesty and integrity. These findings confirm that building credibility is a worthwhile activity for salespeople.

One approach to building credibility through personal behavior is to become a good listener. Obviously, there is a strong correlation between listening and being able to answer customer questions. Both skills are essential for building credibility with the customer. As the benefits of listening become more apparent, popular sales training programs have increased their coverage of this subject. Good listening skills enable the salesperson to learn more about the prospect and also keep the prospect interested in the sales proposition because individuals are usually more interested in listening to someone else when they, too, are given the chance to talk. Moreover, by listening, the salesperson is, in effect, complimenting the prospect and showing respect for the prospect's point of view. The result is a reciprocation process in which the prospect repays the salesperson by listening to the sales presentation more attentively. The platform for credibility is built by the salesperson's willingness and ability to be an effective listener.

We discussed listening as a personal behavior because most effective listeners practice the art all the time, not just during sales presentations. We would not argue, however, with those who propose that listening is a sales technique rather than a personal behavior.

Sales Techniques   One sales technique used to build credibility with prospects is that of **conservative claims** regarding the benefits of the offering. The idea is that prospects may expect claims to be exaggerated, so on discovering that the salesperson has conservatively stated the claims, they tend to rate the credibility of the salesperson higher.

Another technique is to use **third-party evidence** to support a contention. **Testimonials** from satisfied customers are sometimes used for this purpose, as are research reports and product reviews from trade magazines. In the early stages of establishing credibility, salespeople often find that third-party information, particularly if it is written, may be more acceptable than the salesperson's spoken word.

Guarantees and warranties are other sales tools that can improve a salesperson's credibility. A strong warranty without a plethora of fine-print exceptions can go a long way toward eliminating the prospect's perceived risk and elevating the salesperson's credibility. Gregory Brennan of Brennan Communications in California used a strong guarantee to secure a contract with Mervyn's department stores to produce employee-training videos. Mervyn's was reluctant to give Brennan an opportunity to produce the videos because he had not done any work for retailers and thus lacked a desirable level of credibility. Brennan took a cue from Mervyn's liberal return policy, which offers customers refunds with few questions asked. He wrote to the Mervyn's buyer, saying, "Hire me, and if you are not satisfied with my work, I won't bill you." This credibility-building tactic worked, and Brennan earned his first contract with Mervyn's, a $40,000 deal.[13]

Another method is to let the prospect try the product or service under actual usage conditions. This can be as simple as a test-drive in a new automobile or as extensive as installing a computer system on a trial basis. This method permits the prospect to raise and answer questions without immediate persuasive pressure from the salesperson.

Even salespeople who work for companies with good reputations cannot assume that source credibility is a given. Further, they cannot assume that it will be easy to establish. They must recognize the skepticism and perceived risk in many sales situations and then combine appropriate personal behavior and sales techniques to overcome it. For a situation in which the salesperson's credibility might be damaged, see "An Ethical Dilemma."

ACHIEVING CLARITY Salespeople begin the task of **achieving clarity** during sales presentation planning. Recall the sales mix model, in which the salesperson plans such presentation elements as depth of inquiry, pace, and visual aids. The sales mix model also includes the presentation scope and the degree of two-way communication to be accomplished. At this point in the sales presentation, we are ready to implement those plans made with the assistance of the sales mix model.

To supplement the forethought given to achieving clarity as implied in the sales mix model, salespeople must adapt to the dynamics of the sales presentation. That is, as changes in the sales situation occur, salespeople must be adept at soliciting, intercepting, and reacting to feedback from the prospect. Again, listening and questioning skills emerge as important.

Sales aids, such as charts, graphs, printed literature, photographs, films, slides, and portable computers, are excellent tools for achieving clarity. Such sales aids should be used only where they can make the presentation more effective, not merely to "put on a show." After all, the medium should not overpower the message.

ADDRESSING CUSTOMER CONCERNS The solicitation of feedback from the prospect will usually raise concerns in the form of questions and objections related to the salesperson's offering. Addressing these concerns is a routine part of the salesperson–customer relationship. In some cases, these concerns represent an unwillingness to buy unless the problem is resolved. In other cases, the buyer is asking for clarification of a point, or seeking information, perhaps reassurance on a particular point. In still other cases, prospects raise objections and ask questions as a bargaining tactic in an attempt to negotiate a more favorable deal.

Regardless of the reasons for raising objections and asking questions, the salesperson must be ready to respond effectively. Veteran salespeople generally look forward to dealing with questions and objections, viewing them as indicators of interest and therefore of an imminent purchase decision. Accordingly, they treat objections and questions with respect, even when they must tell the prospects that he or she is in error on a point.

Gaining Customer Commitment

A successful relationship requires that all parties in the relationship make firm commitments to each other. Assuming that the earlier steps in the sales process have been properly conducted, a joint commitment is the next logical step. In a sales context, this means that both the customer and the salesperson agree to a course of action. This may involve a purchase agreement or other courses of action, such as agreements to continue sales negotiations, to conduct a product usage test, or perhaps to sign a long-term distribution contract.

The reality of a competitive marketplace dictates that salespeople actively seek a commitment, because more than one firm can usually meet the customer's needs adequately. Customers expect salespeople to seek commitments, but they do not appreciate being pressured into premature decisions, nor do they appreciate high-pressure gimmicks designed to force a positive decision.

The question of when to seek commitment remains open. The stock answer in days gone by was "early and often," meaning that salespeople should try to conclude the sale quickly by using repeated closing attempts. This approach is, however, risky; if the closing attempt is inappropriately early, a negative response is more likely; and once a negative response has been voiced by the prospect, principles of *cognitive consistency* dictate that the prospect will tend to reinforce the decision. The question of timing, therefore, is important in seeking commitment.

Although there are no unimpeachable guidelines to timing, if the presentation has been completed without questions or objections from the prospect, it is logical that commitment should be sought without delay. Likewise, if all questions and objections have been satisfactorily handled, seeking commitment is in order. In many instances, salespeople can interpret cues, or signals, from the prospect that indicate that gaining commitment is the next logical step. For example, the prospect might ask, "Can you deliver by next Tuesday?" Such a question would not be asked by an indifferent or unreceptive prospect. In the final analysis, the question of when to seek commitment is a judgment call to be made by the salesperson, sometimes with the assistance of the prospect.

An Ethical Dilemma

Ron Jackson, sales representative for GEONAV, was wrapping up his fourth sales call on JBL Transport, a prospect for GEONAV's satellite-based tracking systems. Ron felt that he would get a commitment for a large purchase order from JBL. But first, he wanted to be sure that he had answered all of Mr. McKenzie's questions: "Frank, I appreciate the time you have spent with me over the past month helping me understand your requirements. Before I recommend our next step, I was wondering if you have any questions." Frank thought for a minute, then replied, "I guess not Ron. You have been very thorough in explaining how your systems work. On second thought, I do have one question: if you were me, would you ask any more questions before making a purchase decision?" Ron was surprised at Frank's question, but replied, "Can't think of a thing, Frank," then proceeded to secure a major purchase order from JBL Transport. As he drove to his next sales call, Ron wondered whether he should have told Frank the system he ordered had been experiencing periodic downtime due to a programming glitch in the satellite. Frank had not specifically asked about reliability of the system, and Ron hoped the problem would soon be solved. Should Ron have disclosed the potential reliability problem to Mr. McKenzie? Justify your answer.

Enhancing Customer Relationships

The importance of a diligent effort to maintain and enhance customer relationships is well understood by Franco DiCarlo, director of sales for Calvin Klein. With such customers as Saks Fifth Avenue, Barneys in New York, and Ultimo in Chicago, DiCarlo says, "Making the sale is only the beginning. After that you have to keep track of the goods every step of the way. You have to make sure they get delivered on time and that the selling staff knows how they should be displayed." DiCarlo continues, "Anybody can move product. I can go out and sell a ton of something, but if it's not right for that particular store, it's just going to end up back on my doorstep at the end of the season."[14]

Clearly, professional salespeople such as Franco DiCarlo view their customer base as far too valuable an asset to risk losing through neglect. In maintaining and enhancing customer relationships, salespeople are involved in performing routine postsale follow-up activities and in enhancing the relationship as it evolves by anticipating and adapting to changes in the customer's situation, competitive forces, and other changes in the market environment.

One objective in this step is to create a strong bond with the customer that will diminish the probability of the customer's terminating the relationship. In effect, the salesperson's firm earns the business through a number of successive trials and strengthens its position as time passes.

RELATIONSHIP ENHANCEMENT ACTIVITIES Specific **relationship enhancement** activities vary substantially from company to company, but some of the more common ones are entering and expediting purchase orders, assisting in product installations, training customer personnel, and resolving problems with shipping and billing. Salespeople should continually add to the value received by customers through an ongoing diagnosis of customer needs and opportunities. Salespeople can then recommend new solutions, products, and services when appropriate. Salespersons could hold formal status-of-the-business reviews with the customer on a regular basis, reinforcing the importance of the customer to the selling firm. During review sessions or regular sales calls or through surveys, salespeople can solicit feedback on how to improve the product and provide better service.

Salespeople can also enhance the relationship by providing the customer with information relating to how expectations have been met. For example, salespeople can identify and quantify contributions to cost savings and quality improvement programs. They should seek acknowledgment from the customer that the benefits and satisfaction that were sought have been delivered.

As mentioned at the beginning of this module, **building trust** is an important element in a buyer–seller relationship. Throughout the sales process, the salesperson works to earn the trust of the customer. Sales technique is part of the trust-earning process, but the central truth of the matter is

> While it is important to consciously work to convince the buyer that you can be trusted, in the long run nothing is likely to work better than doing what you say you will do, keeping all your promises, and always telling the truth. In the short run certain behaviors have been shown to speed this attribute of trustworthiness. But over the long run, nothing will earn the buyer's trust like being a trustworthy individual.[15]

Summary
1. **Distinguish between transaction-focused traditional selling and trust-based relationship selling.** Summarized in Exhibit 3.1, trust-based selling focuses more on the customer than does transaction-focused selling. The salesperson will act as a consultant to the customer in trust-based selling, whereas transaction-based selling concentrates more on making sales calls and closing sales. There is far more emphasis on post-sales follow-up with relationship selling than with transaction selling, and salespeople must have a broader range of skills to practice relationship selling.
2. **Discuss five alternative approaches to personal selling.** Alternative approaches to personal selling include stimulus response, mental states, need satisfaction, problem-solving, and the consultative approach. Stimulus response selling often uses the same

sales presentation for all customers. The mental states approach prescribes that the salesperson lead the buyer through stages in the buying process. Need satisfaction selling focuses on relating benefits of the seller's products or services to the buyer's particular situation. Problem-solving selling extends need satisfaction by concentrating on various alternatives available to the buyer. Consultative selling focuses on helping customers achieve strategic goals, not just meeting needs or solving problems. In consultative selling, salespersons fulfill three primary roles: strategic orchestrator, business consultant, and long-term ally to the customer.

3. **Describe the three primary roles fulfilled by consultative salespeople.** The three roles are strategic orchestrator, business consultant, and long-term ally. As a strategic orchestrator, salespeople coordinate the use of the sales organization's resources to satisfy the customer. As a business consultant, the salesperson becomes an expert on the customer's business and educates the customer on how his or her products can benefit the customer. The consultative salesperson acts as a long-term ally to the customer, acting in the customer's best interest even when an immediate sale is not expected.

4. **Identify five salesperson attributes that are essential for building customer trust.** As indicated in Figure 3.4, to build trust with customers, salespeople must be customer oriented, honest, dependable, competent, and likable. By consistently displaying these attributes over time, salespeople can build mutually beneficial long-term relationships with customers.

5. **Discuss the sales process as a series of interrelated steps.** As presented in Figure 3.4, the sales process has six steps. The first three steps—prospecting, precall planning, and approaching the customer—are concerned with initiating a relationship with the customer. The next two steps—sales presentation delivery and gaining customer commitment—are related to developing the salesperson–customer relationship. The final step in the sales process, and in many cases the most important one, is enhancing the relationship with the customer. It is important to note that one step builds on the previous step and that it usually takes several sales calls to confirm an initial sale to a prospect.

Understanding Sales Management Terms

- Adaptive selling
- Stimulus response selling
- Continued affirmation
- Mental states selling
- AIDA
- Need satisfaction selling
- Problem-solving selling
- Consultative selling
- Strategic orchestrator
- Business consultant
- Long-term ally
- Sales process
- Prospecting
- Screening criteria
- Cold-call reluctance
- Preapproach
- Sales presentation planning
- Sales presentation format
- Canned sales presentation
- Organized sales presentation
- Sales proposal
- Sales mix model
- Presentation pace
- Presentation scope
- Depth of inquiry
- Two-way communication
- Visual aids
- Approaching the customer
- Sales presentation
- Building credibility
- Conservative claims
- Third-party evidence
- Testimonials
- Guarantees and warranties
- Achieving clarity
- Relationship enhancement
- Building trust

Developing Sales Management Knowledge

1. How are need satisfaction and problem-solving selling related? How do they differ?
2. How does the consultative selling approach differ from problem-solving and need satisfaction selling? Explain the three key roles of consultative salespersons.
3. When do you think stimulus response selling would be most effective?

4. How important is teamwork between the customer and the sales organization in practicing consultative selling? How does teamwork within the sales organization factor into consultative selling?
5. Is adaptive selling as important in domestic markets as it is in international markets?
6. What is the purpose of each step in the sales process?
7. Discuss the final step of the sales process as related to the evolution of personal selling, which was covered in Module 2.
8. Discuss the elements of the sales mix model shown in Figure 3.5.
9. Describe the three different sales presentation formats in terms of their advantages and disadvantages.
10. Which do you feel is the most important—planning the sales presentation or delivering it?

Building Sales Management Skills

1. Skillful questioning is an integral part of the sales process. A good way to think about different types of questions is to use the ADAPT model.[16] According to this model, there are five categories of questions:

   <u>A</u>ssessment questions to elicit factual information about the customer's current situation.
   <u>D</u>iscovery questions to uncover problems or opportunities that can be addressed by the salesperson's company.
   <u>A</u>ctivation questions to activate the customer's interest in solving the problem or realizing an opportunity.
   <u>P</u>rojection questions to assist the customer in "projecting" what life would be like if the problem is solved or opportunity realized.
   <u>T</u>ransition questions confirm the customer's desire to move toward problem resolution or opportunity realization.

   A. Where would the following questions fit into the ADAPT model?
      1. To better meet your needs, I need to ask a few questions. First, could you tell me who else in your company will be involved in developing the specifications for your new computer system?
      2. If we installed a new loading system for you, we could cut your damaged goods expenses to practically zero. Even though the initial investment is substantial, you might want to consider a new system. What do you think?
      3. It sounds like you can really benefit from our in-store merchandising program. It will take about 30 minutes to get the information I need to complete your customized proposal. Do you have time now, or would you prefer to book another appointment?
      4. You mentioned that your current supplier is a bit erratic. Could you tell me what you mean?
      5. A lot of companies are focusing on what they do best and outsourcing the rest. If we take over your cafeteria operation, you no longer have to worry about menu development, staffing, or health inspections. You can concentrate on running your manufacturing business. Is that something you would like to pursue?
   B. Assume you are making your first sales call on the general manager of a small hotel chain that is a target customer for your institutional furniture company. The chain has 15 hotels, 50 rooms per hotel. Existing furniture is several years old. An exterior renovation is underway in most of the hotels to be followed by interior renovation (paint and carpet) and updating of furniture. List several assessment and discovery questions for your first sales call that would serve as the basis for future sales calls during which you could use activation, projection, and transition questions to move toward earning a commitment from the general manager.

2. Salespeople routinely use the Internet to learn more about industries, customers, and competitors to develop sales strategy and plan sales presentations. A useful Internet site for information about manufacturers is found at http://mfginfo.com. Go to this site and select Internet Industry Resources. Then select Thomas Register. Now select

Helpful Buying Hints for one of the product/service categories listed. Write a brief analysis of how this information could be used by a salesperson in the selected category.

3. Assume you are selling PACSEAL, an automatic package-sealing device. One of your current prospects is a manufacturer of windshield wiper blades that ships approximately 5,000 boxes of blades per day to its customers. The cost of PACSEAL is $20,000. The customer can expect to save a penny per box shipped if PACSEAL is installed. The PACSEAL system has a guaranteed life of 5 years. How could you use this information in a sales proposal? How would you illustrate the key selling points derived from this information?

Making Sales Management Decisions

CASE 3.1 *Biomod, Inc.*

Background

Biomod, Inc., a California-based manufacturer of educational models of the human body, has been in business since the mid-1960s. The company's products, sold primarily to middle schools in the United States, are available in plastic or as computer images. Accompanying products include lesson plans for teachers and workbooks and computer programs for students. Biomod has enjoyed healthy sales increases in recent years, as schools increasingly integrated computer-assisted instruction into their curricula. Five years ago, Biomod began selling consumer versions of its models through selected specialty educational toy stores and recently began selling on its own Web site. In addition, Biomod is also selling on the Web through Hypermart.com and Ed-Toys. Further, Biomod has had discussions with Toys-R-Us, and the giant retailer seems eager to stock Biomod products.

Current Situation

Biomod has employed Zack Wilson, a recent graduate of San Diego State University, for the past 6 months. He has become familiar with all aspects of marketing the Biomod product line and is now the sales representative for electronic retailing accounts. Zack is truly excited about his job, as he sees the explosive growth potential for selling Biomod products on the Internet. His first big success came when he convinced Hypermart.com to sell Biomod products. After all, Hypermart has the reputation in most circles as the premier electronic retailer. Thirty days after his initial sales to Hypermart, Zack was thrilled to land Ed-Toys as his second electronic retailer.

No doubt about it, Zack Wilson was on a roll. Securing commitments from Hypermart and Ed-Toys within a month was almost too good to be true. In fact, there was only one problem facing Zack Wilson. Hypermart had begun discounting the Biomod product line as much as 20 percent off suggested retail, and Ed-Toys was unhappy with the intense price competition. The following conversation had just taken place between Zack and Ed-Toys buyer Andrea Haughton:

Andrea: Zack, your line looked really promising to us at suggested retail prices, but meeting Hypermart's pricing sucks the profit right out of the equation. Are you selling Hypermart at a lower price than us?

Zack: Absolutely not! Hypermart just decided to promote our line with the discounts.

Andrea: So the discounts are just a temporary promotion? When will Hypermart stop discounting?

Zack: Well, I don't really know. What I mean by that is that Hypermart often discounts, but in the case of the Biomod line, I've got to believe it's just a temporary thing.

Andrea: Why do you think so?

Zack: Because they haven't asked me for a lower price. Like you, they can't be making much of a profit after the discounts.

Andrea: Well, Zack, we need to stop the bleeding! I can't go on meeting their prices. If they're not making money either, maybe it's time you get them to stop the discounting. Can you talk with them about getting up to suggested retail?

Zack: Andrea, you know I can't dictate retail selling prices to them any more than I could to you.

Andrea: Nor I am suggesting you try to dictate prices. I am simply suggesting that you let them know that if they choose to go back to suggested retail, we will surely follow. If we can't sell at suggested retail, we will have little choice but to stop selling the Biomod line. I'm sure you can appreciate the fact that we have profit expectations for every line we sell. At 20 percent off, Zack, the Biomod line just doesn't cut it for us.

Zack: O.K., I will see what I can do.

Later in the day, Zack checked his e-mail and found a disturbing message from Barbara Moore, a Biomod sales representative for the retail store division. Barbara's message informed Zack that one of her key retailers had visited the Hypermart Web site and was extremely upset to see the heavy discounting on the Biomod line. Barbara claimed that she was in danger of losing her account and that she feared a widespread outcry from other specialty stores as word of the Hypermart discounting would quickly spread. Barbara strongly urged Zack to do what he could to get Hypermart back to suggested retail. Zack noted that Barbara had copied both her sales manager and Rebecca Stanley, Zack's sales manager, with her e-mail message.

The following day, Zack called on Warren Bryant, Hypermart's buyer for the Biomod line. He conveyed to Bryant that Ed-Toys and some of the store retailers were upset with the discounting. Bryant shrugged off the news, commenting only that "it's a dog-eat-dog" world and that price competition was part of the game. Zack asked Bryant if he was happy with the profit margins on the Biomod line, and Bryant responded that he was more concerned with growing Hypermart's market share than with profit margins. He told Zack, "Our game plan is grab a dominant share, then worry about margins." At this point, Warren Bryant gave Zack something else to think about:

Warren: Hey, Zack, I noticed you guys are selling the same products on your own Web site as the ones we're selling on ours.

Zack: True, what's the problem?

Warren: Well, I just read in the trade press where Home Depot told their vendors that they don't buy from their (Home Depot's) competitors and that they view vendor Web sites as competitors to their retail business. Maybe we feel the same way. We sell on the Web, and if you do too, then you're really a competitor for us.

Zack: Warren, you know that we only do a little volume on the Web. Our site is really more of an information site.

Warren: But you do offer an alternative to other electronic retailers and us by selling on your own site. And by the way, don't your store retailers oppose your selling on the Web?

Zack: At this point, most of them are small retailers, and frankly speaking, they view you as more of a threat than us selling on our own site. Besides, our store division salesforce is working on a software package that will enable our store retailers to easily set up their own Web sites over the next 6 months or so.

Warren: Unbelievable! What you're saying is that another division in your company is creating even more Web-based competition for me. I thought we had a real future together, but I've got to do some heavy-duty thinking on that. Thanks, Zack, but I'm really busy and need to move on to some other priorities this afternoon. Call me if you have any new thoughts on where we go from here.

Zack left Hypermart and began the hour-long drive back to the office. "Good thing I've a little time to think about this situation," he thought as he drove along. "I need to talk with Rebecca Stanley just as soon as I get to the office."

Questions
1. How do you think Zack got into this dilemma?
2. If you were Rebecca Stanley, Zack's sales manager, what would you advise Zack to do?

CASE 3.2 *Plastico, Inc.*

Background

Plastico, Inc., located in New York, is a manufacturer of plastic components. The company is noted for producing high-quality products. Its salesforce calls on large accounts, such as refrigerator manufacturers who might need large quantities of custom-made products, such as door liners. Recent increases in new-home sales over the past several years have fueled refrigerator sales and, subsequently, sales at Plastico. Moreover, federal regulations requiring that dishwasher liners be made of plastic, rather than porcelain, have enhanced Plastico's sales.

Current Situation

Sharon Stone had recently been assigned to the central Michigan territory. Although this was her first sales job, she felt confident and was eager to begin. She had taken a sales course in college and had just completed the company's training program. The company stressed the use of an organized sales presentation in which the salesperson organizes the key points into a planned sequence that allows for adaptive behavior by the salesperson as the presentation progresses. She was familiar with this approach because she had studied it in her college sales course.

Sharon's first call was on a small refrigerator manufacturer in Ann Arbor. She had called the day before to set up an appointment with materials purchasing manager David Kline at 9:00 a.m. On the morning of her meeting, Sharon was running behind schedule because of an alarm clock malfunction. As a result, she ended up in traffic she did not anticipate and did not arrive for her appointment until 9:10 a.m. When she informed the receptionist she had an appointment with David Kline, she was told he was in another meeting. He did agree, however, to see Sharon when his meeting was finished, which would be about 9:45 a.m. Sharon was upset Kline would not wait 10 minutes for her and let the receptionist know it.

AT 9:50 a.m. Sharon was introducing herself to Kline. She noticed his office was filled with University of Michigan memorabilia. She remembered from her training that the first thing to do was build rapport with the prospect. Thus she asked Kline if he went to the University of Michigan. This got the ball rolling quickly. Kline had graduated from Michigan and was a big fan of the basketball and football teams. He was more than happy to talk about them. Sharon was excited; she knew this would help her build rapport. After about 25 minutes of football and basketball chitchat, Sharon figured it was time to get down to business.

After finally getting Kline off the subject of sports, Sharon began to discuss the benefits of her product. She figured if she did not control the conversation Kline would revert to discussing sports. She went on and on about the material compounds comprising Plastico plastics, as well as the processes used to develop plastic liners. She explained the customizing process, the product's durability, Plastico's ability to provide door liners in any color, and her company's return and credit policies. After nearly 25 minutes, she finally asked Kline if he had any questions.

Kline asked her if she had any product samples with her. Sharon had to apologize—in all the confusion this morning she ran off and left the samples at home. Then Kline asked her about the company's turnaround time from order to delivery. Knowing quick turnaround was important to Kline, and feeling this prospect may be slipping away, she told him it was about 4 weeks, although she knew it was really closer to five. However, she thought, if Kline ordered from them and it took a little longer, she could always blame it on production. When the issue of price emerged, Sharon was not able to clearly justify in Kline's mind why Plastico was slightly higher than the competition. She thought that she had clearly explained the benefits of the product and that it should be obvious that Plastico is a better choice.

Finally, Kline told Sharon he would have to excuse himself. He had a meeting to attend on the other side of town. He thanked her for coming by and told her he would consider her offer. Sharon thanked Kline for his time and departed. As she reflected on her first call she wondered where she went wrong. She thought she would jot down some notes about her call to discuss with her sales manager later.

Questions

1. What problems do you see with Sharon's first sales call?
2. If you were Sharon's sales manager, what would you recommend she do to improve her chances of succeeding?

PART II

Defining the Strategic Role of the Sales Function

The two modules in Part Two discuss the sales function from a strategic perspective. Module 4 investigates strategic decisions at different levels in multibusiness multiproduct firms. The key elements of corporate strategy, business strategy, marketing strategy, and sales strategy are described, and important relationships between each strategy level and the sales function are identified. Special attention is directed toward the role of personal selling in a marketing strategy and sales strategy development. Account targeting strategy, relationship strategy, selling strategy, and sales channel strategy are the key elements of a sales strategy.

Module 5 emphasizes the importance of sales organization design and salesforce deployment in executing organizational strategies successfully. The concepts of specialization, centralization, span of control, management levels, and line/staff positions are critical considerations in sales organization design. Special attention is directed toward the use of different sales organization structures in different selling environments. Salesforce deployment decisions include allocating selling effort to accounts, determining the appropriate salesforce size, and designing sales territories. The key considerations and analytical approaches for each of these decisions are discussed.

MODULE 4

Organizational Strategies and the Sales Function

Strategic Change and the Sales Function: America Online

America Online (AOL) was established 15 years ago. According to founder, chairman, and CEO Steve Case, the mission of AOL is "to build a global medium as central to people's lives as the telephone or television . . . and even more valuable." By the end of 1999, the company is expected to have more than 22 million subscribers who pay $21.95 a month for unlimited electronic access. AOL is also one of the top 10 media brands in the world.

Although the subscription business is extremely important, AOL began to focus more attention on advertising and e-commerce sales in 1996. The interactive marketing department was established to drive this business. Advertising and e-commerce sales were $102 million in 1996 but were expected to exceed $1 billion in 1999.

This tremendous sales growth has been achieved by a sales organization led by Paul Corvino, vice president and general manager for AOL Interactive Marketing. The sales organization consists of 58 outside salespeople and 20 inside sales representatives. Everyone is driven by the sales organization's mission: "To increase the number of targeted, consultative sales calls to increase revenue and have happier, more satisfied customers."

Salespeople focus on specific industries, such as packaged goods or automotive, and are organized into four geographic regions. Each salesperson is assigned approximately 200 accounts that are ranked in order of spending and potential to spend dollars online. Goals, strategies, and action plans are established for each of these accounts. Salespeople make about nine sales calls a week, with roughly 20 percent of the sales calls producing new deals for AOL.

Salespeople listen to the business challenges faced by their accounts and try to uncover needs that AOL can satisfy. Once the needs are identified, the salespeople prepare proposals and make customized sales presentations that emphasize how advertising and e-commerce with AOL can improve the account's business. Customers then work with the marketing, advertising, and media professionals in AOL's account services department. The goal of the account services department is to get results for customers.

Managing these salespeople is largely the job of the four regional sales managers. These managers work with their salespeople to help them plan and execute account strategies. Ongoing training is emphasized on topics such as consultative

Learning Objectives

After completing this module, you should be able to

1 Define the different strategy levels for multibusiness multiproduct firms.

2 Discuss how corporate and business strategy decisions affect the sales function.

3 List the advantages and disadvantages of personal selling as a marketing communications tool.

4 Specify the situations in which personal selling is typically emphasized in a marketing strategy.

5 Describe ways that personal selling, advertising, and other tools can be blended into effective integrated marketing communications programs.

6 Discuss the important concepts behind organizational buyer behavior.

7 Define an account targeting strategy.

8 Explain the different types of relationship strategies.

9 Discuss the importance of different selling strategies.

10 Describe the different sales channel strategies.

selling, presentation skills, teamwork, and negotiating. Salespeople are evaluated and rewarded for doing things that meet the sales organization's mission: generating revenue, practicing consultative selling and teamwork, making sales calls, participating in training programs, doing paperwork, and following through with customers. The compensation plan consists of a base salary, commissions, and stock options.

One reason for AOL's success is the integration of strategies developed at different organizational levels. Especially important is the attention focused on the sales organization and its critical role in implementing these strategies. Although AOL is proud of what it has accomplished, it must guard against complacency as the competition is formidable.

Sources: Malcolm Campbell, "What Makes AOL Click?", *Selling Power* (September 1999): 55–62; Dana Ray, "Hot Performers," *Selling Power* (July/August 1999): 16.

The America Online situation described in the opening vignette illustrates an important reality in the contemporary business world: Many firms consist of multiple business units that market multiple products to different customer groups. Strategy development in these multibusiness multiproduct firms is extremely complex. Different types of strategic decisions must be made at different levels of the organization. However, the different strategies must be consistent with each other and integrated for the firm to perform successfully. For example, AOL's success depends on developing consistent corporate, business, marketing, and sales strategies and executing them effectively.

Organizational Strategy Levels

The key strategy levels for multibusiness multiproduct firms are presented in Exhibit 4.1. **Corporate strategy** consists of decisions that determine the mission, business portfolio, and future growth directions for the entire corporate entity. A separate **busienss strategy** must be developed for each **strategic business unit** (SBU) (discussed later in this module) in the corporate family, defining how that SBU plans to compete effectively within its industry. Because an SBU typically consists of multiple products serving different markets, each product/market combination

EXHIBIT 4.1 Organizational Strategy Levels

Strategy Level	Key Decision Areas	Key Decision Makers
Corporate strategy	Corporate mission Strategic business unit definition Strategic business unit objectives	Corporate management
Business strategy	Strategy types Strategy execution	Business unit management
Marketing strategy	Target market selection Marketing mix development Integrated marketing communications	Marketing management
Sales strategy	Account targeting strategy Relationship strategy Selling strategy Sales channel strategy	Sales management

---

SALES MANAGEMENT IN THE 21ST CENTURY

Integrating Organizational Strategies

Jane Hrehocik Clampitt, marketing process manager at DuPont, discusses the importance of integrating strategies at different levels in a company:

It is extremely important for large companies to develop effective strategies at different organizational levels. We focus a lot of attention on this process at DuPont. The corporate strategy defines business units and determines strategic objectives and basic resource allocations for each business unit. Then, each business unit follows a detailed process to create a business strategy that will achieve its objectives. Next, another rigorous process is used to develop specific marketing strategies for the business unit's product/markets. Finally, strategies for selling to specific customer groups within each product/market are determined. This type of sequential process is intended to develop effective and consistent strategies at each organizational level.

---

requires a specific **marketing strategy.** Each marketing strategy includes the selection of target market segments and the development of a marketing mix to serve each target market. A key consideration is the role that personal selling will play in the marketing communications mix for a particular marketing strategy.

The corporate, business, and marketing strategies represent strategy development from the perspective of different levels within an organization. Although sales management may have some influence on the decisions made at each level, the key decision makers are typically from higher management levels outside the sales function. Sales management does, however, play the key role in sales strategy development. An example of one approach for strategy development at different organizational levels is presented in "Sales Management in the 21st Century: Integrating Organizational Strategies."

Corporate Strategy and the Sales Function

Strategic decisions at the topmost level of multibusiness multiproduct firms determine the corporate strategy for a given firm, which is what provides direction and guidance for activities at all organizational levels. Developing a corporate strategy requires the following steps:[1]

1. Analyzing corporate performance and identifying future opportunities and threats
2. Determining corporate mission and objectives
3. Defining business units
4. Setting objectives for each business unit

Once the corporate strategy has been developed, management is concerned with implementation, evaluation, and control of the corporate strategic plan. Although the corporate strategy has the most direct impact on business-level operations, each element does affect the sales function.

Corporate Mission

The development of a statement of the corporate mission is an important first step in the strategy formulation process. This mission statement provides direction for strategy development and execution throughout the organization. For example,

AOL's corporate mission is "to build a global medium as central to people's lives as the telephone or television . . . and even more valuable." This statement is intended to communicate the basic purpose of AOL to all employees and to drive the development of business, marketing, and sales strategies.

Sales managers and salespeople must operate within the guidelines presented in the corporate mission statement. Furthermore, they can use these corporate guidelines as a basis for establishing specific policies for the entire sales organization. Thus, in this way, the corporate mission statement has a direct effect on sales management activities.

Definition of Strategic Business Units

Defining business units, often called SBUs, is an important and difficult aspect of corporate strategy development. The basic purpose is to divide the corporation into parts to facilitate strategic analysis and planning. Cravens defines an SBU as "a single product or brand, a line of products, or a mix of related products that meets a common market need or a group of related needs, and the unit's management is responsible for all (or most) of the basic business functions."[2]

The definition of SBUs is an important element of corporate strategy. Changes in SBU definition may increase or decrease the number of SBUs, and these changes typically affect the sales function in many ways. Salesforces may have to be merged, new salesforces may have to be established, or existing salesforces may have to be reorganized to perform different activities. These changes may affect all sales management activities from the type of salespeople to be hired to how they should be trained, motivated, compensated, and supervised.

The establishment of the interactive marketing group represented a new business unit for AOL. Instead of focusing on getting consumers to subscribe to AOL's electronic service, the company is also engaged in getting organizations to use AOL for advertising and e-commerce. The two businesses are, however, consistent and complementary, because the larger the AOL subscription base, the easier it is to sell advertising and e-commerce services. Nevertheless, the new business requires more of a focus on personal selling and the establishment and management of field and inside salesforces.

Objectives for Strategic Business Units

Once SBUs have been defined, corporate management must determine appropriate strategic objectives for each. Many firms view their SBUs collectively as a portfolio of business units. Each business unit faces a different competitive situation and plays a different role in the **business unit portfolio.** Therefore, specific strategic objectives should be determined for each SBU. Corporate management has ultimate responsibility for establishing strategic objectives for each SBU. As illustrated in Exhibit 4.2, the strategic objective assigned to a business unit has a direct effect on personal selling and sales management activities.

Determining strategic objectives for each SBU is an important aspect of corporate strategy. These strategic objectives affect the development of the sales organization's objectives, the selling tasks performed by salespeople, and the activities of sales managers. AOL's subscription and advertising/e-commerce businesses are both focused on building market share. Therefore, the AOL sales organization emphasizes expanding business with current accounts and winning new accounts. All sales organization policies, especially the incentive compensation plan, are designed to help salespeople achieve the market share growth objective. However, too much emphasis on business unit objectives can place salespeople in uncomfortable situations as illustrated in "An Ethical Dilemma."

EXHIBIT 4.2 SBU Objectives and the Sales Organization

Market Share Objectives	Sales Organization Objectives	Primary Sales Tasks	Recommended Compensation System
Build	Build sales volume Secure distribution	Call on prospective and new accounts Provide high service levels, particularly presale service Product/market feedback	Salary plus incentive
Hold	Maintain sales volume Consolidate market positions through concentration on targeted segments Secure additional outlets	Call on targeted current accounts Increase service levels to current accounts Call on new accounts	Salary plus commission or bonus
Harvest	Reduce selling costs Target profitable accounts	Call on and service most profitable accounts only and eliminate unprofitable accounts Reduce service levels Reduce inventories	Salary plus bonus
Divest/Liquidate	Minimize selling costs and clear out inventory	Dump inventory Eliminate service	Salary

An Ethical Dilemma

The personal computer business unit of Modern Technologies is reaching the end of its fiscal year and is very close to meeting its sales growth objective. Herb Smith, your sales manager, is rallying the troops to "get over the top" so everyone can earn a substantial performance bonus. You are motivated to do your share. Your first call today is to ABC Enterprises. ABC Enterprises purchased a number of computers from you last year. Mary Faulds, purchasing manager at ABC Enterprises, indicates that her information technology people want to upgrade these computers. You know this sale could be critical to meeting your quota and the business unit's sales growth objective. However, you also know that a new, more powerful personal computer will be available in 3 months. This new personal computer is exactly what ABC Enterprises needs, but the sale cannot be made until after the fiscal year ends. What would you do? Why?

Corporate Strategy Summary

Strategic decisions at the topmost levels of multibusiness corporations provide guidance for strategy development at all lower organizational levels. Even though the sales function is often far removed from the corporate level, corporate strategy has both direct and indirect impacts on personal selling and sales management. The corporate mission, definition of SBUs and determination of SBU objectives all affect sales organization operations. However, corporate strategy decisions have their most immediate impact on business unit strategies.

Business Strategy and the Sales Function

Whereas corporate strategy addresses decisions across business units, a separate strategy must be designed for each SBU. The essence of business strategy is competitive advantage: How can each SBU compete successfully against competitive products and services? What differential advantage will each SBU try to exploit in the marketplace? What can each SBU do better than competitors? Answers to these questions provide the basis for business strategies.

EXHIBIT 4.3 Generic Business Strategies and Salesforce Activities

Strategy Type	Role of the Salesforce
Low-cost supplier Aggressive construction of efficient-scale facilities, vigorous pursuit of cost reductions from experience, tight cost and overhead control, usually associated with high relative market share.	Servicing large current customers, pursuing large prospects, minimizing costs, selling on the basis of price, and usually assuming significant order-taking responsibilities
Differentiation Creation of something perceived industrywide as being unique. Provides insulation against competitive rivalry because of brand loyalty and resulting lower sensitivity to price.	Selling nonprice benefits, generating orders, providing high quality of customer service and responsiveness, possibly significant amount of prospecting if high-growth industry, selecting customers based on low price sensitivity; usually requires a high-quality salesforce
Niche Service of a particular target market, with each functional policy developed with this target market in mind. Although market share in the industry might be low, the firm dominates a segment within the industry.	To become experts in the operations and opportunities associated with the target market Focusing customer attention on nonprice benefits and allocating selling time to the target market

Business Strategy Types

Although developing a business unit strategy is a complex task, several classification schemes have been developed to aid in this endeavor. One of the most popular is Porter's **generic business strategies**,[3] presented in Exhibit 4.3. Each of these generic strategies—**low cost, differentiation,** or **niche**—emphasizes a different type of competitive advantage and has different implications for a sales organization. America Online uses a differentiation for its business. Although AOL's pricing is competitive, its focus is on providing services that differ from the competition and create meaningful value for customers.

The sales function plays an important role in executing a specific business strategy.[4] As indicated in Exhibit 4.3, the activities of sales managers and salespeople differ depending on whether the business unit is using a low-cost, differentiation, or niche business strategy. The sales function can often provide the basis for differentiation. For example, AOL salespeople try to customize offerings to meet the specific needs of each customer. And the account services department is driven to help customers achieve the desired results from using AOL for advertising and e-commerce. The success of AOL's business strategy is dependent on how well the salespeople can differentiate AOL in the marketplace.

Business Strategy Summary

Business strategies determine how each SBU plans to compete in the marketplace. Several strategic approaches are available, placing different demands on the sales function. The role of the sales function depends on how an SBU plans to compete in the marketplace, with the activities of sales managers and salespeople being important in executing a business strategy successfully.

Marketing Strategy and the Sales Function

Because SBUs typically market multiple products to different customer groups, separate marketing strategies are often developed for each of an SBU's target markets. These marketing strategies must be consistent with the business strategy. For example, marketers operating in an SBU with a differentiation business strategy would probably not develop marketing strategies that emphasize low price. The marketing strategies for each target market should reinforce the differentiation competitive advantage sought by the SBU.

Figure 4.1 illustrates the major components of a marketing strategy and highlights the position of personal selling within the marketing communications portion of a marketing strategy. The key components of any marketing strategy are the selection of a **target market** and the development of a **marketing mix.** Target market selection requires a definition of the specific market segment to be served. The marketing mix then consists of a marketing offer designed to appeal to the defined target market. This marketing offer contains a mixture of product, price, distribution, and marketing communications strategies. The critical task for the marketing

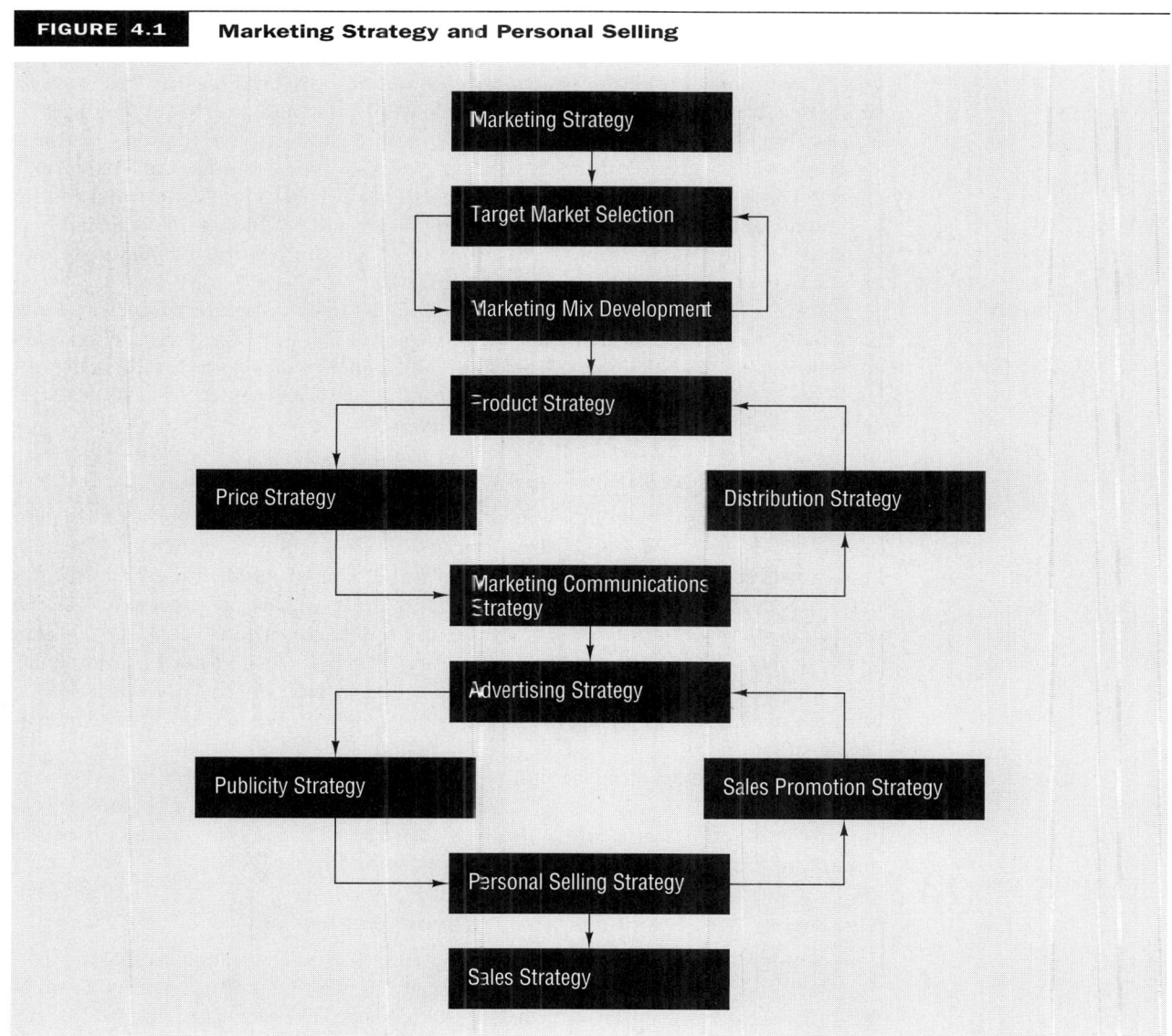

FIGURE 4.1　Marketing Strategy and Personal Selling

Personal selling is an important element of a marketing communications strategy. The marketing communications strategy is one element of a marketing mix designed to appeal to a defined target market. A marketing strategy can be defined in terms of target market and marketing mix components.

strategist is to develop a marketing mix that satisfies the needs of the target market better than competitive offerings.

Personal selling may be an important element in the marketing communications portion of the marketing mix. The marketing communications strategy consists of a mixture of personal selling, advertising, sales promotion, and publicity, with most strategies emphasizing either personal selling or advertising as the main tool. Sales promotion and publicity are typically viewed as supplemental tools. Thus, a key strategic decision is to determine when marketing communications strategies should be driven by personal selling or advertising. This decision should capitalize on the relative advantages of personal selling and advertising for different target markets and different marketing mixes.

Advantages and Disadvantages of Personal Selling

Personal selling is the only promotional tool that consists of personal communication between seller and buyer, and the advantages and disadvantages of personal selling thus accrue from this personal communication. The personal communication between buyer and seller is typically viewed as more credible and has more of an impact (or impression) than messages delivered through advertising media. Personal selling also allows for better timing of message delivery, and it affords the flexibility of communicating different messages to different customers or changing a message during a sales call based on customer feedback. Finally, personal selling has the advantage of allowing a sale to be closed. These characteristics make personal selling a powerful tool in situations in which the benefits of personal communication are important (see Figure 4.2).

The major disadvantage of personal selling is the high cost to reach each member of the audience. Contrast this with the pennies that it costs to reach an audience member through mass advertising. The benefits of personal selling do not come cheap. They may, however, outweigh its costs for certain types of target market situations and for specific marketing mixes.

Target Market Situations and Personal Selling

The characteristics of personal selling are most advantageous in specific target market situations. Personal selling–driven strategies are appropriate when (1) the market consists of only a few buyers that tend to be concentrated in location, (2) the buyer needs a great deal of information, (3) the purchase is important, (4) the product is complex, and (5) service after the sale is important. The target market characteristics that favor personal selling are similar to those found in most business purchasing situations. Thus, personal selling is typically the preferred tool in **business marketing,** whereas advertising is normally emphasized in consumer marketing situations (see Figure 4.3).

An effective marketing communications mix capitalizes on the advantages of each promotional tool. Moreover, characteristics of the target must be considered, and the promotional mix must also be consistent with the other elements of the marketing mix to ensure a coordinated marketing offer.

Marketing Mix Elements and Personal Selling

One of the most difficult challenges facing the marketing strategist is making sure that decisions concerning the product, distribution, price, and marketing communications areas result in an effective marketing mix. There are any number of different ways that these elements can be combined to form a marketing mix. However, some combinations tend to represent logical fits. Exhibit 4.4 shows when a personal selling emphasis might fit well with the other marketing elements. Again, these

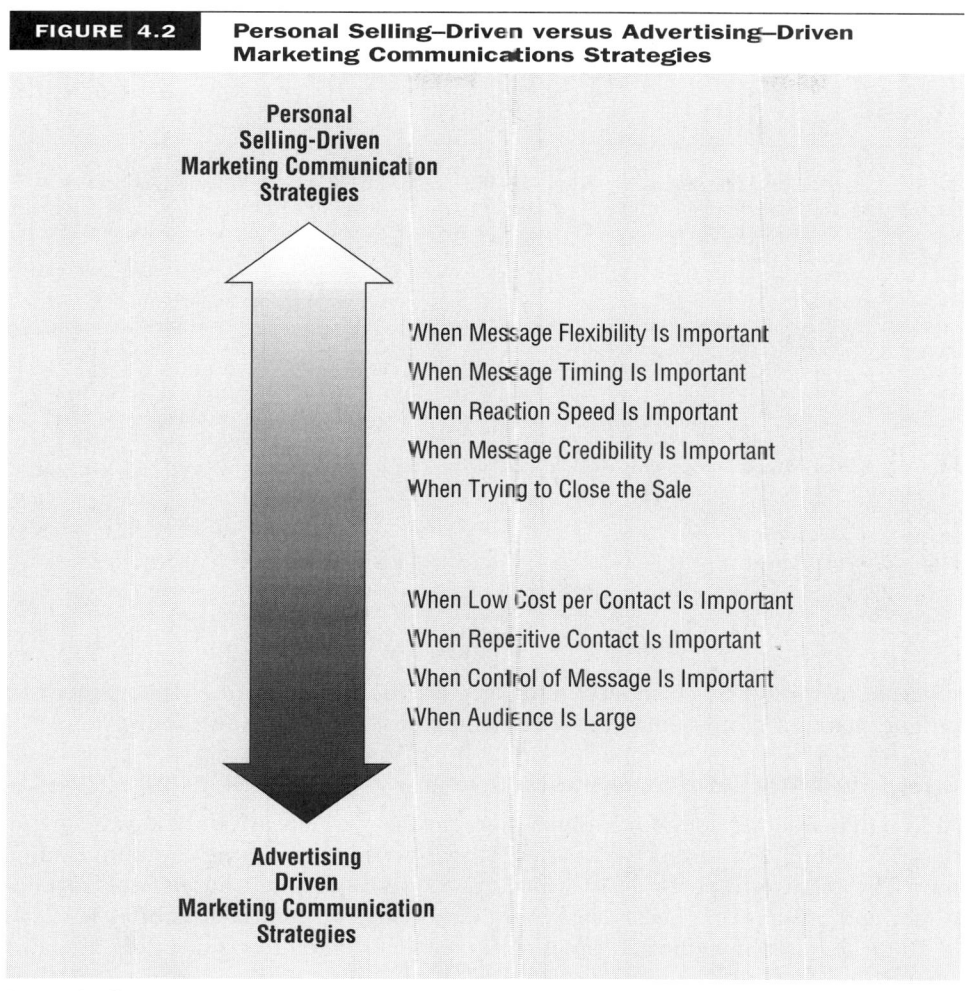

Personal selling–driven marketing communications strategies are most appropriate in situations in which the benefits of personal communication are important.

Personal selling–driven marketing communications strategies are most appropriate for target markets that have the typical characteristics of business markets.

EXHIBIT 4.4 Marketing Mix Elements and Personal Selling

Marketing Mix Area	Characteristics	Marketing Mix Area	Characteristics
Product or service	Complex products requiring customer application assistance (computers, pollution control systems, stream turbines) Major purchase decisions, such as food items purchased by supermarket chains Features and performance of the product requiring personal demonstration and trial by the customer (private aircraft)	Channels	Channel system relatively short and direct to end users Product and service training and assistance needed by channel intermediaries Personal selling needed in "pushing" product through channel Channel intermediaries available to perform personal selling function for supplier with limited resources and experience (brokers or manufacturers' agents)
Price	Final price negotiated between buyer and seller (appliances, automobiles, real estate) selling price or quantity purchased enable an adequate margin to support selling expenses (traditional department store compared with discount house)		

suggestions should be considered only as guidelines, because the development of unique marketing mixes may produce competitive advantages in the marketplace.

Integrated Marketing Communications

Although marketing communications strategies are typically driven by advertising or personal selling, most firms use a variety of tools in their marketing communications mix. The relative importance of various marketing communications tools in consumer and business markets is shown in the rankings presented in Exhibit 4.5.[5]

The key task facing both business and consumer marketers is deciding how and when to use these different tools. **Integrated marketing communications (IMC)** is the increasingly popular term used by many firms to describe their approach. IMC is the strategic integration of multiple marketing communications tools in the most effective and efficient manner. The objective is to use the most cost-effective tool to achieve a desired communication objective and to ensure a consistent message is being communicated to the market.

A typical approach is to use some form of advertising to generate company and product awareness and to identify potential customers. These sales leads might then be contacted and qualified by telemarketers. The best prospects are then turned over to the salesforce to receive personal selling attention. This approach uses relatively inexpensive tools (advertising and telemarketing) to communicate with potential customers early in the buying process and saves the more expensive tools (personal selling) for the best prospects later in the buying process.

Marketing Strategy Summary

Selecting target markets and developing marketing mixes are the key components in marketing strategy development. Marketing strategies must be developed for the target markets served by an SBU and must be consistent with the business unit strategy. One important element of the marketing mix is marketing communications. The critical task is designing a mix that capitalizes on the advantages of each tool. Personal selling has the basic advantage of personal communication and is emphasized in target market situations and marketing mixes in which personal communication is important.

EXHIBIT 4.5 Ranking of Marketing Communications Tools

Consumer Markets	Business Markets
Television ads	Personal selling
Literature, coupons, and point-of-purchase displays	Print ads
Print ads	Direct mail
Direct mail	Trade shows and exhibits catalogs/directories
Radio ads	Literature, coupons, and point-of-purchase displays
Catalogs/directories	Public relations
Public relations	Dealer and distributor materials
Trade shows and exhibits	

Sales Strategy Framework

Corporate, business, and marketing strategies view customers as aggregate markets or market segments. These organizational strategies provide direction and guidance for the sales function, but then sales managers and salespeople must translate these general organizational strategies into specific strategies for individual customers.

A sales strategy is designed to execute an organization's marketing strategy for individual accounts. For example, a marketing strategy consists of selecting a target market and developing a marketing mix. Target markets are typically defined in broad terms, such as the small business market or the university market. Marketing mixes are also described broadly in terms of general product, distribution, price, and marketing communications approaches. All accounts within a target market (e.g., all small businesses or all universities), however, are not the same in terms of size, purchasing procedures, needs, problems, and other factors. The major purpose of a sales strategy is to develop a specific strategic approach for selling to individual accounts within a target market. A sales strategy capitalizes on the important differences among individual accounts or groups of similar accounts.

A firm's sales strategy is important for two basic reasons. First, it has a major impact on a firm's sales and profit performance. Second, it influences many other sales management decisions. Salesforce recruiting/selecting, training, compensation, and performance evaluations are all affected by the sales strategies used by a firm as discussed in "Sales Management in the 21st Century: The Importance of Sales Strategy."

SALES MANAGEMENT IN THE 21ST CENTURY

The Importance of Sales Strategy

Jane Hrehocik Clampitt, marketing process manager at DuPont, emphasizes the importance of having a specific sales strategy for different account groups:

Having an effective sales strategy is so important for a sales organization to be aligned with its business and marketing strategies. The sales strategy provides direction for executing the business and marketing strategies. At DuPont we identify a specific customer interface strategy for each account segment. The customer interface strategy defines how we plan to interact with each customer group. Different customer interface strategies require different selling skills and affect all aspects of sales management. The customer interface strategies determine the types of salespeople to hire, how to develop these individuals and the support systems needed, and how to measure success. Our aim is to maximize the effectiveness, efficiency, and productivity of everyone involved at the customer interface.

Because personal selling–driven promotion strategies are typical in industrial marketing, our discussion of sales strategy focuses on organizational (also called industrial or business) customers. Specific customers are referred to as *accounts*. Thus, a sales strategy must be based on the important and unique aspects of organizational buyer behavior. A framework that integrates organizational buyer behavior and sales strategy is presented in Figure 4.4.

Organizational Buyer Behavior

Organizational buyer behavior refers to the purchasing behavior of organizations. Although there are unique aspects in the buying behavior of any organization, specific types of organizations tend to share similarities in their purchasing procedures (see Exhibit 4.6). Most of our attention is focused on business organizations classified as **users** or **original equipment manufacturers (OEM)**. However, we provide examples of **resellers, government organizations,** and **institutions** throughout the book.

As indicated in Figure 4.4, the development of sales strategy requires an understanding of organizational buyer behavior. The unique aspects of organizational buyer behavior revolve around the buying situation, buying center, buying process, and buying needs.

Buying Situation

One key determinant of organizational buyer behavior is the buying situation faced by an account. Three major types are possible, each representing its own

FIGURE 4.4 **Sales Strategy Framework**

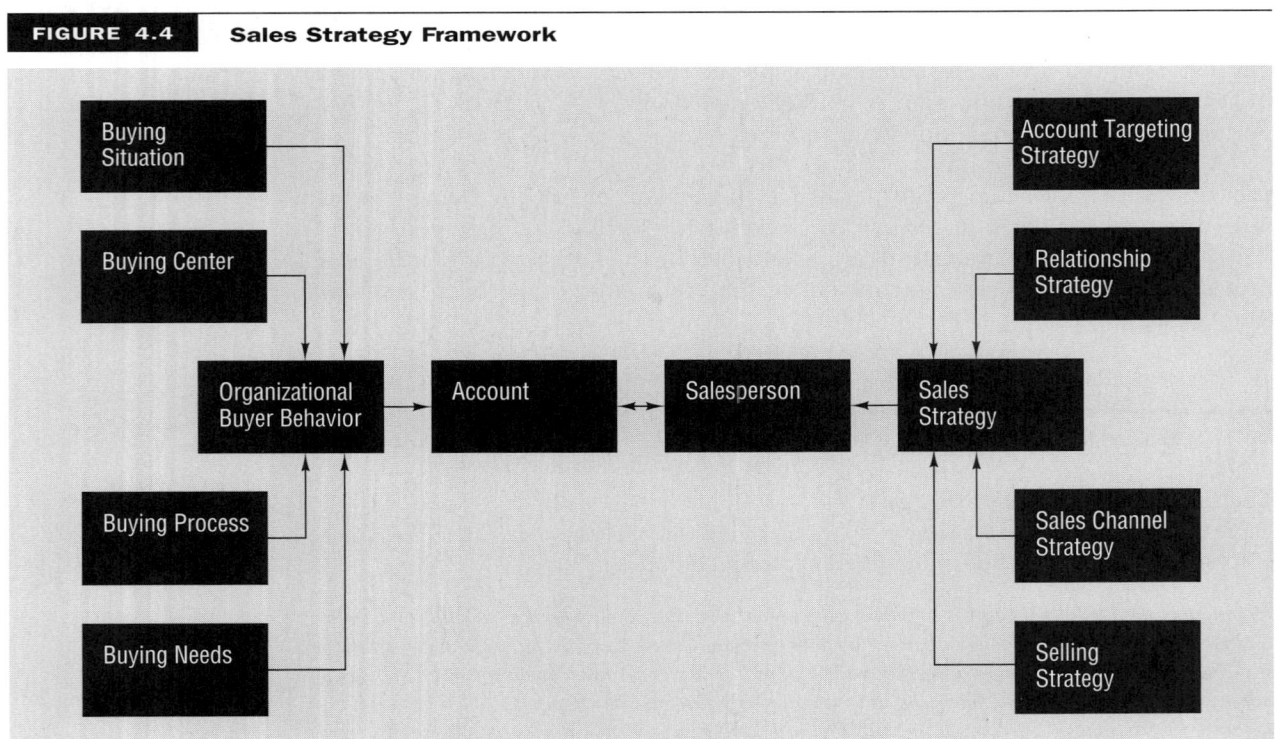

Salesperson interaction with different accounts is directed by a sales strategy. The sales strategy, which defines how specific accounts are to be managed and covered, must be based on an understanding of the buying situation, buying center, buying process, and buying needs of the account.

EXHIBIT 4.6 Types of Organizations

Major Category	Types	Example
Business or industrial organizations	Users—purchase products and services to produce other products and services	IBM purchasing facsimile machines from Sharp for their corporate offices
	Original equipment manufacturers (OEM)—purchase products to incorporate into products	IBM purchasing microcomputer chips from Intel to incorporate into their personal computers
	Resellers—purchase products to sell	Businessland purchasing IBM personal computers to sell to organizations
Government organizations	Federal, state, and local government agencies	Virginia State Lottery purchasing IBM personal computers for managers
Institutions	Public and private institutions	Untied Way purchasing IBM personal computers for their offices

problems for the buying firm and each having different strategic implications for the selling firm.

A **new task buying situation,** in which the organization is purchasing a product for the first time, poses the most problems for the buyer. Because the account has little knowledge or experience as a basis for making the purchase decision, it will typically use a lengthy process to collect and evaluate purchase information. The decision-making process in this type of situation is often called **extensive problem solving.**

A **modified rebuy buying situation** exists when the account has previously purchased and used the product. Although the account has information and experience with the product, it will usually want to collect additional information and may make a change when purchasing a replacement product. The decision-making process in this type of situation is often referred to as **limited problem solving.**

The least complex buying situation is the **straight rebuy buying situation,** wherein the account has considerable experience in using the product and is satisfied with the current purchase arrangements. In this case, the buyer is merely re-ordering from the current supplier and engaging in **routinized response behavior.**

Buying Center

One of the most important characteristics of organizational buyer behavior is the involvement of the many individuals from the firm that participate in the purchasing process. The term *buying center* has been used to designate these individuals. The buying center is not a formal designation on the organization chart but rather an informal network of purchasing participants. (However, members of the purchasing department are typically included in most buying centers and are normally represented in the formal organizational structure.) The difficult task facing the selling firm is to identify all the buying center members and to determine the specific role of each.

The possible roles that buying center members might play in a particular purchasing decision are

- *initiators,* who start the organizational purchasing process
- *users,* who use the product to be purchased
- *gatekeepers,* who control the flow of information between buying center members
- *influencers,* who provide input for the purchasing decision
- *deciders,* who make the final purchase decision
- *purchasers,* who implement the purchasing decision

Each buying center role may be performed by more than one individual, and each individual may perform more than one buying center role.

Buying Process

Organizational buyer behavior can be viewed as a **buying process** consisting of several phases. Although this process has been presented in different ways, the following phases represent a consensus.[6]

Phase 1. Recognition of problem or need
Phase 2. Determination of the characteristics of the item and the quantity needed
Phase 3. Description of the characteristics of the item and quantity needed
Phase 4. Search for and qualification of potential sources
Phase 5. Acquisition and analysis of proposals
Phase 6. Evaluation of proposals and selection of suppliers
Phase 7. Selection of an order routine
Phase 8. Performance feedback and evaluation

These buying phases may be formalized for some organizations and/or for certain purchases. In other situations, this process may only be a rough approximation of what actually occurs. For example, government organizations and institutions tend to have more formal purchasing processes than most business or industrial organizations. Viewing organizational buying as a multiple-phase process is helpful in developing sales strategy. A major objective of any sales strategy is to facilitate an account's movement through this process in a manner that will lead to a purchase of the seller's product.

Buying Needs

Organizational buying is typically viewed as goal-directed behavior intended to satisfy specific **buying needs.** Although the organizational purchasing process is made to satisfy organizational needs, the buying center consists of individuals who are also trying to satisfy individual needs throughout the decision process. Exhibit 4.7 presents examples of individual and organizational needs that might be important in a purchase situation. Individual needs tend to be career related, whereas organizational needs reflect factors related to the use of the product.

Even though organizational purchasing is often thought to be almost entirely objective, subjective personal needs are often extremely important in the final purchase decision. For example, an organization may want to purchase a computer to satisfy data-processing needs. Although a number of suppliers might be able to provide similar products, some suppliers at lower cost than others, buying center members might select the most well-known brand to reduce purchase risk and protect job security.

We discussed how the influence of buying center members varies at different buying phases in the preceding section. Couple this with the different needs of

EXHIBIT 4.7 Personal and Organizational Needs

Personal Goals	Organizational Goals
Want a feeling of power	Control cost in product use situation
Seek personal pleasure	Few breakdowns of product
Desire job security	Dependable delivery for repeat purchases
Want to be well liked	Adequate supply of product
Want respect	Cost within budget limit

different buying center members, and the complexity of organization buying behavior is evident. Nevertheless, sales managers must understand this behavior to develop sales strategies that will satisfy the personal and organizational needs of buying center members.

Sales Strategy

Sales managers and salespeople are typically responsible for strategic decisions at the account level. Although the firm's marketing strategy provides basic guidelines—an overall game plan—the battles are won on an account-by-account basis. Without the design and execution of effective sales strategies directed at specific accounts, the marketing strategy cannot be successfully implemented.

Our framework suggests four basic sales strategy elements: account targeting strategy, relationship strategy, selling strategy, and sales channel strategy. We consider each of these as a separate, but related, strategic decision area. Sales strategies are ultimately developed for each individual account; however, the strategic decisions are often made by classifying individual accounts into similar categories.

Account Targeting Strategy

The first element of a sales strategy is defining an account targeting strategy. As mentioned earlier, all accounts within a target market are not the same. Some accounts might not be good prospects because of existing relationships with competitors. Even those that are good prospects or even current customers differ in terms of how much they buy now or might buy in the future, how they want to do business with sales organizations, and other factors. This means that all accounts cannot be effectively or efficiently served in the same way.

An **account targeting strategy** is the classification of accounts within a target market into categories for the purpose of developing strategic approaches for selling to each account or account group. The account targeting strategy provides the foundation for all other elements of a sales strategy. Just as different marketing mixes are developed to serve different target markets, sales organizations need to use different relationship, selling, and sales channel strategies for different account groups.

The account targeting strategy used by IBM for small and medium-sized businesses is illustrative. IBM targets four different types of small and medium-sized business accounts:

1. the largest customers whose business problems need a complex solution
2. the smaller customers that do not need as much attention
3. prospective customers
4. the very smallest customers

Each of these account segments has different needs, and IBM satisfies these needs in different ways.[7]

Relationship Strategy

As discussed in previous modules, there is a clear trend toward a relationship orientation between buyers and sellers, especially in business markets. However, some accounts want to continue in a transaction mode whereas others want various types of relationships between buyer and seller. A **relationship strategy** is a determination of the type of relationship to be developed with different account groups. A specific relationship strategy is developed for each account group identified by a sales organization's account targeting strategy.

Any number of relationship strategies might be developed, but typically an account targeting strategy defines three to five target groups, each requiring a specific relationship strategy. We illustrate with the general approach established by a large industrial manufacturer. The firm's account targeting strategy identified four different account groups and determined a specific relationship strategy for each group. Exhibit 4.8 presents the characteristics of each relationship strategy.

The relationship strategies range from a transaction relationship based on selling standardized products to a collaborative relationship in which the buyers and sellers work closely together for the benefit of both businesses. In between these extremes are intermediate types of relationships. A solutions relationship emphasizes solving customer problems, and a partnership relationship represents a preferred supplier position over the long term. As a sales organization moves from transaction to collaborative relationships, the time frame becomes longer, the focus changes from buying/selling to creating value, and the products and services offered move from simple and standardized to more complex and customized.

The different characteristics of the different relationship strategies are further illustrated in Figure 4.5. The move from transaction to collaborative relationships requires a greater commitment between buyer and seller, because they will be working together much more closely. Some buyers and sellers are not willing to make the required commitments. In addition, the selling costs are increased to serve accounts with higher-level relationships. Therefore, sales organizations must consider the sales and costs associated with using different relationship strategies for different account groups. The critical task is balancing the customer's needs with the cost to serve the account.

Selling Strategy

Successfully executing a specific relationship strategy requires a different selling approach. A **selling strategy** is the planned selling approach for each relationship strat-

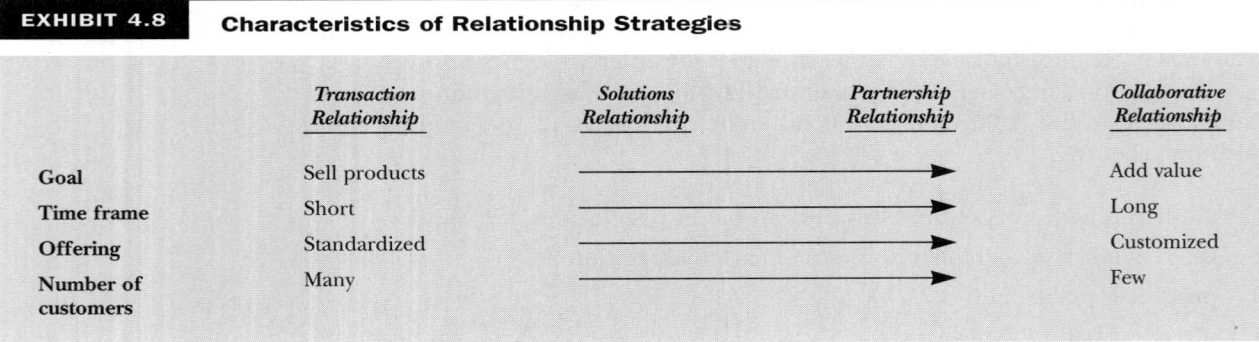

EXHIBIT 4.8 **Characteristics of Relationship Strategies**

	Transaction Relationship	*Solutions Relationship*	*Partnership Relationship*	*Collaborative Relationship*
Goal	Sell products	→	→	Add value
Time frame	Short	→	→	Long
Offering	Standardized	→	→	Customized
Number of customers	Many	→	→	Few

egy. Module 3 presented five basic selling approaches: stimulus response, mental states, need satisfaction, problem solving, and consultative. These selling approaches represent different selling strategies that might be used to execute a specific relationship strategy. We illustrate this by continuing the example of the large industrial manufacturer and the relationship strategies presented in Exhibit 4.8 and Figure 4.5.

Exhibit 4.9 matches the appropriate selling strategy with the appropriate relationship strategy. As indicated, the stimulus response and mental states

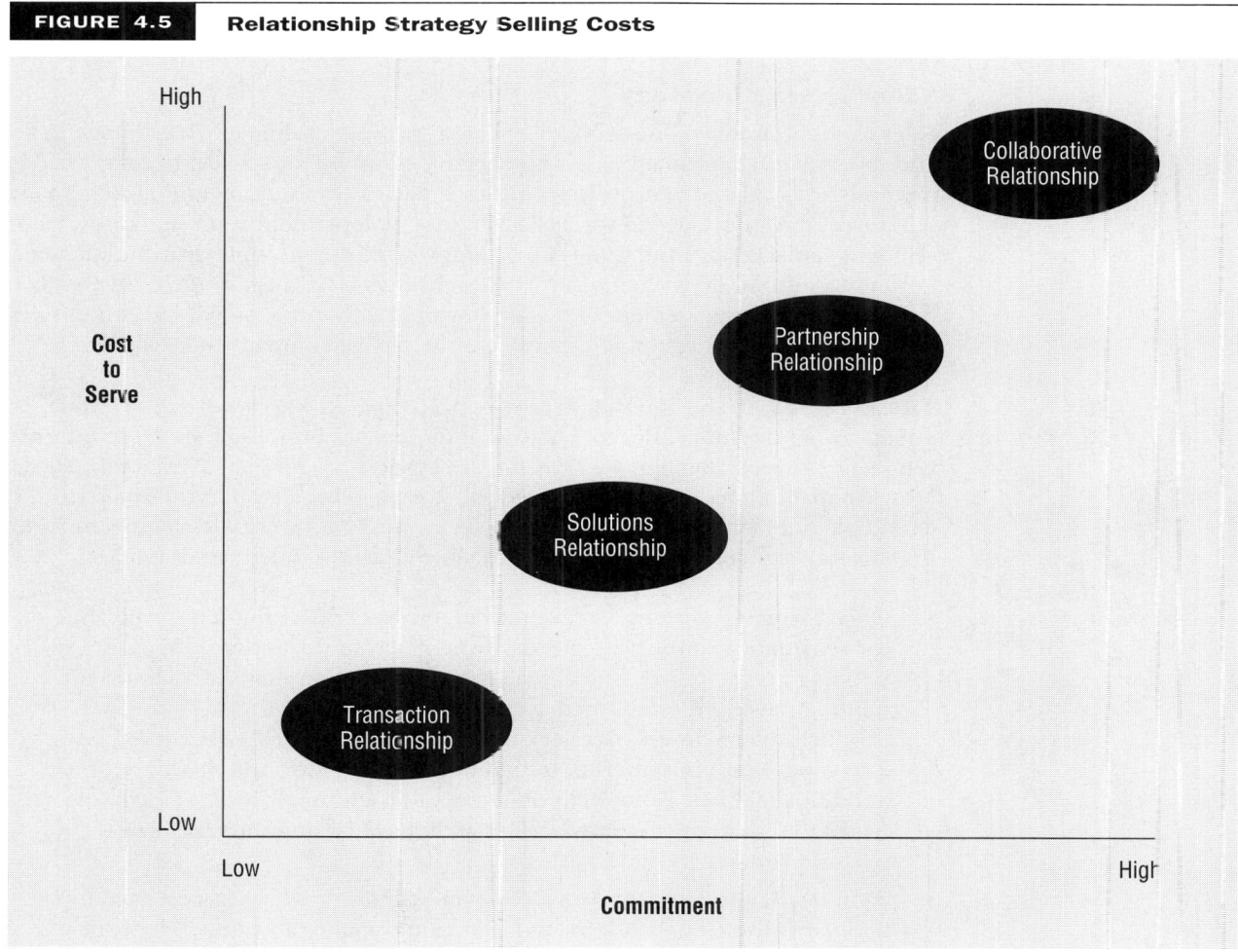

FIGURE 4.5 Relationship Strategy Selling Costs

Each relationship strategy represents an increasing commitment between the buyer and seller and a higher cost to serve the customer.

EXHIBIT 4.9 Matching Selling and Relationship Strategies

	Relationship Strategy		
Transaction	*Solutions*	*Partnership*	*Collaborative*
Stimulus Response Mental States	Need Satisfaction Problem Solving	Consultative	Consultative Customized

approaches typically fit with a transaction relationship strategy. The need satisfaction and problem-solving selling strategies are normally used with a solutions relationship strategy. The consultative approach is most effective with the partnership and collaborative relationship strategies. Sometimes, a collaborative relationship strategy requires a selling strategy that is completely customized to the specific buyer-seller situation. The important point is that achieving the desired type of relationship in a productive manner requires using different selling strategies. Matching selling strategies and relationship strategies is an important sales management task.

Sales Channel Strategy

Sales channel strategy—ensuring that accounts receive selling effort coverage in an effective and efficient manner—is a necessary component of sales strategy. Various methods are available to provide selling coverage to accounts, including a company salesforce, the Internet, industrial distributors, independent representatives, team selling, telemarketing, and trade shows. Many firms use multiple distribution channels and multiple sales channels for their products. Because most of this book is concerned with management of a company field salesforce, our discussion of sales channel strategy focuses on alternatives to the typical company field salesforce.

THE INTERNET The Internet is rapidly becoming an important sales channel in selling to organizations. Recent statistics indicate that business-to-business Internet transactions were $43 billion in 1998 and are expected to reach $1.3 trillion by 2003.[8] Most companies are not replacing field salesforces but integrating the Internet into a multiple sales channel strategy. The focus is using this electronic channel in a way that meets customer needs and reduces selling costs. Consider two examples:

- Cisco Systems has Internet revenues in excess of $9.5 billion annually. But new customers cannot buy directly from Cisco's Internet site. New customers must first work with a dealer to negotiate purchases. Once this initial relationship is established, a customer can go to the Web to research products, place orders, or check the status of orders. This networked business model uses the Internet to handle routine selling and service activities and frees salespeople to focus on more value-adding activities. Cisco estimates that this approach saves $800 million a year and increases salesperson productivity by 15 percent.[9]
- National Semiconductor uses a company salesforce for its largest accounts and a distributor network for the remaining smaller accounts. The company is, however, integrating the Internet as another sales channel for each segment. The objective is to streamline the sales and service process. For the largest accounts, National Semiconductor sets up private Extranets for each customer so the customer can access relevant purchasing information. The smaller accounts have access to an open Web site and can use it to determine which distributors to buy from and to coordinate these purchases. The Internet sales channel has allowed National Semiconductor to develop closer relationships with customers and distributors and to reduce selling costs.[10]

These examples illustrate how the Internet is being used as an electronic sales channel by two different companies. These and most other companies are focusing on ways to integrate the Internet into a multiple sales channel strategy that provides value to customers in a cost-effective manner. Thus, the Internet is being blended with field selling effort but also with other sales channels such as industrial distributors, independent representatives, and telemarketing.

INDUSTRIAL DISTRIBUTORS   One alternative sales channel is to employ **industrial distributors**—channel middlemen that take title to the goods that they market to end users. These distributors typically employ their own field salesforce and may carry (1) the products of only one manufacturer, (2) related but noncompeting products from different manufacturers, or (3) competing products from different manufacturers. Firms that use industrial distributors normally have a relatively small company salesforce to serve and support the efforts of the distributor.

The use of industrial distributors adds another member to the distribution channel. Although these distributors should not be considered as final customers, they should be treated like customers. Developing positive long-term relationships with distributors is necessary for success. Indeed, the development of a partnership with distributors can be the key to success.

Herman Miller, the furniture manufacturer, has 300 direct salespeople and 240 distributors. Herman Miller salespeople call on customers directly but also work with distributors to make sure customers are satisfied. In large markets, the salespeople are usually the lead on accounts, with the distributors responsible for smaller accounts. Herman Miller also provides the distributors with market information to help them succeed, and the salespeople maintain continuous contact to motivate the distributors to emphasize Herman Miller products.[11]

INDEPENDENT REPRESENTATIVES   Firms using personal selling can choose to cover accounts with **independent representatives** (also called *manufacturers' representatives* or just *reps*). Reps are independent sales organizations that sell complementary, but noncompeting, products from different manufacturers. In contrast to industrial distributors, independent representatives do not normally carry inventory or take title to the products they sell. Manufacturers typically develop contractual agreements with several rep organizations. Each rep organization consists of one or more salespeople and is assigned a geographic territory. It is compensated on a commission basis for products sold.

Why would so many manufacturers use reps instead of company salesforces? As indicated in Exhibit 4.10, reps have certain advantages over company salesforces, especially for small firms or for smaller markets served by larger firms. Because reps

---

EXHIBIT 4.10   **Advantages of Independent Representatives**

Independent sales representatives offer several advantages over company salesforces:
- Reps provide a professional selling capability that is difficult to match with company salespeople.
- Reps offer in-depth knowledge of general markets and individual customers.
- Reps offer established relationships with individual customers.
- The use of reps provides improved cash flow because payments to reps are typically not made until customers have paid for their purchases.
- The use of reps provides predictable sales expenses because most of the selling costs are variable and directly related to sales volume.
- The use of reps can provide greater territory coverage because companies can employ more reps than company salespeople for the same cost.
- Companies can usually penetrate new markets faster by using reps because of the reps' established customer relationships.

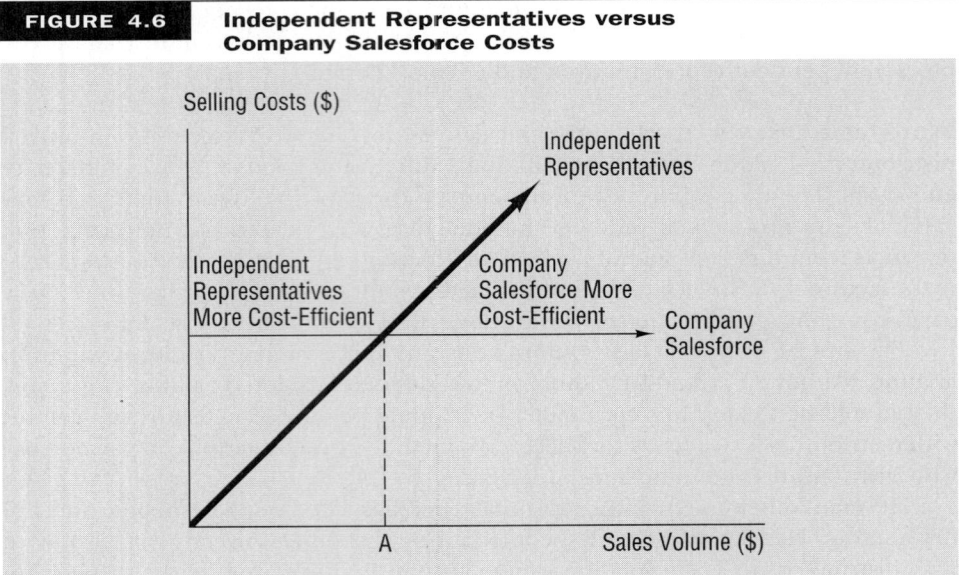

FIGURE 4.6 Independent Representatives versus Company Salesforce Costs

Independent representatives are typically more cost-efficient at lower sales levels, because most of the costs associated with reps are variable. However, at higher sales levels (beyond point A) a company salesforce becomes more cost-efficient.

are paid on a commission basis, selling costs are almost totally variable, whereas a large percentage of the selling costs of a company salesforce are fixed. Thus, at lower sales levels a rep organization is more cost-efficient to use than a company salesforce. However, at some level of sales the company salesforce will become more cost-efficient, because reps typically receive higher commission rates than company salespeople (see Figure 4.6).

Marley Cooling Tower capitalizes on the different cost structure between company salesforces and independent reps. Tim Wigger, vice president of sales, manages a company salesforce of 40, plus 70 manufacturers' reps. The company started with only a field salesforce but began adding reps to capitalize on growth outside the original salesperson territories. This approach has been a cost-effective way for Marley to grow in new geographic areas.[12]

Although reps may cost less in many situations, management also has less control over their activities. The basic trade-off is cost versus control. There are two aspects to control. First, because reps are paid a commission on sales, it is difficult to get them to engage in activities not directly related to sales generation. Thus, if servicing of accounts is important, reps may not perform these activities as well as a company salesforce. Second, the typical rep represents an average of 10 different manufacturers or principals. Each manufacturer's products will therefore receive 10 percent of the rep's time if it is divided equally. Usually, however, some products receive more attention than others. The biggest complaints that manufacturers seem to have with reps is that they do not spend enough time with their products and thus do not generate sufficient sales. The use of reps limits the amount of control that management has over the time spent selling their products. The relationship with manufacturer's representative organizations can also produce some complex situations as indicated in "An Ethical Dilemma."

An Ethical Dilemma

You are national sales manager for Specialty Chemicals. The company serves various types of manufacturers with different types of specialty chemicals. Most of your customers are in Michigan, Illinois, and Indiana. These customers are served by a company salesforce. Other customers in adjoining states are the responsibility of Thompson & Associates, a manufacturer's representative agency. Thompson has done a good job in building your business in this area. You think it might be time to hire company salespeople for these areas. When you indicate to Mr. Thompson that you do not think you will renew the contract with his agency, he gets very mad. He talks about all of the hard work his salespeople did to sell your products and now that business is good you are taking it away from him. What would you do? Why?

TEAM SELLING Our earlier discussion of organizational buyer behavior presented the concepts of buying centers and buying situations. If we move to the selling side of the exchange relationship, we find analogous concepts. As discussed in Module 1, firms often employ multiple-person sales teams to deal with the multiple-person buying centers of their accounts. Figure 4.7 illustrates the basic relationships between sales teams and buying centers. A company salesperson typically coordinates the activities of the sales team, whereas the purchasing agent typically coordinates the activities of the buying center. Both the sales team and buying center can consist of multiple individuals from different functional areas. Each of these individuals can play one or more roles in the exchange process.

The use of team selling is increasing in many firms. Developing successful relationships with accounts often requires the participation of many individuals from the selling firm. One study found that team selling was important at 42 percent of the responding companies. The importance varied by industry, however. Team selling was most important to firms in the petroleum, chemical, industrial machinery,

FIGURE 4.7   Team Selling and Buying Centers

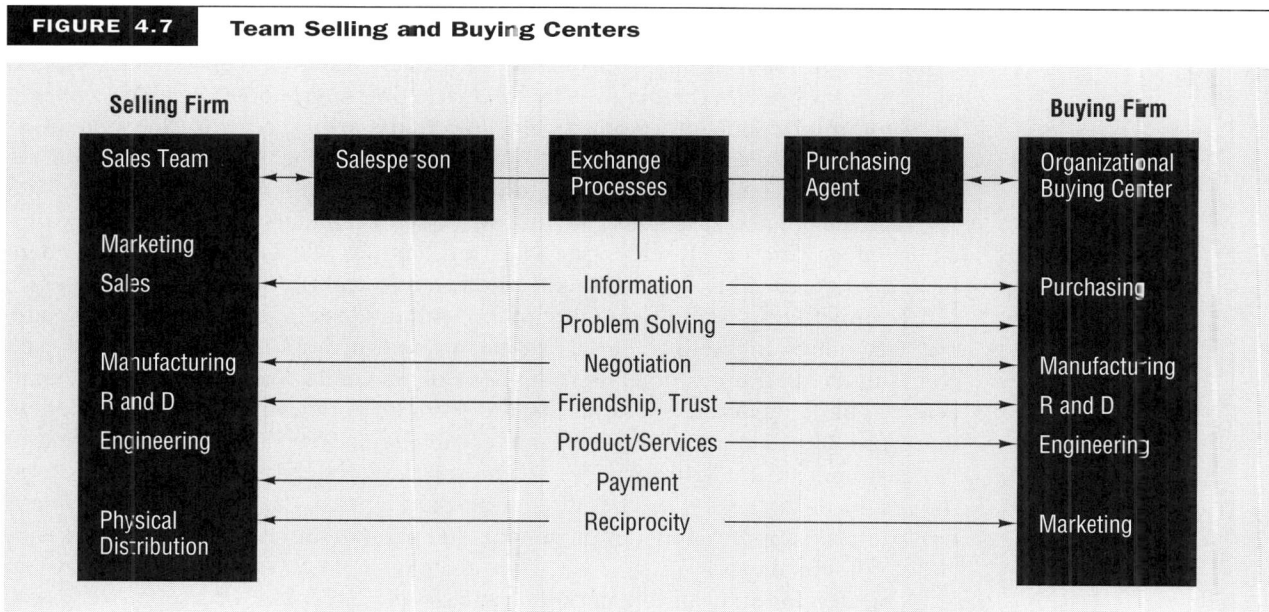

The salesperson coordinates the activities of a sales team to interact with the members of an account's buying center. The size, composition, and activities of the sales team depend on the buying situation faced by the seller.

and electronics industries and less important to those in the food and beverage, retail, and wholesale industries.[13] Another study of global sales leaders indicated that such companies as Sony, Xerox, Hewlett-Packard, Siemens, 3M, and NEC were involved extensively in team selling. Customers like team selling, because they think their needs are better met.[14]

Two specific types of **team selling** deserve mention. **Multilevel selling** is a variation of team selling in which the emphasis is to match functional areas between the buying and selling firms. Thus, individuals from a specific functional area or management level in the selling firm deal with their counterparts in the buying firm. For example, the Polyethylene Division of Atlantic Packaging Products Ltd. uses multifunctional sales teams to add value to customer relationships. Sales teams typically include members from sales, marketing, manufacturing, research and development, division management, management information systems, and purchasing. The team is usually led by a salesperson. Team members focus on their areas of expertise, especially when communicating with individuals in similar positions in buying firms. The emphasis is on selling the whole company and its capabilities rather than simply selling a product.[15]

Major account selling represents the development of specific programs to serve a firm's largest and most important accounts. Although different approaches to major account selling are presented in Module 5, one increasingly popular approach to serve global customers is through global sales teams. For example, Texas Instruments assigns a team of salespeople spread across the globe to serve certain key accounts. The team is headed by a worldwide account manager. Salespeople in Asia, Europe, and the United States coordinate efforts with one another. The salespeople keep in constant touch through electronic communications networks.[16]

TELEMARKETING An increasingly important sales channel is **telemarketing** (also called *telesales*), which consists of using the telephone as a means for customer contact, to perform some of or all the activities required to develop and maintain account relationships. This includes both outbound telemarketing (the seller calls the account) and inbound telemarketing (the account calls the seller).

Firms typically use telemarketing to replace field selling for specific accounts or integrate telemarketing with field selling to the same accounts (see Figure 4.8). The major reason for replacing field selling with telemarketing at specific accounts is the low cost of telemarketing selling. Telemarketing salespeople are able to serve a large number of smaller accounts. This lowers the selling costs to the smaller accounts and frees the field salesforce to concentrate on the larger accounts. For example, Merrell Dow Pharmaceutical found that its cost of a field sales call was $225 but that a telemarketing sales call cost only $20. A telemarketing program was established in which each telephone sales rep handles 500 of the smaller independent drugstores. This frees the field salesforce to call on 10,000 new accounts.[17]

Telemarketing is also being integrated with field selling operations. For example, Shachihata Inc. sells pre-inked rubber stamps through independent reps. The company created a customer development department consisting of 10 telemarketers. The telemarketers take leads and generate appointments for the independent reps. Once an appointment is made, the telemarketer faxes a profile sheet of the customer to the appropriate rep. The rep later returns it with information on the results of the sales call. The integration of independent reps and telemarketers has increased appointments by more than 400 percent and reduced selling costs by about 60 percent.[18]

The development of telemarketing salesforces to replace or support field selling operations can be a difficult task for sales managers. One of the keys to success appears to be consistent communication with the field salesforce throughout all stages of telemarketing development. Field salespeople must be assured that the

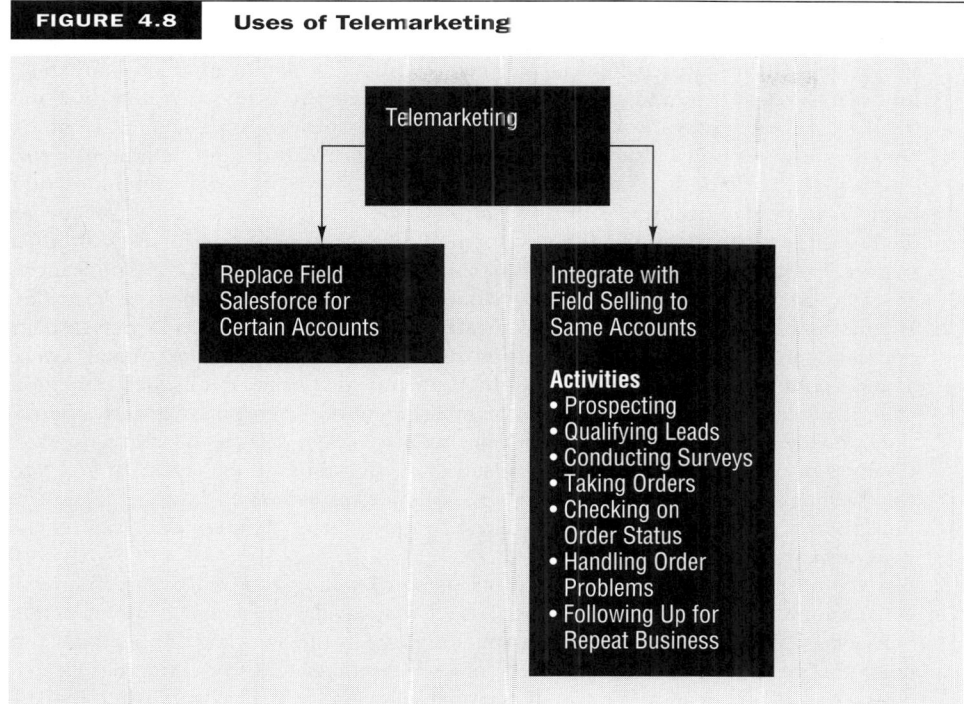

FIGURE 4.8 Uses of Telemarketing

Telemarketing is typically used to either replace field selling or be integrated with field selling by performing specific activities.

telemarketing operations will help them improve their performance. Specific attention must also be directed toward developing appropriate compensation programs for both salesforces and devising training programs that provide the necessary knowledge and skills for the telemarketing and field salesforces to be able to work effectively together.

TRADE SHOWS The final sales channel to be discussed here, **trade shows,** is a typically industry-sponsored event in which companies use a booth to display products and services to potential and existing customers. Because a particular trade show is held only once a year and lasts only a few days, trade shows should be viewed as supplemental methods for account coverage, not to be used by themselves but integrated with other sales channels.

Statistics show that trade shows are popular. During 1996, 101 million persons attended approximately 4,400 trade shows in the United States. Trade shows are most popular in the medical and health care, home furnishings and interior design, computer and computer applications, education, sporting goods and recreation, and building and construction industries. About 91 percent of attendees find trade shows to be extremely useful sources of purchasing information. The average cost to reach a trade show visitor is estimated to be $185.[19]

Trade shows are used to achieve both selling and nonselling objectives. Relevant selling objectives are to test new products, to close sales, and to introduce new products. Nonselling objectives include servicing current customers, gathering competitive information, identifying new prospects, and enhancing corporate image. Successful trade shows tend to be those where firms exhibit a large number of products to a large number of attendees, where specific written objectives for the trade show are established, and where attendees match the firm's target market.

Summary

1. **Define the different strategy levels for multibusiness multiproduct firms.** Multibusiness multiproduct firms must make strategic decisions at the corporate, business, marketing, and sales levels. Corporate strategy decisions determine the basic scope and direction for the corporate entity through formulating the corporate mission statement, defining strategic business units, setting strategic business unit objectives, and determining corporate growth orientation. Business strategy decisions determine how each business unit plans to compete effectively within its industry. Marketing strategies consist of the selection of target markets and the development of marketing mixes for each product market. Personal selling is an important component of the marketing communications mix portion and business of marketing strategies and a key element in sales strategies.

2. **Discuss how corporate strategy decisions affect the sales function.** Corporate strategy decisions provide direction for strategy development at all organizational levels. The corporate mission statement, definition of strategic business units, determination of strategic business unit objectives, and establishment of the corporate growth orientation provide guidelines within which sales managers and salespeople must operate. Changes in corporate strategy typically lead to changes in sales management and personal selling activities. Business strategy decisions determine how each strategic business unit intends to compete. Different business strategies place different demands on the sales organization.

3. **List the advantages and disadvantages of personal selling as a marketing communications tool.** Personal selling is the only tool that involves personal communication between buyer and seller. As such, personal selling has the advantage of being able to tailor the message to the specific needs of each customer and to deliver complicated messages. The major disadvantage of personal selling is the high cost to reach individual buyers.

4. **Specify the situations in which personal selling is typically emphasized in a marketing strategy.** Marketing strategies tend to be either personal selling driven or advertising driven. Personal selling is normally emphasized in business markets where there are relatively few buyers, usually in concentrated locations, who make important purchases of complex products and require a great deal of information and service. Personal selling is also typically emphasized in marketing mixes for complex expensive products that are distributed through direct channels or through indirect channels by using a "push" strategy and when the price affords sufficient margin to support the high costs associated with personal selling.

5. **Describe ways that personal selling, advertising, and other tools can be blended into effective integrated marketing communications strategies.** Effective strategies typically consist of a mixture of personal selling, advertising, and other tools. Firms often use advertising to generate company and brand awareness and to identify potential customers. Personal selling is then used to turn these prospects into customers of the firm's products or services. Other tools are normally used to supplement the advertising and personal selling efforts.

6. **Discuss the important concepts behind organizational buyer behavior.** The key concepts behind organizational buyer behavior are buying situation, buying center, buying process, and buying needs. Buying situations can be characterized as new task, modified rebuy, or straight rebuy. The type of buying situation affects all other aspects of organizational buyer behavior. The buying center consists of all the individuals from a firm involved in a particular buying decision. These individuals may come from different functional areas and may lay the role of initiators, users, gatekeepers, influencers, deciders, and/or buyers. Organizational purchasing should be viewed as a buying process with multiple phases. Different members of the buying center may be involved at different phases of the buying process. Organizational purchases are made to satisfy specific buying needs, which may be both organizational and personal. These concepts are highly interrelated and interact to produce complex organizational purchasing phenomena.

7. **Define an account targeting strategy.** An account targeting strategy is the classification of accounts within a target market into categories for the purpose of developing strategic approaches for selling to each account or account group.

8. **Explain the different types of relationship strategies.** A sales organization might use any number of different relationship strategies to serve targeted accounts. Transaction, solutions, partnership, and collaborative relationship strategies are examples used by some sales organizations.
9. **Discuss the importance of different selling strategies.** A selling strategy is the planned selling approach for each relationship strategy. Different selling strategies might include stimulus response, mental states, need satisfaction, problem-solving, consultative, or a completely customized strategy. Different selling strategies are needed to execute successfully different relationship strategies.
10. **Describe the different sales channel strategies.** A sales channel strategy consists of decisions as to how to provide selling effort coverage to accounts. The sales channel strategy depends on the firm's marketing strategy. If indirect distribution is used, then industrial distributors become the main focus of selling effort coverage. Firms might decide to employ independent representatives instead of having a company salesforce. The concept of team selling is analogous to the buying center concept. Depending on whether the seller faces a new task selling situation, a modified resell situation, or a routine resell situation, different individuals will be included in the sales team. Multilevel selling and major account selling are different types of team selling strategies. Telemarketing is a sales channel that can be used to replace or support field selling operations. Finally, trade shows can be used to achieve specific objectives and supplement the other sales channels.

Understanding Sales Management Terms

- Corporate strategy
- Business strategy
- Marketing strategy
- Corporate mission statement
- Strategic business unit (SBU)
- Business unit portfolio
- Generic business strategies
- Low-cost strategy
- Differentiation strategy
- Niche strategy
- Target market
- Marketing mix
- Business marketing
- Integrated marketing communications
- User
- Original equipment manufacturer (OEM)
- Reseller
- Government organization
- Institution
- New task buying situation
- Extensive problem solving
- Modified rebuy buying situation
- Limited problem solving
- Straight rebuy buying situation
- Routinized response behavior
- Buying center
- Buying process
- Buying needs
- Account targeting strategy
- Relationship strategy
- Selling strategy
- Sales channel strategy
- Industrial distributors
- Independent representatives
- Team selling
- Multilevel selling
- Major account selling
- Telemarketing
- Trade shows

Developing Sales Management Knowledge

1. How does the corporate mission statement affect personal selling and sales management activities?
2. How can sales promotion and publicity be used to supplement a personal selling–driven strategy?
3. Why is personal selling typically emphasized in business markets and advertising emphasized in consumer markets?
4. Why do most firms use both personal selling and advertising in their strategies?
5. How would sales management activities differ for an SBU following a differentiation strategy versus an SBU using a low-cost strategy?

6. Discuss how the type of buying situation affects the buying center, the buying process, and buying needs.
7. How is the management of relationships with industrial distributors different from the management of relationships with end-user customers?
8. How can trade shows be used to supplement other sales channels?
9. How might telemarketing be used when accounts are covered by distributors?
10. What are the most important organizational buyer behavior trends, and how might these trends affect sales strategies in the future?

Building Sales Management Skills

1. Visit the library or use the Internet to find the annual report or similar information about a company of your choice. Try to choose a firm with whom you might like to work after graduation. Use the information in the annual report to describe the firm's corporate strategy, marketing strategy, and sales function.
2. You are the sales manager for WorldPub, a textbook publishing company. You believe it would be a good idea to get involved in the Internet to help move your company's line of college business textbooks. Discuss your strategy for using the Internet and other sales channels to sell textbooks.
3. Protech Athletics Manufacturing currently markets a line of sporting goods equipment through independent sales representatives. The company has grown considerably since its inception 7 years ago. Recently, Protech has become frustrated with its independent reps. It believes its products are not getting the attention they deserve. Protech is wondering if there is something it can do to help motivate the reps. However, given its recent disappointment with the reps, Protech is entertaining the idea of developing its own salesforce. What do you suggest Protech do and why? What are the advantages and disadvantages associated with your solution?

Making Sales Management Decisions

CASE 4.1 *Pronto Retail Centers*

Background

Pronto Retail Centers is a well-established company with 125 outlets in the northeastern United States. Each outlet is a combination convenience store, car wash, and Pronto-Lube oil change center. Of the 125 stores, 31 are company-owned with the remaining stores leased to independent dealers in a quasi-franchising arrangement. The independent dealers agree to buy gasoline and motor oil from Pronto's designated distributors. They also agree to uphold uniformity and facilities appearance standards as set by Pronto. The independent dealers are encouraged to buy their convenience store merchandise from Pronto's designated distributors, but they are not required to do so. Lease payments are collected from independent dealers when gasoline deliveries are made.

Current Situation

In the past 12 months, Pronto's growth rate has slowed considerably. This has been a major concern to Pronto's upper management, including John Rickles, vice president for sales. Rickles has analyzed the declining growth rate and found that sales volume at company-owned stores is growing at a very acceptable 12 percent on an annualized basis. In contrast, stores run by independent dealers are lagging behind with an annual growth rate of only 2 percent. Rickles believes the independent category is under-performing for three basic reasons. First, the independent stores are generally not kept as clean and professional looking as the company-owned stores. Second, many of the larger independent operators have begun buying a larger share of their convenience store merchandise from low-cost distributors other than Pronto's designated distributors. This hurts sales volume results since Pronto's retail operation gets rebates from their designated distributors which counts as sales volume in the Pronto financial system. Third, Pronto has suffered volume losses from closed outlets. Competition had intensified, and turnover among dealers was becoming more commonplace. It was taking Pronto an average of 60 days to find new dealers when existing dealers decided to leave the business. When a dealer operation closed, Pronto rarely converted it to a company-owned store, as their aggressive growth strategy at the corporate level left precious little capital for acquisition of existing outlets.

John Rickles had called his five regional managers into his New York headquarters office to discuss the problem with declining sales volume and possible remedies to the problem. Given that the corporate strategy would continue to be to build market share and sales volume, Rickles outlined the following five-point plan:

1. Each salesperson would continue to supervise company-owned stores and independent dealers.
2. Salespeople would be given specific objectives for facilities appearance and percentage of sales of convenience store merchandise purchases from Pronto's designated distributors.
3. Salespeople would be given mandates that no retail outlet would remain closed for more than 30 days.
4. Sales volume objectives for salespeople would remain in place. Current year volume objectives would not change.
5. Regional sales managers' annual objectives would be revised to be consistent with salespeople's new objectives.

The regional managers saw the need for the revised strategy, but raised several concerns. They felt that the corporate strategy focused on building market share, but that the sales organization was expected to both build and hold market share. They complained that the new-dealer team, a corporate group, should be adding new dealers at a faster rate, and that part of the volume short-fall was due to poor performance of the new dealer team, not the salesforce. They also pointed out that Pronto salespeople were paid on a straight salary basis, primarily because they had previously functioned more as managers of multiple retail outlets than as pure salespeople. The discussion became heated, and finally Mary McCarthy spoke for the regional managers: "Look, John, we know that corporate strategy can shift, and we know we have to adapt when that happens. But this drop in sales volume is partly the fault of the corporate new-dealer team. We don't see them having to change their ways. And we are really concerned that without some incentive pay, it will be hard to redirect our salespeople." Rickles, having heard enough at this point, replied, "Tell your salespeople that their incentive is that if they succeed, they get to keep their jobs!" With that the meeting quickly came to a conclusion.

Questions

1. Is it reasonable to charge Pronto's salesforce with simultaneously building and holding market share?
2. What are the pros and cons of John Rickles' five-point plan?
3. Since the meeting with the regional managers ended on a sour note, what should Rickles do now? What should the regional managers do?

CASE 4.2 National Communications Manufacturing

Background

National Communications Systems (NCM) is a Minneapolis-based manufacturer of consumer communications devices, most notably portable two-way radios commonly called walkie-talkies. In recent years, these devices have exploded in popularity as prices dropped to affordable levels. This is due to advancing technology and low-cost production outside the United States. Although NCM continues to manufacture a few of its own products, most production is outsourced to manufacturers in Taiwan.

A key element in the NCM success story is the growth of dominant retail chains such as Wal-Mart, Target, and Best Buy. NCM uses major account teams to serve these and other large discounters, which accounts for 70 percent of NCM's annual sales. The remaining 30 percent of NCM's sales come from smaller retail accounts that buy either from NCM's manufacturers' reps or directly from NCM's Web site.

Current Situation

Ann Culligan, NCM's national sales manager, is working on two major isuses. First, she is fighting a losing battle to keep NCM's direct cost of sales at 5 percent of total sales. The 5 percent target has been part of NCM's sales culture for more than 20 years, reflecting a belief that a low-cost operation translates into a more competitive position in the marketplace. Over the past few years, Ann's sales organization had reduced costs in various ways. E-mail, instead of long-distance phone calls, staying in budget motels, cutting overnight travel to a minimum, and Saturday night stayovers were just a few of the measures taken to stay within the 5 percent guideline. In spite of diligent efforts, cost of sales was running at 7 percent for the major account sales teams. Commissions paid to the independent reps had remained fixed for several years at 4½ percent.

The second issue currently demanding Ann's attention ironically stemmed from an NCM cost-cutting measure that was implemented 12 months ago. In an attempt to reduce manufacturers' representative costs, NCM had established a Web site as an alternative channel for smaller retail customers. The reps had protested vigorously, but NCM insisted that selling on the Internet was an essential part of a contemporary sales strategy. Not all NCM products were available on the Web, a fact that did little to appease the disgruntled reps. Cost of sales on the Web site was a modest 2 percent of sales. Sales volume on the Web amounted to 3 percent of NCM's total sales during the past year, but current projections were for volume to increase to 5 percent of the total this year, and perhaps as much as 10 percent the following year. Some of the stronger reps were threatening to leave NCM in favor of a major competitor, which offered its reps a partial commission on all Web sales.

As Ann pondered the situation, she began to wonder if she could hit the 5 percent cost-of-sales target this year. Ninety percent of the cost of her major account teams was compensation-related—salaries and incentive pay. Good people were hard to find, and Ann had found that NCM had to pay the going rate or else NCM's top performers would look for new opportunities. Ann still regretted the recent loss of Byron Schuster, a major account manager, to a competitor who offered a better pay package. Sales volume at Byron's former account had dropped 10 percent since his departure.

Ann didn't like to think about changing her major account team strategy, but she wondered if she could move some of her large retail chain accounts to the manufacturers' rep organization. After all, rep commissions ran only 4½ percent, and essentially there were no other direct sales costs associated with the reps. As she headed home after a long day at the office, Ann thought that the next morning she would try to build a case with the CEO of NCM to revise the 5 percent cost-of-sales target to reflect reality. If the answer is no, Ann thought she just might explore the idea of consolidating her major account teams and handing over selected large retail accounts to some of the more capable rep firms. She hated the idea of laying people off, but, she told herself, it may be necessary in this case.

Questions

1. Should Ann request a revision of the 5 percent cost-of-sales target? If so, what sort of information would she need to convince her CEO?
2. What factors should Ann consider as she contemplates a change in major account sales strategy, especially a change that assigns independent reps to some major accounts?
3. How would you assess NCM's alternative sales channel on the Web? Can you recommend any changes to minimize conflict with the independent reps?

MODULE 5

Sales Organization Structure and Salesforce Deployment

Reorganizing the Salesforce: Pinacor

Pinacor is a technology distributor with $5 billion in annual sales and more than 650 sales representatives worldwide. The company serves more than 25,000 resellers, dealers, and systems integrators with customized technology solutions in areas ranging from software and networking to computer telephony and imaging. The technology distribution industry is very competitive, but most competitors offer similar products, pricing, and distribution capabilities.

David Canham, vice president of sales and marketing, realized that for a company to stand out in this industry, its salesforce would need to go beyond the traditional focus on products, pricing, and distribution:

> Many of our customers are looking for a partner that can deliver solutions to their customers as opposed to someone who will just ship a certain box to a certain place. So we help our resellers roll out products across the U.S. to national organizations, handling delivery during a certain time window, coordinating with installation teams where the product has been custom configured with the end users, their own software and any number of other constraints. This is one of the areas where Pinacor shines.

But for Pinacor to "shine" in this area, it had to restructure its sales organization. The Pinacor sales organization previously consisted of one salesforce organized by geography, with each salesperson responsible for many different types of customers within a defined geographic area. Although this type of organizational structure kept costs down, it was difficult for Pinacor salespeople to understand the unique needs of customers in different industries. A salesperson might, for example, serve five systems integrators, three corporate resellers, and six small to medium-sized business customers. This situation would make it impossible for the salesperson to be an expert about any industry or customer type. Thus, the salesperson would treat each customer the same, even though different customer groups had different needs and problems.

The new sales organization structure consists of separate salesforces for each of 10 customer segments, such as solutions integrators, corporate resellers, small and medium-sized companies, and strategic markets. This organizational structure is designed so that each salesperson can concentrate on one specific type of customer. This allows the salesperson to gain a much better understanding of the unique needs of the customer and its industry and to use this understanding to develop customized solutions for these customers.

Learning Objectives

After completing this module, you should be able to

1. Define the concepts of specialization, centralization, span of control versus management levels, and line versus staff positions.

2. Describe the different ways that salesforces might be specialized.

3. Evaluate the advantages and disadvantages of different sales organization structures.

4. Name the important considerations in organizing major account management programs.

5. Explain how to determine the appropriate sales organization structure for a given selling situation.

6. Discuss the different areas involved in salesforce deployment.

7. Explain three different analytical approaches for determining allocation of selling effort.

8. Describe three different methods for calculating salesforce size.

9. Explain the importance of sales territories and list the steps in the territory design process.

10. Discuss the important "people" considerations in salesforce deployment.

The result of the sales organization restructuring has been lasting partnerships with companies such as EDS and Apple. As the Pinacor salespeople get to know their customers and industries better, the customers offer more business to Pinacor. Many Pinacor salespeople are closely integrated into the customer's day-to-day processes. This helps to expand business opportunities but also makes it very difficult for competitors to take business away from Pinacor.

Source: "Bold Goals," *Selling Power* (June 1999): 55–58.

Module 4 discussed the close relationships among corporate, business, marketing, and sales strategies. The different strategic levels must be consistent and integrated to be effective. Strategic changes at one organizational level typically require strategic changes at other organizational levels.

The development of effective strategies is one thing, successfully implementing them another. In one sense, the remainder of this book is concerned with the development and management of a sales organization to implement organizational strategies successfully. This module begins the journey into successful implementation by investigating the key decisions required in sales organization structure and salesforce deployment.

The Pinacor example in the opening vignette illustrates the close link between organizational strategy and sales organization structure. The initial sales organization structure was appropriate for organizational strategies that focused on the typical produce, price, and distribution competition within the technology distribution industry. When the Pinacor strategy was changed to emphasize customized solutions to specific customer problems, the geographic sales organization structure was not suited to implement this strategy. The change to a sales organization structure based on the unique needs of specific customer segments was needed to execute the strategy effectively. This type of structure helps Pinacor salespeople satisfy the needs and solve the problems of individual customers.

Sales Organization Concepts

The basic problem in sales organization structure can be presented in simple terms. The corporate, business, marketing, and sales strategies developed by a firm prescribe specific activities that must be performed by salespeople for these strategies to be successful. Sales managers are also needed to recruit, select, train, motivate, supervise, evaluate, and control salespeople. In essence, the firm has salespeople and sales managers who must engage in a variety of activities for the firm to perform successfully. A sales organization structure must be developed to help salespeople and sales managers perform the required activities effectively and efficiently. This structure provides a framework for sales organization operations by indicating what specific activities are performed by whom in the sales organization. The sales organization structure is the vehicle through which strategic plans are translated into selling operations in the marketplace.

The important role of a sales organization structure for a firm has been described as follows:

> The role of organization in sales has been compared to that of the skeleton in the human body; it provides a framework within which normal functions must take place. There is, however, a degree of uniformity in the human skeleton that does not characterize the sales organization. Each firm has its own objectives and problems, and the structure of the sales organization reflects this diversity.[1]

Developing a sales organization structure is difficult. Many different types of structures might be used, and many variations are possible within each basic type. Often the resultant structure is complex, with many boxes and arrows. The basic concepts involved are specialization, centralization, span of control versus management levels, and line versus staff positions.[2]

Specialization

Our earlier discussion suggested that a sales organization structure must ensure that all required selling and management activities are performed. In the simplest case, each salesperson could perform all selling tasks, and each sales manager could perform all management activities. Most sales organizations, however, are too complex for this structure and require instead some degree of **specialization,** in which certain individuals concentrate on performing some of the required activities to the exclusion of other tasks. Thus, certain salespeople might sell only certain products or call on certain customers. Some sales managers might concentrate on training, others on planning. The basic idea behind specialization is that, by concentrating on a limited number of activities, individuals can become experts on those tasks, leading to better performance for the entire organization.

A useful way to view salesforce specialization is from the perspective of the continuum presented in Figure 5.1. At one extreme, salespeople act as generalists, performing all selling activities for all the company's products to all types of customers. Moving toward the right of the continuum, salespeople begin to specialize by performing only certain selling tasks, selling only certain types of products, or calling on only specific types of accounts.

Centralization

An important characteristic of the management structure within a sales organization is its degree of **centralization**—that is, the degree to which important decisions and tasks are performed at higher levels in the management hierarchy. A centralized structure is one in which authority and responsibility are placed at higher management levels. An organization becomes more decentralized as tasks become the responsibility of lower-level managers. Centralization is a relative concept in that no organization is totally centralized or totally decentralized. Organizations typically centralize some activities and decentralize others. However, most organizations tend to have a centralized or decentralized orientation.

The trends from transactions to relationships, from individuals to teams, and from management to leadership are producing a more decentralized orientation in many sales organizations. Salespeople and other sales team members who have contact with customers must be able to respond to customer needs in a timely manner. They must be empowered to make decisions quickly. A decentralized structure

FIGURE 5.1   **Salesforce Specialization Continuum**

A broad range of alternatives exists for specializing salesforce activities.

facilitates decision making in the field and encourages the development of relationships with customers. This approach can produce difficult situations as indicated in "An Ethical Dilemma."

> ### An Ethical Dilemma
> *Universal Internet Services recently redesigned its sales organization. One objective was to decentralize the sales organization. This was accomplished by eliminating two layers of sales management and increasing the span of control for field sales managers. Salespeople were also given more authority in making decisions needed to serve assigned accounts and were given an overall budget that could be spent as deemed appropriate by the salesperson. District manager Mary Swenson noticed that soon after these changes were made, one of her poorest performers had suddenly increased sales dramatically. The salesperson, Fred Williams, had apparently landed three new, large accounts. Mary was delighted about this development, until she began to hear rumors that Fred had bought these accounts by giving lavish gifts to key decision makers at each account. Universal had strict guidelines about giving gifts. Mary did not want to violate the recent empowerment of salespeople, but she was concerned about Fred's situation. What should Mary do? Why?*

Span of Control versus Management Levels

Span of control refers to the number of individuals who report to each sales manager. The larger the span of control, the more subordinates a sales manager must supervise. **Management levels** define the number of different hierarchical levels of sales management within the organization. Typically, span of control is inversely related to the number of sales management levels. This relationship is illustrated in Figure 5.2.

In the flat sales organization structure, there are relatively few sales management levels, with each sales manager having a relatively large span of control. Conversely, in the tall structure, there are more sales management levels and smaller spans of control. Flat organization structures tend to be used to achieve decentralization, whereas tall structures are more appropriate for centralized organizations. The span of control also tends to increase at lower sales management levels. Thus, as one moves down the organization chart from national sales manager to regional sales manager to district sales manager, the number of individuals to be supervised directly increases.

Line versus Staff Positions

Sales management positions can be differentiated as to line or staff positions. **Line sales management** positions are part of the direct management hierarchy within the sales organization. Line sales managers have direct responsibility for a certain number of subordinates and report directly to management at the next highest level in the sales organization. These managers are directly involved in the sales-generating activities of the firm and may perform any number of sales management activities. **Staff sales management** positions, however, are not in the direct chain of command in the sales organization structure. Instead, those in staff positions do not directly manage people, but they are responsible for certain functions (e.g., recruiting and selecting, training) and are not directly involved in sales-generating activities. Staff sales management positions are more specialized than line sales management positions.

A comparison of line and staff sales management positions is presented in Figure 5.3. The regional and district sales managers all operate in line positions. The district sales managers directly manage the field salesforce and report to a specific regional sales manager. The regional sales managers manage the district sales

FIGURE 5.2 Span of Control versus Management Levels

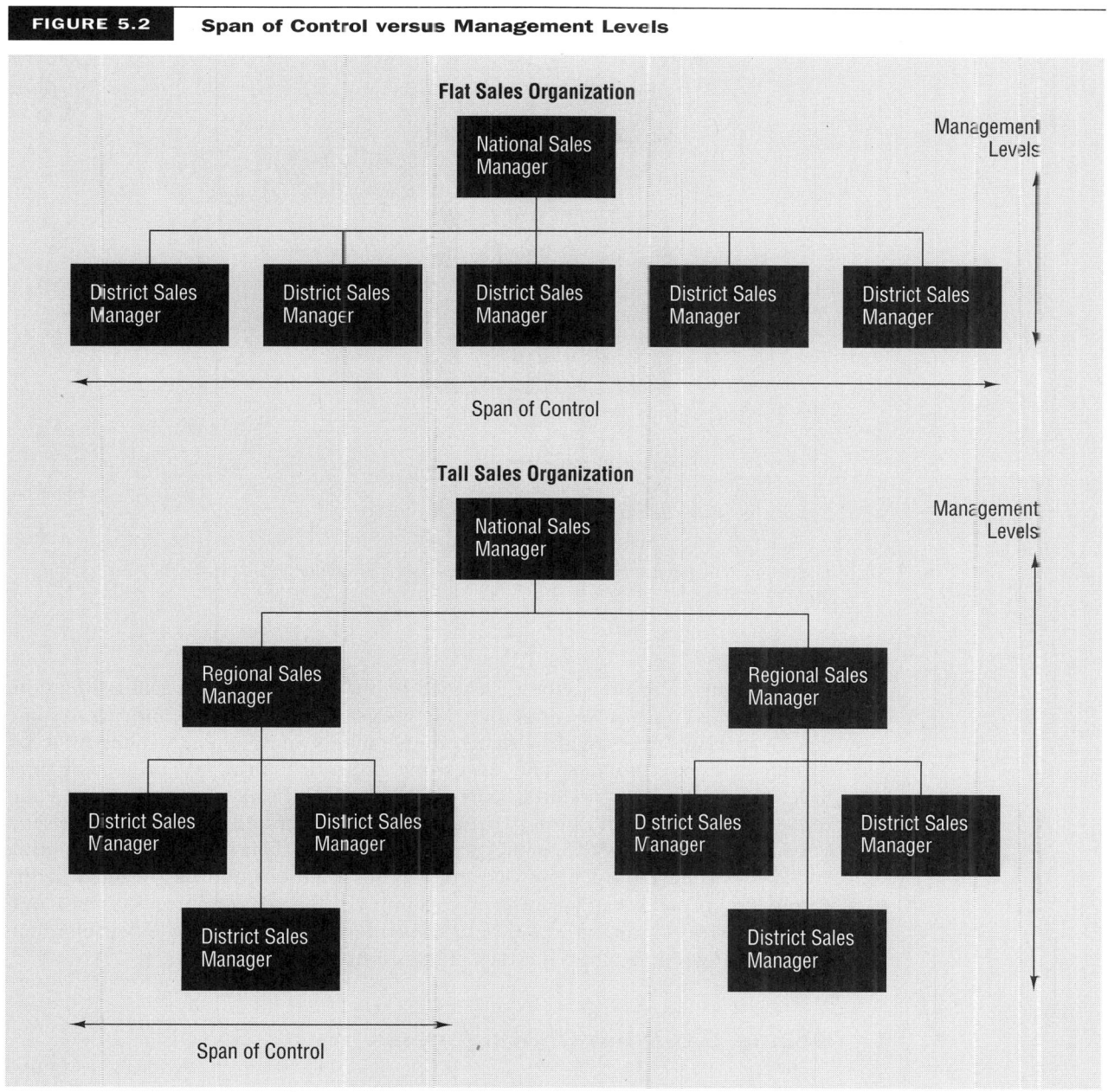

The flat sales organization has only two sales management levels, giving the national sales manager a span of control of 5. The tall sales organization has three sales management levels, giving the national sales manager a span of control of only 2.

managers and report to the national sales manager. Two staff positions are represented in the figure. These training managers are located at both the national and regional levels and are responsible for sales training programs at each level. The use of staff positions results in more specialization of sales management activities. Staff managers specialize in certain sales management activities.

In sum, designing the sales organization is an extremely important and complex task. Decisions concerning the appropriate specialization, centralization, span of control versus management levels, and line versus staff positions are difficult.

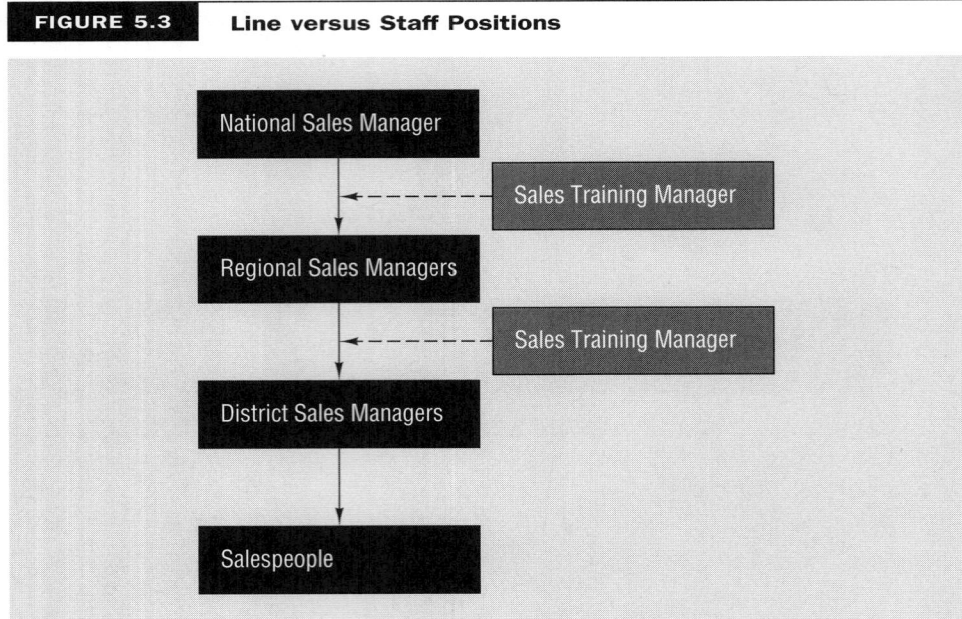

FIGURE 5.3 Line versus Staff Positions

The national, regional, and district sales managers occupy line positions, whereas the sales training managers represent staff positions.

Although these decisions should be based on the specifics of each selling situation, several trends appear to be emerging. Many sales organizations are moving to some type of specialization, usually a structure that allows salespeople to concentrate on specific types of customers. The downsizing and restructuring of entire companies have affected the sales function. Sales management levels have been eliminated and replaced by sales organization structures that are flatter and that increase the span of control exercised by the remaining sales managers. This restructuring has influenced the trend toward more decentralized orientations and has resulted in the elimination of some staff positions. For example, some sales organizations have outsourced the sales training function to sales training firms, thereby either eliminating or greatly reducing the number of sales training staff positions.

Selling Situation Contingencies

Determining the appropriate type of sales organization structure is as difficult as it is important. There is no one best way to organize a salesforce. The appropriate organization structure depends or is contingent on the characteristics of the selling situation. As a selling situation changes, the type of sales organization structure may also need to change. The Pinacor reorganization provides a good illustration of the way one firm altered its sales organization in response to changes in organizational strategies.

One key decision in sales organization design relates to specialization. Two basic questions must be addressed:

1. Should the salesforce be specialized?
2. If the salesforce should be specialized, what type of specialization is most appropriate?

The decision on specialization hinges on the relative importance to the firm of selling skill versus selling effort. Thus, if sales management wants to emphasize the amount of selling contact, a generalized salesforce should be used. If sales management wants to focus on specific skills within each selling contact, then a specialized salesforce should be used. Obviously, there must be some balance between selling effort and selling skill in all situations. But sales management can skew this balance toward selling effort or selling skill by employing a generalized or specialized salesforce.

Some guidelines for sales organization structure and selling situation factors are presented in Exhibit 5.1. This exhibit suggests that a specialized structure is best when there is a high level of environmental uncertainty, when salespeople and sales managers must perform creative and nonroutine activities, and when adaptability is critical to achieving performance objectives. Centralization is most appropriate when environmental uncertainty is low, sales organization activities are routine and repetitive, and the performance emphasis is on effectiveness.

Two of the most important factors in determining the appropriate type of specialization are the similarity of customer needs and the complexity of products offered by the firm. Figure 5.4 illustrates how these factors can be used to suggest the appropriate type of specialization. For example, when the firm has a simple product offering but customers have different needs, a market-specialized salesforce is recommended. If, however, customers have similar needs and the firm sells a complex range of products, then a product-specialized salesforce is more appropriate.

Decisions concerning centralization, span of control versus management levels, and line versus staff positions require analysis of similar selling situation factors. Decisions in these areas must be consistent with the specialization decision. For example, decentralized organization structures with few management levels, large spans

EXHIBIT 5.1 Selling-Situation Factors and Organizational Structure

Organization Structure	Environmental Characteristics	Task Performance	Performance Objective
Specialization	High environmental uncertainty	Nonroutine	Adaptiveness
Centralization	Low environmental uncertainty	Repetitive	Effectiveness

FIGURE 5.4 Customer and Product Determinants of Salesforce Specialization

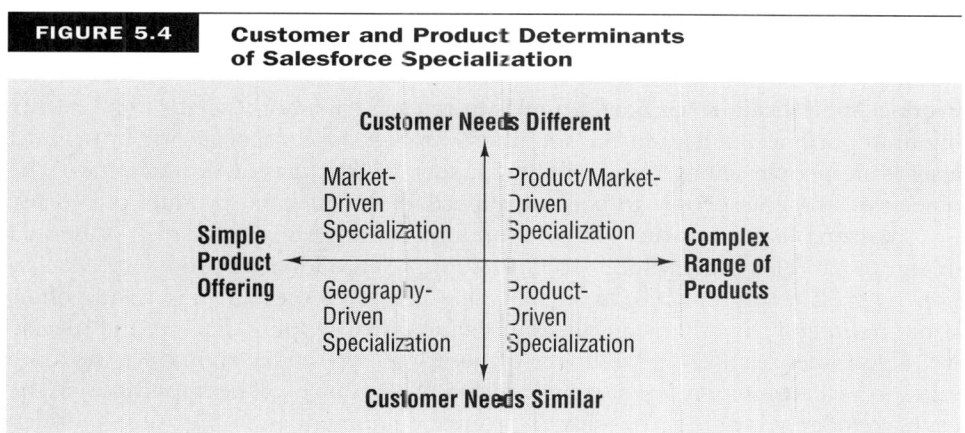

Analysis of the similarity of customer needs and the complexity of a firm's product offering can provide general guidelines for determining the appropriate type of salesforce specialization.

of control, and the use of staff positions may be consistent with a specialized salesforce in some selling situations but not in others. The appropriate sales organization structure depends on the specific characteristics of a firm's selling situation.

Sales Organization Structures

Designing the sales organization structure requires integration of the desired degree of specialization, centralization, span of control, management levels, line positions, and staff positions. Obviously, there are a tremendous number of different ways that a sales organization might be structured. Our objective is to review several of the basic and most often used ways and to illustrate some variations in these basic structures.

To provide continuity to this discussion, each type of sales organization is discussed from the perspective of the ABC Company. The ABC Company markets office equipment (e.g., typewriters, furniture) and office supplies (e.g., paper, pencils) to commercial and government accounts. The firm employs 200 salespeople who operate throughout the United States. The salespeople perform various activities that can be characterized as being related either to sales generation or account servicing. Examples of different types of sales organization structures that the ABC Company might use are presented and discussed.

Geographic Sales Organization

Most salesforces use some type of **geographic specialization.** This is the least specialized and most generalized type of salesforce. Salespeople are typically assigned a geographic area and are responsible for all selling activities to all accounts within the assigned area. There is no attempt to specialize by product, market, or function. An example of a geographic sales organization for the ABC Company is presented in Figure 5.5. Again, note that this type of organization provides no salesforce specialization except by geographic area. Because of the lack of specialization, there is no duplication of effort. All geographic areas and accounts are served by only one salesperson.

The structure in this example is a rather tall one and thus somewhat centralized. There are four levels of line sales management with relatively small spans of control, indicated in parentheses: national sales manager (2), regional sales managers (4), zone sales managers (5), and district sales managers (5). Note the sales management specialization in the sales training staff position. Because this staff position is located at the national sales manager level, training activities tend to be centralized.

Product Sales Organization

Product specialization has been popular in recent years, but it seems to be declining in importance, at least in certain industries. Salesforces specializing by product assign salespeople selling responsibility for specific products or product lines. The objective is for salespeople to become experts in the assigned product categories.

An example of a product sales organization for the ABC Company is presented in Figure 5.6. This organization structure indicates two levels of product specialization. There are two separate salesforces: One salesforce specializes in selling office equipment, and the other specializes in selling office supplies. Each of the specialized salesforces performs all selling activities for all types of accounts. The separate salesforces are each organized geographically. Thus, there will be duplication in the coverage of geographic areas, with both office equipment and office supplies salespeople operating in the same areas. In some cases, the salespeople may call on the same accounts.

FIGURE 5.5 Geographic Sales Organization

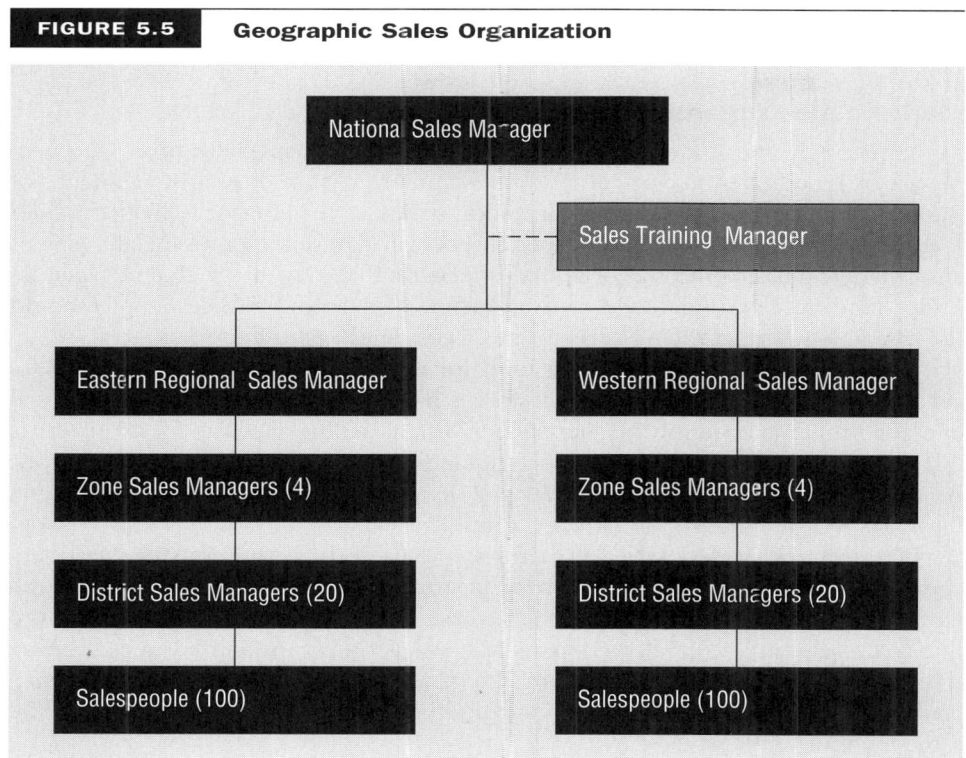

This geographic sales organization structure has four sales management levels, small spans of control, and a staff position at the national level.

FIGURE 5.6 Product Sales Organization

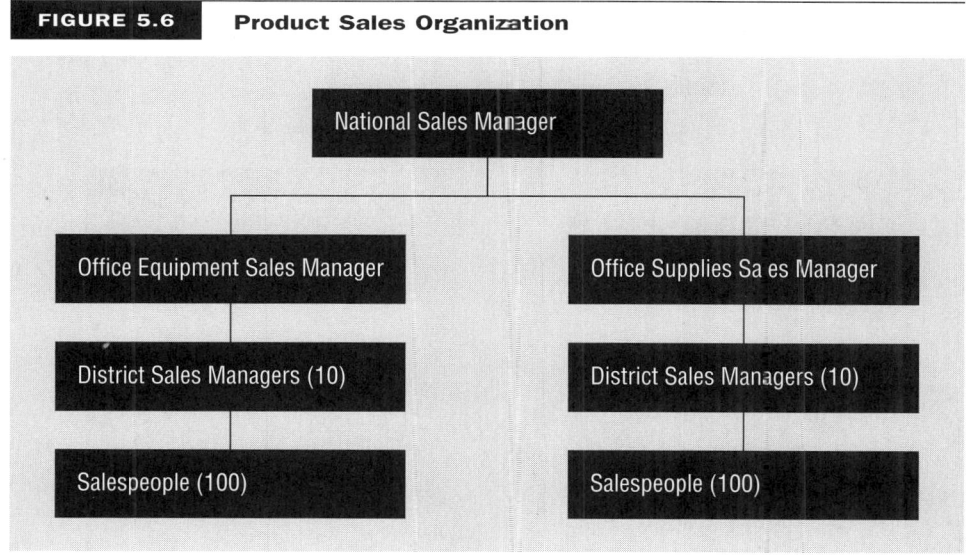

This product sales organization structure has three sales management levels, large spans of control, and no staff positions.

The example structure in Figure 5.6 is flat and decentralized, especially when compared with the example presented in Figure 5.5. There are only three line management levels with wide spans of control: national sales manager (2), product sales managers (10), and district sales managers (10). This structure has no staff positions and thus no management specialization beyond product specialization. The office equipment and office supplies salesforces are organized in exactly the same manner.

Market Sales Organization

An increasingly important type of specialization is **market specialization.** Salespeople are assigned specific types of customers and are required to satisfy all needs of these customers. The new sales organization structure for Pinacor is an example of market specialization, because salespeople specialize in serving one specific type of customer. The basic objective of market specialization is to ensure that salespeople understand how customers use and purchase their products. Salespeople should then be able to direct their efforts to satisfy customer needs better.

The market sales organization shown for the ABC Company in Figure 5.7 focuses on account types. Separate salesforces have been organized for commercial and government accounts. Salespeople perform all selling activities for all products but only for certain accounts. This arrangement avoids duplication of sales effort, because only one salesperson will ever call on a given account. Several salespeople may, however, operate in the same geographic area.

The example in Figure 5.7 presents some interesting variations in sales management organization. The commercial accounts salesforce is much more centralized than the government accounts salesforce. This centralization is due to more line management levels, shorter spans of control, and a specialized sales training staff position. This example structure illustrates the important point that the specialized salesforces within a sales organization do not have to be structured in the same manner.

FIGURE 5.7   Market Sales Organization

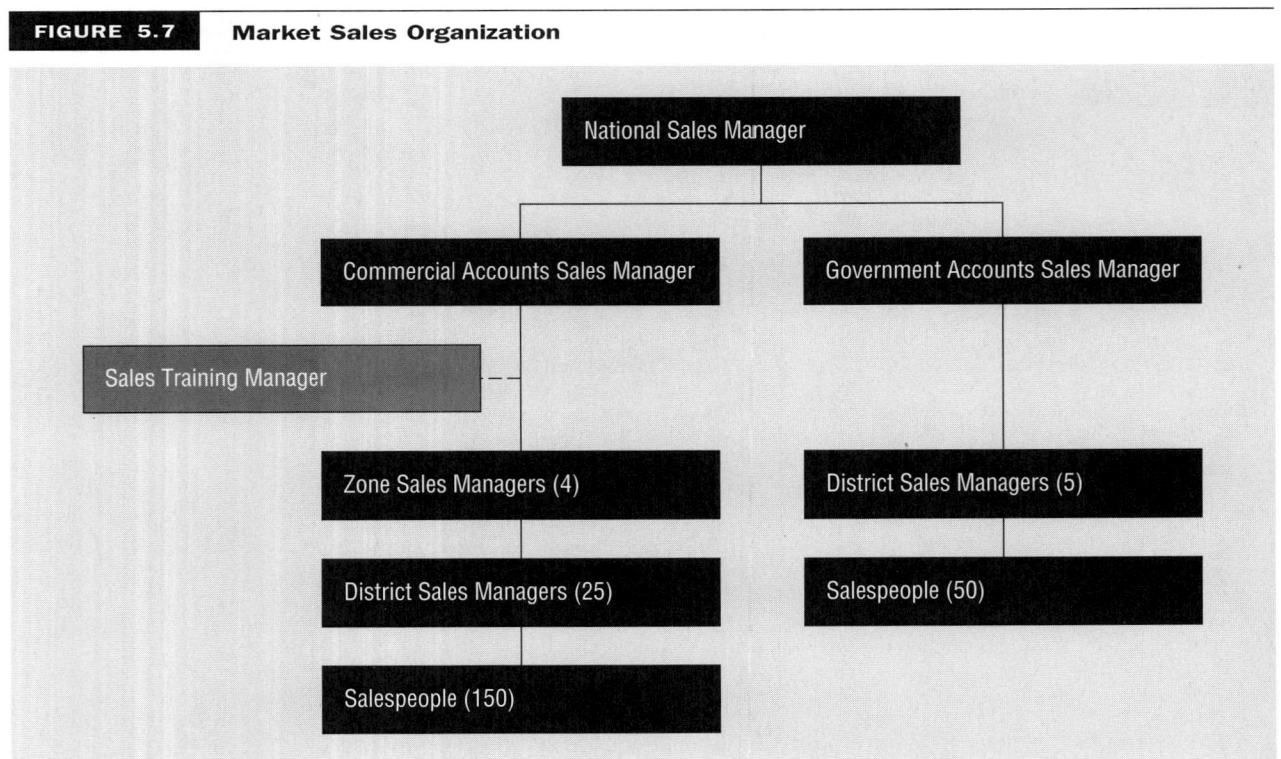

This market sales organization structure organizes its commercial accounts salesforce differently from its government accounts salesforce. The commercial accounts salesforce has three sales management levels, small spans of control, and a staff position. The government accounts salesforce has two sales management levels, large spans of control, and no staff positions.

Functional Sales Organization

The final type of specialization is **functional specialization.** Most selling situations require a number of selling activities, so there may be efficiencies in having salespeople specialize in performing certain of these required activities. As already discussed in Module 4, many firms are using a telemarketing salesforce to generate leads, qualify prospects, monitor shipments, and so forth, while the outside salesforce concentrates on sales-generating activities. These firms are specializing by function.

An example of a functional sales organization for ABC Company is presented in Figure 5.8. In this structure, a field salesforce performs sales-generating activities and a telemarketing salesforce performs account-servicing activities. Although the salesforces will cover the same geographic areas and the same accounts, the use of telemarketing helps to reduce the cost of this duplication of effort. The more routine and repetitive activities will be performed by the inside telemarketing salesforce. The more creative and nonroutine sales-generating activities will be performed by the outside field salesforce.

The field salesforce is more centralized than the telemarketing salesforce, but both salesforces tend to be decentralized. The cost-effectiveness of telemarketing is illustrated by the need for only two management levels and three managers to supervise 40 salespeople. This example does not include any staff positions for sales management specialization.

Major Account Organization

Many firms receive a large percentage of their total sales from relatively few accounts. These large-volume accounts are obviously extremely important and must be considered when designing a sales organization. The term *major account* is used

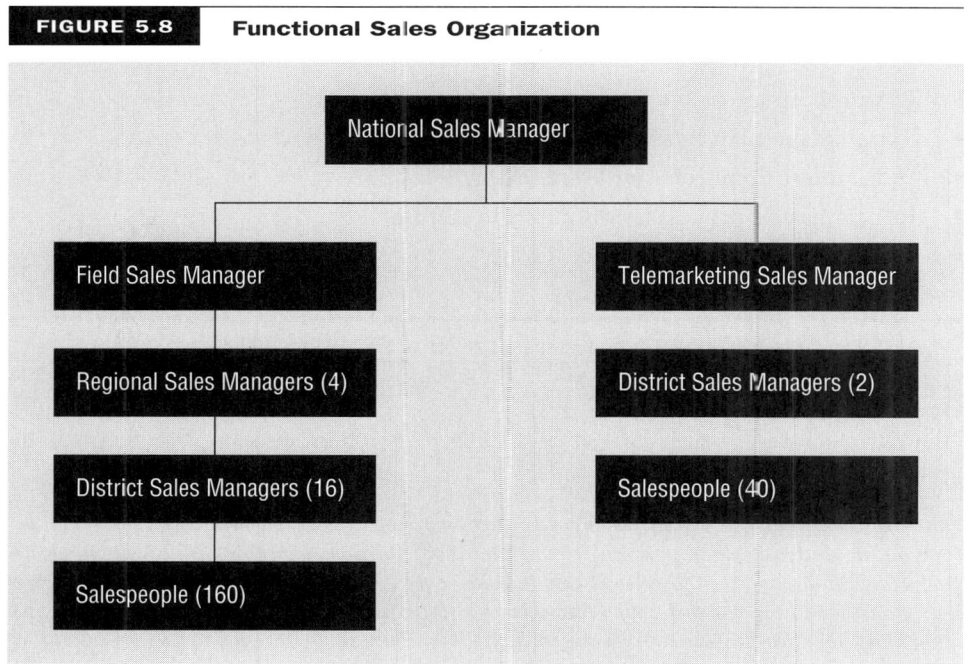

FIGURE 5.8 Functional Sales Organization

This functional sales organization structure organizes its field salesforce differently from its telemarketing salesforce. The field salesforce has three sales management levels with small spans of control, and the telemarketing salesforce has two sales management levels with large spans of control. Neither salesforce uses staff positions.

to refer to large, important accounts that should receive special attention from the sales organization. Some firms use the term *key account* instead. We use the term *major account* to refer to all large, important accounts in this text. One approach for serving major accounts is presented in "Sales Management in the 21st Century: Organizing for Major Accounts."

A **major account organization** represents a type of market specialization based on account size and complexity. Two types of major account organizations are of particular importance. **National account management (NAM)** focuses on meeting the needs of specific accounts with multiple locations throughout a large region or entire country. For example, the distribution company Unisource has a formal national account management program for major accounts that have many locations nationwide. Major accounts from the printing, publishing, retail grocery, manufacturing, and food processing industries are provided special services, pricing, and delivery schedules. These major accounts have a single contact point within Unisource and the same contract for all their locations.[3]

Global account management (GAM), by contrast, serves the needs of major customers with locations around the world. Typically, a global account manager will be located at the customer's headquarters. This manager directs the activities of account representatives in that customer's other locations worldwide. Often, a global account management team is assigned to each customer. This team might consist of product specialists, applications specialists, sales support specialists, and others.[4]

Major account organization has become increasingly important in both domestic and international markets. Although major account programs differ considerably across firms, all firms must determine how to identify their own major accounts and how to organize for effective coverage of them.

IDENTIFYING MAJOR ACCOUNTS All large accounts to not qualify as major accounts. As illustrated in Figure 5.9, a major account should be of sufficient size and complexity to warrant special attention from the sales organization. An account can be considered complex under the following circumstances:[5]

- Its purchasing function is centralized.
- Top management heavily influences its purchasing decisions.
- It has multisite purchasing influences.
- Its purchasing process is complex and diffuse.
- It requires special price concessions.

SALES MANAGEMENT IN THE 21ST CENTURY

Organizing for Major Accounts

John Carey, district manager for Harcourt College Publishers, discusses an interesting approach for serving major accounts:

Harcourt College Publishers considers large and complex universities as major accounts. These universities require special attention from our sales organization. Our sales organization structure integrates product and functional specialization to meet the specific needs of each university. Two sales representatives are assigned to each of these major accounts. One specializes in textbooks for the social sciences and humanities, the other for business and science disciplines. There is also a regional sales consultant for each major account. This consultant helps the sales representatives in planning and executing sales presentations, and with follow-up service after the sale. My job is to coordinate the efforts of salespeople and the consultant at each major account.

FIGURE 5.9 Identifying Major Accounts

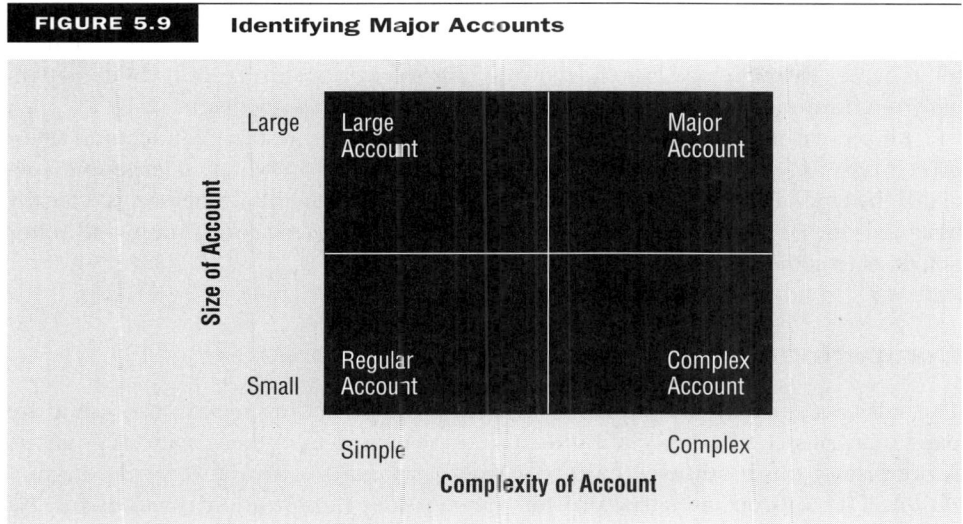

Major accounts are both large and complex. They are extremely important to the firm and require specialized attention.

FIGURE 5.10 Major Account Options

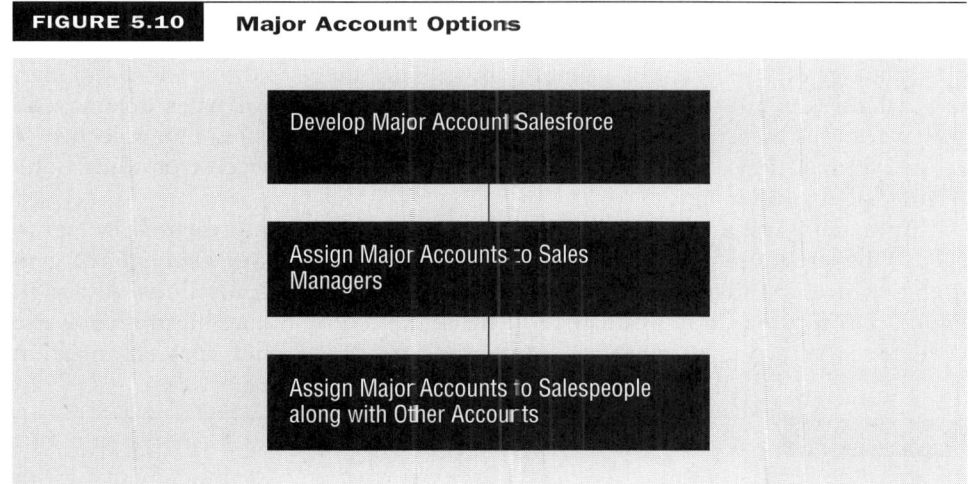

Once identified, major accounts can be served in three basic ways. The development of a major account salesforce is the most comprehensive approach and is being used increasingly often for customers in domestic and international markets.

- It requires special services.
- It purchases customized products.

ORGANIZING FOR MAJOR ACCOUNT COVERAGE Accounts that are not both large and complex are typically served adequately through the basic sales organization structure, but those identified as major accounts pose problems for organization design that might be handled in a variety of ways. The basic options are shown in Figure 5.10. In one option, major accounts, although identified, are assigned to salespeople, as are other accounts. This approach may provide some special attention to these accounts but is not a formal major account management program.

Many firms have found that formal major account management programs can strengthen account relationships and improve communications between buyers and sellers. These formal programs are designed in several ways. One approach is to assign major accounts to sales executives, who are responsible for coordinating all activities with each assigned account. This major account responsibility is typically in addition to the executives' normal management activities.

An increasingly popular approach is to establish a separate major account salesforce. This approach is a type of market specialization in which salespeople specialize by type of account based on size and complexity. Each salesperson is typically assigned one or more major accounts and is responsible for coordinating all seller activities to serve the assigned accounts.

Comparing Sales Organization Structures

The sales organization structures described in the preceding section represent the basic types of salesforce specialization and some examples of the variations possible. A premise of this module is that no one best way exists to structure a sales organization. The appropriate structure for a given sales organization depends on the characteristics of the selling situation. Some structures are better in some selling situations than in others. Exhibit 5.2 summarizes much of what has been discussed previously by directly comparing the advantages and disadvantages of each basic sales organization structure.

As is evident from this exhibit, the strengths of one structure are weaknesses in other structures. For example, the lack of geographic and customer duplication is an advantage of a geographic structure but a disadvantage of the product and market structures. Because of this situation, many firms use **hybrid sales organization** structures that incorporate several of the basic structural types. The objective of these hybrid structures is to capitalize on the advantages of each type while minimizing the disadvantages.

An example of a hybrid sales organizational structure is presented in Figure 5.11. This structure is extremely complex in that it includes elements of geographic, product, market, function, and major account organizations. Although Figure 5.11 represents only one possible hybrid structure, it does illustrate how the different structure types might be combined into one overall sales organization

EXHIBIT 5.2 Comparison of Sales Organization Structures

Organization Structure	Advantages	Disadvantages
Geographic	• Low cost • No geographic duplication • No customer duplication • Fewer management levels	• Limited specialization • Lack of management control over product or customer emphasis
Product	• Salespeople become experts in product attributes and applications • Management control over selling effort allocated to products	• High cost • Geographic duplication • Customer duplication
Market	• Salespeople develop better understanding of unique customer needs • Management control over selling effort allocated to different markets	• High cost • Geographic duplication
Functional	• Efficiency in performing selling activities	• Geographic duplication • Customer duplication • Need for coordination

FIGURE 5.11 Hybrid Sales Organization Structure

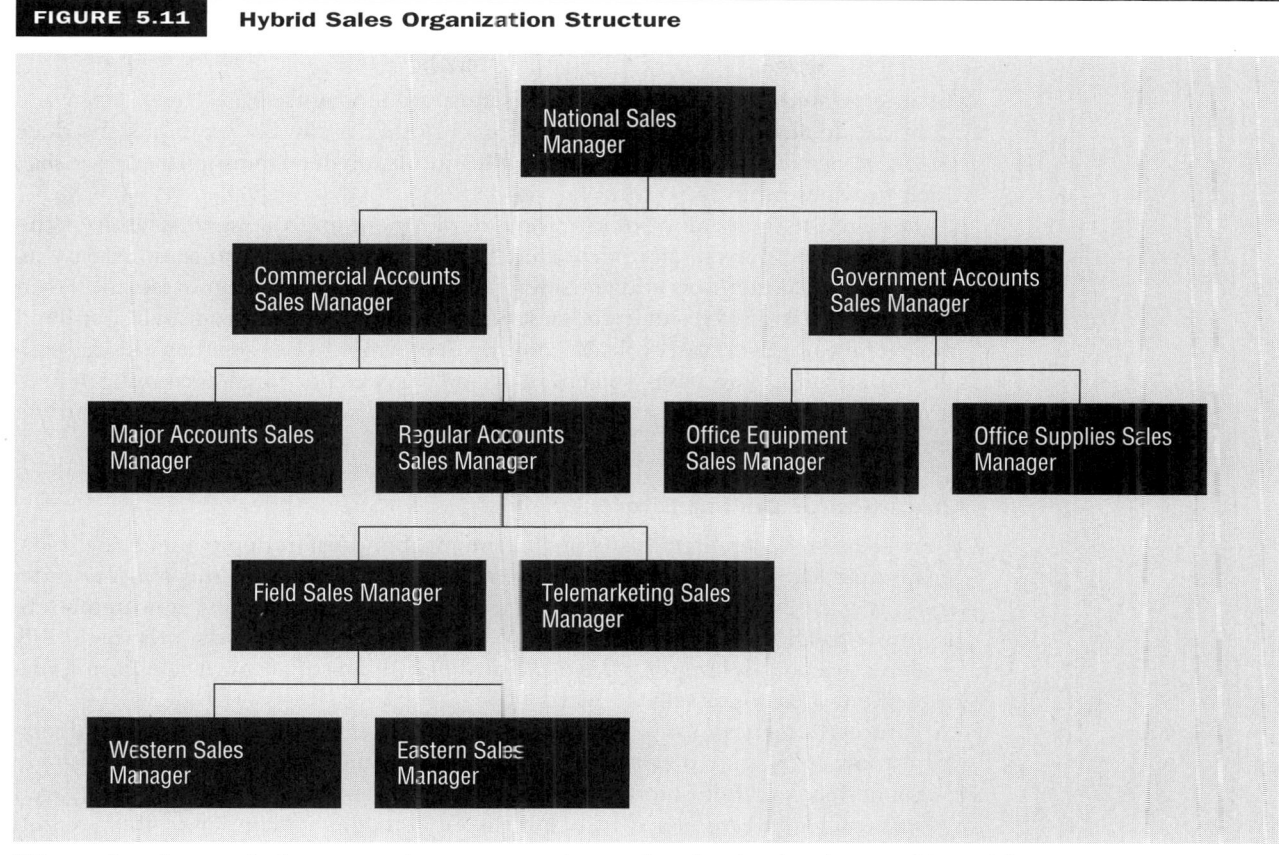

This complex sales organization structure incorporates market, product, functional, and geographic specialization.

structure. The example also illustrates the complex nature of the task of determining sales organization structure. As noted before, the task is an extremely important one; sales management must develop the appropriate sales organization structure for its particular selling situation to ensure the successful implementation of organizational and account strategies. This task becomes increasingly more difficult as firms operate globally.

Salesforce Deployment

The important sales management decisions involved in allocating selling effort, determining salesforce size, and designing territories are often referred to as **salesforce deployment.** These decisions are closely related to the sales organization structure decisions. Changes in structure often require adjustments in all three areas of salesforce deployment—selling effort allocation, salesforce size determination, and territory design.

Salesforce deployment decisions can be viewed as providing answers to three interrelated questions.

1. How much selling effort is needed to cover accounts and prospects adequately so that sales and profit objectives will be achieved?
2. How many salespeople are required to provide the desired amount of selling effort?

3. How should territories be designed to ensure proper coverage of accounts and to provide each salesperson with a reasonable opportunity for success?

The interrelatedness of these decisions is illustrated in Figure 5.12. Decisions in one salesforce deployment area affect decisions in other areas. For example, the decision on allocation of selling effort provides input for determining salesforce size, which provides input for territory design.

Despite the importance of salesforce deployment and the need to address the deployment decisions in an interrelated manner, many sales organizations use simplified analytical methods and consider each deployment decision in isolation—an approach not likely to result in the best deployment decisions. Even such simplified approaches, however, can typically identify deployment changes that will increase sales and profits. The basic objectives of and approaches for determining selling effort allocation, salesforce size, and territory design are discussed separately in the remainder of this module.

Allocation of Selling Effort

The allocation of selling effort is one of the most important deployment decisions, because the salesforce size and territory decisions are based on this allocation decision. Regardless of the method of account coverage, determining how much selling effort to allocate to individual accounts is an important decision strategically speaking, because selling effort is a major determinant of account sales and a major element of account selling costs.

Although decisions on the allocation of selling effort are difficult, several analytical tools are available to help. The three basic analytical approaches are single factor models, portfolio models, and decision models. These three are compared in Figure 5.13 and discussed in detail throughout the remainder of this section.

SINGLE FACTOR MODELS Easy to develop and use, **single factor models** do not, however, provide a very comprehensive analysis of accounts. The typical procedure is to classify all accounts on one factor, such as market potential, and then to assign all accounts in the same category the same number of sales calls. An example of using a single factor model for sales call allocation is presented in Exhibit 5.3.

Although single factor models have limitations, they do provide sales managers with a systematic approach for determining selling effort allocation. Sales managers

FIGURE 5.12   Interrelatedness of Salesforce Deployment Decisions

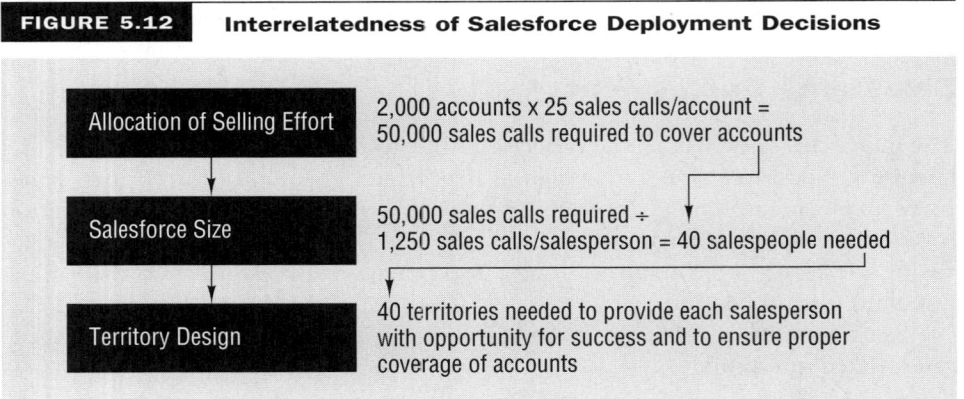

Determining how much selling effort should be allocated to various accounts provides a basis for calculating the number of salespeople required to produce the desired amount of selling effort. The salesforce size decision then determines the number of territories that must be designed. Thus, decisions in one deployment area affect decisions in other deployment areas.

FIGURE 5.13   Analytical Approaches to Allocation of Selling Effort

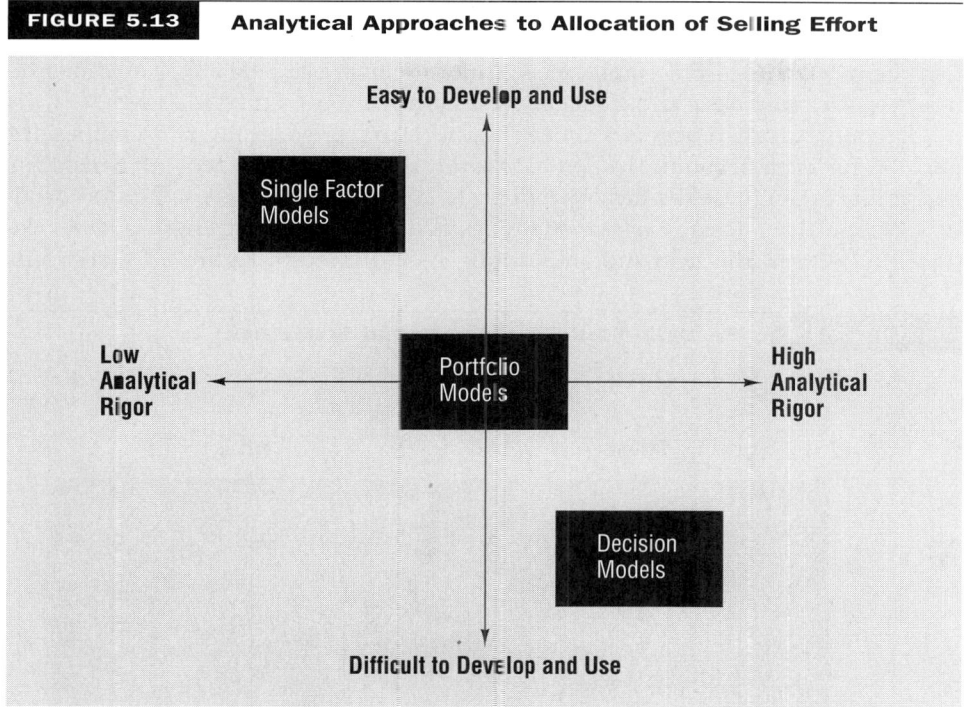

The single factor, portfolio, and decision model approaches for performing a deployment analysis differ in terms of analytical rigor and in ease of development and use. Typically, the more rigorous the approach, the more difficult it is to develop and use.

EXHIBIT 5.3   Example of Single Factor Model

The single factor model was applied to evaluate the market potential of each account and then classify all accounts into A, B, C, and D market potential categories. The average number of sales calls to an account in each market potential category was calculated and evaluated. Based on this analysis, changes in the account effort allocation strategy were made. A summary of the results follows:

Market Potential Categories	Average Sales Calls to an Account Last Year	Average Sales Calls to an Account Next Year
A	25	32
B	23	24
C	20	16
D	16	8

are likely to make better allocation decisions by using single factor models than when relying totally on judgment and intuition. Because of their ease of development and usage, single factor models are probably the most widely used analytical approach for making these allocation decisions.

PORTFOLIO MODELS   A more comprehensive analysis of accounts is provided by **portfolio models,** but they are somewhat more difficult to develop and use than single factor models. In a portfolio model, each account served by a firm is considered as part of an overall portfolio of accounts. Thus, accounts within the portfolio represent different situations and receive different levels of selling effort attention. The typical approach is to classify all accounts in the portfolio into categories of similar attractiveness for receiving sales call investment. Then, selling effort is allocated so that the more attractive accounts receive more selling effort. The typical attractiveness segments and basic effort allocation strategies are presented in Figure 5.14.

Account attractiveness is a function of account opportunity and competitive position for each account. *Account opportunity* is defined as an account's need for and ability to purchase the firm's products (e.g., grocery products, computer products, financial services). *Competitive position* is defined as the strength of the relationship between the firm and an account. As indicated in Figure 5.14, accounts

FIGURE 5.14 Portfolio Model Segments and Strategies

	Competitive Position	
Account Opportunity	**Strong**	**Weak**
High	**SEGMENT 1** **Attractiveness:** Accounts are very attractive because they offer high opportunity, and sales organization has strong competitive position. **Selling Effort Strategy:** Accounts should receive a heavy investment of selling effort to take advantage of opportunity and maintain/improve competitive position.	**SEGMENT 2** **Attractiveness:** Accounts are potentially attractive due to high opportunity, but sales organization currently has weak competitive position. **Selling Effort Strategy:** Additional analysis should be performed to identify accounts where sales organization's competitive position can be strengthened. These accounts should receive heavy investment of selling effort, while other accounts receive minimal investment.
Low	**SEGMENT 3** **Attractiveness:** Accounts are moderately attractive due to sales organization's strong competitive position. However future opportunity is limited. **Selling Effort Strategy:** Accounts should receive a selling effort investment sufficient to maintain current competitive position.	**SEGMENT 4** **Attractiveness:** Accounts are very unattractive; they offer low opportunity, and sales organization has weak competitive position. **Selling Effort Strategy:** Accounts should receive minimal investment of selling effort. Less costly forms of marketing (for example, telephone sales calls, direct mail) should replace personal selling efforts on a selective basis, or the account coverage should be eliminated entirely.

Accounts are classified into attractiveness categories based on evaluations of account opportunity and competitive position. The selling effort strategies are based on the concept that the more attractive an account, the more selling effort it should receive.

are more attractive the higher the account opportunity and the stronger the competitive positions.

Using portfolio models to develop an account effort allocation strategy requires that account opportunity and competitive position be measured for each account. Based on these measurements, accounts can be classified into the attractiveness segments. The portfolio model differs from the single factor model in that many factors are normally measured to assess account opportunity and competitive position. The exact number and types of factors depend on a firm's specific selling situation. Thus, the portfolio approach provides a comprehensive account analysis that can be adapted to the specific selling situation faced by any firm.

Portfolio models can be valuable tools for helping sales managers improve their account effort allocation strategy. They are relatively easy to develop and use (although more difficult than single factor models) and provide a more comprehensive analysis than single factor models.

DECISION MODELS The most rigorous and comprehensive method for determining an account effort allocation strategy is by means of a **decision model.** Because of their complexity, decision models are somewhat difficult to develop and use. However, today's computer hardware and software make decision models much easier to use than before. Research results have consistently supported the value of decision models in improving effort allocation and salesforce productivity.[6]

Although the mathematical formulations of decision models can be complex, the basic concept is simple—to allocate sales calls to accounts that promise the highest sales return from the sales calls. The objective is to achieve the highest level of sales for any given number of sales calls and to continue increasing sales calls until their marginal costs equal their marginal returns. Thus, decision models calculate the optimal allocation of sales calls in terms of sales or profit maximization.

Salesforce Size

Research results have consistently shown that many firms could improve their performance by changing the size of their salesforce. In some situations, the salesforce should be increased. In other situations, however, firms are employing too many salespeople and could improve performance by reducing the size of their salesforces. Determining the appropriate salesforce size requires an understanding of several key considerations as well as a familiarity with different analytical approaches that might be used.

KEY CONSIDERATIONS The size of a firm's salesforce determines the total amount of selling effort that is available to call on accounts and prospects. The decision on salesforce size is analogous to the decision on advertising budget. Whereas the advertising budget establishes the total amount that the firm has to spend on advertising communications, the salesforce size determines the total amount of personal selling effort that is available. Because each salesperson can make only a certain number of sales calls during any period, the number of salespeople times the number of sales calls per salesperson defines the total available selling effort. For example, a firm with 100 salespeople who each make 500 sales calls per year has a total selling effort of 50,000 sales calls. If the salesforce is increased to 110 salespeople, then total selling effort is increased to 55,000 sales calls. Two of the key considerations in determining salesforce size are productivity and turnover.

Productivity In general terms, *productivity* is defined as a ratio between outputs and inputs. One way the **sales productivity** of a salesforce is calculated is the ratio of sales generated to selling effort used. Thus, productivity is an important consideration for all deployment decisions. However, selling effort is often expressed in terms of number of salespeople. This suggests that the critical consideration is the *relationship* between selling effort and sales, not just the total amount of selling effort or the total level of sales. For example, sales per salesperson is an important sales productivity measure.

Sales will generally increase with the addition of salespeople, but not in a linear manner. With some exceptions, costs tend to increase directly with salesforce size. This produces the basic relationship presented in Figure 5.15. In early stages, the addition of salespeople increases sales considerably more than the selling costs. However, as salespeople continue to be added, sales increases tend to decline until a point is reached when the costs to add a salesperson are more than the revenues that salesperson can generate. In fact, the profit maximization point is when the marginal costs of adding a salesperson are equal to the marginal profits generated by that salesperson. It typically becomes more difficult to maintain high sales productivity levels at larger salesforce sizes. This makes it imperative that management consider the relationship between sales and costs when making decisions on salesforce size.

Turnover Salesforce turnover is extremely costly. Because some turnover is going to occur for all firms, it should always be considered when determining salesforce size. Once the appropriate salesforce size is determined—that is, one sufficient for salespeople to call on all the firm's accounts and prospects in a productive manner—this figure should be adjusted to reflect expected turnover. If an increase or maintenance of current salesforce size is desired, excess salespeople should be in the recruiting-selecting-training pipeline. If a decrease is desired, turnover might be all that is necessary to accomplish it. For example, a grocery products marketer that found that its salesforce should be reduced from 34 to 32 salespeople achieved the two-salesperson reduction through scheduled retirements in the near future instead of firing two salespeople.

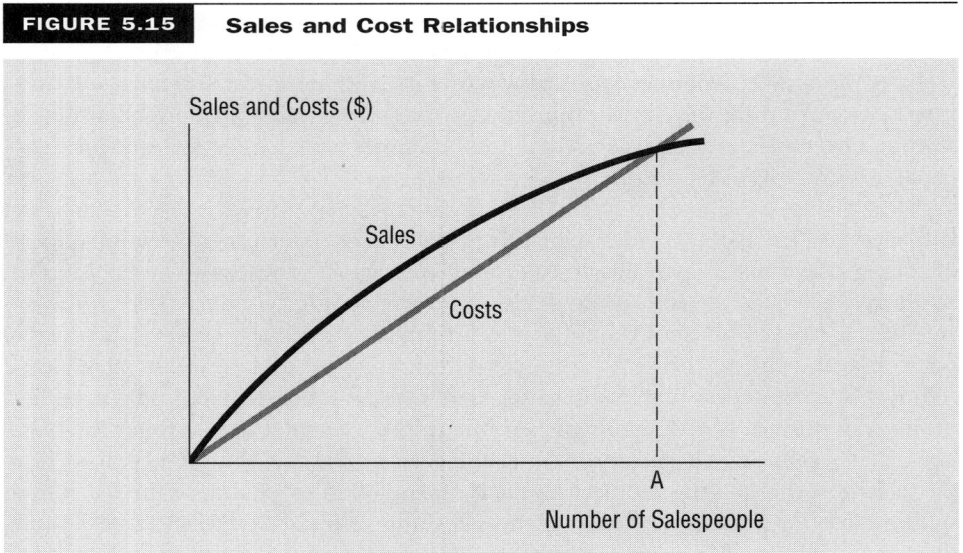

FIGURE 5.15 **Sales and Cost Relationships**

Although costs tend to increase in a linear manner with the addition of salespeople, the associated sales increases are typically nonlinear. In general, the increases in sales tend to decrease as more salespeople are added. A point (A) is reached when the sales from adding a salesperson are not sufficient to cover the additional costs.

ANALYTICAL TOOLS The need to consider sales, costs, productivity, and turnover makes salesforce size a difficult decision. Fortunately, some analytical tools are available to help management process relevant information and evaluate salesforce size alternatives more fully. Before describing these analytical tools, we want to make it clear that there are different types of salesforce size decisions (see Figure 5.16). The most straightforward situation is when a firm has one generalized salesforce. However, as discussed earlier, many firms employ multiple specialized salesforces, in which case both the total number of salespeople employed by the firm and the size of each individual salesforce are important. Both generalized and specialized salesforces are normally organized into geographic districts, zones, regions, and so on. The number of salespeople to assign to each district, zone, region, and so on is a type of salesforce size decision.

These different types of decisions are similar conceptually and can be addressed by the same analytical tools, provided that the type of salesforce size decision being addressed is specified. Unless stated otherwise, you can assume the situation of one generalized salesforce in the following discussion.

Breakdown Approach A relatively simple approach for calculating salesforce size, the **breakdown approach** assumes that an accurate sales forecast is available. This forecast is then "broken down" to determine the number of salespeople needed to generate the forecasted level of sales. The basic formula is

$$\text{Salesforce size} = \text{Forecasted sales}/\text{Average sales per salesperson}$$

Assume that a firm forecasts sales of $50 million for next year. If salespeople generate an average of $2 million in annual sales, then the firm needs 25 salespeople to achieve the $50 million sales forecast:

$$\text{Salesforce size} = \$50,000,000/\$2,000,000 = 25 \text{ salespeople}$$

The basic advantage of the breakdown method is its ease of development. The approach is straightforward, and the mathematical calculations are simple.

FIGURE 5.16   Different Salesforce Size Decisions

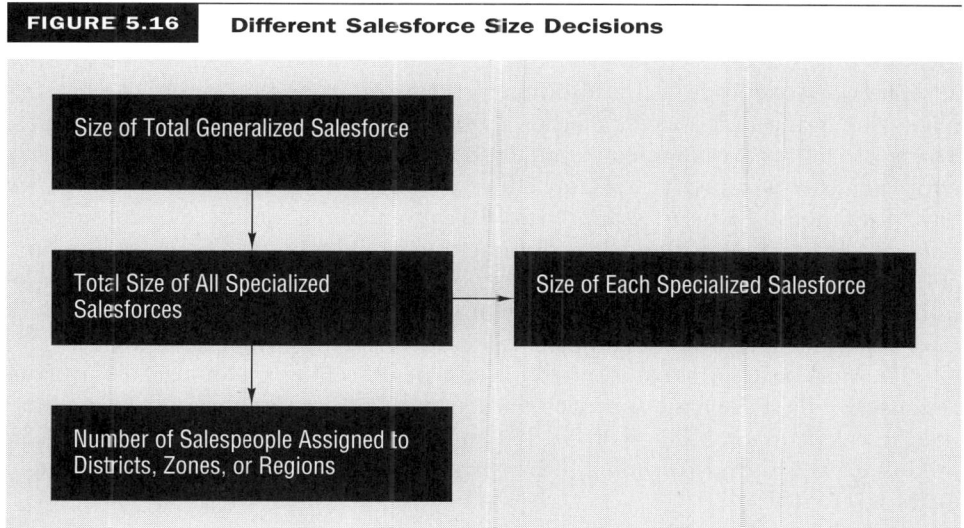

Depending on the sales organization structure of a firm, sales managers may be faced with several different types of salesforce size decisions. Each requires the same basic concepts and analytical methods.

However, the approach is weak conceptually. The concept underlying the calculations is that sales determine the number of salespeople needed. This puts "the cart before the horse," because the number of salespeople employed by a firm is an important determinant of firm sales. A sales forecast should be based on a given salesforce size. The addition of salespeople should increase the forecast, and the elimination of salespeople should decrease it.

Despite this weakness, the breakdown method is probably the most often used for determining salesforce size. It is best suited for relatively stable selling environments in which sales change in slow and predictable ways and no major strategic changes are planned and for organizations that use commission compensation plans and keep their fixed costs low. However, in many selling situations the costs of having too many or too few salespeople are high. More rigorous analytical tools are recommended for calculating salesforce size in these situations.

Workload Approach The first step in the **workload approach** is to determine how much selling effort is needed to cover the firm's market adequately. Then the number of salespeople required to provide this amount of selling effort is calculated. The basic formula is

$$\text{Number of salespeople} = \frac{\text{Total selling effort needed}}{\text{Average selling effort per salesperson}}$$

For example, if a firm determines that 37,500 sales calls are needed in its market area and a salesperson can make an average of 500 annual sales calls, then 75 salespeople are needed to provide the desired level of selling effort:

$$\text{Number of salespeople} = 37{,}500/500 = 75 \text{ salespeople}$$

The key factor in the workload approach is the total amount of selling effort needed. Several workload methods can be used, depending on whether single factor, portfolio, or decision models were used for determining the allocation of effort to accounts. Each workload method offers a different way to calculate how many sales calls to make to all accounts and prospects during any time period. When the sales call allocation strategies are summed across all accounts and prospects, the total amount of selling effort for a time period is determined. Thus, the workload approach integrates the salesforce size decision with account effort allocation strategies.

The workload approach is also relatively simple to develop, although this simplicity depends on the specific method used to determine total selling effort needs. The approach is also sound conceptually, because salesforce size is based on selling effort needs established by account effort allocation decisions. Note, however, we have presented the workload approach in a simplified manner here by considering only selling effort. A more realistic presentation would incorporate nonselling time considerations (e.g., travel time, planning time) in the analysis. Although incorporating these considerations does not change the basic workload concept, it does make the calculations more complex and cumbersome.

The workload approach is suited for all types of selling situations. Sales organizations can adapt the basic approach to their specific situation through the method used to calculate total selling effort. The most sophisticated firms can use decision models for this purpose, whereas other firms might use portfolio models or single factor approaches.

Incremental Approach The most rigorous approach for calculating salesforce size is the **incremental approach.** Its basic concept is to compare the marginal profit contribution with the marginal selling costs for each incremental salesperson. An example of these calculations is provided in Exhibit 5.4. At 100 salespeople, marginal profits exceed marginal costs by $10,000. This relationship continues until salesforce size reaches 102. At 102 salespeople, the marginal profit equals marginal cost, and total profits are maximized. If the firm added one more salesperson, total profits would be reduced, because marginal costs would exceed marginal profits by $5,000. Thus, the optimal salesforce size for this example is 102.

The major advantage of the incremental approach is that it quantifies the important relationships between salesforce size, sales, and costs, making it possible to assess the potential sales and profit impacts of different salesforce sizes. It forces management to view the salesforce size decision as one that affects both the level of sales that can be generated and the costs associated with producing each sales level.

The incremental method is, however, somewhat difficult to develop. Relatively complex response functions must be formulated to predict sales at different salesforce sizes (sales = f [salesforce size]). Developing these response functions requires either historical data or management judgment. Thus, the incremental approach cannot be used for new salesforces where historical data and accurate judgments are not possible.

Turnover All the analytical tools incorporate various elements of sales and costs in their calculations. Therefore, they directly address productivity issues but do not directly consider turnover in the salesforce size calculations. When turnover considerations are important, management should adjust the recommended salesforce size produced by any of the analytical methods to reflect expected turnover rates. For example, if an analytical tool recommended a salesforce size of 100 for a firm that experiences 20 percent annual turnover, the effective salesforce size should be adjusted to 120. Recruiting, selecting, and training plans should be based on the 120 salesforce size.

Failure to incorporate anticipated salesforce turnover into salesforce size calculations can be costly. Evidence suggests that many firms may lose as much as 10 percent in sales productivity due to the loss in sales from vacant territories or low initial sales when a new salesperson is assigned to a territory. Thus, the sooner that sales managers can replace salespeople and get them productive in their territories, the less loss in sales within the territory.

Designing Territories

As discussed earlier, the size of a salesforce determines the total amount of selling effort that a firm has available to generate sales from accounts and prospects. The effective use of this selling effort often requires that sales **territories** be developed and each salesperson be assigned to a specific territory. A territory consists of whatever specific accounts are assigned to a specific salesperson. The overall objective is to ensure that all accounts are assigned salesperson responsibility and that each

EXHIBIT 5.4   Incremental Approach

Number of Salespeople	Marginal Salesperson Profit Contribution	Marginal Salesperson Cost
100	$85,000	$75,000
101	$80,000	$75,000
102	$75,000	$75,000
103	$70,000	$75,000

salesperson can adequately cover the assigned accounts. Although territories are often defined by geographic area (e.g., the Oklahoma territory, the Tennessee territory), the key components of a territory are the accounts within the specified geographic area.

The territory can be viewed as the work unit for a salesperson. The salesperson is largely responsible for the selling activities performed and the performance achieved in a territory. Salesperson compensation and success are normally a direct function of territory performance; thus, the design of territories is extremely important to the individual salespeople of a firm as well as to management. An example of trying to balance company and salesperson needs is presented in "Sales Management in the 21st Century: Designing Sales Territories."

TERRITORY CONSIDERATIONS The critical territory considerations are illustrated in Exhibit 5.5. In this example, Andy and Sally are salespeople for a consumer durable goods manufacturer. They have each been assigned a geographic territory consisting of several trading areas. The exhibit compares the percentage of their time currently spent in each trading area with the percentages recommended from

---

SALES MANAGEMENT IN THE 21ST CENTURY

Designing Sales Territories

John Carey, district manager for Harcourt College Publishers, discusses the important factors in designing effective sales territories:

Each of our salespeople is responsible for a sales territory defined by assigned accounts and geographic area. Designing effective sales territories is a difficult, but important, task. Our goal is to ensure that each territory receives optimal coverage of accounts and provides each sales representative with an equitable chance for success. This is a tough balancing act. We consider a number of different factors when establishing sales territories. These include geography, number and location of accounts, account size and sales potential, and the characteristics of each sales representative. We integrate our analyses of these factors to generate sales territories most likely to meet our goals.

EXHIBIT 5.5 Territory Design Example

	Trading Area[a]	Present Effort (%)[b]	Recommended Effort (%)[b]
Andy	1	10	4
	2	60	20
	3	15	7
	4	5	2
	5	10	3
Total		100	36
Sally	6	18	81
	7	7	21
	8	5	11
	9	35	35
	10	5	11
	11	30	77
Total		100	236

[a] Each territory is made of up several trading areas.
[b] The percentage of salesperson time spent in the trading area (100% = 1 salesperson). Thus, the deployment analysis suggests that Andy's territory requires only 0.36 salespeople, whereas Sally's territory needs 2.36 salespeople for proper coverage.

a decision model analysis. A review of the information provided in the exhibit highlights territory design problems from the perspective of the firm and of each salesperson.

The current territory design does not provide proper selling coverage of the trading areas. The decision model analysis suggests that the trading areas in Andy's territory should require only 36 percent of his time, yet he is spending all his time there. Clearly, the firm is wasting expensive selling effort in Andy's territory. The situation in Sally's territory is just the opposite. Proper coverage of Sally's trading areas should require more than two salespeople, yet Sally has sole responsibility for these trading areas. In this situation the firm is losing sales opportunities because of a lack of selling attention.

From the firm's perspective, the design of Andy's and Sally's territories limits sales and profit performance. Sales performance in Sally's territory is much lower than it might be if more selling attention were given to her trading areas. Profit performance is low in Andy's territory because too much selling effort is being expended in his trading areas. The firm is not achieving the level of sales and profits that might be achieved if the territories were designed to provide more productive market coverage. Thus, one key consideration in territory design is the productive deployment of selling effort within each territory.

From the perspective of Andy and Sally, the poor territory design affects their level of motivation. Andy is frustrated. He spends much of his time making sales calls in trading areas where little potential exists for generating additional sales. Andy's motivational level is low, and he may consider resigning from the company. By contrast, Sally's territory has so much sales potential that she can limit her sales calls to the largest accounts or the easiest sales. She is not motivated to develop the potential of her territory but can merely "skim the cream" from the best accounts. The situations facing Andy and Sally illustrate how territory design might affect salesperson motivation, morale, and even turnover. These potential effects are important considerations when designing territories.

PROCEDURE FOR DESIGNING TERRITORIES A general procedure for designing territories is presented in Figure 5.17. Each step in the procedure can be performed manually or by using computer models. The procedure is illustrated manually by using Andy's and Sally's territories as an example application. The basic problem is to organize the 11 trading areas into three territories that provide proper market coverage of accounts in each territory and equal performance opportunities for each salesperson. Three territories are developed because the decision model results presented in Exhibit 5.5 indicate that two salespeople cannot adequately cover these trading areas. The data needed to design the sales territories are presented in Exhibit 5.6.

FIGURE 5.17 Territory Design Procedure

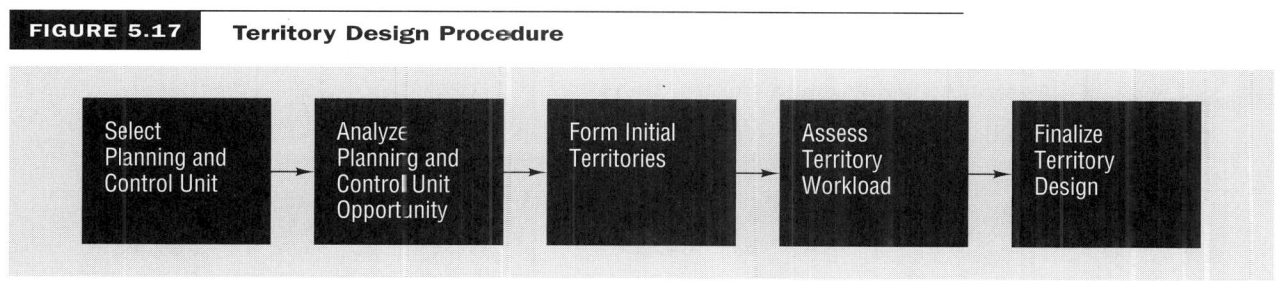

Designing territories requires a multiple-stage approach. Although most territory design approaches follow the stages presented in this figure, the methods used at each stage differ considerably, depending on the analytical tools used.

EXHIBIT 5.6 Territory Design Data

Trading Area	Market Potential	Number of Sales Calls
1	$ 250,000	25
2	$ 700,000	100
3	$ 350,000	35
4	$ 150,000	15
5	$ 200,000	20
6	$2,000,000	175
7	$ 750,000	65
8	$ 500,000	50
9	$1,000,000	100
10	$ 500,000	50
11	$1,750,000	175

Select Planning and Control Unit The first step in territory design is to select the **planning and control unit** that will be used in the analysis—that is, some entity that is smaller than a territory. The total market area served by a firm is divided into these planning and control units, then they are analyzed and grouped together to form territories.

Examples of potential planning and control units are illustrated in Figure 5.18. In general, management should use the smallest unit feasible. However, data are often not available for small planning and control units, and the computational task becomes more complex as more units are included in the analysis. The selection of the appropriate planning and control unit therefore represents a trade-off between what is desired and what is possible under the given data or computational conditions. In our example, trading areas have been selected as the planning and control unit.

Analyze Opportunity of Planning and Control Unit First, determine the amount of opportunity available from each planning and control unit. Specific methods for performing these calculations will be covered in Appendix 5. However, the most often used measure of opportunity is *market potential*. The market potentials for the 11 trading areas in our example are provided in Exhibit 5.6. Everything else being equal, the higher the market potential, the more opportunity is available.

Form Initial Territories Once planning and control units have been selected and opportunity evaluated, initial territories can be designed. The objective is to group the planning and control units into territories that are as equal as possible in opportunity. This step may take several iterations as there are probably a number of feasible territory designs. It is also unlikely that any design will achieve complete equality of opportunity. The best approach is to design several different territory arrangements and evaluate each alternative. Each alternative must be feasible in

FIGURE 5.18 Potential Planning and Control Units

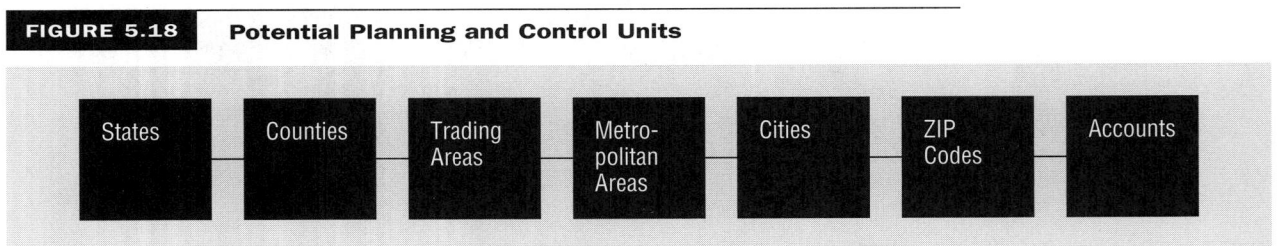

Planning and control units represent the unit of analysis for territory design. Accounts are the preferred planning and control unit. However, often it is not possible to use them as such, in which case a more aggregate type of planning and control unit is used.

that planning and control units grouped together are contiguous. This can be a cumbersome task when done manually but is much more efficient when computer modeling approaches are used.

Two alternative territory designs for our example are presented and evaluated in Exhibit 5.7. Although the first design is feasible, the territories are markedly unequal in opportunity. However, a few adjustments produce reasonably equal territories.

Assess Territory Workloads The preceding step produces territories of nearly equal opportunity. It may, however, take more work to realize this opportunity in some territories than in others. Therefore, the workload of each territory should be evaluated by (1) the number of sales calls required to cover the accounts in the territory, (2) the amount of travel time in the territory, (3) the total number of accounts, and (4) any other factors that measure the amount of work required by a salesperson assigned to the territory. In our example, workload for each trading area and territory is evaluated by the number of sales calls required. This information is presented in Exhibit 5.8.

EXHIBIT 5.7 Initial Territory Design

	Alternative 1		Alternative 2	
	Trading Area	Market Potential	Trading Area	Market Potential
Territory 1	1	$ 250,000	1	$ 250,000
	2	$ 700,000	2	$ 700,000
	3	$ 350,000	5	$ 200,000
	4	$ 150,000	8	$ 500,000
	5	$ 200,000	9	$1,000,000
		$1,650,000		$2,650,000
Territory 2	6	$2,000,000	6	$2,000,000
	7	$ 750,000	7	$ 750,000
	8	$ 500,000		$2,750,000
		$3,250,000		
Territory 3	9	$1,000,000	3	$ 350,000
	10	$ 500,000	4	$ 150,000
	11	$1,750,000	10	$ 500,000
		$3,250,000	11	$1,750,000
				$2,750,000

EXHIBIT 5.8 Workload Evaluations

	Trading Area	Sales Calls
Territory 1	1	25
	2	100
	5	20
	8	50
	9	100
		295
Territory 2	6	175
	7	65
		240
Territory 3	3	35
	4	15
	10	50
	11	175
		275

EXHIBIT 5.9 Final Territory Design

	Trading Area	Market Potential	Sales Calls
Territory 1	1	$ 250,000	25
	5	$ 200,000	20
	7	$ 750,000	65
	8	$ 500,000	50
	9	$1,000,000	100
		$2,700,000	260
Territory 2	2	$ 700,000	100
	6	$2,000,000	175
		$2,700,000	275
Territory 3	3	$ 350,000	35
	4	$ 150,000	15
	10	$ 500,000	50
	11	$1,750,000	175
		$2,750,000	275

Finalize Territory Design   The final step is to adjust the initial territories to achieve equal workloads for each salesperson. The objective is to achieve the best possible balance between equal opportunity and equal workload for each territory. Typically, both of these objectives cannot be completely achieved, so management must decide on the best trade-offs for its situation. Any inequalities in the final territories can be addressed when quotas are established as discussed in Module 11.

Achieving workload and opportunity balance for our example is illustrated in Exhibit 5.9. The equal opportunity territories resulted in somewhat unequal workloads (see Exhibit 5.8). The final territory design moved trading area 7 to territory 1 and trading area 2 to territory 2. This produces territories that are reasonably equal in both opportunity and workload.

Performing territory design analyses manually is difficult and time consuming. Fortunately, advances in computer hardware and software make it possible to consider multiple factors and rapidly evaluate many alternatives when designing territories.

ASSIGNING SALESPEOPLE TO TERRITORIES   Once territories have been designed, salespeople must be assigned to them. Salespeople are not equal in abilities and will perform differently with different types of accounts or prospects. Some sales managers consider their salespeople to be either farmers or hunters. *Farmers* are effective with existing accounts but do not perform well in establishing business with new accounts. *Hunters* excel in establishing new accounts but do not fully develop existing accounts. Based on these categories, farmers should be assigned to territories that contain many ongoing account relationships, and hunters should be assigned to territories in new or less-developed market areas.

"People" Considerations

Our discussion of salesforce deployment decisions has, to this point, focused entirely on analytical approaches. This analytical orientation emphasizes objective sales and cost considerations in evaluating different allocations of sales calls to accounts, different salesforce sizes, different territory designs, and different assignments of salespeople to territories. Although such analytical approaches are valuable and should be used by sales managers, final deployment decisions should also be based on "people" considerations. These "people" considerations can produce some problems as presented in "An Ethical Dilemma."

> **An Ethical Dilemma**
>
> *Business is booming at Lunsford Electronics. The economy is growing and new electronic products are being introduced on a regular basis. The company has decided to add one salesperson to each district. The southeastern district manager, Terry Bearden, will now have 10 salespeople to cover all accounts and prospects in the district. He has spent days examining alternative sales territory designs and thinks one option is best for the company and fair to all salespeople. However, he is considering another option that would give Cathy Swift a better territory and Fred Mangold a poorer one. Terry has always liked Cathy and thinks the better territory will help improve her sales. Fred has been a star performer for years and doesn't mind telling everyone how much money he makes. Terry thinks Fred will still perform well in the new territory and maybe this will eliminate some of his "bragging." Which territory design should Terry decide to use? Why?*

Statistics are numbers, whereas sales managers, salespeople, and customers are people. Analysis of statistical data provides useful but incomplete information for deployment decisions. Models are only representations of reality, and no matter how complex, no model can incorporate all the people factors that are important in any salesforce deployment decision. Accordingly, while using the appropriate analytical approaches, sales managers should temper the analytical results with people considerations before making final deployment decisions.

What are the important people considerations in salesforce deployment? The most important ones concern personal relationships between salespeople and customers and between salespeople and the sales organization. Consider the allocation of selling effort to accounts. The analytical approaches for making this decision produce a recommended number of sales calls to each account based on some assessment of expected sales and costs for different sales call levels. Although these approaches may incorporate a number of factors in developing the recommended sales call levels, there is no way that any analytical approach can use the detailed knowledge that a salesperson has about the unique needs of individual accounts. Therefore, an analytical approach may suggest that sales calls should be increased or decreased to a specific account, whereas the salesperson serving this account may know that the account will react adversely to any changes in sales call coverage. In this situation, a sales manager would be wise to ignore the analytical recommendation and not change sales call coverage to the account, because of the existing relationship between the salesperson and customer.

Salesforce size decisions also require consideration of people issues. A decision to reduce the size of a salesforce means that some salespeople will have to be removed from the salesforce. How this reduction is accomplished can affect the relationship between salespeople and the sales organization. Achieving this reduction through attrition or offering salespeople other positions is typically a better approach than merely firing salespeople.

Increasing salesforce size means that the new salespeople must be assigned to territories. Consequently, some accounts will find themselves being served by new salespeople. These changes in assignment can have a devastating effect on the existing customer-salesperson relationship. Not only should that relationship be considered but also the issue of fairness in taking accounts from one salesperson and assigning them to another. The situation can be a delicate one, requiring careful judgment as to how these people considerations should be balanced against analytical results.

In sum, sales managers should integrate the results from salesforce deployment analysis with people considerations before implementing changes in sales call allocation, salesforce size, or territory design. A good rule of thumb is to make salesforce deployment changes that are likely to have the least disruptive effect on existing personal relationships.

Summary

1. **Define the concepts of specialization, centralization, span of control versus management levels, and line versus staff positions.** *Specialization* refers to the division of labor such that salespeople or sales managers concentrate on performing certain activities to the exclusion of others. *Centralization* refers to where in the organization decision-making responsibility exists. Centralized organizations locate decision-making responsibility at higher organizational levels than decentralized organizations. Any sales organization structure can be evaluated in terms of the types and degrees of specialization and centralization afforded by the structure. Sales management organization design also requires decisions concerning the number of management levels, spans of control, and line versus staff positions. In general, more *management levels* result in smaller *spans of control* and more *staff positions* result in more sales management specialization.

2. **Describe the different ways that salesforces might be specialized.** A critical decision in designing the sales organization is determining whether the salesforce should be specialized and, if so, the appropriate type of specialization. The basic types of salesforce specialization are geographic, product, market (including major account organization), and functional. The appropriate type of specialization depends on the characteristics of the selling situation. Important selling situation characteristics include the similarity of customer needs, the complexity of the firm's product offering, the market environment, and the professionalism of the salesforce. Specific criteria of importance are affordability and payout, credibility and coverage, and flexibility. The use of different types and levels of specialization typically requires the establishment of separate salesforces.

3. **Evaluate the advantages and disadvantages of different sales organization structures.** Because each type of sales organization structure has certain advantages and disadvantages, many firms use hybrid structures that combine the features of several types. Usually, the strengths of one structure are weaknesses in other structures.

4. **Name the important considerations in organizing major account management programs.** Identifying major accounts (which should be both large and complex) and organizing for coverage of them are the important considerations in major account management.

5. **Explain how to determine the appropriate sales organization structure for a given selling situation.** There is no one best way to structure a sales organization. The appropriate way to organize a salesforce and sales management depends on certain characteristics of a particular selling situation. Also, because the sales organization structure decision is dynamic, it must be adapted to changes in a firm's selling situation that occur over time.

6. **Discuss the different areas involved in salesforce deployment.** Salesforce deployment decisions entail allocating selling effort, determining salesforce size, and designing territories. These decisions are highly interrelated and should be addressed in an integrated sequential manner. Improvements in salesforce deployment can produce substantial increases in sales and profits.

7. **Explain three different analytical approaches for determining allocation of selling effort.** Single factor, portfolio, and decision models can be used as analytical tools to determine appropriate selling effort allocations. The approaches differ in terms of analytical rigor and ease of development and use. Sales organizations should use the approach that best fits their particular selling situation.

8. **Describe three different methods for calculating salesforce size.** The breakdown method for calculating salesforce size is the easiest method to use but the weakest conceptually. It uses the expected level of sales to determine the number of salespeople. The workload approach is sounder conceptually, because it bases the salesforce size decision on the amount of selling effort needed to cover the market appropriately. The incremental method is the best approach, although it is often difficult to develop. It examines the marginal sales and costs associated with different salesforce sizes.

9. **Explain the importance of sales territories from the perspective of the sales organization and from the perspective of the salespeople and list the steps in the territory design process.** Territories are assignments of accounts to salespeople. Each becomes

the work unit for a salesperson, who is largely responsible for the performance of the assigned territory. Poorly designed territories can have adverse effects on the motivation of salespeople. From the perspective of the firm, territory design decisions should ensure that the firm's market area is adequately covered in a productive manner. The first step in the territory design process is to identify planning and control units. Next, the opportunity available from each planning and control unit is determined, initial territories are formed, and the workloads of each potential territory are assessed. The final territory design represents management's judgment concerning the best balance between opportunity and workload.

10. **Disucss the important "people" considerations in salesforce deployment.** Although analytical approaches provide useful input for salesforce deployment decisions, they do not address people considerations adequately. Sales managers should always consider existing relationships between salespeople and customers and between salespeople and the sales organization before making salesforce deployment changes. Many of these people considerations have ethical consequences.

Understanding Sales Management Terms

- Specialization
- Centralization
- Span of control
- Management levels
- Line sales management
- Staff sales management
- Geographic specialization
- Product specialization
- Market specialization
- Functional specialization
- Major account organization
- National account management (NAM)
- Global account management (GAM)
- Hybrid Sales organization
- Sales productivity
- Breakdown approach
- Salesforce deployment
- Single-factor models
- Portfolio models
- Decision models
- Workload approach
- Incremental approach
- Territory
- Planning and control unit

Developing Sales Management Knowledge

1. Discuss the situational factors that suggest the need for specialization and centralization. Provide a specific example of each factor discussed.
2. Why do you think there is a trend toward more salesforce specialization?
3. What are the advantages and disadvantages of structuring a sales organization for major account management?
4. What are some problems that a firm might face when undertaking a major restructuring of its sales organization?
5. What are the important relationships between span of control, management levels, line positions, staff positions, specialization and centralization?
6. How are salesforce deployment decisions related to decisions on sales organization structure?
7. How can the incremental method be used to determine the number of salespeople to assign to a sales district?
8. How are salesforce size decisions different for firms with one generalized salesforce versus firms with several specialized salesforces?
9. How can computer modeling assist sales managers in designing territories?
10. Should firms always try to design equal territories? Why or why not?

Building Sales Management Skills

1. Assume that you are the national sales manager for Replica Inc., a manufacturer and marketer of photocopy equipment and supplies. The firm's products are sold both nationally and internationally by a salesforce of 5,000. Replica sells to accounts of various

sizes across several industries. Prepare a proposal that illustrates your recommended sales organization structure. Be sure to justify your recommended structure.

2. As an organization, your university has a specified structure. Identify this structure (draw it or obtain a copy of it). How specialized is this structure? What is its degree of centralization? What does the span of control look like and how appropriate is it? How many levels of management exist? Is this enough or too much? What are the relationships between line and staff positions? Are they appropriate? Assuming you would like the university to run as efficiently and effectively as possible, what changes would you recommend making to this structure and why? If no changes are recommended, why not?

3. Using the following information, calculate the total salesforce size necessary by using each of the following approaches: breakdown, workload, and incremental. (Your answers may vary because each piece of information does not apply to the same company.) Be sure to show your work. Also, explain the advantages and disadvantages of each approach. Which approach would you recommend using to determine salesforce size? Why?

- Sales of $80 million are forecast for next year.
- Fifteen thousand calls are needed in the market area to be covered.
- Salespeople generate an average of $2 million in annual sales.
- A salesperson can make an average of 500 annual sales calls.
- Marginal salesperson cost is $65,000. With 88 salespeople, the marginal salesperson profit contribution is $75,000. This profit contribution decreases by $5,000 with each additional salesperson added to the base of 88 salespeople. Marginal salesperson cost remains constant
- Turnover is 10 percent annually.

Making Sales Management Decisions

CASE 5.1   Protek Packaging, Inc.

Background

Protek Packaging, Inc. (PPI) is a national manufacturer of a wide variety of polyethylene and polystyrene packaging products, including food and ice bags; styrofoam egg cartons, meat trays, and food service products; laundry and dry cleaning packaging; trash bags; construction film and plastic shipping pallets. PPI is a strong competitor in all of its product lines. Not an innovative company, PPI leverages its large manufacturing capacity to drive its costs down, which allows the company to sell its products at highly attractive price levels.

PPI operates five regional offices in Atlanta, New York, Chicago, Dallas, and Los Angeles. These offices are located at manufacturing plants that serve each region. PPI is organized by product line, with each product line run by a regional product manager and a regional sales manager. Eight to ten sales representatives report to each of the five regional sales managers. The product managers and sales managers in each region report to a regional marketing manager. The key products and customers for each product line are shown in Exhibit 1.

Current Situation

John Lovett, Western Region marketing manager, has called his four sales managers and four product managers to Los Angeles to discuss alternative approaches to organizing the PPI salesforce. Thirty days earlier, Lovett and his managers had hosted a key customer roundtable at the annual meeting of the Plastics Packaging Manufacturers' Association. Lovett was troubled by several themes that emerged from the roundtable. Some of the most influential paper and plastic distributors are disturbed by the fact that PPI sells to grocery chains, garment manufacturers, egg packers/processors, and uniform rental companies on a direct basis. This is puzzling to Lovett, since PPI has always sold through distributors when feasible. Further, distributors are informed before stocking PPI products that if end-users meet certain sales volume requirements and request that they be sold on a direct basis, PPI will sell direct rather than risk losing the business.

Lovett is also concerned that many of the grocery chain buyers and paper and plastic distributors complained about the amount of time it takes for them to see several different PPI salespeople. These customers wanted to deal with a single PPI representative, not one from each product line. An additional concern was that PPI did not allow aggregation of products across product lines to make it easier for these buyers to achieve the maximum quantity discounts.

To prepare for the meeting, John Lovett asked each product manager/sales manager team to come ready to discuss these issues:

1. Is it time for PPI to reconsider its salesforce organization by product line?

EXHIBIT 1   PPI Product Lines and Key Customer Types

Product Line	Key Products	Key Customer Types
Food Packaging	produce bags	grocery chains food co-ops paper and plastic distributors
	foam meat trays	grocery chains meat and poultry processors food co-ops paper and plastic distributors
Institutional	trash bags	paper and plastic distributors restaurant wholesalers janitorial wholesalers
	food service (plastic plates, bowls)	restaurant wholesalers grocery store delis institutional food wholesalers paper and plastic distributors
Agricultural	egg cartons	grocery chains egg packers/processors
Garment	poly bags	laundries and dry cleaners uniform rental companies garment manufacturers paper and plastic distributors

2. What are the advantages and disadvantages of organizing the PPI salesforce by product line?
3. What are the advantages and disadvantages of developing a new sales organization for the Western Region that would organize according to these customer types: (a) grocery chains and food co-ops; (b) distributors, including paper and plastic distributors, restaurant wholesalers, institutional food wholesalers, and janitorial wholesalers; and (c) end-users, including meat and poultry processors, grocery store delis, egg packers/processors, laundries and dry cleaners, uniform rental companies, and garment manufacturers?

Assume you are the sales manager for the food packaging product line. Address the preceding questions as if you will attend the upcoming meeting. In addition, outline your thoughts on other alternatives for organizing the salesforce.

CASE 5.2 *Opti-Tax Consulting*

Background

Opti-Tax Consulting (OTC) is a 20-year-old company, which specializes in providing small businesses with tax and financial management expertise. OTC focuses on businesses that handle significant amounts of cash in their daily operations, such as service stations, bars, coffee shops, and small restaurants. OTC has three sales representatives serving the Lexington, Kentucky, metropolitan market.

Dave Mason, OTC's founder and current president, was the company's first salesperson. When the company grew to the point that Mason had a hard time servicing all of his accounts, he added Steve Tremaine as a sales representative. Mason gave Tremaine ten of his existing accounts and instructed him to go after potential customers not yet under contract with OTC. Five years later, Donna Armstrong was hired as a sales representative and added in much the same fashion. Mason and Tremaine turned over 10 accounts each to Armstrong, and she was instructed to add new customers not already doing business with OTC. Both Donna Armstrong and Steve Tremaine report directly to Dave Mason. Of OTC's total sales volume, Dave Mason accounts for approximately half. The remainder is split almost equally between Donna Armstrong and Steve Tremaine. Armstrong and Tremaine are paid a percentage of OTC's billings to their clients.

Current Situation

Mason is planning to enter semi-retirement in another year, and he has brought his son Franklin into the business. Franklin will learn the business over the next several months, then step into a sales role. Dave Mason will continue to function as sales manager and president of the company, but will give up the sales responsibilities for all of his accounts.

Dave Mason is compiling information that will help him decide how to design OTC's sales territories after he gives up his sales responsibilities. He is not comfortable turning over all of his accounts to his son Franklin. Although talented and hard working, Franklin is inexperienced in the financial consulting industry. A recent graduate of the University of Kentucky with a double major in finance and marketing, Franklin's career goal is to become president of OTC, then expand company operations into other markets.

Mason has also been contemplating the sales performance of Donna Armstrong and Steve Tremaine. Both had been solid, dependable performers over the years, but Steve had recently slowed down a bit. While his sales volume compared favorably to Donna's, Steve was selling in a higher potential sales territory. Further, he had a five-year head start on Donna in developing new accounts, yet Donna had brought in almost as much new business as had Steve during the past year. Mason had talked with Tremaine about the lack of sales growth in his territory, but had not learned much. Tremaine made no excuses, and acknowledged that his sales levels had been relatively stable in recent years. He promised to try harder to bring in new business. Mason suspected that Tremaine was comfortable with his earnings and simply did not want to work a lot harder, even if he could make more money.

After several weeks of analysis, Dave Mason finally had a rough draft of a new territory design policy that would go into effect in 90 days. The key points of the new policy are:

1. Half of Dave Mason's accounts will be split between Steve Tremaine and Donna Armstrong. Dave Mason's remaining accounts will be assigned to Franklin Mason.
2. After one year, sales territories will be redesigned so that the three territories will be comparable in terms of workload and sales potential.
3. For the current year, OTC salespeople will continue to earn a commission based on OTC billings to their clients.
4. After the sales territories are redesigned in a year, the commission rate for existing clients will be reduced, and a higher commission rate will be implemented for new accounts added within the past year.

Dave Mason distributed the draft plan to Donna, Steve, and Franklin. Both Donna and Steve questioned the idea of assigning half of Dave's accounts to Franklin. Steve came right to the point, saying, "Look, Dave, he's your son and he will do just fine with some seasoning. But I think he ought to start with a smaller group of accounts. He'll learn the business a lot faster if he has to build it by adding his own accounts."

Donna and Steve were also concerned that they would have some of Dave's former accounts for a year, and then lose them to Franklin. Franklin remained neutral on these issues, and voiced neither support nor opposition to the draft plan.

Questions

1. What are the implications for Donna Armstrong and Steve Tremaine if the draft plan is implemented?
2. What are the implications for OTC's customers if the draft plan is implemented?
3. What are the pros and cons of Mason's draft plan?
4. What changes and additions would you make to the draft plan?

APPENDIX 5

Developing Forecasts

A meterologist used all the latest technology to predict a bright and sunny day in the mid-80s. It rained most of the day and never got warmer than 70 degrees. The weather forecast missed the mark on this particular occasion, but the meterologist will continue to make weather forecasts and to work on improving weather forecasting procedures.

Sales managers face a situation similar to that of the meterologist. The business environment is complex and dynamic, there are a number of forecasting methods available, and often forecasts are incorrect. Nevertheless, sales managers must continue to forecast and to work on improving their forecasting procedures.

Why is forecasting so important to sales managers? In one sense, all sales management decisions are based on some type of forecast. The sales manager decides on a certain action because he or she thinks that it will produce a certain result. This expected result is a **forecast,** even though the sales manager may not have quantified it or may not have used a mathematical forecasting procedure. More specifically, forecasts provide the basis for the following sales management decisions:

1. determining salesforce size
2. designing territories
3. establishing sales quotas and selling budgets
4. determining sales compensation levels
5. evaluating salesperson performance
6. evaluating prospective accounts

Forecasting by Sales Managers

Although top management levels are most concerned with total firm forecasts, sales managers are typically interested in developing and using forecasts for specific areas, such as accounts, territories, districts, regions, and/or zones. For example, a district sales manager would be concerned with the district forecast as well as forecasts for individual territories and accounts within the district. There are, however, different types of forecasts that sales managers might use in different ways, and different approaches and methods might be used to develop these forecasts.

Types of Forecasts

The term *forecast* is ordinarily used to refer to a prediction for a future period. Although this usage is technically correct, it is too general for managerial value. As illustrated in Figure 5A.1, at least three factors must be defined when referring to a forecast: the product level, the geographic area, and the time period. The figure presents 90 different forecasts that might be made, depending on these factors. Thus, when using the term *forecast*, sales managers should be specific in defining exactly what is being forecast, what geographic area is being targeted, and what period is being forecast.

A useful way for viewing what is being forecast is presented in Exhibit 5A.1. This exhibit suggests that it is important to differentiate between industry and firm levels and to determine whether the prediction is for the best possible results or for the expected results given a specific strategy. Four different types of forecast emerge from this classification scheme:

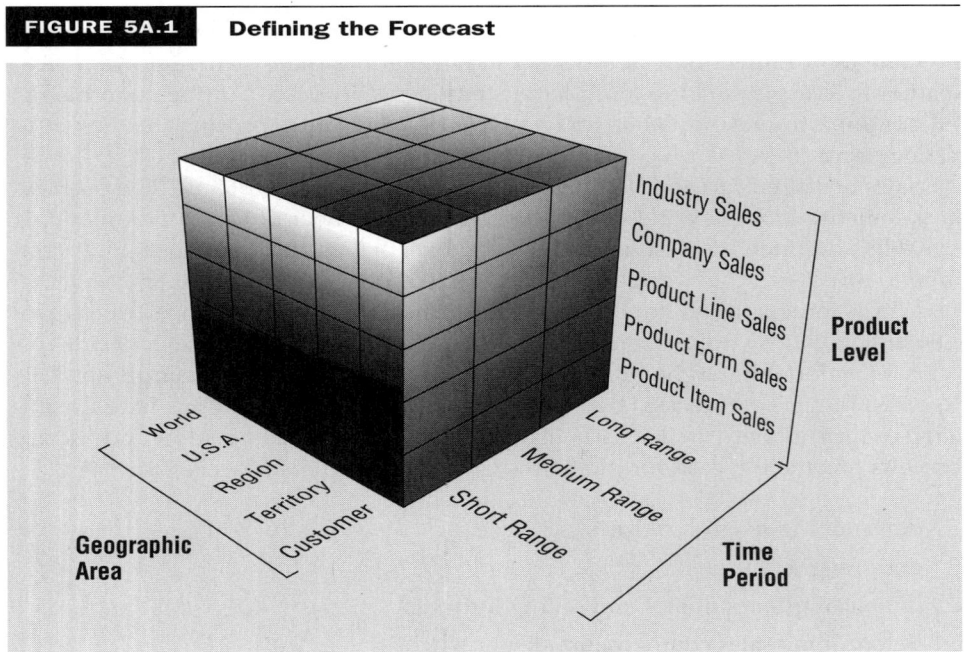

FIGURE 5A.1   Defining the Forecast

Many different types of forecasts are possible. Every forecast should be defined in terms of geographic area, product level, and period.

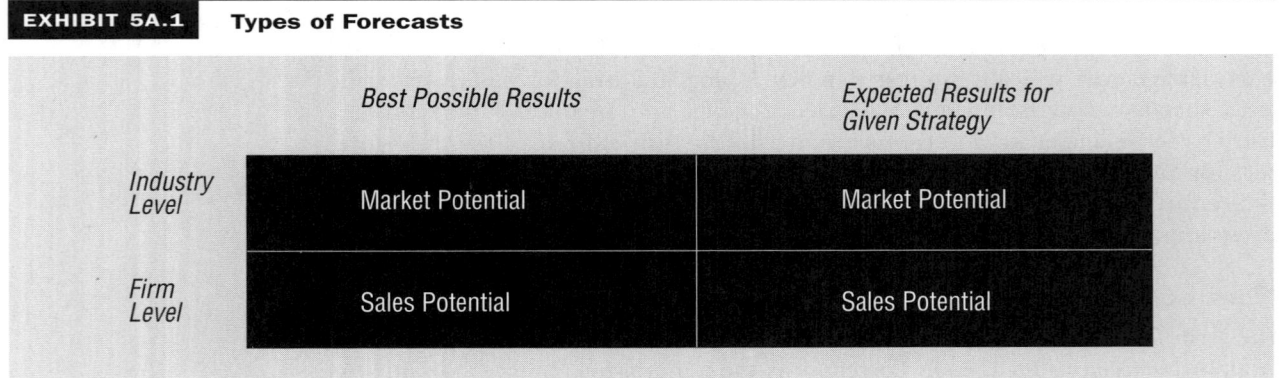

EXHIBIT 5A.1   Types of Forecasts

	Best Possible Results	Expected Results for Given Strategy
Industry Level	Market Potential	Market Potential
Firm Level	Sales Potential	Sales Potential

Four different types of forecasts are typically important to sales managers, depending on whether a forecast is needed for the industry or the firm and whether the best possible or expected results are to be forecast.

1. **market potential**—the best possible level of industry sales in a given geographic area for a specific period
2. **market forecast**—the expected level of industry sales given a specific industry strategy in a given geographic area for a specific period
3. **sales potential**—the best possible level of firm sales in a given geographic area for a specific period
4. **sales forecast**—the expected level of firm sales given a specific strategy in a given geographic area for a specific period

Notice that the geographic area and period are defined for each of these terms and that a true *sales forecast* must include the consideration of a specific strategy. If a firm changes this strategy, the sales forecast should change also.

As an example, assume that you are the district sales manager for a firm that markets microcomputers to organizational buyers. Your district includes Missouri, Kansas, Iowa, and Nebraska. You are preparing forecasts for 2001. You might first try to assess market potential. This market potential forecast would be an estimate of the highest level of microcomputer sales by all brands in your district for 2001. Then, you might try to develop a market forecast, which would be the expected level of industry microcomputer sales in your district for 2001. This forecast would be based on an assumption of the strategies that would be used by all microcomputer firms operating in your district. If you think that new firms are going to enter the industry or that existing firms are going to leave it or change their strategies, your industry forecast will change. Another type of forecast might be a determination of the best possible level of 2001 sales for your firm's microcomputers in the district. This would be a sales potential forecast. Finally, you would probably want to predict a specific level of district sales of your firm's microcomputers given your firm's expected strategy. This would result in a sales forecast that would have to be revised whenever strategic changes were made.

Uses of Forecasts

Because different types of forecasts convey different information, sales managers use specific types for specific sales management decisions. Forecasts of market potential and sales potential are most often used to identify opportunities and to guide the allocation of selling efforts. Market potential provides an assessment of overall demand opportunity available to all firms in an industry. Sales potential adjusts market potential to reflect industry competition and thus represents a better assessment of demand opportunity for an individual firm. Both of these forecasts of potential can be used by sales managers to determine where selling effort is needed and how selling effort should be distributed. For example, as discussed earlier, designing territories requires an assessment of market potential for all planning and control units. Specific territories are then designed by grouping planning and control units together and evaluating the equality of market potential across the territories.

Market forecasts and sales forecasts are used to predict the expected results from various sales management decisions. For example, once territories are designed, sales managers typically want to forecast expected industry and company sales for each specific sales territory. These forecasts are then used to set sales quotas and selling budgets for specific planning periods.

Top-Down and Bottom-Up Forecasting Approaches

Forecasting methods can be classified in a variety of ways.[1] Specific examples of two basic approaches are presented in Figure 5A.2. **Top-down approaches** typically consist of different methods for developing company forecasts at the business unit

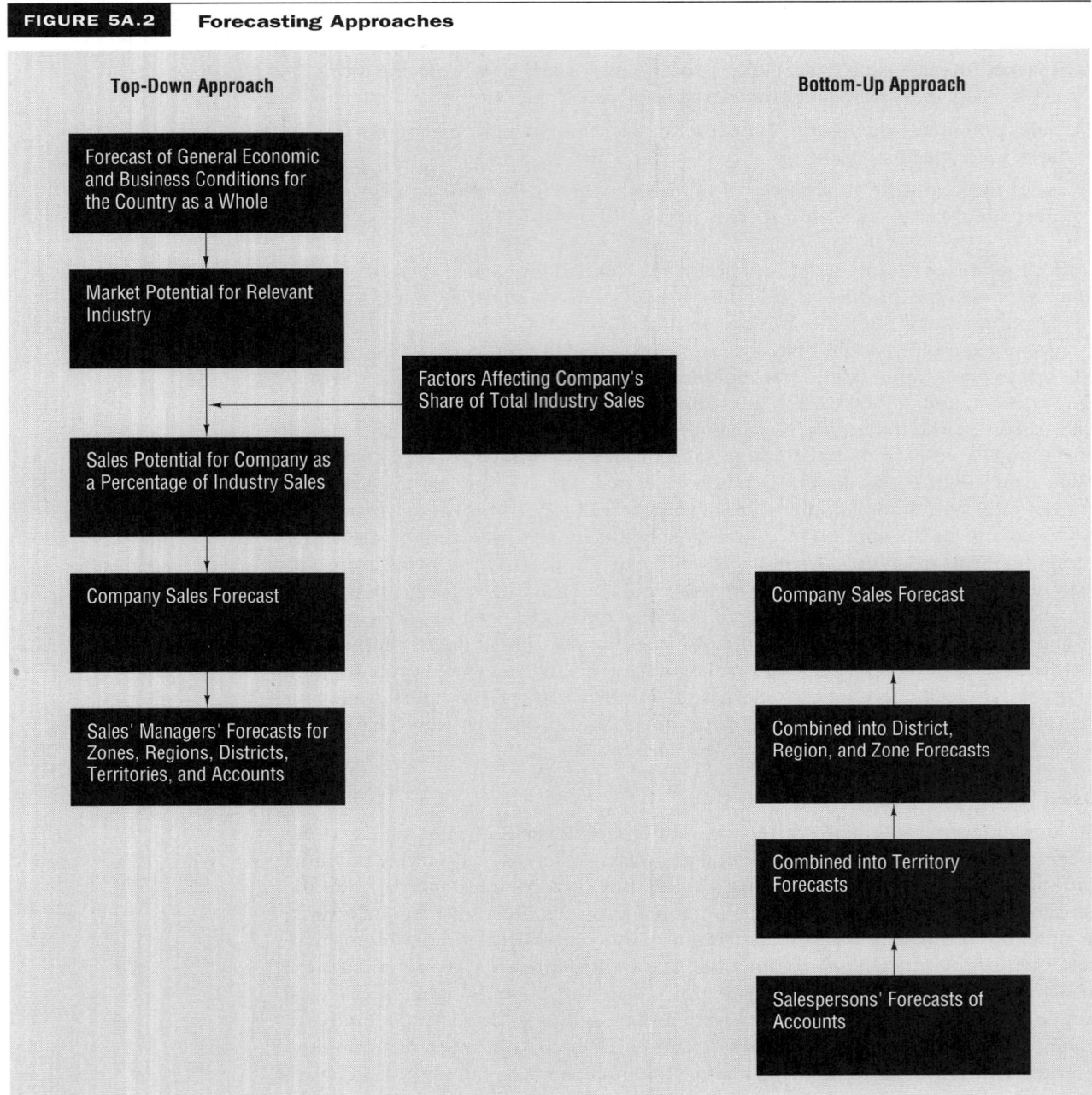

FIGURE 5A.2   Forecasting Approaches

In top-down approaches, company personnel provide aggregate company forecasts that sales managers must break down into zone, region, district, territory, and account forecasts. In bottom-up approaches, account forecasts are combined into territory, district, region, zone, and company forecasts.

level. Sales managers then break down these company forecasts into zone, region, district, territory, and account forecasts. **Bottom-up approaches,** by contrast, consist of different methods for developing sales forecasts for individual accounts. Sales managers then combine the account forecasts into territory, district, region, zone, and company forecasts. The top-down and bottom-up approaches represent entirely different perspectives for developing forecasts, although some forecasting methods can be used in either approach. However, the focus is on the most popular forecasting methods for each approach.

TOP-DOWN APPROACH Implementing the top-down approach requires the development of company forecasts and their breakdown into zone, region, district, territory, and account levels. Different methods are used to develop company forecasts and break them down to the desired levels.

Company Forecasting Methods Although a variety of methods is available for developing company forecasts, this discussion is limited to three popular time series methods: moving averages, exponential smoothing, and decomposition methods.

Moving averages is a relatively simple method that develops a company forecast by calculating the average company sales for previous years. Thus, the company sales forecast for next year is the average of actual company sales for the past 3 years, past 6 years, or some other number of years. An example of calculating a moving averages company sales forecast for 2- and 4-year time frames is presented in Exhibit 5A.2. As illustrated in this example, the moving averages method is straightforward and requires simple calculations. Management must, however, determine the appropriate number of years to include in the calculations. In addition, this method weights actual company sales for previous years equally in generating the forecast for the next year. This equal weighting may not be appropriate if company sales vary substantially from year to year or if there are major differences in the business environment between the most recent and past years. Nevertheless, one survey of managers found this to be the most popular technique for short-range and medium-range forecasts in U.S. corporations.[2]

Exponential smoothing is a type of moving averages method, except that company sales in the most recent year are weighted differently from company sales in past years.[3] An example of the exponential smoothing method is provided in Exhibit 5A.3. A critical aspect of this method involves determining the appropriate weight (α) for this year's company sales. This is typically accomplished by examining different weights for historical sales data to determine which weight would have generated the most accurate sales forecasts in the past. Based on the analysis in Exhibit 5A.3, management should probably use a weight of 0.8 for this year's company sales.

Decomposition methods involve different procedures that break down previous company sales data into four major components: trend, cycle, seasonal, and erratic events. These components are then reincorporated to produce the sales forecast. An example of a decomposition method is presented in Exhibit 5A.4. Notice that

EXHIBIT 5A.2 Moving Averages Example

Year	Actual Sales	Moving Averages Forecast 2-Year	4-Year
1992	$ 8,400,000		
1993	8,820,000		
1994	8,644,000	$8,610,000	
1995	8,212,000	8,732,000	
1996	8,622,000	8,428,000	$8,520,000
1997	9,484,000	8,418,000	8,574,000
1998	9,674,000	9,054,000	8,740,000
1999	10,060,000	9,579,000	8,998,000
2000		9,868,000	9,460,000

where

$$\text{Sales forecast for next year} = \frac{\text{Actual sales for past 2 or 4 years}}{\text{Number of years (2 or 4 years)}}$$

EXHIBIT 5A.3   Exponential Smoothing Example

		Sales Forecast for Next Year		
Year	Actual Sales	$\alpha = 0.2$	$\alpha = 0.5$	$\alpha = 0.8$
1992	$ 8,400,000			
1993	8,820,000	$8,400,000	$8,400,000	$8,400,000
1994	8,644,000	8,484,000	8,610,000	8,736,000
1995	8,212,000	8,516,000	8,626,000	8,664,000
1996	8,622,000	8,456,000	8,420,000	8,302,000
1997	9,484,000	8,488,000	8,520,000	8,558,000
1998	9,674,000	8,686,000	9,002,000	9,298,000
1999	10,060,000	8,882,000	9,338,000	9,600,000
2000		9,118,000	9,698,000	9,968,000

where

Sales forecast for next year = (α) (actual sales this year) + $(1 - \alpha)$ (this year's sales forecast)

EXHIBIT 5A.4   Decomposition Method Example

Assume that various analyses have decomposed previous sales data into the following components:

A 5 percent growth in sales is predicted due to basic developments in population, capital formation, and technology (trend component). A 10 percent decrease in sales is expected due to a business recession (cycle component). Increased tensions in the Middle East are expected to reduce sales by an additional 5 percent (erratic events component). Sales results are reasonably consistent throughout the year except for the fourth quarter, where sales are expected to be 25 percent higher than the other quarters (seasonal component).

A marketer of consumer products might recombine the different components in the following manner to forecast sales for 2001:

Sales in 2000 were $10,060,000. The trend component suggests that 2001 sales will be $10,563,000 ($10,060,000 × 1.05). However, incorporating the expected business recession represented in the cycle component changes the sales forecast to $9,506,700 ($10,563,000 × 0.90). The annual sales forecast is reduced to $9,031,365 when the erratic events component is introduced ($9,056,700 × 0.95). Quarterly sales forecasts would initially be calculated as $2,257,841 ($9,031,365 ÷ 4). However, incorporating the seasonal component suggests fourth-quarter sales of $2,822,302 ($2,257,841 × 1.25) and sales for the other three quarters of $2,069,688 ($9,031,365 − $2,822,302 ÷ 3).

the trend, cycle, and erratic events components are incorporated into the annual forecast but that the seasonal component is used only when forecasting sales for periods of less than a year, such as months or quarters. Decomposition methods are sound conceptually but often require complex statistical approaches for breaking down the company sales data into the trend components. Once this decomposition has been completed, it is relatively easy to reincorporate the components into the development of a company forecast.

Breakdown methods   Once sales managers receive a company forecast, they can use different market factor methods to break it down to the desired levels. **Market factor methods** typically involve identifying one or more factors that are related to sales at the zone, region, district, territory, or account levels and using these factors to break down the overall company forecast into forecasts at these levels.

A typical approach is to use the **Buying Power Index (BPI)** supplied by *Sales and Marketing Management*.[4] The BPI is a market factor calculated for different areas in the following manner:

$$BPI = (5I + 2P + 3R) \div 10$$

where

I = Percentage of U.S. disposable personal income in the area
P = Percentage of U.S. population in the area
R = Percentage of U.S. retail sales in the area

Performing these calculations for any area produces a BPI for the area. This BPI can be translated as the percentage of U.S. buying power residing in the area: The higher the index, the more buying power in the area. Fortunately, *Sales and Marketing Management* provides these calculations for areas in the United States on an annual basis.

An example of the BPI data provided by *Sales and Marketing Management* is presented in Exhibit 5A.5. BPIs and other data are available for all counties in a state and for the major cities and metropolitan areas. The information in the exhibit suggests that the BPI for the Kansas City metropolitan area is 0.6914; for Jackson County, 0.2557; and for Kansas City, Missouri, 0.1764. This means that 0.6914 percent, 0.2557 percent, and 0.1764 percent of total U.S. buying power resides in the Kansas City metro area, Jackson County, and Kansas City, Missouri, respectively.

Sales managers can use the BPI data to divide the overall company forecast into more disaggregate forecasts. For example, assume that you are the Missouri district sales manager for a marketer of cosmetics. Management has used various methods to forecast total company sales in the United States of $500 million for 2001. The calculations necessary to break down this company forecast into sales forecasts for areas within your district are illustrated in Exhibit 5A.6. Using the appropriate BPIs, you are able to forecast 2001 sales of $3,457,000, $1,278,500, and $882,000 for the Kansas City metro area, Jackson County, and Kansas City, Missouri, respectively.

The BPI is an extremely useful tool for forecasting, because it is readily available and updated on an annual basis. It is most appropriate for often-purchased consumer goods because of the factors used in calculating the index for each area. Marketers of durable consumer goods or industrial products may not find the BPI sufficiently accurate for their needs. In these situations, other market factors must be identified and used. For example, Sherwood Medical uses *total available hospitals* requiring a specific product (based on medical procedures performed at the hospital) as a market factor for forecasting purposes.[5]

Another approach is for a firm to develop a buying power index for its specific situation. For example, a general aviation aircraft marketer developed a buying power index for its products in each county in the United States. The basic formula was

$$Index = (5I + 3AR + 2P) \div 10$$

where

I = Percentage of U.S. disposable income in county
AR = Percentage of U.S. aircraft registrations in county
P = Percentage of U.S. registered pilots in county

EXHIBIT 5A.5 Buying Power Index (BPI) Data

METRO AREA County/City	Total EBI ($000)	Median Household EBI	Effective Buying Income (EBI) — Percentage of Households by EBI Group				Buying Power Index
			(A) $10,000–$19,999	(B) $20,000–$34,999	(C) $35,000–$49,999	(D) $50,000 and More	
COLUMBIA	1,992,259	33,873	16.1	22.4	18.1	30.4	.0516
Boone	1,992,259	33,873	16.1	22.4	18.1	30.4	.0516
Columbia	1,241,418	29,645	18.7	21.0	15.2	28.3	.0378
Suburban Total	750,841	39,208	11.7	25.0	23.2	33.9	.0138
JOPLIN	1,928,856	27,823	20.2	27.1	18.7	19.2	.0520
Jasper	1,270,128	27,079	20.9	26.9	18.5	18.2	.0373
Joplin	601,136	25,413	22.5	26.6	16.7	17.5	.0225
Newton	658,728	29,348	18.7	27.6	18.8	21.4	.0147
Suburban Total	1,327,720	28,931	19.1	27.4	19.5	20.1	.0295
KANSAS CITY	30,987,132	40,963	12.4	20.7	19.8	38.4	.6914
Cass	1,163,582	39,979	13.2	22.2	22.1	35.3	.0243
Clay	2,978,457	41,735	11.8	22.1	22.4	37.9	.0748
Clinton	260,091	33,954	18.0	23.2	19.2	29.3	.0055
Jackson	11,052,639	36,936	14.4	21.6	19.6	33.1	.2557
Blue Springs	860,954	51,044	7.4	14.4	21.9	51.6	.0206
Independence	1,919,067	37,782	15.8	22.3	21.2	32.9	.0462
Kansas City	7,482,105	35,483	14.8	21.7	19.1	31.6	.1764
Lee's Summit	1,190,035	49,815	9.1	16.3	18.9	49.8	.0237
Lafayette	474,375	32,757	17.1	26.2	20.3	25.9	.0103
Platte	1,265,415	45,520	9.9	19.8	21.4	43.9	.0256
Ray	305,948	34,906	15.7	23.5	22.4	27.5	.0061
Johnson, Kans.	9,979,906	54,758	6.8	15.7	18.3	55.5	.2118
Olathe	1,333,636	50,929	7.3	16.9	20.4	51.3	.0321
Overland Park	3,314,864	56,241	6.8	15.5	17.3	57.2	.0765
Leavenworth, Kans.	1,162,130	43,140	10.9	19.7	21.7	40.2	.0235
Leavenworth	726,671	39,967	12.1	21.5	21.6	35.4	.0154
Miami, Kans.	392,606	37,473	15.1	22.3	20.9	32.7	.0081
Wyandotte, Kans.	1,951,983	29,202	18.3	25.9	19.8	20.6	.0457
Kansas City	1,791,288	28,711	18.7	25.5	19.7	19.9	.0419
Suburban Total	19,653,432	44,951	10.8	19.6	20.1	43.6	.4256
ST. JOSEPH	1,397,897	30,847	18.2	23.7	19.4	24.2	.0349
Andrew	209,843	32,952	16.9	22.7	21.6	25.3	.0045
Buchanan	1,188,054	30,476	18.4	23.8	19.0	24.1	.0304
St. Joseph	1,014,905	29,567	19.0	23.4	18.7	23.0	.0274
Suburban Total	382,992	34,530	15.9	24.3	21.3	27.9	.0075

These calculations produced an index for each county that could be translated and used like the BPI. The firm could take U.S. forecasts provided by the industry trade association and convert them to market and sales forecasts for each county by using their calculated indices and market shares.

The use of market factor methods is widespread in the sales management area. Indices such as the BPI or those developed by specific firms and other market factor methods can be extremely valuable forecasting tools for sales managers. These indices and market factors should be continually evaluated and improved. They can be assessed by comparing actual sales in an area to the market factor value for the area. For example, the general aviation aircraft marketer found high correlations

EXHIBIT 5A.6   Market Factor Calculations

	Kansas City Metro Area	Jackson County	Kansas City, Missouri
2001 company sales forecast	$500,000,000	$500,000,000	$500,000,000
BPI	0.6914%	0.2557%	0.1764%
2001 area sales forecast	$3,457,000	$1,278,500	$882,000

between actual aircraft sales in a county and the county indices. This finding provided support for the use of the calculated index as an indirect forecasting tool.

BOTTOM-UP APPROACH Implementing the bottom-up approach requires various methods to forecast sales to individual accounts and the combination of these account forecasts into territory, district, region, zone, and company forecasts. This section focuses on the survey of buyer intentions, jury of executive opinion, Delphi, and salesforce composite methods as used in a bottom-up approach.

The **survey of buyer intentions method** is any procedure that asks individual accounts about their purchasing plans for a future period and translates these responses into account forecasts. The intended purchases by accounts might be obtained through mail surveys, telephone surveys, personal interviews, or other approaches. For example, at Dow Chemical's Basic Chemical Division, salespeople provide forecast data based on customers' business plans.[6] Similarly, Hewlett-Packard Company's major customers supply its marketing centers with input concerning future needs.[7] At times, forecasts based on customer intentions may be distorted due to buyers' unwillingness to put much effort into predicting future needs. Moreover, buyers are often unwilling to reveal plans for selling a vendor's product out of fear competitors may retaliate if they find out.[8]

The **jury of executive opinion method** involves any approach in which executives of the firm use their expert knowledge to forecast sales to individual accounts. Separate forecasts might be obtained from managers in different functional areas. These forecasts are then averaged or discussed by the managers until a consensus forecast for each account is reached. Team-based approaches such as this are believed to result in more accurate long-range industry-level forecasts than individually based approaches.[9]

The **Delphi method** is a structured type of jury of executive opinion method. The basic procedure involves selection of a panel of managers from within the firm. Each member of the panel submits anonymous forecasts for each account. These forecasts are summarized into a report that is sent to each panel member. The report presents descriptive statistics concerning the submitted forecasts with reasons for the lowest and highest forecasts. Panel members review this information and then again submit anonymous individual forecasts. The same procedure is repeated until the forecasts for individual accounts converge into a consensus. Because this procedure involves written rather than verbal communication, such negatives as domination, undue conservatism, and argument are eliminated, while team members benefit from one another's input.[10]

The **salesforce composite method** involves various procedures by which salespeople provide forecasts for their assigned accounts, typically on specially designed forms (see Figure 5A.3) or electronically via computer. At Ricoh Corporation, an office products manufacturer, salespeople are asked to provide a 3-month rolling forecast for each product and model.[11] Similarly, salespeople at Pfizer Animal

FIGURE 5A.3 Quarterly Forecasting Form for Salespeople

Account	Projected Sales by Product Group for Quarter Beginning 7/5/2000						Totals
	364-60	364-80	28B	460	28		
Ace	1,250	960	1,400	2,100	160		5,870
Sentry	950	1,250	1,930	470	968		5,568
Cutter	—	2,110	—	960	1,750		4,820
Grossman	—	—	—	—	364		364
Paycass	400	1,800	—	—	720		2,920
American	—	—	—	—	1,230		1,230
Pro	—	—	—	—	—		700
Totals	2,600	6,820	3,330	3,530	5,192		21,472

This is an example of a form used by a firm to get salespeople to forecast sales for each account and product group.

Health Care are asked to forecast account sales based on their familiarity with each account's business.[12] Research results suggest that salesperson forecasts can be improved by developing detailed instructions about the forecasting procedures and providing salespeople with detailed information about their accounts and feedback concerning the accuracy of previous forecasts.[13]

Using Different Forecasting Approaches and Methods

This discussion of top-down and bottom-up approaches and several forecasting methods is illustrative of the forecasting procedures used by many sales organizations. However, all available forecasting methods have not been introduced, and some sales organizations may use the approaches and methods in different ways than discussed here. For example, some sales organizations use statistical methods, such as regression analysis, to develop sales forecasts for accounts, territories, districts, regions, zones, and/or the company. In the next section, the use of regression procedures for developing sales forecasts as a means for establishing sales quotas is examined.

The actual usage of specific forecasting methods is presented in Exhibit 5A.7. Although this study did not ask respondents their degree of usage of either the survey of buyer intentions approach or the Delphi method, previous research indicates these two approaches are fairly popular.[14] Study results indicate that the bottom-up approaches are more popular than the top-down approaches. Notice the differences that exist in the frequency of usage depending on the forecast period.

Because forecasting is such a difficult task and each approach and method has certain advantages and disadvantages, most firms use multiple forecasting approaches and methods. Then, various approaches are used to combine the results from each method into a final forecast.[15] If different approaches and methods produce similar sales forecasts, sales managers can be more confident in the validity of the forecast. If extremely divergent forecasts are generated from the different approaches and methods, additional analysis is required to determine the reasons for the large differences and to make the adjustments necessary to produce an accurate sales forecast.

EXHIBIT 5A.7 Usage of Forecasting Methods

	Percentage of Firms Using Method by Forecast Period			
Forecasting Method	Immediate (less than 1 month)	Short (1–6 months)	Medium (6 months–1 year)	Long (more than 1 year)
Top-Down				
Moving average	17.7	33.5	28.3	8.7
Exponential smoothing	12.9	19.6	16.8	4.2
Decomposition	0.0	6.8	11.9	9.3
Regression	13.4	25.1	25.4	16.5
Bottom-Up				
Jury of executive opinion	17.5	28.9	40.1	26.2
Salesforce composite	28.6	17.5	33.1	8.7

Even though firms use multiple forecasting methods, research evidence indicates that several criteria are used to select specific forecasting methods.[16] The most important criterion identified in this study was the accuracy of the forecasting method. Other criteria that were considered in decreasing importance were ease of use, data requirements, cost, and familiarity with methods. These results suggest that the selection of forecasting methods often represents a trade-off between the accuracy of the method and the ease with which it can be implemented. Some of the more accurate forecasting methods are difficult to use and have substantial data requirements. Thus, firms may have to sacrifice some accuracy by selecting methods that they are able to readily implement. This situation is illustrated in Exhibit 5A.7, where some of the more accurate methods (e.g., decomposition) are not used by many firms. Strengths and weaknesses of each forecasting method are found in Exhibit 5A.8.

EXHIBIT 5A.8 Strengths and Weaknesses of Forecasting Methods

Technique	Strengths	Weaknesses
Moving averages	Well suited to situations in which sales forecasts are needed for a large number of products	Requires a large amount of historical data
		Adjusts slowly to changes in sales
	Good for products with fairly stable sales	Assigns equal weight to each period, ignoring the fact that more recent periods usually have more impact on future sales
	Smoothes out small random fluctuations	
	Can compensate to some degree for trend if double moving average model is used	Results cannot be tested statistically
Exponential smoothing	Fairly simple to understand and use	Much searching may be needed to find appropriate weight
	Provides more weight to recent data points	
	Requires little data storage	Poor for medium- and long-term forecasts
	Generally accessible software packages are available	Erroneous forecasts can result due to large random fluctuations in recent data
	Fairly good accuracy for short-term forecasts	

continued

EXHIBIT 5A.8 *continued*

Technique	Strengths	Weaknesses
Decomposition method	Simple to understand	Requires a large amount of past data
	Included in most computer packages	Does not lend itself to longer-range forecasts
	Acknowledges three key factors affecting sales—trend, seasonal, cycles	Does not lend itself to statistical analysis of forecast values (no confidence limits or tests of significance)
	Breaks past sales into component parts making it easier to understand the sales pattern	
Survey of buyer intentions	Forecasts are based on customers' buying plans	Intentions frequently do not culminate in actual purchases
	Contacts with customers can also provide feedback about possible problems with the firm's products	Some firms may not be willing to disclose buying intentions, especially if they are not regular customers
	Relatively inexpensive if only a few key customers need to be contacted	
Jury of executive opinion	Provides input from the firm's key functional areas	May require excessive amounts of executives' time
	Executives usually have a solid understanding of broad-based factors and how they affect sales	Executives removed from the marketplace may not understand the firm's sales situation
	Can provide fairly quick forecasts	Not well suited to firms with a large number of products
		One or two influential people may dominate the process
Delphi method	Eliminates the need for committee or group meetings	Participants are often selected more on their willingness to participate and their accessibility than on their real knowledge or representativeness
	Eliminates group decision-making pitfalls, such as specious persuasion or a bandwagon effect	Can take a great deal of time to arrive at a consensus. Process may suffer because of high dropout rate of participants
	Participants receive input from other "experts" in an isolated environment	
	Allows for voicing of unusual opinions and anonymous mind changing	
	Proper facilities (e-mail) enable rapid exchange of ideas	
Salesforce composite	Uses input from persons closest to actual markets	Salespeople may underestimate sales when their forecasts are being used to set sales quotas
	Provides reasonably detailed forecasts (by product, customer, or territory)	Can take excessive amounts of salespeople's time if done too often
	May enhance salesforce morale by letting their input guide decisions	Salespeople often lack the knowledge to evaluate the economic situation and how it might affect future sales

PART III

Developing the Salesforce

The two modules in Part Three concentrate on the development of a productive salesforce. In Module 6, we review the process of staffing the salesforce through recruitment and selection. Standard recruitment and selection tools such as advertising, job interviews, and tests are discussed. Legal and ethical issues are also raised, and the topic of salesforce socialization is introduced.

Module 7 focuses on the continual development of salespeople through sales training. A model of the sales training process provides a framework for discussing needs assessment, training objectives, alternatives for training, and the design, performance, and evaluation of sales training.

MODULE 6

Staffing the Salesforce: Recruitment and Selection

Finding Successful Salespeople at Edward Jones

Hiring the right salespeople for the job is critical to a firm's success. Consequently, companies such as Edward Jones are taking actions to enhance their chances of hiring salespeople who will be successful with the company.

St. Louis–based Edward Jones is a highly decentralized financial services company with 4,200 investment representatives who work in one-person offices throughout the United States. Salespeople essentially run their own businesses and are responsible for the profitability of their offices. However, salespeople use the company's support systems.

Edward Jones believes that to hire the best reps, it must first understand the competencies of its successful reps. To determine the profile of successful reps, Edward Jones employed the Gallup Organization's management consulting unit in Lincoln, Nebraska, to conduct focus groups with top Edward Jones salespeople and high-level sales managers. The investigation allowed Gallup to create a composite profile that identified Jones's sales pros as persistent, self-reliant, and "willing to bet it all on themselves."

The recruitment process at Edward Jones is geared toward finding salespeople who possess competencies identified in this composite profile. Each month the company examines approximately 1,000 applications, 80 percent of which are referrals from the salesforce. The company looks for those who have excelled in their current occupation and have risen in both rank and pay level, but who are upset with their current compensation. Resumes that make it past the initial screening are given to Gallup, where a consultant conducts a phone interview with each applicant. The consultant asks 60 questions in an attempt to uncover three key personality traits: strong work ethic, high degree of motivation, and the ability to build rapport. Jones' hiring team then personally interviews salespeople that Gallup identified with those qualities. During this stage, interviewers try to identify past behaviors that may reveal competencies identified in the composite profile. Ultimately, 200 salespeople are hired.

This process has proved highly successful for Edward Jones. Since implementing the program 4 years ago, its attrition rate has fallen from 20.8 percent to 9 percent. According to Chris Gilkison, a general partner responsible for sales hiring, "We got better at hiring the right people."

Source: Michelle Marchetti, "Hiring," *Sales & Marketing Management* 150 (December 1998): 32.

Learning Objectives

After completing this module, you should be able to

1 Explain the critical role of recruitment and selection in building and maintaining a productive salesforce.

2 Describe how recruitment and selection affect salesforce socialization and performance.

3 Identify the key activities in planning and executing a program for salesforce recruitment and selection.

4 Discuss the legal and ethical consideration in salesforce recruitment and selection.

The account of Edward Jones's hiring practices illustrates the importance of hiring the right individuals for the job. Recruiting and selecting those best qualified for a position can make the difference between a firm's long-run ultimate success and failure. By clearly identifying the competencies necessary for sales success and then identifying salespeople with those competencies, Jones is able to reduce its turnover and grow its company.

Although many factors influence sales performance, sales managers cannot survive without doing a competent job in recruiting and selecting salespeople. The vital and complex nature of the job is summarized by Munson and Spivey:

> The process is complicated by various conflicting factors—the need to select applicants with characteristics related to job success, the difficulty of determining these characteristics, inadequacies inherent in the various selection techniques themselves, and the need to simultaneously insure that the selection process satisfies existing governmental regulations pertaining to discrimination in hiring practices.[1]

As we move into the next millennium, the recruitment and selection process will have to be adjusted to new demographics of an older salesforce with a higher proportion of women and minorities than in the past.[2] Seventy-five percent of U.S. population growth will come from Asians, Hispanics, and African-Americans.[3] Sales managers also face challenges associated with staffing an international salesforce, as well as with recruiting and selecting for team selling. Proper staffing of the salesforce is critical given the strong impact of the recruiting process on a firm's performance and profits.[4]

Today's sales manager's role in recruitment and selection is explored in this module. Before examining a basic model of the process, let's discuss further the importance of recruitment and selection.

Importance of Recruitment and Selection

In most sales organizations, sales managers with direct supervisory responsibilities for salespeople have the ultimate responsibility for recruitment and selection. They may have the support of top management, or perhaps they coordinate their efforts with human resource personnel or other managers within the firm. But it is the sales manager who generally retains primary recruitment and selection responsibilities. To emphasize the importance of recruitment and selection, consider only a few of the potential problems associated with its inadequate implementation:

1. inadequate sales coverage and lack of customer follow-up
2. increased training costs to overcome deficiencies
3. more supervisory problems
4. higher turnover rates
5. difficulty in establishing enduring relationships with customers
6. suboptimal total salesforce performance

Clearly, salesforce performance will suffer if recruitment and selection are poorly executed. Other sales management functions become more burdensome when the sales manager is handicapped by a multitude of "bad hires." The full costs of unsuccessful recruitment and selection are probably impossible to estimate. In addition to sales trainee salaries and employment agency fees, there are hidden costs associated with salesforce turnover, such as the loss of the relationships that salespeople build with their customers over time, and increased managerial problems that defy calculation. It is estimated that it costs anywhere from 50 to 150 percent of an employee's salary to replace that person.[5] For a bad hire, such an investment represents sunk costs that may be nonrecoverable. And in view of studies that tell us that a significant number of salespeople should not be in sales for one reason or another,[6] it is apparent that recruitment and selection are among the most challenging and important responsibilities of sales management.

Introduction to Salesforce Socialization

Salesforce socialization refers to the process by which salespeople acquire the knowledge, skills, and values essential to perform their jobs. The process begins when the sales recruit is first exposed to the organization and may extend for several years. A model of salesforce socialization is shown in Figure 6.1. This model suggests that important job outcomes such as job satisfaction, job involvement and commitment, and performance are directly and indirectly affected by recruitment and selection procedures.

The socialization process is discussed again in subsequent modules. For now, accept the idea that socialization affects salesforce performance and that recruitment and selection procedures play a major role in the socialization process. The two stages of socialization relevant to recruitment and selection are (1) **achieving realism**, which is giving the recruit an accurate portrayal of the job, and (2) **achieving congruence**, which is matching the capabilities of the recruit with the needs of the organization. From the candidates' perspective, they are more likely to choose an organization if they perceive its goals and values to be congruent with theirs.[7] Accurate job descriptions, matching candidates to the job and organization, and perhaps offering a **job preview** through a field visit with a salesperson are suggested for

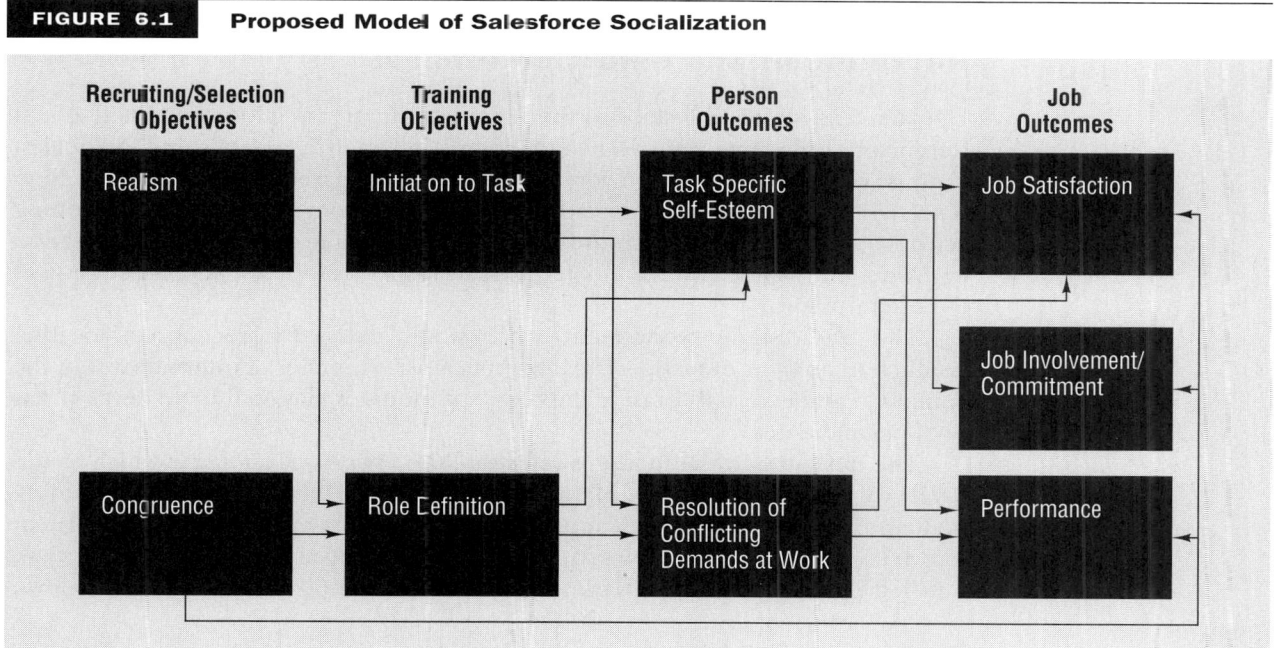

FIGURE 6.1 Proposed Model of Salesforce Socialization

Sales organizations must present accurate portrayals of the sales job (achieving realism) to sales recruits, who must possess skills and needs compatible with the needs and offerings of the organization (achieving congruence). If these objectives of recruiting and selection are met, salesforce socialization is enhanced, and ultimately, salesforce performance, job satisfaction, and job involvement and commitment are improved.

> **SALES MANAGEMENT IN THE 21ST CENTURY**
>
> **Finding a Fit at Hershey Chocolate**
> Douglas Clopton, district sales manager for Hershey Chocolate U.S.A., comments on the importance of congruence:
>
> *We have identified 15 traits or dimensions that we feel individuals should possess in order to be successful sales representatives with Hershey Chocolate. A few of these are planning and organizing skills, personal leadership, persuasiveness, initiative, and communication skills. We determine if sales candidates possess these dimensions through extensive questioning and testing of each during the interview process. Having most of these, however, is no guarantee of success. A candidate also must possess what we refer to as motivational fit. This fit occurs when the individual is one who enjoys the selling process. Thus, it is important for candidates to not only possess certain characteristics, but to enjoy the selling process to be successful at Hershey.*

achieving realism and congruence in recruitment and selection. For a closer look at the importance of obtaining congruence at Hershey Chocolate, see "Sales Management in the 21st Century: Finding a Fit at Hershey Chocolate."

Companies take several approaches to achieve realism and congruence in the recruiting process. For instance, RE/MAX International, Inc., has four different videotapes that franchise owners can provide to recruits to help them understand the company and its sales process.[8] Dictaphone, Inc., gives students an opportunity to view what a career in sales at the company entails by providing a videocassette to college placement centers. Companies such as Hershey Chocolate, Federated Insurance, and Motorola, Inc., provide candidates with a comprehensive brochure describing the company, its philosophy, and its products.

Recruitment and Selection Process

Figure 6.2 illustrates the steps in the recruitment and selection process. The first step involves **planning activities:** conducting a job analysis, establishing job qualifications, completing a written job description, setting recruitment and selection objectives, and developing a recruitment and selection strategy. These planning activities are conducted within the overall planning framework of the organization to ensure consistency with the objectives, strategies, resources, and constraints of the organization.

The second step is **recruitment,** which, simply put, is the procedure of locating a sufficient number of prospective job applicants. A number of internal (within the company) and external (outside the company) sources may be used to develop this pool of candidates.

The next step in the model is **selection,** the process of choosing which candidates will be offered the job. Many screening and evaluation methods, including evaluation of resumes and job application forms, interviews, tests, assessment centers, background investigations, and physical exams, are used in this step. A more detailed discussion of each step in the recruitment and selection process follows.

Planning for Recruitment and Selection

Given the critical nature of recruitment and selection, it would be difficult to overstate the case for careful planning as part of the process. Sales managers are concerned with the current staffing needs of their organizations; but perhaps more

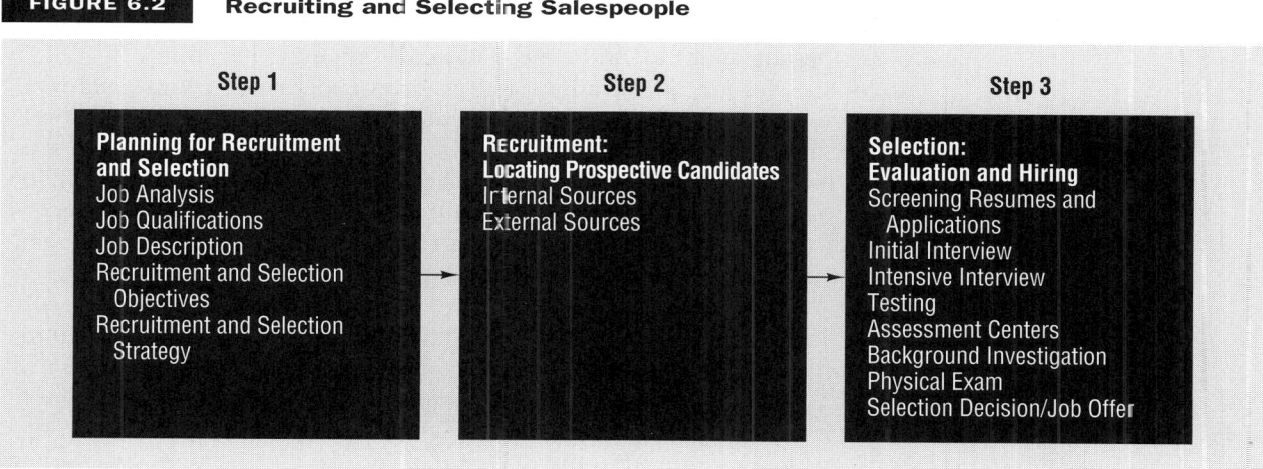

FIGURE 6.2 Recruiting and Selecting Salespeople

Three main steps are involved in recruiting and selecting salespeople: planning activities are followed by recruiting activities, which are followed by selection activities.

important, they are also concerned with future staffing needs, which is what makes planning so essential.

Proper planning provides more time for locating the best recruits. Upper management can be alerted in advance to probable future needs, rather than having to be convinced quickly when the need becomes imminent. Also, training can be planned more effectively when the flow of new trainees into the organization is known. Overall, the main benefit of adequate planning for the recruitment and selection process is that it helps prevent the kind of poor decisions that often prove so expensive both emotionally and financially. The key tasks in planning for recruitment and selection are the following.

JOB ANALYSIS To effectively recruit and select salespeople, sales managers must have a complete understanding of the job for which candidates are sought. Because most sales managers have served as salespeople in their companies before entering management, it is reasonable to think that they would have a good understanding of the sales jobs for which they recruit. However, some have lost touch with changing conditions in the field and thus have an obsolete view of the current sales task to be accomplished.

To ensure an understanding of the sales job, the sales manager may need to conduct, confirm, or update a **job analysis**, which entails an investigation of the tasks, duties, and responsibilities of the job. For example, will the selling tasks include responsibilities for opening new accounts as well as maintaining existing accounts? Will the salesperson be responsible for collecting accounts receivable or completing administrative reports? The job analysis defines the expected behavior of salespeople, indicating which areas of performance will be crucial for success. In most larger companies, the job analysis is completed by human resource managers or other corporate managers, but even then, the sales manager may have input into the job analysis.

JOB QUALIFICATIONS The job analysis indicates what the salespeople are supposed to do on the job, whereas **job qualifications** refer to the aptitude, skills, knowledge, personal traits, and willingness to accept occupational conditions necessary to perform the job. For example, Schein Pharmaceutical, Inc., looks for candidates who are college educated; have 2 years of pharmaceutical sales experience;

understand the pharmaceutical industry and the buying process; have good computer, oral and written communication, and negotiation skills; are problem solvers; and possess strong analytical and conceptual skills, among other things.[9]

Common sales job qualifications address sales experience, educational level, willingness to travel, willingness to relocate, interpersonal skills, listening skills, self-motivation, and ability to work independently. Consistent with our earlier discussion of the diversity of personal selling jobs, there is a corresponding variance in job qualifications for different sales jobs. Therefore, each sales manager should record the pertinent job qualifications for each job in the salesforce. Recall from the opening vignette that Edward Jones identified sales pros at its company as persistent, self-reliant, and "willing to bet it all on themselves" and thus looked for salespeople with these qualifications. A generic list of job qualifications for all the salespeople in the organization may not be feasible. Doug Clopton explains key job qualifications necessary for a position in sales at Hershey Chocolate U.S.A. in "Sales Management in the 21st Century: Key Job Qualifications at Hershey Chocolate."

For a given sales job within the same company, the qualifications may vary in different selling situations. For example, a multinational company whose salespeople sell the same products to the same types of customers may require different qualifications in different countries. Qualifications considered unimportant, and even discriminatory, in hiring salespeople in the United States, such as social class and religious and ethnic background, are important in hiring overseas.[10] In general, when sending salespeople on international assignments, it is helpful if they are patient, flexible, confident, persistent, motivated, and tolerant of new ways of doing things; have a desire to work abroad; and have a sense of humor.[11]

JOB DESCRIPTION Based on the job analysis and job qualifications, a written summary of the job, the **job description,** is completed by the sales manager or, in many cases, the human resource manager. Job descriptions for salespeople could contain any of or all the following elements:

1. job title (e.g., sales trainee, senior sales representative)
2. duties, tasks, and responsibilities of the salesperson

SALES MANAGEMENT IN THE 21ST CENTURY

Key Job Qualifications at Hershey Chocolate
Douglas Clopton, district sales manager for Hershey Chocolate U.S.A., comments on key sales job qualifications:

Selling has evolved from a feature and benefit based selling process to a consultative selling process. In the past, we would attempt to address the customer's needs by providing an arsenal of features and benefits included in the "sales presentation." Today, however, our first goal is to uncover customer wants, needs, or problems; then we tailor our promotional solutions to best satisfy them. For example, most people don't want to deal with a doctor that "has all the answers" even before discussing their health concerns with him/her. They would rather have the physician thoroughly question and seek out all the symptoms and problems and then write a prescription. At Hershey Chocolate, sales reps' first step is to conduct a want/need analysis with the customer, extensively utilizing their questioning skills; then they write a prescription (promotional program) that will serve as the solution to the patient's (customer's) needs. In light of this change, Hershey Chocolate's recruiting efforts have been revised to place much greater emphasis on listening skills *as well as* problem solving skills. *Our recruiting efforts no longer focus on candidates that can sell but on individuals that can help our customers buy.*

3. administrative relationships indicating to whom the salesperson reports
4. types of products to be sold
5. customer types
6. significant job-related demands, such as mental stress, physical strength or stamina requirements, or environmental pressures to be encountered

Job descriptions are an essential document in sales management. Their use in recruitment and selection is only one of their multiple functions. They are used to clarify duties and thereby reduce role ambiguity in the salesforce, to familiarize potential employees with the sales job, to set objectives for salespeople, and eventually, to aid in evaluating performance. A typical job description for a sales representative is shown in Exhibit 6.1.

RECRUITMENT AND SELECTION OBJECTIVES To be fully operational, recruitment and selection objectives should be specifically stated for a given period. The following general objectives of recruitment and selection could be converted to specific operational objectives in a given firm:

- Determine present and future needs in terms of numbers and types of salespeople (as discussed in Module 5).
- Meet the company's legal and social responsibilities regarding composition of the salesforce.
- Reduce the number of underqualified or overqualified applicants.
- Increase the number of qualified applicants at a specified cost.
- Evaluate the effectiveness of recruiting sources and evaluation techniques.

By setting specific objectives for recruitment and selection, sales managers can channel resources into priority areas and improve organizational and salesforce effectiveness.

RECRUITMENT AND SELECTION STRATEGY After objectives have been set, a **recruitment and selection strategy** can be developed. Formulating this strategy requires the sales manager to consider the scope and timing of recruitment and selection activities as follows:

- When will the recruitment and selection be done?
- How will the job be portrayed?
- How will efforts with intermediaries, such as employment agencies and college placement centers, be optimized?
- What type of salespeople will be hired when developing an international salesforce?
- How much time will be allowed for a candidate to accept or reject an offer?
- What are the most likely sources for qualified applicants?

Recruitment and selection are perpetual activities in some sales organizations but in others are conducted only when a vacancy occurs. Most sales organizations could benefit by ongoing recruitment to facilitate selection when the need arises. Some recruit seasonally. For example, large companies often concentrate their efforts to coincide with spring graduation dates on college campuses.

A strategic decision must be made in terms of how the job will be portrayed, particularly in advertisements. Initial descriptions of the job in the media are

> **EXHIBIT 6.1** **Schein Pharmaceutical, Inc., Position Description**
>
> **Job Title:** Corporate Account Manager
> **Department:** Sales
> **Reports To:** Regional Sales Manager
>
> *Job Function/Purpose:*
>
> Continually develop and enhance Schein's base of sales opportunities within assigned accounts by negotiating sound contracts and programs to ensure availability of products, and maximizing the business derived from these accounts. Develop ongoing relationships between Schein and assigned CAM accounts to ensure product sales. Classes of trade include, but are not limited to, Warehousing Chains, Nonwarehousing Chains, Regional Wholesalers, Buying Groups, Long-Term Care, Drug Stores, and Managed Care Accounts.
>
> *Principal Activities/Objectives:*
>
> 1. Effectively negotiate mutually beneficial purchasing arrangements and contracts that are within Schein guidelines to maximize business opportunities, usage, and distribution of Schein products.
> 2. Initiate and develop relationships with key decision makers within assigned accounts through frequent contact and communication. Establish a consistent communication network with the customer, including all key corporate personnel.
> 3. Develop mutually beneficial contract proposals that are tailored to customers' needs by using the approved programs provided by and in cooperation with marketing.
> 4. Initiate and implement creative value-added programs or trade promotion tools within assigned budget to ensure sales on contracted and other core products.
> 5. Actively communicate customer programs and contracts to the field and inside salesforce by participating in meetings and developing tactical implementation plans to ensure the utilization and/or distribution of products and pull through.
> 6. Maintain a current understanding of industry changes and trends, with an insight to the future needs of those customers that offer the greatest potential business gains.
> 7. Analyze and interpret all pertinent sales, marketing, and financial information with assigned accounts to develop and implement account specific business plans that are consistent with the overall plans of the District and Sales and marketing organization.
> 8. Establish effective communications to solve problems for the customer to promote internal teamwork, long-term partnerships, and effective customer relations.
> 9. Maintain and increase profitability of identified and overall CAM accounts.
>
> *Qualifications*
>
> The CAM position requires a college degree and a minimum of 2 years of successful pharmaceutical sales or sales management experience. The incumbent must possess a complete understanding of Schein Pharmaceutical products, as well as competitive products. Incumbent must possess a thorough understanding of distribution for pharmaceutical products as well as an understanding of external forces that ultimately affect the purchase decision. A macro and comprehensive knowledge of the company's goals, policies, and structure is required. Additionally, the CAM must be knowledgeable of goals, policies, and structures of customer organizations and be able to identify the key decision makers and work with these customers for mutually beneficial programs. The CAM must have thorough knowledge of marketing techniques and the legalities of contracting. Incumbent must possess a thorough understanding of the multisource marketplace, reimbursement, state governments, public health care policy, and negotiating skills.
>
> Computer, oral/written communication, and negotiation skills are critical to the success in the CAM job. Successful incumbent will demonstrate problem-solving skills in overcoming obstacles, be able to anticipate change, and possess highly developed persuasive sales skills.
>
> *Problem Solving*
>
> Incumbent must possess strong analytical and conceptual skills to analyze data and situations, show familiarity with various customer organizational structures and their policies/procedures, identify problems, develop priorities, and implement appropriate solutions to meet both short- and long-term objectives. The CAM will be challenged to resolve problems that will require judgment and creativity and be aware of impact. The problems/opportunities and solutions will be customer driven and will require a high degree of creativity/practicality for resolution and stay within the legal parameters and Schein policies.

necessarily limited. Should earnings potential be featured, or perhaps the opportunity for advancement? Or is this job correctly portrayed as ideal for the career salesperson? Consider how the advertisement in Exhibit 6.2 portrays the salesperson's job at a pharmaceutical company.

Strategy also involves coordinating recruiting needs and activities with employment agencies and college placement centers. For instance, dates and times for interviewing on campus must be arranged. If an employment agency is to be used, it will need a job description and job qualifications for the position to be filled.

When developing an international salesforce, the sales manager must consider the type of salesperson best suited for selling outside the home country. Options include hiring expatriates, who are salespeople from the firm's home country, hiring host-country nationals, or hiring third-country nationals. Advantages and disadvantages of hiring each type of salesperson are shown in Exhibit 6.3.

Another strategic decision is the length of time a candidate will be given to accept an offer. This time element is important because other recruitment and selection activities may be temporarily suspended until the decision is made. Strategy

---

EXHIBIT 6.2 Example of an Individual Company's Advertisement to Recruit Salespeople

He can enjoy an active lifestyle

It's our solid dedication, vision and constant search for answers that allow us to touch millions of people around the world every day. As a major division of Fortune 100 American Home Products Corporation, we help people lead healthier lives through the development of innovative pharmaceutical, vaccine and nutritional products. We achieve this through our superior research, manufacturing, sales and marketing capabilities. Enjoy the freedom to develop your own career while having the support of a valuable team. We are recruiting for territories in the New York Metropolitan area, New Jersey and Connecticut.

Pharmaceutical Sales Representative

Great training. And a piece of the business.
As we build on our history of developing successful products and people, you can play an important role in our future, with responsibilities for promotion and sales of pharmaceutical products to physicians, pharmacists and hospitals. You'll begin by completing a comprehensive training program that prepares you for immediate challenges and development on our career advancement ladder.
A Bachelor's degree is required, preferably in a business or life science discipline. Ideally, you also will have a strong record of relevant sales experience. Outstanding communication and presentation skills are also a must. In return, we offer an excellent compensation package that includes bonuses, comprehensive benefits, a company car and stock options—along with support of members who are among our industry's most accomplished professionals.
Wyeth-Ayerst offers other benefits, including child-care subsidies, educational assistance and professional development programs. Please forward your resume with salary requirements to **Wyeth-Ayerst. Reference ONNYT-0199, P.O. Box 7886, Philadelphia, PA 19101-7886. Fax in fine mode to: (610) 989-4854. E mail: jobs@RAMAIL1.wyeth.com** (ASCII format, no attachments, subject: resume. For more information, visit our website at **www.ahp.com/wyeth.htm** Principals only.
Equal Opportunity Employer. M/F/D/V

EXHIBIT 6.3 Advantages and Disadvantages of Salesperson Types for International Salesforce Development

Salesperson Type	Advantages	Disadvantages
Expatriates	High product knowledge Good follow-up service Good training for promotion Greater home-country control	Highest maintenance costs High turnover rates High training costs
Host-Country Nationals	Easy and inexpensive to hire Significant market knowledge Speak the native language Cultural understanding Quickly penetrate market	Need extensive product training Sales often considered low-esteem position Difficult to instill organization's culture Hard to ensure organizational loyalty
Third-Country Nationals	Possible cultural understanding and language skills if from similar region Economical labor force Allows regional sales coverage May allow sales to country in conflict with home country	Nationality unrelated to organization or place of work Low promotion potential Need extensive product and company training Sales often considered low-esteem position Potential difficulty of adapting to new environments Difficult to instill organization's culture Hard to ensure organizational loyalty

also involves identifying the sources that look most promising for recruitment. This subject is discussed in detail in the following section.

Recruitment: Locating Prospective Candidates

As Figure 6.2 showed, the next step in recruitment and selection is to locate a pool of prospective job candidates. This step, the actual recruiting, may use a variety of sources. Some of the more popular ones are advertising, employee referrals, and private employment agencies.

INTERNAL SOURCES One of the most popular methods of locating sales recruits is through **employee referral programs.** These programs are relatively quick and inexpensive compared with other recruiting methods, such as advertising, using employment agencies, and visiting college campuses. Referral programs also may be very effective. In a survey of more than 200 sales managers, 47 percent indicated that they found their best salespeople through referrals.[12] An employee who furnishes a referral may be paid a "finder's fee." For example, Vantive Corporation, a customer-service software provider, pays employees $2,500 for each inside rep they recruit and $5,000 for each field seller.[13] Existing salespeople are obviously good sources for referral programs because they have a good understanding of the type of person sought for a sales position. Purchasing agents within the company may also be helpful in identifying prospective sales candidates. Employee referral programs can be enhanced by publicly recognizing successful referrals, by regularly providing incentives and promptly rewarding successful referrals, by offering a proactive program that encourages employee participation, and by providing feedback concerning the status of referrals to those making them.[14]

Other internal methods include announcing sales job openings through newsletters, in meetings, or on the bulletin board. Internal transfers or promotions may result from announcing an opening on the salesforce. One study found that employees of the firm who transfer to sales positions can be expected to yield more long-run profits than salespeople from any other source.[15]

EXTERNAL SOURCES Although it is a good idea to include internal sources as part of a recruitment and selection program, there may not be enough qualified persons inside the organization to meet the human resource needs of the salesforce. The search then must be expanded to external sources.

Advertisements One way to produce a large pool of applicants in a short time is by advertising. On a cost-per-applicant basis, advertising is generally inexpensive. However, a large number of the applicants may not be qualified for the job, even when the ads carefully spell out job qualifications. As a result, advertising usually requires extensive screening procedures to identify a reasonable number of prospective candidates. Exhibit 6.4 offers sound advice on how to use print ads to recruit salespeople.

Advertisements in trade publications can attract those already in a specified field. In the case of trade magazines, lead time to place an advertisement in the next issue is longer than with newspapers—typically 6 to 8 weeks. Other specialty publications are nationally distributed employment listings, such as the one published by *The Wall Street Journal.*

A potentially effective and relatively inexpensive way to advertise involves the Internet. Companies can list job openings on bulletin boards or in job banks such as Career Resource Center (**www.careers.org**) or Career Mosaic (**www.careermosaic.com**) for 30 days.[16] Candidates seeking a position can reply to an ad online. Newspapers, such as the *New York Times,* have added Web versions of their classified sections. Because a large number of job seekers accessing the Inter-

| EXHIBIT 6.4 | Using Print Advertising to Recruit Salespeople |

The sales recruiting ads you run depend on the job, the speed needed to fill it, availability of the applicant, and competition. Here are some tips for maximizing advertising effectiveness:
- Use business publications to recruit those with business experience.
- Use display ads in the business pages for sales management and top selling posts.
- Use classified newspaper advertising when speed is important.
- Advertise on Sunday when running a classified ad.
- Use the ad as a sales tool to motivate candidates to reply.
- Focus on prospective candidates' needs and interests rather than on company characteristics.
- Emphasize the unique aspects of the job.
- Do not exaggerate earnings estimates. This may cause distrust.
- Add restrictions (e.g., bachelor's degree) to avoid being flooded with unqualified applicants.
- Provide a telephone number where the reader can call on Sunday, if possible.
- Add art (e.g., a border) to copy for greater effect.
- Use a box number to screen telephone calls and surprise visits. However, many employed people will not answer box number ads.
- Provide a fax number.
- Answer inquiries immediately before they cool off.

The ad in Exhibit 6.2 attempts to use many of these suggestions.

net are college students, such advertising may provide an alternative for reaching the college market.[17]

Private Employment Agencies A commonly used source is the **private employment agency.** The fee charged by the agency may be paid by the employer or the job seeker, as established by contract before the agency begins work for either party. Fees vary but typically amount to 15 to 20 percent of the first-year earnings of the person hired through the agency. The higher the caliber of salesperson being sought, the greater the probability the employer will pay the fee.

Many agencies, such as SALESworld and Sales Consultants, specialize in the placement of salespeople and have offices across the country. Such agencies can be extremely useful in national searches, particularly if the sales manager is seeking high-quality, experienced salespeople. This is true because high-performing salespeople are usually employed but may contact an agency just to see if a better opportunity arises.

Employment agencies usually work from a job description furnished by the sales manager and can be instructed to screen candidates based on specific job qualifications. The professionalism of private employment agencies varies widely, but there are enough good agencies that a sales manager should not tolerate an agency that cannot refer qualified candidates.

Employment agencies that specialize in part-timers are sometimes used when a need arises to hire part-time salespeople to support or supplant the full-time salesforce. For example, when Prudential HMO wanted to win new customers for its healthcare product in the Northeast, it used Sales Staffers International to recruit about 75 insurance salespeople with healthcare experience to blanket the area.[18] In most cases, part-time salespeople are not eligible for fringe benefits, so the cost of sales coverage can be reduced by using them. However, when considering using temporaries internationally, keep in mind that many western European countries restrict or even ban their use.[19]

Colleges and Universities A popular source for sales recruits, especially for large companies with extensive training programs, are colleges and universities. College students usually can be hired at lower salaries than experienced salespeople, yet they have already demonstrated their learning abilities. Companies seeking future managers often look here for sales recruits.

Campus placement centers can be helpful in providing resumes of applicants, arranging interviews, and providing facilities for screening interviews. Some campus placement centers now offer videoconferencing systems that allow corporate recruiters to interview students from the home office.[20] Most placement centers also provide access to alumni in addition to the current student body. In some instances, contacts with faculty members may provide sales recruits. Another campus recruiting method is to offer sales internships, which allow both the company and the student an opportunity to see whether a match exists. The internship as a recruiting vehicle is gaining popularity. Northwestern Mutual Life's internship program is designed to develop college students personally and professionally. Approximately 75 percent of the 800 to 900 student interns participating each year continue working until they graduate, and a third of those become full-time agents.[21] Mutual of Omaha has even gone as far as sponsoring a university's selling program to enable closer contact with students in hopes of recruiting them.[22] College campuses are also common sites for career conferences in which multiple companies participate in trade show fashion to familiarize students with sales job opportunities.

On the international scene, college campuses are gaining in popularity as a source of sales recruits. College students in foreign countries are beginning to see United States–based firms as viable alternatives to home-country firms.

Job Fairs Several employers are brought together in one location for recruiting purposes by **job fairs.** Candidates visit the booths of employers they are interested in, or companies request a meeting with a candidate based on a favorable reaction to the candidate's resume. Job fairs are best conducted in the evening hours so that currently employed salespeople can attend. However, virtual job fairs on the Internet circumvent this problem. Companies can participate in online career fairs hosted by Monster Board (www.monster.com) or the Online Career Center (www.occ.com). Employers' banner ads are grouped in common areas. When candidates click on a banner, they are treated to company information, position descriptions, and electronic applications.[23]

Professional Societies Another worthwhile source of sales recruits is **professional societies.** A primary reason sales executives join professional organizations is to establish a network of colleagues who have common interests. Organizations such as Sales and Marketing Executives International meet regularly and provide the opportunity to establish contacts with professional sales executives, who may provide the names of prospective salespeople. Some professional organizations publish newsletters or operate a placement service, which could also be used in recruiting.

Computer Rosters Locating prospective salespeople through **computerized matchmaking** services is becoming a more important recruiting method each day. Computer technology is being used by an increasing number of college placement centers and employment agencies. For instance, at Central Missouri State University, employers can post job vacancies directly to the career services Web site, which is accessible by all students. Independent computer recruiting services are also widely available. For example, Wonderlic Personnel Test, Inc. (www.wonderlic.com), offers sales managers an automated application service that allows them to screen applicants before taking a phone call or handling a resume or application. Applicants call a special toll-free phone number included in the firm's recruiting ad and respond to questions related to the job. Wonderlic forwards the completed applications to the client company the next day for their review. American Linen Supply used this service to recruit good customer service reps quickly and credits it with helping them raise the standards and expectations of candidates they recruit.[24]

Resume-search services are also useful for finding qualified candidates. These services sort through thousands of resumes they have on file looking for candidates who match the specific qualifications a firm desires. They generally guarantee qualified candidates and charge only when a match is made. For example, SkillSearch (www.skillsearch.com), a resume-search service, has a databank composed predominantly of experienced degreed professionals who are currently employed but who are searching for a better career opportunity.

Selection: Evaluation and Hiring

The third step in the recruitment and selection model shown in Figure 6.2 is selection. As part of the selection process, various tools are used to evaluate the job candidate in terms of job qualifications and to provide a relative ranking compared with other candidates. In this section, commonly used evaluation tools are presented and some of the key issues in salesforce selection are discussed.

SCREENING RESUMES AND APPLICATIONS The pool of prospective salespeople generated in the recruiting phase often must be drastically reduced before engaging in time-consuming expensive evaluation procedures such as personal interviews. Initially, sales recruits may be screened based on a review of a resume or an application form.

In analyzing resumes, sales managers check job qualifications (e.g., education or sales experience requirements), the degree of career progress by the applicant, and the frequency of job change. Depending on the format and extensiveness of the resume, it may be possible to examine salary history and requirements, travel or relocation restrictions, and reasons for past job changes. Also, valuable clues about the recruit may be gathered from the appearance and completeness of the resume.

A **job application form** can be designed to gather all pertinent information and exclude unnecessary information. There are three additional advantages of application forms as a selection tool. First, the application form can be designed to meet antidiscriminatory legal requirements, whereas resumes often contain such information. For example, if some applicants note age, sex, race, color, religion, or national origin on their resumes and others do not, a legal question as to whether this information was used in the selection process might arise. A second advantage of application forms is that the comparison of multiple candidates is facilitated because the information on each candidate is presented in the same sequence. This is not the case with personalized resumes. Finally, job applications are usually filled out in handwriting, so the sales manager can observe the attention to detail and neatness of the candidate. In some sales jobs, these factors may be important for success.

INTERVIEWS Interviews of assorted types are an integral part of the selection process. Because interpersonal communications and relationships are a fundamental part of sales jobs, it is only natural for sales managers to weigh interview results heavily in the selection process.

Although sales managers agree that interviews are important in selecting salespeople, there is less agreement on how structured the interviews should be and how they should be conducted. For example, some sales managers favor unstructured interviews, which encourage the candidates to talk freely about themselves. Others favor a more structured approach in which particular answers are sought, in a particular sequence, from each candidate.

Initial Interviews Interviews are usually designed to get an in-depth look at the candidate. In some cases, however, they merely serve as a screening mechanism to support or replace a review of resumes or application forms. These **initial interviews** are typified by the on-campus interviews conducted by most sales recruiters. They are brief, lasting less than an hour. The recruiter clarifies questions about job qualifications and makes a preliminary judgment about whether a match exists between the applicant and the company.

A promising time-saving technique for initially interviewing candidates involves them responding to a series of questions over the phone. Gallup, Inc., developed "Life Themes," a series of 50 to 200 structured questions that assess patterns of thoughts, feelings, and behaviors commonly occurring among top-performing salespeople. Questions are structured to determine candidates' strengths and weaknesses in such areas as ego drive, competition, intensity, focus, discipline, empathy, courage, ethics, and self-knowledge. These interviews, lasting from 45 to 90 minutes, alleviate some of the costs involved in conducting a personal interview.[25]

Computer-assisted interviewing is an emerging device that also can be used for screening candidates. For example, Nike used it to hire 250 retail salespeople for its Niketown outlet in Las Vegas. After seeing an ad in the newspaper and responding to eight questions over the phone, applicants who were not screened out were invited to the store for a computer-assisted interview, followed by a personal interview. As part of the computer interview, applicants viewed a video showing three scenarios for helping a customer and were asked to pick the best one. The computer flagged applicants' strengths, weaknesses, and areas that needed further probing. Although Nike used on-site computer-assisted interviewing, the Internet now provides another venue for this option, allowing greater flexibility for both employers and prospective employees.[26]

During this phase of selection, sales managers should be careful to give the candidate an accurate picture of the job and not oversell it. Candidates who are totally "sold" on the job during the first interview only to be rejected later suffer unnecessary trauma.

Intensive Interviews One or more **intensive interviews** may be conducted to get an in-depth look at the candidate. Often, this involves multiple sequential interviews by several executives or several managers at the company's facilities. Another variation on the theme, used less often, is to interview several job candidates simultaneously in a group setting.

When a candidate is to be interviewed in succession by several managers, planning and coordination are required to achieve more depth and to avoid redundancy. Otherwise, each interviewer might concentrate on the more interesting dimensions of a candidate and some important areas may be neglected. An interviewing guide such as the one in Exhibit 6.5 could be used with multiple interviewers, each of whom would delve into one or more of the seven categories of information about the candidate.

Interviews, like any other single selection tool, may fail to predict adequately applicants' future success on the job.[27] **Interviewer bias,** or allowing personal opinions, attitudes, and beliefs to influence judgments about a candidate, can be a particularly acute problem with some interviewers. Sales managers, like other human beings, tend to have preferences in candidates' appearances and personalities—and any number of other subjective feelings that may be irrelevant for a given interview situation.

Research confirms the subjective nature of interviewing, concluding that different interviewers will rate the same applicant differently unless there is a commonly accepted stereotype of the ideal applicant.[28] For instance, recent research

EXHIBIT 6.5   **Interview Guide**

Meeting the Candidate

At the outset, act friendly but avoid prolonged small talk—interviewing time costs money.
- Introduce yourself by using your name and title.
- Mention casually that you will make notes. (You don't mind if I make notes, do you?)
- Assure the candidate that all information will be treated in confidence.

Questions:
- Ask questions in a conversational tone. Make them both concise and clear.
- Avoid loaded and negative questions. Ask open-ended questions that will force complete answers: "Why do you say that?" (Who, what, where, when, how?)
- Don't ask direct questions that can be answered "Yes" or "No."

Analyzing:
- Attempt to determine the candidate's goals. Try to draw the candidate out, but let him or her do most of the talking. Don't sell—interview.
- Try to avoid snap judgments.

Interviewer Instructions

You will find two columns of questions on the following pages. The left-hand column contains questions to ask yourself about the candidate. The right-hand column suggests questions to ask the candidate. During the interview it is suggested that you continually ask "yourself" What is this person telling me about himself or herself? What kind of person is he or she?" In other parts of the interview, you can cover education, previous experience, and other matters relating to specific qualifications.

Ask Yourself

I. Attitude
- Can compete without irritation?
- Can bounce back easily?
- Can balance interest of both company and self?
- What is important to him or her?
- Is he or she loyal?
- Takes pride in doing a good job?
- Is he or she a cooperative team player?

II. Motivation
- Is settled in choice of work?
- Works from necessity, or choice?
- Makes day-to-day and long-range plans?
- Uses some leisure for self-improvement?
- Is willing to work for what he or she wants in face of opposition?

III. Initiative
- Is he or she a self-starter?
- Completes own tasks?
- Follows through on assigned tasks?
- Works in assigned manner without leaving own "trademark?
- Can work independently?

IV. Stability
- Is he or she excitable or even-tempered?
- Impatient or understanding?
- Uses words that show strong feelings?
- Is candidate poised or impulsive; controlled or erratic?
- Will he or she broaden or flatten under pressure?
- Is candidate enthusiastic about job?

Ask the Candidate

1. Ever lose in competition? Feelings?
2. Ever uncertain about providing for your family?
3. How can the American way of business be improved?
4. Do you think that you've made a success of life to date?
5. Who was your best boss? Describe the person.
6. How do you handle customer complaints?

1. How does your spouse (or other) feel about a selling career?
2. When and how did you first develop an interest in selling?
3. What mortgages, debts, etc., press you now?
4. How will this job help you get what you want?
5. What obstacles are most likely to trip you up?

1. How (or why) did you get into (or want) into sales?
2. Do you prefer to work alone or with others?
3. What do you like most, like least about selling?
4. Which supervisors let you work alone? How did you feel about this?
5. When have you felt like giving up on a task? Tell me about it.

1. What things disturb you most?
2. How do you get along with customers (people) you dislike?
3. What buyers' actions irritate you?
4. What were your most unpleasant sales (work) experiences?
5. Most pleasant sales (work) experiences?
6. What do you most admire about your friends?
7. What things do some customers do that are irritating to other people?

continued

EXHIBIT 6.5 continued

Ask Yourself

V. Planning
- Ability to plan and follow through? Or will depend on supervisor for planning?
- Ability to coordinate work of others?
- Ability to think of ways of improving methods?
- Ability to fit into company methods?
- Will he or she see the whole job or get caught up in details?

VI. Insight
- Realistic in appraising self?
- Desire for self-improvement?
- Interested in problems of others?
- Interested in reaction of others to self?
- Will he or she take constructive action on weaknesses?
- How does he or she take criticism?

VII. Social Skills
- Is he or she a leader or follower?
- Interested in new ways of dealing with people?
- Can get along best with what types of people?
- Will wear well over the long term?
- Can make friends easily?

Ask the Candidate

1. What part of your work (selling) do you like best? like least?
2. What part is the most difficult for you?
3. Give me an idea of how you spend a typical day.
4. Where do you want to be 5 years from today?
5. If you were manager, how would you run your present job?
6. What are the differences between planned and unplanned work?

1. Tell me about your strengths and weaknesses?
2. Are your weaknesses important enough to do something about them? Why or why not?
3. How do you feel about those weaknesses?
4. How would you size up your last employer?
5. Most useful criticism received? From whom? Tell me about it. Most useless?
6. How do you handle fault finders?

1. What do you like to do in your spare time?
2. Have you ever organized a group? Tell me about it.
3. What methods are effective in dealing with people? What methods are ineffective?
4. What kind of customers (people) do you get along with best?
5. Do you prefer making new friends or keeping old ones? Why?
6. How would you go about making a friend? developing a customer?
7. What must a person do to be liked by others?

suggests that race bias is a potential concern.[29] Sales managers must not let race interfere with the hiring decision.

TESTING To overcome the pitfalls of subjectivity and a potential lack of critical analysis of job candidates, many firms use tests as part of the selection process. Selection tests may be designed to measure intelligence, aptitudes, personality, and other interpersonal factors.

Historically, the use of such tests has been controversial. In the late 1960s, it appeared that testing would slowly disappear from the employment scene under legal and social pressure related to the lack of validity and possible discriminatory nature of some testing procedures. Instead, selection tests have changed, and perhaps managers have learned more about how to use them as a legitimate part of the selection process. Therefore, they are still used today.

Those who have had success with tests suggest they are useful for identifying candidates' strengths and weaknesses, as well as for revealing candidates who possess key personality traits associated with successful salespeople.[30] For example, the trait "conscientiousness" appears to be a valid predictor of sales performance.[31] Sales Success Profile, a 50-question, multiple-choice test, measures salespeople's strengths and weaknesses in 13 critical areas, including the ability to approach, involve, and build rapport; the ability to identify a buyer's needs and motivations; skill at overcoming objections; and time management.³² Valid tests measuring certain personality traits or sale skills may be used to supplement other salesforce selection tools.

Those who remain reluctant to use tests ask three questions: (1) Can selection tests really predict future job performance? (2) Can tests give an accurate, job-related profile of the candidate? (3) What are the legal liabilities arising from testing? In addressing the first question, one must admit it is sometimes difficult to correlate performance on a test at a given point in time with job performance at a later date. For example, how can sales managers account for performance variations caused primarily by changes in the uncontrollable environment, as might be the case in an unpredictable economic setting?

Question 2 really is concerned with whether the tests measure the appropriate factors in an accurate fashion. The precise measurement of complex behavioral variables such as motivation is difficult at best, so it is likely that some tests do not really measure what they purport to measure.

Answers to question 3 depend largely on the complete answers to questions 1 and 2. The capsule response to the third question is that unless test results can be validated as a meaningful indicator of performance, there is strong possibility that the sales manager is in a legally precarious position.

Suggestions to improve the usefulness to sales managers of tests as selection tools follow.³³

1. Do not attempt to construct tests for the purpose of selecting salespeople. Leave this job to the testing experts and human resource specialists.
2. If psychological tests are used, be sure the standards of the American Psychological Association have been met.
3. Use tests that have been based on a job analysis for the particular job in question.
4. Select a test that minimizes the applicant's ability to anticipate desired responses.
5. Use tests as part of the selection process, but do not base the hiring decision solely on test results.

Tests can be useful selection tools if these suggestions are followed. In particular, tests can identify areas worthy of further scrutiny if they are administered and interpreted before a final round of intensive interviewing. For example, prospective candidates who enter Northwestern Mutual Life's Web page take an examination that is scored and forwarded to agents in geographic areas close to that student's school or desired place of residence before further interviewing.³⁴

Sales managers may use commercial testing services in selecting salespeople. For example, Wonderlic Personnel Test, Inc., offers a computer-scored test called the Comprehensive Personality Profile that "assesses personality from a job compatibility perspective.³⁵ This extensively validated test can be used to analyze candidates' strengths and weaknesses related to a position in sales.

Tests may prove useful for selecting among local candidates when operating in a foreign country. For example, when United States–based Caliper wanted to hire salespeople for its operations in the Czech Republic, it successfully translated and administered to Czech candidates the same examination it gives to American candidates to assess such qualities as ego drive, empathy, and leadership.³⁶

ASSESSMENT CENTERS An **assessment center** offers a set of well-defined procedures for using techniques such as group discussion, business game simulations, presentations, and role-playing exercises for the purpose of employee selection or development. The participant's performance is evaluated by a group of assessors, usually members of management within the firm. Although somewhat expensive because of the high cost of managerial time to conduct the assessments, such centers are being used more often in the selection of salespeople.

An interesting report on the use of an assessment center to select salespeople comes from the life insurance industry, well known for its continual need for new salespeople. Traditional selection methods used in this industry apparently leave something to be desired because turnover rates are among the highest for salespeople. An assessment-center approach was used by one life insurance firm to select salespeople based on exercises simulating various sales skills, such as prospecting, time management, and sales presentation skills. Results of the study indicated that this program was superior to traditional methods of selecting salespeople in the insurance industry in terms of predicting which salespeople would survive and which would drop out within 6 months of being hired.[37] Chemical Bank has had success in hiring its salespeople by using an assessment exercise that involves trading and phone sales simulations.[38]

BACKGROUND INVESTIGATION Job candidates who have favorably emerged from resume and application screening, interviewing, testing, and perhaps an assessment center may next become the subjects of a **background investigation.** This may be as perfunctory as a reference check or comprehensive if the situation warrants it. In conducting background investigations, it is advisable to request job-related information only and to obtain a written release from the candidate before proceeding with the investigation.

If a reference check is conducted, two points should be kept in mind. First, persons listed as references are biased in favor of the job applicant. As one sales manager puts it, "Even the losers have three good references—so I don't bother checking them." Second, persons serving as references may not be candid or may not provide the desired information. This reluctance may stem from a personal concern (i.e., Will I lose a friend or be sued if I tell the truth?) or from a company policy limiting the discussion of past employees.

Despite these and other limitations, a reference check can help verify the true identity of a person and possibly confirm his or her employment history. With personal misrepresentation and resume fraud being very real possibilities, a reference check is recommended.[39]

PHYSICAL EXAMINATION Requiring the job candidate to pass a physical examination is often a formal condition of employment. In many instances, the insurance carrier of the employing firm requires a physical examination of all incoming employees. The objective is to discover any physical problem that may inhibit job performance.

In recent years, drug and communicable disease testing has made this phase of selection controversial. Although the courts will undoubtedly have a major role in determining the legality of testing in these areas in the future, the current rules, at least in the case of drug testing of potential employees, are fairly simple. A company can test for drug use if the applicant is informed of the test before taking it, if the results are kept confidential, and if the need for drug testing is reasonably related to potential job functions.[40] If a drug testing program is in place, all applicants should be required to be tested.[41]

SELECTION DECISION AND JOB OFFER When making the selection decision, the sales manager must evaluate candidates' qualifications relative to characteristics considered most important for the job. A decision must be made about whether a candidate's strength in one characteristic can compensate for a weakness in another characteristic, whether a characteristic is so important a weakness in it cannot be tolerated, or whether the candidate must meet certain minimum levels to be successful.[42] At times, the sales manager may face a dilemma, similar to that found in "An Ethical Dilemma."

> ### An Ethical Dilemma
> *You are the district sales manager for an electronics manufacturing company and are responsible for all the recruitment and selection decisions in your district. The company's national sales manager has asked you to interview his son for a sales position that has just opened up in your district. Coincidentally, he mentions that a regional sales manger position (which you desire very much) is about to open up. On interviewing the national sales manger's son, along with several other candidates, you find that he is not the best qualified for the position. What do you do? Explain.*

After evaluating the available candidates, the sales manager may be ready to offer a job to one or more candidates. Some candidates may be "put on hold" until the top candidates have made their decisions. Another possibility is that the sales manager may decide to extend the search and begin the recruitment and selection process all over again.

In communicating with those offered jobs, it is now appropriate for the sales manager to "sell" the prospective salesperson on joining the firm. In reality, top salespeople are hard to find, and the competition for them is intense. Therefore, a sales manager should enthusiastically pursue the candidate once the offer is extended. As always, an accurate portrayal of the job is a must.

In addition to standard enticements, such as salary, performance bonuses, company car, and fringe benefits, certain extra incentives are sometimes offered to prospective salespeople. Bonuses for relocation are one type of incentive, especially with today's sentiment for less mobile lifestyles. Another is the **market bonus** paid on hiring to salespeople having highly sought-after skills and qualifications. This one-time payment recognizes an existing imbalance in supply and demand in a given labor market. Using a market bonus could be a reasonable alternative if the supply-demand imbalance is thought to be temporary because the bonus is a one-time payment and not a permanent addition to base compensation. For instance, IBM offered some high-tech sales reps who were in high demand as much as $50,000 to join its organization.[43]

The offer of employment should be written but can be initially extended in verbal form. Any final contingencies, such as passing a physical examination, should be detailed in the offer letter. Candidates not receiving a job offer should be notified in a prompt, courteous manner. A specific reason for not hiring a candidate need not be given. A simple statement that an individual who better suits the needs of the company has been hired is sufficient.

Legal and Ethical Considerations in Recruitment and Selection

Key Legislation

The possibility of illegal discrimination permeates the recruitment and selection process, and a basic understanding of pertinent legislation can be beneficial to the sales manager. Some of the most important legislation is summarized in Exhibit 6.6. The legislative acts featured in Exhibit 6.6 are federal laws, applicable to all firms engaged in interstate commerce. Companies not engaging in interstate commerce are often subject to state and local laws that are similar to these federal laws.

EXHIBIT 6.6 Legislation Affecting Recruitment and Selection

Legislative Act	Purpose
Fifth and Fourteenth Amendments to the U.S. Constitution	Provides equal protection standards to prevent irrational or unreasonable selection methods.
Equal Pay Act (1963)	Requires that men and women be paid the same amount for performing similar job duties.
Civil Rights Act (1964)	Prohibits discrimination based on age, race, color, religion, sex, or national origin.
Age Discrimination in Employment Act (1967)	Prohibits discrimination against people of ages 40 to 70.
Fair Employment Opportunity Act (1972)	Founded the Equal Employment Opportunity Commission to ensure compliance with the Civil Rights Act.
Rehabilitation Act (1973)	Requires affirmative action to hire and promote handicapped persons if the firm employs 50 or more employees and is seeking a federal contract in excess of $50,000.
Vietnam Veterans Readjustment Act (1974)	Requires affirmative action to hire Vietnam veterans and disabled veterans of any war. Applicable to firms holding federal contracts in excess of $10,000.
Americans with Disabilities Act (1990)	Prohibits discrimination against qualified disabled people in all areas of employment. Prohibits the use of employment tests, qualification standards, and selection criteria that tend to screen out individuals with disabilities unless the standard is job related or consistent with business necessity.
Civil Rights Act (1991)	Prohibits employers from adjusting scores of, using different cutoff scores for, or otherwise altering the results of employment-related tests on the basis of race, color, religion, sex, or national origin.
Amendment to Fair Credit Reporting Act (1997)	When seeking background information from a reporting service company, employers must inform job applicants or employees in writing that a report on them will be procured and must obtain their signature authorizing the move.

Guidelines for Sales Managers

The legislation reviewed in Exhibit 6.6 is supported by various executive orders and guidelines that make it clear that sales managers, along with other hiring officials in a firm, have legal responsibilities of grave importance in the recruitment and selection process. In step 1 of the process, planning for recruitment and selection, sales managers must take care to analyze the job to be filled in an open-minded way, attempting to overcome any personal mental biases. For example, in the 1980s, many sales organizations overcame biases against women in sales positions. These organizations are practically unanimous in reporting that women have performed as well as, and in some cases better than, their male counterparts.

Job descriptions and job qualifications should be accurate and based on a thoughtful job analysis. The planning stage may also require that the sales manager consider fair employment legislation and affirmative action requirements before setting recruitment and selection objectives.

In step 2 of the process, recruitment, the sources that serve as intermediaries in the search for prospective candidates should be informed of the firm's legal position. The firm must be careful to avoid sources that limit its hiring from protected classes.[44] It is also crucial that advertising and other communications be devoid of potentially discriminatory content. For example, companies that advertise for "young, self-motivated salesmen" may be inviting an inquiry from the Equal Employment Opportunity Commission.

Finally, all selection tools must be related to job performance. Munson and Spivey summarize legal advice for selection by stating, "At each step in the selection process, it would be advisable to be as objective, quantitative, and consistent as possible, especially because present federal guidelines are concerned with all procedures suggesting employment discrimination.[45] Such advice should be considered, particularly when facing a situation similar to one found in "An Ethical Dilemma."

> **An Ethical Dilemma**
>
> *Sales manager John Brown was interviewing several candidates for a sales position with the XYZ company. After interviewing, testing, and assessing several candidates, two clearly stood out above the rest, one male and the other female. Although the male was slightly more qualified, John suspected that his male customers might enjoy the "looks" of the female and thus be more willing to give XYZ their business. What should John do? Explain.*

To more fully appreciate the sensitivity necessary in these matters, consider the following list of potentially troublesome information often found on employment applications.[46]

- age or date of birth
- length of time at present address
- height and/or weight
- marital status
- ages of children
- occupation of spouse
- relatives already employed by the firm
- person to notify in case of an emergency
- type of military discharge

Not only are these topics open to charges of discrimination, but so is a request for a photograph of the applicant, a birth certificate, or a copy of military discharge papers. Further questions to avoid are those concerning the original name of the applicant, race or color, religion (including holidays observed), nationality or birthplace of the applicant, arrests, bankruptcy or garnishments, disabilities, handicaps and health problems, and memberships in organizations that may suggest race, religion, color, or ancestral origin of the applicant.

Ethical Issues

Two ethical issues of particular importance are (1) how the job to be filled is represented and (2) how interviews are conducted. **Misrepresentation** of the job does not always extend into the legal domain. For example, earnings potential may be stated in terms of what the top producer earns, not expected first-year earnings of the average salesperson. Or perhaps the opportunities for promotion are somewhat overstated but no completely false statements are used. As simple as it may sound, the best policy is a truthful policy if the sales manager wants to match the applicant to the job and avoid later problems from those recruited under false pretenses.

Some ethical issues also arise in interviewing, especially regarding the **stress interview.** This technique is designed to put job candidates under extreme, unexpected, psychological duress for the purpose of seeing how they react. A common tactic for stress interviewing in the sales field is to demand an impromptu sales presentation for a convenient item such as a ballpoint pen or an ashtray. Such requests may seem unreasonable to a professional salesperson who is accustomed to planning a presentation before delivering it. Another stress interviewing tactic is to ridicule the responses of the job candidates or to repeatedly interrupt the candidates' responses to questions before they have an adequate opportunity to provide a complete response.

Sales managers who use stress interviewing justify its use by pointing out that salespeople must be able to think on their feet and react quickly to unanticipated questions from customers. Although this is true, there would seem to be better ways of assessing a candidate's skills. The stress interview may create an unfavorable image of the company, and it may alienate some of the better candidates.[47] It appears to be a risky, and ethically questionable, approach.

Summary

1. **Explain the critical role of recruitment and selection in building and maintaining a productive salesforce.** Recruitment and selection of salespeople can be an expensive process, characterized by uncertainty and complicated by legal considerations. If the procedures are not properly conducted, a multitude of managerial problems can arise, the worst of which being that salesforce performance is suboptimal. The sales manager is the key person in the recruitment and selection process, although other managers in the hiring firm may share responsibilities for staffing the salesforce.

2. **Describe how recruitment and selection affect salesforce socialization and performance.** Socialization, the process by which salespeople adjust to their jobs, begins when the recruit is first contacted by the hiring firm. Two stages of socialization should be accomplished during recruitment and selection: achieving realism and achieving congruence. Realism means giving the recruit an accurate portrayal of the job. Congruence refers to the matching process that should occur between the needs of the organization and the capabilities of the recruit. If realism and congruence can be accomplished, future job satisfaction, involvement, commitment, and performance should be improved. These relationships are shown in a model of the socialization process in Figure 6.1.

3. **Identify the key activities in planning and executing a program for salesforce recruitment and selection.** Figure 6.2 depicts a model of the recruitment and selection process. There are three steps in the process: planning, recruitment, and selection. *Planning* consists of conducting a job analysis, determining job qualifications, writing a job description, setting objectives, and formulating a strategy. *Recruitment* involves locating prospective job candidates from one or more sources within or outside the hiring firm. The third step, *selection,* entails an evaluation of the candidates culminating in a hiring decision. Major methods of evaluating candidates include resume and job-application analysis, interviews, tests, assessment centers, background investigations, and physical examinations.

4. **Discuss the legal and ethical considerations in salesforce recruitment and selection.** Every step of the recruitment and selection process has the potential to discriminate illegally against some job candidates. Federal laws and guidelines provide the basic antidiscriminatory framework, and state and local statutes may also be applicable. The most important legislation that applies are the Civil Rights Act and the Fair Employment Opportunity Act. Two primary ethical concerns are (1) misrepresentation of the job to be filled and (2) using stress interviews in the selection stage.

Understanding Sales Management Terms

- Salesforce socialization
- Achieving realism
- Achieving congruence
- Private employment agency
- Job fairs
- Computerized matchmaking

- Job preview
- Planning activities
- Recruitment
- Selection
- Job analysis
- Job qualifications
- Job description
- Recruitment and selection strategy
- Employee referral programs
- Job application form
- Initial interviews
- Intensive interviews
- Interviewer bias
- Assessment center
- Background investigation
- Market bonus
- Misrepresentation
- Stress interview

Developing Sales Management Knowledge

1. What are some of the problems associated with improperly executed recruitment and selection activities?
2. To enhance salesforce socialization, recruitment and selection should ensure realism and congruence. How can this be accomplished?
3. Refer to Sales Management in the 21st Century: Finding a Fit at Hershey Chocolate." What are important factors for achieving congruence at Hershey?
4. Describe the relationship between conducting a job analysis, determining job qualifications, and completing a written job description.
5. Refer to "Sales Management in the 21st Century: Key Job Qualifications at Hershey Chocolate." What is the relationship between job qualifications and a company's personal selling approach?
6. What are the advantages of using employee referral programs to recruit salespeople? Can you identify some disadvantages?
7. How can private employment agencies assist in the recruitment and selection of salespeople? Who pays the fee charged by such agencies, the hiring company or the job candidate?
8. What can be learned about a job candidate from analyzing a job application that cannot be learned from the candidate's resume?
9. Summarize the primary legislation designed to prohibit illegal discrimination in the recruitment and selection process.
10. What is stress interviewing? How do some sales managers justify using stress interviews?

Building Sales Management Skills

1. Find three different advertisements for sales positions (one from a newspaper, one from a trade magazine, and one from the Internet). After examining each ad, list the job qualifications for the position being advertised. Then, develop a job description based on the ad's contents. Finally, using Exhibit 6.4 as a guide, provide your suggestions for improving each ad.
2. Find job qualifications and a position description for a sales position at a company of your choice. Design a series of questions that you could use as a guide to interview a candidate for this position. Now, find a classmate who also has found job qualifications and a position description for a sales position, and swap this information with him or her. Using your interview guide, take turns interviewing each other. (The information you swapped with your classmate serves as a guide for the interviewee.) Record your interview on audiotape or videotape. Finally, listen to or view your tape and write a critique of your interview, explaining what went well and what did not.
3. The World Wide Web is filled with many sites that could be beneficial in the recruitment and selection process. One site that has been designed to make getting around in cyberspace easier for human resource development professionals is WorkIndex (www.workindex.com). Access this site; then go to the "search" line and type in "recruitment." This will provide you with several sites that could be useful in the recruitment and selection process. Explore some of these sites, and then choose three that you believe would be helpful to a sales manager involved in recruitment and selection. First, provide each site address. Second, provide a description of each site. Finally, explain how each site or the information it contains could be useful in the recruitment and selection process.

Making Sales Management Decisions

CASE 6.1   Sweet-Treats, Inc.

Background

Sweet-Treats, Inc., one of the leading manufacturers and marketers of chocolate and cocoa products, has several plants located throughout the United States. Its products can be divided into two major categories: confectionery products, which include several brands of candy bars and assorted candy treats, and grocery products, such as cocoa, syrup, and baking chips. In the United States, Sweet-Treats' products are distributed through a network of strategically located warehouses, with volume customers receiving direct shipment from the manufacturing plants. The method of shipment and warehousing is determined by customer location and quantity ordered.

Sweet-Treats uses a field sales organization to sell products to retailers and wholesalers nationwide. Its overriding goals are to distribute a high-quality product and to provide optimum consumer value. To ensure that these goals are met, the company hires salespeople who possess outstanding planning and organizing skills, have the ability to lead, are persuasive, show initiative, and possess strong communication skills, including the ability to write, speak, and listen.

At Sweet-Treats, salespeople represent the company and carry its image. A crucial responsibility, this calls for salespeople to be consummate professionals. Major responsibilities of the salesperson include selling and maintaining distribution of all products, ensuring the salability of all Sweet-Treat items in an assigned territory, implementing promotional programs, introducing new items, and presenting proper merchandising techniques to both headquarter and retail accounts. In addition, salespeople must act as "sales consultants" to customers. This involves maintaining good customer rapport while developing accounts in an assigned territory. Salespeople work with their sales managers and team members to achieve specific sales and merchandising objectives.

Current Situation

Sweet-Treats' Kansas City district sales manger, Rob Gum, recently lost one of his top-performing salespeople, Arlene Oellermann, who left for a sudden career change. Although other salespeople in his district are covering Arlene's accounts, Rob fears that an extended absence will make it difficult on these salespeople and may affect the quality of service they provide to their accounts as well as to Arlene's.

Rob is presently undergoing an intensive search to locate Arlene's replacement. He placed a classified ad in the local newspaper, the *Kansas City Star*. In addition, he contacted the career placement offices of local colleges and universities to see whether they had any leads on potential candidates. Through these efforts, Rob received several resumes. After examining the resumes, Rob decided to interview two candidates. What follows are excerpts from those interviews:

Excerpts from an interview with Christine Pirrone who is currently a sales rep with an industrial products company in the Kansas City area and who has 3 years of sales experience.

Rob: Why did you get into sales?

Christine: I chose sales as a career for several reasons. First, I like dealing with other people and helping them to solve their problems. I view sales as a way to accomplish this. Second, sales provides me with a certain level of independence. I am self-motivated so I like being able to get things accomplished without being closely supervised. Third, there is decent money to be made in sales. I might as well get my share of the pie.

Rob: In general, how do you get things accomplished?

Christine: Simple, planning. I set certain goals for each day. Then I plan how I will achieve them. Planning helps me to stay organized, and I feel that by being organized I am able to accomplish many things.

Rob: This position requires some degree of travel. How do you feel about that?

Christine: Currently I travel quite extensively. I enjoy the travel, so it would not bother me.

Rob: Have you ever organized a group?

Christine: Yes. When I was a junior in college I started a new organization on campus, the Entrepreneurship Club. I was the organization's president for 2 years. When I graduated we had more than 40 members. I was very proud! I am currently a member of several civic groups, although I did not organize any of these.

Excerpts from an interview with Joe Stein who is from Minnesota, but just received his B.S.B.A. from a local university with a 3.8 (4.0 scale) G.P.A. His major was marketing.

Rob: Why do you want a career in sales?

Joe: I think sales is a very flexible job. You basically manage your own time, and I like the idea of this. Also, it is more exciting than sitting behind a desk. You get to meet and interact with people. Also, I understand that there is a fair amount of money to be made in sales.

Rob: In general, how do you get things accomplished?

Joe: I've found that the best way to get things done is to jump right in and tackle them. Take the bull by the horns, so to speak. Procrastinating only makes things worse.

Rob: This position requires some degree of travel. How do you feel about that?

Joe: I traveled a lot with the track team in college. I also travel back to Minnesota quite frequently to visit family and friends. I don't think the travel will bother me.

Rob: Have you ever organized a group?

Joe: In college, we worked in several groups. Sometimes I was the group leader, but I always tried to carry my load. I was also a member of the American Marketing Association.

Rob decided that additional searching at this point might not prove worthwhile. With his salespeople getting restless, he decided he would make a decision between Christine and Joe and make one an offer.

Questions

1. Based on the information you have about Christine and Joe, how do they stack up against Sweet-Treats' job qualifications?
2. Who should Rob hire and why? Explain.
3. How could Rob improve his recruiting and selecting process? Explain.
4. What key concepts of salesforce socialization are related to this situation? Explain.

CASE 6.2 *Titan Industries*

Background

Titan Industries manufactures and markets industrial equipment throughout the United States. In 1999, Titan did more than $2 billion in sales and appeared to be in an upward growth trend. The company has grown considerably since its inception in 1964. Founder and CEO Carman Pulte is proud of the progress the company has achieved over the years, despite considerable aggressive competition. He attributes much of Titan's success to his management team, most of whom have been with him since the company's founding.

David Winston had been vice president of sales and marketing at Titan since 1968. Two months ago, he retired and was replaced by Duane Blankenship. Blankenship had been in product design and engineering at Titan since 1979. Well-educated, articulate, and likable, Blankenship was believed to be the best candidate for the position.

Blankenship, a very methodical individual, set as his first task an assessment of the marketing program. One of the main things concerning him was the composition of the salesforce. In particular, he was concerned about two items. First, the salesforce was aging, with the average age being 51. Several salespeople were nearing retirement. Only a small percentage were in their twenties or thirties. Second, he noticed that the salesforce did not include any minorities or women. Blankenship scheduled a meeting to discuss these issues with Titan's national sales manager, Tommy Angotti.

Angotti loves his job. He has been with Titan for nearly 25 years. He began as a salesperson and worked his way up to national sales manager. Surprisingly, many of his salespeople have been with the company for 20 years or more. Angotti takes pride in the accomplishments of his salesforce. He believes they have been instrumental in Titan's growth over the years.

Current Situation

At their scheduled meeting, Blankenship explained to Angotti his ideas concerning the composition of the salesforce. The following are excerpts from their meeting:

Angotti: I realize we will have several salespeople soon retiring, but could you explain why it is necessary to hire women and minorities to replace these individuals?

Blankenship: Many of the companies we sell equipment to are now being closely monitored and regulated by federal and state governments. Several companies in our industry have recently come under attack from the Equal Employment Opportunity Commission. The commission is putting pressure on these companies to hire women and minorities. It is only a matter of time before they take aim at us. We need to get women and minorities into the salesforce so that they can eventually work their way up into management positions.

Angotti: I can't imagine a woman going into the field trying to sell a large piece of industrial equipment. How seriously do you think a woman will be taken in this business? Not very, I can assure you. Our customers want to speak to someone who really understands how this equipment operates.

Blankenship: Women can learn to sell our equipment. Just because they may not operate it doesn't mean they can't understand how it works. As a matter of fact, a few months ago a woman was involved in selling us a piece of manufacturing equipment for our operations. She did an outstanding job.

Angotti: Maybe so. However, when we hire a replacement, we try to find the best person for the job. As a result, I believe we currently have some of the best salespeople in the business.

Blankenship: Unfortunately, that person always seems to be a white male. There are plenty of intelligent and motivated women and minorities graduating from business schools today who are capable of performing the job. Regardless of governmental threats, it is still the right thing to do, and the profitable one. I would like to see us take a leadership role in this area in our industry and begin to make an effort to hire women and minorities.

Angotti was not convinced. He was very concerned that minorities, and women in particular, would not be positively accepted by buyers. The industrial equipment business is largely male dominated. This, in turn, could have a negative impact on sales. Moreover, given that much of his salesforce was composed of "old-timers," he was concerned about how hiring these groups might affect salesforce morale.

Turnover in the salesforce was relatively low. Thus, specific hiring procedures were not well developed. Angotti decided he would recruit women and minorities to appease Blankenship but would develop an entrance test that would be difficult for women and minorities to pass. This way he could actively recruit women and minorities but tell Blankenship they did not qualify because they did not pass the entrance test. Angotti was only a few years from retirement and was unwilling to change his current practices at this juncture, particularly in light of the success his salesforce had experienced over the years.

Questions

1. Should Blankenship be concerned about the present composition of the salesforce? Explain.
2. How do you evaluate Angotti's method for dealing with the salesforce composition issue?
3. What steps could be taken to effectively bring about a salesforce comprised of more women and minorities?

MODULE 7

Continual Development of the Salesforce: Sales Training

Training Wheels: How Raleigh USA Bicycle Company Peddled Its Way to Success

Facing strong competition from mass-market sporting goods dealers, independent bike dealers are looking for salespeople who can help them grow their business. Enter Joe Shannon, director of national sales for Raleigh USA Bicycle Company. When he joined the company in 1997, he realized that to help Raleigh's customer base grow he needed to make his salespeople the best and most consultative salespeople to walk through a dealer's door. Because Raleigh sells primarily to independent bike dealers, Shannon believes his salespeople not only must possess product knowledge but also must know something about accounting and inventory so that they can help customers run their businesses better. According to Shannon, the goal is to "create a value-added partnership between ourselves and our dealers."

To accomplish this goal, Shannon determined that his 31 field salespeople and 10 inside reps needed training. First, he determined his training goals. Topping the list was the need to form a base of understanding and dialog between salespeople and customers to allow salespeople to develop a more consultative selling approach. Second, he determined that an outside trainer should be used because of the many other responsibilities demanding his attention as a new manager. Shannon went through the process of interviewing several training firms before choosing STI International, a sales training institute based in Bellevue, Washington. Besides having a good curriculum, STI was chosen because it was local, which would allow follow-up training, and Shannon believed that its trainer, Conrad Elnes, STI's chairman, would relate well to his salesforce.

In March 1998, STI's Elnes began working with Raleigh's three regional sales managers. Together they identified 12 areas in which reps could improve (e.g., resolving dealer objections) and incorporated Raleigh-centric examples into the lesson plan. Elnes then conducted regional training seminars for Raleigh's reps. In June and September, Elnes returned to Raleigh's headquarters to conduct day-long follow-up sessions to review the skills he had taught, offer feedback, and introduce new techniques.

The training appears to have achieved its goals. According to one of Raleigh's top reps, Herb Hart, who has 18 years of sales experience, "When we came out of the training, as a company we were more focused." Hart believes the training taught him to listen to the needs of his dealers better and ask more qualifying questions. Since the training began, Raleigh has doubled its number of dealers and increased

Learning Objectives

After completing this module, you should be able to

1 Understand the role of sales training in salesforce socialization.

2 Explain the importance of sales training and the sales manager's role in sales training.

3 Describe the sales training process as a series of six interrelated steps.

4 Discuss six methods for assessing sales training needs and identify typical sales training needs.

5 Name some typical objectives of sales training programs, and explain how setting objectives for sales training is beneficial to sales managers.

6 Identify the key issues in evaluating sales training alternatives.

7 Identify key ethical and legal issues in sales training.

sales 35 percent during a period in which industry growth was 3 percent or less. Shannon credits sales increases to the training. "Nothing has really changed in terms of how good our bikes are," he explains. "They [salespeople] took what they learned and applied it. Our dealers are sensing that there's a new salesforce walking through their doors."

Source: Erika Rasmusson "Getting Schooled in Outsourcing," *Sales & Marketing Management* 151 (January 1999): 48–53.

As the opening vignette illustrates, companies often believe sales training is the key to success. Raleigh believes its people determine its success and is willing to invest considerable time and money in developing its salesforce. As illustrated at Raleigh, sales training can be outsourced when it is believed that doing so will lead to more effective sales management. Another important point illustrated in the vignette is that training is an ongoing process that continues beyond the initial training period. Moreover, training must be evaluated to ensure its effectiveness.

Today's salespeople must be prepared to meet the demands of value-conscious customers. Salespeople must do their part by providing solutions to problems and meeting service requirements expected to satisfy customer needs. Proper training can prepare salespeople to meet these challenges.

In this module several training issues and methods are discussed. First, the role of sales training in salesforce socialization is examined. Then the importance of sales training is considered and management of the sales training process is discussed.

Role of Sales Training in Salesforce Socialization

Recall from Module 6 that salesforce *socialization* refers to the process by which salespeople acquire the knowledge, skills, and values essential to perform their jobs. Training plays a key role in this process. Newly hired salespeople usually receive a company orientation designed to familiarize them with company history, policies, facilities, procedures, and key people with whom salespeople interact. Some firms go well beyond a perfunctory company orientation in an effort to enhance salesforce socialization. By referring to Figure 6.1 in Module 6, you can see how sales training can affect salesforce socialization. During initial sales training, it is hoped that each salesforce member will experience a positive **initiation to task**—the degree to which a sales trainee feels competent and accepted as a working partner—and satisfactory **role definition**—an understanding of what tasks are to be performed, what the priorities of the tasks are, and how time should be allocated among the tasks.[1]

The need for socialization as part of the training process is supported by expected indirect linkages between socialization and beneficial job outcomes. As suggested in Figure 6.1, trainees who have been properly recruited and trained tend to be more confident on the job and have fewer problems with job conflicts, leading to higher job satisfaction, involvement, commitment, and performance.

The positive relationships between salespeople's job-related attitudes and perceptions and their commitment to their companies have been supported in empirical studies. For example, a study of 102 salespeople in the food industry found that "among approaches within a company's control, programs aimed at minimizing new salespeople's role ambiguity and improving their satisfaction are most likely to be most effective in building commitment to the company."[2] Another study of 120 manufacturers' salespeople found a positive relationship between job satisfaction and salespeople's commitment to the organization.[3] In addition, a study of 301 industrial salespeople found that when salespeople believe the company is taking certain actions to support the salesforce and reduce the difficulties associated with a sales position, they are more committed to and satisfied with the job.[4] These studies reinforce the importance of sales managers taking an active role in socializing their salespeople to maximize overall salesforce productivity.

Newly hired salespeople should be extremely interested in learning about their jobs, peers, and supervisors. A basic orientation may be insufficient to provide all the information they desire, so more extensive socialization may be indicated. At Federated Insurance, trainees participate in a 2-week seminar that introduces them to the company's products, the corporate mission, the Federated business plan, functions and departments within the company, and many of the support people with whom they will work.[5]

The need for salesforce socialization is especially likely to extend past the initial training period. This is particularly true if salesforce members have limited personal contact with peers, managers, and other company personnel.

Sales Training as a Crucial Investment

A comprehensive review of sales management research concludes that whom one recruits is important but it is probably not as important in determining salesforce performance as what sales managers do with the recruits—and to the recruits—after they have been hired.[6]

The importance of sales training in achieving the highest levels of sales performance is shown in *Sales and Marketing Management* magazine's annual survey of the best salesforces in the United States. The accounts of sales successes for the top salesforces often reveal that the winning salesforces had to adapt to changes in marketing and sales strategies. This obviously requires some degree of salesforce training or retraining. The value of sales training is apparent at Intel and Nabisco. Intel contributes increases in sales from its highly ranked salesforce to its heavy investment in sales training.[7] At Nabisco, an extensive return-on-investment analysis of its "Professional Selling Program" found its sales training resulted in a 122-1 sales increase and a 20-1 increase in corporate profits. Furthermore, its investment in training resulted in improved morale, reduced turnover, a spirit of teamwork, and improved customer satisfaction.[8]

Most organizations have a need for sales training of some type. This enduring need exists in part because of inadequacies of current training programs and in part because new salespeople join the organization on a regular basis.

Thus, an ongoing need exists to conduct sales training to improve salesforce performance. It should be stressed that the need for sales training is continual, if for no other reason than that the sales environment is constantly changing. One survey found that managers believe salespeople should attend at least one training course per quarter.[9]

Companies view training as an important means for protecting their investments in their salesforces.[10] U.S. companies spend approximately $7.1 billion annually to provide salespeople with training and devote more than 33 hours per year to the average salesperson.[11] Because salespeople are so vital to its business, reps at Lands' End receive 80 hours of training initially, and they receive an additional 3 hours each month in areas such as product knowledge, new systems, and customer service.[12]

EXHIBIT 7.1 Time and Money Investments in Sales Training

	Training Period for New Hires (Months)	Cost per Salesperson	Ongoing Training (Hours per Year)	Cost per Salesperson
Company Size				
Less than $5 million	4.4	$5,500	30.1	$3,752
$5 million–$24.9 million	4.2	8,141	36.1	3,947
$25 million–$99.9 million	3.7	8,091	31.0	3,902
$100 million–$249.9 million	1.7	7,400	25.2	5,365
More than $250 million	3.6	7,000	38.0	4,824
Type of Sales				
Consumer products	3.4	5,354	35.8	4,039
Consumer services	3.3	4,537	33.9	3,623
Industrial products	4.8	9,894	31.6	5,149
Industrial services	4.8	9,061	30.8	4,867
Office products	3.8	6,269	41.8	4,261
Office services	3.2	6,200	33.3	3,470

Note: Time and costs are averages.

Time and money invested in sales training are considerable. Each year, salespeople receive roughly 164 million hours of training, about 37 hours per salesperson, ranking them first in average number of training hours per year among all professional and managerial groups.[13] As Exhibit 7.1 shows, costs and time vary depending on the size of the organization, the types of sales, and the experience of the salesperson.

One aspect of the investment in sales training is the amount of time required of the sales manager. Usually, sales managers are involved not only in the "big picture" of planning but also in the time-consuming details of implementing training, such as the following:[14]

- Arranging for salespeople to work with key personnel in various departments in the firm to familiarize them with the functions of those departments
- Selecting literature, sales aids, and materials for study
- Enrolling salespeople in professional workshops
- Accompanying salespeople in the field to critique their sales behavior and reinforce other training
- Conducting periodic training meetings and professional training conferences

Sales training is indeed expensive, and sales managers should take special care to see that time and money are wisely spent. With these thoughts in mind, let's examine a model for the judicious analysis, planning, and implementation of a sales training program.

Managing the Sales Training Process

The sales training process is depicted as six interrelated steps in Figure 7.1: assess training needs, set training objectives, evaluate training alternatives, design the sales training program, perform sales training, and conduct follow-up and evaluation.

FIGURE 7.1 Sales Training Process

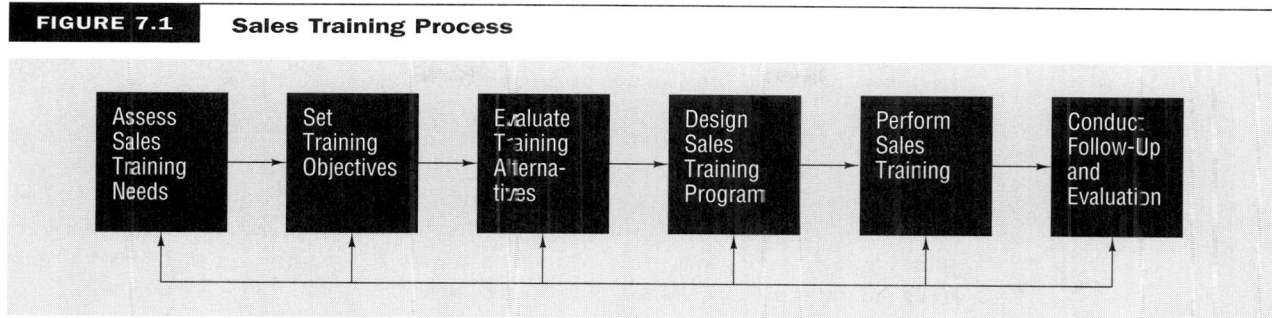

The sales training process is performed in six steps, beginning with an assessment of training needs. The process is continual, with the follow-up and evaluation step providing feedback that may alter the other steps in future sales training activities.

Assess Training Needs

The purpose of sales training **needs assessment** is to compare the specific performance-related skills, attitudes, perceptions, and behaviors required for salesforce success with the state of readiness of the salesforce. Such an assessment usually reveals a need for changing or reinforcing one or more determinants of salesforce performance.

All too often, the need for sales training becomes apparent only after a decline in salesforce performance is revealed by decreasing sales volume, rising expenses, or perhaps low morale. Sales training for correcting such problems is sometimes necessary, but the preferred role of sales training is to prevent problems and improve salesforce productivity on a proactive, not reactive, basis.

Needs assessment requires that sales managers consider the training appropriate for both *sales trainees* and regular salespeople. A sales trainee is an entry-level salesperson who is learning the company's products, services, and policies in preparation for a regular sales assignment. For example, entry-level salespeople may need basic training in sales techniques, whereas experienced salespeople could benefit from training in advanced sales techniques. In addition, the training needs of selling teams must be considered. For a comment on teamwork and sales training at Automatic Data Processing (ADP), which ranked second in *Sales & Marketing Management Magazine*'s ranking of top sales forces in 1997, see "Sales Management in the 21st Century: Team Training at ADP."

SALES MANAGEMENT IN THE 21ST CENTURY

Team Training at ADP

Sandy Apple, sales manager at ADP, comments on team training:

At ADP, having a well-trained, highly motivated sales force is crucial to our overall success. ADP places a tremendous emphasis on training from the moment a salesperson is hired. Training encompasses some self-study and may be computer based; however, most training is conducted on a group level with focus on product knowledge, marketplace, and selling skills. Training is mostly interactive, often with a district manager cofacilitating. Role playing is a big part of most training sessions. When training is conducted within the whole team, trainees learn new techniques from each other and become more supportive of one another's and the team's goals. The greater the individual involvement in training, the greater the understanding and implementation in the field.

METHODS OF NEEDS ASSESSMENT Proactive approaches to determining sales training needs include a salesforce audit, performance testing, observation, a salesforce survey, a customer survey, and a job analysis.

Salesforce Audit A **salesforce audit** is "a systematic, diagnostic, prescriptive tool which can be employed on a periodic basis to identify and address sales department problems and to prevent or reduce the impact of future problems."[15] The salesforce audit (discussed fully in Module 10) includes an appraisal of all salesforce activities and the environment in which the salesforce operates. In the sales training area, the audit examines such questions as follow:

- Is the training program adequate in light of objectives and resources?
- Does the training program need revision?
- Is an ongoing training program available for senior salespeople?
- Does the training program positively contribute to the socialization of sales trainees?

To be effective, a salesforce audit should be conducted annually. More frequent audits may be warranted in some situations, but the comprehensive nature of an audit requires a considerable time and money investment. As a result, other periodic assessments of sales training are suggested.

Performance Testing Some firms use **performance testing** to help determine training needs. This method specifies the evaluation of particular tasks or skills of the salesforce. For example, salespeople may be given periodic examinations on product knowledge to check retention rates and uncover areas for retraining. Salespeople may be asked to exhibit particular sales techniques, such as demonstrating the product or using the telephone to set up sales appointments while the sales trainer evaluates their performance.

Observation First-level sales managers spend a considerable amount of time in the field working with salespeople. They also may have direct responsibility for some accounts, acting as a salesperson or as a member of a sales team. Through these field selling activities, sales managers often **observe** the need for particular sales training. In some instances, the training need is addressed instantaneously by critiquing the salesperson's performance after the sales call has been completed. In other situations, frequent observation of particularly deficient or outstanding sales behavior may suggest future training topics.

Salesforce Survey The salesforce may be surveyed in an attempt to isolate sales training needs. Such a **salesforce survey** may be completed as an independent activity or combined with other sales management activities such as field visits or even included as part of the routine salesforce reporting procedures. The weekly reports submitted by many salespeople to their sales managers often have sections dealing with problems to be solved and areas in which managerial assistance is requested. For example, a faltering new-product introduction may signal the need for more product training, additional sales technique sharpening, or perhaps training needs specific to an individual salesperson.

By surveying the salesforce, the task of assessing training needs may become more complex than if sales management alone determines training needs. To ignore the salesforce in this step of the training process, however, could be a serious sin of omission. For example, Lucent Technologies conducted phone interviews, lasting 3 to 4 hours each, with all 2,400 of its reps to determine their experience, skills, and knowledge. Salespeople were then each assigned a training program to fit their needs.[16] If sales managers and their salespeople should disagree on training needs, it is far better to discover this disagreement and resolve it before designing and delivering specific sales training programs.

Customer Survey Intended to define customer expectations, a **customer survey** helps determine how competitive the salesforce is compared with other salesforces in the industry. If personal selling is prominent in the firm's marketing strategy, some sort of customer survey to help determine sales training needs is highly recommended. At 3M, salespeople provide their customers with a questionnaire used to assess their selling skills in six key areas and the importance of these skills to the selling relationship. It then measures the difference between performance and expectations and develops a curriculum to address deficiencies.[17] Sometimes information gathered from a customer survey may have ethical implications as seen in "An Ethical Dilemma."

> **An Ethical Dilemma**
>
> *Your salespeople have been reaching or exceeding their sales goals for the year, and your region is on pace to set a new company sales record, putting you in line for a big bonus. When conducting a recent customer survey to use as input for developing a training program, you discover that some customers are upset about promises salespeople are making but not fulfilling. Is this cause for alarm? What should you do and when?*

Job Analysis The **job analysis,** defined in Module 6, is an investigation of the task, duties, and responsibilities of the sales job. In a well-run sales organization, a job analysis will be part of the recruitment and selection process and then will continue to be used in sales training and other managerial functions. For instance, NBC bases its hiring and training goals for sales teams on a competency model it developed that describes characteristics of its ideal salespeople in 12 areas, including team orientation and communication skills.[18] Because the job analysis defines expected behavior for salespeople, it is a logical tool to be used in assessing training needs. Because sales jobs may vary within the same salesforce, job analyses may also help in determining individualized sales training needs or the needs of different groups of salespeople.

TYPICAL SALES TRAINING NEEDS As the preceding discussion implies, the need for sales training varies over time and across organizations. However, the need for salesforce training on certain topics is widespread. A discussion of some of the more popular sales training topics follows.

Sales Techniques There is a universal, ongoing need for training on "how to sell." Research has indicated that salespeople sometimes sell despite themselves; that is, many salespeople do not competently execute fundamental **sales techniques.**[19] Common mistakes identified in this research include the following:

- ineffective listening and questioning
- failure to build rapport and trust
- poor job of prospecting for new accounts
- lack of preplanning of sales calls
- reluctance to make cold calls (without an appointment)

- lack of sales strategies for different accounts
- failure to match call frequency with account potential
- spending too much time with old customers
- overcontrolling the sales call
- failure to respond to customers' needs with related benefits
- giving benefits before clarifying customers' needs
- ineffective handling of negative attitudes
- failure to effectively confirm the sale

This rather lengthy list of common shortcomings is remarkable in that proper training could erase these problems entirely. In fact, most formal sales training programs spend considerable time on sales techniques. One survey of sales trainers, sales managers, and salespeople concluded that more than 31 percent of the time spent in training programs for salespeople was dedicated to sales skills.[20]

As mentioned previously, the basic nature of sales techniques training is changing, and more emphasis is being placed on developing trusting, enduring relationships with customers. Salespeople are receiving more training on listening and questioning skills so that they may be more effective in learning the customer's needs. For example, one survey of managers found that 47 percent believe that their salespeople should receive training in consultative selling, whereas 29 percent believe training in listening skills is necessary.[21] Limited research supports the idea that effective listening skills are positively associated with sales performance and work satisfaction.[22] Furthermore, high-pressure sales techniques are declining in popularity and are being replaced with sales techniques based on need satisfaction, problem solving, and partnership forming with the customers' best interests as the focus.[23] At ACCO World Corporation, a manufacturer of office and school supplies, salespeople are trained in relationship building and negotiation.[24] A survey assessing training needs found that more than 92 percent of those responding cited training in customer relations as "very important," whereas approximately 87 percent indicated that training on methods for retaining current customers is "very important."[25] To learn how ADP trains its salespeople to build relationships, see "Sales Management in the 21st Century: Training for Relationship Building at ADP."

Product Knowledge Salespeople must have thorough **product knowledge,** including its benefits, applications, competitive strengths, and limitations. Product knowledge

---

SALES MANAGEMENT IN THE 21ST CENTURY

Training for Relationship Building at ADP

Sandy Apple, sales manager at ADP, comments on training for relationship building:

ADP salespeople are responsible for building and maintaining relationships both outside and within the organization. Training focuses on how to conduct fruitful meetings to maximize customers' and sales representatives' opportunities resulting in trust and rapport, which will be key ingredients to a mutually beneficial relationship. Relationships develop when the sales representative has a genuine interest in the "business partners'" business and provides valuable resources to them. Salespeople develop relationships with clients, prospects, accountants, and other persons in the business community for networking opportunities. It is very important for a salesperson to be trained on what each of those partners' business needs are so that a relationship can thrive. There is also a strong emphasis on building relationships between departments within the ADP organization. There are joint training sessions conducted so that each party can learn more about the other and how working together ultimately results in clients receiving "world class service." The more astute salespeople are in relationship building, the more successful they are.

may need updating in the event of new-product development, product modification, product deletions, or the development of new applications for the product.

Generally speaking, product knowledge is one of the most commonly covered topics in sales training programs. As expected, the more complex the product or service, the higher the likelihood that detailed knowledge about the offering will be stressed in the training program.

Although it is an essential requirement, adequate product knowledge will not necessarily lead to sales success. Studies have shown that product knowledge levels of high-performing salespeople are not significantly different from those of moderate performers.[26] Having product knowledge is not enough—the salesperson must know the customer and have the necessary sales skills to apply the knowledge of the product to the customer's situation.

Customer Knowledge Sales training may include information relating to customers' needs, buying motives, buying procedures, and personalities (i.e., **customer knowledge**). For example, at A+ Network, new salespeople spend 2 weeks in a training course focused exclusively on understanding customers and establishing relationships.[27] Faced with situational and individual differences among customers, some firms use classification methods to categorize buyers according to personality and the buying situation. An example of different types of buyers and suggested sales training topics is presented in Exhibit 7.2.

As companies expand their global selling efforts, training programs must address cultural differences and business protocol in foreign countries. For example, gift giving is a sensitive area because well-intentioned expressions of goodwill can backfire and instead become personal insults to a prospective customer. It is also important that salespeople are trained in intercultural communication to improve

EXHIBIT 7.2 Sales Training for Different Types of Buyers

Kind of Buyer	Sales Training Topic
1. Hard Bargainer (a difficult person to deal with)	1. Teach psychologically oriented sales strategies (e.g., transactional analysis). 2. Teach sales *negotiation* strategies (e.g., the use of different bases of power). 3. Teach listening skills and the benefits of listening to the prospect. 4. Emphasize how to handle objections. 5. Emphasize *competitive* product knowledge.
2. Sales Job Facilitator (attempts to make the sales transaction go smoothly)	1. Teach importance of a *quid pro quo*. 2. Communicate advantages of having a satisfied customer base. 3. Show how customers can assist salespeople (e.g., by pooling orders, providing leads).
3. Straight Shooter (behaves with integrity and propriety)	1. Teach importance of selling the "substance" of the product offering and not just the "sizzle." 2. Teach straightforward techniques for handling objections (e.g., a direct denial approach).
4. Socializer (enjoys personal interaction with salespeople)	1. Communicate company policy information about giving gifts and entertaining and socializing with customers. 2. Discuss ethical and legal implications of transacting business. 3. Emphasize importance of salespeople maintaining an appropriate balance between socializing with customers and performing job responsibilities.
5. Persuader (attempts to "market" his or her company)	1. Communicate importance of qualifying prospects. 2. Teach techniques for qualifying customers.
6. Considerate (shows compassion for salesperson)	1. Communicate importance of obtaining market information from customers. 2. Teach importance of a *quid pro quo*.

> **EXHIBIT 7.3** **Understanding Foreign Customers**
>
> Many selling skills that are successful in the United Sates will also work in other countries. However, one must be aware of cultural variations that can make the difference between closing a deal and losing a customer. Here is some advice for conducting business in certain countries around the world.
>
> *Arab Countries:*
>
> Don't use your left hand to hold, offer, or receive materials because Arabs use their left hands to touch toilet paper. If you must use your left hand to write, apologize for doing so.
>
> *China:*
>
> Don't refuse tea during a business discussion. Always drink it, even if you're offered a dozen cups a day.
> Printed materials presented to Chinese business leaders should be in black and white because colors have great significance for the Chinese.
> Never begin to eat or drink before your host does in China.
>
> *France:*
>
> Don't schedule a breakfast meeting—the French tend not to meet until after 10 AM.
>
> *Germany:*
>
> Don't address a business associate by his or her first name, even if you have known each other for years. Always wait for an invitation to do so.
> Breakfast meetings are unheard of here also.
>
> *Latin America:*
>
> People here don't take the clock too seriously—scheduling more than two appointments in the same day can prove disastrous.
>
> *Japan:*
>
> Don't bring up business on the golf course—always wait for your host to take the initiative.
> Don't cross your legs in Japan—showing the bottom of the foot is insulting.
>
> *Mexico:*
>
> Don't send a bouquet of red or yellow flowers as a gift—Mexicans associate those colors with evil spirits and death. Instead, send a box of premium chocolates.
>
> *Miscellaneous:*
>
> The thumbs-up gesture is considered offensive in the Middle East, rude in Australia, and a sign of "OK" in France.
> It is rude to cross your arms while facing someone in Turkey.
> In the Middle East don't ask, "How's the family?"—it is considered too personal. Also, don't show the bottom of your foot.

their chances of developing international buyer–seller relationships.[28] Insights for understanding foreign customers are provided in Exhibit 7.3.

Competitive Knowledge Salespeople must know competitive offerings in terms of strengths and weaknesses to plan sales strategy and sales presentations effectively and to be able to respond effectively to customer questions and objections. This area is extremely important for salespeople who are new to the industry because the competitor's salespeople may have years of experience and be quite knowledgeable. Furthermore, customers may exploit a salesperson's lack of **competitive**

knowledge to negotiate terms of sale that may be costly to the selling firm. For example, salespeople who are not familiar with a competitor's price structure may unnecessarily reduce their own price to make a sale, thereby sacrificing more revenue and profits than they should have.

Time and Territory Management The quest for an optimal balance between salesforce output and salesforce expenditures is a perennial objective for most sales managers. Therefore, training in **time and territory management** (TTM), introduced in Module 3, is often included in formal sales training programs. Essentially, the purpose of TTM training is to teach salespeople how to use time and efforts for maximum work efficiency.

TTM training is important for all sales organizations but especially for those in declining, stagnant, or highly competitive industries. In such situations, salespeople are often overworked, and there comes a point when working harder to improve results is not realistic. Such circumstances call for "working smarter, not harder," an idea that is receiving considerable discussion in sales management circles.[29]

Efforts to make more efficient use of time and increase salesperson productivity have been bolstered by salesforce automation. Salesforce automation can boost productivity by as much as 20 to 40 percent.[30] To do so, salespeople often need training in computer and software applications. For example, at Sebastiani Winery, 70 salespeople were trained in a 3-day crash course on PC and networking basics, Windows 95, e-mail, how to retrieve real-time data from the company's mainframe computer, and how to create custom reports and presentations. Some reps claim the training has resulted in as much as a 50 percent time savings.[31] Furthermore, as electronic data interchange (a method for transferring information electronically between selling firms and buying firms) becomes more prominent, the need for computer literacy in the salesforce will increase.[32]

Set Training Objectives

Having assessed the needs for sales training, the sales manager moves to the next step in the sales training process shown in Figure 7.1: setting specific **sales training objectives.** Because training needs vary from one sales organization to the next, so do the objectives. In general, however, one or more of the following are included:

1. Increase sales or profits.
2. Create positive attitudes and improve salesforce morale.
3. Assist in salesforce socialization.
4. Reduce role conflict and ambiguity.
5. Introduce new products, markets, and promotional programs.
6. Develop salespeople for future management positions.
7. Ensure awareness of ethical and legal responsibilities.
8. Teach administrative procedures (e.g., expense accounts, call reports).
9. Ensure competence in the use of sales and sales support tools, such as portable computers.
10. Minimize salesforce turnover rate.
11. Prepare new salespeople for assignment to a sales territory.
12. Improve teamwork and cooperative efforts.

These objectives are interrelated. For example, if salespeople gain competence in the use of a new sales tool, sales and profit may improve, salesforce morale may be positively affected, and other beneficial outcomes may occur. By setting objectives for sales training, the manager avoids the wasteful practice of training simply for training's sake. Furthermore, objectives force the sales manager to define the reasonable expectations of sales training rather than to view training as a quick-fix panacea for all the problems faced by the salesforce. Additional benefits of setting objectives for sales training are as follows:[33]

- Written objectives become a good communications vehicle to inform the salesforce and other interested parties about upcoming training.
- Top management is responsive to well-written, specific objectives and may be more willing to provide budget support for the training.
- Specific training objectives provide a standard for measuring the effectiveness of training.
- By setting objectives, the sales manager finds it easier to prioritize various training needs, and the proper sequence of training becomes more apparent.

Evaluate Training Alternatives

In the third step of the sales training process, the sales manager considers various approaches for accomplishing the objectives of training. Certainly, many more alternatives exist today than in the past, thanks to such technologies as computer-assisted instruction, videotape, and videotext. The number of sales training professionals for hire also seems to be increasing, or perhaps such trainers are just doing a better job of promoting their services. Even a casual examination of a typical shopping mall bookstore will reveal a number of titles related to building sales skills, along with audiotapes and videotapes on the subject.

Critiquing all these alternatives is a monumental job, so it is recommended that fairly stringent criteria, including cost, location of the training, flexibility of prepackaged materials, opportunity for reinforcement training, and time required to implement an alternative, be established for preliminary screening.

The evaluation of alternatives for training inevitably leads to three key questions. First, who will conduct the training? An answer to this question will require the consideration of internal (within the company) and external (outside the company) trainers. The second question deals with location for the training. Sales training may be conducted in the field, in the office, at a central training location, at hotels and conference centers, or at other locations. The third question is which method (or methods) and media are best suited for conducting the training?

SELECTING SALES TRAINERS In general, companies rely most heavily on their own personnel to conduct sales training. In this endeavor, the sales manager is the most important **sales trainer.** Senior salespeople are also often involved as trainers. For example, Landis & Staefa, a manufacturer of building management systems, often pulls top reps from the field to facilitate training classes.[34] In larger companies, a full-time sales trainer is often available. According to surveys of training practices, only a small percentage of firms use outside training consultants, and these are primarily larger firms. The training staff is most often responsible for conducting training in large companies, whereas in small companies, the sales manager is most likely to conduct sales training.[35]

What factors lead to the dominance of internal sources in sales training? First, and perhaps most important, sales managers and senior salespeople are intimately aware of job requirements and can communicate in very specific terms to the sales trainee. However, outside consultants may be only superficially informed about a specific sales job and often offer generic sales training packages. Second, sales man-

EXHIBIT 7.4 Choosing an Outside Training Program

Several training organizations, such as the Corvey Leadership Center, the Center for Creative Leadership, Decker Communications, and the American Society of Training and Development, provide their input on what makes a useful training program.

1. The program should make it easy to master content by lessening the participant's struggle to learn new skills and knowledge and change old work habits. Content and delivery must consider the skill level, education level, and learning style of participants.
2. The program should anticipate and deal with obstacles to long-term behavior modification. It should motivate participants to drop old habits, adopt new skills, and desire continued training.
3. The program's content should be limited to what has been shown to help participants most on the job.
4. The program's development and delivery should stay within the constraints of time, money, logistics, and repeatability. Only technology that enhances training should be used.
5. Participants should be actively involved in the program to preserve the excitement that comes from self-development.
6. The trainer must clearly understand the program's objectives, as well as the concepts, behaviors, and attitudes to be acquired by participants.
7. When appropriate, the program should accommodate group dynamics and promote a sense of group membership and shared purpose.

---

agers are the logical source for training to be conducted in the field, where valuable learning can occur with each sales call. It is extremely difficult to turn field training over to external trainers. Finally, using internal trainers simplifies control and coordination tasks. It is easier to control the content of the program, coordinate training for maximum impact, and provide continuity for the program when it is the sales manager who does the training or who designates other company personnel to do the training.

At some point, a sales manager's effectiveness may be improved by using external trainers. Internal resources, including time, expertise, facilities, and personnel, may be insufficient to accomplish the objectives of the sales training program. Also, outside trainers might be looked to for new ideas and methods. Large training firms such as The Forum Corporation, U.S. Learning Inc., and Learning International often customize their generic programs for use within specific companies. Exhibit 7.4 outlines attributes to consider when shopping for an outside training program.

SELECTING SALES TRAINING LOCATIONS Most sales training is conducted in home, regional, or field offices of the sales organization. Manufacturing plants are also popular training sites, and some firms use noncompany sites such as hotels or conference centers to conduct training.

Central training facilities are another possibility, used extensively by Noxell Corporation, Xerox, IBM, General Electric, Armstrong World Industries, and scores of other large firms. One of the largest training facilities in the country is Xerox Document University, located on the banks of the Potomac River in Leesburg, Virginia. At this facility, trainees stay in dormlike confines while being indoctrinated into the company. Xerox offers a training program that focuses on understanding the thought processes of buyers. Salespeople learn a seven-stage process that teaches them how to match their actions to buyers' needs.[36]

As video broadcasting and teleconferencing become more prevalent, many firms are enjoying some of the benefits of a centralized training facility without incurring the travel costs and lost time to transport the salesforce to and from training. Field offices arrange for video hook-up, either in-house or at video-equipped conference hotels, and trainees across the country share simultaneously in training emanating from a central location. RE/MAX uses a satellite television network to offer agents 800 different training sessions that cover such topics as effective communication and sales skills.[37]

SELECTING SALES TRAINING METHODS A variety of methods can be selected to fit the training situation. Indeed, the use of multiple methods is encouraged over the course of a training program to help maintain trainee attention and enhance learning. There are four categories of training methods: classroom/conference, on-the-job, behavioral simulations, and absorption.

Classroom/Conference Training The **classroom** or **conference** setting features lectures, demonstrations, and group discussion with expert trainers serving as instructors. This method is often used for training on basic product knowledge, new-product introductions, administrative procedures, and legal and ethical issues in personal selling. The format often resembles a college classroom, with regularly scheduled examinations and overnight homework assignments. In addition to using internal facilities and personnel, some companies send their salespeople to seminars sponsored by the American Management Association, American Marketing Association, Sales and Marketing Executives International, and local colleges and universities. These organizations offer training on practically any phase of selling and sales management.

On-the-Job Training In the final analysis, salespeople can be taught only so much about selling without actually experiencing it. Consequently, **on-the-job training (OJT)** is extremely important and is the most prevalent method of training salespeople.[38] OJT puts the trainee into actual work circumstances under the observant (it is hoped) eye of a supportive **mentor** or sales manager. Other OJT methods approximate a "sink or swim" philosophy and often produce disastrous results when the trainee is overwhelmed with unfamiliar job requirements.

Mentors have different objectives from company to company, but they usually strive to make the new hires feel at home in their jobs, relay information about the corporate culture, and be available for discussion and advice on topics of concern to the trainee. Coworker mentoring is popular among salesforces, and in some companies, the sales manager serves as the mentor. At GE Capital, which has one of the top-ranked salesforces in the country, junior sales reps are assigned to senior sales reps as a way of mentoring. Besides providing junior reps with guidance, it offers senior reps a chance to develop leadership skills.[39] The mentoring concept is yet another way that companies are striving to improve salesforce socialization, especially the role definition and initiation-to-task steps explained earlier in this module.

Other than working with a senior salesperson or a mentor, common OJT assignments include the trainee's filling in for a vacationing salesperson, working with a sales manager who acts as a "coach," and job rotation. When senior salespeople act as mentors, they too are undergoing continual training as their ideas and methods are reassessed, and sometimes refined, with each trainee. For example, Ricoh Corporation, a copier manufacturer, uses a checklist as a tool to guide sales trainees' observations when accompanying senior sales reps in the field. The checklist represents key selling behaviors trainees should develop and serves as a feedback device for senior salespeople on their sales call behavior.[40] The sales manager's role as *coach* is discussed in Module 8 on supervision and leadership of the salesforce. **Job rotation,** the exposure of the sales trainee to different jobs, may involve stints as a customer service representative, a distribution clerk, or perhaps in other sales positions. For instance, Applied Materials has recent graduates who are hired spend a few months as product marketing engineers, another few in a manufacturing role, and some in customer service, all in an attempt to give them a feel for everything the company does.[41] Job rotation is often used to groom salespeople for management positions.

Behavioral Simulations Methods that focus on behavioral learning by means of business games and simulations, case studies, and role playing, where trainees portray a specified role in a staged situation, are called **behavioral simulations.** They focus on defining desirable behavior or in correcting behavioral mistakes.

An example of a simulation is one developed by AchieveGlobal called "Selling beyond Quota." This is an off-the-shelf CD-ROM simulation for companies that want to teach their salespeople that success comes from showing customers how to be successful. It focuses on a firm that is introducing a new product and needs a marketing firm to help it. The trainee follows three salespeople who apply needs satisfaction selling techniques with varying degrees of success. Testing is included as a part of the simulation.[42] Such simulations provide the advantage of reaching large populations at once via the Internet, Intranet, or CD-ROM.

Along with OJT, **role playing** is extremely popular for teaching sales techniques. Typically, one trainee plays the role of the salesperson and another trainee acts as the buyer. The role playing is videotaped or performed live for a group of observers who then critique the performance. This can be an extremely effective means of teaching personal selling, without the risk of a poor performance in the presence of a real customer. It is most effective when promptly critiqued with emphasis on the positive points of the performance as well as suggestions for improvement. A good way to maximize the benefits of the critique is to have the person who has played the role of the salesperson offer opinions first and then solicit opinions from observers. After role playing, the "salesperson" is usually modest about his or her performance, and the comments from observers may bolster this individual's self-confidence. In turn, future performance may be improved.[43] While role playing offers the opportunity for a positive learning experience, this may not always be the case as seen in "An Ethical Dilemma."

An Ethical Dilemma

During a recent training session, national sales manager Joe Smith was not happy with trainee Jill Horner's performance in a role-playing exercise. Upon conclusion of the exercise, Joe began to mock Jill's role-playing behavior in front of the other trainees to illustrate how inadequate her performance was. He informed Jill and the others that if they performed like that on a sales call, they would be looking for a new job very soon. What do you think about Joe's actions? How would you have handled this situation?

Absorption Training As the name implies, **absorption training** involves furnishing trainees or salespeople with materials that they peruse (or "absorb") without opportunity for immediate feedback and questioning. Product manuals, direction-laden memoranda, and sales bulletins are used in absorption training. This method is most useful as a supplement to update salesforce knowledge, reinforce previous training, or introduce basic materials to be covered in more detail at a later date.

One method of absorption training that has become widespread recently is to furnish the salesforce with audiocassettes so that driving time can be used as training time.[44] At NIBCO, Inc., a fluid distribution company based in Indiana, salespeople are given 20-minute audiocassettes containing humorous skits that teach valuable sales lessons. Salespeople listen to the cassettes while traveling on the road between calls. NIBCO contracted a recording studio and theater company to produce different cassettes monthly.[45]

SELECTING SALES TRAINING MEDIA Communications and computer technology have expanded the range of **sales training media** dramatically in the past decade. Sales trainers warn against the tendency to be overly impressed with the glamorous aspects of such training media, but they agree that it is advisable to evaluate new media continually to see whether they should be incorporated into the sales training program. The most promising new media are found at the communications/computer technology interface.

An example of how video technology can improve sales training comes from Frito-Lay. Frito-Lay's Priority One video series involves its CEO and senior vice president of field operations role playing a Frito-Lay salesperson and a store owner, respectively, in a variety of situations. Each month, the 15-minute videos are distributed to reps who get together with their district managers to view them. The videos suggest one new tactic that reps should try that month.[46]

Computer and communications equipment are combined for training in the Simulation System Trainer developed by Performax Inc. This system features a personal computer, videodisc player, videotape camera and recorder, video monitor, equipment interfaces, and computer programs that enable the trainee to "talk" to a customer on the screen. Realistic dialogs are accomplished, and the trainee has the opportunity to analyze the outcomes of sales behaviors and improve presentation skills.

The Performax interactive video training system is being used by several major companies, including IBM, BellSouth, Motorola, and Massachusetts Mutual Life Insurance. It is also being used to supplement instruction in sales fundamentals at the University of Memphis, Ball State University, and Illinois State University, where they are using computer software and laser disk programs made available to them from BellSouth and Massachusetts Mutual Life Insurance.[47]

The merging of communications and computer technologies is being used to conduct training at remote locations. Salespeople at Sun Microsystems Computer Company log on to a centralized computer server from remote locations and call up a browser that steps them through a training program developed specifically for Sun by Lifecycle Selling Inc., a sales training firm. Sun also has the program available on CD-ROMs and intends to place it on the Internet.[48] Another emerging technology, desktop personal computer videoconferencing, allows sales managers and salespeople to see each other and trade information via their personal computers. Similarly, audiographics connects the instructor simultaneously with several sites via computer displays and audio link.[49] Or sales managers may want to set up an online chat room to train salespeople interactively at remote locations.[50] These technologies can be used to simultaneously train salespeople dispersed in several remote locations.

Sales training software is increasingly available for a few hundred dollars per program or less. Programs cover time and territory management, sales analysis, and the entire sales process. For example, Wilson Learning Corporation offers 2- to 3-hour interactive CD-ROMs that include motion video, graphics, business simulations, and games. The company offers CD-ROM titles such as "No Trust? No Sale!" which focuses on building relationships; "Sell to Needs," a consultative program; and "Start to Sell," which examines introductory issues of selling. Walman Optical, an optical supply wholesaler, uses Wilson's CDs to reinforce sales skills and as a coaching tool. More than one-third of its sales team uses the programs regularly.[51]

Design the Sales Training Program

The fourth step in the sales training process is a culmination of, and condensation of, the first three steps shown in Figure 7.1. Working toward selected objectives based on needs assessment and having evaluated training alternatives, the sales manager now commits resources to the training to be accomplished. At this point in the process, sales managers may have to seek budget approval from upper management.

In this step of designing the training program, the necessary responses to what, when, where, and how questions are finalized. Training is scheduled, travel arrangements made, media selected, speakers hired, and countless other details arranged. Certainly this can be the most tedious part of the sales training process, but attention to detail is necessary to ensure successful implementation of the process.

Perform Sales Training

The fifth step in the process, actually performing the training, may take only a fraction of the time required by the previous steps. This is particularly true in better sales training programs. As the training is being conducted, the sales manager's primary responsibility is to monitor the progress of the trainees and to ensure adequate presentation of the training topics. In particular, sales managers should assess the clarity of training materials. It is also recommended that some assessment of the trainees' continuing motivation to learn be made. Feedback from the trainees might be solicited on everything from the effectiveness of external trainers to the adequacy of the physical training site.

Conduct Follow-Up and Evaluation

It is always difficult to measure the effectiveness of sales training. This is a long-standing problem, due in some cases to a lack of clearly stated sales training objectives. Even with clearly stated objectives, however, it is hard to determine which future performance variations are a result of sales training. Other factors, such as motivation, role perceptions, and environmental factors, may affect performance more or less than training in different situations.

Although scientific precision cannot be hoped for, a reasonable attempt must nevertheless be made to assess whether current training expenditures are worthwhile and whether future modification is warranted. Evaluations can be made before, during, and after the training occurs.[52] For example, the pretraining evaluation might include an examination for sales trainees to assess their level of knowledge, corroborate or deny the need for training, and further define the objectives of the training. As suggested earlier, training can be evaluated while it is being conducted, and adjustments may be made at any point in the delivery of training. Post-training evaluations might include reactions or critiques of the trainees, "final examinations," retention examinations at later dates, observations by sales managers as they work in the field with salespeople, and in some cases, an examination of actual performance indicators such as sales volume. At Nabisco sales training is evaluated in a variety of ways. For one, it determines which parts of its programs are most satisfying to trainees and graphs these on a chart. Nabisco also uses quizzes, role playing, and open discussions to assess whether its training has improved attitudes, knowledge, or skills. Moreover, to measure how well salespeople use their training on the job, it observes sales reps on call, conducts focus groups, and administers customer questionnaires.[53] Exhibit 7.5 summarizes the sales training evaluation practices of 129 companies.

Despite the inherent difficulty in relating subsequent sales performance to previously conducted sales training, the effectiveness of sales training is increasingly being measured in dollars and cents. This return-on-investment approach seeks to define training effectiveness in terms of incremental sales volume from existing accounts or volume generated by new accounts. At Nabisco, training is evaluated based on its impact on both sales and profits.[54]

EXHIBIT 7.5 Sales Training Evaluation Practices Ranked by Importance and Frequency

Source	Mean Importance*			Frequency of Use Percentage		
	All Companies	Service Companies	Manufacturing Companies	Often	Sometimes	Never
Reaction Measures						
Trainee feedback	3.42	3.39	3.39	86	14	0
Supervisor's feedback	3.15	3.14	3.12	68	24	8
Training staff comments	2.95	2.92	2.85	93	7	0
Learning Measures						
Performance tests	3.10	3.31	2.85	63	29	8
Pretraining versus post-training Measurements	2.72	2.71	2.56	31	51	18
Behavior Measures						
Supervisory appraisal	3.38	3.50	3.29	64	26	10
Self-appraisal	3.25	3.37	3.10	61	30	9
Customer appraisal	3.17	3.42	2.78	41	35	23
Subordinate appraisal	2.73	2.93	2.37	32	45	23
Coworker appraisal	2.52	2.63	2.33	33	45	22
Result Measures						
Bottom line measurement	3.20	3.34	2.94	40	46	14

*Mean importance is based on a 1 to 5 scale, with five indicating the most importance.

It is also important to reinforce the training in subsequent weeks. According to one training company, in the 16-week period following training, four or five coaching intervention sessions are needed or learning will decay by 80 percent.[55]

A reasonable approach to sales training is to ensure that it is not prohibitively expensive by carefully assessing training needs, setting objectives, and evaluating training alternatives before designing the training program and performing the training. Furthermore, the sales training process is incomplete without evaluation and follow-up.

Ethical and Legal Issues

Ethical and legal issues are being included in sales training programs more often than in the past. One catalyst for this change has been product liability litigation that has awarded multimillion-dollar judgments to plaintiffs who have suffered as a result of unsafe products. Research has found that salespeople face a number of ethical and legal dilemmas on the job and that salespeople want more direction from their managers on how to handle such dilemmas.[56] Exhibit 7.6 lists situations or practices that some salespeople find to be ethically troubling and would like to see addressed by a company policy.

Training in the legal area is extremely difficult because laws are sometimes confusing and subject to multiple interpretations. Training salespeople in ethics is even more difficult because ethical issues are often "gray," not black or white. Companies that address ethics and legal issues in their sales training programs usually rely on straightforward guidelines that avoid complexity. Salespeople should be provided with the company's code of ethics and informed of the organization's policies concerning ethical behavior. Furthermore, by providing salespeople with potentially troubling ethical scenarios, having them respond, and then explaining how a simi-

EXHIBIT 7.6   Ethically Troubling Situations and Practices Salespeople Would Like Addressed by Company Policy*

1. Making statements to an existing purchaser that exaggerate the seriousness of his or her problem to obtain a bigger order or other concessions.
2. Soliciting low-priority or low-volume business that the salesperson's firm will not deliver or service in an economic slowdown or periods of resource shortages.
3. Allowing personalities—liking one purchaser and disliking another—to affect price, delivery, and other decisions regarding the terms of sale.
4. Seeking information from purchasers on competitor's quotations for the purpose of submitting another quotation.
5. Having less competitive prices or other terms for buyers who use your firm as the sole source of supply than for firms for which you are one of two or more suppliers.
6. Giving physical gifts such as free sales promotion prizes or "purchase-volume incentive bonuses" to a purchaser.
7. Providing free trips, free luncheons or dinners, or other free entertainment to a purchaser.
8. Using the firm's economic power to obtain premium prices or other concessions from buyers.
9. Gaining information about competitors by asking purchasers.
10. Giving preferential treatment to purchasers whom higher levels of the firm's own management prefer or recommend.
11. Giving preferential treatment to customers who are also good suppliers.
12. Attempting to reach and influence other departments (e.g., engineering) directly rather than going through the purchasing department when such avoidance of the purchasing department increases the likelihood of a sale.

*Ranked from most to least troubling in a survey of industrial salespeople.

EXHIBIT 7.7   Legal Reminders for Salespeople

1. Use factual data rather than general statements of praise during the sales presentation. Avoid misrepresentation.
2. Thoroughly educate customers before the sale on the product's specifications, capabilities, and limitations. Remind customers to read all warnings.
3. Do not overstep authority because the salesperson's actions can be binding to the selling firm.
4. Avoid discussing these topics with competitors: prices, profit margins, discounts, terms of sale, bids or intent to bid, sales territories or markets to be served, and rejection or termination of customers.
5. Do not use one product as bait for selling another product.
6. Do not try to force the customer to buy only from your organization.
7. Offer the same price and support to all buyers who purchase under the same set of circumstances.
8. Do not tamper with a competitor's product.
9. Do not disparage a competitor's product, business conduct, or financial condition without specific evidence of your contentions.
10. Avoid promises that will be difficult or impossible to honor.

lar situation could be handled, it may be possible to lessen salespeople's concerns about such situations. Salespeople are given basic training on applicable legal dimensions and advised simply to tell the truth and seek management assistance should problems arise. Another possibility includes role playing, in which trainees learn to develop consistently legal interactive scripts.[57] These guidelines may sound simplistic, but such training can greatly reduce salesperson conflict on the job, help develop profitable long-term relationships with customers, and reduce the liability of the salesperson and the organization.

The legal framework for personal selling is extensive. Some of the key components of this framework are antitrust legislation, contract law, local ordinances governing sales practices, and guidelines issued by the Federal Trade Commission dealing with unfair trade practices. A partial listing of important legal reminders that should be included in a sales training program is shown in Exhibit 7.7. Salespeople must be made aware of changes in the legal environment as soon as they occur.

Summary

1. **Understand the role of sales training in salesforce socialization.** Newly hired salespeople usually receive a company orientation designed to familiarize them with company history, policies, facilities, procedures, and key individuals with whom they will interact. During initial sales training, it is hoped that each salesforce member will experience a positive initiation to task and satisfactory role definition.

2. **Explain the importance of sales training and the sales manager's role in sales training.** Most organizations have a continual need for sales training as a result of changing business conditions, the influx of new salespeople into the organization, and the need to reinforce previous training. Sizable investments in training are likely in larger companies. The sales manager has the overall responsibility for training the salesforce, although other people may also conduct sales training.

3. **Describe the sales training process as a series of six interrelated steps.** Figure 7.1 presents the sales training process in six steps: assess sales training needs, set training objectives, evaluate training alternatives, design the sales training program, perform sales training, and conduct follow-up and evaluation. The time spent to perform sales training may be only a fraction of the time spent to complete the other steps in the process, especially in well-run sales organizations.

4. **Discuss six methods for assessing sales training needs and identify typical sales training needs.** Sales managers may assess needs through a salesforce audit, performance testing, observation, a salesforce survey, a customer survey, or a job analysis. It is recommended that salesforce training needs be assessed in a proactive fashion; that is, needs should be assessed before performance problems occur rather than after problems occur. Typical sales training needs include product, customer, and competitive knowledge; sales techniques; and time and territory management.

5. **Name some typical objectives of sales training programs, and explain how setting objectives for sales training is beneficial to sales managers.** The objectives of sales training vary over time and across organizations, but they often include preparing sales trainees for assignment to a sales territory, improving a particular dimension of performance, aiding in the socialization process, or improving salesforce morale and motivation. By setting objectives, the sales manager can prioritize training, allocate resources consistent with priorities, communicate the purpose of the training to interested parties, and perhaps gain top management support for sales training.

6. **Identify the key issues in evaluating sales training alternatives.** Evaluation of alternatives is a search for an optimal balance between cost and effectiveness. One key issue is the selection of trainers, whether from outside the company (external) or inside the company (internal). Another is the potential location or locations for training. Still another important factor is the method or methods to use for various topics. Sales training methods include classroom/conference training, on-the-job training, behavioral simulations, and absorption training. The sales manager must also consider whether to use various sales training media, such as printed material, videotape, and computer-assisted instruction.

7. **Identify key ethical and legal issues in sales training.** Because of increasing product liability litigation, legal and ethical issues are being incorporated into salesforce training. Exhibits 7.6 and 7.7 point out several issues that should be covered in sales training. Lectures and role playing provide useful means for training in this area.

Understanding Sales Management Terms

- Initiation to task
- Role definition
- Needs assessment
- Salesforce audit
- Performance testing
- Observation
- Salesforce survey
- Sales trainer
- Central training facility
- Classroom/conference training
- On-the-job training (OJT)
- Mentor
- Job rotation
- Behavioral simulations

- Customer survey
- Job analysis
- Product knowledge
- Customer knowledge
- Sales training objectives
- Role playing
- Absorption training
- Sales training media
- Competitive knowledge
- Time and territory management

Developing Sales Management Knowledge

1. How is sales training related to recruiting and selecting salespeople? How can sales training contribute to salesforce socialization?
2. Why is it important to invest in sales training?
3. Refer to "Sales Management in the 21st Century: Team Training at ADP." Why is teamwork important in sales training?
4. What are six methods of assessing sales training needs? Can each of these methods be used in either a proactive or reactive approach to determining training needs?
5. Refer to "Sales Management in the 21st Century: Training for Relationship Building at ADP." How can training salespeople in relationship building help a company?
6. How is the process of setting objectives for sales training beneficial to sales managers?
7. When the sales manager is evaluating sales training alternatives, what four areas should he or she consider?
8. Discuss four methods for delivering sales training.
9. What is the purpose of the follow-up and evaluation step in the sales training process? When should evaluation take place?
10. What are some of the important ethical and legal considerations that might be included in a sales training program?

Building Sales Management Skills

1. There is a universal ongoing need for training on "how to sell." For instance, knowing how to listen effectively is an extremely important skill that contributes to the success of salespeople. Find several articles on listening. Use this information to design a training program to improve salespeople's listening skills. Assume that you will conduct the training session. Determine what you will teach, along with the methods and media you will use. Also, decide how you will assess whether the training was successful. If possible, conduct your training program on a small group such as your fraternity, sorority, student American Marketing Association chapter, or any other student group.
2. As the sales manger for ABC company, you have decided that as part of your training program you would like to use role playing to achieve three objectives: (1) teach salespeople how to set appointments with prospects properly via the phone, (2) teach salespeople how to approach prospects and build rapport, and (3) teach salespeople how to question prospects effectively. Design three role plays (one of each objective) to achieve these goals. Then, have a classmate play the salesperson and you play the buyer and act out each role play. On completing each role play, critique the salesperson's performance, being sure to emphasize the positive points and to make suggestions for improvements. Consider soliciting self-assessment feedback from the salesperson before making your own critique.
3. Access SalesPro Online Training at **http://4moresales.com**. Click on "guests." Address the following questions:
   A. What types of sales training needs does this company address with its online training?
   B. What are some potentially important training needs that are not addressed?
   C. Examine the example of a SalesPro Seminar: "Selling to Different Personality Types." What are the advantages and disadvantages of using this type of online training?
   D. What does it cost to use this training?

Making Sales Management Decisions

CASE 7.1 Solutions Software, Inc.

Background

Solutions Software, Inc., develops and markets software through office and computer software retailers throughout the United States. Established in 1982, the company has been successful competing against larger companies because it offers a quality product at an affordable price. Moreover, it has a reputation of providing a high level of service through a knowledgeable and efficient salesforce.

On entering the salesforce, reps are given formal training at the company's headquarters in St. Louis, Missouri. There they are taught various sales techniques, product knowledge, and competitive knowledge. In addition, they learn about company policies and the company's code of ethics. Each of the company's four regional sales managers is responsible for any additional training, to occur as each deems necessary. Regional sales managers typically have attempted, at a minimum, to keep their salespeople up to speed on product knowledge.

Current Situation

More than one-third of the way into the fiscal year, sales in the Midwest region at Solutions Software are running about 10 percent behind last year. Regional Sales Manager Clara Halter is concerned. National Sales Manager Ken Raft has been pushing Clara hard since last year when her region's sales came in just under the yearly sales target. This year, Clara is determined to exceed her goal. If she does not, she fears she might not be around to make an attempt again next year.

Clara has been the Midwest regional sales manager for 4 years, having formerly been a salesperson with Solutions for 6 years. During her tenure as sales manger, she has yet to conduct any formal training beyond keeping her salespeople abreast of new products. Now, she thinks, might be the time for some additional training. Perhaps this would provide her salespeople with the tools they need to increase their sales.

First, Clara thinks, she must decide what the training should include. She recalls that salespeople's initial training did not address time and territory management or customer knowledge. Perhaps her salespeople are not using their time as efficiently and effectively as they should be. She figures that salespeople could always use some additional training in this area. Furthermore, she surmises that her salespeople might benefit from understanding different buyer types along with techniques for handling each. Finally, Clara believes that her salespeople might gain from brushing up on some sales techniques. Clara believes that because building relationships is such an important part of the business, salespeople could use some additional training on how to build rapport and trust, as well as effectively listen and question.

Having determined what she wants her salespeople to learn, Clara sets out to decide on the methods that will be most suitable for teaching her salespeople. She decides that she will develop a two-page handout on time and territory management to deliver to salespeople during their training session. They can review these materials at their leisure and use the information to make them more efficient. With regard to customer knowledge, Clara thinks she will design a series of role-playing exercises involving different customer types. Salespeople will form teams of two. One salesperson will play the role of a specific type of buyer and the other salesperson will attempt to identify and appropriately sell to this buyer type. Salespeople will then critique the performance. Finally, Clara believes that the best way for salespeople to improve their selling skills is for her to lecture on the topics of rapport and trust building, and listening and questioning.

Next, Clara has to decide when and where to hold the training. As far as she is concerned, it cannot be soon enough. She decides to hold a 2-day training seminar in sunny Orlando, Florida, at the beginning of next month. She thinks this change in scenery might be conducive to learning. She sends a company memo via e-mail to all her salespeople explaining the program and the date.

On completion of the sales training, Clara feels more upbeat. Surely, she thinks this will help her salespeople pick up the pace. Only time will tell.

Questions

1. Assess the sales training processes used by Clara Halter. What would you do differently if you were she? (That is, how could the process be improved?)
2. Do you think this program will improve sales? Explain.
3. Do you think that salespeople will find this program useful? Explain.

CASE 7.2 Compusystems, Inc.

Background

Beth Barnes joined Compusystems, Inc., 1½ years ago. She was interested in working for a progressive company with growth potential. Compusystems, Inc., appeared to be such a company. The company sold a variety of business computing systems. Beth was assigned to sell computerized cash register systems.

The salesforce was taught to practice adaptive selling in which salespeople learned how to probe for customer needs and respond to customer wants. This method of selling has proven to be very successful for the company. In fact, the company credits its move in market position from number five to number three in the last 3 years to its implementation of adaptive selling and its salesforce's ability to build strong customer relationships.

Current Situation

Beth was running behind as usual. She had a major presentation scheduled with a well-qualified prospect that could bring a substantial payoff to both her and her company. As a result, she had to cancel her first scheduled appointment of the day so that she could finish preparing her presentation for this prospect. This was not the first time she had to cancel an appointment. Just last week she canceled an appointment because she realized she would be unable to make it to the client's firm before it closed. She had failed to budget enough time into her schedule to allow her to travel from one appointment to the next.

Beth arrived at Handyman Hardware 5 minutes late. Luckily for Beth the owner of Handyman, Joshua Jones, had been on an important conference call that ran a little longer than anticipated. Jones was hoping to purchase a new cash register system that could track his inventory. He was concerned about inventory loss, particularly in terms of pilferage and the possibility of employees inaccurately (both on purpose and otherwise) ringing up sales. Moreover, he hoped to implement a system that would allow him to track sales better, while at the same time expedite the check-out process. Currently, he is using fairly antiquated equipment that does not provide him with the ability to scan merchandise or systematically track inventory and sales.

After introducing herself and her company, Beth got right down to business. She went into a 30-minute presentation explaining the CR2000, a cash register system she believed would be appropriate for Jones' store. What follows are excerpts from her meeting with Jones:

Beth: Although we sell several systems, Mr. Jones, I believe the CR2000 cash registers would be good for you. They are relatively inexpensive, provide a more rapid system for checking out customers, and are superior to what you now have.

Jones: As I mentioned earlier, I want a system that provides me with the ability to track inventory and total sales. Does this system do that?

Beth: No, it doesn't. We sell systems that can monitor inventory, but they are more expensive. You presently have some type of system for tracking inventory, don't you?

Jones: Yes, but it is time-consuming and I have always been concerned about its accuracy.

Beth: We could provide you with an inventory tracking system. But, in your case, it may not be worth the extra cost.

Jones: I'd really be interested in a system that is quicker than my present system and can track sales and inventory. I would also like to begin using barcodes, rather than individually pricing each item.

Beth: We carry the CR2500. This system would provide you with the ability to do these things. However, this system runs quite a bit more.

Jones: Will this system allow me to monitor sales hourly?

Beth: I believe it will. This is a fairly new system. It's an update of an earlier model. Some changes were made, and I'm not sure exactly what has been changed.

Jones: Can the system break out sales by department?

Beth: The older version of this system could. I am sure the new version can also. If you would like, Mr. Jones, I can write you a proposal for installing the CR2500. When I finish the proposal we can meet again to further discuss the CR2500.

Questions

1. With regard to Beth, what sales training needs can you identify?
2. If you were Beth's sales manager and you discovered that several of your salespeople had training needs similar to those of Beth, what methods would you suggest for training the salesforce to improve in deficient areas?
3. What are the effects of sales training on salesforce motivation and morale?

PART IV

Directing the Salesforce

This part contains two modules dealing with the direction of the activities of the salesforce. Module 8 presents a model of sales management leadership. Contemporary views of sales leadership are discussed, along with important leadership functions such as coaching. The critical role of ethics in leadership is investigated, and coverage is provided on dealing with problems such as sexual harassment, conflicts of interest, and disruptive salespeople.

Module 9 deals with motivating the salesforce to work hard on the right activities over a sustained period of time. Reward systems, with an emphasis on financial and nonfinancial compensation are discussed. Special issues related to team compensation and compensating a global salesforce are presented. Guidelines for motivating and rewarding salespeople are offered.

MODULE 8

Sales Management Leadership and Supervision

Hands-on Leadership at SAS Brings Great Success

SAS Institute, a software manufacturer that supplies nearly 17,000 companies, government offices, and universities around the world, can credit much of its success to Barrett Joyner, vice president of North American sales and marketing. Joyner is in charge of a division of 350 people who sell, service, and support these products. Due in large part to his leadership ability, SAS earned $750 million in revenue in fiscal year 1997.

Joyner is a hands-on leader who tries to be accessible to his managers and salespeople by establishing some link between him and them. His goal is to "establish a win–win situation with everybody I encounter." He accomplishes this through a process called Double D, Double M—dialog, development, mentoring, and measurement. He uses dialog to find mutually beneficial goals. He will sit across from someone and say, "This is what I need. What do you need?" Joyner claims, "That sounds like management from Mayberry, but I think it works. Most people want to find common ground." Another part of his dialog involves the use of e-mail and his Web site, where he posts daily updates on sales, hot topics, sales tips, and best practices case studies. During development, planning takes place in which he and his colleagues discuss strategies. Joyner uses mentoring as a way to establish two-way helping relationships. Finally, measurement affords him the opportunity to assess whether both sides received what they wanted from the process. Then it all circles back to dialog.

According to Joyner, "This process is different with every individual, and at different times in their lives." Joyner gives an example of a situation that might involve a rep who has been with the company for 6 years. When she started she may have been single and loved to travel. Now that she is married and has a family, she no longer finds those trips appealing. Joyner would be happy to talk to this rep and arrange for her to travel less. He would then find someone who is looking for some extra trips. "That way, everybody wins. Reps are happy and clients get the attention they need," says Joyner.

Joyner also has the leadership ability to make his vision a reality. In 1994, Joyner launched a program titled "$100 million in 1,000 days." His goal was to increase his division's new business by $100 million in 3 years. To accomplish this goal, Joyner determined that the company needed to acquire capital to develop new products and services and that his department needed to hire more rapidly and train employees with broader skills. His ideas worked. By the end of 1997, Joyner's

Learning Objectives

After completing this module, you should be able to

1 Distinguish between salesforce leadership and supervision.

2 Discuss how salesforce socialization can be enhanced through supervision and leadership.

3 Explain how the LMX model, transformational leadership, and behavioral self-management concepts contribute to contemporary sales leadership.

4 List the six components of a sales leadership model.

5 Discuss five bases of power that affect leadership.

6 Explain five influence strategies used in leadership.

7 Discuss issues related to coaching the salesforce, holding integrative meetings, and practicing ethical management.

8 Identify some of the problems encountered in leading and supervising a salesforce.

197

noncommission salesforce topped $100 million by 17 percent. Then in 1998, his division grew by another 20 percent over 1997. According to Joyner, "Everybody here has the same job—to move the account forward in a win–win fashion."

Source: Chris Glass, "Success Sure Is a Lot of Fun," *Sales & Marketing Management* 151 (January 1999): 54–59.

This module deals with the leadership and supervisory roles of sales managers. As illustrated in the opening vignette, successful sales leadership calls for working effectively with salespeople by empowering them. It also involves developing a vision and determining the means for achieving it.

Leadership involves the use of influence with other people through communication processes to attain specific goals and objectives. Even though sales managers have a fair amount of authority by virtue of their positions in the organizational hierarchy, it is their skill to influence rather than dictate the actions of others that determines whether they are effective leaders.

As mentioned in the opening module of this book, today's sales managers are more involved in leadership than were their predecessors. They use collaboration with others more than control over others to achieve sales objectives, and they are more apt to coach than to deliver one-way criticism. Sales leadership increasingly requires that managers equip and empower salespeople, rather than dominate them. It is also important to treat salespeople as individuals, while still fostering teamwork.

Supervision is the day-to-day control of the salesforce under routine operating conditions. It is obviously an integral part of leadership; however, it is not the sum total of leadership. For one thing, supervision is concerned only with the sales manager–salesperson relationship, whereas leadership extends to all interpersonal relationships in which the sales manager is engaged. Furthermore, leadership requires more foresight and intuition than supervision. This is true because supervision deals more with maintenance and improvement of the status quo, whereas leadership often requires redefinition of major objectives and operations of the salesforce.

This module is organized into four sections. First, the previously discussed concept of salesforce socialization is reviewed to see how it relates to supervision and leadership. Next, a leadership model is discussed. The third section deals with three important leadership functions: coaching, holding integrative meetings, and practicing ethical sales management. The last section addresses some problems in leading and supervising a salesforce—namely, conflicts of interest; chemical abuse and dependency; disruptive, rule-breaking salespeople; termination of employment; and sexual harassment.

Salesforce Socialization Revisited

As you will recall, a model of salesforce socialization (the process by which salespeople acquire the knowledge, skills, and values essential to do their job) was introduced as Figure 6.1. Note that recruiting/selection and training objectives that relate to salesforce socialization have been discussed in Modules 6 and 7, respectively. Through leadership, supervision, and motivation, sales managers can further socialize the salesforce, contributing to a strong sales culture and positive job-related outcomes.[1] For example, research has demonstrated the importance of salespeople having high levels of job-related, **task-specific self-esteem,** which has been linked to improved performance and job satisfaction.[2]

Sales managers can positively affect their salesforce by reducing on-the-job conflicts and role stress (introduced in Module 2) for their salespeople (i.e., they can help achieve the congruence objective shown in Figure 6.1). For example, research shows that by reducing salespeople's stress on the job, sales managers could increase not only salespeople's job satisfaction but, ultimately, their **organizational commitment** as well.[3] Organizational commitment can be defined variously but is usually thought of in one of two ways: (1) as a psychological bond to the organization or (2) as demonstrated through behavior over time.

Despite whether salespeople might like to have freedom on the job, one study suggests that salespeople's job stress was reduced by higher levels of **formalization**—the extent to which work activity is directed by rules, regulations, and directives. The reduction in job stress led to higher levels of organizational commitment and lower levels of **work alienation**, which is described as an individual's psychological separation from the activities of the job.[4] Work alienation might be thought of as the opposite of **job involvement**, which is a strong attachment by the salesperson to the job itself. Recent research suggests that similar associations hold internationally, at least among Japanese and Korean salespeople.[5]

Understandably, most sales managers would like to have a salesforce composed of people who are highly committed to the organization and highly involved in the job itself. This module considers how sales managers, through effective leadership and supervision, can affect overall salesforce performance and other desirable job outcomes, such as satisfaction, involvement and commitment on the part of their salespeople.

Contemporary Views of Sales Leadership

In recent years, sales researchers have advanced three especially relevant views of sales leadership: the Leader–Member Exchange (LMX) model, transformational leadership, and behavioral self-management. Each of these views offers useful aspects for the contemporary sales manager.

The **Leader–Member Exchange (LMX) model,** in existence for more than two decades but only recently applied in sales management, focuses on the salesperson–sales manager dyad as a reciprocal influence process. LMX proposes that sales managers interact uniquely with individual salespeople rather than prescribing one style or set of behaviors to be used in standardized "situations." Studies have shown that reciprocal trust between sales managers and salespeople influences the leader–member exchange and can generate positive job attitudes and perceptions in the salesforce.[6] In addition, one study found that the higher the quality of exchange relationship between salesperson and sales manager, the greater the salesperson's goal commitment and ultimately performance.[7]

One appealing notion of the LMX model is that many organizations are reorienting their sales processes toward more long-term, trust-based customer relationships. In organizations where this is occurring, both sales managers and salespeople are learning the benefits of building and earning trust; thus their motivation to engage in trust building in the salesperson–sales manager dyad may well be present.

Transformational leadership is another emerging concept of interest to sales managers and researchers.[8] Transformational leaders are charismatic, inspirational, and driven by a sense of mission. They provide intellectual stimulation, often by showing employees new ways of thinking or completing tasks. In this capacity, transformational leaders act as change agents. Another aspect of transformational leadership is individualized consideration, through which employees are given personalized attention.

With early studies offering limited empirical support in the sales management context, interest in transformational leadership remains high.[9] This is in part because of the perceived role of the transformational leader as a change agent and the high level of prescribed change in many of today's sales organizations.

Behavioral self-management (BSM) involves self-imposed planning, behavior, evaluation, rewards, and punishment.[10] Given the unique nature of the sales role, BSM offers some advantages. First, many salespeople work without constant supervision, so self-control and self-discipline are important for success. Second, individuals usually work more enthusiastically when they have had significant input into planning and prioritizing their work. In addition, sales managers who work only periodically in the field with salespeople may not be capable of fully assessing all important behaviors.

Furthermore, sales managers who work only occasionally in the field may become a cue for desirable sales behaviors that are not reinforced in the manger's absence. In other words, the sales rep plays the game while the manager is in the field, then reverts to less-than-desirable behaviors when the manager departs. BSM can help address this problem, and it is also an alternative worth considering for the many sales organizations that are cutting out layers of management in the quest to improve sales productivity.

A Leadership Model for Sales Management

The LMX model, transformational leadership, and behavioral self-management approaches capture some of the key thoughts in contemporary sales leadership: Build a strong, trust-based relationship with individual salespeople. Be an active stimulus for change, and work with salespeople and others to accomplish the mission. Expect salespeople to take an active role in managing themselves. To pull these and other leadership approaches together, we now offer a leadership model for sales management.

Figure 8.1 shows the model with six components:

1. *Power*—of the salesperson, salespeople, or other party with whom the sales manager is interacting
2. *Power*—of the sales manager
3. *Situation*—including time constraints, nature of the task, organizational history, and group norms
4. *Needs*—of the salesperson, salespeople, or other people with whom the sales manager is interacting
5. *Goals and objectives*—of the individuals and the organization
6. *Leadership skills*—anticipation, diagnostic, selection and matching, and communications

Power and Leadership

In most job-related interpersonal situations, sales managers and the parties with whom they interact hold power in some form or another. As the model in Figure 8.1 suggests, the possession and use of this power will have a major impact on the quality of leadership achieved by a sales manager. To simplify discussion, the sales manager–salesperson relationship is focused on here, but keep in mind that sales managers must use their leadership skills in dealing with other personnel in the firm, as well as outside parties such as employment agencies, external trainers, customers, and suppliers.

FIGURE 8.1 A Leadership Model for Sales Management

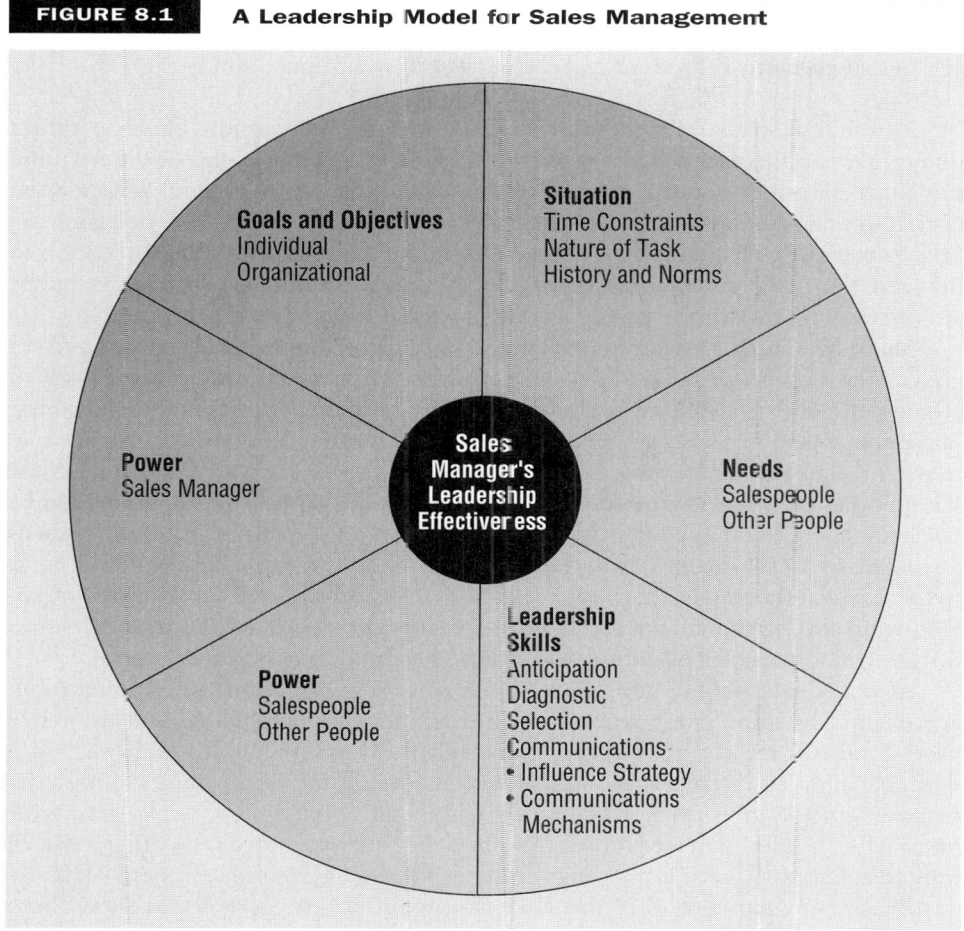

A sales manager's leadership effectiveness is a function of six factors: the power of the salesperson and other people, the power of the sales manager, the situation, human needs, individual and organizational goals and objectives, and the leadership skills of the sales manager.

The power held by an individual in an interpersonal relationship can be of one or more of the following five types.[11] For each type, a sample comment from a salesperson recognizing the sales manager's power is shown in parentheses.[12]

1. **Expert power**—based on the belief that a person has valuable knowledge or skills in a given area. ("I respect her knowledge and good judgment because she is well trained and experienced.")
2. **Referent power**—based on the attractiveness of one party to another. It may arise from friendship, role modeling, or perceived similarity of personal background or viewpoints. ("I like him personally and regard him as a friend.")
3. **Legitimate power**—associated with the right to be a leader, usually as a result of designated organizational roles. ("She has a legitimate right, considering her position as sales manager, to expect that her suggestions will be followed.")
4. **Reward power**—stems from the ability of one party to reward the other party for a designated action. ("He is in a good position to recommend promotions or permit special privileges for me.")

5. **Coercive power**—based on a belief that one party can remove rewards and provide punishment to affect behavior. ("She can apply pressure to enforce her suggestions if they are not carried out fully and properly.")

It should be stressed that it is the various individuals' perceptions of power, rather than a necessarily objective assessment of where the power lies, that will determine the effects of power in interpersonal relationships. For example, a newly appointed district sales manager may perceive the legitimate power associated with being a manager to be extremely high, whereas the salespeople may not share this perception in the least. Such differences in perceptions regarding the nature and balance of power are often at the root of the problems that challenge sales managers.

Many sales managers have been accused of relying too much on reward and coercive power. This is disturbing for three reasons. First, coercive actions are likely to create strife in the salesforce and may encourage turnover among high-performing salespeople who have other employment opportunities. Second, as salespeople move through the career cycle, they tend to self-regulate the reward system. Senior salespeople are often seeking rewards that cannot be dispensed and controlled by sales managers, such as a sense of accomplishment on the job. As a result, rewards lose some of their impact. Third, research has demonstrated that other power bases (expert and referent) are positively related to salespeople's satisfaction with supervision and with sales managers.[13] Thus, it is recommended that sales managers who wish to become effective leaders develop referent and expert power bases.

At times, salespeople have more power in a situation than the sales manager. For example, senior salespeople may be extremely knowledgeable and therefore have dominant expert power over a relatively inexperienced sales manager. Or a sales manager with strong self-esteem needs may be intent on winning a popularity contest with the salesforce, which could give salespeople a strong referent power base. When a sales manager senses that the salesperson is more powerful in one of these dimensions, there is a strong tendency to rely on legitimate, coercive, or reward power to gain control of the situation. Again, it is suggested that these three power bases be used sparingly, however, and that the sales manger work instead toward developing more expert and referent power.

This recommendation is getting results in progressive sales organizations. For example, since being promoted to national sales manager for Century Maintenance Supply, Theresa Cullens has used a personal approach to leadership to bring about double-digit sales increases. One of her coworkers at Century explains, "She doesn't direct her team from a throne, she gets down in the trenches with you."[14]

The concepts of teamwork and employee participation in management decision making are gaining popularity and are largely incompatible with the heavy-handed use of coercive and legitimate power. Sales managers interested in developing an effective power base might consider the advice given in Exhibit 8.1 by Robert Dilenschneider, president of Hill and Knowlton, the world's largest public relations firm.

One additional point on sales managers' use of power is that a combination of power bases may be used in a given situation. For example, it might be a sales manager's referent and expert power that allow him or her to conduct a highly effective leadership function, such as an annual sales meeting. Previous research that focused on food brokers suggests that the use of combinations of power bases more accurately reflects reality than does the exclusive use of one power base in a given situation.[15]

Situational Factors

Scores of studies have tried to uncover what makes an effective leader. One popular category of this research is called the **trait approach,** which attempts to determine the personality traits of an effective leader. To date, trait research, however, has not

EXHIBIT 8.1 How Sales Managers Can Develop Power

The president of Hill and Knowlton, the world's largest public relations firm, offers sales managers several suggestions for developing their power bases:

- Decide on overall objectives.
- Listen to your sales team's wants, needs, and dreams.
- Align the sales team with the firm's corporate culture.
- Meet key customers and industry leaders.
- Make appearances at image-enhancing events.
- Secure support of upper management for sales management programs and activities.
- Use one-on-one meetings to motivate salespeople.
- Develop an information management system to minimize the flow of irrelevant information.

been enlightening. The **behavior approach**, which seeks to catalog behaviors associated with effective leadership, has likewise failed to identify what makes an effective leader. As the behavior and trait studies continue inconclusive, it has become increasingly apparent that the *situation* could have a strong impact on leadership. The model in Figure 8.1 of a **contingency approach** to leadership recognizes the importance of the interaction between situational factors and other factors. Situational contingency factors include the firm's market orientation; sales organization culture; company policies and procedures; the importance of the issue requiring attention; the time available to react; and the power, resources, and interdependencies of the parties involved.[16] When time is at a premium, crisis management is called for, which requires totally different leadership behaviors than usual. For example, a sales manager might rely on legitimate power, or even coercive power, to get immediate, undisputed support of the salesforce if time is constrained.

Certainly the nature of the task is an important part of the situation. If the situation is concerned with the top priority of the sales organization, a more calculated approach to leadership may be called for than when the situation is of minor importance.

The history, culture, and policies of the company may also affect a particular situation and thus the leadership action that would be most suitable. For example, Oscar Mayer has a long-standing history as a market leader offering high-quality products at premium prices. Despite intense competitive pressures to reduce prices, Oscar Mayer sales leadership is bolstered by the tradition of high-quality products, and what might be viewed as a crisis in price competition by another firm is hardly worthy of managerial attention at Oscar Mayer.

Needs and Wants of Salespeople

Continuing the discussion of the model shown in Figure 8.1, it should be stressed that leadership is an interactive process requiring one or more individuals to assume the role of followers or constituents. If coercive power-based behavior is cast aside, the needs and wants of salespeople must be given due consideration to ensure a supporting constituency for effective sales management leadership. Obviously the needs and wants of salespeople cannot be met on a carte blanche basis. Furthermore, a sales manager cannot become overly sensitive to the point of paranoia or managerial paralysis brought on by the fear that necessary actions will alienate the salesforce. But on balance, the needs and wants of salespeople must be constantly weighed as an important determinant of leadership behavior.

In assessing the needs and wants of salespeople, it is important to consider each salesperson as a unique individual. Although it is true that individual salespeople are typically part of a work group (i.e., the salesforce), sales managers should attempt to tailor their actions to individual salespeople when feasible. A study of retail and insurance salespeople provides support for these ideas, concluding that sales managers' supervisory behaviors are related to sales performance and that sales managers should manage salespeople individually in terms of supervisory behaviors.[17]

Goals and Objectives

If salespeople's needs and wants are consistent with the organization's goals and objectives, leadership is an easier task for sales managers. To this end, some companies hold extensive training and development sessions on "life planning" for their salespeople. In these sessions, salespeople define their short- and long-term personal goals. In subsequent sessions, company management attempts to show how the salespeople's personal goal achievement can also assist in organizational goal achievement.

One firm that uses life planning is Combustion Engineering, a large industrial company. Combustion Engineering conducts these sessions on college campuses such as MIT with the assistance of industrial psychologists. The sessions are taken seriously. Company management believes that such goal clarification is beneficial not only to the personal development of their employees, but also because it helps produce a supportive constituency for the leaders of the firm.

Leadership Skills

As previously suggested, no one has been able to identify the exact personality traits or leadership behaviors that make an effective sales management leader. Likewise, there is no magic combination of skills that ensures effective leadership. Next, several skill areas that may be related to effective leadership are reviewed; keep in mind, however, that possession of a particular skill is no more important than knowing when to use it. The skill areas covered include anticipation and seeking feedback, diagnostic skills, selection and matching, and communication skills. See how sales executive Anthony Lockhart uses various skills to accomplish several activities necessary for leading a salesforce in "Sales Management in the 21st Century: Using Leadership Skills to Build Sales Teams at FirstEnergy."

SALES MANAGEMENT IN THE 21ST CENTURY

Using Leadership Skills to Build Sales Teams at FirstEnergy

Anthony Lockhart, director, central region sales of FirstEnergy, shares his opinions about how to build and lead sales teams:

Sales leadership in a rapidly changing environment is the challenge of the new millennium. The challenge includes building a strong sales team, developing the team, setting clear goals and expectations for the team, establishing a solid work ethic for team members, and recognizing the team's accomplishments. A major role of leadership in building a strong sales team is a commitment to a rigorous selection process that identifies individuals with excellent relationship building skills and a strong desire to sell. Once the team is in place, a sales leader must provide encouragement to team members and assure them that they are headed in the right direction. The growth and confidence building of team members comes by helping them find ways to achieve results more effectively and by empowering team members to take charge within clearly defined limits. This can be accomplished by maintaining an environment that welcomes new ideas and new ways of doing things. Furthermore, a sales leader can create focus and increase the likelihood of achieving the team's objectives by clearly delineating and communicating members' expectations. Finally, a sales leader in the new millennium can create a solid work ethic by assuming a do as I do, rather than do as I say, attitude. Plan your day, get an early start, make the extra effort, insist on honesty and integrity, and give recognition to the team's successes.

ANTICIPATION AND SEEKING FEEDBACK The business press is full of examples of leadership crises that could have been avoided by **anticipation** of a potential problem. Consider the case of Frontier Corporation, a telecommunications company based in Rochester, New York, whose goal is to be as familiar to businesses and consumers as AT&T, MCI, and Sprint. With revenues sliding, the fifth largest telecommunications company in the United States decided to revamp its misguided sales compensation plan that paid salespeople against the total revenue they generated in a new account over a 3-month period. With proper anticipation, management at Frontier might have foreseen that this system provided reps with little reason to further customer relationships beyond the third month. The new plan rewards reps for increasing business in a 1-year period and provides them roughly 3 percent of the total revenue in the account each month after that period. Salespeople have embraced the new system because they find that it is easier to sell additional products to a current customer than it is to open a new account.[18]

The Frontier case illustrates how even the best-run companies can benefit from better anticipation of problems to avert leadership crises. It is unfair to expect unerring clairvoyance of sales managers, but it is reasonable to expect that responsible leaders will try to extend their vision into the future. One way they can do this is to **seek feedback** from customers, salespeople, and other important sources regularly. Feedback can be gathered regularly through field visits, salesforce audits, and conscientious reviews of routine call reports submitted by salespeople. The idea of sales managers spending more time in the field, whether or not they are accompanied by salespeople, is increasingly being advocated.

One option is for the sales manager to actually spend time in the field in the role of the salesperson. Some sales managers have actual sales responsibilities; others visit the field as temporary salespeople. While in the sales role, the manager can assess sales support, customer service, availability of required information, job stress, workload factors, and other variables of interest. For example, the national sales manager at Century Maintenance Supply spends half her time making sales calls with reps.[19]

DIAGNOSTIC SKILLS Effective leaders must be able to determine the specific nature of the problem or opportunity to be addressed. Although this sounds simple, it is often difficult to distinguish between the real problem and the more visible symptoms of the problem. Earlier it was noted that sales managers have relied too heavily on reward and coercive power to direct their salesforces. A primary reason for this is a recurring tendency to attack easily identified symptoms of problems, not the core problems that need resolution. Reward and coercive power are also expedient ways to exercise control, and they suit the manager who likes to react without deliberation when faced with a problem.

For example, a sales manager may react to sluggish sales volume results by automatically assuming the problem is motivation. What follows from this hasty conclusion is a heavy dose of newly structured rewards, or just the opposite, a strong shot of coercion. Perhaps motivation is not the underlying problem; perhaps other determinants of performance are actually the source of the problem. But a lack of **diagnostic skills** (discussed further in Module 11) has led the sales manager to attack the easiest target, the symptom of the problem, rather than fully examine the root cause of the problem. As we all know from our experiences with the common cold, treating the symptoms will not solve the problem permanently.

SELECTION AND MATCHING As already mentioned, no specific inventory of skills exists for effective leadership. Rather, there is a range of behaviors that should be matched to a particular situation. For example, aspersions have been cast on the use of coercive power in sales management, but its use may be entirely appropriate in some situations. In the case of a problem employee whose insubordination is creating morale problems for the remainder of the salesforce, for example, a "shape up or ship out" ultimatum may be the best response.

The importance of *selecting* appropriate leadership responses to *match* the situation is highlighted in the research dealing with salespeople's concerns as they move through career stages. A study of one company's salespeople found entry-level salespeople to be unhappy with their sales managers and the aspects of the sales jobs over which the manager had considerable control.[20] For example, they did not perceive their sales managers to be open and supportive, and they believed they had little opportunity to make important decisions. More experienced salespeople in this company held positive perceptions toward their sales managers and toward aspects of their jobs heavily influenced by management. Obviously, either a change in managerial behavior toward the discontented entry-level salespeople was called for in this case, or the company's recruitment and selection methods should have been changed. Either way, being able to match managerial actions to the situation, rather than responding within a narrowly defined range of behaviors, would be a big advantage to effective leadership.

Communication

Recall the definition of leadership from the beginning of this module. At the heart of the definition is the phrase "the use of influence through communication processes." In this section, various influence strategies and communications mechanisms involved in leadership and supervision are discussed. Effective leaders deliver clear, timely information through appropriate media or interpersonal communications. By contrast, the best plans and intentions can be destroyed by faulty communication. All too often, sales operations are damaged by premature leakage of information, inconsistent and conflicting communication, tardy messages, or poorly conceived strategies for influencing the salesforce.

INFLUENCE STRATEGIES Because sales managers have power from different sources to use in dealing with salespeople, peers, and superiors, they have the opportunity to devise different **influence strategies** according to situational demands. Influence strategies can be based on threats, promises, persuasion, relationships, and manipulation.[21] All are appropriate at some time with some salespeople but not necessarily with superiors or peers.

Threats In a strategy based on **threats,** a manager might specify a desired behavior and the punishment that will follow if the behavior is not achieved. "If you do not call on your accounts at least once a week, you will lose your job," is an example. Because threats are used only in cases of noncompliance to operational guidelines, their use requires a monitoring system to see whether the threatened person is engaging in the desired behavior. This can be time-consuming and annoying for the manager. Threats should be viewed as a last resort, but they should not be eliminated as a viable influence strategy. Research has indicated that salespeople, contrary to common wisdom, do not appear to react unfavorably to appropriate punishment and that managers "need to overcome their own reluctance in meting out punishment."[22]

Promises Sales managers can use reward power as a basis for developing influence strategies based on **promises.** Research has indicated that promises produce better compliance than threats.[23] This would seem to be especially true for well-educated mobile employees as typified by a large portion of professional salespeople. Furthermore, influence strategies based on promises as opposed to threats help foster positive feelings among salespeople and boost salesforce morale.

Persuasion An influence strategy based on **persuasion** can work without the use of reward or coercive power. Because persuasive messages must be rational and reasonable, however, expert and referent power bases are necessary to make them effective. Persuasion implies that the target of influence must first change his or her attitudes and intentions to produce a subsequent change in behavior. For example, a sales manager might persuade the salesforce to submit weekly activity reports by first convincing them of the importance of the reports in the company's marketing information system.

Sales managers are almost always former salespeople and therefore are comfortable with influence through persuasion. Generally speaking, persuasion is preferred to threats and promises, but it does require more time and skill.

Relationships Two types of **relationships** can affect influence processes. The first type is based on referent power. It builds on personal friendships, or feelings of trust, admiration, or respect. In short, one party is willing to do what the other party desires, simply because the former likes the latter. In a salesforce setting, these kinds of relationships are consistent with the notion of the salesforce as a cooperative team.

To develop relationships based on referent power, sales managers can take several actions. First, they should recognize that, generally speaking, they will be better liked by others if they can cope effectively with their own job pressures. Being calm and pleasant under pressure will bring a sales manager more power than caving in to the pressure, which might result in temper tantrums and impulsive reactions. Second, sales managers can take a genuine interest in the people with whom they interact and can learn to show that interest through conversation and other means of communication. Another suggestion is to initiate reciprocation with other parties by being the first to offer information or to provide a service.[24] For example, a sales manager might provide a production manager with a timely sales forecast on a voluntary basis to help schedule future manufacturing processes. In turn, this may lead the production manager to reciprocate with valuable information for the sales manager at some future date.

In the second type of relationship, one party has legitimate power over the other party by virtue of position in the organizational hierarchy. Sales managers have legitimate power in dealing with salespeople. As a result, they can influence salespeople in many situations without the use of threats, promises, or persuasion.

Manipulation Unlike the other influence strategies, **manipulation** does not involve direct communications with the target of influence. Rather, circumstances are controlled to influence behavior. For example, a salesperson lacking self-confidence might be assigned to work on temporary assignment with a confident senior salesperson. In team selling, the sales manger might control the group dynamics within teams by carefully selecting compatible personality types to compose the teams. Manipulation might also involve "office politics" and the use of third parties to influence others. For example, a sales manager might use the backing of his or her superior in dealing with peers on the job.

COMMUNICATION MECHANISMS A critical part of using communication in leadership processes is knowing how to use appropriate **communication mechanisms** effectively. It is beyond the scope of this book to discuss fully fundamental business communication topics, such as letter and memo writing, report writing, and the use of e-mail. Instead, consider how a communications mechanism called the *hub concept* could contribute to effective leadership. This concept is contrasted with the traditional linear approach to communications in Figure 8.2.

The hub concept is only one example of how communication mechanisms can facilitate leadership functions. In today's productivity-driven environment, sales managers are using every conceivable device to improve the efficiency of their communication with the salesforce. Car phones, pagers, fax machines, voice mail, e-mail, and companywide video networks are some of the more popular tools being used to speed communication to salesforces in far-flung locations. For example, Hewlett-Packard's 5,000 salespeople have access to the Electronic Sales Partner, a massive Intranet filled with product data, competitive intelligence, and ideas for winning pitches. This system allows the company's geographically scattered sales teams to more quickly and easily gather all important materials about a particular account to ensure that sales presentations will be as competitive as possible.[25]

FIGURE 8.2   Hub Concept and Salesforce Communications

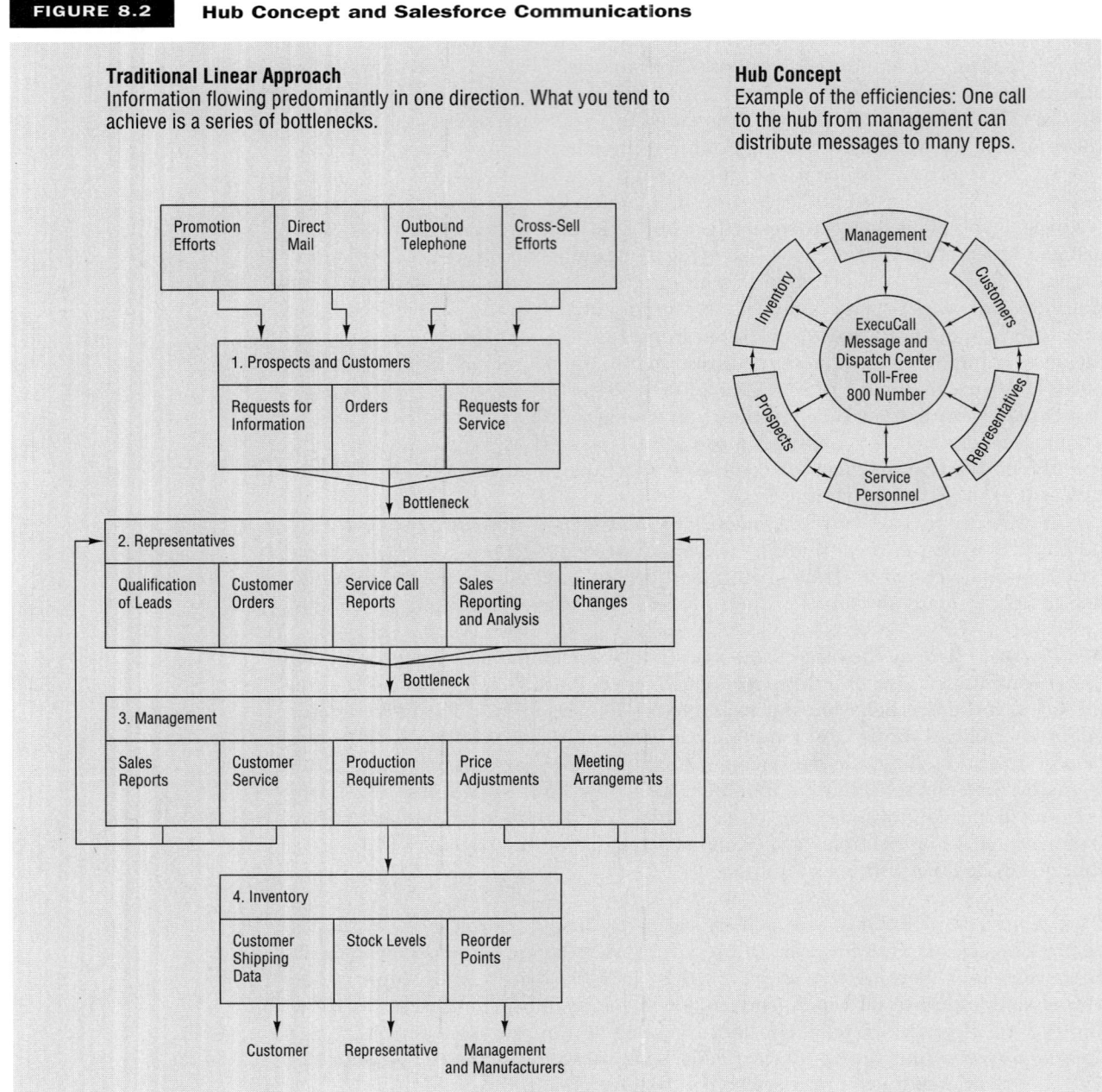

The traditional linear approach to salesforce communications is often plagued by inefficiencies, or so-called bottlenecks. The hub concept allows direct communication among all parties.

All communication with the salesforce must be carefully planned to ensure accuracy and clarity. And remember, although the latest developments such as the hub offer exciting features, the simple spoken word between a sales manager and a salesperson is still of prime importance in effective leadership.

Selected Leadership Functions

In this section, three particularly important leadership functions of sales management are discussed: coaching the salesforce, planning and conducting integrative sales meetings, and striving for ethical (or moral) leadership behavior.

Coaching

In the **coaching** role, a sales manager concentrates on continuous development of salespeople through supervisory feedback and role modeling.[26] The importance of coaching is illustrated in this passage:

> To many a sales manager, a seller either has or hasn't got what it takes to sell. This attitude reduces sales management to a problem of finding the right seller. The difficulty with that approach is that seller turnover rates are often horrendous, leaving many territories poorly covered or not covered at all. . . . Sales managers should be in the field with their low producers, and their new sellers, as much as possible. Like good athletic coaches, they should constantly remind the sellers of the fundamentals, constantly encourage, and constantly praise good performance.[27]

Although coaching may entail the sales manager's interactions with a group of salespeople, its most crucial activities are those conducted with individual salespeople. Coaching sessions may take place in the office or during the sales manager's field visits with salespeople. In the field, such sessions often take the form of "curbstone conferences" immediately before or after each sales call.

Because salespeople often have considerable latitude to plan and execute work activities, coaching is extremely important for most sales managers. Furthermore, the boundary-role demands of sales jobs and the frequent geographic isolation of salespeople from other company personnel add to the significance of coaching activities.

The essence of coaching is providing guidance and feedback as close as possible to the occurrence of an appropriate event related to developing salespeople's skills, attitudes, or behaviors. By ensuring a close link between the coaching session and the appropriate event (e.g., a sales call) the sales manager is using the principle of *recency* to assist the developmental, or learning, process. Essentially this principle holds that learning is facilitated when it is immediately applied. By making a practice of holding coaching sessions before and after each sales call, sales managers are also using *repetition*, another powerful learning tool.

In addition to using repetition and recency to facilitate learning, sales managers should consider the type of feedback they offer to salespeople during coaching sessions. Feedback can be described as either outcome feedback or as cognitive feedback.[28] **Outcome feedback** is information about whether a desired outcome is achieved. By contrast, **cognitive feedback** is information about how and why the desired outcome is achieved. Post–sales call coaching focusing on outcome feedback might feature such comments as, "Your response to the question on pricing was totally inadequate," whereas cognitive feedback might focus on why the pricing question was poorly handled, how a better response could have been made, and how the proper handling of the question could have facilitated the desired outcome for the sales call.

Researchers have suggested that cognitive feedback can be helpful to salespeople and that outcome feedback can be dysfunctional in the complex dynamic environments faced by many salespeople.[29] The importance of cognitive feedback is reaffirmed in several of the points in Exhibit 8.2.

| EXHIBIT 8.2 | Coaching Suggestions |

1. Take a "we" approach instead of a "you" approach. Instead of telling the salesperson, "You should do it this way next time," try, "On the next call, we can try it this way."
2. Address only one or two problems at a time. Prioritize problems to be attacked, and deal with the most important ones first.
3. Instead of criticizing salespeople during coaching, help them improve by giving "how to" advice. Repeatedly tell them what you like about their performance.
4. Ask questions to maximize the salesperson's active involvement in the coaching process.
5. Recognize differences in salespeople and coach accordingly. Although salespeople should work together as a team, direct some efforts toward meeting individual needs.
6. Coordinate coaching with more formal sales training. Coaching is valuable, but it cannot replace formal sales training. Train regularly to enhance skills, then reinforce with coaching.
7. Encourage continual growth and improvement of salespeople. Use team or one-on-one sessions to evaluate progress and celebrate accomplishments.
8. Insist that salespeople evaluate themselves. Self-evaluation helps develop salespeople into critical thinkers regarding their work habits and performance.
9. Reach concrete agreements about what corrective action is to be taken after each coaching session. Failure to agree on corrective action may lead to the salesperson's withdrawal from the developmental aspects of coaching.
10. Keep records of coaching sessions specifying corrective action to be taken, objectives of the coaching session, and a timetable for accomplishing the objective. Follow up to ensure objectives are accomplished.

Successful coaching occurs in an environment of trust and respect between the sales manager and salesperson. By demonstrating honesty, reliability, and competency and by listening to salespeople's needs, sales managers can earn the trust and respect of salespeople and enhance their own chances of being a successful coach.[30] One study suggested that sales managers also can enhance salespeople's trust in them by being good role models.[31] As coaches, sales managers must be role models that set positive examples through their behavior. This is crucial because salespeople will emulate the work habits, positive attitudes, and goals of their managers.[32] See how Steve Randazzo at Schein Pharmaceutical uses collaboration and coaching to help his salespeople achieve their goals in "Sales Management in the 21st Century: Collaboration and Coaching at Schein Pharmaceutical."

Planning and Conducting Integrative Meetings

One of the best opportunities for sales managers to demonstrate leadership ability comes when they plan and execute an **integrative meeting,** one in which several sales and sales management functions are achieved. Although multiple objectives are accomplished at such meetings, their overall purpose is to unite the salesforce

SALES MANAGEMENT IN THE 21ST CENTURY

Collaboration and Coaching at Schein Pharmaceutical

Steve Randazzo, regional director for Schein Pharmaceutical, Inc., shares his strategy for using collaboration and coaching to help his salespeople achieve their goals:

We believe that our salespeople are also our customers. Therefore, we listen closely to their needs and then work with them to develop strategies to best serve their accounts. I sit down with salespeople, and together we analyze their current product mix and relationship development strategy for each account. We then determine a strategy for developing a product mix and cultivating relationships that will grow each account to achieve desired sales goals. Besides helping salespeople with strategy, we use coaching to help salespeople improve their sales presentations. After a sales call, I will conduct a post-call analysis. First, salespeople provide a self-critique of the call. Then I give my analysis, letting the salespeople know what they did well or not so well and offering suggestions for improving future calls. Although salespeople are still held fully accountable for reaching their goals, we believe that they will be in a better position to achieve them if we can provide them with direction for doing so.

in the quest for common objectives, a key part of the leadership model discussed earlier in this module. Such meetings may combine training, strategic planning, motivational programs, recognition of outstanding sales performance, and recreation and entertainment for the attendees. In large sales organizations, the entire salesforce may attend a major integrative sales meeting each year to review the past year's performance and unite for the upcoming year. According to John Mackenzie, a meeting consultant for Coca-Cola, Du Pont, and General Foods, such events allow "psychic bonding" among salespeople; that is, salespeople can share common experiences and feel more like team members than isolated employees.[33] Sales managers can use integrative meetings to ensure that salespeople gain a better understanding of their important revenue production role. Mackenzie also stresses that such meetings provide an excellent means for sales managers to reinforce their own visibility, reputation, and image with top management and the salesforce.

As is true with all leadership functions, the needs and wants of the salesforce should be given some consideration in the planning and execution of integrative meetings. Some suggestions from salespeople are given in Exhibit 8.3.

Planning and conducting an integrative sales meeting involves creative, sometimes glamorous, activities, such as selecting a theme for the meeting, arranging for the appearance of professional entertainers, or even assisting in the production of special films and other audiovisual materials. For example, Northwestern Mutual Life held a meeting that included a 10-K run, a garden party at the Milwaukee Zoo, a concert featuring country music star Wynonna Judd, and an opening to the meeting that involved a videotape of the company's senior vice president of agencies playing catch with Green Bay Packers' quarterback Brett Favre.[34] However, the ultimate success of all meetings depends on the planning and execution of rather detailed activities, such as communicating with all parties before the meeting, checking site arrangements, preparing materials for the meeting, arranging for audiovisual support, and ensuring that all supplies are on hand when the meeting begins. To increase the effectiveness of a major meeting, sales managers would be well served to heed the advice given in Exhibit 8.4.

Increasingly, communication technology allows off-site meeting participants to join in meetings. This is often an attractive option for salesforces that are geographically dispersed. Computer networks groupwork software such as Lotus Notes, and videoconferencing can replace some face-to-face meetings without any loss in meeting effectiveness. The cost is often lower as well. Nonetheless, face-to-face meetings remain a crucial sales leadership activity.

Meeting Ethical and Moral Responsibilities

In recent years, increased attention has been paid to the subject of ethical responsibilities of business leaders. As pointed out in a prize-winning *Harvard Business*

EXHIBIT 8.3   **Suggestions from Salespeople on Conducting Meetings**

1. Keep technical presentations succinct, and use visual aids and breakout discussion groups to maintain salespeople's interest
2. Keep salespeople informed of corporate strategy and their role in it.
3. Minimize operations reviews unless they are directly related to sales. Use a combination of face-to-face exchanges and written handouts to introduce key people in advertising and customer service.
4. Set a humane schedule. Overscheduling can deter learning. Allow time for salespeople to share experiences so they learn from each other.
5. Let salespeople know what's planned. Be sure they are briefed on the purpose and content of the meeting. Distribute a written agenda.
6. Ask salespeople for their ideas on topics, speakers, and preferred recreational activities, if applicable.
7. Generate excitement with contests. Reward effort and results so that all participants can enjoy the chance to win.

EXHIBIT 8.4 Sales Manager's Meeting Review List

Before your meeting
1. Distribute meeting notice/agenda.
2. Plan and prepare the meeting content, both words and visuals, in terms of the needs of your audience.
3. Rehearse.
4. Check out room and equipment.

At the start of the meeting
1. Review the agenda.
2. Review meeting objectives.
3. Explain what role the participants will have in the meeting.

During the meeting (encouraging participation)
1. Ask open-end questions . . . that is, questions that can't be answered with yes or no.
2. Ask one or two participants to bring specific relevant information to share at the meeting.
3. Reinforce statements that are on-target with meeting objectives.
4. When questions are asked of you, redirect them to the group or to the questioner.
5. Use examples from your own personal experience to encourage the group to think along similar lines.

During the meeting (maintaining control)
1. Ignore off-target remarks. Do not reinforce.
2. Ask questions specifically related to the task at hand.
3. Restate relevant points of the agenda when the discussion veers from objectives.
4. When one person is dominating the discussion, tactfully, but firmly, ask him or her to allow others to speak.
5. Ask the group's opinion about whether a certain subject is on-target or not with the agenda.

At the end of the meeting
1. Summarize
2. State conclusions and relate to original meeting objectives.
3. Outline actions to be taken as a result of the meeting (who is expected to do what and by when).

Cautions
1. Encourage, don't resent, questions.
2. Be a facilitator and not a monopolizer of discussion.
3. A little humor is welcome at most any meeting, but don't attempt to be a constant comic.
4. Don't put anybody down in public. If you have a problem participant, take him or her aside at a break and ask for cooperation.
5. Coming unprepared is worse than not coming.

Review article, "Most business decisions involve some degree of ethical judgment; few can be taken solely on the basis of arithmetic."[35] In previous modules, ethical concerns have been highlighted to stress their importance in practically every sales management function. In this section, three approaches to management ethics are discussed: **immoral management, amoral management,** and **moral management.** The key points distinguishing these three approaches are shown in Exhibit 8.5. The author of the material shown in the exhibit contends that most managers fit into the amoral category and that the number of moral managers roughly equals the number of immoral managers.[36]

As you review the information in Exhibit 8.5, examples of immoral management may come to mind easily, whereas examples of amoral and moral management are probably harder to recall. This is partially a function of what types of business practices have been deemed most topical by the business and popular press. However, that press coverage could also indicate a deep concern throughout society about ethics in management.

Before discussing the features of moral, or ethical, sales management, some examples of seemingly immoral management (as described in Exhibit 8.5) might be helpful.[37]

- Agents at Prudential Insurance Company of America convinced customers to purchase new policies, promising that they would practically pay for themselves. Agents failed to inform customers that cash value in an older policy was being used to pay for the new, more expensive one. Agents' actions cost the company $435 million to settle a class-action suit.
- Two men were indicted in Federal District Court in Brooklyn on charges that they solicited the murder of rivals who tried to secure part of the cash they received selling the stock of a fake company.

EXHIBIT 8.5   Approaches to Management Ethics

		Immoral Management	*Amoral Management*	*Moral Management*
Organizational Characteristics	**Ethical Norms**	Management decisions, actions, and behavior imply a positive and active opposition to what is moral (ethical). Decisions are discordant with accepted ethical principles. An active negation of what is moral is implied.	Management is neither moral nor immoral, but decisions lie outside the sphere to which moral judgments apply. Management activity is outside or beyond the moral order of a particular code. May imply a lack of ethical perception and moral awareness.	Management activity conforms to a standard of ethical, or right, behavior. Management activity conforms to accepted professional standards of conduct. Ethical leadership is common on the part of management.
	Motives	Selfish. Management cares only about its or the company's gains.	Well-intentioned but selfish in the sense that impact on others is not considered.	Good. Management wants to succeed but only within the confines of sound ethical precepts (fairness, justice, due process).
	Goals	Profitability and organizational success at any price.	Profitability. Other goals are not considered.	Profitability within the confines of legal obedience and ethical standards.
	Orientation toward Law	Legal standards are barriers that management must overcome to accomplish what it wants.	Law is the ethical guide, preferably the letter of the law. The central question is what we can do legally.	Obedience toward letter and spirit of the law. Law is a minimal ethical behavior. Prefer to operate well above what law mandates.
	Strategy	Exploit opportunities for corporate gain. Cut corners when it appears useful.	Give managers free rein. Personal ethics may apply but only if managers choose. Respond to legal mandates if caught and required to do so.	Live by sound ethical standards. Assume leadership position when ethical dilemmas arise. Enlightened self-interest.

- At ALC Communications Corporation, several reps cut the account number off invoices and pasted them onto other invoices. They were trying to prove that an account was bringing in a particular level of revenue or had an acceptable credit history to collect commissions. Before the accounting department caught on, the reps had been paid and quit the company.
- The owner of a Los Angeles promotion company looked his customer directly in the eye and asked, "Is there anything more you need from me?" The innuendo was clear—if his customer, a Hollywood film executive, wanted anything, such as cash or a trip, he could take care of it. The day after the meeting, the promotion company owner sent a limousine to pick up the customer to take him to a private party involving two prostitutes and a hotel room.
- In a survey of 200 sales managers, 49 percent indicated that their sales reps have lied on a sales call, and 34 percent say that they have heard their reps make unrealistic promises on a sales call.

These examples are in sharp contrast to moral management as described in Exhibit 8.5. Corporate training can help sensitize managers to ethical issues and may be able to convert amoral, and even immoral, managers to the moral school of thought.

Tighter financial controls and closer supervision of sales activities may help achieve ethical sales management practices. Bribery, for example, is hard to commit when sales expenditures are closely monitored. Many sales organizations are adopting a **code of ethics.** One survey found that 84 percent of the companies surveyed have a code of conduct and 45 percent have an ethics office.[38] Associations also develop ethical codes and urge members to adhere to standards of ethical business behavior. For an example, refer to Module 2 (Exhibit 2.2).

Certainly, the development of a code of ethics is a positive action, although it is probably not enough to ensure ethical management. Sales managers must be willing to evaluate their own behavior and ask themselves if they consistently act in an ethical manner in dealing with their coworkers, employees, customers, and other parties.[39] This process of self-evaluation could be very revealing, as suggested in a study of how sales managers react to unethical sales behavior.[40] The study concluded that sales managers would be more likely to use harsher disciplinary measures if the salesperson were male instead of female or a poor performer rather than a top performer and if negative consequences (e.g., losing a major account) were to follow the unethical action by the salesperson. In an ideal world, sales managers would react to unethical sales behavior without regard for individual characteristics of the salesperson involved or the consequences of the unethical act.

In examining their own behavior and that of the salesforce, sales managers should be aware of three particularly relevant types of unethical acts, as shown in Exhibit 8.6. The first type of unethical act is termed a **nonrole act.** This type of act (e.g., cheating on an expense account) would not relate to a sales manager's or a salesperson's specific job role but rather is a calculated attempt to gain something at the expense of the company. A **role failure act** involves a failure to perform job responsibilities. For example, a sales manager may do a superficial job on a salesperson's performance appraisal. The third type of unethical act is the **role distortion act** (e.g., committing bribery), which may put the individual at risk, presumably to benefit the company and the individual's own job objectives.

Researchers suggest that it is most likely that a given organization will concentrate attention on nonrole acts by implementing financial controls and employee monitoring systems. Interestingly, these researchers conclude that role distortion and role failure acts seldom receive systematic attention in most organizations.[41] Perhaps these findings offer direction to sales managers who are determined to manage their salesforce according to principles of moral, or ethical, conduct.

Those interested in achieving moral management will undoubtedly face some challenges because competitive pressures and the premium placed on expedient action often encourage unethical behavior. As one observer puts it,

> The central nature of selling—a negotiation between buyer and seller—is inherently a laboratory of ethical scenarios. Sales managers likewise face many ethical is-

EXHIBIT 8.6 **Types of Morally Questionable Managerial Acts**

Type	Direct Effect	Examples
Nonrole	Against the firm	• Expense account cheating • Embezzlement • Stealing supplies
Role failure	Against the firm	• Superficial performance appraisal • Not confronting expense account cheating • Palming off a poor performer with inflated praise
Role distortion	For the firm	• Bribery • Price fixing • Manipulation of suppliers

sues stemming from the discretion they must exercise in adjusting resources for variations in territories, salesperson ability, competitor strength, and social, political, and regulatory climates in the various markets served.[42]

For a long-term horizon for success, we urge you to use a framework for moral, ethical management as described in the last column of Exhibit 8.5 and to embrace, when available, codes of ethics, training to sensitize salespeople and their mangers to ethical issues, and legal instruction. Those who become sales managers will have the added responsibility of providing ethical leadership by setting an example.

Problems in Leadership

Any managerial position involving the direct supervision of employees will require periodic handling of personnel management problems. As indicated earlier, personnel problems can be minimized through proper recruitment and selection, training, motivation and compensation, and the establishment of clearly stated salesforce plans, policies, and procedures.

Examples of the problems that sales managers may have to deal with include conflicts of interest, chemical abuse and dependency, salespeople who will not conform to guidelines, salespeople whose employment must be terminated, and sexual harassment.

Conflicts of Interest

Because salespeople assume a boundary-role position, they cannot help but encounter **conflicts of interest.** Such conflicts are part of the job, and problem-solving skills are often tested. In some cases, meeting customer demands could violate company policy. In an even more serious vein, the salesperson could have a vested interest or ownership in a customer's business, or even in a competitor's business. The use of confidential information for individual profit, as in the case of Wall Street insider trading, is also an example of serious—in fact, criminal—conflict of interest. At times, sales managers may be asked to put the company's interest ahead of customers' interests, as seen in "An Ethical Dilemma." Many companies require that employees periodically sign an agreement not to engage in specified situations that may represent conflicting interests.

> **An Ethical Dilemma**
>
> *You recently received a promotion to district sales manager. You are eager to show your leadership ability and ready to implement a strategy to make your company successful. Your boss has come to you to explain a new selling strategy that he would like to see you implement. It involves having your salespeople be a little more aggressive with their customers. Essentially, he would like them to oversell their customers. For instance, a salesperson should attempt to convince a customer that he needs an $8,000 copier, even if a $4,000 copier would satisfy his needs. Your boss explains that customers will still be receiving what they need, albeit perhaps a little more, and the company will reap greater profits, resulting in larger bonuses for you. What would you do and why?*

Chemical Abuse and Dependency

Salespeople may be no more susceptible to chemical dependency than any other occupational group, nor is there any hard evidence that chemical abuse and dependency are worse among their ranks now than in the past. However, these problems do exist. A report by the U.S. Department of Health and Human Services found that approximately 10 percent of salespeople younger than age 50 admitted to doing illicit drugs regularly. In another study, 61 percent of the respondents indicated that they knew someone who went to work under the influence of drugs or alcohol. Estimates indicate that drug abuse in the workplace costs employees more than $160 billion annually.[43] Awareness of this problem is increasing, and sales managers are taking a more active role in identifying individuals with problems and in assisting rehabilitative efforts.

Sales managers have historically played a key role as counselors to salespeople with chemical dependency problems. In today's environment, sales managers might be well advised to leave the counseling to professionals. Many companies have assistance programs to help employees deal with emotional distress, alcoholism, and drug dependency. Such programs take sales managers out of the role of counselor, allowing them to focus on other aspects of their job for which they are better equipped.[44]

Problem Salespeople: A Disruptive Influence

Sales managers must be able to deal effectively with problem salespeople. In most cases, problems can be remedied by identifying the behavior or attitude to be corrected, then encouraging a change through motivation, supervision, and further training and development. Several caricatures of problem salespeople and the recommended sales management actions are shown in Exhibit 8.7.

Perhaps the most infamous of the "problem salespeople" is the nonconforming "maverick" who breaks all the rules in the quest for sales results. Although mavericks often are high achievers, their flouting of the rules can be disruptive to sales managers and can adversely affect the remainder of the salesforce. A maverick who fails to produce will not survive in most sales organizations, but a rule-breaker who can produce often thrives as the center of attention.

EXHIBIT 8.7 Examples of Problem Salespeople and Remedies

	Behavior	Nonverbal Signals	Motivated by	Strengths	Problems	How to Manage	Growth Programs
Grandstand George	Aggressive	Exuberant	Big awards	Great closer	Overpowering at times	Clip his wings	Team-building program
Fearful Fred	Low enthusiasm	Scared	Support	Honesty	Low sales volume	Set/support activity goals	Dale Carnegie course
Slumped Sally	Burned out	Depressed	Coaching	Past success experience	Pessimistic attitude	Focus on future goals	Positive attitude programs
Excited Eddie	High enthusiasm	Wired	Exotic incentives	Opening new territories	Poor follow-up	Supply new challenges; monitor carefully	Relaxation training
Disorganized Debbie	Inconsistent	Frustrated	Meaning	Good team player	Unfinished business	Prioritize; assign specific tasks, deadlines	Time/territory management
Perfectionist Pete	Overcontrolled	Rigid	Control	Detail oriented	Lack of flexibility	Relax pressure; reward growth	Stress management
Worried Walter	Low enthusiasm	Hesitant	Stability	Amiable, understanding	Tendency to start rumors	Build self-confidence	Self-esteem program

In terms of organizational commitment and job involvement discussed earlier in this module, mavericks are often very enthusiastic about their selling jobs (high involvement) but are not bound to their organizations (low commitment). This high–low combination in terms of involvement and commitment produces a salesperson type sometimes called a **lone wolf.**[45] In some sales environments, for example, if the company sold through independent sales contractors, so-called lone wolves would not present substantial problems. In others, especially when team efforts are required, they would represent a sales management challenge.

Salespeople who are highly committed to the organization but who do not strongly identify with their selling roles might be called **corporate citizens.** They, too, may represent supervisory problems for sales managers, particularly if aggressive sales growth objectives are in place.

Most sales managers would prefer to have a high proportion of salespeople who are both highly committed to the organization and highly involved in their selling jobs. Such salespeople have been called **institutional stars,** and they are the primary targets of retention and reward programs.

Continuing the involvement/commitment typology, salespeople who are low on both dimensions would represent another problem category for sales managers. These salespeople have been referred to as **apathetics** and may be candidates for termination of employment if they cannot be resurrected.

Termination of Employment

In some cases, problems cannot be overcome, and it is necessary to terminate the employment of a salesperson. When performance consistently fails to meet standards and coaching, training, and retraining are unsuccessful, termination or reassignment may be the only remaining alternatives. Also, a salesperson's insubordination or lack of effort may damage the overall effectiveness or morale of the salesforce, in which case termination could be justified.

The current environment dictates that sales managers pay close attention to the legal ramifications of terminating a salesperson's employment. A permanent record of performance appraisals, conditions of employment, and any deviations from expected performance or behavior should be carefully maintained throughout the salesperson's term of employment. Attempts to correct performance deficiencies should be noted and filed when they occur.

Before firing the salesperson, the sales manager should carefully review all relevant company policies to ensure his or her own adherence to appropriate guidelines. Finally, the actual communication of termination should be written, and any verbal communication of the termination should be witnessed by a third party. At all times, sales managers should respect the dignity of the person whose employment is being terminated while firmly communicating the termination notice.

Sexual Harassment

In 1980, the Equal Employment Opportunity Commission (EEOC) formally addressed a long-standing workplace problem by issuing guidelines for minimizing **sexual harassment.**[46] Defining this term is not an easy matter, but EEOC guidelines indicate that sexual harassment could include lewd remarks, physical and visual actions, and sexual innuendos. Companies are expected to have guidelines for dealing with this offense, including a written policy prohibiting all forms of sexual harassment, training on this policy, and a method for responding to sexual harassment complaints.[47]

Since the establishment of EEOC guidelines, there have been numerous instances of reported sexual harassment, most often with a woman being the target of the harassment. A survey of 200 sales professionals revealed that 63 percent of the female respondents had been sexually harassed, compared with 9 percent of the men surveyed. Almost three-fourths (74 percent) of the women said that sexual harassment was most likely to occur during job-related travel.[48] Charges filed with the EEOC have gone from less than 7,000 to nearly 16,000 during the 1990s.[49]

Policies and procedures for dealing with sexual harassment should be developed for the entire company, and sales managers must strive to implement them in a conscientious manner. Furthermore, sales managers must become familiar with EEOC guidelines so that they can serve as role models and communicate clearly to their salespeople the important issues involved in sexual harassment. The job of protecting salespeople from sexual harassment is complicated by the fact that salespeople work with customers away from the office and in social situations.

It is important to take action immediately if a sexual harassment problem comes to light. Employers may be legally accountable, for example, if they ignore sexual harassment of their salespeople by customers or others in the workplace. In a landmark case by the Supreme Court, Burlington Industries was held liable for sexual harassment in a suit filed by a former employee who claimed that her sales manager constantly harassed her. The sales manager reportedly advised her to "loosen up" in the office and told her that he could make her life very hard or very easy at Burlington.[50] As illustrated in "An Ethical Dilemma," similar situations may occur among salespeople.

An Ethical Dilemma

It has recently come to your attention that your star salesperson, Bob Smith, has been making sexual innuendos to some of the female salespeople on your salesforce. You have known Bob and his family for more than 5 years, and during this period, he never struck you as the type of guy who would do this. He has been an outstanding performer for you, being your top salesperson each year. You are afraid that if you falsely accuse Bob of these actions, you might damage your relationship with him, hurt his family, and possibly drive him off. You would hate to lose Bob. Perhaps these women are just overly sensitive. What should you do and why?

The examples of conflicts of interest, chemical dependency, rule-breaking salespeople, the need to terminate employment of unsatisfactory salespeople, and sexual harassment are offered here to remind you of the complex human issues of managing a salesforce. Realities dictate that sales managers be able to confront and handle personnel problems as adeptly as strategic sales management issues to be effective leaders of their salesforces.

Summary

1. **Distinguish between salesforce leadership and supervision.** Supervision is part of leadership. It deals with the day-to-day operations of the salesforce and is primarily concerned with the maintenance and improvement of the status quo. Leadership requires more foresight and intuition than mere supervision, however, and may involve major changes in salesforce objectives and operations. Leadership involves the sales manager's interactions with a variety of parties, including salespeople, customers, other company personnel, external trainers, and employment agencies. Supervision, however, is concerned only with the relationships between the sales manager and the salesforce.
2. **Discuss how salesforce socialization can be enhanced through supervision and leadership.** The concept of salesforce socialization was first introduced in Module 6 (refer to Figure 6.1). Through effective supervision and leadership, sales managers can build the task-specific self-esteem of their salespeople and help resolve on-the-job conflicts. This should lead to desirable job outcomes: higher levels of organizational commitment, job involvement, job satisfaction, and performance.

3. **Explain how the LMX model, transformational leadership, and behavioral self-management concepts contribute to contemporary sales leadership.** These views of sales leadership offer several important thoughts for today's sales managers. The Leader–Member Exchange (LMX) model encourages sales managers and salespeople to build a relationship on mutual trust. Transformational leadership recognizes the necessity and importance of change in most sales organizations. Behavioral self-management offers an alternative to close supervision, an important concept for many salespeople who do not work under close supervision.
4. **List the six components of a sales leadership model.** A model for sales leadership, shown in Figure 8.1, identifies six components: power of the sales manager, power of salespeople, situational factors, needs of salespeople and other parties, goals and objectives, and leadership skills.
5. **Discuss five bases of power that affect leadership.** Five power bases are coercive, reward, legitimate, referent, and expert. Coercive power is associated with punishment and is the opposite of reward power. Legitimate power stems from the individual's position in the organizational hierarchy. Referent power is held by one person when another person wants to maintain a relationship with that person. Expert power is attributed to the possession of information. A sales manager and those with whom he or she interacts may use one or more power bases in a given situation.
6. **Explain five influence strategies used in leadership.** Influence strategies used by sales managers could be based on threats, promises, persuasion, relationships, or manipulation. Unlike the other four strategies, manipulation does not involve face-to-face interactions with the target of influence. Threats use coercive power, whereas promises stem from the reward power base. Persuasion uses expert and referent power. Legitimate and referent power are used when influence strategy is based on interpersonal relationships.
7. **Discuss issues related to coaching the salesforce, holding integrative meetings, and practicing ethical management.** Coaching involves the continual development of the salesforce. A most critical part of coaching is one-on-one sessions with a salesperson. Coaching relies on the learning principles of recency and repetition and is often conducted in the field before and after sales calls. Integrative meetings accomplish multiple sales management functions. Sales managers are involved in creative aspects of planning integrative meetings, but paying attention to detail is the key to successful meetings. Meeting ethical responsibilities is not necessarily easy but is essential to long-term success in a sales career.
8. **Identify some of the problems encountered in leading and supervising a salesforce.** Some of the problems encountered in salesforce management are conflicts of interest; chemical abuse and dependency; disruptive, rule-breaking salespeople; salespeople whose employment must be terminated; and sexual harassment.

Understanding Sales Management Terms

- Leadership
- Supervision
- Task-specific self-esteem
- Organizational commitment
- Formalization
- Work alienation
- Job involvement
- Leader–Member Exchange (LMX) model
- Transformational leadership
- Behavioral self-management (BSM)
- Expert power
- Referent power
- Legitimate power
- Reward power
- Coercive power
- Trait approach
- Behavior approach
- Contingency approach
- Anticipation
- Seek feedback
- Diagnostic skills
- Influence strategies
- Threats
- Promises
- Persuasion
- Relationships
- Manipulation
- Communication mechanisms
- Coaching
- Outcome feedback
- Cognitive feedback
- Integrative meeting
- Immoral management
- Amoral management
- Moral management
- Code of ethics

- Nonrole act
- Role failure act
- Role distortion act
- Conflicts of interest
- Lone wolf
- Corporate citizens
- Institutional stars
- Apathetics
- Sexual harassment

Developing Sales Management Knowledge

1. Explain why the following views of leadership are relevant for sales organizations: Leader–Member Exchange (LMX) model, transformational leadership, and behavioral self-management.
2. Briefly describe the six components of the sales leadership model shown in Figure 8.1.
3. Describe five types of power that affect leadership. What are the problems associated with overreliance on reward and coercive power?
4. How does the contingency approach to leadership differ from the trait approach and the behavior approach?
5. What are four categories of skills that could be useful in leadership?
6. Describe five influence strategies, including the power bases related to each strategy.
7. What is the difference between outcome feedback and cognitive feedback? Which is most important in coaching?
8. Sales managers may learn a lot about their organizations and salespeople simply by spending time observing activities in the office or in the field and talking with the people involved. To maximize their own learning while simultaneously providing leadership, which power bases would be especially important?
9. Refer to "Sales Management in the 21st Century: Collaboration and Coaching at Schein Pharmaceutical." How does Schein use collaboration and coaching to help its salespeople succeed?
10. Refer to "Sales Management in the 21st Century: Using Leadership Skills to Build Sales Teams at FirstEnergy." Explain how leadership skills are used to build sales teams at FirstEnergy.

Building Sales Management Skills

1. Sid Cox has been a steady contributor as an automotive parts representative with Premier Auto Parts for the past 5 years. Conscientious and hardworking, he has always been willing to pull his weight and then some. Customers and coworkers find that his cheerful and pleasant demeanor make him a joy to be around. Over the past month, his sales manager, Randy Ross, has noticed a significant change in Sid's behavior. Sid appears to be worn down, less than enthusiastic, and reluctant to make as many sales calls as he has in the past. His positive, upbeat demeanor seems to have been replaced with a more pessimistic attitude about things. His generally steady sales results have been on the decline. If you were Randy Ross, what would you do? Explain.
2. Choose an individual who is considered to be (or to have been) a great leader (e.g., Lee Iacocca, J.F.K.). Use library resources, the Internet, and so on, to examine this individual to determine what makes (or made) this person such a good leader. In your analysis, explain this leader's traits or characteristics and the leadership skills that contributed to his or her success. Also, attempt to identify and explain the sources of power generally used by this leader. Finally, explain what you learned about this leader that you could use to help you become a more successful leader.
3. "What Would You Do?" Each month *Sales & Marketing Management* magazine poses this question to its readers for a real-life scenario containing a sales-related problem. Readers are asked to submit their responses, and the most noteworthy appear in the following month's issue. This same feature can be accessed at their World Wide Web site (**www.salesandmarketing.com**). Access this address. Click "magazine content" on the menu bar found at the top of the screen. Then click on "contest." Study the situation described and write a short paper that answers the following: (1) What has happened? (2) What would you do and why? You also may want to submit your response to *Sales & Marketing Management* (methods for doing so are provided). Remember, some reader responses will be featured in the following month's issue.

Making Sales Management Decisions

CASE 8.1 Tasti-Fresh Bakery Products

Background

Tasti-Fresh Bakery Products has been very successful at selling breads, rolls, and other bakery products to small and medium-sized retailers throughout the Midwest. It has built its reputation on quality products, strong service, honesty, and integrity. The company credits much of its success to its salespeople, who provide the main link between it and its customers. The ability of Tasti-Fresh's salespeople to build strong customer relationships has helped keep the company profitable despite increasing competition.

Current Situation

Tasti-Fresh district sales manager Laurel Brown recently received the following letter from one of the company's biggest customers.

February 22, 2000
3242 Grand Avenue
St. Louis, MO 65441

Ms. Laurel Brown
District Sales Manager
Tasti-Fresh Bakery Products
1675 Main
St. Charles, MO 63301

Dear Laurel:

We have always been pleased with your company's products and service. The sales rep who calls on us, Curt Stanford, has gone out of his way to ensure our satisfaction. Lately, however, I have noticed some changes in Curt's behavior. Normally I would not complain, but the treatment we have been getting recently is dramatically different from that to which we are accustomed, and I am concerned about Curt.

Over the past couple of months, I have noticed a dramatic shift in Curt's behavior. Usually steady and dependable, his behavior has become erratic. He has been late, or not shown up at all, for some of his scheduled appointments. Curt also has failed to follow through on several occasions. Sometimes he visits us and he is so enthusiastic it is almost unbearable, whereas on other visits he appears very tired and worn down. I suspect and fear that he may be on drugs.

As I said earlier, over the years we have been happy with your products and service. However, if this type of behavior persists, we will be forced to look for another supplier. We simply cannot afford to jeopardize our business.

Sincerely,

Janice Miller

Janice Miller
Purchasing Agent, Flanders Groceries, Inc.

Laurel was perplexed. Curt is one of her top performers. He has worked for the company for 4 years and has been salesperson of the year the past 2 years. She had not noticed a change in Curt. Then again, she has not had much direct contact with Curt lately because she has been concentrating her efforts on three newly hired sales reps. She wonders if she should confront Curt or simply ignore it. He is making the company a lot of money, and she has not heard any other complaints. If she confronts him, he might quit. Perhaps Janice is simply exaggerating and is really upset about something else. Maybe Janice needs to be confronted. Ignoring her may result in the loss of a big customer.

Questions

1. Should Laurel confront Curt? If not, why? If so, how should she handle the situation?
2. Should Laurel speak to Janice? Why or why not? If so, what should she say to her?
3. If Curt is taking drugs, what do you recommend that Laurel do? How can she prevent problems like this in the future?

CASE 8.2 Global Enterprise

Background

Rock Madd was a drill sergeant in the U.S. Marine Corps for 5 years before joining Global Enterprise 7 years ago as a sales representative. In the Corps, he had been through some tough times and was always willing to face a challenge. A disciplined man, he rapidly became one of the company's best salespeople. However, his goal was to move into sales management. Because of his strong determination and hard work, he was eventually promoted to district sales manager where he replaced Lucille Fagan, who recently retired.

Lucille had done an outstanding job with the district. Her district's sales figures were consistently among the top in the company. She was well liked and respected by her salespeople. Lucille practiced good management skills and was adept at planning, organizing, controlling, and leading. Although she always took the ultimate responsibility for planning she often consulted salespeople when she thought their ideas might be helpful. When it came to organizing, her goal was to motivate her salespeople to work as a team. As a result, she was able to get salespeople to help each other when the needs arose. She had control over her salespeople, but it was primarily through self-control. By setting realistic and individual-specific goals, she was able to motivate her salespeople not only to commit to those goals but also to supervise their own efforts effectively. Finally, Lucille had a real knack for leadership.

She had the ability to get salespeople to realize their true potential and then help them achieve it. It was her contention that a leader should develop people, and she did. In fact, over the years, her salespeople were consistently promoted into management positions.

Rock took a different approach to managing, primarily as a result of his military background. He was a hard-working individual who demanded respect from those around him. He wanted to make sure those he supervised knew he was the boss. His attitude toward planning was that he made the plans and others carried them out. He did not need or seek input from others. He ran a tight organization, calling all the shots. When it came to control, he liked to scrutinize his salespeople closely, making sure they were doing what they were supposed to do.

Current Situation

On Monday afternoon, Rock completed a sales call with Electra Aveshon, a 3-year veteran at Global Enterprise. Although not the most outstanding salesperson in the district, Electra was a good performer. She credited much of her success to Lucille who had helped bring her along. It was Electra's opinion that Lucille could have easily let her go after her rocky start but instead invested the time in coaching her to become a better salesperson. After the call, Rock indicated that he would like to meet with Electra on Friday to discuss the sales call. He had some other business he had to attend to right away, so they could not meet that afternoon. She agreed and an appointment was scheduled for Friday afternoon.

After finishing her appointments Friday morning, Electra met with Rock as scheduled. Following are excerpts from their meeting:

Rock: I was disappointed with your sales call on Monday. It surprised me to see a veteran such as yourself perform so sloppily. You should be ashamed.

Electra: I realize I didn't make the sale. But for the first visit, I felt I made progress in beginning to establish trust and build a relationship.

Rock: You spent too much time attempting to build rapport. You wasted valuable time that could be spent calling on other prospects or servicing current customers.

Electra: I always spend a little more time building rapport. I think it pays off in the long run.

Rock: Your handling of objections was poor. Your response to the question on pricing was totally inadequate. Your response to the question on delivery time was likewise inept. You need to work on handling objections.

Electra: My responses may not have been perfect, but I did not sense the prospect was unsure about what I was saying or had a problem with my responses.

Rock: And where did you learn to close? You need to drive the sale home. You played it a little too soft. I expect to see some real improvement on our next outing. If you can't do any better than this, maybe I'll have to find someone who can.

That evening after work Electra met with a few of her colleagues for some drinks and dinner. The following conversation ensued:

Electra: I'm sick of Madd bossing us around like we are a bunch of his soldiers. This isn't the army. We deserve to be treated with a little more respect.

Andrew: I hear you. The other day Madd went with me on a sales call. All I heard was what a horrible job I was doing. It was as if nothing I did on my call was right.

Colette: Madd always has something to say, and it's usually negative. He doesn't have any problem telling me what's wrong, but he never offers any advice on how to improve.

Matt: Come on, you guys. Give the guy a break. He's just doing what he thinks is right. He's trying to impress upper management by showing them he has everything under control down here. Once he sees this hard-guy stuff doesn't work, he'll loosen up.

Andrew: Yeah, if half the salesforce doesn't quit first. I don't like working for a guy like him. Why should I bust my tail to make him look good? I won't put up with it for long. I've heard some of the others (salespeople) talking and they aren't happy either. Morale really seems to be down.

Colette: Maybe Matt's right. Perhaps soon, Madd will loosen up a bit.

Electra: I don't know, Colette. It's been 8 months now. Once a sergeant, always a sergeant.

Questions

1. How would you characterize Rock's management style? How would you assess his sales management performance thus far?
2. What suggestions can you provide to Rock regarding coaching?
3. What would you recommend Rock do differently?

MODULE 9

Motivation and Reward System Management

Motivating and Rewarding: A Tale of Large and Small

Although sales managers at both large and small companies are interested in motivating and rewarding their salespeople, the approach is not always the same. Typically, larger companies have more resources available with which to reward their salespeople. Smaller companies, with limited budgets, often have to find creative ways to motivate and reward their salespeople. The case of American Express and KXKT-FM illustrates some differences between large and small companies when it comes to motivating and rewarding salespeople.

At American Express, teamwork is considered critical for making the company successful. According to David House, president of worldwide establishment services for American Express, a winning team must stay close to its customers, be committed to excellence, make a difference every day, be accountable for results, and share with peers. Team members who follow this prescription are rewarded. Besides receiving a bonus for every new account opened and a percentage of every dollar charged on that account for 6 years, each rep has an opportunity to be one of the top 75 salespeople in House's division who are taken on a lavish excursion each year. For instance, one year winners received a 4-day trip to Napa Valley, $2,000 in prize money, a plaque, and a book that highlighted their achievements. Former winner Toni-Marie Beccia exemplifies the team spirit that makes a winner. Noted for her stellar track record of signing up car dealerships, Beccia's spot on the trip was achieved by sending copies of her winning presentation to everyone in the company, and accompanying some salespeople on calls to dealerships in her region.

It is not only the stars who get recognized. House often motivates and rewards his salespeople in more subtle ways. He once left a voice mail message commending a rep for closing a small but challenging deal. It was obvious that the message had an impact on the rep from a message House received in return: "I had my mom and dad over for dinner last night, and I played the voice mail for them. Thanks for making my night."

Efforts taken to reward and motivate at American Express are paying off. In one year, its salesforce opened 353,000 U.S. accounts, a 27 percent increase from the previous year.

Sometimes, it is necessary to motivate on a tight budget. Such was the case for Colleen McCoy Hitz, former sales manager at KXKT-FM, a radio station in Omaha, Nebraska. Unable to afford snazzy cars or a lucrative pay plan for her six

Learning Objectives

After completing this module, you should be able to

1 Explain the key components of motivation: intensity, persistence, and direction.

2 Explain the difference between compensation rewards and noncompensation rewards.

3 Describe the primary financial and nonfinancial compensation rewards available to salespeople.

4 Describe salary, commission, and combination pay plans in terms of their advantages and disadvantages.

5 Explain the fundamental concepts in sales-expense reimbursement.

6 Discuss issues associated with sales contests, equal pay for equal work, team compensation, global compensation, and changing a reward system.

7 List the guidelines for motivating and rewarding salespeople.

salespeople, Hitz had to rely on other methods to motivate. Having a small salesforce, Hitz was able to develop relationships with her salespeople, allowing her to understand what motivated each one. For example, she motivated one of her reps, a single working mother, by offering her the flexibility to design her own schedule. She also offered some incentives aimed at the entire salesforce. Unable to provide recognition via money, she honored outstanding reps with "Salesperson of the Month" plaques. Moreover, she kept a board in her office that listed each rep and the percentage of goal each achieved in the past 3 months. According to Hitz, "Nobody wants to be last on the board." She held a proposal-writing contest each week for 3 months in an attempt to improve reps' literary skills. Each week, the salesperson with the best proposal received a $25 bonus. Last, she held her weekly sales meeting every Monday afternoon at a nearby restaurant, where she purchased 99-cent dessert specials to thank her reps for a job well done.

Source: Michele Marchetti, "Master Motivators," *Sales & Marketing Management* 150 (April 1998): 38–44.

The opening vignette introduces several topics regarding the management of salesforce job rewards. A salesforce reward system, because of its impact on motivation and job satisfaction, is one of the most important determinants of both short- and long-term sales performance. The vignette illustrates that there are many effective ways to motivate and reward the salesforce. However, the needs of both the salespeople and the budget must be considered in doing so. The vignette also illustrates the importance of encouraging teamwork in motivating the salesforce, as was the case at American Express.

This module examines the sales manager's role in motivating the salesforce through the use of reward systems. We first define motivation and explain some key concepts in reward system management. In the next section of this module, the characteristics of an effective reward system along with the reward preferences of salespeople in general are discussed. The following section concentrates on financial rewards, such as salaries, commissions, and bonuses. Expense reimbursement is also covered.

Nonfinancial rewards, such as opportunities for growth, recognition, and promotion, are reviewed. Current issues in reward system management, such as the use of sales contests, equal pay for equal work, team compensation, global compensation, and changing reward systems, are presented. This module concludes with summary guidelines for managing salesforce reward systems.

Motivation and Reward Systems

Defining **motivation** has been a tedious job for psychologists, sales management researchers, and sales managers. After decades of study, the most commonly used definitions of motivation include three dimensions—intensity, persistence, and direction.[1] **Intensity** refers to the amount of mental and physical effort put forth by the salesperson. **Persistence** describes the salesperson's choice to expend effort over time, especially when faced with adverse conditions. **Direction** implies that salespeople choose where their efforts will be spent among various job activities.[2]

Because salespeople are often faced with a diverse set of selling and nonselling job responsibilities, their choice of which activities warrant action is just as important as how hard they work or how well they persist in their efforts. The motivation task is incomplete unless salespeople's efforts are channeled in directions consistent with the overall strategic role of the salesforce within the firm. These ideas are supported in two studies of salespeople: one in the direct selling industry and the other of a national manufacturer's salesforce.[3] Both studies indicate that higher levels of effort, or intensity, are not necessarily associated with higher levels of performance.

Motivation is an unobservable phenomenon, and the terms *intensity, persistence,* and *direction* are concepts that help managers explain what they expect from their salespeople. It is important to note that although sales managers can observe salespeople's behavior, they can only infer their motivation. Indeed, it is the personal, unobservable nature of motivation that makes it such a difficult area to study.

Motivation can also be viewed as intrinsic or extrinsic. If salespeople find their job to be inherently rewarding, they are **intrinsically motivated.** If they are motivated by the rewards provided by others, such as pay and formal recognition, they are **extrinsically motivated.** Although a salesperson's overall motivation could be a function of both intrinsic and extrinsic motivation, some will have strong preferences for extrinsic rewards, such as pay and formal recognition awards, whereas others will seek intrinsic rewards, such as interesting, challenging work.[4]

Reward system management involves the selection and use of organizational rewards to direct salespeople's behavior toward the attainment of organizational objectives. An organizational reward could be anything from a $5,000 pay raise to a compliment for a job well done.

Organizational rewards can be classified as compensation and noncompensation rewards. **Compensation rewards** are those that are given in return for acceptable performance or effort. Compensation rewards can include nonfinancial compensation, such as recognition and opportunities for growth and promotion.

Noncompensation rewards include factors related to the work situation and well-being of each salesperson. Sales jobs that are interesting and challenging can increase salespeople's motivation, as can allowing salespeople some control over their own activities. Sales managers can also improve salesforce motivation by providing performance-enhancing feedback to salespeople. Other examples of noncompensation rewards are (1) providing adequate resources so that salespeople can accomplish their jobs and (2) practicing a supportive sales management leadership style. In this module, the focus is on compensation rewards, including financial and nonfinancial compensation.

Optimal Salesforce Reward System

The optimal reward system balances the needs of the organization, its salespeople, and its customers against one another. From the organization's perspective, the reward system should help accomplish the following results:

1. Provide an acceptable ratio of costs and salesforce output in volume, profit, or other objectives.
2. Encourage specific activities consistent with the firm's overall, marketing, and salesforce objectives and strategies. For example, the firm may use the reward system to encourage the selling of particular products or to promote teamwork in the salesforce.
3. Attract and retain competent salespeople, thereby enhancing long-term customer relationships.
4. Allow the kind of adjustments that facilitate administration of the reward system. A clearly stated, reasonably flexible plan assists in the administration of the plan.

EXHIBIT 9.1	Salesforce Rewards Ranked in Order of Preference
PayPromotionSense of AccomplishmentPersonal Growth OpportunitiesRecognitionJob Security	

From the perspective of the salesperson, reward systems are expected to meet a somewhat different set of criteria than from the sales manager's perspective. As indicated in the previous module, salespeople expect to be treated equitably, with rewards comparable to those of others in the organization doing a similar job—and to the rewards of competitors' salespeople. Most salespeople prefer some stability in the reward system, but they simultaneously want incentive rewards for superior performance. Because the most productive salespeople have the best opportunities to leave the firm for more attractive work situations, the preferences of the salesforce regarding compensation must be given due consideration.

In recent years, the needs of the customer have become more important than the needs of the salesforce in determining the structure of reward systems in sales organizations. Companies such as IBM, Eastman Kodak, and Xerox tie compensation to customer satisfaction. Some automobile dealers have tried to reduce customer dissatisfaction stemming from high-pressure sales techniques by paying their salespeople a salary instead of a commission based on sales volume. Others adjust the salesperson's commission based on customer satisfaction with the salesperson's handling of the sale.

Meeting the needs of customers, salespeople, and the sales organization simultaneously is indeed a challenging task. As you might suspect, compromise between sometimes divergent interests becomes essential for managing most salesforce reward systems As noted by Greenberg and Greenberg, "A salesforce is comprised of individual human beings with broadly varying needs, points of view, and psychological characteristics who cannot be infallibly categorized, measured, and punched out to formula.[5]

Types of Salesforce Rewards

For discussion purposes, the countless number of specific rewards available to salespeople are classified into six categories (ranked in order of salespeople's preferences), as shown in Exhibit 9.1: pay, promotion, sense of accomplishment, personal growth opportunities, recognition, and job security. Each of these reward categories is discussed in the next two sections of this module. The financial compensation section focuses on pay, and the nonfinancial compensation section on the other rewards shown in Exhibit 9.1. Keep in mind that these preferences may differ internationally. For example, one study found that Japanese salespeople prefer being a member of a successful team with shared goals and values over receiving financial rewards.[6]

Financial Compensation

In many sales organizations, financial compensation is composed of current spendable income, deferred income or retirement pay, and various insurance plans that

EXHIBIT 9.2 Types of Financial Compensation for Salespeople

Survey Position	Straight Salary	Straight Commission	Commission and Bonus	Salary and Commission	Salary and Bonus	Salary, Bonus and Commission
1. Top marketing executive	15.43%	3.35%	1.30%	8.18%	37.36%	34.39%
2. Top sales executive	9.17	2.81	1.63	10.80	12.28	63.02
3. Regional sales manager	8.21	0.65	0.52	23.47	26.08	41.07
4. District sales manager	36.72	0.19	0.00	7.57	29.05	26.46
5. Senior sales rep	17.05	14.23	2.15	29.53	21.30	15.72
6. Intermediate sales rep	16.78	19.49	0.99	19.96	24.28	18.49
7. Entry-level sales rep	23.56	5.70	2.46	22.47	13.83	31.98
8. National/major account manager	15.08	0.00	1.41	25.71	10.73	44.07
9. National account rep	36.99	3.47	0.87	4.62	11.27	42.77
10. Major (key) account rep	19.69	8.29	8.29	16.06	16.06	31.61

EXHIBIT 9.3 Summary of Financial-Compensation Plans

Type of Plan	Advantages	Disadvantages	Common Uses
Salary	Simple to administer; planned earnings facilitates budgeting and recruiting; customer loyalty enhanced; more control of nonselling activities	No financial incentive to improve performance; pay often based on seniority, not merit; salaries may be a burden to new firms or to those in declining industries	Sales trainees; sales support
Commission	Income linked to results; strong financial incentive to improve results; costs reduced during slow sales periods; less operating capital required	Difficult to build loyalty of salesforce to company; less control of nonselling activities	Real estate; insurance; wholesaling; securities; automobiles
Combination	Flexibility allows frequent reward of desired behavior; may attract high-potential but unproven recruits	Complex to administer; may encourage crisis-oriented objectives	Widely used—most popular type of financial pay plan

may provide income when needed. The discussion here is limited to the current spendable income because it is the most controllable, and arguably most important, dimension of a salesforce reward system. The other components of financial compensation tend to be dictated more by overall company policy rather than by sales managers.

Current spendable income includes money provided in the short term (weekly, monthly, and annually) that allows salespeople to pay for desired goods and services. It includes salaries, commissions, and bonuses. Bonus compensation may include noncash income equivalents, such as merchandise and free-travel awards. A comprehensive study of salesforce financial compensation practices found salaries, commissions, and bonuses to be used widely to pay salespeople. The study concluded that financial compensation plans including a salary and one or more incentives (commission and/or bonus) are the most popular. These conclusions are summarized in Exhibit 9.2.

The three basic types of salesforce financial compensation plans are straight salary, straight commission, and a salary plus incentive, with the incentive being a commission and/or a bonus. A discussion of each type follows (summarized in Exhibit 9.3).

Straight Salary

As indicated in Exhibit 9.2, paying salespeople a **straight salary** (exclusively by a salary) is uncommon. Such plans are well suited for paying sales support personnel and sales trainees.

Sales support personnel, including missionaries and detailers, are involved in situations in which it is difficult to determine who really makes the sale. Because missionaries and detailers are concerned primarily with dissemination of information rather than direct solicitation of orders, a salary can equitably compensate for effort. Compensation based on sales results might not be fair.

Salaries are also appropriate for sales trainees, who are involved in learning about the job rather than producing on the job. In most cases, a firm cannot recruit sales trainees on a college campus without the lure of a salary to be paid at least until training is completed.

ADVANTAGES OF SALARY PLANS One advantage of using salary plans is that they are the simplest ones to administer, with adjustments usually occurring only once a year. Because salaries are fixed costs, **planned earnings** for the salesforce are easy to project, which facilitates the salesforce budgeting process. The fixed nature of planned earnings with salary plans may also facilitate recruitment and selection. For example, some recruits may be more likely to join the sales organization when their first-year earnings can be articulated clearly in salary terms rather than less certain commission terms.

Salaries can provide control over salespeople's activities, and reassigning salespeople and changing sales territories is less a problem with salary plans than with other financial compensation plans. There is general agreement that salesforce loyalty to the company may be greater with salary plans and that there is less chance that high-pressure, non-customer-oriented sales techniques will be used.

Salaries are also used when substantial developmental work is required to open a new sales territory or introduce new products to the marketplace. Presumably, the income stability guaranteed by a salary allows the salesperson to concentrate on job activities rather than worry about how much the next paycheck will be. In general, salary plans allow more control over salesforce activities, especially nonselling activities.

DISADVANTAGES OF SALARY PLANS The most serious shortcoming of straight-salary plans is that they offer little financial incentive to perform past a merely acceptable level. As a result, the least productive members of the salesforce are, in effect, the most rewarded salespeople. Conversely, the most productive salespeople are likely to think salary plans are inequitable.

Differences in salary levels among salespeople are often a function of seniority on the job instead of true merit. Even so, the constraints under which many salary plans operate may cause **salary compression,** or a narrow range of salaries in the salesforce. Thus sales trainees may be earning close to what experienced salespeople earn, which could cause perceptions of inequity among experienced salespeople.

Salaries represent fixed overhead in a sales operation. If the market is declining or stagnating, the financial burden of the firm is greater with salary plans than with a variable expense such as commissions based on sales.

Straight Commission

Unlike straight-salary plans, commission-only plans (or **straight commission**) offer strong financial incentives to maximize performance. However, they also limit control of the salesforce. Some industries—real estate, insurance, automobiles, and securities—traditionally have paid salespeople by straight commission. In these industries, the primary responsibility of the salespeople is simply to close sales; non-selling activities are less important to the employer than in some other industries.

Manufacturers' representatives, who represent multiple manufacturers, are also paid by commission. Wholesalers, many of whom founded their businesses with limited working capital, also traditionally pay their salesforce by commission.

The huge direct-sales industry, including such companies as Mary Kay Cosmetics, Tupperware, and Avon, also pays by straight commission. The large number of salespeople working for these organizations makes salary payments impractical from an overhead and administrative standpoint.

COMMISSION PLAN VARIATIONS There are several factors to be considered in developing a commission-only plan:

1. **Commission base**—volume or profitability
2. **Commission rate**—constant, progressive, regressive, or a combination
3. **Commission splits**—between two or more salespeople or between salespeople and the employer
4. **Commission payout event**—when the order is confirmed, shipped, billed, paid for, or some combination of these events

Commissions may be paid according to sales volume or some measure of profitability, such as gross margin, contribution margin, or in rare cases, net income. Recently, there has been more experimentation with profitability-oriented commission plans in an effort to improve salesforce productivity. Despite the gradual adoption of profitability-based commission plans by various companies, the most popular commission base appears to be sales volume.

Commission rates vary widely, and determining the appropriate rate is a weighty managerial task. The commission rate, or percentage paid to the salesperson, may be a **constant rate** over the pay period, which is an easy plan for the salespeople to understand and provides incentive for them to produce more sales or profits (because pay is linked directly to performance). A **progressive rate** increases as salespeople reach prespecified targets. This provides an even stronger incentive to the salesperson, but it may result in overselling and higher selling costs. A **regressive rate** declines at some predetermined point. Regressive rates might be appropriate when the first order is hard to secure but reorders are virtually automatic. Such is the case for many manufacturer salespeople who sell to distributors and retailers.

Some circumstances might warrant a combination of a constant rate with either a progressive or regressive rate. For example, assume that a manufacturer has limited production capacity. The manufacturer want to use capacity fully (i.e., sell out) but not oversell, because service problems would hamper future marketing plans. In such a case, the commission rate might be fixed, or perhaps progressive up to the point at which capacity is almost fully used, then regressive to the point of full use.

When salespeople are paid on straight commission, the question of splitting commissions is of primary concern. To illustrate this point, consider a company with centralized purchasing, such as Delta Airlines. Delta may buy from a sales representative in Atlanta, where its headquarters are located, and have the product shipped to various hubs across the country. The salespeople in the hub cities are expected to provide local follow-up and be sure the product is performing satisfactorily. Which salespeople will receive how much commission? Procedures for splitting commissions are best established before such a question is asked.

No general rules exist for splitting commissions; rather, company-specific rules must be spelled out to avoid serious disputes. A company selling to Delta Airlines in the situation just described might decide to pay the salesperson who calls on the Atlanta headquarters 50 percent of the total commission and split the remaining 50 percent among the salespeople who serve the hub cities. The details of how commissions are split depend entirely on each company's situation.

Another issue in structuring straight-commission plans is when to pay the commission. The actual payment may be at any time interval, although monthly and quarterly payments are most common. The question of when the commission is earned is probably just as important as when it is paid. The largest proportion of companies operating on the basis of sales-volume commissions declare the commission earned at the time the customer is billed for the order, rather than when the order is confirmed, shipped, or paid for.

Salesforce automation has made it easier to keep track of complicated commission systems. For instance, Trilogy Development Group offers a software application, SC Commission, that enables companies to rapidly design, process, and communicate sophisticated commission programs. By communicating sales credit, performance, and earnings information directly to each salesperson's laptop, the software allows salespeople to keep abreast of their compensation status.[7]

ADVANTAGES OF COMMISSION PLANS One advantage of straight-commission plans is that salespeople's income is linked directly to desired results and therefore may be perceived as more equitable than salary plans. In the right circumstances, a strong financial incentive can provide superior results, and commission plans provide such an incentive.

From a cost-control perspective, commissions offer further advantages. Because commissions are a variable cost, operating costs are minimized during slack selling periods. Also, working capital requirements are lessened with commission-only pay plans. Before choosing a straight-commission plan, however, the disadvantages of such plans should be considered.

DISADVANTAGES OF COMMISSION PLANS Perhaps the most serious shortcoming of straight-commission plans is that they contribute little to company loyalty, which may mean other problems in controlling the activities of the salesforce, particularly nonselling and administrative activities. A lack of commitment may lead commission salespeople to leave the company if business conditions worsen or sales drop. Another potential problem can arise if commissions are not limited by an earnings cap, in that salespeople may earn more than their managers. Not only do managers resent this outcome, but the salespeople may not respond to direction from those they exceed in earnings.

Performance Bonuses

The third dimension of current spendable income is the **performance bonus,** either group or individual. Both types are prevalent, and some bonus plans combine them. As an example, the Plastics Division of Mobil Chemical pays a cash bonus of 10 percent of salary to any salesperson achieving his or her sales volume target. If the operating group achieves its overall profit objectives, the salesperson receives another percentage point in bonus for every percentage point by which he or she exceeds the sales volume target.

Bonuses are typically used to direct effort toward relatively short-term objectives, such as introducing new products, adding new accounts, or reducing accounts receivable. They may be offered in the form of cash or income equivalents, such as merchandise or free travel. Although commissions or salary may be the financial-compensation base, bonuses are used strictly in a supplementary fashion.

Combination Plans (Salary plus Incentive)

The limitations of straight-salary and straight-commission plans have led to increasing use of plans that feature some combination of salary, commission, and bonus—in other words, **salary plus incentive.** Combination pay plans usually feature salary as the major source of salesperson income. Exhibit 9.2 indicates that salary-plus-bonus and salary-plus-commission-plus-bonus plans are popular.

When properly conceived, combination plans offer a balance of incentive, control, and enough flexibility to reward important salesforce activities. The most difficult part of structuring combination plans is determining the **financial compensation mix,** or the relative amounts to be paid in salary, commission, and bonus. Exhibit 9.4 enumerates a number of factors related to determining the appropriate ratio of salary to total financial compensation.

As indicated in Exhibit 9.4, the compensation mix should be tilted more heavily toward the salary component when individual salespeople have limited control over their own performance. When well-established companies rely heavily on advertising to sell their products in highly competitive markets, the salesforce has less direct control over job outcomes. Then a salary emphasis is logical. Furthermore, if the provision of customer service is crucial as contrasted with maximizing short-term sales volume or if team selling is used, a compensation mix favoring the salary dimension is appropriate. As suggested in Exhibit 9.4, conditions contrary to those favorable to a high salary-to-total-compensation ratio would dictate an emphasis on commissions in the compensation mix.

ADVANTAGES OF COMBINATION PLANS The primary advantage of combination pay plans is their flexibility. Sales behavior can be rewarded frequently, and specific behaviors can be reinforced or stimulated quickly. For example, bonuses or additional commissions could be easily added to a salary base to encourage such activities as selling excess inventory, maximizing the sales of highly seasonal products, introducing new products, or obtaining new customers. For example, when manufacturer Scottsker Inc. wanted to boost its first quarter sales, it instituted an incentive plan that awarded its top three sellers from January through March a 10 percent of salary bonus. The program was a success, increasing sales by 23 percent over the same period from the previous year.[8]

Combination plans can also be used to advantage when the skill levels of the salesforce vary, assuming that the sales manager can accurately place salespeople into various skill-level categories and then formulate the proper combination for each category.[9] In effect, this is done with sales trainees, regular salespeople, and

EXHIBIT 9.4 Conditions That Influence the Proportion of Salary to Total Pay for Salespeople

Condition	Proportion of Salary to Total Pay Should Be	
	Lower	Higher
1. Importance of salesperson's personal skills in making sales	Considerable	Slight
2. Reputation of salesperson's company	Little known	Well known
3. Company's reliance on advertising and other sales promotion activities	Little	Much
4. Competitive advantage of product in terms of price, quality, and so forth	Little	Much
5. Importance of providing customer service	Slight	Considerable
6. Significance of total sales volume as a primary selling objective	Greater	Lesser
7. Incidence of technical or team selling	Little	Much
8. Importance of factors beyond the control of salesperson that influence sales	Slight	Considerable

senior salespeople in some companies, with each category of salespeople having a different combination of salary and incentive compensation.

Combination pay plans are attractive to high-potential but unproven candidates for sales jobs. College students nearing graduation, for example, might be attracted by the security of a salary and the opportunity for additional earnings from incentive-pay components.

DISADVANTAGES OF COMBINATION PLANS As compared with straight-salary and straight-commission plans, combination plans are more complex and difficult to administer. Their flexibility sometimes leads to frequent changes in compensation practices to achieve short-term objectives. Although flexibility is desirable, each change requires careful communication with the salesforce and precise coordination with long-term sales, marketing, and corporate objectives. A common criticism of combination plans is that they tend to produce too many salesforce objectives, many of which are of the crisis resolution "fire-fighting" variety. Should this occur, more important long-term progress can be impeded.

Nonfinancial Compensation

As indicated early in this module, compensation for effort and performance may include nonfinancial rewards. Examples of **nonfinancial compensation** include career advancement through promotion, a sense of accomplishment on the job, opportunities for personal growth, recognition of achievement, and job security. Sometimes, nonfinancial rewards are coupled with financial rewards—for example, a promotion into sales management usually results in a pay increase—so one salesperson might view these rewards as primarily financial, whereas another might view them from a nonfinancial perspective. The value of nonfinancial compensation is illustrated by the considerable number of salespeople who knowingly take cuts in financial compensation to become sales managers. The prevalence of other nonfinancial rewards in salesforce reward systems also attests to their important role.

Opportunity for Promotion

As shown in Exhibit 9.1, **opportunity for promotion** ranks second only to pay as the most preferred reward among salespeople. Among younger salespeople, it often eclipses pay as the most valued reward.[10] Given the increasing number of young to middle-aged people in the workforce, the opportunities for promotion may be limited severely in nongrowth industries. (Growth industries, such as financial services and direct sales, offer reasonably good opportunities for advancement through promotion.) Because opportunities for promotion are not easily varied in the short run, the importance of matching recruits to the job and its rewards is again emphasized.

It should be noted that a promotion need not involve a move from sales into management. Some career paths may extend from sales into management, whereas others progress along a career salesperson path.

Sense of Accomplishment

Unlike some rewards, a **sense of accomplishment** cannot be delivered to the salesperson from the organization. Because a sense of accomplishment emanates from the salesperson's psyche, all the organization can do is facilitate the process by which it develops. Although organizations cannot administer sense-of-accomplishment rewards as they would pay increases, promotions, or formal recognition rewards, the converse is not true—they do have the ability to withhold this reward, to deprive individuals of feeling a sense of accomplishment. Of course, no organization chooses this result; it stems from poor management practice.

Several steps can be taken to facilitate a sense of accomplishment in the salesforce. First, ensure that the salesforce members understand the critical role they fulfill in revenue production and other key activities within the company. Second, personalize the causes and effects of salesperson performance. This means that each salesperson should understand the link between effort and performance and between performance and rewards. Third, strongly consider the practice of management by objectives or goal setting as a standard management practice. Finally, reinforce feelings of worthwhile accomplishment in communication with the salesforce.

Opportunity for Personal Growth

Opportunities for personal growth are routinely offered to salespeople. For example, college tuition reimbursement programs are common, as are seminars and workshops on such topics as physical fitness, stress reduction, and personal financial planning. Interestingly, many sales job candidates think the major reward available from well-known companies is the opportunity for personal growth. This is particularly true of entrepreneurially oriented college students who hope to "learn then earn" in their own business. In a parallel development, many companies showcase their training program during recruitment and selection as an opportunity for personal growth through the acquisition of universally valuable selling skills.

Recognition

Recognition, both informal and formal, is an integral part of most salesforce reward systems. Informal recognition refers to "nice job" accolades and similar kudos usually delivered in private conversation or correspondence between a sales manager and a salesperson. Informal recognition is easy to administer, costs nothing or practically nothing, and can reinforce desirable behavior immediately after it occurs.

Formal recognition programs have long been popular in sales organizations. The insurance industry has the Million Dollar Roundtable, and 100% clubs for those who exceed 100 percent of their sales quota are common. GTE annually inducts its top performers into the Winner's Circle, and the ultimate recognition for Xerox's sales elite is to be named a member of the President's Club.

Formal recognition programs are typically based on group competition or individual accomplishments representing improved performance. Formal recognition may also be associated with monetary, merchandise, or travel awards but is distinguished from other rewards by two characteristics. First, formal recognition implies public recognition for accomplishment in the presence of peers and superiors in the organization. Second, it includes a symbolic award of lasting psychological value, such as jewelry or a plaque. Sound advice for conducting formal recognition programs is offered in Exhibit 9.5.

EXHIBIT 9.5 **Guidelines for Formal Programs**

Formal recognition programs have a better chance of success if sales managers

1. Remember that recognition programs should produce results well beyond the expected and that the program should make sense from a return-on-investment perspective.
2. Publicize the program before it is implemented. Build momentum for the program while it is under way with additional communiqués, and reinforce the accomplishments of the winners with postprogram communications both inside and outside the company.
3. Ensure that the celebration for winners is well conceived and executed. Consider the possibility of having customers and teammates join in with brief congratulatory testimonials or thanks.
4. Arrange for individual salespeople or sales teams to acknowledge the support of others who helped them win the award—as is the case with the Grammy Awards, for example. This builds the teamwork orientation.
5. Strive for fairness in structuring recognition programs so that winners are clearly superior performers, not those with less difficult performance goals.

SALES MANAGEMENT IN THE 21ST CENTURY

Recognition Programs at FirstEnergy

Anthony Lockhart, director, central region sales for FirstEnergy, discusses how the company uses recognition programs:

Most of us in the energy industry are familiar with the concept of motivation and the personal intangible reward of serving our customers. However, the concept of tangible rewards that reward high performance in sales is new to our industry. As we move from the regulated arena to a deregulated environment, I've found that recognition programs that motivate and reward can be excellent tools to help facilitate and sustain the transition. They represent an opportunity to build morale, increase focus, and inject some fun into the day-to-day activities of salespeople. It is key to keep the program simple, fair, and fun. Participants need to understand how and what it takes to be successful with the program, and each participant must feel they have a chance to win. In other words, don't just build the program around those that already get the highest sales. That would limit your program to the same people that usually win that particular game, particularly when all territories are not created equal. The fun part of the program is limited only by your imagination. The results can be astounding. Your sales organization will be energized to find new ways to achieve this recognition. Some may say, why bother? After all, salespeople get a salary and bonus, anyway. The simple answer is that we all appreciate positive recognition.

As formal recognition, programs often feature lavish awards banquets and ceremonies to culminate the program and set the stage for future recognition programs. Because lavish expenditures for any salesforce activity ultimately must be well justified in this era of emphasis on productivity improvement, it is evident that many companies believe that money spent on recognition is a good investment. For more on recognition programs, see "Sales Management in the 21st Century: Recognition Programs at FirstEnergy."

Job Security

Job security, although valued highly by salespeople nearing retirement age, is the least-valued reward among those shown in Exhibit 9.1. High-performing salespeople may sense they have job security, if not with their present employer then with another employer.

With the current wave of mergers, acquisitions, and general downsizing of corporations, it is becoming more difficult to offer job security as a reward. In the past, job security was easier to assure, at least as long as performance contingencies were met. Another factor that will make it difficult to offer job security with a given company is the lack of unionization of salespeople in most fields.

Sales Expenses

Most sales organizations provide full reimbursement to their salespeople for legitimate **sales expenses** incurred while on the job. As shown in Exhibit 9.6, typical reimbursable expenses include travel, lodging, meals, entertainment of customers, telephone, and personal entertainment. Dartnell Corporation, generally recognized as the leading source of information about selling costs, reports that companies are beginning to reverse a recent trend of reducing their selling expenses as a percentage of sales. Selling expenses are a substantial amount in most companies, averaging more than $1,000 a month for an experienced salesperson across a wide variety of industries.[11] Given the magnitude of sales expenses, it is easy to under-

EXHIBIT 9.6	**Percentage of Companies Paying 100 Percent of Various Expense Items**
Automobile (company-leased)	31%
Automobile (company-owned)	35%
Mileage allowance	63%
Other travel reimbursement	78%
Lodging	86%
Telephone	85%
Entertainment	75%
Product samples	80%
Local promotions	80%
Office and/or clerical	81%
Car phone	61%
Home photocopier	47%
Home fax machine	53%
Laptop PC	65%

stand why most companies impose tight controls to ensure judicious spending by the salesforce.

Controls used in the sales expense reimbursement process include (1) a definition of which expenses are reimbursable, (2) the establishment of expense budgets, (3) the use of allowances for certain expenditures, and (4) documentation of expenses to be reimbursed.

Covered expenses vary from company to company, so it is important for each company to designate which expenses are reimbursable and which are not. For example, some firms reimburse their salespeople for personal entertainment, such as the cost of movies and reading material while traveling, and others do not.

Expense budgets may be used to maintain expenses as a specified percentage of overall sales volume or profit. Expenditures are compared regularly to the budgeted amount, and expenditure patterns may change in response to budgetary pressures.

Allowances for automobile expenses, lodging, and meal costs are sometimes used to control expenditures. For example, one common practice is to reimburse personal automobile use on the job at a cents-per-mile allowance. Many firms use a per-diem allowance for meals and lodging.

Because of more stringent tax laws, extensive documentation in the form of receipts and other information concerning the what, when, who, and why of the expenditure has become standard procedure. Salespeople whose companies do not reimburse expenses must also provide such documentation to deduct sales expenses in calculating their income taxes. A typical form for documenting sales expenses is shown in Exhibit 9.7.

The job of reporting and tracking sales expenses has become less burdensome for companies that use expense-report software programs. Portable Software's Xpense Management Solution and Extensity Inc.'s Expense Reports make it easier for salespeople to file expense reports and for sales managers to process the reports and analyze expenditures. These programs allow salespeople to access their corporate credit card information that has been downloaded to their account by the company's credit card company. Salespeople access their information via the company's Intranet and then match the credit card company's posting with their business expenses. The report is then forwarded to the manager for approval and sent directly to the accounts payable department. With these programs, sales managers can easily audit salespeople's expenditures, focus on expenses in a particular area, and compare selling costs with selling budgets. It is also possible to track expenditures

| EXHIBIT 9.7 | Sales Expense Report Form |

with particular hotels or rental car companies, which may enable the sales organization to negotiate more favorable rates.[12]

The area of expense reimbursement is the cause of some ethical and legal concern in sales organizations. Certainly **expense account padding,** in which a salesperson seeks reimbursement for ineligible or fictional expenses, is not unknown. There are countless ways for an unscrupulous salesperson to misappropriate company funds. A common ploy of expense account "padders" is to entertain friends rather than customers, then seek reimbursement for customer entertainment. Another tactic is to purchase equipment such as video players or slide projectors for personal use by applying company-paid rental fees in a lease-to-buy agreement with the dealer. As illustrated in "An Ethical Dilemma," at times sales managers are confronted with these situations.

Tight financial controls, requirements for documentation of expenditures, and periodic visits by highly trained financial auditors help deter expense account abuse. Although it may sound extreme, many companies have a simple policy regarding misappropriation of company funds—the minimum sanction is termination of employment, and criminal charges are a distinct possibility.

> **An Ethical Dilemma**
>
> *You have been hired by a copier supply company to replace their sales manager. Although a small company, its salesforce has always performed well, allowing it to hold its own against much larger competitors. The former sales manager had a unique way of motivating his salesforce. Each year all salespeople were rank ordered, and the bottom three performers were fired, despite having performed very profitably for the company. Will you change this system? Why, or why not?*

Additional Issues in Managing Salesforce Reward Systems

In addition to the managerial issues raised thus far, five other areas of salesforce reward systems are currently receiving considerable attention: sales contests, equal pay for equal work, team compensation, global considerations, and changing an existing reward system.

Sales Contests

Sales contests are temporary programs that offer financial and/or nonfinancial rewards for accomplishing specified, usually short-term, objectives. Contests may involve group competition among salespeople, individual competition whereby each salesperson competes against past performance standards or new goals, or a combination of group and individual competition. Sales contests can be instituted without altering the basic financial compensation plan.

Despite the widespread use of sales contests and the sizable expenditures for them, very little is known about their true effects. In fact, many contests are held to correct bad planning and poor sales performance, and others are held with the belief that contests must have positive effects, despite the difficulty in pinpointing these effects. There is always a concern about whether sales contests have any lasting value or simply boost short-term sales. If contests merely pulls sales from a future period into the contest period, little is gained—and the expenses of running contests can be substantial.

To optimize the use of sales contests, the following guidelines are recommended.[13]

1. Minimize potential motivation and morale problems by allowing multiple winners. Salespeople should compete against individual goals and be declared winners if those goals are met.
2. Recognize that contests will concentrate efforts in specific areas, often at the temporary neglect of other areas. Plan accordingly.
3. Consider the positive effects of including nonselling personnel in sales contests.
4. Use variety as a basic element of sales contests. Vary timing, duration, themes, and rewards.
5. Ensure that sales contest objectives are clear, realistically attainable, and quantifiable to allow performance assessment

Sales contests can also be linked with improving the skills and knowledge of salespeople, as was illustrated in the opening vignette. Recall that the sales manager at KXKT-FM held a proposal-writing contest each week for 3 months in an attempt to improve reps' literary skills. Each week, the salesperson with the best proposal received a $25 bonus.

It is hard to design a sales contest that will maximally motivate every member of the salesforce. It is even more difficult to measure precisely the effectiveness of most sales contests. Even so, sales contests will doubtless continue to be a commonly used tool. By following the five guidelines previously mentioned, sales managers can improve the odds of making justifiable investments in sales contests.

Equal Pay

In addition to the motivational aspects of equity in financial compensation systems, there is a legal responsibility to ensure that salespeople are paid on an equitable basis. The Equal Pay Act, mentioned in Module 6, requires that equal pay be given for jobs requiring the same skills, efforts, responsibilities, and working conditions.

Sad to say, some sales managers attempt to pay female salespeople less than males because they think women's family responsibilities will cause them to leave the salesforce, or they think women will be less willing to travel or relocate than male salespeople. The dangers of such thinking are not limited to legal ramifications, but the Equal Pay Act of 1963 does provide a strong reminder for those who consider paying one group of people less than another.

Team Compensation

Most salespeople are still paid based on their individual performance. As mentioned throughout this textbook, however, teamwork in selling and team selling are growing in importance. As a result, many sales organizations are adjusting their compensation plans to recognize team performance. This represents a real challenge to sales managers for several reasons. Existing reward systems for individual salespeople typically are not easy to adapt to team selling situations.[14] Salespeople who are accustomed to earning commissions based on their individual efforts may not respond enthusiastically to team-based compensation. They may be concerned that rewards for high performers might be diminished by lower-performing team members. Furthermore, it is difficult to determine an individual salesperson's contribution to overall team performance.

Given these challenges, it is easy to see that experimentation is often required to find the right compensation plan for sales teams. Pittsburg-based Mine Safety Appliances devised a three-part compensation plan for its 28-team, 100-member

---

SALES MANAGEMENT IN THE 21ST CENTURY

Team Rewards at Pitney Bowes Office Systems

Charlie Kowalczyk, former branch sales manager at Pitney Bowes Office Systems, discusses how the company rewards both individuals and groups:

At Pitney Bowes, both individual and group rewards are used to motivate the salesforce. The company runs a contest that rewards individual salespeople and managers who achieve or exceed their yearly quota. Those who win are rewarded with a trip to places such as Maui, Puerto Rico, or Bermuda. In addition, teams have an opportunity to earn rewards. Each month, salespeople choose a sales activity goal that goes beyond their assigned weekly activities. For instance, this goal might be to make five in-person calls after 5:00 PM, or to increase in-house demonstrations by five, or perhaps to develop and distribute a creative mail piece. When each member of the sales team achieves his or her individual monthly goal, the team is rewarded. Members of the team and I will take a half day on a Friday, and I will treat them to some activity. Activities have included golfing, bowling, laser tag, volleyball, dinner, and the movies, among others. The use of team rewards helps build a sense of comradery and creates an atmosphere in which salespeople motivate each other to achieve their goals so that the team will be rewarded.

salesforce: a base salary, revenue-based incentives, and non–revenue-based incentives. Initially, the company decided on a uniform base salary for all salespeople. This was changed because of the strong feelings among salespeople that multiple salary levels were a better idea. Salary levels are reevaluated each year, based in part on peer evaluations. In many cases, discussion among team members determines how incentive pay is distributed.[15]

There are no easy answers for structuring team pay. In general, it is a good idea to reward both individual and team performance. As one expert says, "Team pay does not mean that all team members must be measured and paid alike!"[16] In most cases, the majority of compensation will be in salary form, but bonuses and commissions also play an important role in team compensation. For example, at Scottsdale Plaza Resort, salespeople get monthly checks for 0.5 percent of the business they book. Also, the staff is divided into three teams, each led by a senior rep who receives another 0.1 percent of what the members of their teams book. Furthermore, salespeople receive a year-end bonus based on business booked by the sales team.[17] Team recognition rewards are also important because they can build excitement and motivation and lead to higher performance levels. For more of team recognition, see "Sales Management in the 21st Century: Team Rewards at Pitney Bowes Office Systems."

Global Considerations

Global compensation issues are receiving more attention. In many cases, sales representation in other countries is secured through a distributor or sales agent. These situations are not so complex from a compensation management point of view because commissions or discounts from list price provide the income basis for the sellers. The compensation of native salespeople is more difficult. In many countries, political or cultural factors may have a strong influence on salesforce pay practices. For example, salespeople in the United States are less often paid by straight salary than their counterparts in any other part of the world.[18] It has been suggested that this practice is linked to cultural norms; for example, in the United States, we prize individualism, whereas in many other cultures, collectivism is valued.

The compensation of expatriate salespeople presents a different set of problems.[19] Often, the company is in the position of offering additional incentives to encourage salespeople to take assignments abroad. This pattern is changing somewhat as awareness increases that overseas assignments can enhance career opportunities. It is also changing as companies scale back the once-lucrative incentives for foreign-based employment.[20] Nonetheless, arriving at equitable pay for salespeople deployed around the world requires knowledge of living costs, taxes, and other factors that are not typically dealt with by sales managers. In fact, sales managers often rely on human resource professionals to assist in global compensation planning. These professionals point out that expatriates should not lose or gain in spending power as a result of an international assignment. They also point out the importance of tying a deployment plan to the sales growth strategy and specifying the particulars of the job before addressing compensation issues.[21]

Changing the Reward System

The need to change the salesforce reward system for a given company may arise periodically as companies strive for improved performance and productivity. Changes in sales compensation are often made to bring the salesforce more in line with a shift in strategy or to maximize corporate resources. International Data Corporation (IDC), a publisher of market research for the technology industry, used a compensation system that worked well for motivating salespeople during the first quarter of the year. However, it was discovered that once salespeople hit their goals, many slowed down, resulting in year-end cash flow problems for the company. As a result, IDC fixed the amount of compensation reps earn at quota and provided additional incentive pay beyond quota to ensure that its reps continue to be motivated after reaching early sales targets.[22] Reward systems should be closely monitored and should be changed when conditions warrant. A situation similar to the one in "An Ethical Dilemma" may warrant consideration.

> **An Ethical Dilemma**
>
> *You have been Sherry Smith's sales manager for more than 6 years. Her dedication to the company, her sales team, and her customers is beyond reproach. For the past 2 years, she has been named salesperson of the year at your company. Besides being an outstanding performer, she is a genuinely nice person with a great personality. Looking over Sherry's latest expense report, you noticed that she had meal expenses for her and a customer last Thursday. However, you recall making a call to this customer on that very day to follow up with some information he had requested and being informed that he was out of town. Your company has very strict policies regarding business expenses. What should you do? Explain.*

Minor adjustments in reward systems can be made relatively painlessly, and sometimes even pleasurably, for all concerned parties. For example, the sales manager might plan three sales contests this year instead of the customary two, or could announce a cash bonus instead of a trip to Acapulco for those who make quota.

However, making major changes in reward systems can be traumatic for salespeople and management alike if not properly handled. Any major change in financial compensation practices is likely to produce a widespread fear among the salesforce that their earnings will decline. Because many changes are precipitated by poor financial performance by the company or inequitable earnings among salesforce members, this fear is often justified for at least part of the salesforce.

To implement a new or modified reward system, sales managers must, in effect, sell the plan to the salesforce. To do this, the details of the plan must be clearly communicated well in advance of its implementation. Feedback from the salesforce should be encouraged and questions promptly addressed. Reasons for the change should be discussed openly, and any expected changes in job activities should be detailed.

It is recommended that, if possible, major changes be implemented to coincide with the beginning of a new fiscal year or planning period. It is also preferable to institute changes during favorable business conditions, rather than during recessionary periods.

The dynamic nature of marketing and sales environments dictates that sales managers constantly monitor their reward systems. It is not unreasonable to think that major changes could occur every few years or even more frequently.

Guidelines for Motivating and Rewarding Salespeople

Sales managers should realize that practically everything they do will influence salesforce motivation one way or another. The people they recruit, the plans and policies they institute, the training they provide, and the way they communicate with and supervise salespeople are among the more important factors. In addition, sales managers should realize that environmental factors beyond their control may also influence salesforce motivation. Like other managerial functions, motivating salespeople requires a prioritized, calculated approach rather than a futile attempt to address all motivational needs simultaneously. If for no other reason, the complexity of human nature and changing needs of salesforce members will prohibit the construction of motivational programs that run smoothly without periodic adjustment. Guidelines for motivating salespeople are as follows:

1. Recruit and select salespeople whose personal motives match the requirements and rewards of the job.
2. Attempt to incorporate the individual needs of salespeople into motivational programs.
3. Provide adequate job information and assure proper skill development for the salesforce.
4. Use job design and redesign as motivational tools.
5. Concentrate on building the self-esteem of salespeople.
6. Take a proactive approach to seeking out motivational problems and sources of frustration in the salesforce.

Recruitment and Selection

The importance of matching the abilities and needs of sales recruits to the requirements and rewards of the job cannot be overstated. This is especially critical for sales managers who have little opportunity to alter job dimensions and reward structures. Investing more time in recruitment and selection to ensure a good match is likely to pay off later in terms of fewer motivational and other managerial problems.

Incorporation of Individual Needs

At the outset of this module, motivation was described as a complex personal process. At the heart of the complexity of motivation is the concept of individual needs. Although there is considerable pressure and, in many cases, sound economic rationale for supporting mass approaches to salesforce motivation, there may also be opportunities to incorporate individual needs into motivational programs. When possible, individual consideration should be taken into account when motivating and rewarding salespeople.

Information and Skills

Salespeople must have high skill levels and be well equipped with the right information to do their jobs well. If sales managers train their people properly and give them the right information, salespeople can see how their efforts lead to the desired results. If salespeople's understanding of how their efforts produce results is consistent with that of the sales manager, reasonable goals can be set that allow performance worthy of rewards. Providing adequate information to the salesforce also enhances salesforce socialization (discussed in earlier modules), thereby reducing role conflict and role ambiguity.

Job Design

Given the nature of sales jobs, one would expect good opportunities to stimulate intrinsic motivation without major changes in the job. Sales jobs allow the use of a wide range of skills and abilities; boredom is thus not a typical problem. And given the unique contributions of personal selling to the organization, as discussed in Module 2, salespeople can readily see that their jobs are critical to the organization's success. Most salespeople have considerable latitude in determining work priorities and thus experience more freedom on the job than do many other employees. Finally, feedback from sales managers or through self-monitoring is readily available. In many ways, the motivational task is easier for sales managers than for other managers. The sales job itself can be a powerful motivator.

Building Self-Esteem

Sales managers increase salesforce motivation by building salespeople's self-esteem. Positive reinforcement for good performance should be standard procedure. This may be done with formal or informal communications or recognition programs designed to spotlight good performance. When performance is less than satisfactory, it should not be overlooked but addressed in a constructive manner.

Proactive Approach

Sales managers should be committed to uncovering potential problems in motivation and eliminating them before they develop. For example, if some members of the salesforce perceive a lack of opportunity for promotion into management and are demotivated as a result, the sales manager might take additional steps to clearly define the guidelines for promotion into management and review the performance of management hopefuls in light of these guidelines. If promotion opportunities are indeed limited, the matching function of recruitment and selection again shows its importance.

Summary

1. **Explain the key components of motivation: intensity, persistence, and direction.** A variety of ways exist to define motivation. Our definition includes the qualities of intensity, persistence, and direction. Intensity is the amount of mental and physical effort the salesperson is willing to expend on a specific activity. Persistence is a choice to expend effort over time, especially in the face of adversity. Direction implies that, to some extent, salespeople choose the activities on which effort is expended.
2. **Explain the difference between compensation rewards and noncompensation rewards.** Compensation rewards are those given by the organization in return for the salesperson's efforts and performance. They may include both financial and nonfinancial rewards. Noncompensation rewards are related to job design and work environment. The opportunity to be involved in meaningful interesting work is an example of a noncompensation reward. The provision of adequate resources to do the job and a supportive management system are other examples. The focus in this module has been on the management of compensation rewards.
3. **Describe the primary financial and nonfinancial compensation rewards available to salespeople.** As shown in Exhibit 9.1, six major rewards are available to salespeople: pay (or financial compensation), opportunity for promotion, a sense of accomplishment, personal growth opportunities, recognition, and job security (the last five being nonfinancial). Pay is usually current spendable income generated by salary, commissions, and bonuses.
4. **Describe salary, commission, and combination pay plans in terms of their advantages and disadvantages.** Straight-salary plans and straight-commission plans represent the two extremes in financial compensation for salespeople. Straight salary offers maximum control over salesforce activities but does not provide added incentive for exceptional performance. The opposite is true for straight-commission plans. The limitations of both plans have made combination plans the most popular with sales organizations. Although such plans can become too complex for easy administration, when properly conceived, they offer a balance of control and incentive.
5. **Explain the fundamental concepts in sales-expense reimbursement.** Job-related expenses incurred by salespeople are reimbursed by a large majority of sales organizations. Sales expenses are usually substantial, averaging 20 to 30 percent of total financial com-

pensation paid to salespeople. Companies use budgets, allowances, and documentation requirements to control sales expenses.

6. **Discuss issues associated with sales contests, equal pay for equal work, team compensation, global compensation, and changing a reward system.** Sales contests are used widely to achieve short-term results, but little is known about their true effects. The Equal Pay Act of 1963 reinforces an ethically desirable behavior—paying those who do equal work an equal amount of money. Companies that are new to team selling may find it difficult to move from individual-based compensation to team-based compensation. It is a challenge to determine how much of each team member's pay should be based on individual performance and how much on team performance. In most team selling situations, salary is the major compensation component, although bonuses, commissions, and other team rewards can have a positive influence on motivation. Global compensation may be dependent on different cultures and other business environment factors in varying locations around the world. Sales managers often rely heavily on human resource professionals to structure global compensation plans. Changing a reward system is a delicate procedure, requiring careful communication to the salesforce, who must "buy" the new system much like a customer would buy a product.

7. **List the guidelines for motivating and rewarding salespeople.** Six managerial guidelines for motivating salespeople are as follows: First, match the recruit to the requirements and rewards of the job. Second, incorporate individual needs into motivational programs when feasible. Third, provide salespeople with adequate information and ensure proper skill development to facilitate job performance. Fourth, cultivate salespeople's self-esteem. Fifth, take a proactive approach to uncovering motivational problems. Sixth, try to eliminate problems before they become serious.

Understanding Sales Management Terms

- Motivation
- Intensity
- Persistence
- Direction
- Intrinsic motivation
- Extrinsic motivation
- Reward system management
- Compensation rewards
- Noncompensation rewards
- Current spendable income
- Straight salary
- Planned earnings
- Salary compression
- Straight commission
- Commission base
- Commission rate
- Commission splits
- Commission payout event
- Constant rate
- Progressive rate
- Regressive rate
- Performance bonus
- Salary plus incentive
- Financial compensation mix
- Nonfinancial compensation
- Opportunity for promotion
- Sense of accomplishment
- Opportunities for personal growth
- Recognition
- Job security
- Sales expenses
- Expense account padding
- Sales contests

Developing Sales Management Knowledge

1. Identify and explain the three key dimensions of motivation.
2. Distinguish between compensation rewards and noncompensation rewards.
3. Describe an optimal salesforce reward system.
4. What are the nonfinancial compensation rewards discussed in this module? What suggestions can you make for administering recognition rewards?
5. Evaluate straight-salary, straight-commission, and combination pay plans in terms of their advantages and disadvantages. When should each be used?
6. Refer to "Sales Management in the 21st Century: Team Rewards at Pitney Bowes Office Systems." What are some advantages of team rewards?
7. What concerns should a sales manager have regarding the use of sales contests?

8. Refer to "Sales Management in the 21st Century: Recognition Programs at FirstEnergy." What makes a good recognition program?
9. What challenges do sales mangers face when using team-based compensation? What guidelines can sales managers follow when using team-based compensation?
10. Discuss several guidelines to improve the effectiveness of salesforce motivation and reward system management.

Building Sales Management Skills

1. Assume you have been hired as the national sales manager for a newly formed electronics distributor. Your salesforce will sell directly to electronics retailers. Although the company is not widely known, it will use little other than the salesforce to promote its products in a highly competitive market. Thus, salespeople's skills are very important. Salespeople will be responsible for providing complete customer service, including handling damage claims, helping with merchandising, providing advice, and following up after the sale to ensure the customer is completely satisfied. Devise a reward system for your salesforce, being sure to address the type of financial compensation plan you will use and why, as well as the types of nonfinancial compensation you will provide. What role will recruitment and selection play in this process? Explain.

2. Most student organizations are looking for ways to raise funds. Choose a student (or any other) organization and determine a fundraising activity that involves some form of personal selling (e.g., a raffle). Then, devise a sales contest that would be appropriate for achieving predetermined fundraising objectives. Explain your fundraiser, the contest, and the rationale behind the contest's incentives.

3. Understanding industry and market factors is critical when designing a salesforce compensation plan. For instance, the compensation system must consider compensation levels for similar positions in the same industry. One way to do this is through salary surveys. Access Job Smart (www.jobsmart.org), a resource designed to help job seekers get a job. Click on "Salary Info," and then scroll to the bottom of the page and click on "salary survey basics." Read this and answer the following questions:
   A. What is a salary survey and what are the advantages of conducting one?
   B. How could one go about conducting a salary survey?
   C. Is it always necessary for a company to conduct its own salary survey to get comparable salary information? Explain.

   Moreover, it is important to consider cost of living differences if a company has salespeople who will be located in several different places. Assume that you will pay salespeople a base salary of $32,000 based on the cost of living in St. Louis, Missouri. Click the "back" button to return to the "Salary Information" page, scroll to the top of the page and click on "Salary Surveys," then click on "General Salary Surveys" and scroll down and click on "careers.wsj.com-salaries and profiles." Now click on the "Salary Calculator" and use the calculator to determine what an equivalent base salary of $32,000 would be in the following places:

Washington, DC	_____	Jacksonville, FL	_____
San Diego, CA	_____	Seattle, WA	_____
Houston, TX	_____	Syracuse, NY	_____
Chicago, IL	_____	Paris, France	_____
London, England	_____	Athens, Greece	_____

Making Sales Management Decisions

CASE 9.1 Stalwart Industrial Products

Background

Stalwart Industrial Products manufactures and sells a wide variety of industrial tools to various resellers and end users. Founded in 1935, the company prides itself on producing high-quality, durable tools. The company's salesforce has always been an integral part of its success. Sales reps at Stalwart work hard and are rewarded accordingly.

Current Situation

Stalwart's national sales manager, Tom Beesman, has enjoyed a great deal of success with his salesforce. Since being promoted to his position 3 years ago, things have gone relatively smoothly, until now. "When it rains, it pours," Tom thinks to himself as he sits at his desk and contemplates two issues confronting him. For starters, one of his star salespeople, Charlie Davidson, seems to be slowing down at a time when his help is desperately needed. Second, the company has added a new Web page, and the reps are upset.

Charlie Davidson has worked for Stalwart for almost 3 years. His first year he generated $850,000 in revenues, hitting 112 percent of quota. He followed this by racking up sales of $1.29 million, for 119 percent of quota. He accomplished this by prospecting and meeting with customers 14 hours a day during the week, and completing reports and writing proposals on the weekends. At this pace, Davidson looked as if he would exceed quota again this year—that is, until he had his first child 2 months ago. Currently, he's down to 50 to 60 hours per week, and his sales reflect this.

Beesman is worried. Stalwart currently is undertaking an ambitious growth program. Next month alone, it plans to introduce four new products. Beesman had hoped to make Davidson a member of the management team. In casual conversation with Davidson, however, Beesman discovered that Davidson was not interested in becoming a manager at Stalwart because the big money is in sales. Davidson is still earning a hefty paycheck despite working fewer hours. To be successful, Beesman realizes that he needs to get back the energetic, hard-charging Davidson he hired, but he is not sure how.

In the meantime, the salesforce, including Davidson, is upset. As part of its aggressive growth strategy, the company began accepting orders through its Web site. Although customers are happy about this, the salesforce is not. Although salespeople earn commissions on current customers who order through the Web site, they do not receive commissions on any new Web customers in their territories. The company's president, Thurston Howell III, views the Web site as an additional "rep." However, salespeople see it as competition. Consequently, productivity and morale are down. Beesman is caught in the middle. He needs to find a solution to please both his salesforce and Howell.

Questions

1. How do you suggest that Beesman handle Davidson?
2. Assess the situation regarding Stalwart's use of the Web. What would you suggest that Beesman do to please both Howell and his salesforce?

Source: This case is developed from information in "What Would You Do?" *Sales & Marketing Management* 150 (June 1998): 100–101.

CASE 9.2 Floor-Shine Cleaning Products

Background

Floor-Shine Cleaning Products has been manufacturing and selling household floor cleaning products for more than 60 years. The company offers several brands that can be used to clean a variety of floor surfaces. It stands behind all its products with a "customer satisfaction guarantee." Any consumer who is not fully satisfied with the floor cleaner on applying it properly may return it to the place of purchase and receive a refund or have the product replaced with another of equal value.

Floor-Shine's products are distributed in a variety of outlets, ranging from small grocery and convenience stores to huge discounters such as Wal-Mart and Home Depot. Each customer is highly valued regardless of size. According to the company's founder, Arthur Worthington, "Every customer should be treated as if they are our only customer." For this reason, the company takes pride in establishing long-term customer relationships. In fact, several of the company's current customers have been distributing its products since the company was founded. The company's salesforce was built around this idea and to this day is well noted for its commitment to building strong and satisfying customer relationships.

Current Situation

Vince Coleman, Floor-Shine's national sales manager, recently asked regional sales manager Bob Herman to coordinate a special fourth-quarter sales push to achieve projected year-end sales goals. Herman, a committed sales manager, was confident he could develop a program that would succeed. He thought a sales contest would be an excellent way to boost fourth-quarter sales in his region. By developing a contest, he could avoid altering the current compensation package, which he believed to be satisfactory to his salespeople.

Herman has 100 salespeople in his region, about 20 percent of whom are women. The region is divided into five districts, each comprised of 20 salespeople. Rather than have all 100 salespeople compete against each other, Herman decided to have five winners, one for each district. Salespeople within each district would compete against each other, and the salesperson with the highest number of sales during the contest period would be declared the winner.

Herman recently heard about a new approach being taken by some companies to motivate their salespeople. Contest winners were awarded a trip to a fantasy baseball camp. Award winners spent a week with baseball legends who taught and coached them. The award proved to be a highly successful motivator. Herman liked this idea and decided to offer this trip to each district winner as the prize for winning the sales contest.

Herman contacted the company's marketing communications group to ask them to design a set of promotional materials to be distributed to each salesperson. He then visited each district explaining the contest rules to its salespeople. At the same time, he delivered pep talks. "Each of you has an equal chance at victory. Now is the time to seize the moment and go for the gold!"

After all the preplanning was completed, the contest finally went into effect. Most salespeople realized that they could increase their sales either by selling more to current customers or by finding new accounts. One method for increasing sales to current customers was to help them in merchandising so that they could sell more product. This seemed to work well for many salespeople. However, several concentrated on their large customers at the expense of their smaller accounts. The larger customers had much more potential and the input-to-output ratio with these customers had a much higher payoff. Several salespeople's obsession with their larger accounts got in the way of providing their smaller customers with the service they had come to expect. Some customers even threatened to take their business elsewhere. In fact, Ray's Groceries, a small but long-standing customer, was so upset with the decline in service that it dropped Floor-Shine as a supplier.

Numerous salespeople got wise to the idea that they could increase their sales by loading their customers with product toward the end of the contest period. Some salespeople asked customers to purchase and take delivery of their next scheduled order early. Others offered customers special incentives if they agreed to order more product than usual. One salesperson went so far as to offer a small kickback.

In an attempt to gain new customers, some salespeople took on customers that were poor credit risks. For instance, salesman Larry Lynn knew a medium-sized hardware store in his territory was in financial trouble, so much so that the store had lost its paint supplier because of its inability to pay. Larry figured he could enhance his sales during the contest period by taking the customer's order. If the customer was unable to pay, it would not show up until after the contest was over, and Larry would already have these sales added to his total for the period.

About one-third of the way into the contest, Dan Tate, a sales rep in District 3, was able to land a new major account, which meant a tremendous increase in sales for him. At that point, the other salespeople in his district seemed to lose enthusiasm for the contest. As Saul Weber put it, "I don't stand a prayer of winning the contest now. The only way I would have a chance is to land a similar account. Given my present territory, that is impossible. Doug has this contest wrapped up. He might as well grab his mitt and pack his bags—he's heading for fantasy baseball camp."

As the contest was drawing to a close, Herman noticed that sales had not increased nearly as much as he had anticipated. Moreover, most of the women in the salesforce did not significantly increase their sales figures. In fact, they were about the same as usual. Herman knew Coleman would want a full assessment of the contest on its completion. As he sat at his desk, he began to think about what went wrong.

Questions

1. How would you evaluate this contest?
2. How could this contest be designed to have a better chance of success?

PART V

Determining Salesforce Effectiveness and Performance

The two modules in Part Five focus on determining salesforce effectiveness and performance. Module 10 addresses the evaluation of sales organization effectiveness. Methods for analyzing sales, costs, profitability, and productivity at different sales organization levels are reviewed. Module 11 addresses the evaluation of salespeople's individual performance and job satisfaction. Ways of determining the appropriate performance criteria and methods of evaluation, and of using the evaluations to improve salesperson performance and job satisfaction, are discussed.

MODULE 10

Evaluating the Effectiveness of the Organization

Focus on Productivity at Dealer Truck Accessory Warehouse

Dealer Truck Accessory Warehouse (DTAW) is a rapidly growing truck accessory wholesale distributor located in Stephenville, Texas. Founded in 1994, the small family-run business primarily serves large automobile, truck, and hot rod retail outlets. The company relies on inside sales reps to maintain regular contact with customers and to route drivers to deliver the goods.

The company credits its recent growth in part to a new software accounting system, Visual AccountMate SQL, which has allowed its salespeople to become more productive. Before implementing the new system, salespeople had a difficult time tracking product inventory. Although they began each day with current inventory status, as time passed, they lost track of it as parts were delivered to customers and new shipments arrived at the warehouse. When a customer would call to inquire about the availability of a product, the salesperson would have to get off the phone with the customer, check the inventory in the warehouse, and then call the customer back. Salespeople often had difficulty reaching customers on the return call and sometimes lost the sale by the time they finally reached the customer who had already ordered from a competing vendor.

The new software has provided sales reps with easy access to all the information they need to deal with customers. They have instant access to customer balances, sales histories, and inventory, eliminating the need to run to the warehouse when customers call. The new system allows them to answer customer queries on the spot, and its ability to provide a picture of the product and a textual description are a tremendous help when talking to customers. Reps can now track orders with confidence because the system will not close sales orders until every item has been shipped or every back order has been canceled.

The system provides several other useful features that allow reps to be more productive. It has eliminated the need for paper price lists, allowing reps to save time by accessing pricing information more quickly. The system warns salespeople if a customer's order exceeds their credit limit. It also helps prevent salespeople from fulfilling duplicate orders by signaling to them if a customer's order has already been created on a particular day. Moreover, the system contains multiple shipping and billing addresses for each customer, eliminating the need for retyping a drop-ship location that differs from the billing address.

Learning Objectives

After completing this module, you should be able to

1 Differentiate between sales organization effectiveness and salesperson performance.

2 Define a sales organization audit and discuss how it should be conducted.

3 Define benchmarking and discuss how it should be conducted.

4 Describe how to perform different types of sales analysis for different organizational levels and types of sales.

5 Describe how to perform a cost analysis for a sales organization.

6 Describe how to perform an income statement analysis, activity-based costing, and return on assets managed to assess sales organization profitability.

7 Describe how to perform a productivity analysis for a sales organization.

The new system has resulted in a substantial increase in salesforce productivity. Reps now have more time to spend on the phone with customers. In addition, salespeople are providing better customer service by being able to attend to customer needs more quickly. Subsequently, DTAW has been able to increase its sales and customer loyalty without an increase in salesforce size.

The system has likewise improved management reporting. Because the old system did not tie the company's computers together, management could not determine the financial performance of the business until its accounting firm closed the books several weeks after month-end. The new system allows management up-to-the-minute reports. For instance, the company was able to identify unintentional overspending and misappropriation of funds before they became serious problems.

Besides enabling salespeople to be more productive, the new system allows sales managers to better analyze sales, more carefully track salesforce productivity, pinpoint problems, and define opportunities. As such, it helps improve salesforce effectiveness.

Source: Peggy Allison, "System Helps WD Increase Sales," *Automotive Marketing* 27 (November 1998): 126–128.

Assessing the success of a sales organization is difficult because of the many factors that must be considered. For example, the success of the sales organization must be differentiated from the success of individual salespeople (see Figure 10.1).[1]

FIGURE 10.1   Sales Organization Effectiveness versus Salesperson Performance

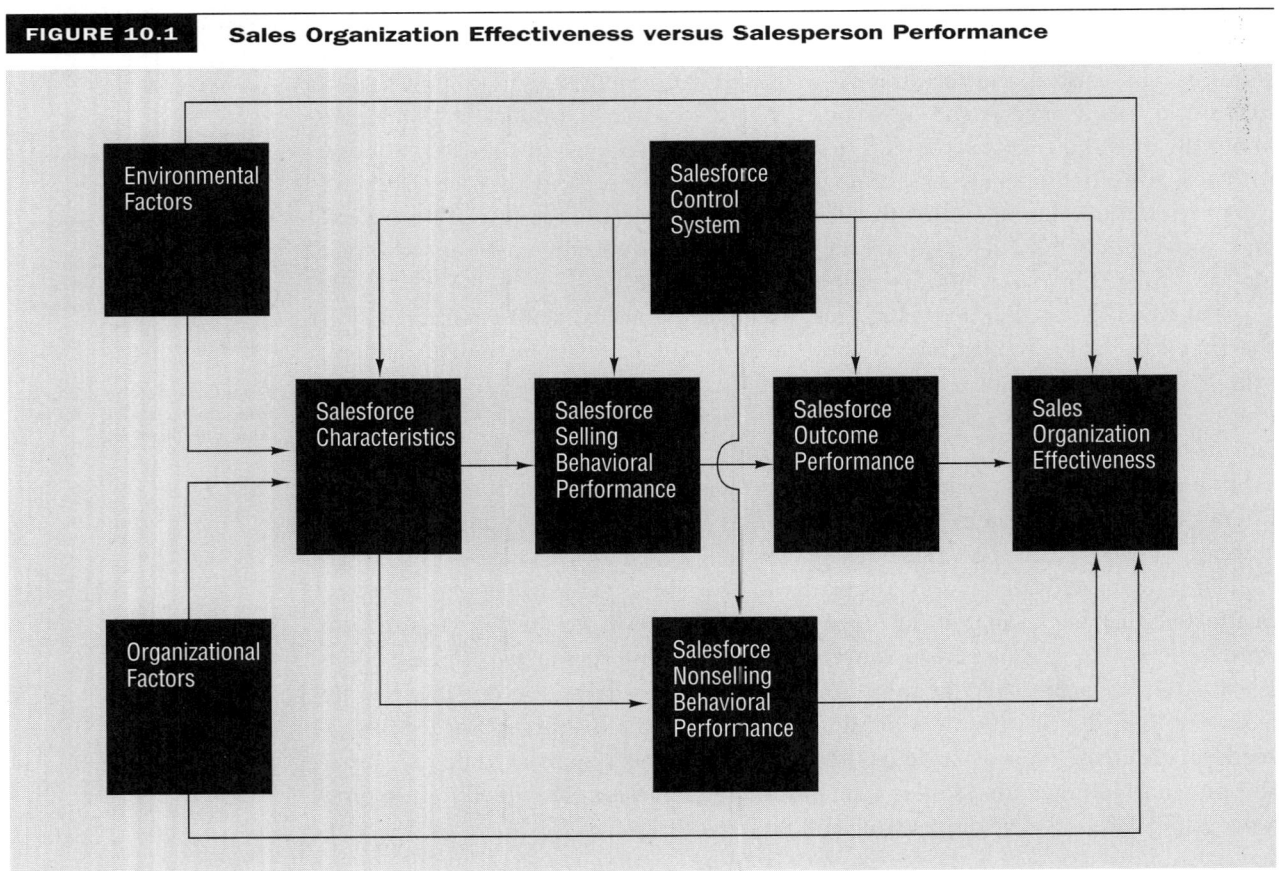

Whereas sales organization effectiveness is a function of how well the sales organization achieved its goals and objectives overall, salesperson performance is a function of how well each salesperson performed in his or her particular situation. Thus, salesperson performance contributes to, but does not completely determine, sales organization effectiveness.

As indicated by the DTAW example in the opening vignette, sales organization effectiveness must be evaluated to determine means for improving performance and productivity. The focus is on the overall sales organization as well as the different levels within the sales organization (territories, districts, regions, and zones). The results of such evaluations are normally general strategic or policy changes. However, analyzing and improving salesperson performance is typically paramount to improving sales organization effectiveness.

Evaluations of salesperson performance are confined to the individuals themselves, not the sales organization or sales organization levels. The results of these evaluations are typically tactical in nature. In other words, they lead a sales manager to take specific actions to improve the performance of an individual salesperson. Generally, different actions are warranted for different salespeople, depending on the areas that need improvement.

Evidence for the difference between sales organization effectiveness and salesperson performance is provided in a study of 144 sales organizations in the United States. A comparison of the more-effective and less-effective sales organizations indicated that those that were more effective had achieved much better results in many areas, compared with their less-effective counterparts. For example, the more-effective sales organizations generated much higher sales per salesperson ($3,988,000 versus $1,755,000) and much lower selling expenses as a percentage of sales (13 percent versus 18 percent) than the less-effective sales organizations. The salespeople in the more-effective organizations also outperformed salespeople in the less-effective ones in several areas. However, the differences in salesperson performance were not sufficient to completely explain the differences in sales organization effectiveness. Thus, sales organization effectiveness is the result of salesperson performance as well as many other factors (e.g., sales organization structure and deployment, and sales management performance).[2]

This module addresses the evaluation of sales organization effectiveness, and Module 11 addresses the evaluation of salesperson performance. This module begins with a discussion of a sales organization audit, examines benchmarking, then describes more specific analyses of sales, costs, profits, and productivity to determine sales organization effectiveness.

Sales Organization Audit

Although the term *audit* is most often used in reference to financial audits performed by accounting firms, the audit concept has been extended to different business functions in recent years. In Module 7, a **sales organization audit** was described as a comprehensive, systematic, diagnostic, and prescriptive tool.[3] The purpose of a sales organization audit is

> to assess the adequacy of a firm's sales management process and to provide direction for improved performance and prescription for needed changes. It is a tool that should be used by all firms whether or not they are achieving their goals.

This type of audit is the most comprehensive approach for evaluating sales organization effectiveness.

A framework for performing a sales organization audit is presented in Figure 10.2. As indicated in the figure, the audit addresses four major areas: sales organization environment, sales management evaluation, sales organization planning system, and sales management functions. The purpose of the audit it to investigate, systematically and comprehensively, each of these areas to identify existing or potential problems, determine their causes, and take the necessary corrective action. For example, EPR, an air pollution and control device manufacturer, used an audit to gain insights into customer relationships and trouble areas that were not being expressed or received any other way. The company credits a sales increase from $40 million to $130 million in less than 2 years to the implementation of recommendations resulting from the audit.[4]

The sales organization audit should be performed regularly, not just when problems are evident. One of the major values of an audit is its generation of diagnostic information that can help management correct problems in early stages or eliminate potential problems before they become serious. Because auditing should be objective, it should be conducted by someone from outside the sales organiza-

FIGURE 10.2　Sales Organization Audit Framework

The sales organization audit is the most comprehensive evaluation of sales organization effectiveness. The audit typically provides assessments of the sales organization environment, sales management evaluation, sales organization planning system, and sales management functions.

tion. This could be someone from another functional area within the firm or an outside consulting firm.

Although outsiders should conduct the audit, members of the sales organization should be active participants in it. Both sales mangers and salespeople often provide much of the information collected. Exhibit 10.1 presents some sample questions that should be addressed in a sales organization audit. Answers to these types of questions typically come from members of the sales organization and company records.

Although obviously an expensive and time-consuming process, the sales organization audit generates benefits that usually outweigh the monetary and time costs. This is especially true when audits are conducted regularly because the chances of identifying and correcting potential problems before they become troublesome increase with the regularity of the auditing process.

Benchmarking

Although the sales audit can help identify areas in the sales organization that need improvement, an increasingly popular technique for improving sales organization

---

EXHIBIT 10.1   **Sample Questions from a Sales Organization Audit**

IV. Sales Management Functions
   A. Salesforce Organization
      1. How is our salesforce organized (by product, by customer, by territory)?
      2. Is this type of organization appropriate given the current intraorganizational and extraorganizational conditions?
      3. Does this type of organization adequately service the needs of our customers?
   B. Recruitment and Selection
      1. How many salespeople do we have?
      2. Is this number adequate in light of our objectives and resources?
      3. Are we serving our customers adequately with this number of salespeople?
      4. How is our salesforce size determined?
      5. What is our turnover rate? What have we done to try to change it?
      6. Do we have adequate sources from which to obtain recruits? Have we overlooked some possible sources?
      7. Do we have a job description for each of our sales jobs? Is each job description current?
      8. Have we enumerated the necessary sales job qualifications? Have they been recently updated? Are they predictive of sales success?
      9. Are our selection screening procedures financially feasible and appropriate?
     10. Do we use a battery of psychological tests in our selection process? Are the tests valid and reliable?
     11. Do our recruitment and selection procedures satisfy employment opportunity guidelines?
   C. Sales Training
      1. How is our sales training program developed? Does it meet the needs of management and sales personnel?
      2. Do we establish training objectives before developing and implementing the training program?
      3. Is the training program adequate in light of our objectives and resources?
      4. What kinds of training do we currently provide our salespeople?
      5. Does the training program need revising? What areas of the training program should be improved or deemphasized?
      6. What methods do we use to evaluate the effectiveness of our training program?
      7. Can we afford to train internally or should we use external sources for training?
      8. Do we have an ongoing training program for senior salespeople? Is it adequate?
   D. Compensation and Expenses
      1. Does our sales compensation plan meet our objectives in light of our financial resources?
      2. Is the compensation plan fair, flexible, economical, and easy to understand and administer?
      3. What is the level of compensation, the type of plan, and the frequency of payment?
      4. Are the salespeople and management satisfied with the compensation plan?
      5. Does the compensation plan ensure that the salespeople perform the necessary sales job activities?
      6. Does the compensation plan attract and retain enough quality sales performers?
      7. Does the sales expense plan meet our objectives in light of our financial resources?
      8. Is the expense plan fair, flexible, and easy to administer? Does it allow for geographical, customer, and/or product differences?
      9. Does the expense plan ensure that the necessary sales job activities are performed?
     10. Can we easily audit the expenses incurred by our sales personnel?

effectiveness is **benchmarking.** Benchmarking is an ongoing measurement and analysis process that compares an organization's current operating practices with the "best practices" used by world-class organizations. It is a tool for evaluating current business practices and finding a way to do them better, more quickly, and less expensively to better meet customer needs.[5] Using benchmarking, Hewlett-Packard improved on-time delivery 150 percent, and one division of General Electric had a 54 million drop in inventory.[6] Xerox claims that benchmarking has allowed them to reduce total costs by up to $1 billion.[7] A research study of more than 1,600 U.S. and Canadian organizations found that those companies willing to learn from the best practices of others are more successful at improving customer satisfaction than those that are more reluctant. Perhaps this explains why such firms as IBM, AT&T, Du Pont, Ford, Eastman-Kodak, Milliken, Motorola, and Xerox use benchmarking.[8]

Figure 10.3 outlines steps in the benchmarking process. A pivotal part of this process is identifying the company or salesforce to benchmark. Literature search and personal contacts are means for identifying companies that perform the process in an exceptional manner. Winning an industry award, being recognized for functional excellence, and receiving a national quality award are three indicators of excellence.[9] Eastman Chemical Company and IBM have used the Malcolm Baldrige National Quality Award criteria as bases on which to evaluate their salesforce, map processes leading to desired results, and focus efforts on continuously improving these processes.[10] Those processes that have the greatest impact on salesforce productivity should be benchmarked. Companies such as Best Practices, LLC (www.best-in-class.com), The Benchmarking Network (www.well.com), Arthur Andersen LLP (www.arthurandersen.com/gbp), and American Productivity and Quality Center (www.apqc.org) provide useful Web sites for initiating a benchmarking program.[11]

A benchmarking study should provide several outputs. First, it should provide a measure that compares performance for the benchmarked process relative to the organization studied. Second, it should identify the organization's performance gap relative to benchmarked performance levels. Third, it should identify best practices and facilitators that produced the results observed during the study. Finally, the study should determine performance goals for the process studied and identify areas in which action can be taken to improve performance.[12] Exhibit 10.2 provides

FIGURE 10.3   **Benchmarking Process**

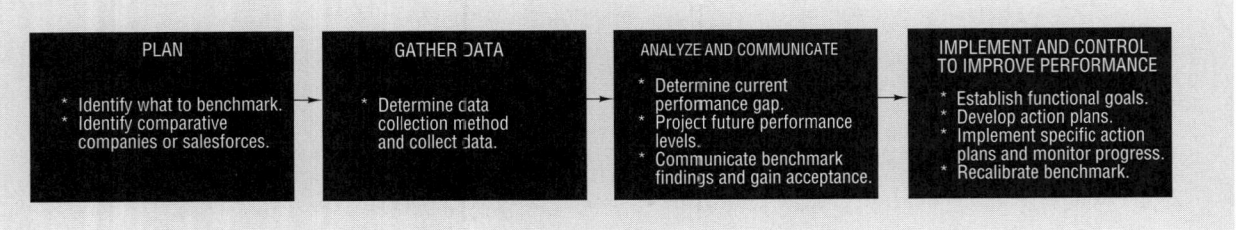

EXHIBIT 10.2   **Keys to Successful Benchmarking**

- Clearly identify critical activities that will improve quality or service or reduce cost.
- Properly prepare and benchmark *only one activity at a time.*
- Make sure that you thoroughly understand your own process first.
- Create a "seek, desire, and listen" environment by choosing curious and knowledgeable people for your benchmark team.
- Verify that your benchmark partner company is the best in its class, and clearly understand your partner's process.
- Provide adequate resources, not only financial, but most important, knowledgeable personnel.
- Be diligent in selecting the correct partner—be sure not to use a company that may not provide advantages to you.
- Implement the benchmarking action plan.

some keys to successful benchmarking. To see how benchmarking can be used to improve sales organization performance, see "Sales Management in the 21st Century: Using Benchmarking to Succeed."

Sales Organization Effectiveness Evaluations

There is no one summary measure of sales organization effectiveness. Sales organizations have multiple goals and objectives, and thus, multiple factors must be assessed. As illustrated in Figure 10.4, four types of analyses are typically necessary to develop a comprehensive evaluation of any sales organization. Conducting analyses in each of these areas is a complex task for two reasons. First, many different types of analyses can be performed to evaluate sales, cost, profitability, and productivity results. For example, a sales analysis might focus on total sales, sales or specific products, sales to specific customers, or other types of sales and might include sales comparisons to sales quotas, to previous periods, to sales of competitors, or other types of analyses. Second, separate sales analyses need to be performed for the different levels in the sales organization. Thus, a typical evaluation would include separate sales analyses for sales zones, regions, districts, and territories.

SALES MANAGEMENT IN THE 21ST CENTURY

Using Benchmarking to Succeed

Andre Wickham, food service region manager and national accounts sales manager for Hormel Foods Corporation, comments on his company's use of benchmarking:

The marketplace today is fast paced and constantly changing. As a result, sales organizations are continuously challenged to develop a structure that will allow them to effectively meet customer needs and fully penetrate all competitive market segments. At Hormel, we use benchmarking to help us achieve this goal. With benchmarking, we gauge our practices against the "best practices" of others in the marketplace. This evaluation helps us to assess our current and future course, which may range anywhere from no change to a major overhaul. Importantly, however, this practice allows us to clearly understand our strengths, weaknesses, opportunities, and threats.

FIGURE 10.4   Sales Organization Effectiveness Framework

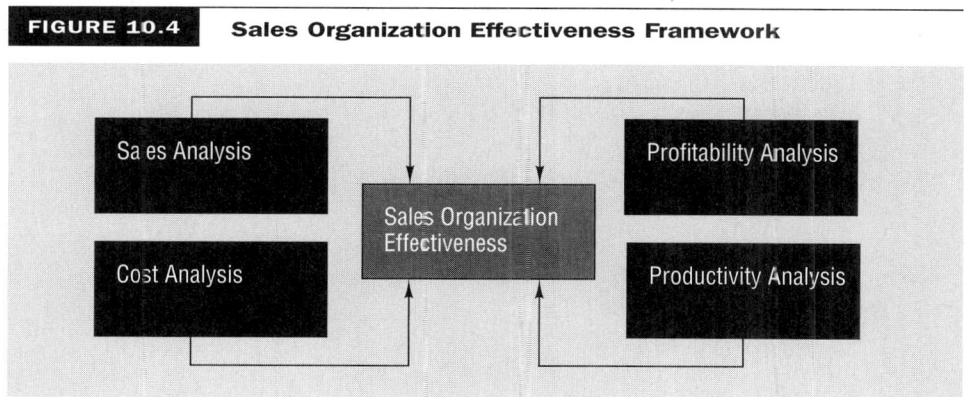

Evaluating sales organization effectiveness requires analyses of sales, cost, profitability, and productivity. Each type of analysis can be performed in different ways, should be performed at different sales organization levels, and produces different evaluative and diagnostic information for sales managers.

Many sales organizations focus their sales organization assessments on sales analysis.[13] The results from one study are presented in Exhibit 10.3. Although many firms in this study report using several forms of sales analyses, fewer report the use of cost, profit contribution, net profit, or return on assets analyses. Each area that should be addressed to evaluate sales organization effectiveness is discussed separately here.

Sales Analysis

Because the basic purpose of a sales organization is to generate sales, **sales analysis** is an obvious and important element of evaluating sales organization effectiveness. The difficulty, however, is in determining exactly what should be analyzed. One key consideration is in defining what is meant by a *sale*. Definitions include a placed order, a shipped order, and a paid order. Defining a sale by when an order is shipped is probably most common. Regardless of the definition used, the sales organization must be consistent and develop an information system to track sales based on whatever sales definition is used.

Another consideration is whether to focus on *sales dollars* or *sales units*. This can be extremely important during times when prices increase or when salespeople have substantial latitude in negotiating selling prices. The sales information in Exhibit 10.4 illustrates how different conclusions may result from analyses of sales dollars or sales units. If just sales dollars are analyzed, all regions in the exhibit would appear to be generating substantial sales growth. However, when sales units are introduced, the dollar sales growth for all regions in 1998 can be attributed almost entirely to price increases, because units sold increased only minimally during this period. The situation is somewhat different in 1999, because all regions increased the number of units sold. However, sales volume for region 2 is relatively flat, even though units sold increased. This could be caused either by selling more lower-priced products or by using larger price concessions than the other regions. In either case, analysis of

EXHIBIT 10.3 Use of Sales Organization Effectiveness Analyses

Quantitative Measures	*Mean Score*[1]
Sales volume in dollars	3.77
Sales volume versus previous year	3.60
Number of accounts lost	3.36
New accounts sales	3.23
Net profit in dollars	3.23
Sales volume versus quotas	3.21
Net profit margin	3.21
Number of new accounts	3.18
Sales volume versus market potentials	3.16
Number of customer complaints	3.15
Sales volume in units	3.14
Gross profit margin	3.06
Gross profit margin as percentage of sales	3.02
Selling expense/sales budget	2.93
Return on sales cost	2.87
Percentage of market share achieved	2.84
Selling expense as percentage of sales	2.65
Accounts buying full line	2.65
Number of reports turned in	2.63
Payments overdue	2.62
Sales volume by product type	2.62
Sales volume by customer type	2.52

[1]Means are calculated from a 5-point scale, with higher scores indicating greater importance.

EXHIBIT 10.4 Sales Dollars versus Sales Units

	1997		1998		1999	
	Sales Dollars	Sales Units	Sales Dollars	Sales Units	Sales Dollars	Sales Units
Region 1	$50,000,000	500,000	$55,000,000	510,000	$62,000,000	575,000
Region 2	$55,000,000	550,000	$60,000,000	560,000	$62,000,000	600,000
Region 3	$45,000,000	450,000	$50,000,000	460,000	$58,000,000	520,000
Region 4	$60,000,000	600,000	$65,000,000	610,000	$73,000,000	720,000

FIGURE 10.5 Sales Analysis Framework

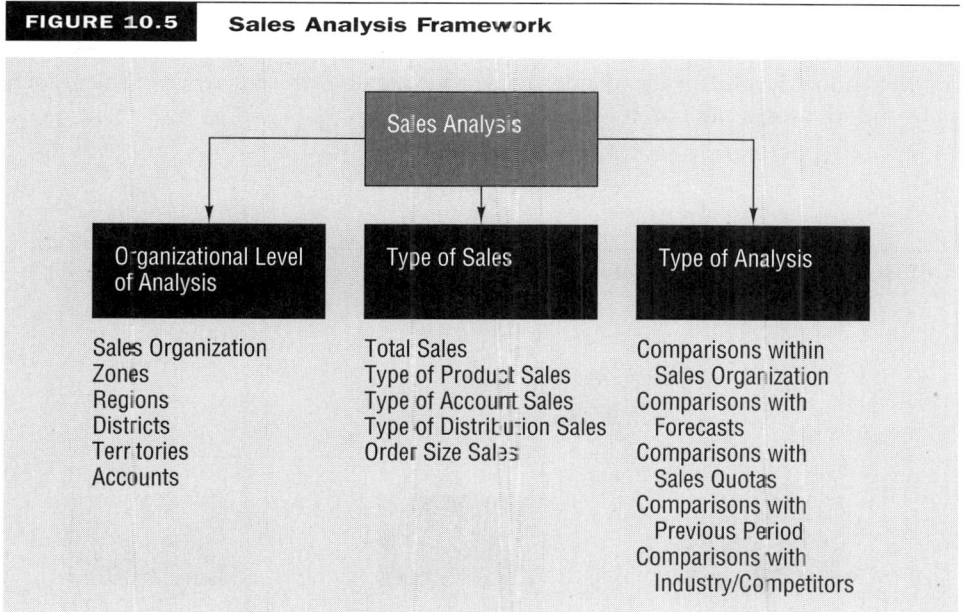

A sales analysis can be performed at different organization levels and for different types of sales and can use different types of analysis.

sales dollars or sales units provides different types of evaluative information, so it is often useful to include both dollars and units in a sales analysis.

Given a definition of sales and a decision concerning sales dollars versus units, many different sales evaluations can be performed. Several alternative evaluations are presented in Figure 10.5. The critical decision areas are the organizational level of analysis, the type of sales, and the type of analysis.

ORGANIZATIONAL LEVEL OF ANALYSIS Sales analyses should be performed for all levels in the sales organization for two basic reasons. First, sales managers at each level need sales analyses at their level and the next level below for evaluation and control purposes. For example, a regional sales manager should have sales analyses for all regions as well as for all districts within his or her region. This makes it possible to assess the sales effectiveness of the region and to determine the sales contribution of each district.

Second, a useful way to identify problem areas in achieving sales effectiveness is to perform a **hierarchical sales analysis,** which consists of evaluating sales results throughout the sales organization from a top-down perspective. Essentially, the analysis begins with total sales for the sales organization and proceeds through each successively lower level in the sales organization. The emphasis is on identifying potential problem areas at each level and then using analyses at lower levels to pinpoint the specific problems. An example of a hierarchical sales analysis is presented in Figure 10.6.

In this example, sales for region 3 appear to be much lower than those for the other regions, so the analysis proceeds to investigate the sales for all the districts in region 3. Low sales are identified for district 4; then district 4 sales are analyzed by territory. The results of this analysis suggest potential sales problems within territory 5. Additional analyses would be performed to determine why sales are so low for territory 5 and to take corrective action to increase sales from this territory. The hierarchical approach to sales analysis provides an efficient way to conduct a sales analysis and to identify major areas of sales problems.

TYPE OF SALES The analysis in Figure 10.6 addresses only total firm sales at each organizational level. It is usually desirable to evaluate different types of sales, such as by the following categories:

FIGURE 10.6 Example of Hierarchical Sales Analysis

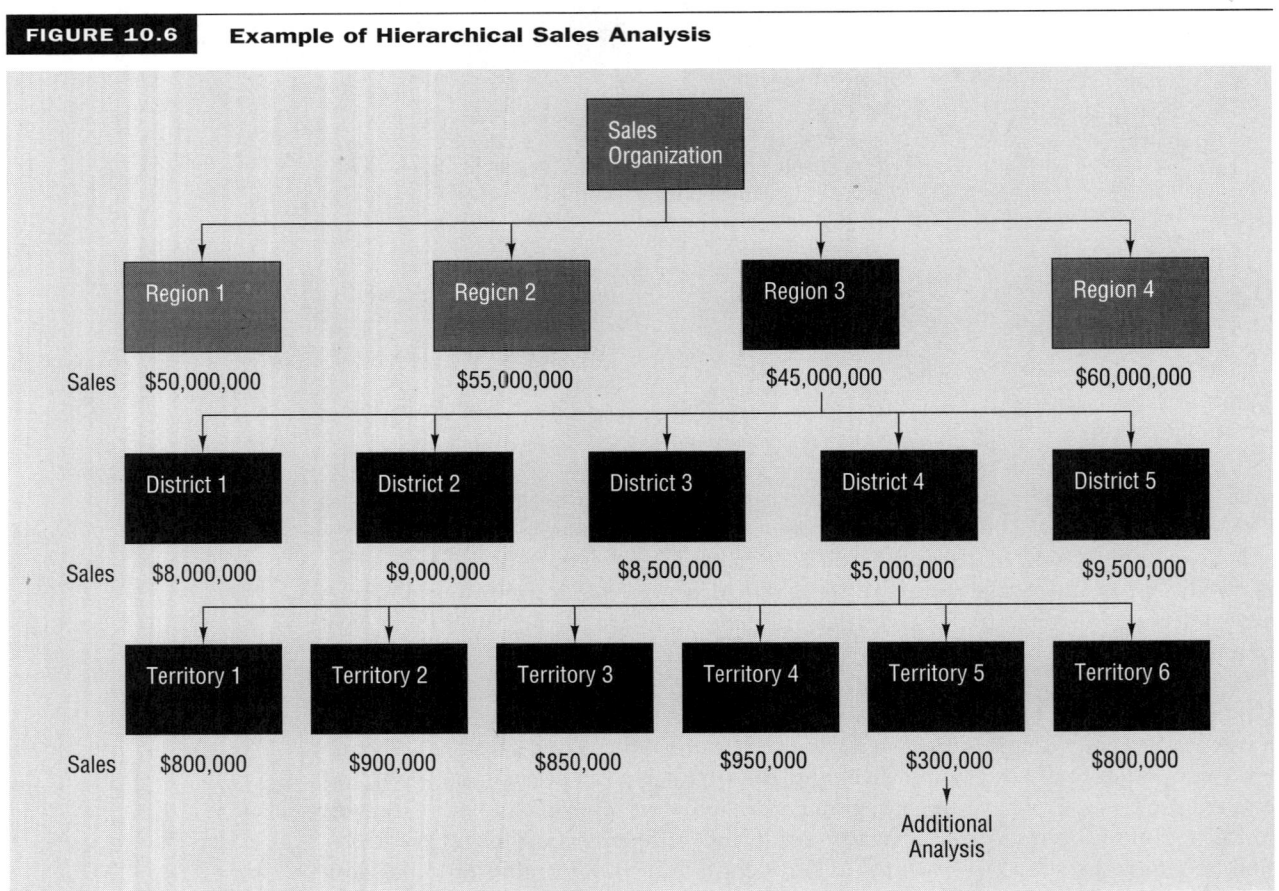

This multistage analysis proceeds from one sales organization level to the next by identifying the major deviations and investigating them in more detail at the next lower level. In the present example, region 3 has the lowest sales, so all districts in region 3 are examined. District 4 has poor sales results, so all the territories in district 4 are examined. Additional analysis is indicated for territory 5.

- product type or specific products
- account type or specific accounts
- type of distribution method
- order size

The hierarchical analysis in Figure 10.6 could have included sales by product type, account type, or other type of sales at each level. Or once the potential sales problem in territory 5 has been isolated, analysis of different types of sales could be performed to define the sales problem more fully. An example analysis is presented in Figure 10.7. This example suggests especially low sales volume for product type A and account type B. Additional analyses within these product and account types would be needed to determine why sales are low in these areas and what needs to be done to improve sales effectiveness.

The analysis of different types of sales at different organizational levels increases management's ability to detect and define problem areas in sales performance. However, incorporating different sales types into the analysis complicates the evaluation process and requires an information system capable of providing sales data concerning the desired breakdowns.

TYPE OF ANALYSIS The discussion to this point has focused on the actual sales results for different organizational levels and for different types of sales. However, the use of actual sales results limits the analysis to comparisons across organizational levels or sales types. These within-organization comparisons provide some useful information but are insufficient for a comprehensive evaluation of sales effectiveness. Several additional types of analysis are recommended and presented in Exhibit 10.5.

Comparing actual sales results with sales forecasts and quotas is extremely revealing. A *sales forecast* represents an expected level of firm sales for defined products, markets, and time periods and for a specified strategy. Based on this

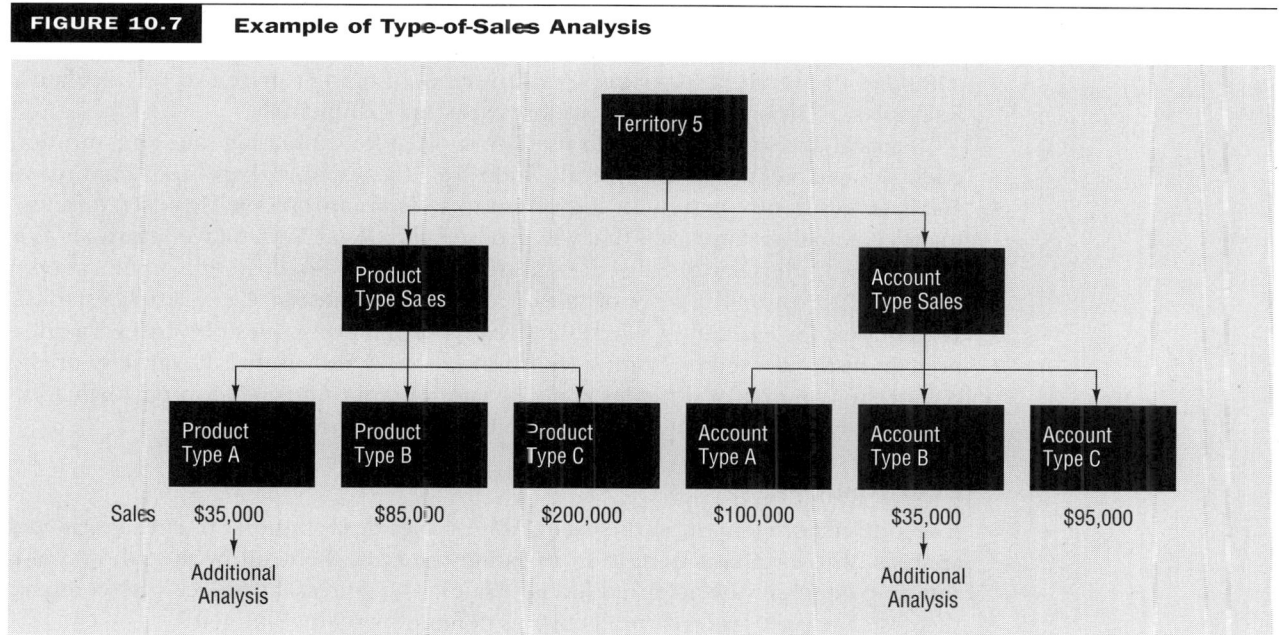

FIGURE 10.7 Example of Type-of-Sales Analysis

This is a continuation of the hierarchical sales analysis presented in Figure 10.6. Sales in territory 5 are analyzed by both product type and account type. The analysis suggests poor sales results for product type A and account type B.

EXHIBIT 10.5 Types of Analysis Examples

	District 1	District 2	District 3	District 4	District 5
Sales	$8,000,000	$9,000,000	$8,500,000	$5,000,000	$9,500,000
Sales quota	$8,250,000	$8,500,000	$8,250,000	$8,000,000	$8,500,000
Effectiveness index	97	106	103	63	112
Sales last year	$7,750,000	$8,250,000	$8,000,000	$4,850,000	$8,250,000
Sales growth	3%	9%	6%	3%	15%
Industry sales	$32,000,000	$32,000,000	$35,000,000	$30,000,000	$35,000,000
Market share	25%	28%	24%	17%	27%

definition, a sales forecast provides a basis for establishing specific *sales quotas* and reasonable sales objectives for a territory, district, region, or zone (methods for establishing sales quotas are discussed in Module 11). An **effectiveness index** can be computed by dividing actual sales results by the sales quota and multiplying by 100. As illustrated in Exhibit 10.5, sales results in excess of quota will have index values greater than 100, and results lower than quota will have index values less than 100. The sales effectiveness index makes it easy to compare directly the sales effectiveness of different organizational levels and different types of sales.

Another type of useful analysis is the comparison of actual results to previous periods. As illustrated in Exhibit 10.5, this type of analysis can be used to determine sales growth rates for different organizational levels and for different sales types. And incorporating sales data for many periods makes it possible to assess long-term sales trends.

A final type of analysis to be considered is a comparison of actual sales results to those achieved by competitors. This type of analysis can again be performed at different organizational levels and for different types of sales. If the comparison is extended to overall industry sales, various types of market share can be calculated. Examples of these comparisons are presented in Exhibit 10.5.

Sales analysis is the approach used most often for evaluating sales organization effectiveness. Sales data are typically more readily available than other data types, and sales results are extremely important to sales organizations. However, developing a sales analysis approach that will produce the desired evaluative information is a complex undertaking. Sales data must be available for different organizational levels and for different types of sales. Valid sales forecasts are needed to establish sales quotas for evaluating sales effectiveness in achieving sales objectives. In addition, industry and competitor sales information is also useful. Regardless of the comprehensiveness of the sales analysis, sales organizations need to perform additional analyses to evaluate sales organization effectiveness adequately.

Cost Analysis

A second major element in the evaluation of sales organization effectiveness is **cost analysis.** The emphasis here is on assessing the costs incurred by the sales organization to generate the achieved levels of sales. The general approach is to compare the costs incurred with planned costs as defined by selling budgets.

Corporate resources earmarked for personal selling expenses for a designated period represent the total **selling budget.** The key sales management budgeting task is to determine the best way to allocate these sales resources throughout the sales organization and across the different selling activities. The budgeting process is intended to instill cost consciousness and profit awareness throughout the organization, and it is necessary for establishing benchmarks for evaluating selling costs.

Selling budgets are developed at all levels of the sales organization and for all key expenditure categories. Our discussion focuses on the major selling expense categories and methods for establishing specific expenditure levels within the budget.

Firms differ considerably in how they define their selling expense categories. Nevertheless, all sales organizations should plan expenditures carefully for the major selling and sales management activities and for the different levels in the sales organization structure. The selling budget addresses controllable expenses, not uncontrollable ones. Typical selling budget expense categories are presented in Exhibit 10.6.

Both the total expenditures for each of these categories and sales management budget responsibility must be determined. Sales management budget responsibility depends on the degree of centralization or decentralization in the sales organization. In general, more centralized sales organizations will place budget responsibility at higher sales management levels. For example, if salesforce recruitment and selection take place at the regional level, then the regional sales managers will have responsibility for this budget category. Typically, the sales management activity occurs at all management levels. For example, training activities might be performed at national, zone, regional, and district levels. In this case, the budgeting process must address how much to spend on overall training and how to allocate training expenditures to the different organizational levels.

The basic objective in budgeting for each category is to determine the lowest expenditure level necessary to *achieve the sales quotas*. Notice that we did not say the lowest possible expenditure level. Sales managers might cut costs and improve profitability in the short run, but if expenditures for training, travel, and so forth are too low, long-run sales and profits will be sacrificed. However, if expenses can be reduced by more effective or more efficient spending, these productivity improvements can produce increased profitability in the long run. Achieving productivity

EXHIBIT 10.6 Selling Expense Categories in Budget

Classification	Actual 1999	Original 2000 Budget	April Revision	July Revision	October Revision
Compensation expenses					
Salaries					
Commissions					
Bonuses					
Total					
Travel expenses					
Lodging					
Food					
Transportation					
Miscellaneous					
Total					
Administrative expenses					
Recruiting					
Training					
Meetings					
Sales offices					
Total					

improvements has been one of the most demanding tasks facing sales managers in recent years because increases in field selling costs and extremely competitive markets have put tremendous pressure on firm profitability.

Determining expenditure levels for each selling expense category is extremely difficult. Although there is no perfect way to arrive at these expenditure levels, two approaches warrant attention: the percentage of sales method and the objective and task method.[14]

Probably the most often used, the **percentage of sales method** calculates an expenditure level for each category by multiplying an expenditure percentage times forecasted sales. The effectiveness of the percentage of sales method depends on the accuracy of sales forecasts and the appropriateness of the expenditure percentages. If the sales forecasts are not accurate, the selling budgets will be incorrect, regardless of the expenditure percentages used. If sales forecasts are accurate, the key is determining the expenditure percentages. Fortunately, typical expenditure percentages for different industries are available from published sources. Some general industry information is presented in Exhibit 10.7. These typical percentages should be viewed as guidelines only. Sales management should adjust them up or down to reflect the unique aspects of their sales organization.

The **objective and task method** takes an entirely different approach. In its most basic form, it is a type of zero-based budgeting. In essence, each sales manager prepares a separate budget request that stipulates the objectives to be achieved, the tasks required to achieve these objectives, and the costs associated with performing the necessary tasks. These requests are reviewed, and through an iterative process, selling budgets are approved. Many variations of the objective and task method are used by different sales organizations.

EXHIBIT 10.7 Typical Sales Costs by Industry

Industry Group	Cost per Call*	Number of Calls Needed to Close a Sale	Average Number of Calls per Day	Salesforce Costs as a Percentage of Total Sales
Banking	274.04	3.5	2.5	0.9
Business	202.09	4.2	2.2	10.5
Chemicals	137.92	5.4	3.2	3.4
Communication	109.75	4.0	3.1	9.9
Construction	140.66	6.2	2.2	7.1
Educational services	243.10	5.0	1.8	12.7
Electronics	195.74	5.0	2.5	12.6
Electronic components	191.21	5.0	2.6	4.9
Fabricated metals	195.72	3.7	2.5	7.2
Health services	133.76	4.0	3.5	13.4
Hotels and other lodging	121.51	3.8	2.8	1.9
Instruments	195.43	4.6	2.8	14.8
Insurance	112.15	2.8	3.1	NA
Machinery	281.20	4.0	2.6	11.3
Manufacturing	144.69	3.5	2.9	6.6
Office equipment	174.80	3.8	2.7	2.4
Pharmaceuticals	152.59	4.2	4.0	5.6
Printing and publishing	168.10	4.9	2.5	22.2
Real estate	NA	3.8	2.7	2.8
Retail	87.92	3.5	4.2	15.3
Rubber and plastics	119.30	3.8	3.8	3.6
Transportation equipment	NA	4.0	3.2	6.2
Wholesale (consumer goods)	96.28	2.6	3.9	11.2

*Average cost of a sales call is determined by dividing average industry total yearly compensation for an average performing salesperson with 3 years' experience, field expenses, and benefits, by the average number of sales calls made per year per sales representative (average calls per day x 225, which is the average number of days worked in a year). NA = not available.

EXHIBIT 10.8 Cost Analysis Examples

	Compensation Costs			Training Costs		
	Actual Cost	Budgeted Cost	Variance	Actual Cost	Budgeted Cost	Variance
Region 1	$3,660,000	$3,600,000	+$ 60,000	$ 985,000	$1,030,000	−$ 45,000
Region 2	$3,500,000	$3,700,000	−$200,000	$2,110,000	$2,040,000	+$ 70,000
Region 3	$3,150,000	$3,400,000	−$250,000	$ 830,000	$1,060,000	−$230,000
Region 4	$4,200,000	$3,900,000	+$300,000	$2,340,000	$2,160,000	+$180,000

	Compensation Costs		Training Costs	
	Actual % Sales	Budgeted % Sales	Actual % Sales	Budgeted % Sales
Region 1	6.1	6	2.9	3
Region 2	5.8	6	3.1	3
Region 3	5.4	6	2.6	3
Region 4	6.0	6	3.1	3

In reality, the process of establishing a selling budget is an involved one that typically incorporates various types of analysis, many meetings, and much politicizing. However, the process has been streamlined in many firms through the use of computer technology to rapidly evaluate alternative selling budgets.

After determining a budget, cost analysis can then be performed. Examples of two types of cost analysis are presented in Exhibit 10.8. The first analysis calculates the variance between actual costs and budgeted costs for the regions in a sales organization. Regions with the largest variation, especially when actual costs far exceed budgeted costs, should be highlighted for further analysis, Large variations are not necessarily bad, but the reasons for the variations should be determined. For example, the ultimate purpose of selling costs is to generate sales. Therefore, the objective is not necessarily to minimize selling costs but to ensure that a specified relationship between sales and selling costs is maintained. Evaluate one sales manager's method for determining budgeted costs in "An Ethical Dilemma."

An Ethical Dilemma

At the Alpha company, a contest is held each year among sales regions. Salespeople in the region deemed to be the most effective, based in large part on a cost analysis, receive a weekend trip to an exotic island. As manager of the southeastern region, Karen has finished as runner-up in the contest the past 3 years. She thinks her salespeople are long overdue. This year Karen is considering setting budgeted costs higher than she actually anticipates so that her year-end costs will look significantly lower than budgeted. What do you think Karen should do? Why?

One way to evaluate this relationship is to calculate the various selling costs as a percentage of sales achieved. Translating actual selling costs into percentages of sales achieved provides a means for assessing whether the cost–sales relationship has been maintained, even though the actual costs may exceed the absolute level in the selling budget. This situation is illustrated by region 4 in Exhibit 10.8.

Sales and cost analyses are the two most direct approaches for evaluating sales organization effectiveness. Profitability and productivity analyses extend the evaluation by assessing relationships between sales and costs. These analyses can be quite complex but may provide very useful information.

Profitability Analysis

Sales and cost data can be combined in various ways to produce evaluations of sales organization profitability for different organizational levels of different types of sales. This section covers three types of **profitability analysis:** income statement analysis, activity-based costing, and return on assets managed analysis.

INCOME STATEMENT ANALYSIS The different levels in a sales organization and different types of sales can be considered as separate businesses.[15] Consequently, income statements can be developed for profitability analysis. One of the major difficulties in **income statement analysis** is that some costs are shared between organizational levels or sales types.

Two approaches for dealing with the shared costs are illustrated in Exhibit 10.9. The **full cost approach** attempts to allocate the shared costs to individual units based on some type of cost allocation procedure. This results in a net profit figure for each unit. The **contribution approach** is different in that only direct costs are included in the profitability analysis; the indirect or shared costs are not included. The net contribution calculated from this approach represents the *profit contribution* of the unit being analyzed. This profit contribution must be sufficient to cover indirect costs and other overhead and to provide the net profit for the firm.

An example that incorporates both approaches is presented in Exhibit 10.10. This example uses the direct approach for assessing sales region profitability and the contribution approach for evaluating the districts within this region. Notice that the profitability calculations for each district include only district sales, cost of

EXHIBIT 10.9 Full Cost versus Contribution Approaches

Full Cost Approach	Contribution Approach
Sales	Sales
Minus: Cost of good sold	Minus: Cost of goods sold
Gross margin	Gross margin
Minus: Direct selling expenses	Minus: Direct selling expenses
Minus: Allocated portion of shared expenses	Profit distribution
Net profit	

EXHIBIT 10.10 Profitability Analysis Example

| | Full Cost Approach | Contribution Approach | | |
	Region	District 1	District 2	District 3
Sales	$300,000,000	$180,000,000	$70,000,000	$50,000,000
Cost of goods sold	235,000,000	168,500,000	58,500,000	28,000,000
Gross margin	45,000,000	11,500,000	11,500,000	22,000,000
District selling expenses	11,000,000	5,000,000	3,500,000	2,500,000
Region direct selling expenses	10,000,000	—	—	—
Profit contribution	24,000,000	6,500,000	8,000,000	19,500,000
Allocated portion of shared zone costs	16,000,000			
Net profit	8,000,000			

goods sold, and district direct selling expenses. A *profit contribution* is generated for each district. The profitability calculations for the region include district selling expenses, region direct selling expenses that have not been allocated to the districts, and an allocated portion of shared zone costs. This produces a net profit figure for a profitability evaluation of the region.

Although either approach might be used, there seems to be a trend toward the contribution approach, probably because of the difficulty in arriving at a satisfactory procedure for allocating the shared costs. Different cost allocation methods produce different results. Thus, many firms feel more comfortable with the contribution approach because it eliminates the need for cost allocation judgments and is viewed as more objective. For a look at how Hormel Foods focuses on selling costs to achieve profitable sales, see "Sales Management in the 21st Century: Focus on Profits at Hormel."

ACTIVITY-BASED COSTING Perhaps a more accountable method for allocating costs is **activity-based costing (ABC)**. ABC allocates costs to individual units on the basis of how the units actually expend or cause these costs. Costs are accumulated and then allocated to the units by the appropriate drivers, factors that drive costs up or down.[16]

Exhibit 10.11 illustrates how the profitability picture changed for a building supplies company that switched to ABC to assess distribution channel profitability. Notice that with ABC, selling expenses are no longer allocated to each channel based on a percentage of that channel's sales revenues. Instead, costs associated with each activity used to generate sales for a specific channel are allocated to that channel. Using ABC, a clearer picture of operating profits per channel emerges. In particular, the original equipment manufacturer channel appears to be much more profitable than the firm's prior accounting system indicates.

ABC places greater emphasis on more accurately defining unit profitability by tracing activities and their associated costs directly to a specific unit. For example, using ABC analysis, Diamant Boart found that a major customer who contributed 6 to 7 percent of total sales was very unprofitable when all the special efforts for that customer were considered.[17] As such, ABC helps foster an understanding of resource expenditures, how customer value is created, and where money is being made or lost.[18]

RETURN ON ASSETS MANAGED ANALYSIS The income statement approach to profitability assessment produces net profit or profit contribution in dollars or

---

SALES MANAGEMENT IN THE 21ST CENTURY

Focus on Profits at Hormel

Andre Wickham, food service region manager and national accounts sales manager for Hormel Foods Corporation, comments on his company's focus on profitable selling:

In today's sales environment, simply making the sale is not enough. We are interested in making profitable sales that mutually benefit our company and our customers. Our sales organization's ability to achieve desired profit targets is often manifested in two ways: by controlling our selling costs and improving our product mix. An attempt is made to control sales costs by holding salespeople accountable for managing controllable expenses such as travel, entertainment, and product samples. Further, we believe that by selling our customers a balanced mix of products our sales organization benefits from higher profits. When these tasks are effectively accomplished, the objectives of the customer and our company are met in a very efficient manner.

> [!NOTE] EXHIBIT 10.11 Activity-Based Costing Example

Profits by Commercial Distribution Channel (Old System)

	Contrast	Industrial Suppliers	Government	OEM	Total Commercial
Annual sales (in thousands of dollars)	$79,434	$25,110	$422	$9,200	$114,166
Gross margin	34%	41%	23%	27%	35%
Gross profit	$27,375	$10,284	$136	$2,461	$ 40,256
SG&A allowance[1] (in thousands of dollars)	$19,746	$ 6,242	$105	$2,287	$ 31,814
Operating profit (in thousands of dollars)	$ 7,629	$ 4,042	$ 31	$ 174	$ 11,876
Operating margin	10%	16%	7%	2%	10%
Invested capital allowance[2] (in thousands of dollars)	$33,609	$10,624	$179	$3,893	$ 48,305
Return on investment	23%	38%	17%	4%	25%

[1]SG&A allowance for each channel is 25 percent of that channel's revenues.
[2]Invested capital allowance for each channel is 42 percent of that channel's revenues.

Profits by Commercial Distribution Channel (New System: ABC)

	Contrast	Industrial Suppliers	Government	OEM	Total Commercial
Gross profit (from previous table)	$27,375	$10,284	$136	$2,461	$40,256
Selling expenses[1] (all in thousands of dollars)					
Commission	$ 4,682	$ 1,344	$ 12	$ 372	$ 6,410
Advertising	132	38	0	2	172
Catalog	504	160	0	0	664
Co-op advertising	416	120	0	0	536
Sales promotion	394	114	0	2	510
Warranty	64	22	0	4	90
Sales administration	5,696	1,714	20	351	7,781
Cash discount	892	252	12	114	1,270
Total	$12,780	$ 3,764	$ 44	$ 845	$17,433
G&A (in thousands of dollars)	$ 6,740	$ 2,131	$ 36	$ 781	$ 9,688
Operating profit (in thousands of dollars)	$ 7,855	$ 4,389	$ 56	$ 835	$13,135
Operating margin	10%	17%	13%	9%	12%
Invested capital[1]	$33,154	$10,974	$184	$2,748	$47,060
Return on investment	24%	40%	30%	30%	28%

[1]Selling expenses and invested capital estimated under an activity-based system.

expressed as a percentage of sales. Although necessary and valuable, the income statement approach is incomplete because it does not incorporate any evaluation of the investment in assets required to generate the net profit or profit contribution.

The calculation of **return on assets managed (ROAM)** can extend the income statement analysis to include asset investment considerations. The formula for calculating ROAM is

$$\text{ROAM} = \text{Profit contribution as percentage of sales} \times \text{Asset turnover rate}$$
$$= (\text{Profit contribution}/\text{Sales}) \times (\text{Sales}/\text{Assets managed})$$

Profit contribution can be either a net profit figure from a direct approach or profit contribution from a contribution approach. Assets managed typically include inventory, accounts receivable, or other assets at each sales organizational level.

An example of ROAM calculations is presented in Exhibit 10.12. The example illustrates ROAM calculations for sales districts within a region. Notice that district

EXHIBIT 10.12	Return on Assets Managed (ROAM) Example				
		District 1	District 2	District 3	District 4
Sales		$24,000,000	$24,000,000	$24,000,000	$24,000,000
Cost of goods sold		12,000,000	12,000,000	14,000,000	14,000,000
Gross margin		12,000,000	12,000,000	10,000,000	10,000,000
Direct selling expenses		7,200,000	9,600,000	5,200,000	8,800,000
Profit contribution		4,800,000	2,400,000	4,800,000	1,200,000
Accounts receivable		8,000,000	4,000,000	16,000,000	4,000,000
Inventory		8,000,000	4,000,000	16,000,000	4,000,000
Total assets managed		16,000,000	8,000,000	32,000,000	8,000,000
Profit contribution percentage		20%	10%	20%	5%
Asset turnover		1.5	3.0	.75	3.0
ROAM		30%	30%	15%	15%

1 and district 2 produce the same ROAM but achieve their results in different ways. District 1 generates a relatively high profit contribution percentage, whereas district 2 operates with a relatively high asset turnover. Both district 3 and district 4 are achieving poor levels of ROAM but for different reasons. District 3 has an acceptable profit contribution percentage but very low asset turnover ratio. This low asset turnover ratio is the result of both inventory accumulations or problems in payments from accounts. District 4, however, has an acceptable asset turnover ratio but low profit contribution percentage. This low profit contribution percentage may be the result of selling low margin products, negotiating low selling prices, or accruing excessive selling expenses.

As illustrated in the preceding example, ROAM calculations provide an assessment of profitability and useful diagnostic information. ROAM is determined by both profit contribution percentage and asset turnover. If ROAM is low in any area, the profit contribution percentage and asset turnover ratio can be examined to determine the reason. Corrective action (e.g., reduced selling expenses, stricter credit guidelines, lower inventory levels) can then be taken to improve future ROAM performance.

Productivity Analysis

Although ROAM incorporates elements of productivity by comparing profits and asset investments, additional **productivity analysis** is desirable for thorough evaluation of sales organization effectiveness. Productivity is typically measured in terms of ratios between outputs and inputs. For example, as discussed in Module 5, one often-used measure of salesforce productivity is sales per salesperson. A major advantage of productivity ratios is that they can be compared directly across the entire sales organization and with other sales organizations. This direct comparison is possible because all the ratios are expressed in terms of the same units.

Because the basic job of sales managers is to manage salespeople, the most useful input unit for productivity analysis is the salesperson. Therefore, various types of productivity ratios are calculated on a per-salesperson basis. The specific ratios depend on the characteristics of a particular selling situation but often include important outputs such as sales, expenses, calls, demonstrations, and proposals. An example of a productivity analysis is presented in Exhibit 10.13.

Exhibit 10.13 illustrates how productivity analysis provides a different and useful perspective for evaluating sales organization effectiveness. As the exhibit reveals, absolute values can be misleading. For example, the highest sales districts are not necessarily the most effective. Although profitability analyses would likely detect this also, productivity analysis presents a vivid and precise evaluation by highlighting specific areas of both high and low productivity. Take the information concerning district 2. Although sales per salesperson is reasonable and expenses per salesperson is relatively low, both calls per salesperson and proposals per salesperson are much lower than those for the other districts. This may explain why selling expenses are low, but it also suggests that the salespeople in this district may not be covering the district adequately. The high sales may be due to a few large sales to large customers.

In any case, the productivity analysis provides useful evaluative and diagnostic information that is not directly available from the other types of analyses discussed in this module. Sales productivity and profitability are highly interrelated. However, profitability analysis has a financial perspective, whereas productivity analysis is more managerially oriented. Improvements in sales productivity should translate into increases in profitability.

Productivity improvements are obtained in one of two basic ways:

1. increasing output with the same level of input
2. maintaining the same level of output but using less input

Productivity analysis can help determine which of these basic approaches should be pursued.

Ethical Issues

The value of comparing actual expenses with budgeted expenses depends on the accuracy of the expense information provided by salespeople. Although most sales organizations have prepared forms with the expense categories and instructions for

EXHIBIT 10.13 **Productivity Analysis Example**

	District 1	District 2	District 3	District 4
Sales	$20,000,000	$24,000,000	$20,000,000	$24,000,000
Selling expenses	$ 2,000,000	$ 2,400,000	$ 3,000,000	$ 3,000,000
Sales calls	9,000	7,500	8,500	10,000
Proposals	220	180	260	270
Number of salespeople	20	30	20	30
Sales/salesperson	$ 1,000,000	$ 800,000	$ 1,000,000	$ 800,000
Expenses/salesperson	$ 100,000	$ 80,000	$ 150,000	$ 100,000
Calls/salesperson	450	250	425	333
Proposals/salesperson	11	6	13	9

salespeople, salespeople often face ethical problems in reporting their expenses. Consider the following situations:

- A salesperson has been on the road for a week and incurs laundry expenses. He knows that if he places the laundry expenses under the miscellaneous expense category in his expense report, he will have to provide receipts. He decides that he can include them under the meals category because receipts are not required for this category as long as he stays under his per-diem allowance.
- A salesperson is trying to get a customer to purchase a new product. He decides to take three individuals from the customer's firm to dinner and a basketball game, even though he knows that he has exceeded his entertainment budget for the month. He thinks about hiding these entertainment expenses in different categories in his expense report.

The decisions that salespeople make in these and similar situations affect the ability of sales managers to evaluate actual and budgeted expenses in an accurate manner. Sales managers themselves, however, may have opportunities to act unethically when evaluating salesforce effectiveness as illustrated in "An Ethical Dilemma."

An Ethical Dilemma

As regional sales manager for International Enterprises, Janice has been passed over several times for a promotion. Although her region performs as well as others within the company, she believes she may be getting overlooked because she is female. She has been told that if her region ranks above the other regions in the company in terms of effectiveness (based on sales, costs, profitability, productivity) this year that she will finally get her promotion. To ensure that her salesforce fares well, Janice is considering doing a little "creative bookkeeping." She reasons that her salesforce might look a little more effective than it actually is, but no harm will be done, and she will finally get the promotion the company owes her. If you were Janice, what would you do and why?

Concluding Comments

As is obvious from the discussion in this module, there is no easy way to evaluate the effectiveness of a sales organization. Our recommendation is to perform separate analyses of sales, costs, profitability, and productivity to assess different aspects of sales organization effectiveness. In addition, salesperson performance, which is discussed in the next module, must also be evaluated and considered. Each type of analysis offers a piece of the puzzle. Sales managers must put these pieces together for comprehensive evaluations. The objective underlying each of the analyses is to be able to evaluate effectiveness, identify problem areas, and use this information to improve future sales organization effectiveness.

Summary

1. **Differentiate between sales organization effectiveness and salesperson performance.** Sales organization effectiveness is a summary evaluation of the overall success of a sales organization in meeting its goals and objectives in total and at different organizational levels. By contrast, salesperson performance is a function of individual salesperson performance in individual situations.

2. **Define a sales organization audit and discuss how it should be conducted.** The most comprehensive type of evaluation is a sales organization audit, which is a systematic assessment of all aspects of a sales organization. The major areas included in the audit are sales organization environment, sales management evaluation, sales organization planning system, and sales management functions. The audit should be conducted regularly by individuals outside the sales organization. It is intended to identify existing or potential problems early so that corrective action can be taken before the problems become serious.
3. **Define benchmarking and discuss how it should be conducted.** Benchmarking is an ongoing measurement and analysis process that compares an organization's current operating practices with the "best practices" used by world-class organizations. It involves identifying the sales organization processes to be benchmarked and whom to benchmark, collecting data on the benchmarked firm, analyzing performance gaps and communicating them to the salesforce, and establishing goals and implementing plans. Its purpose is to improve processes to improve performance.
4. **Describe how to perform different types of sales analysis for different organizational levels and types of sales.** Sales analysis is the most common evaluation approach, but it can be extremely complex. Specific definitions of a sale are required, and both sales dollars and units typically should be considered. A hierarchical approach is suggested as a top-down procedure to address sales results at each level of the sales organization with an emphasis on identifying problem areas. Sales analysis is more useful when sales results are compared with forecasts, quotas, previous time periods, and competitor results.
5. **Describe how to perform a cost analysis for a sales organization.** Cost analysis focuses on the costs incurred to generate sales results. Specific costs can be compared with the planned levels in the selling budget. Areas with large variances require specific attention. Costs can also be evaluated as percentages of sales and compared to comparable industry figures.
6. **Describe how to perform an income statement, analysis, activity-based costing, and return on assets managed to assess sales organization profitability.** Profitability analysis combines sales and cost data in various ways. The income statement approach focuses on net profit or profit contributions from the different sales organization levels. Activity-based costing allocates costs to individual units on the basis of how the units actually expend or cause these costs. The return on assets managed approach assesses relationships between profit contributions and the assets used to generate these profit contributions. Residual income analysis combines the return on assets managed concept with sales growth objectives to produce a very useful evaluative tool. The different profitability analyses address different aspects of profitability that are of interest to sales managers.
7. **Describe how to perform a productivity analysis for a sales organization.** Productivity analysis focuses on relationships between outputs and inputs. The most useful input is the number of salespeople, whereas relevant outputs might be sales, expenses, proposals, and so on. The productivity ratios calculated in this manner are versatile because they can be used for comparisons within the sales organization and across other sales organizations. Productivity analysis not only provides useful evaluative information but also provides managerially useful diagnostic information that can suggest ways to improve productivity and increase profitability.

Understanding Sales Management Terms

- Sales organization audit
- Benchmarking
- Sales analysis
- Hierarchical sales analysis
- Effectiveness index
- Cost analysis
- Selling budget
- Percentage of sales method
- Objective and task method
- Profitability analysis
- Income statement analysis
- Full cost approach
- Contribution approach
- Activity-based costing (ABC)
- Return on assets managed (ROAM)
- Productivity analysis

Developing Sales Management Knowledge

1. Discuss why it is important to differentiate between sales organization effectiveness and salesperson performance.
2. Discuss what is involved in conducting a sales management audit.
3. What is the purpose of benchmarking? Discuss what is involved in benchmarking.
4. Refer to "Sales Management in the 21st Century: Using Benchmarking to Succeed." How can benchmarking be used to improve performance?
5. What is meant by a hierarchical sales analysis? Can a hierarchical approach be used in analyzing costs, profitability, and/or productivity?
6. What is the difference between the full cost and contribution approaches to income statement analysis for a sales organization? Which would you recommend for a sales organization? Why?
7. Refer to "Sales Management in the 21st Century: Focus on Profits at Hormel." How can a company achieve more profitable sales?
8. What are the two basic components of return on assets managed? How is each component calculated, and what does each component tell a sales manager?
9. Identify five different sales organization productivity ratios that you would recommend. Describe how each would be calculated and what information each would provide.
10. Discuss how you think new computer and information technologies will affect the evaluations of sales organization effectiveness in the future.

Building Sales Management Skills

1. Using the following information, conduct a sales analysis to evaluate sales organization effectiveness. Explain your findings.

	Region 1 ($000)	Region 2 ($000)	Region 3 ($000)	Region 4 ($000)
Sales	$ 4,050	$ 4,750	$ 4,250	$ 2,500
Sales quota	$ 4,125	$ 4,250	$ 4,075	$ 3,900
Sales last year	$ 3,925	$ 4,375	$ 4,000	$ 2,425
Industry sales	$11,500	$12,500	$13,500	$10,500

2. Sales and cost data can be combined in various ways to produce evaluations of sales organization profitability for different organizational levels or different types of sales. Three types of profitability analysis are useful for evaluating effectiveness: activity-based costing, income statement analysis, and return on assets managed analysis. Examining Exhibit 10.11, point out differences in operating profits by commercial distribution channel between the company's old and new (ABC) system, and explain why they differ. What would the ABC system lead you to believe regarding the effectiveness of each channel? Using the information in Exhibit 10.11 and the information below, conduct an income statement analysis and return on assets managed analysis. Explain the results of your analyses.

	Contract ($000)	Industrial Suppliers ($000)	Government ($000)	OEM ($000)
Accounts receivable	$26,478	$16,740	$70	$1,533
Inventory	$26,478	$16,740	$71	$1,534

3. Several sites are available on the World Wide Web that provide benchmarking services. One such site is Best Practices, LLC (www.best-in-class.com), a research and consulting firm that provides business insight and analysis of how world-class companies achieve exceptional economic and operational performance. Access this site and review its services.
    A. How can a company such as this be useful to a sales manager attempting to improve the sales organization?
    B. From the Best Practices home page, click on "Practice of the Day." Read and briefly summarize the information you find. Could this information be used by a sales

manager to improve the sales organization? If so, how? (It is best if this can be accessed on Monday, the day in which a sales and marketing best practice is featured.)
C. From the Best Practices home page, click on "Best Practice Database." Next, click "Sample & Free Reports." Now click on "Sales & Marketing." You will find several reports. Indicate which reports might be helpful for improving a sales organization's effectiveness, and briefly explain how each report's information might be used.
D. Locate another benchmarking service on the World Wide Web. Identify its address and briefly describe its services. Compare and contrast its services to those of Best Practices, LLC.

Making Sales Management Decisions

CASE 10.1   Beauty Glow Cosmetics Company

Background

Beauty Glow Cosmetics Company manufactures and markets a line of cosmetics products to retailers throughout the United States. The salesforce is organized into five regions, each comprised of five districts. A national sales manager oversees the five regional sales managers. Each regional manager is responsible for the effectiveness of his or her region and is compensated accordingly.

Current Situation

Kate Flower is the regional sales manager for the northern region. The fiscal year just ended, and Kate has compiled data to help her analyze her region's effectiveness. Although her region has had what she believes to be a very successful year, she wants to closely analyze each district. She hopes to use her analysis to identify and correct problems. Moreover, she needs to complete her analysis for her upcoming meeting with her national sales manager, Calvin Cline.

Market shares for each district were fairly sizable (29 percent, 31 percent, 33 percent, 30 percent, and 27 percent for districts 1 through 5, respectively) at the beginning of the fiscal year. Kate had expected these to remain relatively stable over the past year. The company had anticipated a sales growth of 2 percent. In addition, selling costs were budgeted at 10 percent of sales. If Kate's region did not increase sales by 2 percent and stay within the sales budget, her performance appraisal, and subsequently her compensation, would suffer.

Kate knew her boss would carefully scrutinize her analysis. She hoped to be able to identify any problem areas so that she could develop solutions and implement them in the upcoming year. She was scheduled to meet with Cline in 3 days.

Kate compiled the following information:

	District 1 ($000)	District 2 ($000)	District 3 ($000)	District 4 ($000)	District 5 ($000)
Sales	$8,200	$8,500	$10,450	$13,750	$8,400
Cost of goods sold	4,920	5,510	6,479	8,250	4,620
Compensation	615	810	735	1,140	630
Transportation	41	67	42	70	50
Lodging and meals	17	30	16	41	21
Telephone	8	10	12	14	9
Entertainment	10	8	15	12	12
Training	80	95	105	125	110
District accounts receivable	1,170	1,400	1,450	2,420	1,150
District inventory	2,000	3,500	3,200	5,250	2,500
Number of salespeople	8	9	11	12	10
Sales quota	8,100	9,750	10,250	14,125	3,300
Sales last year	7,500	9,250	10,250	13,925	8,200
Industry sales	26,452	29,689	30,736	45,834	30,000

Questions

1. What analyses should Kate perform with this data? Perform these analyses.
2. What problems can you identify from your analyses?
3. What solutions do you recommend to solve these problems and improve results in the future?

CASE 10.2   Induplicate Copiers, Inc.

Background

Induplicate Copiers, Inc., manufactures and markets photocopiers. The company operates throughout the United States and is divided into four regions, each consisting of four districts with a district sales manager in charge of each. A regional sales manager is assigned ultimate responsibility for each region. The company manufactures its copiers in San Diego, California, and ships them directly to regional warehouses.

For the most part, salespeople at Induplicate are well qualified and experienced. All its salespeople have a college degree, and several have prior sales experience. The average salesperson tenure at Induplicate is 7 years.

Current Situation

Despite competing with major copier manufacturers such as Xerox and Minolta, Induplicate has done well. It continues to produce some of the most innovative and advanced machines on the market. However, Induplicate's president, Alicia Doubleit, believes that the company can do much better. The following is a conversation she recently had with her national sales manager, Rich Getmore:

Alicia: I believe that the key to our growth lies in having a successful salesforce.

Rich: Absolutely. We have made great strides over the past 3 years, consistently increasing our sales volume.

Alicia: Sales growth is a must. However, we need to measure up to the performance of our competition in other ways.

Rich: What do you mean?

Alicia: If we want to reach the top, we have to have a salesforce that performs like those at the top. How convenient and quick is our service? How long does it take from order to delivery and setup?

Rich: I suppose we could always improve our service. However, our salespeople are well qualified and do a competent job.

Alicia: What about our user training program? Can it be made more convenient for customers? Is it possible to accomplish it more quickly and less expensively without sacrificing the quality of the training?

Rich: We seem to be doing okay in this area. There haven't been a lot of complaints that I am aware of, so I assume everything is going well.

Alicia: If we are going to be the best, we have to have the best salesforce. Rich, I'm counting on you to lead our salesforce to the top. I can't stress how important it is for us to have a high performing salesforce. I'd like to meet with you in 2 weeks to discuss your plan for addressing these issues.

Rich: Perhaps it's time to take a closer look at our sales organization. I'll do my best.

Questions

1. How could Rich use benchmarking to address Alicia's concerns?
2. Outline a benchmarking study that could be used to help make Induplicate's salesforce more effective.
3. What else can be done to ensure that Induplicate's salesforce is performing effectively?

MODULE 11

Evaluating the Performance of Salespeople

Changing Environment Prompts Changes in Salesperson Evaluation

Deregulation is resulting in changes in the way utility companies compete. Take the case of Entergy, an electric utility serving the mid-southern United States. Facing increased competition, the utility company found its salesforce had become more vital to its success. The salesforce would actually have to sell its products and services.

Given this new environment, Entergy turned to Bryan Associates, Inc. (BAI), a management consulting company, for help in defining performance standards for its salesforce. Together, Entergy and BAI developed highly customized models defining the competencies necessary for successful salespeople at Entergy. To accomplish this, they used focus groups to collect information from the utility's salespeople, management, and customers. They also interviewed Entergy's top sales performers, along with salespeople and sales managers from top performing salesforces of other companies. What emerged from the process was the precise attributes against which Entergy's salespeople could be measured and developed.

The competency model serves as a measure against which to evaluate salespeople's performance. Using a 360-degree feedback process, salespeople are evaluated on model competencies by their managers, their colleagues, and their customers. Results are then reviewed with their manager, and methods for improving competencies are determined.

Another facet of Entergy's sales performance evaluation process revolves around its sales certification process. This assessment effort recognizes and rewards salespeople for demonstrating core competencies. As part of the process, salespeople are required to appear before a Board of Review consisting of key executives, sales managers, and a certified peer of the salesperson being evaluated. Armed with two real sales situations having occurred during the year, the salesperson being evaluated appears before the board, which uses a data-based interviewing technique to walk salespeople through these situations and assess their demonstration of actual competencies. Using standardized assessment forms, the board provides feedback to sales managers regarding salespeople's strengths and areas for improvement.

The competency model approach has allowed Entergy to develop a successful salesforce in a changing environment. Although exact figures are difficult to attain, measurable results have been achieved in sales and productivity.

Source: Joel Cohn, "A Model Sell," *Management Review* 86 (March 1997): 55–59.

Learning Objectives

After completing this module, you should be able to

1 Discuss the different purposes of salesperson performance evaluations.

2 Differentiate between an outcome-based and a behavior-based perspective for evaluating and controlling salesperson performance.

3 Describe the different types of criteria necessary for comprehensive evaluations of salesperson performance.

4 Compare the advantages and disadvantages of different methods of salesperson performance evaluation.

5 Explain how salesperson performance information can be used to identify problems, determine their causes, and suggest sales management actions to solve them.

6 Discuss the measurement and importance of salesperson job satisfaction.

Whereas Module 10 focused on evaluating sales organization effectiveness, this module examines the task of evaluating salesperson performance and job satisfaction. Evaluations of sales organization effectiveness concentrate on the overall results achieved by the different units within the sales organization, with special attention given to determining the effectiveness of territories, districts, regions, and zones and identifying strategic changes to improve future effectiveness. These effectiveness assessments examine sales organization units and do not directly evaluate individuals; however, sales managers are responsible for the effectiveness of their assigned units.

The Entergy utility company example in the opening vignette illustrates a relatively new approach for examining salesperson performance that includes input from several sources. The more typical situation is when sales managers evaluate the performance of the salespeople assigned to them. To do so, sales managers must understand both why and how performance evaluations are conducted, as well as how to use information gained from these evaluations. As the opening vignette demonstrates, Entergy developed a system for evaluating salespeople's performance and used it to improve not only salespeople's individual performance but subsequently the overall performance of its company.

The purpose of this module is to investigate the key issues involved in evaluating and controlling the performance and job satisfaction of salespeople. The different purposes of salesperson performance evaluations are discussed initially. Then, the performance evaluation procedures currently used by sales organizations are examined. This is followed by a comprehensive assessment of the different areas in salesperson performance evaluation. The assessment addresses the criteria to be used in evaluating salespeople, the methods for evaluating salespeople against these criteria, and the outcomes of salesperson performance evaluations. The module concludes by discussing the importance and measurement of salesperson job satisfaction and relationships between salesperson performance and job satisfaction.

Purposes of Salesperson Performance Evaluations

As the name suggests, the basic objective of salesperson performance evaluations is to determine how well individual salespeople have performed. However, the results of salesperson performance evaluations can be used for many sales management purposes:[1]

1. To ensure that compensation and other reward disbursements are consistent with actual salesperson performance.
2. To identify salespeople who might be promoted.
3. To identify salespeople whose employment should be terminated and to supply evidence to support the need for termination.
4. To determine the specific training and counseling needs of individual salespeople and the overall salesforce.
5. To provide information for effective human resource planning.
6. To identify criteria that can be used to recruit and select salespeople in the future.
7. To advise salespeople of work expectations.
8. To motivate salespeople.
9. To help salespeople set career goals.
10. To improve salesperson performance.

These diverse purposes affect all aspects of the performance evaluation process. For example, performance evaluations for determining compensation and special rewards should emphasize activities and results related to the salesperson's current job and situation. Performance evaluations for the purpose of identifying salespeople for promotion into sales management positions should focus on criteria related to potential effectiveness as a sales manager and not just current performance as a salesperson. The best salespeople do not always make the best sales managers. Thus, salesperson performance appraisals must be carefully developed and implemented to provide the types of information necessary to accomplish all the desired purposes.

Salesperson Performance Evaluation Approaches

Although it is impossible to determine with precision all the performance evaluation approaches used by sales organizations, several studies have produced sufficiently consistent information to warrant some general conclusions.[2]

1. Most sales organizations evaluate salesperson performance annually, although many firms conduct evaluations semiannually or quarterly. Relatively few firms evaluate salesperson performance more often than quarterly.
2. Most sales organizations use combinations of input and output criteria that are evaluated by quantitative and qualitative measures. However, emphasis seems to be placed on outputs, with evaluations of sales volume results the most popular.
3. Sales organizations that set performance standards or quotas tend to enlist the aid of salespeople in establishing these objectives. The degree of salesperson input and involvement does, however, appear to vary across firms.
4. Many sales organizations assign weights to different performance objectives and incorporate territory data when establishing these objectives.
5. Most firms use more than one source of information in evaluating salesperson performance. Computer printouts, call reports, supervisory calls, sales itineraries, prospect and customer files, and client and peer feedback are some of the common sources of information.
6. Most salesperson performance evaluations are conducted by the field sales manager who supervises the salesperson. However, some firms involve the manager above the field sales manager in the salesperson performance appraisal.
7. Most sales organizations provide salespeople with a written copy of their performance review and have sales managers discuss the performance evaluation with each salesperson. These discussions typically take place in an office, although sometimes they are conducted in the field.

These results offer a glimpse of current practices in evaluating salesperson performance. Although performance appraisal continues to be primarily a top-down process, changes are taking place in some companies leading to the implementation of a broader-based assessment process. An increasingly popular assessment technique, dubbed **360-degree feedback,** involves performance assessment from multiple raters, including sales managers, internal and external customers, team members, and even salespeople themselves. Recall from the opening vignette that Entergy had managers, colleagues, and customers provide feedback on its salespeople to ascertain their performance on certain core competencies. Vital

Learning, for instance, has developed an assessment procedure that has customers rate salespeople in such areas as interpersonal skills, precall preparation, and selling and communication skills. The managers then rate the salespeople, and the salespeople in turn rate themselves. Responses are reviewed and performance scores are assigned to salespeople in each area relative to the degree of importance customers place in that area.[3] At Xerox and GE, customer satisfaction surveys are part of its sales representatives' performance evaluations.[4] Linking customer satisfaction to salesforce evaluation is becoming increasingly popular. A study of 124 large U.S. corporations found that 34 percent of them link the performance evaluations of their sales departments to customer satisfaction measurement results.[5]

Among its many benefits, 360-degree feedback helps to better understand customer needs, detect barriers to success, assess developmental needs, create job involvement, reduce assessment bias, and improve performance.[6] However, when using the process, keep in mind that bias may still exist. Individuals may be less forthright in giving feedback and less accepting of feedback from others if they believe it will have damaging consequences.[7] Thus, it may be best to use it in conjunction with other appraisal techniques. Exhibit 11.1 provides keys to implementing an effective 360-degree feedback system. To facilitate this process, some companies are using Internet Web sites as an efficient means for distributing and collecting multiple evaluations.[8]

EXHIBIT 11.1 Keys to an Effective 360-Degree Feedback System

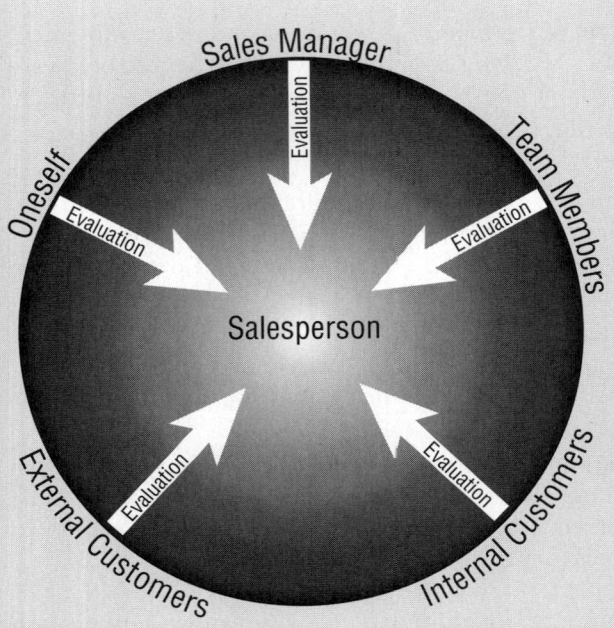

1. Ensure that participants willingly provide honest feedback by distributing the feedback instrument confidentially, aggregating responses by rating source, having rating forms sent directly to the person or group organizing the data, and including feedback from at least three respondents in each rater group (e.g., customers, coworkers, team members).
2. Explain to all participants how the data will be used.
3. Ensure that the data sources remain confidential so those being rated do not know specifically who did the rating.
4. Verify that the data are accurate. The assessment tools used to gather the data should be reliable and valid.
5. Ensure that subjects can use the data to improve their performance. Present the feedback from the different groups (perspectives). Compare feedback from others with one's own perceptions.
6. Determine how the system will affect the organization overall and systematically evaluate its effectiveness.

Another evaluation approach that moves away from the traditional top-down appraisal is referred to as **performance management.** This approach involves sales managers and salespeople working together on setting goals, giving feedback, reviewing, and rewarding.[9] With this system, salespeople create their own development plans and assume responsibility for their careers. The sales manager acts as a partner in the process, providing feedback that is timely, specific, regular, solicited, and focused on what is within the salesperson's control to change. Salespeople are compensated on the value of their contributions to the organization's success. Performance management ultimately focuses on improving organizational performance by finding new and better ways to satisfy customers.[10] A study of 437 U.S. companies in 58 industries reported that companies following a performance management approach had greater financial and productivity performance relative to other companies in their industry.[11]

A performance management approach is consistent with the principles of **total quality management (TQM).** TQM incorporates a strong customer orientation, a team-oriented corporate culture, and the use of statistical methods to analyze and improve all business processes including sales management.[12] TQM programs focus on efforts to continuously monitor and improve performance rather than merely evaluating performance over extended periods. This can be accomplished by mapping the processes that lead to desired results and then concentrating effort on improving these processes. As a result, reengineering may occur, resulting in a simpler process with corresponding savings in time and cost and improvements in quality.[13] For example, FedEx analyzes customer costs and delivery cycle time and uses customer feedback to determine the effects of service failure on customer satisfaction. This information is then used to help them improve their processes.[14]

K/P Corporation, a graphic communications company, incorporates a TQM perspective in salesperson performance evaluation. Sales professionals, comprising customer-focused teams, develop process-related goals consistent with their role in the sales team. Annual performance evaluations consist of career planning sessions in which career goals and plans are established. Emphasis is placed on continuously assessing and improving processes.[15]

BI Performance Services incorporates a TQM perspective via a monthly tracking and measurement report for salespeople. The report includes measures of productivity, efficiency, building customer relationships, and customer satisfaction. Salespeople use the report to compare themselves with previous performance, performance of their peers, or performance of the entire salesforce to manage and continuously improve their performance.[16]

Despite the approach taken, several key decisions concerning the appraisal process must be made. The remainder of this module addresses the key decision areas and alternative methods for developing comprehensive evaluation and control procedures.

Key Issues in Evaluating and Controlling Salesperson Performance

A useful way to view different perspectives for evaluating and controlling salesperson performance is presented in Exhibit 11.2. An **outcome-based perspective** focuses on objective measures of results with little monitoring or directing of salesperson behavior by sales managers. By contrast, a **behavior-based perspective** incorporates complex and often subjective assessments of salesperson characteristics and behaviors with considerable monitoring and directing of salesperson behavior by sales managers.[17]

EXHIBIT 11.2   Perspectives on Salesperson Performance Evaluation

Outcome-Based Perspective	Behavior-Based Perspective
• Little monitoring of salespeople • Little managerial direction of salespeople • Straightforward, objective measures of results	• Considerable monitoring of salespeople • High levels of managerial direction of salespeople • Subjective measures of salesperson characteristics, activities, and strategies

The perspectives that a sales organization might take toward salesperson performance evaluation and control lie on a continuum. The two extremes are the outcome-based and behavior-based perspectives.

The outcome-based and behavior-based perspectives illustrated in Exhibit 11.2 represent the extreme positions that a sales organization might take concerning salesperson performance evaluation. Although our earlier review of current practice indicates a tendency toward an outcome-based perspective, most sales organizations operate somewhere between the two extreme positions. However, emphasis on either perspective can have far-reaching impacts on the salesforce and important implications for sales managers. Several of these key implications are presented in Exhibit 11.3. See how placing too much focus on outcomes may lead to undesirable behavior as illustrated in "An Ethical Dilemma."

An Ethical Dilemma

It is performance appraisal time again. Dollar sales volume is an important criterion on which salespeople's performance is evaluated. You just found out that your star sales performer is making statements to customers that exaggerate the seriousness of their problem to obtain a bigger order or other concessions. Your yearly bonus is based on how well your salesforce performs. What do you do? Why?

EXHIBIT 11.3   Outcome-Based versus Behavior-Based Implications

The more behavior-based (versus outcome-based) a salesperson performance evaluation is:

- The more professionally competent, team-oriented, risk averse, planning-oriented, sales support-oriented, and customer-oriented salespeople will be.
- The more intrinsically and recognition-motivated salespeople will be.
- The more committed to the sales organization salespeople will be.
- The more likely salespeople will be to accept authority, participate in decision making, and welcome management performance reviews.
- The less the need for using pay as a control mechanism.
- The more innovative and supportive the culture is likely to be.
- The more inclined salespeople are to sell smarter rather than harder.
- The better salespeople will perform on both selling (e.g., using technical knowledge, making sales presentations) and nonselling (e.g., providing information, controlling expenses ethically) behavioral performance dimensions.
- The better salespeople will perform on outcome (e.g., achieving sales objectives) performance dimensions.
- The better the sales organization will perform on sales organization effectiveness dimensions (e.g., sales volume and growth, profitability, and customer satisfaction).
- The greater salespeople's job satisfaction will be.

On balance, these implications provide strong support for at least some behavior-based evaluations in most selling situations. In the absence of any behavior-based measures and limited monitoring and direction from sales management, salespeople are likely to focus on the short-term outcomes that are being evaluated. The process of obtaining the desired outcomes may be neglected, causing some activities that produce short-term results. (e.g., selling pressure, unethical activities) to be emphasized and activities related to long-term customer relationships (e.g., customer orientation, postsale service) to be minimized.

A reasonable conclusion from this discussion is that sales organizations should use both outcome-based and behavior-based measures when evaluating salesperson performance. Research indicates that some firms use a hybrid approach to controlling the salesforce. The hybrid form was found to place considerable emphasis on the following: supervision; evaluation of attitude, effort, and quantitative results; and complete, accurate paperwork.[18] However, the relative emphasis on outcome-based and behavior-based measures depends on environmental, firm, and salesperson considerations. Establishing the desired emphasis should be the initial decision in developing a salesperson performance evaluation and control system. Once this emphasis has been established, the sales organization can then address the specific criteria to be evaluated, the methods of evaluation, and how the performance information will be used. For an example of how Pitney Bowes uses outcome-based and behavior-based measures, see "Sales Management in the 21st Century: Outcome-Based and Behavior-Based Measures at Pitney Bowes Office Systems."

Criteria for Performance Evaluation

The typical salesperson job is multidimensional. Salespeople normally sell multiple products to diverse customers and perform a variety of selling and nonselling activities. Therefore, any comprehensive assessment of salesperson performance must include multiple criteria.

Although the specific criteria depend on the characteristics of a given selling situation and the performance evaluation perspective, the four performance dimensions illustrated in Figure 11.1 should be considered: behavioral and professional development (behavior-based perspective) and results and profitability (outcome-based perspective). Regardless of the specific evaluative criteria chosen, it is important that salespeople know and understand the criteria to achieve desired performance.

BEHAVIOR The behavioral dimension consists of criteria related to activities performed by individual salespeople. The emphasis is on evaluating exactly what

---

SALES MANAGEMENT IN THE 21ST CENTURY

Outcome-Based and Behavior-Based Measures at Pitney Bowes Office Systems

Charlie Kowaczyk, former branch sales manager Pitney Bowes Office Systems, discusses performance measures:

We use several criteria when evaluating salespeople's performance. Each month salespeople are evaluated on quota achievement. They are provided with a status report on their year-to-date quota so that they will know if they are on target to achieve yearly quota. Salespeople are evaluated weekly on various sales activities such as the number of direct mail pieces distributed, cold calls made, or product demonstrations given. Moreover, each week salespeople are evaluated on the number of prospects generated. Customers also are used to evaluate salespeople. Each quarter, customers fill out an account management report that details their satisfaction with service, salesperson follow-up, and equipment performance.

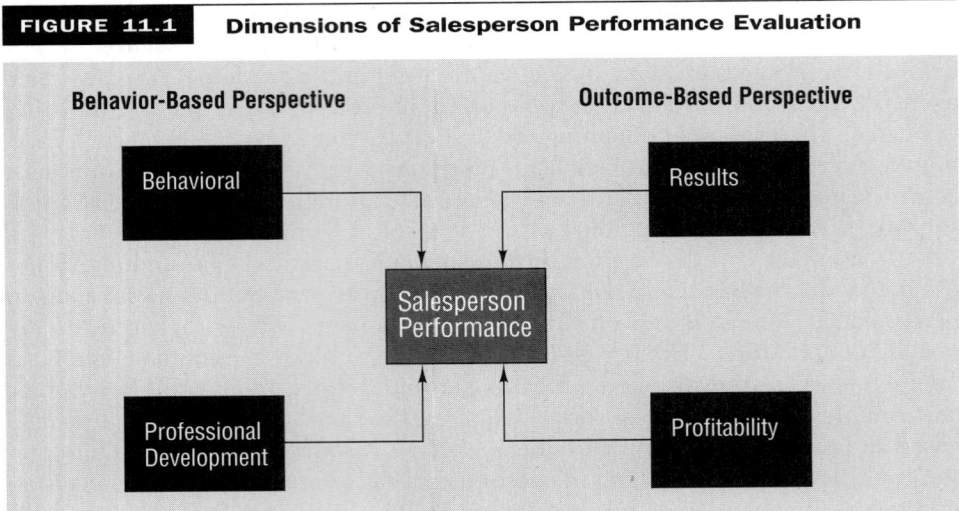

FIGURE 11.1 Dimensions of Salesperson Performance Evaluation

A comprehensive evaluation of salesperson performance should incorporate criteria from these different dimensions. Sales organizations using a behavior-based perspective would focus on behavioral and professional development criteria, whereas those using an outcome-based perspective would emphasize results and profitability criteria.

each salesperson does. These **behavioral criteria** should not only address activities related to short-term sales generation but should also include nonselling activities needed to ensure long-term customer satisfaction and to provide necessary information to the sales organization. Examples of typical behavioral criteria are presented in Exhibit 11.4.

As might be expected, most sales organizations focus on the number of sales calls made as the key behavioral criterion. However, other activities are also important to at least some sales organizations. At IBM, for instance, customer satisfaction plays a role in salespeople's evaluation. Part of their paycheck is based on how customers rate them.[19] When salespeople's rewards are based on customer satisfaction rating, salespeople are likely to demonstrate a higher level of customer service activity.[20]

Salespeople have the most control over what they do, so evaluations of their performance should include some assessment of their behaviors. As discussed in Exhibit 11.3, the use of behavior-based criteria will also facilitate the development of a professional, customer-oriented, committed, and motivated salesforce.

PROFESSIONAL DEVELOPMENT Another dimension of considerable importance in evaluating the performance of individual salespeople relates to professional development. **Professional development criteria** assess improvements in certain characteristics of salespeople that are related to successful performance in the sales job. For example, if product knowledge is critical in a particular selling situation, then evaluations of the product knowledge of individual salespeople over various periods should be conducted. Interestingly, foreign subsidiaries of U.S.–based multinationals appear to rely more heavily than U.S. firms on behavioral criteria for evaluating salesperson performance.[21] Examples of professional development criteria are presented in Exhibit 11.5.

Many sales organizations incorporate multiple professional development criteria into their salesperson performance evaluations. For instance, at AT&T, salespeople are evaluated on their knowledge of the product line being sold as well as competitive products, knowledge of customers' businesses, the development of plans to assist customers, and the development of their professional skills.[22] This is appropriate, because salespeople have control over the development of personal

EXHIBIT 11.4 Behavioral Criteria

Base	Percentage Reporting Using
Calls	
Number of customer calls	48
Number of calls per day (or period)	42
Number of planned calls	24
Number of calls per account	23
Number of calls per number of customers—by product class (call frequency ratio)	18
Average time spent per call	8
Number of unplanned calls	7
Planned to unplanned call ratio	3
Ancillary Activities	
Number of required reports turned in	38
Number of days worked (per period)	33
Selling time versus nonselling time	27
Training meetings conducted	26
Number of customer complaints	25
Number of formal presentations	22
Number of quotes	21
Percentage of goods returned	17
Number of dealer meetings held	17
Number of service calls made	15
Number of formal proposals developed	15
Advertising displays set up	13
Number of demonstrations conducted	12
Dollar amount of overdue accounts collected	10
Number of letters/phone calls to prospects	9

EXHIBIT 11.5 Professional Development Criteria

Base	Percentage Reporting Using
Communication skills	88
Product knowledge	85
Attitude	82
Selling skills	79
Initiative and aggressiveness	76
Appearance and manner	75
Knowledge of competition	71
Team player	67
Enthusiasm	66
Time management	63
Judgment	62
Cooperation	62
Motivation	61
Ethical/moral behavior	59
Planning ability	58
Pricing knowledge	55
Report preparation and submission	54
Creativity	54
Punctuality	49
Resourcefulness	49
Knowledge of company policies	48
Customer goodwill generation	41
Self-improvement efforts	40
Care of company property	39
Degree of respect from trade and competition	38
Use of promotional materials	37
New product ideas	35
Use of marketing/technical backup teams	33
Good citizenship	22

characteristics related to success in their selling situation. The professional development criteria introduce a long-term perspective into the process of salesperson performance evaluation. Salespeople who are developing professionally are increasing their chances of successful performance over the long run. Although the professional development and behavioral criteria might be combined into one category, we prefer to keep them separate to reflect their different perspectives.

RESULTS The results achieved by salespeople are extremely important and should be evaluated. Examples of **results criteria** used in salesperson performance evaluations are listed in Exhibit 11.6.

A potential problem with the use of results criteria in Exhibit 11.6 is that the overall results measures do not reflect the territory situations faced by individual salespeople. The salesperson with the highest level of sales may have the best territory and may not necessarily be the best performer in generating sales. In fact, some research shows that rewards for achieving results have a negative effect on performance and satisfaction because salespeople may view the rewards as arbitrary if the goals are beyond their control.[23] Aside from the impossible task of developing territories that are exactly equal, the only way to address this potential problem is to compare actual results with standards that reflect the unique territory situation faced by each salesperson. These standards are generally called sales quotas.

A **sales quota** represents a reasonable sales objective for a territory, district, region, or zone. Because a sales forecast represents an expected level of firm sales for a defined geographic area, time period, and strategy, there should be a close relationship between the sales forecast and the sales quota. Bottom-up and/or top-

EXHIBIT 11.6　Results Criteria

Base	Percentage Reporting Using
Sales	
Sales volume in dollars	79
Sales volume to previous year's sales	76
Sales volume by (versus) dollar quota	65
Percentage of increase in sales volume	55
Sales volume by product or product line	48
Sales volume by customer	44
Amount of new account sales	42
Sales volume in units	35
Sales volume to (versus) market potential	27
Sales volume by customer type	22
Sales volume to physical unit quota	9
Sales volume per order	7
Sales volume per call	6
Sales volume by outlet type	4
Percentage of sales made by telephone or mail	1
Market Share	
Market share achieved	59
Market share per quota	18
Accounts	
Number of new accounts	69
Number of accounts lost	33
Number of accounts buying the full line	22
Dollar amount of accounts receivable	17
Number of accounts (payment is) overdue	15
Lost account ratio	6

down approaches might be used to develop sales forecasts that are translated into sales quotas.

Another recommended approach is to use statistical methods such as regression.[24] A market response framework to guide this type of approach is presented in Figure 11.2. Depending on the planning and control unit of interest (territory, district, region, or zone), different determinants of market response (e.g., sales, market share) might be important. However, these determinants can be classified as either environmental, organizational, or salesperson factors. Once the determinant and market response factors are identified, their values for each planning and control unit in the previous period must be measured.

Statistical packages can then be used to estimate the parameters of the regression equation. For example, if you are a district sales manager interested in forecasting territory sales, you would identify and measure specific environmental, organizational, and salesperson factors as well as sales for each territory in the previous year. You could then develop a regression model of the following form:

$$\text{Territory sales} = a + (b1)(\text{environmental factor}) + (b2)(\text{organizational factor}) + (b3)(\text{salesperson factor})$$

The a, $b1$, $b2$, and $b3$ values are the model parameters supplied by the regression procedure to define the relationship between the determinant factors and territory sales.

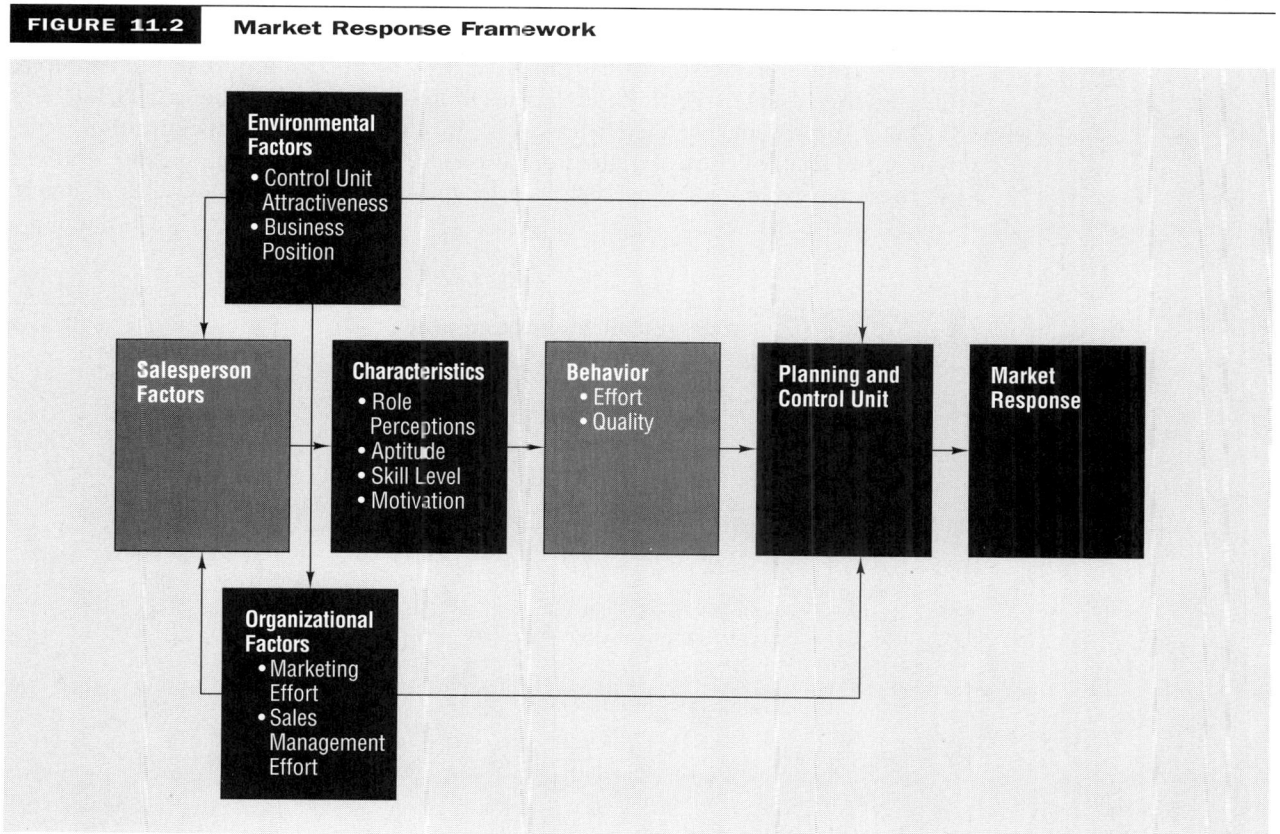

FIGURE 11.2   Market Response Framework

These are the types of factors that affect market response for any planning and control unit, whether it be accounts, territories, districts, regions, or zones. Market response might be profits, market share, or some other response, but sales is usually the market response variable of interest to sales managers.

Although this type of model might be useful, it suffers from two basic weaknesses. First, it incorporates only the independent effects of the determinant variables, yet these variables are highly interrelated. Second, this type of equation is linear, yet the determinant variable relationships are probably nonlinear. These weaknesses can be addressed by performing the linear regression on the logarithms of the actual data, producing a multiplicative power function of the following form:

$$\text{Territory sales} = (a)(\text{environmental factor}^{b1})(\text{organizational factor}^{b2})(\text{salesperson factor}^{b3})$$

This function is nonlinear and incorporates interactions through the multiplication of determinant variables.

A specific example illustrating this type of function is presented in Exhibit 11.7. The environmental factors are *potential* and *concentration,* the salesperson factor is *experience,* and the organizational factor is *span of control.* The data are for three territories and are used in the model to generate sales forecasts for each territory individually. This regression model indicates that the higher the territory potential, account concentration, and level of salesperson experience are, the higher the territory sales will be. The larger the span of control is, the lower the territory sales. The exponents in the model suggest that territory sales are most affected by territory potential and span of control. Thus, the regression model generates a specific sales forecast for each territory, and it also provides information concerning relationships between determinant factors and sales.

The regression forecasting approach develops sales forecasts that explicitly consider the characteristics of a territory or other planning and control unit. Thus, these regression forecasts can be translated directly into sales quotas. For example, the sales forecasts for the three territories in Exhibit 11.7 ($586,000, $238,400, and $173,200) represent expected sales levels given the potential, concentration experience, and span of control evaluations for each territory. Sales management might use these regression sales forecasts as sales quotas for each territory. Alternatively,

EXHIBIT 11.7 Regression Model Example

$\text{Territory sales} = (800.82)(\text{potential}^{.53})(\text{concentration}^{.03})(\text{experience}^{.08})(\text{span of control}^{-.55})$

	Territory 1	Territory 2	Territory 3
Potential (number of persons employed by firms in customer industry located in territory)	114,000	125,000	87,000
Concentration (number of persons employed by the large plants in customer industry located in territory)	94,000	52,000	12,000
Experience (months salesperson has been with company)	30	10	20
Span of control (number of salespeople supervised by sales manager)	5	8	10
Territory sales forecast	$586,000	$238,400	$173,200

EXHIBIT 11.8 Elements Important in Assigning Sales Quotas

Statement	Mean[1,2]	Standard Deviation	Rank
Concentration of businesses within the sales representative's territory is important in determining the amount of quota.	1.82	0.64	1
The geographical size of territory is important in determining the amount of quota.	1.95	0.86	2
Growth of businesses within the sales representative's territory is important in determining the amount of quota.	2.11	0.83	3
Commitment by the sales manager to assisting the sales representative is important in determining the amount of quota.	2.23	1.07	4
Complexity of products sold is important in determining the amount of quota.	2.50	1.12	5
The sales representative's past sales performance is important in determining the amount of quota.	2.54	1.10	6
Extent of product line is important in determining the amount of quota.	2.59	0.88	7
The financial support (e.g., compensation) a firm provides sales representatives is important in assigning quota.	2.76	0.99	8
The relationship of your product line is important in determining the amount of quota.	2.82	1.02	9
The amount of clerical support given to a sales representative is important in determining the amount of quota.	3.13	1.09	10

[1]The rating scale and weights used to rate the importance of each statement were as follows: 1 = strongly agree; 2 = agree; 3 = neutral; 4 = disagree and 5 = strongly disagree.
[2]The responses numbered 186.

sales management might adjust the forecasts up or down based on information about the territories not incorporated in the regression model. Exhibit 11.8 shows results of a survey indicating the relative importance placed on various factors by sales managers when assigning sales quotas.[25] In any case, the territory sales forecasts provide the basis for establishing the territory sales quotas.

The regression approach can be used to develop sales forecasts and establish sales quotas at all sales organization levels.[26] The determinant variables and measures are typically different depending on whether the control unit is a territory, district, region, or zone. Nevertheless, accurate sales forecasts are critical for establishing valid sales quotas at all sales organization levels.

Although forecasts provide the basis for developing quotas, they must be adjusted to determine each individual's quota. Research suggests that salesperson performance can be enhanced by assigning more challenging quotas to experienced salespeople who have demonstrated exceptional competence or to novices who quickly exhibit high potential.[27]

PROFITABILITY A potential problem with focusing on sales results is that the profitability of sales is not assessed. Salespeople can affect profitability in two basic ways. First, salespeople have an impact on gross profits through the specific products they sell and/or through the prices they negotiate for final sale. Thus, two salespeople could generate the same level of sales dollars and achieve the same sales/sales quota evaluation, but one salesperson could produce more gross profits by selling higher margin products and/or maintaining higher prices in sales negotiations.

Second, salespeople affect net profits by the expenses they incur in generating sales. The selling expenses most under the control of salespeople are travel and entertainment expenses. Therefore, two salespeople could generate the same levels of total sales, the same sales/sales quota performance, and even the same levels of gross profits, but one salesperson could contribute more to net profits through lower travel and entertainment costs. Examples of **profitability criteria** are listed in Exhibit 11.9.

Sales organizations are increasingly incorporating profitability criteria into their salesperson performance evaluations. At Tosco, a marketer of gasoline, oil, and fuel refining products, salespeople are rated on the profitability of accounts, among other things.[28] The most frequently used profitability criterion is net profit dollars. Selling expenditures relative to budget is also heavily emphasized. The need to address profitability criteria is especially important during a slow-growth, competitive environment in which sales growth is so difficult and productivity and profitability so important.

COMMENT ON CRITERIA Conducting a comprehensive evaluation of salesperson performance typically requires consideration of behavioral professional development, results, and profitability criteria. Each set of criteria tells a different story as to how well salespeople have performed and provides different diagnostic information for control purposes. Steve Randazzo of Schein Pharmaceutical explains how Schein uses various performance criteria to drive relationship development in "Sales Management in the 21st Century: Performance Criteria at Schein Pharmaceutical." Different methods for evaluating salespeople against these criteria are now discussed.

EXHIBIT 11.9   Profitability Criteria

Base	Percentage Reporting Using
Sales	
Net profit dollars	69
Gross margin per sales (a percentage of sales)	34
Return on investment	33
Net profit as a percent(age) of sales	32
Margin by product category	28
Gross margin (in dollars)	25
Margin by customer type	18
Net profit per sale	14
Return on sales cost	14
Net profit contribution	—
Order(s)	
Number of orders secured	47
Average size of order secured	22
Order per call ratio (aka batting average)	14
Number of orders canceled	11
Net orders per repeat order	10
Number of canceled orders per orders booked	4
Selling Expense	
Selling expense versus budget	55
Total expenses	53
Selling expense to sales	49
Average cost per call	12
Selling expense to quota	12
Expenses by product category	7
Expenses by customer type	3

SALES MANAGEMENT IN THE 21ST CENTURY

Performance Criteria at Schein Pharmaceutical

Steve Randazzo, regional director for Schein Pharmaceutical, Inc., discusses how it uses various performance criteria to drive relationship development:

Our salespeople are evaluated on several criteria: industry/product knowledge, promotion of specified and new products, relationship development skills, territory management/work habits, and sales and profitability. Although achieving sales and profitability goals are important, it is equally as important for our salespeople to be able to develop customer relationships, be creative, and think outside the box. Good sales numbers might be achieved because we launched a new product or offered a very competitive price. However, we want to establish relationships with customers that will enable us to withstand turbulent times in the market. For instance, salespeople are evaluated on their ability to get customers to implement promotional programs developed by our marketing department that are designed to help customers move our products. Customers who use these programs are more likely to see us as a partner. Therefore, we evaluate salespeople's ability to build relationships just as seriously as we do their ability to achieve sales and profits, among other goals.

Performance Evaluation Methods

Sales managers can use a number of different methods for measuring the behaviors, professional development, results, and profitability of salespeople. Ideally, the method used should have the following characteristics.[29]

- *Job relatedness:* The performance evaluation method should be designed to meet the needs of each specific sales organization.
- *Reliability:* The measures should be stable over time and exhibit internal consistency.
- *Validity:* The measures should provide accurate assessments of the criteria they are intended to measure.
- *Standardization:* The measurement instruments and evaluation process should be similar throughout the sales organization.
- *Practicality:* Sales managers and salespeople should understand the entire performance appraisal process and should be able to implement it in a reasonable amount of time.
- *Comparability:* The results of the performance evaluation process should make it possible to compare the performance of individual salespeople directly.
- *Discriminability:* The evaluative methods must be capable of detecting differences in the performance of individual salespeople.
- *Usefulness:* The information provided by the performance evaluation must be valuable to sales managers in making various decisions.

Designing methods of salesperson performance evaluation that possess all these characteristics is a difficult task. As indicated in Exhibit 11.10 each evaluative method has certain strengths and weaknesses. No one method provides a perfect evaluation. Therefore, it is important to understand the strengths and weaknesses of each method so that several can be combined to produce the best evaluative procedure for a given sales organization.

EXHIBIT 11.10 Comparison of Performance Evaluation Methods

Performance Evaluation Method	Evaluation Criteria							
	Job Relatedness	Reliability	Validity	Standardization	Practicality	Comparability	Discriminability	Usefulness
Graphic rating/checklist	Very good	Good	Good	Very good	Very good	Very good	Poor	Good
Ranking	Poor	Poor	Poor	Very good	Poor	Good	Excellent	Poor
Objective-setting/MBO	Very good	Good	Good	Poor	Good	Poor	Good	Poor
Behaviorally Anchored Rating Scale (BARS)	Very good	Good	Good	Poor	Good	Poor	Poor	Good

GRAPHIC RATING/CHECKLIST METHODS Graphic rating/checklist methods consist of approaches in which salespeople are evaluated by using some type of performance evaluation form. The performance evaluation form contains the criteria to be used in the evaluation as well as some means to provide an assessment of how well each salesperson performed on each criterion. An example of part of such a form is presented in Exhibit 11.11.

This method is popular in many sales organizations. It is especially useful in evaluating salesperson behavioral and professional development criteria. As part of its assessment process, Eastman Chemical Company asks its customers to evaluate their satisfaction with the company by using a rating scale. As evident from Exhibit 11.12, Eastman's salespeople are responsible for several behavior-based performance factors. Rating methods have been developed to evaluate all the important salesperson performance dimensions.[30] There are even employee-appraisal software programs, such as Performance Now!, available to assist in the review process. The program asks users to rate employees by goals, development plans, and competencies.[31]

As evident from Exhibit 11.10, graphic rating/checklist methods possess many desirable characteristics, especially in terms of job relatedness, standardization, practicality, and comparability. The reliability and validity of these methods, however, must be continually assessed and the specific rating scales improved over time.

EXHIBIT 11.11 Graphic Rating/Checklist Example

1. Asks customers for their ideas for promoting business
   Almost Never   1   2   3   4   5   Almost Always   NA
2. Offers customers help in solving their problems
   Almost Never   1   2   3   4   5   Almost Always   NA
3. Is constantly smiling when interacting with customers
   Almost Never   1   2   3   4   5   Almost Always   NA
4. Admits when he/she doesn't know the answer, but promises to find out
   Almost Never   1   2   3   4   5   Almost Always   NA
5. Generates new ways of tackling new or ongoing problems
   Almost Never   1   2   3   4   5   Almost Always   NA
6. Returns customers' calls the same day
   Almost Never   1   2   3   4   5   Almost Always   NA
7. Retains his or her composure in front of custsomers
   Almost Never   1   2   3   4   5   Almost Always   NA
8. Delivers what he or she promises on time
   Almost Never   1   2   3   4   5   Almost Always   NA

EXHIBIT 11.12 Eastman Chemical Company Customer Satisfaction Survey

Importance: Rate the importance of each statement (your buying criteria) by asking, "Would I place additional business with a supplier who improved performance in this cathegory from 'average' to 'outstanding'?"

Performance: Rate Eastman performance and your best "other supplier" on each criteria.

Importance:	Performance		
5 - Definitely Would 4 - Probably Would 3 - Uncertain 2 - Probably Would Not 1 - Definitely Would Not NA - Not Applicable	5 - Outstanding 2 - Fair 4 - Good 1 - Poor 3 - Average NA - Not Applicable		
		EASTMAN	BEST OTHER SUPPLIER

Product

1. Product Performance: Supplier provides a product that consistently meets your requirements and performance expectations.
2. Product Mix: Supplier offers a range of products that meets your needs.
3. Packaging: Supplier has the package type, size, and label to meet your needs.
4. New Products: Supplier meets your needs through timely introduction of new products.
5. Product Availability: Supplier meets volume commitments and is also fair and consistent during times of restricted supply.
6. Product Stewardship: Supplier provides information about the transportation, storage, handling, use, recycling, disposal, and regulation of products and product packaging.

Service

7. Order Entry: Supplier has a user-friendly system to place orders that is flexible and responsive to routine order changes as well as urgent or special requests.
8. Delivery: Supplier consistently delivers the right product on time and in satisfactory condition.
9. Technical Service: Supplier provides timely technical support through training, information, problem solving, and assistance in current and new end-use applications.
10. Sharing Information: Supplier is a resource for product, market, industry, and company information that helps you better understand business issues.
11. New Ideas: Supplier offers new ideas that add value to your business.

Pricing/Business Practices

12. Pricing Practices: Supplier is consistent with the marketplace in establishing pricing practices.
13. Paperwork: Supplier provides clear and accurate paperwork and business documents that meet your needs.
14. Commitment to Total Quality Management: Supplier exhibits strong commitment to total quality management in all aspects of their business.
15. Responsiveness: Supplier listens and responds to your business needs in a timely manner.

Relationship

16. Integrity: Supplier is credible, honest, and trustworthy.
17. Dependability: Supplier follows through on agreements.
18. Supplier Contact: Supplier is easy to contact and provides the right amount of interface with the appropriate personnel.
19. Problem Solving: Supplier provides empowered employees to solve your problems.

Supplier Commitment

20. Industry Commitment: Supplier exhibits a strong commitment to your industry.
21. Regional Commitment: Supplier has the appropriate resources in place in your region to provide products and services needed.
22. Customer Commitment: Supplier is strongly committed to helping your business be successful.

The major disadvantage of graphic rating/checklist methods is in providing evaluations that discriminate sufficiently among the performances of individual salespeople or among the performances on different criteria for the same salesperson. For example, some sales managers may be very lenient in their evaluations; they may try to play it safe and give all salespeople ratings around the average. In addition, when evaluating an individual salesperson, some sales managers are subject to a *halo effect,* meaning that their evaluations on one criterion affect their ratings on other criteria.

The advantages of graphic rating/checklist methods clearly outweigh the disadvantages. However, care must be taken to minimize potential sales management biases when the evaluation forms are completed, and continuous attention to reliability and validity issues is necessary.

RANKING METHODS   Otherwise similar to graphic rating/checklist methods, **ranking methods** rank all salespeople according to relative performance on each performance criterion rather than evaluating them against a set of performance criteria. Many different approaches might be used to obtain the rankings. An example of a ranking approach in which salespeople are compared in pairs concerning relative communication skills is presented in Exhibit 11.13.

Ranking methods provide a standardized approach to evaluation and thus force discrimination as to the performance of individual salespeople on each criterion. The process of ranking forces this discrimination in performance. Despite these advantages, ranking methods have many shortcomings, as indicated in Exhibit 11.10. Of major concern are the constraints on their practicality and usefulness. Ranking all salespeople against each performance criterion can be a complex and cognitively difficult task. The ranking task can be simplified by using paired-comparison approaches like the one presented in Exhibit 11.13. However, the computations required to translate the paired comparisons into overall rankings can be extremely cumbersome.

Even if the evaluative and computative procedures can be simplified, the rankings that are obtained are of limited usefulness. Rank data reveal only relative ordering and omit any assessment of the differences between ranks. For example, the actual differences in the communication skills of salespeople ranked first, second, and third may be small or large, but there is no way to tell the degree of these differences from the ranked data. In addition, information obtained from graphic rating/checklist methods can always be transformed into rankings, but rankings cannot be translated into graphic rating/checklist form. Therefore, using ranking methods for salesperson performance evaluations is recommended only as an adjunct to other methods.

OBJECTIVE-SETTING METHODS   The most common and comprehensive goal-setting method is **management by objectives (MBO).** Applied to a salesforce, the typical MBO approach is as follows:[32]

EXHIBIT 11.13   Ranking Method Example

Performance Criterion: Communication Skills

	Much Better	Slightly Better	Equal	Slightly Better	Much Better	
Jane Haynes	X	___	___	___	___	John Evans
Ron Castaneda	___	X	___	___	___	Jane Haynes
Bill Haroldson	___	___	X	___	___	Jane Haynes

1. mutual setting of well-defined and measurable goals within a specified time period
2. managing activities within the specified time period toward the accomplishment of the stated objectives
3. appraisal of performance against objectives

As with all the performance evaluation methods, MBO and other goal-setting methods have certain strengths and weaknesses (see Exhibit 11.10). Although complete reliance on this or any other goal-setting method is inadvisable, the incorporation of some goal-setting procedures is normally desirable. This is especially true for performance criteria related to quantitative behavioral, professional development, results, and profitability criteria. Absolute measures of these dimensions are often not very meaningful because of extreme differences in the territory situations of individual salespeople. The setting of objectives or quotas provides a means for controlling for territory differences through the establishment of performance benchmarks that incorporate these territory differences.

Quotas can be established for other important results criteria and for specific behavioral, professional development, and profitability criteria. Each type of quota represents a specific objective for a salesperson to achieve during a given period. Actual performance can be compared with the quota objective and a performance index calculated for each criterion being evaluated. The individual performance indices can then be weighted to reflect their relative importance and combined to produce an overall performance index. An example of this procedure is shown in Exhibit 11.14.

This example illustrates an evaluation of Kendra, David, and Laura on sales, gross profit, and demonstration quotas. The unequal weights reflect that the firm is placing the most importance on gross profits, followed by demonstrations and then sales. Laura has performed the best overall, but she did not reach her sales quota for this period. David has performed reasonably well on all criteria. Kendra's situation is interesting in that she performed the best on the sales quota but poorly overall due to low performance indices for gross profits and demonstrations. Perhaps she is concentrating too much on short-term sales generation and not concerning herself with the profitability of sales or the number of product demonstrations. In any case, the use of quotas

EXHIBIT 11.14 Quota Evaluation Example

Salesperson	Quota	Weight	Actual Performance	Index	Weighted Performance
Laura					
Sales	600,000	3	552,000	92	276
Gross profits	150,000	6	180,000	120	720
Demonstrations	200	4	250	125	500
Overall performance					115
David					
Sales	700,000	3	710,000	101	303
Gross profits	170,000	6	174,000	102	612
Demonstrations	200	4	200	100	400
Overall performance					101
Kendra					
Sales	550,000	3	650,000	118	354
Gross profits	140,000	6	100,000	71	426
Demonstrations	180	4	150	83	332
Overall performance					86

provides an extremely useful method for evaluating salesperson performance and highlighting specific areas in which performance is especially good or especially poor.

BEHAVIORALLY ANCHORED RATING SCALES The uniqueness of **behaviorally anchored rating scales (BARS)** is due to its focus on trying to link salesperson behaviors with specific results. These behavior–results linkages become the basis for salesperson performance evaluation in this method.

The development of a BARS approach is an iterative process that actively incorporates members of the salesforce.[33] Salespeople are used to identify important performance results and the critical behaviors necessary to achieve those results. The critical behaviors are assigned numbers on a rating scale for each performance result. An example of one such BARS rating scale is presented in Figure 11.3.

The performance result in this example is achieving cooperative relations with sales team members. Seven behaviors have been assigned numbers on a 10-point rating scale to reflect the linkages between engaging in the behavior and achieving the result. This scale can then be used to evaluate individual salespeople. For instance, the example rating of 5 in the figure suggests that the salesperson occa-

FIGURE 11.3 BARS Scale

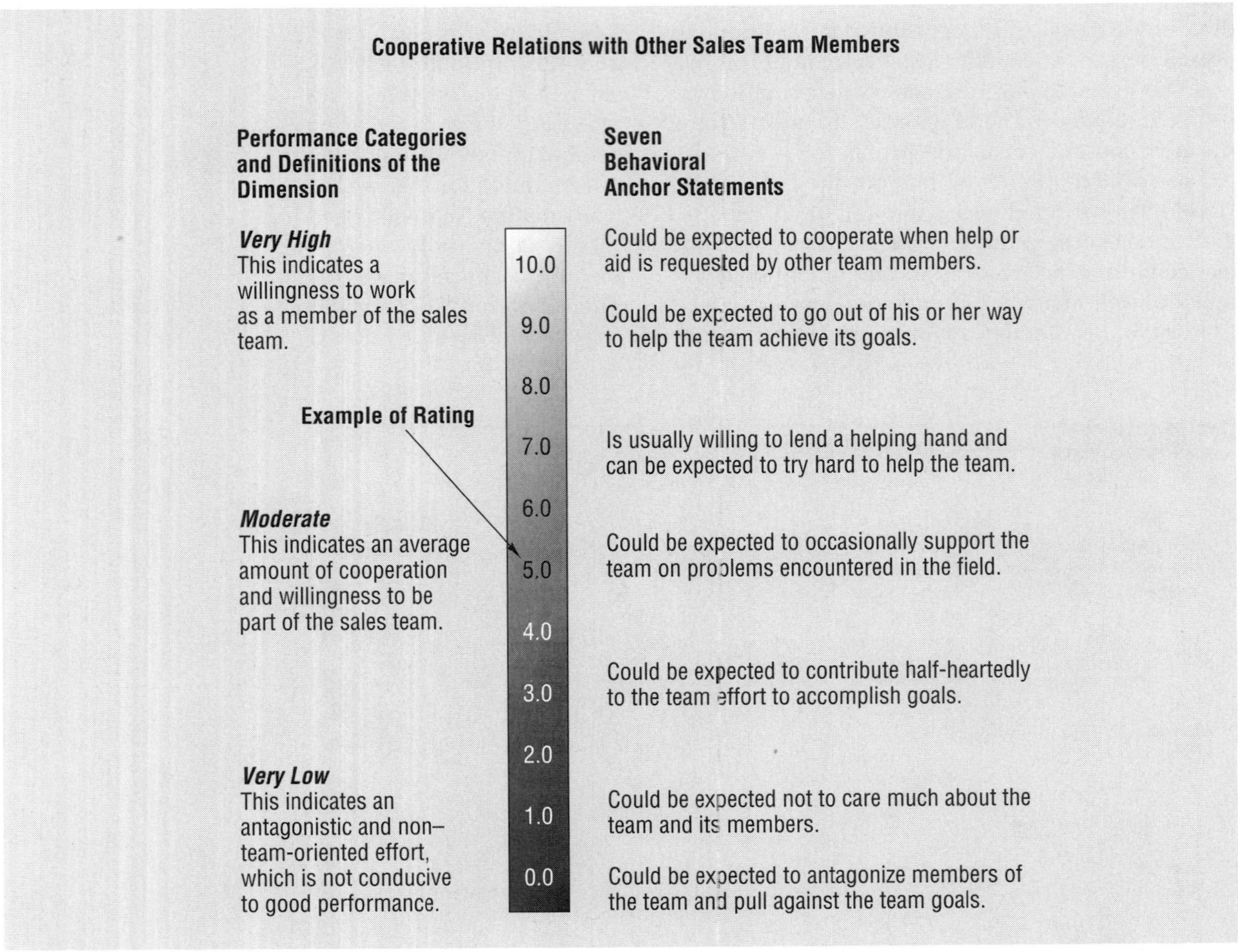

Cooperative Relations with Other Sales Team Members

Performance Categories and Definitions of the Dimension	Rating	Seven Behavioral Anchor Statements
Very High This indicates a willingness to work as a member of the sales team.	10.0	Could be expected to cooperate when help or aid is requested by other team members.
	9.0	Could be expected to go out of his or her way to help the team achieve its goals.
	8.0	
Example of Rating →	7.0	Is usually willing to lend a helping hand and can be expected to try hard to help the team.
	6.0	
Moderate This indicates an average amount of cooperation and willingness to be part of the sales team.	5.0	Could be expected to occasionally support the team on problems encountered in the field.
	4.0	
	3.0	Could be expected to contribute half-heartedly to the team effort to accomplish goals.
	2.0	
Very Low This indicates an antagonistic and non–team-oriented effort, which is not conducive to good performance.	1.0	Could be expected not to care much about the team and its members.
	0.0	Could be expected to antagonize members of the team and pull against the team goals.

This scale evaluates a salesperson's cooperation with other sales team members. The example rating of 5 suggests a moderate level of cooperation in which the salesperson gives only occasional support to the sales team.

sionally supports the sales team on problems encountered in the field and thus achieves only a moderate amount of cooperation with sales team members.

As indicated in Exhibit 11.10, the BARS approach rates high on job relatedness. This is because of the rigorous process used to determine important performance results and critical salesperson behaviors. The results and behaviors identified in this manner are specific to a given selling situation and directly related to the job of the salespeople being evaluated. Research indicates that positive feedback about sales behaviors has a greater impact on salesperson behavior than positive output feedback, perhaps because it gives salespeople direction for improving selling. However, although both have a positive effect on performance, the effect is greater for positive output feedback.[34] The really unique aspect of BARS is the focus on linkages between behaviors and results. No other approach incorporates this perspective.

In sum, the basic methods for evaluating salesperson performance include graphic rating/checklist methods, ranking methods, objective-setting methods, and BARS methods. Each approach has specific strengths and weaknesses that should be considered. Combining different methods into the salesperson performance evaluation process is one way to capitalize on the strengths and minimize the weaknesses inherent in each approach.

Performance Evaluation Bias

Sales managers must be careful to avoid bias when assessing salespeople. For instance, sales managers tend to give more favorable performance ratings to those with whom they have closer personal relationships and less favorable performance ratings to those with whom they maintain formal role-defined relationships.[35] Similarly, sales managers are more likely to discount internal responsibility while bolstering external explanations when appraising salespeople with whom they work well and are socially compatible. In addition, these salespeople are less likely to receive coercive feedback.[36] Sales managers also tend to rate individuals in more difficult territories higher in ability and performance than those in less difficult territories.[37] Sales managers must likewise be careful to avoid **outcome bias.** Outcome bias occurs when the outcome of a decision rather than the appropriateness of the decision influences an evaluator's ratings. When sales managers rate the quality of a salesperson's decision, outcome information (e.g., salesperson did or did not make the sale) often influences their ratings across all criteria when the decision is perceived to have been inappropriate. Using the BARS scale to assess behavioral and professional development criteria helps reduce outcome bias.[38]

Performance evaluation bias not only is harmful to the individual being rated but could result in legal action. Personnel actions that discriminate unfairly are unlawful.[39] A performance appraisal system is more likely to withstand a legal challenge if the guidelines in Exhibit 11.15 are adhered to in developing and implementing the system. "An Ethical Dilemma" illustrates potential difficulties a sales manager may face when evaluating salesperson performance.

An Ethical Dilemma

As district manager for the ABC company, you are responsible for evaluating the performance of all eight of your salespeople. Your performance appraisals play a large role in your salespeoples' bonus and promotion opportunities. Your boss has come to you and "suggested" that you look favorably on one of your salespeople, Ann Anderson, during her upcoming performance appraisal. You understand that a sales management position is opening up in another division next month and suspect that Ann may be next in line, particularly if her latest appraisal looks good. Although Ann is a solid performer, she has not exactly been outstanding. Your star sales performer would actually be a good candidate for the position. However, you would hate to lose him. What would you do? Explain.

EXHIBIT 11.15   Guidelines for Withstanding Discriminatory Appraisal Lawsuits

- Conduct reviews at least once a year, preferably more often.
- Base the appraisal system on a thorough job analysis that identifies the important duties or elements of job performance.
- Base the appraisal system on behaviors or results, not vague or ambiguous salesperson traits or characteristics.
- Observe salespeople performing their work.
- Train performance raters how to use the system, including proper use of the rating forms.
- Use the same rating form, that measures specific criteria, for all salespeople.
- Fill out the rating form *honestly*. Sales managers are asking for trouble if they allow salespeople to think their performances are satisfactory if they are not.
- Address both the salesperson's strengths and weaknesses.
- Carefully document appraisals and their rationale. Both the sales manager and salesperson should sign and date the evaluation after the meeting.
- Develop with the salesperson a plan of action and specific goals for the coming months.
- Bring in a third party for sensitive evaluation meetings.
- Never make reference to a legally protected class of which the salesperson is a member (e.g., racial or religious origin, gender, age).
- Have higher-level managers or human resource managers review appraisals.
- Develop a formal appeal mechanism or system that provides an avenue of appeal to salespeople who are dissatisfied with their evaluations.
- Provide performance counseling, guidance, and/or training to help poor performers improve their performance.

Evaluating Team Performance

Sales organizations employing sales teams must also consider how to evaluate them. When designing the appraisal process for teams, sales managers must still consider the criteria on which members will be evaluated and the methods used to evaluate performance. In addition, it is important that sales managers establish a link between team performance and positive outcomes to promote individual and team effort. The process is fostered by allowing team members to participate in developing team goals and objectives.[40] Furthermore, members are more willing to participate when individual goals are linked to team goals.[41]

Generally, the team as a whole should be evaluated, in addition to assessing individual member performance. Team performance can be measured by team members as well as by the sales manager.[42] Exhibit 11.16 provides an example of a multidimensional approach team members can use to evaluate teammates' critical skills and behaviors. The measurement allows sales managers to develop a composite performance appraisal, merging each team member's viewpoint. The process helps strengthen teams, enhance morale, and contribute to a healthy working climate.[43]

Poor team performance is often not the fault of individual team members but of management. A study of 179 companies found top management commitment and support, appropriate use of teams, provision of training, start-up support, cross-team communication, and accountability for team performance to most influence a team's success.[44]

Using Performance Information

Using different methods to evaluate the behavior, professional development, results, and profitability of salespeople provides extremely important performance information. The critical sales management task is to use this information to improve the performance of individual salespeople, sales teams, and the overall operations of the sales organization. Initially, it should be used to determine the absolute and relative performance of each salesperson. These determinations then provide the basis for reward disbursements, special recognition, promotions, and so forth.

EXHIBIT 11.16 Teamwork Effectiveness/Attitude Measurement (TEAM)

TEAMwork
ALWAYS / USUALLY / OFTEN / SOMETIMES / RARELY / NEVER

1. Is competitive/wants team to "win."
2. Takes reasonable risks.
3. Has confidence in team members' abilities.
4. Places team success before individual recognition.
5. Contributes "extra effort" to team success efforts.
6. Implements or supports all team decisions.
7. Shares "credit" with team members.
8. Works well with team.
9. Has personal "chemistry" with other team members.
10. Is resilient; bounces back and regains momentum after setback.
Totals

MAJOR TEAMWORK STRENGTH:

POSITIVE SUGGESTION FOR IMPROVING TEAMWORK:

TEAM Leadership
ALWAYS / USUALLY / OFTEN / SOMETIMES / RARELY / NEVER

1. Is assertive, persuasive.
2. Has trust and respect of team members.
3. Sets good example, role model.
4. Is consistent in attitude, actions, behavior.
5. Provides recognition/encouragement to others.
6. Volunteers, takes initiative on assignments.
7. Is willing to assume extra responsibility.
8. Makes effective decisions/uses good judgment.
9. Has high, positive expectations of self and team members.
10. Is firm but fair.
Totals

MAJOR LEADERSHIP STRENGTH:

POSITIVE SUGGESTION FOR IMPROVING LEADERSHIP ROLE:

TEAM Productivity
ALWAYS / USUALLY / OFTEN / SOMETIMES / RARELY / NEVER

1. Uses time effectively.
2. Produces quality work.
3. Provides creative ideas and proposals.
4. Is industrious, works at good pace.
5. Meets targets and deadlines.
6. Focuses on high-priority projects.
7. Has discipline and perserverance.
8. Plans and organizes effectively.
9. Produces accurate work.
10. Stays within budget (resources and/or parameters).
Totals

MAJOR PRODUCTIVITY STRENGTH:

POSITIVE SUGGESTION FOR IMPROVING PRODUCTIVITY:

TEAM Relations
ALWAYS / USUALLY / OFTEN / SOMETIMES / RARELY / NEVER

1. Is sensitive to needs of others.
2. Is supportive, concerned.
3. Keeps commitments.
4. Has positive attitude.
5. Is pleasant, courteous, tactful.
6. Maintains control, has high threshold of frustration.
7. Levels with others.
8. Cooperates with team members.
9. Is flexible in approach and relationships.
10. Has patience, accepts team members' shortcomings.
Totals

MAJOR RELATIONS STRENGTH:

POSITIVE SUGGESTION FOR IMPROVING RELATIONS WITH TEAM

TEAM Communication
ALWAYS / USUALLY / OFTEN / SOMETIMES / RARELY / NEVER

1. Communicates clearly and specifically.
2. Allows sufficient time for communication.
3. Listens effectively.
4. Keeps others informed, provides feedback.
5. Is concise, to the point.
6. Organizes written and verbal communication.
7. Initiates discussion on important matters.
8. Is open-minded, receptive to others' ideas.
9. Generates or confirms important communication in writing.
10. Responds promptly to requests for information.
Totals

MAJOR COMMUNICATION STRENGTH:

POSITIVE SUGGESTION FOR IMPROVING COMMUNICATION SKILLS:

The second major use of this performance information is to identify potential problems or areas in which salespeople need to improve for better performance in the future. If salespeople are evaluated against multiple criteria, as suggested in this module, useful diagnostic information will be available. The difficulty exists in isolating the specific causes of low performance areas. A framework for performing this analysis is given in Figure 11.4.

FIGURE 11.4 Framework for Using Performance Information

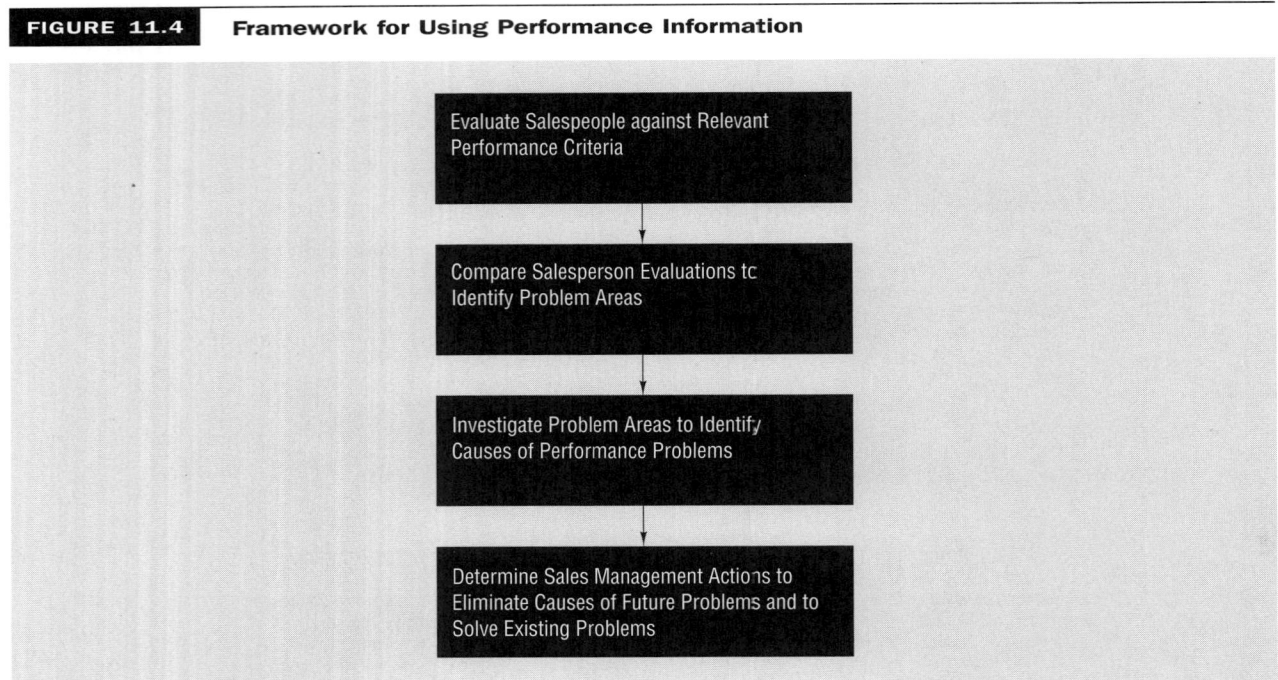

Sales managers need to be able to use the information provided by salesperson performance evaluations in a diagnostic manner. The basic diagnostic approach is to determine problem areas, identify the causes of these problems, and take appropriate action to eliminate the causes and to solve problems that are already present, thus improving future salesperson performance.

The first step in this analysis is to review the performance of each salesperson against each relevant criterion and then to summarize the results across all salespeople being supervised. The purpose of this step is to determine whether there are common areas of low performance. For example, the situation is different when most salespeople are not meeting their sales quotas than when only one or two salespeople are not meeting their sales quotas.

Once the poor performance areas have been identified, the sales manager must work backward to try to identify the cause of the poor performance. Merely determining that most salespeople did not meet their sales quotas is not sufficient to improve future performance; the sales manager must try to uncover the reason for this poor performance. The basic approach is to try to answer the question, "What factors affect the achievement of this performance dimension?" For instance, in regard to achieving sales quotas, the key question is, "What factors determine whether salespeople achieve their sales quotas?" All the factors identified should be reviewed to isolate the cause of any poor performance. Several factors that might cause poor performance in different areas are presented in Exhibit 11.17.

After identifying the potential causes of poor performance, the sales manager must determine the appropriate action to reduce or eliminate the cause of the problem so that performance will be improved in the future. Examples of potential management actions for specific problems are also presented in Exhibit 11.17.

Consider again the poor performance on sales quota achievement. Assume that intense review of this problem reveals that salespeople not meeting sales quotas also do not make many product demonstrations to prospects. This analysis suggests that if salespeople were to make more product demonstrations, they would be

EXHIBIT 11.17 Sample Problems, Causes, and Management Actions

Performance Problems	Potential Causes	Sales Management Actions
Not meeting sales or other results quotas	Sales or other results quotas incorrect; poor account coverage; too few sales calls	Revise sales or other results quotas; revise effort allocation; redesign territories; develop motivational programs; provide closer supervision; increase salesforce size
Not meeting behavioral quotas	Behavioral quotas incorrect; too little effort; poor quality of effort	Revise behavioral quotas; develop motivational programs; increase salesforce size; conduct training programs; provide closer supervision
Not meeting profitability quotas	Profitability quotas incorrect; low gross margins; high selling expenses	Revise profitability quotas; change compensation; devise incentive programs; provide closer supervision; conduct training programs
Not meeting professional development quotas	Professional development quotas incorrect; inadequate training	Revise professional development quotas; conduct training programs; provide closer supervision; develop motivational programs; change hiring practices

able to generate more sales and thus achieve their sales quotas. The sales management task is to determine what management actions will lead to more product demonstrations by salespeople. Possible actions include more training on product demonstrations, direct communication with individual salespeople about the need for more product demonstrations, or some combination of these or other management actions.

This discussion highlights the thought processes that sales managers need to use to identify performance problems, isolate the causes of these problems, and determine the appropriate management actions necessary to solve the problems and improve future salesperson performance. Using this approach successfully requires that sales managers have a detailed understanding of the personal selling and sales management processes and relationships. Such an understanding is essential for them to be able to determine the causes of performance problems and identify the appropriate management actions to solve these problems.

Our discussion and examples have emphasized problems affecting many salespeople. The same basic approach can be used for performance problems that are unique to one individual salesperson. In fact, many sales organizations use performance reviews as a means for a sales manager to meet with each salesperson, analyze the salesperson's performance on each criterion, and suggest ways to improve future performance. These performance reviews provide one means for communicating the *performance feedback* that is so important to salespeople. Performance feedback is also an important determinant of salesperson job satisfaction, which is discussed next.

Salesperson Job Satisfaction

In addition to evaluating salesperson performance, sales managers should be concerned with the **job satisfaction** of salespeople. Research results have consistently found relationships between salesperson job satisfaction and turnover, absenteeism, motivation, and organizational commitment.[45] Salespeople who are satisfied with their job tend to stay with the firm and work harder than those who are not satisfied.

Other research has investigated relationships between salesperson performance and salesperson satisfaction. This research has produced conflicting findings concerning the direction of the relationship between performance and satisfaction.[46] In other words, it has not been established whether achieving high performance causes salesperson satisfaction or whether salesperson satisfaction determines salesperson performance. It is clear, however, that sales managers should be concerned with both the performance and satisfaction of their salespeople. Of importance to sales managers is how salesperson satisfaction might be measured and then how this satisfaction information might be used.

Measuring Salesperson Job Satisfaction

Because job satisfaction is based on individual perceptions, measures of salesperson satisfaction must be based on data provided by individual salespeople. In addition, there are many different aspects of a salesperson's job, and these different areas should be incorporated into the satisfaction evaluation. Fortunately, a scale for evaluating the job satisfaction of salespeople, termed INDSALES, has been developed, validated, and revised. Portions of the revised scale are presented in Exhibit 11.18.[47]

On this scale, salespeople indicate their level of agreement with statements concerning their particular sales job. These statements are designed to measure their satisfaction in seven general areas: satisfaction with the job, fellow workers, supervision, company policy and support, pay, promotion and advancement, and customers. Answers to the specific questions for each area are summed to produce a separate satisfaction score for each job dimension. These individual job dimension scores can then be summed to form an overall salesperson satisfaction score. Sales managers can then view the dimensional or overall satisfaction scores for each salesperson or for specified groups of salespeople.

Using Job Satisfaction Information

INDSALES provides extremely useful evaluative and diagnostic information. Because sales managers can evaluate the degree of salesperson satisfaction with specific aspects of the sales job, areas in which satisfaction is low can be investigated further by looking at the individual questions for that dimension. For example, if salespeople tended to express dissatisfaction with the supervision they were receiving, management could investigate the answers to the specific questions designed to

EXHIBIT 11.18 Example for Revised INDSALES Scale

Component	Total Number of Items	Sample Items
The job	4	My work gives me a sense of accomplishment. My job is exciting.
Fellow workers	4	My fellow workers are selfish. My fellow workers are pleasant.
Supervision	4	My sales manager really tries to get our ideas about things. My sales manager keeps his or her promises.
Company policy and support	4	Top management really knows its job. Management is progressive.
Pay	4	My pay is low in comparison with what others get for similar work in other companies. I'm paid fairly compared with other employees in this company.
Promotion and advancement	4	My opportunities for advancement are limited. I have a good chance for promotion.
Customers	4	My customers are loyal. My customers are trustworthy.

evaluate the supervision dimension (see Exhibit 11.18). The sales manager in this example might find that most salespeople responded negatively to the statement, "My sales manager really tries to get our ideas about things." The sales manager could then try to increase salesperson satisfaction by using a more participative management style and trying to incorporate salesperson input into the decision-making process.

One useful approach is to perform separate analyses of salesperson satisfaction for high-performing and low-performing salespeople. Research results suggest that there may be important differences in job satisfaction between high performers and low performers. Not incorporating these differences could lead sales managers to make changes that would tend to reduce the turnover of low performers but not of high performers.[48]

Research has also found an important relationship between salesperson satisfaction and performance feedback. Interestingly, negative output feedback does not lower satisfaction with supervisors, whereas negative behavioral feedback appears to improve satisfaction marginally.[49] This suggests salespeople are open to feedback that helps improve their sales performance. Further support for this finding comes from studies showing that sales managers' leadership and role modeling behaviors positively affect salespeople's job satisfaction.[50] One of the studies, involving 25,000 employees (2,000 of whom were sales professionals), found that 69 percent of employee job satisfaction stems from the leadership skills of managers. The study suggests a sales manager can become a great leader by doing many of the activities involved in performance appraisal: providing feedback on what salespeople need to improve; offering recognition and rewards in a manner that acknowledges individuals and teams; and helping and supporting salespeople in developing their talents and careers.[51] Carefully evaluating salesperson performance and satisfaction, identifying problem areas, and solving these problems is really what sales management is all about.

Summary

1. **Discuss the different purposes of salesperson performance evaluations.** Performance evaluations can serve many different purposes and should be designed with specific purposes in mind. They may serve to determine appropriate compensation and other reward disbursements, to identify salespeople who should be promoted or fired, to determine training and counseling needs, to provide information for human resource planning to identify criteria for future recruitment and selection of salespeople, to advise salespeople of work expectations, to motivate salespeople, to help salespeople set career goals, and to ultimately improve salesperson performance.

2. **Differentiate between an outcome-based and a behavior-based perspective for evaluating and controlling salesperson performance.** An outcome-based perspective focuses on objective measures of results, with little monitoring or direction of salesperson efforts by sales managers. By contrast, a behavior-based perspective focuses on close supervision of salesperson efforts and subjective measures of salesperson characteristics, activities, and strategies. The perspective taken by a sales organization will affect salespeople and has important implications for sales management.

3. **Describe the different types of criteria necessary for comprehensive evaluations of salesperson performance.** The multifaceted nature of sales jobs requires that performance evaluations incorporate multiple criteria. Although the specific criteria depend on the characteristics of a particular selling situation, comprehensive evaluations of salesperson performance require that four dimensions be addressed: behavioral, professional development, results, and profitability criteria. Addressing each of these areas is necessary to get a complete picture of salesperson performance and to produce the diagnostic information needed to improve future performance.

4. **Compare the advantages and disadvantages of different methods of salesperson performance evaluation.** Sales managers can use four basic methods to evaluate salesperson behaviors, professional development, results, and profitability: graphic rating/checklist

methods, ranking methods, objective-setting methods, and behaviorally anchored rating scales (BARS). Each method has certain strengths and weaknesses that must be understood and can be compensated for by using other methods in combination. Special attention should be directed toward developing performance benchmarks or quotas that reflect the unique characteristics of each territory.

5. **Explain how salesperson performance information can be used to identify problems, determine their causes, and suggest sales management actions to solve them.** The suggested approach is to first identify areas of poor performance, then work backward to try to identify the cause by asking, "What factors affect the achievement of this performance dimension?" Finally, the most effective sales management action to remove the cause of the problem and improve future performance must be decided on. Examples of possible actions are given in Exhibit 11.17.

6. **Discuss the measurement and importance of salesperson job satisfaction.** Dissatisfied salespeople tend to be absent more, leave the firm more, and work less hard than satisfied salespeople. The INDSALES scale can be used to measure salesperson satisfaction in total and for specific job dimensions. Analysis of the satisfaction with individual job dimensions can be used to determine appropriate action to increase salesperson job satisfaction.

Understanding Sales Management Terms

- 360-degree feedback
- Performance management
- Total quality management (TQM)
- Outcome-based perspective
- Behavior-based perspective
- Behavioral criteria
- Professional development criteria
- Results criteria
- Sales quota
- Profitability criteria
- Graphic rating/checklist methods
- Ranking methods
- Management by objectives (MBO)
- Behaviorally anchored rating scales (BARS)
- Outcome bias
- Job satisfaction

Developing Sales Management Knowledge

1. Discuss the different purposes of an evaluation of salesperson performance and how each purpose affects the performance evaluation process.
2. Characterize the salesforce of a firm that uses an outcome-based perspective for evaluating salespeople.
3. Why should sales managers pay more attention to behavioral criteria when evaluating salespeople?
4. Compare and contrast the graphic rating/checklist and ranking methods for evaluating salesperson performance.
5. Refer to "Sales Management in the 21st Century: Performance Criteria at Schein Pharmaceutical." Discuss the different types of performance criteria Schein uses and how these drive relationship development.
6. Discuss the importance of using different types of quotas in evaluating and controlling salesperson performance.
7. What is unique about the BARS method for evaluating salesperson performance?
8. Refer to "Sales Management in the 21st Century: Outcome-Based and Behavior-Based Measures at Pitney Bowes." Identify the outcome-based and behavior-based performance measures used at Pitney Bowes.
9. Why should sales managers be concerned with the job satisfaction of salespeople?
10. How can evaluations of salesperson performance and satisfaction be used by sales managers?

Building Sales Management Skills

1. Develop a method that can be used to evaluate salespeople's performance in the following areas: communication skills, attitude, initiative and aggressiveness, appearance and

manner, knowledge of competition, enthusiasm, cooperation, and time management. Explain any advantages and/or disadvantages associated with your measurement method.

2. Using the following scale (1 to 5, with *1* = "strongly disagree" and *5* = "strongly agree") and the questions in Exhibit 11.18, interview three salespeople and determine the level of job satisfaction of each. Explain areas of dissatisfaction and offer suggestions for improving satisfaction.

3. Below is an evaluation of salesperson Sally from the XYZ Corporation that was filled out by her sales manager. The company requires all its sales managers to use this form when evaluating salespeople.

The following scale was used: Almost never   1   2   3   4   5   Almost Always

Sally's Score

Asks customers for their ideas for promoting business	2
Offers customers help in solving their problems	1
Is constantly smiling when interacting with customers	4
Admits when she does not know the answer, but promises to find out	4
Generates new ways of tackling new or ongoing problems	1
Returns customers' calls the same day	2
Retains her composure in front of customers	5
Delivers what she promises on time	1
Remains positive about company in front of customers	5
Knows the design and specification of company products	4
Knows the applications and functions of company products	2
Submits reports on time	2
Maintains company specified records that are accurate and complete	2
Uses expense accounts with integrity	3
Uses business gift and promotional allowances responsibly	3
Controls costs in other areas of the company (order processing and preparation, delivery, etc.) when taking sales orders	3

Identify any problems that you see with Sally and make suggestions for improving her performance. In your analysis, be sure to consider the reasons why Sally may be doing a poor job in some of these areas. How could information like this be used to improve the performance of the sales organization?

Making Sales Management Decisions

CASE 11.1 Labels Express

Background

Sally Stickum has just completed her first year as a district sales manager for Labels Express, a manufacturer and marketer of a wide variety of labels. Before joining Labels Express, Sally was a salesperson for one of Labels' competitors. She was hired partly because of her philosophy on personal selling.

Sally's philosophy on personal selling is simple and consists of three premises. First, to succeed in sales requires the proper attitude. A salesperson should have a positive, forward-looking, nondefeatist, cooperative attitude. Second, a salesperson should be aggressive and show initiative. According to Sally, "Things don't happen until you make them happen." Third, although salespeople should be aggressive, at no time should their behavior be unethical. It is Sally's opinion that honest and ethical behavior leads to long-term trusting relationships.

Current Situation

Sally is now in the process of a year-end review. When the year began, she met with each salesperson to explain the criteria on which their performance would be judged. Several quotas were determined for each salesperson, including a sales dollar quota, new account quota, and sales call quota. The relative importance of each was determined by the following weight system: 4 for new accounts, 3 for sales, and 2 for sales calls, with 4 being weighted the highest. Salespeople were also told that their performance would be judged by the number of customer complaints received and by the extent to which they submitted required reports. Finally, salespeople would be judged on their ability to meet customer needs. This includes salespeople's ability to suggest ideas for promoting business, helping customers solve problems, finding answers to customer questions not readily known, returning customers' calls, and delivering what is promised.

Sally had heard about a performance appraisal process dubbed 360-degree feedback that involved getting feedback from multiple sources. She thought that this would be a great way to evaluate her salespeople and decided to implement her plan for using it. She decided that she would have each salesperson give a questionnaire to a customer, a team member, and a member of customer service (with whom salespeople worked very closely) to have them evaluate that salesperson's performance. Each questionnaire contained the following questions: (1) How often did you have contact with this salesperson over the course of the year? (2) Were you able to work closely with this salesperson to satisfy your needs? (3) Overall, how would you evaluate this salesperson's performance? (4) How satisfied are you with this salesperson? The questionnaire was to be signed by the respondent and returned to the salesperson who would submit it to Sally for review. Sally decided that if she saw something that she did not like in the feedback, she would discuss it with the salesperson. Sally thought that evaluating quota achievement would be a fairly straightforward process and that she could easily determine discrepancies and make salespeople aware of their shortcomings.

Questions

1. Assess Sally's use of 360-degree feedback for performance appraisal. Can you make any suggestions for improving this process?
2. What do you think about the type of feedback Sally is willing to provide her salespeople? How do you suggest performance feedback be handled?
3. What can Sally do to ensure that her salespeople make efforts to improve their performance in the areas she deems important?

CASE 11.2 Oakmaster Furniture Inc.

Background

Oakmaster Furniture Inc. produces several lines of oak furniture, ranging from traditional to contemporary. The firm has been in business for more than 20 years, serving primarily the western half of the United States. Headquartered in Portland, Oregon, the company employs 360 salespeople. Its salesforce consists of three regions, with four districts in each region. There are three regional sales managers and 12 district sales managers.

About 1 year ago, Roger Acorn was promoted to district sales manager at Oakmaster. He had been a salesperson with a competing firm for 5 years before joining the company 2 years ago. Roger was dissatisfied with the work environment at his previous employer, so when he arrived at Oakmaster, he was eager to take on new challenges with a company he viewed to be progressive.

Current Situation

As Roger reflected on his first year as district sales manager, he was concerned. His district had experienced higher-than-expected turnover among his salesforce during the year, and he was puzzled. In his opinion, Oakmaster offered excellent pay and benefits, a cooperative work environment, a challenging and rewarding job, strong company support, and opportunity for promotion.

Although Roger was very satisfied at Oakmaster, he began to believe that his salespeople might not be as happy. As a salesperson, he had noticed that dissatisfied colleagues' job performance often suffered. However, his salespeople's performance on the whole was not significantly down. Like many salesforces, his salespeople's performances ranged from less than average to outstanding. Nevertheless, he knew the importance of being satisfied. It was job dissatisfaction that led to his departure from his previous job.

In an attempt to measure the level of job satisfaction among his salespeople, Roger administered INDSALES to his salesforce. When the results were tabulated, he was surprised to find several areas in which salespeople expressed dissatisfaction. Salespeople seemed to be dissatisfied with their pay, thinking that it was low in comparison with what others were getting for similar work in other companies. Much to his dismay, Roger's salespeople seemed to be dissatisfied with him. They thought that he did not attempt to solicit their ideas about things and did not live up to his promises. Salespeople also expressed their dissatisfaction with the promotion policy, believing that it was unfair. They did not think that promotion was based on ability.

Although Roger was satisfied with the company's training program, his salespeople were not. Finally, salespeople did not believe they were receiving adequate support from the home office.

Although Roger was surprised and disappointed at the level of dissatisfaction among his salespeople, he was glad he took steps to analyze their job satisfaction. He was eager to take steps to bring about greater satisfaction. Roger decided to draw up plans for improving satisfaction and present them to his boss at their meeting scheduled for next week.

Questions

1. What steps can Roger take to increase the level of satisfaction among his salespeople?
2. What might be a more useful approach to examining salesforce job satisfaction with INDSALES?
3. What do you perceive the relationship to be between job satisfaction and turnover at Oakmaster?

CASES

Businessland Computers, Inc.
Royal Corporation
Topnotch Investment Company
MCI Vision (A)
Morgantown Inc.
Hospital Supply International
Arizonia Company
BSI
Adams Brands
Westinghouse Electric Corporation
Romano Pitesti
Windsor Management Company
Hongkong Bank of Canada
General Electric Appliances
The Dunn Corporation
Modern Plastics
IDS Financial Services
Denman Industrial Products (A)
Denman Industrial Products (B)
Dura-plast Inc. (A)
Dura-plast Inc. (B)
Toronto-Dominion Bank

Businessland Computers, Inc.: What If We Automated Our Salesforce?

Bill Pfaff, Sales Manager for Businessland, was reviewing sales performance and selling expenses from the past fiscal period in preparation of a budget which was due in a couple of weeks. At first glance, Bill was surprised to see that the company's total selling expenses were approaching $300 million. In pursuing initial analysis, he noted two areas in particular that were quite disturbing: First, the average cost of a sales call had been increasing substantially in recent years to where it was near $300 during the previous year. Secondly, nearly 60% of the sales rep's time was spent in non-selling activities. Compounding this was the company's profit trend which last year dropped to an all-time low ending at a loss of $23 million. Bill's thoughts centered upon some of his own company's technology products. He questioned,

> "What if. . . . we were to look toward technology-based solutions. Could Businessland develop new sales systems to bring together data from many sources providing sales reps access to the most up-to-date information? How would the sales reps respond to it; for that matter, how would Businessland's clients respond to it?"

As Bill began to formulate ideas about using technology, he projected that a process could reduce administrative communication tangles so sales professionals would have more time for customers, and improve information accuracy and efficiency for more effective time usage.

> "Maybe we could use our own technology (computers) to provide the salesforce immediate information on order status, pricing, availability of items, electronic mail, spread sheets, account and territory profiles, etc. This would help manage information and improve communications among the sales reps, sales managers, corporate marketing personnel and, most importantly, the customer."

Background

Businessland was founded in the mid 1980s by Bret Lane and Gerald Parsons. They combined knowledge, skill and the experience of marketing and technology to form a company that sells, services, and supports computer and workstation products from leading manufacturing companies. Today, Businessland is a prominent, privately-held company that specializes in building PCs from multiple manufacturers and integrating them into customer environments by using an outside salesforce of 300. In addition, they provide customer training, service, and telephone hotline support.

The personal computer industry is very dynamic and has experienced rapid changes in technology and products that have a relatively short life cycle. By the mid 1980s, hundreds of manufacturers had entered the market and there was a scramble to sell hardware with little attention to applications, systems, or support. There was an industry-wide rush to establish computer stores and retail outlets with the anticipation that personal computers would ultimately be marketed similarly to that of refrigerators. In the latter part of the decade, a large number of those companies ceased to operate either due to failure, mergers, or acquisitions. World sales of personal computers exceeded $150 billion in the mid 1990s up from $12 billion a decade earlier. Similar growth occurred in the US as sales of $5 billion in 1985 exceeded $60 billion in 1995. Sales of personal computers dwarf all other computer markets including mainframes which have plateaued at $50 billion annually.

The companies that did survive discovered the need to emphasize software ahead of hardware and to address user needs. The initial surge for personal computers was limited as most users required education in the applications and selection of both software and hardware. Essentially, it was an evolution. With the development of more sophisticated software and more extensive usage in many different areas of applications, the need for systems and networking became apparent. Thus, a more complex "systems approach" required not only a change in marketing but also a need for service and support. Many of these changes called for greater resources than originally planned. Inventories of equipment and parts were higher than anticipated, the need for knowledge and well-trained personnel increased, and there was an increase in the training of users and in providing after-sale support.

Sales and Earnings

Adding to Bill's dilemma of rising costs and inefficiency in the selling process, was the realization that Businessland's orders for the last year increased only 1% as compared to a 19% increase five years earlier. In a similar pattern, current year revenues increased only 13.8% compared to a revenue growth of 21.1% the previous year and 42.7% two years earlier. Earnings, however, decreased to a negative of −$23 million in the last year as compared to a decreasing growth rate of 91.5% in the previous year and 37% two years earlier. Parallel to this, Bill noted that the category of expenses identified as selling, general, and administrative increased nearly 19% during the past year compared to only 9.6% the previous year. It was immediately apparent that revenues were still increasing but at a decreasing rate but that actual orders had almost become stagnet during the past year. By contrast, operating expenses were running wild and if Businessland were to remain competitive, these would have to be brought back under control. Bill began to focus upon alternatives. Revenues and earnings are shown in Figure 1.

Source: Allen J. Wedell, Colorado State University. This case was prepared for classroom discussion rather than to illustrate either effective or ineffective managerial decisions. Copyright © 1997.

Sales and Marketing Automation

At a recent seminar entitled "Marketing Technology," Bill had been exposed to the concept of Sales and Marketing Automation (SMA) which is a system designed to add efficiency to sales operations. In the words of Steve Husner, a sales rep for Nation's Carriers, "The laptop allows one to follow through with a customer rather than having to get back to them at a later time." It permits a rep to hook right up to a mainframe via a modem and get answers to any question the customer may have right on the spot. SMA also improves salesforce productivity and increases effectiveness by:

- reducing the amount of time a salesperson devotes to administrative tasks such as the preparation of call reports.
- tracking sales leads.
- managing time and territory
- developing proposals and persuasive presentations

Impressed with the opportunities of such a program, Bill began to think about a program that would provide Businessland's salesforce the productivity tools that would increase selling productivity and, at the same time, lower selling costs. Immediately, Bill set up a task group to help him outline the goals and objectives for the project and to identify the resources that would be required—financial, equipment, and support personnel. The group identified three fundamental objectives that would evaluate the effectiveness of such a program:

1. To increase sales productivity and effectiveness by 25 percent.
2. To increase customer visibility of Businessland's automation solutions through the use of their own products (computers).
3. To increase sales rep job satisfaction, confidence and motivation.

In order to evaluate future sales productivity, the group analyzed the past performance of the salesforce. They identified work patterns falling into the following major categories with time spent as shown:

Contact with Customers	26%
Administrative Sales Activities	31%
Travel and waiting	15%
Meetings and training	13%
Office and personal time	15%
Total	100%

The group estimated the automation costs to run about $7500 per salesperson as shown in Figure 2: The task group thought it would be relatively easy to measure

FIGURE 1 Businessland Computers, Inc.

Five-Year Selected Financial Data

(in thousands)	Year 1 (last fiscal period)	Year 2	Year 3	Year 4	Year 5
Net Sales	$1,367,170	$1,200,628	$990,119	$693,828	$501,053
Gross Profit	287,550	313,645	265,868	198,956	136,475
Selling, General, & Administrative Exp.	298,076	250,762	228,673	181,364	139,435
Restructuring Exp.	13,635	—	—	—	—
Income (loss) from Operations	(24,161)	62,884	37,195	17,592	(2,959)
Income (loss) for IRS	(30,880)	56,334	31,663	13,882	(8,044)
Income (loss) before extraordinary item	(24,354)	33,205	17,485	8,078	(10,763)
Net Income (loss)	**(23,297)**	**33,497**	**17,485**	**12,759**	**(2,180)**

FIGURE 2 Estimated SMA Costs

	First Year	Second Year
Basic:		
Hardware	$3,500	
Software	1,000	$1,500
Supplies	500	
Total	$5,000	$1,500
Operational:		
Insurance	$100	$100
Electronic mail	150	150
Software Upgrade	100	100
Extended Warranty	—	350
Total	$350	$700
Implementation:		
Consultant	$300	
Training	400	
Spare Equipment	350	
Total	$1,050	
Overall Total	$6,400	$2,200
Amount added for management support personnel	$1,500	$500
Grand Total	$7,400	$2,700

the second and third objectives by randomly surveying both Businessland's clients and the salesforce once the program was initiated. They proposed that clients could be surveyed as to how they perceived sales automation and the impact Businessland had upon their purchasing decisions. Similarly, they thought that reports could be obtained from the salesforce regarding their satisfaction with the implementation and usage of SMA. The group, however, was much more concerned as to how they would measure the productivity of the sales automation and with the determination of the return on investment. Bill was rather clear that he wanted to know the break even point before he would be willing to include the proposal in the budget.

Royal Corporation

As Mary Jones, a third-year sales representative for the Royal Corporation, reviewed her call plans for tomorrow, she thought about her sales strategy. It was only July, 1993, but Jones was already well on her way toward completing her best year, financially, with the company. In 1992, she had sold the largest dollar volume of copiers of any sales representative in the northeast and was the tenth most successful rep in the country.

But Jones was not looking forward to her scheduled activities for the next day. In spite of her excellent sales ability, she had not been able to sell the Royal Corporate Copy Center (CCC). This innovative program was highly touted by Royal upper management. Jones was one of the few sales reps in her office who had not sold a CCC in 1992. Although Jones had an excellent working relationship with her sales manager, Tom Stein, she was experiencing a lot of pressure from him of late because he could not understand her inability to sell CCCs. Jones had therefore promised herself to concentrate her efforts on selling CCCs even if it meant sacrificing sales of other products.

Jones had five appointments for the day— 9:00 a.m., Acme Computers; 9:45, Bickford Publishing; 11:45, ABC Electronics; 12:30, CG Advertising; and 2:00 p.m., General Hospital. At Acme, Bickford, and ABC, Jones would develop CCC prospects. She was in various states of information gathering and proposal preparation for each of the accounts. At CG, Jones planned to present examples of work performed by a model 750 color copier. At General Hospital, she would present her final proposal for CCC adoption. Although the focus of her day would be on CCCs, she still needed to call and visit other accounts that she was developing.

Royal Introduces CCC Concept

In 1990, Royal had introduced its Corporate Copy Center facilities management program (CCC). Under this concept, Royal offered to equip, staff, operate, and manage a reproduction operation for its clients, on the clients' premises (see Exhibit I). After analyzing the needs of the client, Royal selected and installed the appropriate equipment and provided fully trained, Royal employed operators. The CCC equipment also permits microfilming, sorting, collating, binding, covering, and color copying, in addition to high-volume copying.

The major benefits of the program include: reproduction contracted for at a specified price, guaranteed output, tailor-made capabilities, and qualified operators.

As she pulled into the Acme Computers parking lot, she noticed that an unexpected traffic jam had made her ten minutes late for the 9:00 a.m. appointment. This made her uncomfortable as she valued her time, and assumed that her clients appreciated promptness. Jones had acquired the Acme Computers account the prior summer and had dealt personally with Betty White, Director of Printing Services, ever since. She had approached White six months earlier with the idea of purchasing a CCC but had not pursued the matter further until now because Betty had seemed very unreceptive. For today's call, Jones had worked several hours preparing a detailed study of Acme's present reproduction costs. She was determined to make her efforts pay off.

Jones gave her card to the new receptionist, who buzzed White's office and told her that Jones was waiting.

Source: Copyright © 1994. This case was prepared at Babson College by Professor H. David Hennessey and Barbara Kalunian, graduate student, as the basis for discussion rather than to illustrate either effective or ineffective sales performance. Names and locations have been disguised.

EXHIBIT I

Labor
Operator (Hrs × 4.3 Wks)
Secretary (Hrs × 4.3 Wks)
Executive (Hrs × 4.3 Wks)
Supervisor (Hrs × 4.3 Wks)

CCC provides expert operators and experienced reprographic managers so all labor costs are included in one convenient monthly invoice.

Paid Benefits
Social Security
Vacations
Sick Leave
Pensions
Medical Plans

CCC eliminates all "people problems"—your repro staff is on our payroll, and we pay for their benefits.

Recruiting & Training
Advertising Costs
Personnel Time
Interviewer Time
Operator Time
Supervisor Time

No more recruiting and training . . . we handle that job, and we cover all related expenses!

Administrative Time
Purchase Orders
Filing Work
Calling Service People
Talking to Sales People

We handle all repro management—you receive a single monthly invoice for your entire repro system (and supplies)!

Waste
Operator Negligence
Unauthorized Copies
Equipment Malfunction

You only pay for the copies you use . . .

Downtime
Resulting In . . .
Vendor Charges
Overtime Costs
Missed Deadlines

Comprehensive back-up capabilities at your local Royal Reproduction Center—job turnaround times are guaranteed at no extra cost to you!

Price Increases
Labor
Materials
Overhead
Interest

The CCC price includes everything and it's guaranteed for the length of our agreement!

Space Requirements
Inventory
File Cabinets
Additional Equipment

Equipment and supplies are our responsibility, eliminating the need for anything extra on your part . . .

Chargeback Control
Clients
Departments
Individuals

At no charge, we maintain a log of all copies made . . . for clients, departments and individuals.

To see what Royal Corporate Copy Center can do for you—and for your operating budget—take a minute to explore the *true* cost of your *present* system, outlined in the chart above. As you can see, it includes those "hidden" reprographic expenses that *many* organizations fail to consider . . .

The CCC concept is a familiar one, of course . . . many progressive organizations are now utilizing similar arrangements for their food service and data processing programs.

A few minutes later, Betty appeared and led Jones to a corner of the lobby. They always met in the lobby a situation that Jones found frustrating but it was apparently company policy.

"Good morning, Betty, it's good to see you again. Since I saw you last, I've put together the complete analysis on the CCC that I promised. I know you'll be excited by what you see. As you are aware, the concept of a CCC is not that unusual anymore. You may recall from the first presentation that I prepared for you, the CCC can be a tremendous time and money saver. Could you take a few moments to review the calculations that I have prepared exclusively for Acme Computers?" Betty flipped through the various pages of exhibits that Jones had prepared, but it was obvious that she had little interest in the proposal. "As you can see," Jones continued, "the savings are really significant after the first two years."

"Yes, but the program is more expensive the first two years. But what's worse is that there will be an outsider here doing our printing. I can't say that's an idea I could ever be comfortable with."

Jones realized that she had completely lost the possibility of White's support, but she continued.

"Betty, let me highlight some of the other features and benefits that might interest Acme."

"I'm sorry, Mary, but I have a 10:00 meeting that I really must prepare for. I can't discuss this matter further today."

"Betty, will you be able to go over these figures in more depth a little later?"

"Why don't you leave them with me, I'll look at them when I get the chance," White replied.

Jones left the proposal with White hoping that she would give it serious consideration, but as she pulled out of the driveway to Acme Computers, she could not help but feel that the day had gotten off to a poor start.

The Royal Corporation established the Royal Reproduction Center (RRC) Division in 1956. With 51 offices located in 24 states in the United States, the RRC specializes in high quality quick-turnaround copying, duplicating, and printing on a service basis. In addition to routine reproduction jobs, the RRC is capable of filling various specialized requests including duplicating engineering documents and computer reports, microfilming, color copying, and producing overhead transparencies. In addition, the RRC sales representatives sell the Royal 750 color copier (the only piece of hardware sold through RRCs) and the Royal Corporate Copy Center program (CCC). Although the RRC accepts orders from "walk ins," the majority of the orders are generated by the field representatives who handle certain named accounts which are broken down by geographic territory.

At 9:45 a.m., Jones stopped at Bickford Publishing for her second sales call of the day. She waited in the lobby while Joe Smith, Director of Corporate Services, was paged. Bickford Publishing was one of Jones's best accounts. Last year her commission from sales to Bickford totaled 10 percent of her pay. But her relationship with Joe Smith always seemed to be on unstable ground. She was not sure why, but she had always felt that Smith harbored resentment towards her. However, she decided not to dwell on the matter as long as a steady stream of large orders kept coming in. Jones had been calling on Bickford ever since Tim McCarthy, the sales representative before her, had been transferred. Competition among the RRC sales reps for the Bickford account has been keen. But Stein had decided that Jones's performance warranted a crack at the account, and she had proven that she deserved it by increasing sales 40 percent within six months.

"Good morning, Miss Jones, how are you today?" Smith greeted her. He always referred to her formally as Miss Jones.

"I'm fine Mr. Smith," Jones replied. "Thank you for seeing me today. I needed to drop by and give you some additional information on the CCC idea that I reviewed with you earlier."

"Miss Jones, to be perfectly honest with you, I reviewed the information that you left with me, and although I think that your CCC is a very nice idea, I really don't believe it is something that Bickford would be interested in at this particular point in time."

"But Mr. Smith, I didn't even give you any of the particulars. I have a whole set of calculations here indicating that the CCC could save Bickford a considerable amount of time, effort, and money over the next few years."

"I don't mean to be rude, Miss Jones, but I am in a hurry, I really don't care to continue this conversation."

"Before you go, do you think that it might be possible to arrange to present this proposal to Mr. Ferry [Tony Perry, V.P. of Corporate Facilities, Joe Smith's immediate supervisor] in the near future? I'm sure that he would be interested in seeing it. We had discussed this idea in passing earlier, and he seemed to feel that it warranted serious consideration."

"Maybe we can talk about that the next time you are here. I'll call you if I need to have something printed. Now I really must go."

As Jones returned to her car, she decided that in spite of what Smith had told her about waiting until next time, she should move ahead to contact Mr. Perry directly. He had seemed genuinely interested in hearing more about the CCC when she had spoken to him earlier, even though she had mentioned it only briefly. She decided that she would return to the office and send Perry a letter requesting an appointment to speak with him.

Although Jones was not yet aware of it, Joe Smith had returned to his desk and immediately began drafting the following memo to be sent to Tony Perry:

To: Tony Perry, V.P. Corporate Facilities
From: Joe Smith, Corporate Services
Re: Royal CCC

Tony:

I spoke at length with Mary Jones of Royal this morning. She presented me with her proposal for the adoption of the CCC program at Bickford Publishing. After reviewing the proposal in detail, I have determined that the program: (a) is not cost effective, (b) has many problem areas that need ironing out, and (c) is inappropriate for our company at this time.

Therefore, in light of the above, my opinion is that this matter does not warrant any serious consideration or further discussion at this point in time.

Royal 750 Color Copier

The Royal 750 color copier made its debut in 1983 and was originally sold by color copier specialists in the equipment division of Royal. But sales representatives did not want to sell the color copier exclusively and sales managers did not want to manage the color copier specialists. Therefore, the 750 was not a particularly successful product. In 1989, the sales responsibility for the color copier was transferred to the RRC division. Since the RRC sales representatives were already taking orders from customers needing the services of a color copier, it was felt that the reps would be in an advantageous position to determine when current customer requirements would justify the purchase of a 750.

Jones arrived back at her office at 10:45. She checked her mailbox for messages, grabbed a cup of coffee, and returned to her desk to draft the letter to Tony Perry. After making several phone calls setting up appointments for the next week and checking on client satisfaction with some jobs that were delivered that day, she gathered up the materials that she needed for her afternoon sales calls. Finishing her coffee, she noticed the poster announcing a trip for members of the "President's Club." To become a member, a sales representative had to meet 100% of his or her sales budget, sell a 750 color copier, sell a CCC program, and sell a short-term rental. Jones believed that making budget would be difficult but attainable, even though her superior performance in 1992 led to a budget increase of 20% for 1993. She had already sold a color copier and a short-term rental. Therefore, the main thing standing in her way of making the President's Club was the sale of a CCC. Not selling a CCC this year would have even more serious ramifications, she thought. Until recently, Jones had considered herself the prime candidate for the expected opening for a senior sales representative in her office. But Michael Gould, a sales rep who also had three years experience, was enjoying an excellent year. He had sold two color copiers and had just closed a deal on a CCC to a large semiconductor manufacturing firm. Normally everyone in the office celebrated the sale of a CCC. As a fellow sales rep was often heard saying, "it takes the heat off all of us for a while." Jones, however, found it difficult to celebrate Michael's sale. For not only was he the office "Golden Boy" but now, in her opinion, he was also the prime candidate for the senior sales rep position as well. Michael's sale also left Jones as one of the few reps in the office without the sale of a CCC to his or her credit. "It is pretty difficult to get a viable CCC lead," Jones thought, "but I've had one or two this year that should have been closed." Neither the long discussions with her sales manager, nor the numerous inservice training sessions and discussions on how to sell the CCC had helped. "I've just got to sell one of these soon," Jones resolved.

On her way out, she glanced at the clock. It was 11:33. She had just enough time to make her 11:45 appointment with Sam Lawless, operations manager, at ABC Electronics. This was Jones's first appointment at ABC and she was excited about getting a foot in the door there. A friend of hers was an assistant accountant at ABC. She had informed Jones that the company spent more than $15,000 a month on printing services and that they might consider a CCC proposal. Jones knew who the competition was, and although their prices were lower on low-volume orders, Royal could meet or beat their prices for the kind of volume of work for which ABC was contracting. But Jones wasn't enthusiastic about garnering the account for reproduction work. She believed she could sell ABC a CCC.

Jones's friend had mentioned management dissatisfaction with the subcontracting of so much printing. Also, there had been complaints regarding the quality of work. Investment in an in-house print shop had been discussed. Jones had assessed ABC's situation and had noticed a strong parallel with the situation at Star Electronics, a multi-division electronics manufacturing firm that had been sold CCCs for each of their four locations in the area. That sale, which occurred over a year ago, was vital in legitimizing the potential customers in the Northeast. Jones hoped to sell ABC on the same premise that Fred Myers had sold Star Electronics. Myers had been extremely helpful in reviewing his sales plan with Jones and had given her ideas on points he felt had been instrumental in closing the Star deal. She felt well prepared for this call.

Jones had waited four months to get an appointment with Lawless. He had a reputation for disliking to speak with salespeople, but Jones's friend had passed along to him some CCC literature and he had seemed interested. Finally, after months of being unable to reach him by telephone, or get a response by mail, she had phoned two weeks ago and he had consented to see her. Today she planned to concentrate on how adoption of the CCC program might solve ABC's current reproduction problems. She also planned to ask Lawless to provide her with the necessary information to produce a convincing proposal in favor of CCC. Jones pulled into a visitor parking space and grabbed her briefcase. "This could end up being the one," she thought as she headed for the reception area.

Jones removed a business card from her wallet and handed it to the receptionist. "Mary Jones to see Sam Lawless, I have an appointment," Jones announced.

"I'm sorry," the receptionist replied, "Mr. Lawless is no longer with the company."

Jones tried not to lose her composure, "But I had an appointment to see him today. When did he leave?"

"Last Friday was Mr. Lawless's last day. Mr. Bates is now operations manager."

"May I see Mr. Bates, please?" Jones inquired, knowing in advance, the response.

"Mr. Bates does not see salespeople. He sees no one without an appointment."

"Could you tell him that I had an appointment to see Mr. Lawless? Perhaps he would consider seeing me."

"I can't call him. But I'll leave him a note with your card. Perhaps you can contact him later."

"Thank you, I will." Jones turned and left ABC, obviously shaken. "Back to square one," she thought as she headed back to her car. It was 12:05 p.m.

Jones headed for her next stop, CG Advertising, still upset from the episode at ABC. But she had long since discovered that no successful salesperson can dwell on disappointments. "It interferes with your whole attitude," she reminded herself. Jones arrived at the office park where CG was located. She was on time for her 12:30 appointment.

CG was a large full-service agency. Jones's color copy orders from CG had been increasing at a rapid rate for the past six months, and she had no reason to believe that their needs would decrease in the near future. Therefore she believed the time was ripe to present a case for the purchase of a 750 color copier. Jones had been dealing primarily with Jim Stevens, head of Creative Services. They had a good working relationship, even though on certain occasions Jones had found him to be unusually demanding about quality. But she figured that characteristic seemed to be common in many creative people. She had decided to use his obsession with perfection to work to her advantage.

Jones also knew that money was only a secondary consideration as far as Stevens was concerned. He had seemingly gotten his way on purchases in several other instances, so she planned her approach to him. Jones had outlined a proposal which she was now ready to present to Jim.

"Good morning, Jim, how's the advertising business?"

"It's going pretty well for us here, how's things with you?"

"Great, Jim," Jones lied, "I have an interesting idea to discuss with you. I've been thinking that CG has been ordering large quantities of color copies. I know that you utilize them in the presentations of advertising and marketing plans to clients. I also know that you like to experiment with several different concepts before actually deciding on a final idea. Even though we have exceptionally short turnaround time, it occurred to me that nothing would suit your needs more efficiently and effectively than the presence of one of our Royal 750 color copiers right here in your production room. That way, each time that you consider a revision one of your artists will be able to compose a rough, and you can run a quick copy and decide virtually immediately if that is the direction in which you want to go, with no need to slow down the creative process at all."

"Well, I don't know; our current situation seems to be working out rather well. I really don't see any reason to change it."

"I'm not sure that you're fully aware of all the things that the 750 color copier is capable of doing," Jones pressed on. "One of the technicians and I have been experimenting with the 750. Even I have discovered some new and interesting capabilities to be applied in your field, Jim. Let me show you some of them."

She reached into her art portfolio and produced a wide variety of samples to show Stevens. "You know that the color copier is great for enlarging and reducing as well as straight duplicating. But look at the different effects we got by experimenting with various sizes and colors. Don't you think that this is an interesting effect?"

"Yes, it really is," Stevens said loosening up slightly.

"But wait," Jones added, "I really have the ultimate to show you." Jones produced a sheet upon which she had constructed a collage from various slides that Stevens had given her for enlarging.

"Those are my slides! Hey, that's great."

"Do you think that a potential client might be impressed by something like this? And the best part is you can whip something like this up in a matter of minutes, if the copier is at your disposal."

"Hey, that's a great idea, Mary, I'd love to be able to fool around with one of those machines. I bet I'd be able to do some really inventive proposals with it."

"I'm sure you would, Jim."

"Do you have a few minutes right now, I'd like to bounce this idea off of Bill Jackson, Head of Purchasing, and see how quickly we can get one in here."

Jones and Stevens went down to Jackson's office. Before they ever spoke, Jones felt that this deal was closed. Jim Stevens always got his own way. Besides, she believed she knew what approach to use with Bill Jackson. She had dealt with him on several other occasions. Jackson had failed to approve a purchase for her the prior fall, on the basis that the purchase could not be justified. He was right on that account. Their present 600 model was handling their reproduction needs sufficiently, but you can't blame a person for trying, she thought. Besides, she hadn't had Stevens in her corner for that one. This was going to be different

"How's it going, Bill. You've met Mary Jones before, haven't you?"

"Yes, I remember Miss Jones. She's been to see me several times, always trying to sell me something we don't need," he said cynically.

"Well, this time I do have something you need and not only will this purchase save time, but it will save money, too. Let me show you some figures I've worked out regarding how much you can save by purchasing the 750 color copier." Jones showed Jackson that, at their current rate of increased orders of color copies, the 750 would pay for itself in three years. She also stressed the efficiency and ease of operation.

But she knew that Jackson was really only interested in the bottom line.

"Well, I must admit, Miss Jones, it does appear to be a cost-effective purchase."

Stevens volunteered, "Not only that, but we can now get our artwork immediately, too. This purchase will make everyone happy."

Jones believed she had the order. "I'll begin the paperwork as soon as I return to the office. May I come by next week to complete the deal?"

"Well, let me see what needs to be done on this end, but I don't foresee a problem," Jackson replied.

"There won't be any problem," Stevens assured Jones.

"Fine, then. I'll call Jim, the first of next week to set up an appointment for delivery."

Jones returned to her car at 1:00. She felt much better having closed the sale on the 750. She had planned enough time to stop for lunch.

During lunch, Jones thought about her time at Royal. She enjoyed her job as a whole. If it weren't for the pressure she was feeling to sell the corporate copy center program, everything would be just about perfect. Jones had been a straight "A" student in college where she majored in marketing. As far back as she could remember, she had always wanted to work in sales. Her father had started out in sales, and enjoyed a very successful and profitable career. He had advanced to sales manager and sales director for a highly successful Fortune 500 company and was proud that his daughter had chosen to pursue a career in sales. Often they would get together, and he would offer suggestions that had proven effective for him when he had worked in the field. When Jones's college placement office had announced that a Royal collegiate recruiter was visiting the campus, Jones had immediately signed up for an interview. She knew several recent graduates that had obtained positions with Royal and were very happy there. They were also doing well financially. She was excited at the idea of working for an industry giant. When she was invited for a second interview, she was ecstatic. Several days later, she received a phone call offering her a position at the regional office. She accepted immediately. Jones attended various pre-training workshops for 6 weeks at her regional office preparing her for her 2-week intensive training period at the Royal Training Headquarters. The training consisted of product training and sales training.

She had excelled there, and graduated from that course at the head of her class. From that point on everything continued smoothly . . . until this problem with selling the CCC.

After a quick sandwich and coffee, Jones left the restaurant at 1:30. She allowed extra time before her 2:00 appointment at General Hospital, located just four blocks from the office, to stop into the office first, check for messages, and check in with her sales manager. She informed Tom Stein that she considered the sale of a 750 to CG almost certain.

"That's great, Mary, I never doubted your ability to sell the color copiers, or repro for that matter. But what are we going to do about our other problem?"

"Tom, I've been following CCC leads all morning. To tell you the truth, I don't feel as though I've made any progress at all. As a matter of fact, I've lost some ground." Jones went on to explain the situation that had developed at ABC Electronics and how she felt when she learned that Sam Lawless was no longer with the company. "I was pretty excited about that prospect, Tom. The news was a little tough to take."

"That's okay. We'll just concentrate on his replacement, now. It might be a setback. But the company's still there, and they still have the same printing needs and problems. Besides, you're going to make your final presentation to General Hospital this afternoon, and you really did your homework for that one." Stein had worked extensively with Jones on the proposal from start to finish. They both knew that it was her best opportunity of the year to sell a CCC.

"I'm leaving right now. Wish me luck."

He did. She filled her briefcase with her personals and CCC demonstration kit that she planned to use for the actual presentation and headed toward the parking lot.

Jones's appointment was with Harry Jameson of General Hospital. As she approached his office, his receptionist announced her. Jameson appeared and led her to the board room for their meeting. Jones was surprised to find three other individuals seated around the table. She was introduced to Bob Goldstein, V.P. of

---

EXHIBIT II   Why Royal Corporate Copy Center?

- No Hidden Costs
- No Downtime
- No Capital Investment
- No Recruiting or Training
- No People Problems
- No Inventory Problems
- Increased Quality
- Expert Operators—Plus
- Guaranteed Turnaround Time
- Allows You to Devote Full Time to Your Business
- Departmental Budget Control
- RRC Full Center Support
- Tailor Made System
- Full Write Off
- Guaranteed Cost Per Copy
- Short Term Agreement
- Trial Basis

operations, Martha Chambers, director of accounting, and Dr. J. P. Dunwitty, chairman of the board. Jameson explained that whenever an expenditure of this magnitude was being considered, the hospital's executive committee had to make a joint recommendation.

Jones set up her demonstration at the head of the table so that it was easily viewed by everyone and began her proposal. She presented charts verifying the merits of the CCC (Exhibit II, III) and also the financial calculations that she had generated based upon the information supplied to her by Jameson.

Forty minutes later, Jones finished her presentation and began fielding questions. The usual concerns were voiced regarding hiring an "outsider" to work within the hospital. But the major concern seemed to revolve around the loss of employment on the part of two present printing press operators. One, John Brown, had been a faithful employee for more than five years. He was married and had a child. There had never been a complaint about John personally, or with regard to the quality or quantity of his work. The second operator was Peter Dunwitty, a recent graduate of a nearby vocational school and nephew of Dr. Dunwitty. Although he had been employed by the hospital for only three months, there was no question about his ability and performance.

In response to this concern, Jones emphasized that the new equipment was more efficient, but different, and did not require the skills of experienced printers like Brown and Dunwitty. She knew, however, that this was always the one point about the adoption of a CCC program that even she had the most difficulty justifying. She suddenly felt rather ill.

"Well, Miss Jones, if you'll excuse us for a few minutes, we'd like to reach a decision on this matter," said Jameson.

"There's no need to decide right at this point. You all have copies of my proposal. If you'd like to take a few days to review the figures, I'd be happy to come by then," said Jones, in a last-ditch attempt to gain some additional time.

"I think that we'd like to meet in private for a few minutes right now, if you don't mind," interjected Dunwitty.

"No, that's fine," Jones said as she left the room for the lobby. She sat in a waiting room and drank a cup of coffee. She lit a cigarette, a habit that she seldom engaged in. Five minutes later, the board members called her back in.

"This CCC idea is really sound, Miss Jones," Jameson began. "However, here at General Hospital, we have a very strong commitment to our employees. There really seems to be no good reason to put two fine young men out of work. Yes, I realize that from the figures that you've presented to us, you've indicated a savings of approximately $30,000 over three years. But I would have to question some of the calculations. Under the circumstances we feel that maintaining sound employee relations has more merit than switching to an unproven program right now. Therefore, we've decided against purchasing a CCC."

Jones was disappointed. But she had been in this situation often enough not to show it. "I'm sorry to hear that, Mr. Jameson, I thought that I had presented a very good argument for participation in the CCC program. Do you think that if your current operators decided to leave, before you filled their positions, you might consider CCC again?"

"I can't make a commitment to that right now. But feel free to stay in touch," Jameson countered.

"I'll still be coming in on a regular basis to meet all your needs for other work not capable of being performed in your print shop," Jones replied.

"Then you'll be the first to know if that situation arises," said Jameson.

"Thank you all for your time. I hope that I was of assistance even though you decided against the purchase. If I may be of help at any point in time, don't hesitate to call," Jones remarked as she headed for the door.

Now, totally disappointed, Jones regretted having scheduled another appointment for that afternoon. She would have liked to call it a day. But she knew she had an opportunity to pick up some repro work and develop a new account. So she knew she couldn't cancel.

Jones stopped by to see Paul Blake, head of staff training at Pierson's, a large department store with locations throughout the state. Jones had made a cold call one afternoon the prior week and had obtained a sizable printing order. Now she wanted to see whether Blake was satisfied with the job, which had been delivered earlier in the day. She also wanted to speak to him about some of the other services available at the RRC. Jones was about to reach into her briefcase for her card to offer to the receptionist when she was startled by a "Hello, Mary" coming from behind her.

"Hello, Paul," Jones responded, surprised and pleased that he had remembered her name. "How are you today?"

"Great! I have to tell you that report that you printed for us is far superior to the work that we have been receiving from some of our other suppliers. I've got another piece that will be ready to go out in about an hour. Can you have someone come by and pick it up then?"

"I'll do better than that. I'll pick it up myself," Jones replied.

"See you then," he responded as he turned and headed back towards his office.

"I'm glad I decided to stop by after all," Jones thought as she pressed the elevator button. She wondered how she could best use the next hour to help salvage the day. When the elevator door opened, out stepped Kevin Fitzgerald, operations manager for Pierson's. Jones had met him several weeks earlier when she had spoken with Ann Leibman, a sales rep for Royal Equipment Division. Leibman had been very close to closing a deal that would involve selling Pierson several "casual" copying machines that they were planning to locate in various offices to use for quick copying. Leibman informed Jones that Tom Stein had presented a CCC proposal to Pierson's six months earlier but the plan was flatly refused. Fitzgerald, she explained, had been sincerely interested in the idea. But the plan involved

EXHIBIT III — What Is Royal Corporate Copy Center?

General Hospital Copying Objectives
1. To lower on-hand inventory of forms
2. To be able to upgrade or relocate equipment if needed
3. To have a competent full-time operator as well as back-up operators
4. To increase productivity
5. To be more cost efficient
6. 89-day trial option period
7. To eliminate downtime
8. To eliminate waste
9. To assure fast turnaround
10. To establish an inventory control system for paper and copier supplies
11. To install an accurate departmental charge-back system
12. To improve copy quality
13. To eliminate queuing time
14. To allow administrative support personnel to devote their full time to General Hospital's daily business
15. To eliminate having to worry about service on machines

General Hospital Offset vs. Printing
1. You won't eliminate all your related printing problems such as:
    A. You will still have to keep Savins for short-run lengths.
    B. You will still have waste problems.
    C. You still need plates and printing supplies.
    D. It is messy and complicated.
    E. You must have a dependable operator every day, and someone for vacations.
    F. You will have to vend some printing.
    G. You won't be able to cut down inventory of forms on hand, and you will have to have long-run lengths to be profitable and long turnaround for two-sided copying.
    H. You will be running a copying print shop, but this is still not state of the art.
    I. It is very noisy. You wouldn't be able to put it in this building. You might have to find another location or keep it in the old building.
    J. Only 3 out of about 15 hospitals on the North Shore area have printing presses—those that do have large duplicators that do 100,000 to 200,000 in volume per month besides long-run lengths on presses.
2. You would lose all of the extra benefits the Royal Corporate Copy Center would give you. (See Attached)
3. For the first full year because of expense for press, your cost would be $14,890 higher than Royal Corporate Copy Center, and your estimated price increases over the next two years would not be fixed, thus still costing you more for a less efficient operation.

Royal Corporate Copy Center Will Satisfy These Objectives in the Following Manner:
1. By having a high-speed duplicator and professional operator, you will be able to order forms on an as-needed basis. This will lower your present inventory by at least 80%, thus freeing up valuable space for other use.
2. Because of the flexibility that Royal Corporate Copy Center gives you, you have the opportunity to change or upgrade equipment at any time. If relocation of equipment is necessary because of changes in the hospital's structure, this can be done also.
3. Royal Corporate Copy Center will provide a trained, professional operator whose hours will conform to General Hospital's. Regardless of vacation schedules, sickness, or personal absences, a competent operator will report to General Hospital every day. If these operators do not meet with General Hospital's satisfaction, they can be changed within 24 hours' time. Because Royal will supply the operators, you will be relieved of this person as a staff member. Benefits, sick time, and vacation will be taken care of by Royal. You will receive operators for your facility 52 weeks a year.

Royal Corporate Copy Center Will Satisfy These Objectives in the Following Manner (continued):
4. Our people will report directly to your supervisor for their assignment the same as any other employee under your supervision. These people will be able to sort incoming jobs as we have discussed or may be used for other work in the copy center at non-peak times. These people would also be available to pick up copying work from various central locations throughout General Hospital at specified times, thus eliminating the need for people to come to the copy center. These people may also be used to operate other various types of equipment that General Hospital has.
5. By having a Royal Corporate Copy Center program at General Hospital and letting Royal take care of all your duplicating needs in a professional manner, your copying costs will become much more cost efficient. We believe that the cost savings alone in the first year could be upwards of 10–15% and would increase as your copy volume grows with you. Your present system does not offer several of the important benefits that Royal Corporate Copy Center offers that

Royal Corporate Copy Center is the means whereby Royal will equip, staff, operate and manage a reproduction operation for you on your own premises. First, we analyze your needs, then we select and install the appropriate equipment. Secondly, we provide two fully trained Royal employed operators and professional reproduction management. Finally, we schedule all work, and protect you with comprehensive back-up capabilities at our Royal Reproduction Center . . . and you receive just one monthly bill for the entire package.

now will be included in one fixed cost—in dollars and cents, by not having to pay for these services, this is where the additional 10–15% cost savings per year could come in. We also will give you a fixed reproduction cost so that you can budget more accurately. We will also fix all of your cost for the next three years (that includes supplies, machine, support and operators) if you sign a three-year agreement at the end of the trial period. This will enable you to save upwards of another 10% per year.

6. We at Royal feel very confident about this program and its success. We, therefore, wish to minimize our customers' risk for installing a new program. We feel we are able to do this by offering a trial option period of up to 89 days. This program works in the following way: General Hospital must sign a trial option pricing addendum and a three-year agreement. This will put into action the following:
   A. $1,050.00 per month credit off the original pricing for the first partial month, the first full month, and the second full month (total of $3,150.00).
   B. At the end of the trial option period General Hospital can elect to:
      a. Remain on the three-year agreement date May 1, 1993.
      b. Execute a 90-day, one-year, or two-year agreement with applicable pricing.
      c. Cancel the agreement date May 1, 1993, without liquidation damages.
7. With Royal Corporate Copy Center you will never experience downtime. Your work will always be done timely. We will back up the machines with a back-up copier running the work there or send it to our closest center to be completed and returned. By being a Royal Corporate Copy Center customer, General Hospital will always receive priority on service. Also, our operators will be able to handle more extensive types of service to the equipment.
8. General Hospital will be charged only for the copies ordered. This will eliminate all of your present waste that is involved with offset.
9. Trained Royal operators should reduce turnaround time on work. These operators will know how to run jobs on the equipment properly and in the fastest way so that productivity will increase and turnaround time will decrease.
10. Royal will order all toner and developer, thus eliminating the need for General Hospital to make large commitments and maintain large inventories. We will order paper also for you on a weekly basis if you so choose.
11. Royal will install an accurate departmental charge-back system, allowing General Hospital to accurately account for all copies. You will receive a copy of this breakdown each month.
12. Royal will provide trained operators, guaranteeing high-quality copies. By using a Xerographic process, you will always have consistently high-quality copies.
13. By providing General Hospital with skilled operators, copying and duplicating requirements will be met in a timely fashion, eliminating the need for General Hospital employees to stand and wait to use other equipment. In essence, General Hospital employees will be free to do General Hospital business; Royal will fulfill the copying and duplicating requirements.
14. Administrative personnel will no longer have to worry about sales people, service problems, obtaining purchase orders, or buying supplies.
15. All machines used will be the responsibility of Royal for service and maintenance.

General Hospital Cash Flow (One-Year Period) Royal Corporate Copy Center vs. Present System

Corporate Copy Center		Hospital
Royal 900	Equipment	Obsolete presses & mimeo
$ 6,500.00	Supplies and Paper	$ 42,189.00
Included	Toner and Developer	-0-
Included	Labor	$ 22,496.00
Included	Benefits	$ 2,681.00
Included	Administrative Time	-?-
Included	Management Time	-?-
Included	CCC Benefits	None
Eliminated	Savin 680 Rental	$ 4,534.00
Eliminated	Smaller Savin I Rental	$ 1,080.00
Eliminated	Smaller Savin II Rental	$ 1,320.00
Eliminated	Savin Copying Cost	$ 2,400.00
Eliminated	Vending	$ 7,000.00
	(Forms that could be kept in-house)	
Eliminated	Issuing of P.O.s	$ 500.00
Eliminated	Expense for Present Building	$ 2,500.00
$ 80,310.00	Royal Facilities Management	—
($.029 per copy)	(200,000 copies)	
$ 86,810.00	TOTAL CASH FLOW	$ 86,700.00

(continued)

EXHIBIT III (continued)

	Fixed	Price Increases	Est.	
$ 86,810.00	0	15 months	5%	$ 91,035.00
$ 89,414.00	3%	2nd year	9%	$ 99,228.00
$ 91,202.00	2%	3rd year	9%	$108,158.00
$267,426.00		PROJECTED 3-YEAR COST		$298,421.00
$ 30,995.00		PROJECTED 3-YEAR SAVINGS		None

Recommendation

Royal feels at this time that it would be very beneficial for General Hospital to change from its present reproduction system of two offset presses, mimeograph equipment, several smaller copiers, and a collator to a Royal 900 and a professional operator under the Royal Corporate Copy Center program. Royal feels it would be beneficial for General Hospital to effect this change presently for the following reasons:

1. Professional people would replace a part-time operator (20 hours) and an operator that is on leave (20 hours).
2. State-of-the-art equipment would replace the present presses, which are very old and outdated.
3. The large amount of waste presently experienced would be eliminated.
4. The high maintenance cost for the presses would be eliminated.
5. Hand collating and off-line collating would be eliminated.
6. Poor and inconsistent quality in the copies would be eliminated.
7. The back-up problem would be eliminated.
8. You would have better turnaround and accountability.
9. Some of the smaller copiers, and lower copy volumes on the smaller copiers, would be eliminated.
10. You would receive all other Royal Corporate Copy Center benefits unattainable with your present program.

In the following pages I hope to show you how we will accomplish these goals by installing the Royal Corporate Copy Center at General Hospital.

---

a larger initial expenditure than Pierson's was willing to make. Now, Leibman explained, there would be a much larger savings involved, since the "casual" machines would not be needed if a CCC were involved. Jones had suggested to Fitzgerald that the CCC proposal be reworked to include the new machines so that a current assessment could be made. He had once again appeared genuinely interested and suggested that Jones retrieve the necessary figures from Jerry Query, Head of Purchasing. Jones had not yet done so. She had phoned Query several times, but he had never responded to her messages.

"Nice to see you again, Mr. Fitzgerald. Ann Leibman introduced us, I'm Mary Jones from Royal."

"Yes, I remember. Have you spoken with Mr. Query, yet?"

"I'm on my way to see him right now," Jones said as she thought that this would be the perfect way to use the hour.

"Fine, get in touch with me when you have the new calculations."

Jones entered the elevator that Fitzgerald had been holding for her as they spoke. She returned to the first floor and consulted the directory. Purchasing was on the third floor. As she walked off the elevator on the third floor, the first thing that she saw was a sign that said, "Salespeople seen by appointment only. Tuesdays and Thursdays, 10 a.m.–12 noon."

"I'm really out of luck," Jones thought, "not only do I not have an appointment, but today's Wednesday. But I'll give it my best shot as long as I'm here."

Jones walked over to the receptionist who was talking to herself as she searched through a large pile of papers on her desk. Although Jones knew she was aware of her presence, the receptionist continued to avoid her.

"This could be a hopeless case," Jones thought. Just then the receptionist looked up and acknowledged her.

"Good afternoon. I'm Mary Jones from Royal. I was just speaking to Mr. Fitzgerald who suggested that I see Mr. Query. I'm not selling anything. I just need to get some figures from him."

"Just a minute," the receptionist replied as she walked towards an office with Query's name on the door.

"Maybe this is not going to be so bad after all," Jones thought.

"Mr. Query will see you for a minute," the receptionist announced as she returned to her desk.

Jones walked into Mr. Query's plushly furnished office. Query was an imposing figure at 6 feet, 4 inches, nearly 300 pounds, and bald. Jones extended her hand, which Query grasped firmly. "What brings you here to see me?" Query inquired.

Jones explained her conversations with Ann Leibman and Kevin Fitzgerald. As she was about to ask her initial series of questions, Query interrupted. "Miss Jones, I frankly don't know what the hell you are doing here!" Query exclaimed. "We settled this issue over six months ago, and now you're bringing it up again. I really don't understand. You people came in with a proposal that was going to cost us more money than we were spending. We know what we're doing. No one is going to come in here and tell us our business."

"Mr. Query," Jones began, trying to remain composed, "the calculations that you were presented with were based upon the equipment that Pierson's was utilizing six months ago. Now that you are contemplating additional purchases, I mentioned to Mr. Fitzgerald that a new comparison should be made. He instructed me to speak with you in order to obtain the information needed to prepare a thorough proposal," Jones tried to explain.

"Fitzgerald! What on earth does Fitzgerald have to do with this? This is none of his damn business. He sat at the same table as I six months ago when we arrived at a decision. Why doesn't he keep his nose out of affairs that don't concern him? We didn't want this program six months ago, we don't want it now!" Query shouted.

"I'm only trying to do my job, Mr. Query. I was not part of the team that presented the proposal six months ago. But from all the information that is available now, I still feel that a CCC would save you money here at Pierson's."

"Don't you understand, Miss Jones? We don't want any outsiders here. You have no control over people that don't work for you. Nothing gets approved around here unless it has my signature on it. That's control. Now I really see no need to waste any more of my time or yours."

"I appreciate your frankness," Jones responded, struggling to find something positive to say.

"Well, that's the kind of man I am, direct and to the point."

"You can say that again," Jones thought. "One other thing before I go, Mr Query. I was noticing the color copies on your desk."

"Yes, I like to send color copies of jobs when getting production estimates. For example, these are of the bogs that we will be using during our fall promotion. I have received several compliments from suppliers who think that by viewing color copies they get a real feel for what I need."

"Well, it just so happens that my division of Royal sells color copiers. At some time it may be more efficient for you to consider a purchase. Let me leave you some literature on the 750 copier which you can review at your leisure." Jones removed a brochure from her briefcase. She attached one of her business cards to it and handed it to Query. As she shook his hand and left the office, Jones noted that she had half an hour before the project of Blake's would be ready for pick-up. She entered the donut shop across the street and as she waited for her coffee, she reviewed her day's activities. She was enthusiastic about the impending color copier sale at CG Advertising, and about the new repro business that she had acquired at Pierson's. But the rest of the day had been discouraging. Not only had she been "shot down" repeatedly, but she'd now have to work extra hard for several days to insure that she would make 100% of budget for the month. "Trying to sell the CCC is even harder than I thought it was," Jones thought.

Topnotch Investment Company

Topnotch Investment Company (TICO) is an international money management firm that specializes in the management of institutional portfolios. The Atlanta, Georgia, office was established in 1972 to service institutions in the southern United States and Latin America. TICO Atlanta manages money for several well-known municipalities, endowments, and foundations, each with a combined asset balance of over $85 million.

In the summer of 1991, TICO Atlanta was one of several firms asked to submit information for a search for a money manager for a central Florida municipality (known as Prospect City). TICO believed that one of the firms competing against it (ABC Management) was using false historical investment performance numbers in its presentation in order to win the Prospect City account. If TICO Atlanta did not address the issue, ABC Management was almost certain to be awarded the account based on its exaggerated investment performance track record.

Background Information

TICO was incorporated as a registered investment advisor in 1971 when the founding partners worked in the trust department of the Citizens & Southern National Bank in Atlanta. In 1978, they purchased the national pension fund business from the bank and formed TICO. From a base of approximately $500 million in assets under management, the nine original partners made the firm into one of the largest, most successful investment counseling companies in the United States. In November 1986, TICO entered into a limited partnership with a major British financial services company to pursue the global investment business. TICO was the general partner. In December 1988, the two firms completed a merger, creating a global investment organization with offices worldwide in North America, Europe, and Asia. The holding company's name was changed to Topnotch Investment Company (TICO) in January 1990.

Today TICO manages $22.9 billion in retirement fund assets for 243 clients located throughout the United States, the United Kingdom, and Japan. Exhibit I shows a partial list of TICO's Florida municipal pension plan accounts, and Exhibit II lists some of TICO's well-known corporate and nonprofit accounts. TICO's business is broadly diversified not only by geography and client type but also by investment mandates. The company manages U.S. equity, fixed income, balanced, and cash portfolios for its clients. These are offered as either separate or commingled accounts. TICO also offers discretionary and advisory services to clients—for example, with respect to investment of funds in stocks, bonds, gold, silver, and real estate.

Source: Dalrymple & Crum, *Sales Mgmt: Concepts & Cases* (Wiley 1995). Prepared by Jonathan N. Goodrich of Florida International University.

EXHIBIT I — Sampling of TICO's Florida Municipal Pension Plan Accounts

City of Boca Raton General Employees	City of Okeechobee General Employees, Police and Fire
City of Boynton Beach Firefighters	City of Pompano Beach General Employees
City of Coral Gables General Employees, Police and Fire	City of Riviera Beach Firefighters
City of Daytona Beach Police and Firefighters	City of Riviera Beach Police
City of Deland Police	City of St. Petersburg Police
City of Ft. Lauderdale Police and Firefighters	City of Sarasota General Employees
City of Hollywood General Employees	City of South Miami General Employees and Police
City of Hollywood Firefighters	City of West Palm Beach Police
City of Miramar Police	City of West Palm Beach Employees
City of North Bay Village General Employees and Police	City of Wilton Manors General Employees and Police
City of Oakland Park General Employees	Town of Davie Police
City of Oakland Park Police and Firefighters	Town of Davie Firefighters

Products/Services

TICO's services include management of corporate pension and profit sharing plans, public funds, trusteed plans, and endowment and foundation funds. The company also offers specialized investment programs for insurance companies and taxable investors. Clients entrust TICO with the management of their assets (cash, stocks, and bonds). Given some basic guidelines and objectives by the client and the legal obligations set by the industry, TICO buys and sells assets for the client. TICO is a low risk, value-oriented manager with an emphasis on steady growth and preservation of capital.

Pricing

TICO receives its compensation for money management and investment counseling services through a fee based on a percentage of the market value of the assets under management. Fees are billed on a quarterly basis. Exhibit III shows TICO's fee schedule and a sample fee for a $25 million balanced account.

Advertising and Promotion

Due to the confidential nature of the industry, TICO's services are marketed in a low-key manner. TICO relies a great deal on prior client satisfaction and industry reputation. Most clients are initially referred to TICO by consultants or actuaries. TICO's marketing representatives also call on the administrators of pension plans. They introduce the firm, explain its investment methods, and try to establish name recognition for TICO in the hope that the prospective client will include TICO in its next money manager search. Marketing representatives also call on consulting firms which often handle the money management search for prospective clients.

Distribution

TICO's services are distributed through its many offices worldwide. TICO may obtain new business through consultants, from clients dissatisfied with their present money management firms, or through deliberate selection by a client. The search for a money management firm is as follows. A money manager search is often conducted by the consultant, or potential client, and the needs of the client are matched with several possible money management firms. A detailed questionnaire is then sent to each potential money manager to be completed and returned. Exhibit IV provides a sample questionnaire asking for information on investment philosophy, performance, and other pertinent facts. This information is used to help narrow the field of appropriate money management firms to four or five. Those that remain are asked to make an oral presentation to the trustees of the plan.

The oral presentation generally includes an overview of the money management firm's style and investment performance track record, and provides the trustees with a chance to meet the individuals who would be managing their money. After the presentation, there is normally a question-and-answer session between the trustees and the money management firm. Finally, the trustees vote to hire the firm that they feel would be most appropriate.

The Prospect City Dilemma

In 1992, TICO Atlanta was included in a search for a money manager by a consultant working for the Prospect City Municipal Pension Plan. TICO was included in the search because it had already established a relationship with the chairman of the board of trustees, who felt that TICO's investment philosophy was compatible with the goals and objectives of Prospect City. Also included in the search was a competitor, ABC Management. The consultant sent detailed questionnaires to several different money management firms. In the questionnaire, the consultant asked for specific, detailed historic investment performance data from each prospective management company. From the responses to the questionnaire, the consultant compiled charts that compared the money managers' investment performance records, as well as the volatility of the returns.

EXHIBIT II	Some of TICO's Corporate and Nonprofit Clients

AT&T
Ameritech
BellSouth Corporation
Boeing Company
The Coca-Cola Company

COMSAT Corporation
The Dow Chemical Company
The Ford Foundation
Frank Russell Trust Co.

Fruehauf Trailer Corporation
General Motors Corp.
J. Paul Getty Trust
Household International, Inc.
Inland Steel Company

Levi Strauss & Company
McDonald's Corp.
National Geographic Society
NCR Corp.

Norfolk Southern Corp.
Raytheon Company
Salvation Army
Southern Company Services, Inc.
The Times Mirror Co.
The University of Virginia

EXHIBIT III	Sample of TICO's Fee Schedule

Equity and Balanced Accounts
  0.75 of 1% on the first $10 million
  0.50 of 1% on the next $10 million
  0.25 of 1% thereafter
Fixed Income Accounts
  0.50 of 1% on the first $10 million
  0.25 of 1% thereafter

Sample Fee for $25 Million Balanced Account

$0.0075 \times \$10,000,000 = \$75,000$ (1st $10 million)
$0.0050 \times \$10,000,000 = \$50,000$ (2nd $10 million)
$0.0025 \times 5,000,000 = \underline{\$12,500}$ (thereafter)
                                $137,500 annual total fee

$137,500/4 quarters = $34,375 per quarter

The historical investment performance information ABC Management submitted put them at the top of the performance charts. Their reported performance seemed to be substantially better than the known market leaders' performance.

The consultant sent TICO a copy of ABC's report, which included performance charts. ABC Management's performance was unbelievable. TICO knew that ABC Management was on the verge of losing several accounts because of poor investment performance. TICO's marketing representative spoke with another consultant who monitored ABC Management on two accounts, and the consultant confirmed that ABC Management was doing poorly. TICO was convinced that ABC Management was using false investment performance numbers but was unsure how to proceed. If nothing was done, it seemed likely that ABC would get the account.

EXHIBIT IV	Sample Questionnaire: Guidelines for Submissions/Required Information

1. *Structure/Organization—Experience*
   a. Summarize organizational structure and describe location of main and subsidiary offices.
   b. Describe any affiliation with banks, insurance companies, or brokers.
   c. Describe experience and qualification of managers who would handle this account. Is the manager available to attend quarterly meetings and any additional meetings upon request?
   d. Does your organization or a separate division of your organization devote all of its time to investment management? Describe availability of staff for Board consultation.
   e. How long has your organization managed corporate retirement and municipal plan assets?
   f. What is the approximate current level of assets under management? What percentage of total managed assets do employee benefit assets represent? How many funds do you manage? How many municipalities? How many public funds in Florida?
   g. Do you maintain a "recommended list"? How extensive is it (number of issues)? What are basic criteria for a stock being added to the list? Deleted? Who controls the addition or deletion of securities from the list? Is a recommended percentage distribution of particular stocks or industries given to the portfolio manager? May the manager deviate from the list or a recommended percentage distribution?
   h. How would you characterize your style of management of retirement and/or municipal fund assets?

continued

EXHIBIT IV continued

2. *Research and Client Contact*
   a. Describe briefly research facilities available and how used. In-house capabilities and availability of information; outside support.
   b. Type and frequency of reports (furnish a sample copy). Clearly understandable statement and accountings considered essential.

3. *Investment Performance*
   a. What average annual rate of return can we reasonably expect over the next three to five years (assuming you have sole investment discretion)?
   b. Supply accurate representative performance figures by year over last five-year period concerning:
      (1) Similar discretionary pension fund accounts.
      (2) Other discretionary pension fund accounts.

4. *Fixed Income Assets*
   a. Explain *briefly* your recommendations for handling the fixed income portfolio.
   b. What are the main contributing factors to turnover in one of your bond portfolios?
   c. Please give an indication of your outlook for the bond market in the next quarter. Nest twelve months.
   d. What is a realistic rate of return to expect from a bond fund over the next three to five years?

5. *Accounting Management Process*
   a. Describe *briefly* the manner of handling this account; that is, one investment advisor in charge, daily review, and continuous supervision?
   b. Describe *briefly* investment selection and decision-making process. Committee action? Can qualified investment advisor act without delay?
   c. Describe procedures for measuring investment performance.
   d. Are individual investment advisors evaluated by you on their investment performance?
   e. Describe limitations imposed by you on total assets volume per account manager; also maximum number of accounts handled per manager.
   f. Do you have established operational policies with continuing internal supervision so as to prevent excess workloads on individual account managers?

6. *References*
   a. Please provide five references of similar type accounts: fund name, location, contact person, and phone number.
   b. Please provide representative client list.

7. *Fees*
   Please explain your fee structure and show fees for a fund our size, annual contribution rate, etc. (Show dollar rate as well as formula.)

MCI Vision (A) [Condensed]

In early April 1991, Steven Zecola, vice president of marketing in MCI Communications' Eastern division, was considering what actions to take concerning divisional marketing efforts for MCI Vision, a long-distance service designed for small- and medium-sized businesses. Vision, introduced in July 1990, had surpassed 1990 goals. But 1991 first-quarter results indicated that sales were running 50% below target levels. Zecola was considering options ranging from revised pricing policies to new customer and salesforce promotions. Simultaneously, corporate product management at MCI was developing plans to revitalize Vision sales.

Company and Industry Background

MCI, the second-largest U.S. provider of long-distance telecommunications services, with 1990 revenues of $7.7 billion **(Exhibit I),** offered voice, data, and messaging services including telex, electronic mail, customized facsimile, and advanced network management services. Strategic priorities included growing faster than the industry, competing in all significant long-distance markets, expanding MCI's global presence, and "aggressively driving cost efficiencies through automation, rigorous expense control, [and] organizational efficiencies."

Source: Professor Frank V. Cespedes and Research Associate Laura Goode prepared this case as the basis for class discussion rather than to illustrate either effective or ineffective handling of an administrative situation. Certain company data, while useful for discussion purposes, have been disguised. Copyright © 1993 by the President and Fellows of Harvard College. To order copies, call (617) 495-6117 or write the Publishing Division, Harvard Business School, Boston, MA 02163. No part of this publication may be reproduced, stored, in a retrieval system, used in a spreadsheet, or transmitted in any form or by any means—electronic, mechanical, photocopying, recording, or otherwise—without the permission of Harvard Business School.

EXHIBIT I	MCI Communications Corporation: Selected Financial Information for Years Ended December 31 (in millions, except per common share amounts)				
	1990	1989	1988	1987	1986
Summary of Operations					
Revenue	$ 7,680	$ 6,471	$ 5,137	$ 3,939	$ 3,592
Total operating expenses	(7,060)	(5,489)	(4,553)	(3,704)	(4,036)
Income (loss) from operations	620	982	584	235	(444)
Net interest expense	(192)	(205)	(198)	(169)	(124)
Income (loss) before extraordinary item	299	603	356	78	(481)
Net income (loss)	299	553	346	64	(498)
Earnings (loss) applicable to common shareholders	270	529	334	64	(498)
Earnings (loss) per common share:					
Income (loss) before extraordinary item	1.06	2.26	1.27	.27	(1.75)
Loss on early debt retirements		(.17)	(.04)	(.05)	(.06)
Net income (loss)	1.06	2.09	1.23	.22	(1.81)
Cash dividends per common share	.10				
Balance sheet					
Gross investment in communications system	$8,708	$7,345	$6,577	$5,686	$5,284
Annual investment in communications system	1,283	1,052	896	619	1,074
Total assets	8,249	6,484	5,954	5,380	5,258
Long-term debt	3,147	2,241	2,677	2,663	2,576
Stockholders' equity	2,340	1,995	1,359	1,279	1,212

MCI was founded in 1968 and, for over two decades, had waged legal and regulatory as well as marketing battles with AT&T and others, requiring (as one executive explained) "high leverage and frequent brushes with bankruptcy, a willingness to repeatedly alter plans in the face of new threats and opportunities, and low tolerance for systems and wallflowers." One result, many observers believed, was a distinct organizational environment. Throughout the 1980s, the average age of employees was less than 31 and, while MCI had grown to 24,000 employees by 1991, attrition rates had exceeded 30% in some years. William McGowan, MCI's chairman since 1968, had repeatedly emphasized that "the greatest handicap [in running a company] is that organizations hate to change. You're always at risk for getting chains of committees, manuals, procedures." The 1990 annual report noted that "MCI has succeeded in this fast-changing industry because we put a premium on attracting and developing resourceful, independent, creative people who know how to drive and manage change. . . . We ensure that our people have the work environment to think for themselves and maximize their contributions." One trade journal (*Computerworld*, 8/21/89) stated that "MCI's culture encourages frequent and open communication among all employees . . . the corporate culture of fast action and no bureaucracy borders on anarchy, according to some observers." In comments to the casewriters, MCI managers described the company atmosphere in the following terms:

> There aren't many formal processes or defined career paths here. During my seven years with the company, I've worked in marketing, sales, MIS, finance, and now international operations, and I had offers from legal and engineering. Cross-functional mobility is encouraged, especially for marketing people who, in a high fixed-cost service operation, must work with many groups in developing products, setting prices, and other activities.

* * * * *

> What I both love and hate about MCI is that everybody thinks everything is their job. The positive aspect is that people want to be part of a crisis, not run away from it; and we're able to do things quickly and responsively in the marketplace. The negative aspect is the redundancy and long hours that often result from this "all-hands-on-deck" approach.

* * * * *

> I had worked for GE and then McKinsey, and when I got to MCI it was a week before anyone explained to me how to get an office, payroll number, and other basics, and another week before I realized this place is really a vast sorority and fraternity network that operates on move-or-be-moved principles. Our managers are young and must have a high tolerance for frustration, but they're given good compensation and significant responsibilities for their age and experience. Also, we often have a chance to define those responsibilities and make a real impact on the company and market.

Company Developments

In the 1980s, MCI's revenues grew at a 26% compounded rate as the firm gained market share from about 1% to over 12% by 1990 (see **Exhibit II**). Until the mid-1980s, the

EXHIBIT II The U.S. Long-Distance Industry

Long-Distance Revenues[a] (billions of dollars)

	1985	1986	1987	1988	1989	1990
AT&T	27.5	32.3	35.2	35.4	34.6	35.0
MCI	2.5	3.6	3.9	4.9	6.2	6.7[b]
US Sprint	1.2	2.9	3.3	3.2	5.8	6.0
Others	1.3	2.9	3.3	3.2	5.8	6.0
Total	32.5	41.7	48.7	46.7	52.4	53.7

Long-Distance Market Shares[a] (percent of total)

	1985	1986	1987	1988	1989	1990
AT&T	84.6	78.1	77.9	75.5	68.0	67.2
MCI	7.6	8.7	8.6	10.4	12.2	12.9[b]
US Sprint	3.6	6.2	6.2	7.2	8.4	8.4
Others	4.1	7.0	7.3	6.9	11.4	11.5
Total	100.0	100.0	100.0	100.0	100.0	100.0

Average Rate Per Switched Access Minute ($ per minute)

	1984	1985	1986	1987	1988	1989	1990	84-90 CAGR
AT&T	.279	.276	.260	.227	.211	.191	.176	−7.4%
Other carriers	.159	.173	.191	.154	.151	.172	.170	1.2%
% of AT&T Rate	56.9%	62.9	73.4	67.9	71.3	90.0	96.7	—
Total	.259	.255	.244	.206	.192	.184	.174	−6.4%

1989 Long-Distance Marketplace, by Industry Segment

Industry Segment	Industry Revenues ($ Billions)	Estimated 1989-1995 CAGR	Market Share			
			AT&T	MCI	Sprint	Other
Basic long distance	$24.4	10%	65%	16%	11%	8%
International	6.7	20	80	12	8	0
Private line	5.6	15	87	8	4	0
800	5.0	15	87	8	4	1
WATS	4.1	9	70	15	10	5
Payphone	2.0	10	80	8	7	5
Data	1.0	22	89	7	3	1
900	1.0	30	88	2	4	6
Other	1.5	N/A	N/A	N/A	N/A	N/A
Total	50.9	N/A	68	12	8	12

Source: North American Telecommunications Association, Annual Report 1990.
[a]Excludes local exchange carriers.
[b]Excludes Telecom USA

company focused largely on the residential market where the divestiture of the Bell System allowed all U.S. customers to choose among long-distance companies on an equal-access basis. MCI concentrated much of its marketing and other resources on winning and keeping customers in this $20 billion segment where calls were typically made off-peak when there is ample network capacity. The company also decentralized into seven largely autonomous domestic divisions in order to align with the regional phone companies that provided local exchange connections for customers. Beginning in the mid-1980s, MCI began efforts to attract more large corporate customers (i.e., greater than $50,000/month in long-distance business), a segment where, in 1985, AT&T had an estimated 95% share. Corporate customers were typically located in major urban areas (where MCI had installed new fiber optic capacity), and their traffic ran primarily during business hours (when rates were highest).

The company established a National Accounts Program in 1986 and, by 1991, had an estimated 12% share of the large business/government segment and (according to FCC estimates) a 17% share of the top 250 users of long-distance telecommunications services.

Throughout this period, MCI also expanded its product line and, with more than $7 billion of capital investments, expanded and upgraded its network. One result was improved service (via, by the end of 1991, a completely digital network), operating efficiencies, and new capacity that made the incremental costs of adding customers very low. Another result was the development of software-defined network management services that combined many of the advantages of private networks with the efficiencies of the shared public network. Vnet was MCI's flagship offering in this category, and was targeted at large corporate accounts that sought a variety of network management, accounting, billing and pricing features without the special equipment and setup fees required by a private network. A third result was the increased ability to offer customized billing and other services (previously available only to large telecom users) to the General Business segment (GB), which comprised seven million small- and mid-sized companies with $500-$50,000/month in long-distance usage. Vision was MCI's initial such offering to this segment which, in 1990, represented an estimated $19 billion market.

To help position the firm for the 1990s, MCI undertook in 1990 a major acquisition and reorganization. In April 1990 MCI acquired for $1.25 billion Telecom USA, the fourth-largest U.S. long-distance carrier with a 1.4% market share and over $700 million in revenues. Telecom had grown at nearly 30% per annum since its founding in 1984 by targeting primarily small- and medium-sized businesses with competitive prices and several innovative products such as special calling cards that allowed customers to set up conference calls from any touch-tone telephone.

In November 1990, MCI reorganized from seven geographic regions to a structure aligned by customer segments (**Exhibit III**). Business customers were managed by four regional divisions (primarily responsible for sales and other field marketing activities), with support from a headquarters business marketing unit (primarily responsible for product development and product management). Residential customers, previously the responsibility of each geographic region, were now managed via a headquarters consumer markets unit responsible for nationwide advertising, telemarketing, customer service, and other activities in this segment. In addition, a network services unit addressed the network requirements of both markets. (The company's international operations were unaffected by the reorganization.)

Corporate Product Marketing

Within the Business Markets unit, the Corporate Product Marketing organization was divided into three categories: Large Accounts (over $50,000/month), General Business (under $50,000/month), and a Government Systems unit.

In the Large Accounts unit, there were product management groups for (1) Inbound Products (800 and 900 services); (2) Vnet (an outbound virtual-network service sold by MCI's National Accounts and Major Accounts sales groups to large corporate customers); (3) Network Management Services that provided customers with the ability to monitor, analyze, reconfigure, and control their MCI voice and data services; (4) Data Services (a group of high-speed data and private-line applications); and (5) Integrated Billing Services which managed the billing procedures for other MCI products. Billing and invoicing modifications were generally the most complex product changes for network engineers and, due to MCI's investments in software, considered by management a source of potential competitive advantage.

In the General Business unit, there were product management groups for: (1) Dial 1 (long-distance voice service); (2) PRISM/PRISM PLUS (a volume-discounted package of outbound domestic and international long-distance services targeted at GB accounts with monthly billings under $50); (3) Corporate Account Service (CAS) and CAS PLUS (special discounts and reporting features for GB accounts with over $2,500/month in billings); (4) Operator Services (domestic and international services such as collect calls, third-party charging, person-to-person calls, and calling assistance); (5) Messaging Services (various products including electronic mail, facsimile, and telex services); (6) Vision (see below); and (7) MCI Preferred (the newest GB product, introduced in March 1991 and targeted at accounts with $50-$1,500/month in billings; like MCI Vision, Preferred provided voice, data, fax, calling card, and international services in one package, with a consolidated invoice and combined volume discount).

Individual product managers were measured primarily in terms of revenues, although the president of the Business Markets unit had profit-and-loss responsibility. Product development was a joint function of the product marketing groups (based in Washington, D.C.) and the development group (based in Richardson, Texas) which managed product specifications including the software and associated information systems. At MCI, product development had traditionally been "opportunistic and fast," in the words of one executive. In 1988, for example, William McGowan noticed a surge in ads for fax machines in the *New York Times* and decided MCI should create the first customized fax network which, by 1991, generated substantial revenues for the firm. Product pricing was the joint responsibility of corporate Product Marketing, Business Analysis (a unit within Finance), and Development; the former two groups first generated a joint proposal for a new product or enhancement and then submitted it to Development, which estimated costs for each feature. Commenting on their interaction, a Large Accounts product manager noted:

EXHIBIT III MCI Organization (November 1990)

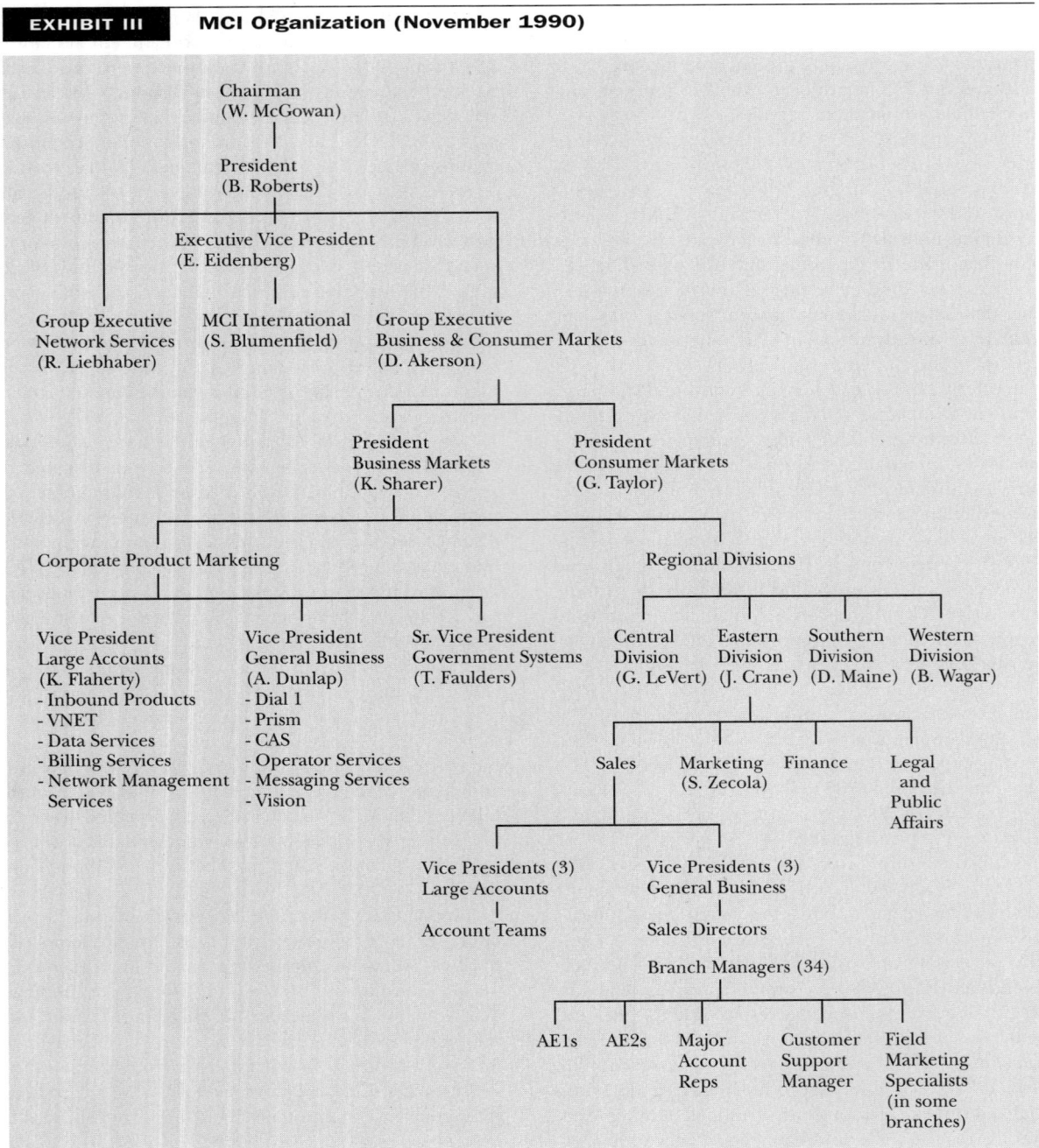

I compete with other product managers for shared Development resources. So, much of my time is spent with Business Analysis rationalizing my list of needs and trying to place my list higher on Development's list of priorities. A key company asset is the shared network, and that means Development must look at the interrelationships implicated by each product introduction or modification. The complexity of this increases as software-based services become a bigger part of the products MCI offers. As a product manager, it's great when you get the attention and frustrating when you don't; in the latter situation, you try to solicit more input and support from divisional managers concerning needed features.

A General Business product manager commented:

I sell my initiatives based on the incremental revenue opportunities in this segment: GB represents a big opportunity, *if* we get to market first with innovative services that leverage our network capabilities. Historically, however, MCI has focused Development attention on residential and then corporate markets, and some still perceive GB as a smaller, "third-class" priority in comparison to those mass-market and large-volume segments.

A Development manager explained:

> Once Product Marketing defines the product need, we assess the product requirements and costs by talking to other functional groups. MCI has few guidelines for program management. The good news is that we have talented, energetic people who cross internal boundaries to get things done. As a result, we've introduced more than 50 products in the past few years. The bad news is that the company is sometimes prey to the "hot project" syndrome, and the rest of the business ticks on while people focus on this project. Also, product overlap becomes more likely as we expand our offerings.

Commenting on product plans, McGowan noted that "you have to be big enough to be recognized as a candidate for anybody's communication needs and to afford the systems, services, support and personnel. Some number, around 25% of the market or more, has got to be within your capability for you to be considered a full-service carrier. We're going to introduce new services as fast as we can. We're going to provide multiple services to multiple market segments, from residential to the most sophisticated multinational [firm]."

Industry Developments

In 1991, AT&T, MCI, and Sprint held about 90% of the long-distance market. About 400 firms accounted for the remainder; most were resellers that purchased services at bulk rates from the major carriers, and competed regionally for small business customers. Three developments were expected to impact industry competition during the coming decade.

First, after double-digit growth through the 1980s, estimates of domestic long-distance growth were 5% annually for the 1990s. International growth was expected to be higher.

Second, pricing pressures and marketing expenditures in many segments were expected to continue increasing. In 1989, the FCC granted AT&T "Tariff 12" permission to offer large accounts volume discounts (often, 10%-30%) under 18-36 month contracts. Competitors, including MCI, responded by offering similar contracts. By 1991, the majority of large corporate accounts were believed to have signed such contracts. Hence, less large-account business was "up for bid," in the words of one executive. In the residential segment, advertising and promotional expenditures had increased dramatically in recent years. In 1990, AT&T was estimated to have doubled its ad spending to nearly $600 million, while MCI and Sprint each increased their ad spending from about $50 million to $75 million. In contrast to earlier years, much of AT&T's advertising was aimed at taking customers away from other carriers rather than increasing usage and primary demand. Ad spending also reflected a need among carriers to introduce and explain a greater variety of services, rather than what industry observers called the POTS products ("plain-old-telephone-service") of past years. Similarly, each carrier had increased its number of field salespeople and telemarketers. one analyst noted that, in recent years "the various players have been employing only one of the four P's in the market share war—price. [But] the industry is now exercising the other three Ps: product, promotion and place [distribution channels]."

Third, technology affected product development and selling requirements. Data communications was a faster-growing percentage of commercial long-distance usage than voice communications. Technology was also making more common enhanced and combined services such as computer transmissions, electronic mail, videotext, teleconferencing, and voice mail; and software-defined network made it more feasible to "down-market" such services to smaller customers as well as corporate accounts. Similarly, an increasingly important source of product differentiation was the billing options provided to customers. Often these were enhancements to existing products (e.g., management reports); but new billing formats had also become the basis for new products. In turn, these developments were expected to alter cost structures in the industry. According to one analyst:

> [In the past] there was little differentiation of products and services across the network; hence, the facilities base overwhelmed all else in the investment process. Barriers to entry were the scale of facilities. [But] software and marketing expenses are beginning to outweigh facility expense. The "down-marketing" of services to the lower end broadens the market for applications. The barriers to entry move up to relative scales of software and sales expense. Brand-name recognition and product differentiation will be important factors.

MCI's Eastern Division

After the 1990 reorganization, the four divisions reporting through the Business Markets unit were structured identically (**Exhibit III**) and measured primarily in terms of contribution (i.e., net revenue minus expenses). The Eastern division covered 13 states and Washington, D.C. It was the largest revenue producer among the four divisions, generating more than $1.5 billion in 1990 and included about 60% of Fortune-1000 headquarters. Its president, Jonathan Crane, noted, "For 20 years MCI necessarily focused on areas such as building a network, hiring a salesforce, making billing work, and getting product out. Now we must use these established strengths in an environment where price competition is less feasible. Service, support, and applications-oriented marketing will increasingly be the basis of competition."

In 1990, Large Account customers accounted for more than 30% of Eastern Division revenues, General Business customers sold via the field salesforce for more than 40%, and General Business customers sold via telemarketing for less than 20%. Divisional plans for 1991 called for a 10% revenue increase, with the growth driven primarily by GB segments.

EASTERN DIVISION MARKETING ORGANIZATION
Steven Zecola became the division's vice president of marketing in January 1991. The marketing department was responsible for (1) achieving budget and revenue plans for Silver segment (under $500/month in telecom billings) which, for 1991, was $290 million; and (2) providing support to the field sales organization in achieving Large Account and GB revenue plans. Reporting to Zecola (see **Exhibit IV**) were the following functions.

Commercial Telemarketing was responsible for achieving Silver segment goals. It sold primarily outbound products such as Prism, Vision, 800 services, and Preferred via three telemarketing centers. Target accounts were classified as Silver or Gold ($500-$2,500/month in billings). Average monthly billings were $1,400. Telemarketing reps were compensated via a base salary and commissions tied to customers' line usage. Two types of sales were tracked and rewarded: services to new accounts and new services to current accounts.

Commercial Customer Service provided free 800 access to small businesses to answer questions regarding MCI's services and to resolve service problems. Separately, this unit also assigned Customer Service Engineers (CSEs) to accounts generating at least $3,000/month. CSE's reported to branch managers and had dotted-line reporting relationships with marketing.

Technical Services provided technical sales support for larger customers involved in complex installations or voice-and-data enhancements.

Sales Operations was created in late 1990 and included sales-reporting (installations, disconnects, and backlogs by product and segment), and sales compensation administration.

Planning and Analysis identified new business opportunities and helped to coordinate various sales and marketing programs.

Training was responsible for sales training which, in 1991, was being revised and expanded.

Alternate Channel Marketing was responsible for negotiating co-marketing agreements to sell MCI services with other organizations. The group also pursued Sales Agent programs with authorized third parties to sell MCI services on commission. Agents included office equipment vendors, telecommunications consultants, financial planners, and others.

Product Marketing was responsible for coordinating product plans with corporate marketing units, developing strategies for assigned products, intrastate pricing, competitive analysis, and field sales support. One product manager explained:

> Product development and interstate pricing are corporate marketing responsibilities. We are supposed to take the product and price as a given and then get field support and execution. But we do have some input and, if Corporate won't make changes we perceive as necessary or fund a division-specific promotion, I can make my case with Steve Zecola or Jonathan Crane for divisional money. There's no formalized process. I must convince the right people it's the right thing to do.

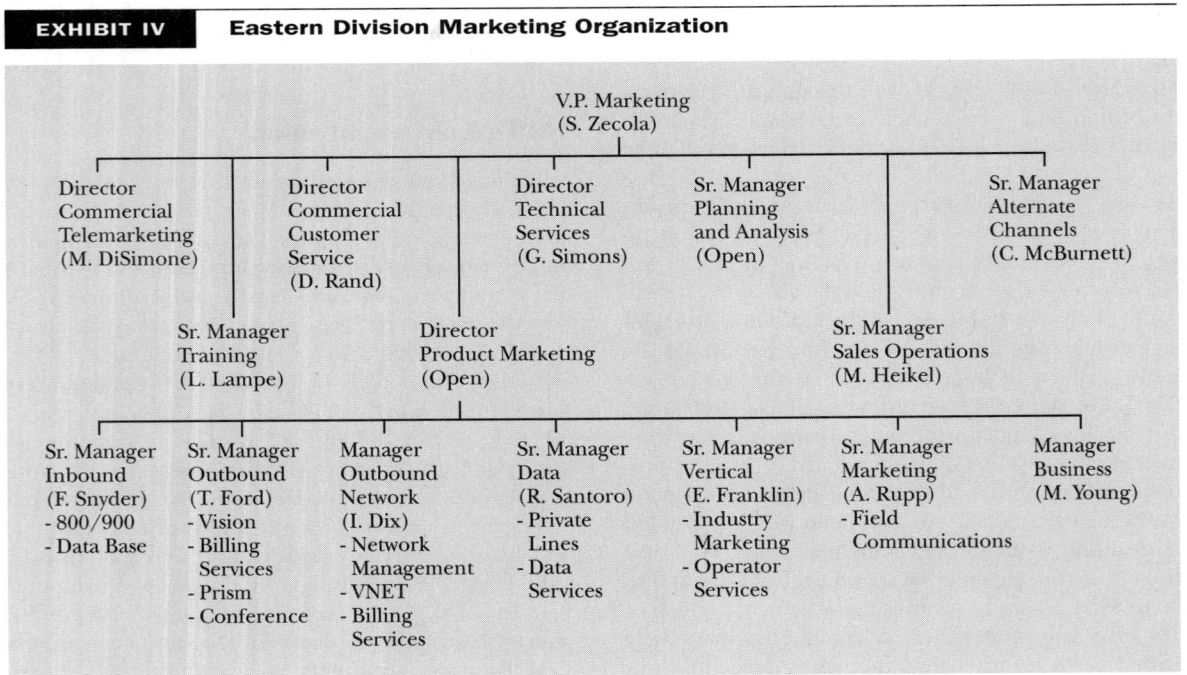

EXHIBIT IV Eastern Division Marketing Organization

MCI placed its products into four categories: Commercial Outbound, Inbound, Network Services, and Data/Private Line. Each category had a division product manager and assistant product managers who were measured on revenue contribution.

Commercial Outbound included products (Dial 1, PRISM Plus, CAS/CAS Plus, MCI Card, Fax, Vision, and Preferred) that generated about 50% of divisional revenues, with the older Dial 1 and PRISM products as the largest contributors. Dial 1 was traditional WATS service, and PRISM was a long-distance service based on the actual distance of each call, targeted at accounts generating less than $50/month. Preferred was targeted at accounts generating $50-$1,500/month, and Vision at accounts of $1,500-$50,000/month. Terri Ford, senior manager for Outbound products, noted that "Dial 1 and Prism are now commodities with little feature differentiation from competing offers. Our field salesforce is comfortable selling them. But Preferred and Vision must be marketed on the basis of their application and enhanced-service benefits."

Commercial Inbound included 800 and 900 inbound services. Fran Snyder, senior manager for Inbound, noted that these services "are not commodities and imply big switching costs to customers," in contrast to Outbound products where customer switching costs were generally lower: "For example, a credit card company has its 800 number printed on each card. You must demonstrate significant new applications or features to get them to switch." To encourage more attention to Inbound products, Fran Snyder often implemented division promotions and sales incentives, beyond those offered by corporate marketing.

Network Services was managed by Ian Dix whose primary responsibility was Vnet. Vnet was traditionally targeted at large accounts with billings of more than $50,000 a month. However, Dix noted that "in the past three years, probably 80% of national and major accounts in the division have signed multiyear agreements. Short-term, that revenue is untouchable: either I already have it or can't get it. So, I have geared my 1991 plan to focus more on GB accounts and the field salesforce that sells to those accounts, because that's where the potential business is. However, Vnet is more complex than most GB sales efforts."

Data Products included private networks and high-speed data services that generated about 5% of the division's 1990 revenues. Richard Santoro, senior manager for Data, explained that "Data has been a second-class citizen at MCI: the sales cycle is long-term, technically complex, applications-oriented, involves both Telecom and MIS managers, and AT&T has been embedded at most accounts. So, our salespeople have not devoted much time to these products. But data communications are especially important for the many multinational accounts headquartered in the Eastern Division, and our enhanced network gives us more technical capability here."

Also part of the Product Marketing unit was Field Communications, which distributed and coordinated information from corporate and divisional product managers to field sales. Meg Reilly, manager of divisional field communications, noted, "Part of my job is to protect the field from information overload. Every product group is vying for field attention." A key vehicle for internal communications was MCI Mail, an electronic mail service which connected every employee and generated more than 400,000 messages daily throughout the company.

Eastern Division Sales Organization

The division's sales organization had 34 branches, each headed by a branch manager who reported to the division director of sales. Starting in 1990, the National Account salespeople had a separate structure and reported directly to corporate headquarters. There were 1,800 salespeople in the Eastern Division, and 100 National Account managers.

Branch managers were paid a salary and incentive compensation tied to two factors: 60% of the incentive depended upon Net Revenue Increase (NRI) and 40% on New Growth Revenue (NGR). NRI had recently been instituted to focus attention on customer retention and usage levels; NGR had previously been the sole component of branch incentives and was calculated by multiplying the branch sales headcount by the quota assigned to each sales rep level. One branch manager explained: "If a branch starts the year at $20 million in usage revenues, it must be at, say, $24 million by year end. It's not that difficult to gain 20% in business from new accounts, but now we must also be sure not to lose business from existing customers."

Reporting to each branch manager were two to five sales managers, each of whom had four to eight salespeople as direct reports. Most salespeople were assigned geographic territories, but some were responsible for Major Accounts. Sales managers were assigned monthly quotas based on sales headcount in each of three categories: (1) Account Executive 1 (AE1s) called on businesses with billings of $500-$2,500/month; this was the entry-level field sales position, and was staffed by people in their early to mid-20s with about two years' previous sales experience (either with another firm or in MCI telemarketing); (2) Account Executive 2 (AE2s) called on businesses with billings of $2,500-$30,000/month; AE2s were typically AE1s with one to two years of successful performance; (3) Major Account reps called on businesses with billings of $30,000-$400,000/month (i.e., up to National Account status); about half of Major Account reps were outside hires and half were AE2s with two to three years of successful performance.

All salespeople were paid a salary plus commission. Two types of revenue were tracked for all rep levels: New Revenue was business produced from a new account during its first year of usage, and commissions were established at a flat rate but uncapped; Growth Revenue was additional business generated from an existing account, and an accelerated commission rate structure provided for higher levels of incentive pay as higher levels of Growth Revenue were achieved. AE2s and Major Account reps were also paid incentives for Retention Revenue (the billings MCI received monthly from the account) and were responsible for ensuring that Retention Revenue was equal to or above the prior month's.

While incentive earnings opportunities were uncapped, at target the average AE1 had total compensation of $34,000, about one-third of which was incentive compensation; the average AE2 had total compensation of $45,000, about one-half of which was incentive compensation (with 20% of the incentive tied to Retention Revenue); and the average Major Account rep had total compensation of $68,000, about one-half of which was incentive compensation (with 30% of the incentive tied to Retention Revenue). In 1990, 28% of the division's salespeople achieved assigned quota targets and the turnover rate among salespeople was 35%.

Also reporting to each branch was a Customer Support Manager who managed branch CSEs, who were organized in three levels comparable to those of the salesforce. All CSEs were responsible for post-sale support, including managing the installation process, conducting account reviews, and dealing with any reporting or billing issues that might arise. CSE1s and CSE2s were each assigned 30-50 accounts; Major Account CSEs had an average of 10, and were typically involved in account planning as well as post-sales activities. CSEs also sold add-on features and additional customer sites for MCI services at established accounts, and received revenue credit (along with the assigned salesperson) for such sales. CSE compensation was primarily base salary, but as of 1990 they were also paid bonuses for new sales, and about 10% of CSE compensation was tied to selling activities.

In the industry, according to one magazine, "MCI's salespeople have earned a reputation as tigers, which they need to be." In recent years, moreover, MCI had recruited numerous salespeople and sales managers from leading computer, business equipment, and other firms. One branch manager, previously with IBM and Raytheon Data Systems, noted that "the youth, vitality, and aggressiveness in the field are a delight, and absolutely necessary when you have about a 15% share in a consolidating business. But MCI is now the dominant vendor in many accounts, and a focus on customer retention and net revenue increase is a change-of-pace for many in the field." A Major Account manager commented: "AT&T is definitely more aggressive lately. They're cutting more special deals and changing prices, things they were very rigid about in the past. Also, their traditional attitude was to focus on the biggest users. But now they're putting in more people at the Major Account level and, to a lesser extent, at GB accounts as well. But we still are more flexible in responding to customers, have an advantage in billing and many other 'soft cost' areas, and in my opinion still out-hustle the competition."

FIELD MARKETING SPECIALIST   In mid-1990, the Eastern Division established in certain branches a field marketing specialist position (FMS). The initial goal was to provide a field generalist position to assist salespeople with product questions and cross-selling strategies, while also developing managers with both marketing and sales experience. The first FMSs were mid-level salespeople with strong track records, and the anticipated career path was from FMS to a product manager and/or branch manager position. However, due to Vision support requirements, FMSs soon focused efforts on this product, providing technical and applications support during the introduction. One salesperson noted:

> The FMS position is great. It helps me make sense of a broad line and, when I make an important customer presentation, I can focus on the products I'm comfortable with and have the FMS present the more specialized products. I often learn more from listening to the FMS talk to a customer than from a formal product training session. Also, because the FMS has field sales experience, they're accessible and I know many of them personally.

Based on this feedback (and funding requirements), management in August 1990 changed the FMS from a generalist position to one focused on specific products. In 1990, there were twelve FMS positions and the key products were Vision, 800 and Private Line services.

Beginning in 1991, FMSs reported directly to branch managers with dotted-lines to appropriate division product managers (who, with the branch manager, had input into FMS hiring decisions). FMS compensation (a combination of salary and incentive pay) was based on the branch's sales performance in the FMS's assigned products. Deciding whether to hire an FMS was made the branch manager's prerogative. One branch manager noted that "my branch quota remains the same if I hire an FMS, so the decision is based largely on whether I believe an FMS will help generate more revenue than an additional salesperson would. We have five FMSs in this region, and what's evolving is that each has a product-group specialty which we share among the participating branches. My FMS probably spends 90% of her time on branch-specific activities and 10% as the product specialist for other branches." Another commented that "having the field pay for a resource like the FMS has a long history at MCI where cash constraints, decentralization, and monthly quotas taught field managers not to expect centralized supports or subsidies. Also, paying for the FMS drives accountability and forces branch managers to look closely at how the resource is used and whether it contributes to goals."

While the FMS position continued to receive favorable feedback, some marketing managers were concerned that, with branch funding and a product specialty emphasis, the FMS "will become another tactical, short-term position. Branch managers won't allocate money for products requiring longer-term FMS support activities, and some will use the position as a slot to place field reps who are not meeting quota."

Vision

By mid-1989, many MCI managers were concerned about the company's position in the GB market. In addition, as one corporate product manager noted, "Our development priorities and monies had been going to our Vnet virtual network service for a few years, and [like other carriers] we had no product designed specifically for GB accounts who [unlike corporate customers] have not traditionally viewed telecom services as a strategic investment."

Having identified this gap, debate then ensued about how to address it. Some managers argued for bringing Vnet down market by repackaging and repricing the product for smaller-volume users. In addition to rapid development time, they cited the advantages of keeping growing GB accounts on the same product as their usage increased. The other option was to develop a new product, based on the Vnet platform but with features and pricing structures customized for GB market needs. By late 1989, the latter option had been chosen for a number of reasons. It was determined that current Vnet software could not easily handle the additional volume of transactions, invoices and reports that GB customers would require. In addition, as one corporate marketing manager involved in the Vision development process explained:

> MCI had worked hard to establish Vnet as a high-end product for large corporate accounts, and we didn't want to dilute that positioning. Conversely, by 1989, Vnet had many features not needed by GB customers, and we wanted a simple product that could be sold in two or three sales calls without all the analyses that a Vnet sale to a large account requires. We also needed a very different billing approach. Vnet accounts have in-house telecom staffs that can analyze telecom usage. But GB accounts don't, and our market research had determined that simple, visible management controls such as call detail reports would be key features in a GB-oriented product. We also needed to establish an identify for MCI in the GB segment and a stand-alone product that the salesforce selling into GB customers could rally around.

Development of Vision took nine months from establishment of a project team to product introduction. In late 1989, corporate management set an announcement date of June 1990 in order to coincide with a national sales meeting. In addition, as one corporate marketing manager noted, "The key with Vision was getting to market quickly: it would be a unique offering in this segment. So we wanted to keep it a competitive secret and maximize the first-mover advantages inherent in an applications-driven product." As a result, most divisional product managers learned about specific Vision features at the time of introduction.

When introduced, Vision offered customers a variety of features and management reports (**Exhibit V**). Vision pricing was set at a simple flat rate per minute domestically and with a single invoice that aggregated into a volume discount usage across an account's locations. Initially targeted at GB customers spending between $500 and $50,000 per month, Vision altered MCI's product portfolio as indicated in **Exhibit VI**.

INTRODUCTION AND 1990 RESULTS   In June 1990, Vision was introduced to 300 branch managers and sales managers at the national sales meeting in Washington, D.C. Several senior executives addressed the group about Vision, emphasizing its many unique features, the opportunity it represented among small-business customers who spent more than $500/month, and its status as MCI's flagship offering in the GB segment, designed to replace PRISM as the product of choice and focus of sales attention at qualified GB accounts. An MCI mail message describing the product release and associated customer benefits was also sent that evening to all branches and a TV ad campaign (with the theme, "Big-business long distance for your business") was begun. In addition, a number of customer promotions were included as part of the introduction, including one free month of service, a credit of up to $1,000 to customers that signed up by August 31, and MCI's assumption of any PIC costs (i.e., fees paid by users to local Bell operating companies for changing carriers), as well as a sales bonus for Vision installations through August 31, 1990.

The field's response was immediate and positive. In the Eastern Division, a number of significant Vision sales were made the day after the product announcement. One sales manager noted, "Our people were hungry for a good GB-oriented product, and we could all see that Vision had many features that competing products didn't have." R. Santoro, who in 1990 helped to establish the division's new FMS position, explained:

> Vision was the perfect product to roll out with the FMS program. The salesperson's key task is finding the right customer application for Vision functionality. This means the rep must often deal with issues that go beyond telecommunications. It became crucial to have someone in the branch who knew the product in detail and could help develop application selling skills. Vision and our FMS program were developed independently, but the timing coincided perfectly. So, by late July of 1990, we had put together a Vision presentation that makes most rock concerts look boring and, over the next six weeks, our new FMSs took that show on the road to every branch office.

A division marketing manager noted, "When Vision was introduced, everything else was put on hold for weeks because we didn't have any real advance notice yet realized fast movement was essential. Every product manager was assigned to work on the project exclusively for the first month, and we implemented a training program which included product features and detailed application training." Sharon Lovit was appointed divisional product manager for Vision and, in addition to customer calls, conducted numerous "roundtable" sessions in branch offices where she discussed rep feedback concerning customer responses

EXHIBIT V MCI Vision

Features	Benefits	Applications
Flat rate	Provide simple, easy-to-follow pricing structure	Allows company to forecast expenditures and control costs
Consolidate invoice access methods	Combines traffic and access methods from all locations, for optimum telecom savings	Communications between headquarters, division salesforces, distributors, plants, customers, etc.
Accounting codes	Allows customers to allocate costs	Trace projects and administer project chargebacks
Universal calling range privileges	Allows customers to restrict calling privileges at the location and/or user levels	Reduce costs and improve productivity
Vision card	With an 800 access, it allows calls from any domestic location while contributing to total usage for volume discounts	Personnel travelling between offices and customer locations
Call detail (paper/mag type)	Offers complete summary of activity by personal ID code or accounting code	Manage multiple projects, departments, locations, and organizations
Personal ID codes	Provides verifiable security and cost-allocation capabilities by location or individual	Controls telephone abuse, particularly in remote locations
Six-second billing	Provides additional savings with accurate call pricing	Compete internationally while reducing costs
Remote exchange	Provides customers with a "local number" presence in one place, while handling the calls at a distant site	Market new services and expand client base
Instant ringdown	Eliminates expensive point-to-point private-line charges	Credit card verification

By year-end 1990, companywide sales of Vision had exceeded plan. A Vision Customer Satisfaction survey, conducted in December 1990 by The Gallup Organization, found high levels of satisfaction across all types of installed customer groups (see **Exhibit VII** for survey excerpts).

For 1991, corporate marketing established a $425 million sales goal for Vision, making this product's performance the key determinent of the corporate GB unit's 1991 plan. It was anticipated that half of this goal would be generated by customer migrations from PRISM and half from new Vision acquisitions. For the Eastern Division, the 1991 Vision plan called for $150 million in sales, making it a key component of the division's GB goals and the Commercial Outbound marketing unit's revenue plan.

1991 During the first quarter of 1991, companywide sales of Vision were down 20% from fourth-quarter 1990 sales and, in terms of usage, Vision minute growth had stabilized at about 650,000 per week. Dedicated Vision locations (i.e., customer locations where circuits were installed for Vision service, rather than "switched" on to the network) were running about 30% below plan; dedicated locations represented "anchors" that spurred multilocation penetration of accounts. Rather than migrating customers "up-service," moreover, sales statistics indicated that Prism 1 installations were being sold at nearly twice the rate of Vision dedicated services. At current trends, Vision generated about $1 million/day in revenues but represented about 8% of 1991 MCI revenues (versus a planned 17%) and would fall short of goal. Further, AT&T and Sprint were expected to introduce competing products within the coming months.

Eastern Division sales reflected companywide results. In late March, Terri Ford (division marketing manager for Outbound services) sent a memo to Steven Zecola and corporate product marketing managers. Among the reasons cited for Vision's stalled sales growth was competitive activity in the GB segment and MCI's response. In early 1991, AT&T launched a large ad campaign to promote its Pro Wats product for small-business customers. This product was the feature equivalent of MCI's PRISM product (regular outbound domestic and international long-distance service based on the size of the business and its calling patterns). But AT&T revised its pricing to duplicate the Vision

EXHIBIT VI — MCI Product Positioning: Before and After Introduction of MCI Vision

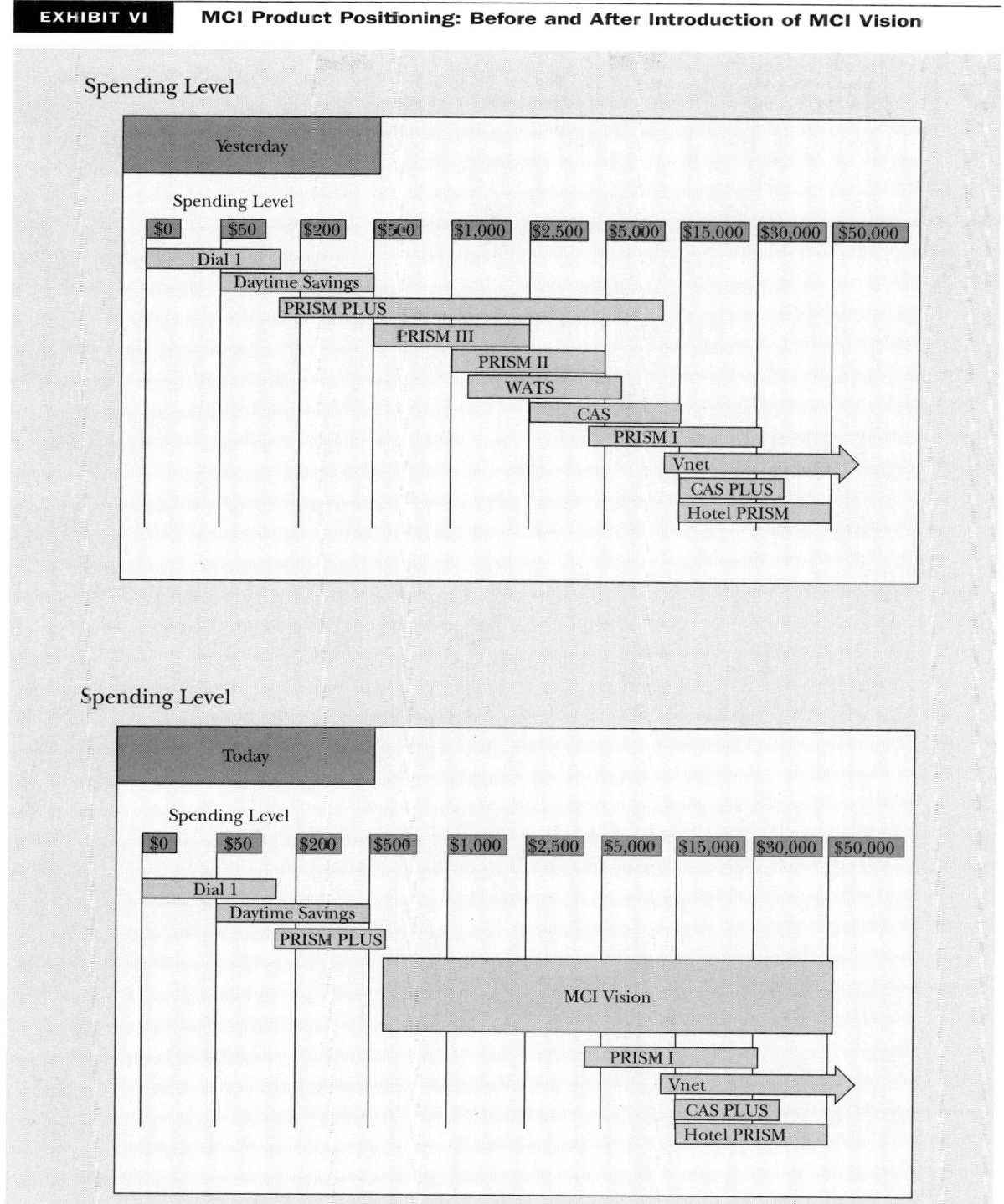

discount structure and initial free month of service for new customers, and also offered reduced international prices on Pro Wats service. In response, MCI during the first quarter of 1991 increased its advertising and promotions for PRISM (including reduced international fees on this product) and substantially cut advertising for Vision.

In February 1991, moreover, MCI had introduced a new product (MCI Preferred) which offered flat per-minute rates, volume and time-of-day discounts, and features such as calling cards, voice messaging and conference calling. Preferred was based on technology and software made possible by MCI's acquisition of U.S. Telecom, and

EXHIBIT VII Vision Customer Satisfaction Survey (Excerpts)

Methodology Gallup interviewers contacted by telephone a random sample of Vision customers during December 1990. A total of 807 interviews were conducted. Sample characteristics were:

Male: 56% (n = 452)   Female: 44%   (n = 355)

Division: Eastern (33%), Southern (37%), Central (13%), Western (17%)

Which of the following best describes your role in choosing MCI Vision?

Sole decision maker: 42%
One of the primary decision makers: 32%
Played a major role in researching and recommending MCI Vision, but the final decision was approved by someone else: 26%

What were the primary reasons why your company became an MCI Vision customer?

Response	1st Response	All Responses
Low rates	50%	70%
Type of billings reports/opt	8	14
Sales representative	7	12
Previous experience with MCI	6	8
Good service	5	12
Dissatisfied with previous carrier	4	5
Features/specific services	2	6
Recommended by someone else	2	3
Accounting codes	1	3
Security codes	1	1
Consolidation	1	3
Other	10	23

Overall, how satisfied would you say your company is with MCI Vision?

Very Satisfied: 52%
Somewhat Satisfied: 35
Somewhat Dissatisfied: 6
Very Dissatisfied: 1
Don't Know: 6

With regard to your expectations for the product, would you say it has:

Met all of your expectations: 34%
Met most of your expectations: 45
Met some of your expectations: 8
Met only a few of your expectations: 3
Not met your expectations: 1
Don't know: 8

MCI Vision customers have a wide variety of product service options to choose from. Please tell me whether you currently utilize the following.

MCI Vision Calling Card	73%	Remote Exchange	5%
Accounting Codes	39	Custom Calling	5
Personal ID Codes	26	10-Digit Restriction	5
Universal Calling	14	Call Detail Information on Magnetic Tape	3
Instant Ringdown	8		

Source: The Gallup Organization, December 1990.

For each service option, how satisfied are you with this aspect of MCI Vision?

MCI Vision Service Option	Very Satisfied	Somewhat Satisfied	Somewhat Dissatisfied	Very Dissatisfied	Don't Know
Accounting codes (3.53)	58%	29%	4%	2%	7%
Universal calling range privileges (3.55)	53	31	3	1	12
Call detail information on magnetic tape (3.67)	46	23	0	0	27
Personal ID Codes (3.62)	60	26	3	0	10
10-digit restrict (3.53)	60	29	5	2	13
Instant ringdown (3.73)	66	32	0	0	2
Remote exchange (3.68)	66	32	0	0	2
Custom calling range privileges (3.49)	58	32	5	3	3
Calling card (3.36)	41	29	8	2	21
Combined volume discounts (3.39)	40	32	4	2	20
Flat rate pricing (3.43)	37	36	3	1	23
International calls (3.43)	27	20	2	2	47
One consolidated monthly billing invoice (3.61)	65	17	5	3	10

[Numbers in parentheses refer to mean ratings. Scale: 1 = very dissatisfied; 2 = somewhat dissatisfied; 3 = somewhat satisfied; 4 = very satisfied]

How important is each service option as part of your total Vision package?

MCI Vision Service Option	Among the Most Important	Important	Not that Important	Not at all Important
Accounting codes (3.37)	47%	41%	8%	1%
Personal ID codes (3.33)	44	43	8	2
10-digit restrict (3.15)	29	55	10	2
Call detail information on magnetic tape (3.08)	27	50	12	4
Custom calling range privileges (2.95)	18	58	18	3
Remote exchange (2.93)	20	54	22	2
Instant ringdown (2.90)	23	39	27	3
Calling card (2.88)	23	47	23	6
Universal calling range privileges (2.82)	18	46	27	5

[Numbers in parentheses refer to mean ratings. Scale: 1 = not at all important; 2 = not that important; 3 = an important service; 4 = among the most important services]

How responsive has MCI support staff (excludes salespeople) been to your questions, comments, or complaints with regard to MCI Vision?

Very responsive	63%	
Somewhat responsive	21	
Not very responsive	5	[Mean = 3.59]
Not at all responsive	2	
Don't know	9	

was targeted at Telecom's traditional customer base: GB customers spending $50-$1,500/month on long-distance services. Preferred lacked many report and other capabilities of Vision, but its introduction revised Vision's ztarget segment upwards to GB customers generating $1,500/month or more. Preferred was introduced with an extensive ad campaign, a $1,000 credit to customers who signed up for Preferred by April 1, and extensive product training and attention in field branch offices.

Terri Ford noted at the beginning of the year, "We told the field to concentrate on Vision, but then offered promotions on PRISM and international services." She also noted that the increased promotional activity among all vendors had "encouraged customers to switch between carriers to take advantage of first-free-month offers. Many existing customers feel that there is no incentive for loyalty." However, she emphasized that any Vision promotions should "facilitate revenue acquisition and maintenance but *not* position MCI as a discount company having a 'fire sale' for Vision."

In reviewing this memo, Steven Zecola considered several questions: Was Vision's first-quarter results fundamentally a reflection of product/feature issues, competitive activity, or marketing/sales programs? Did the division's sales organization have the required skills and support to be effective with this product? What roles should the division and/or corporate marketing organizations play in a plan to revitalize Vision sales performance? And what would be the impact of any Vision promotions on other products sold by the salesforce, on Steven Zecola's ability to achieve his Silver segment goals, and on precedents established for the introduction and management of other feature-rich products like Vision?

Morgantown Inc.

In November 1995 Morgantown Inc. merged with Lea-Meadows Industries, a manufacturer of upholstered furniture for living and family rooms. The merger was not planned in a conventional sense. Charlton Bates's father-in-law died suddenly in August 1995, leaving his daughter with controlling interest in the firm. The merger proceeded smoothly, since the two firms were located on adjacent properties and the general consensus was that the two firms would maintain as much autonomy as was economically justified. Moreover, the upholstery line filled a gap in the Morgantown product mix, even though it would retain its own identity and brand names.

The only real issue that continued to plague Bates was merging the selling effort. Morgantown had its own salesforce, but Lea-Meadows Industries relied on sales agents to represent it. The question was straight-forward, in his opinion: "Do we give the upholstery line of chairs and sofas to our salesforce, or do we continue using the sales agents?" Mr. John Bott, Morgantown's sales vice-president, said the line should be given to his sales group; Mr. Martin Moorman, national sales manager of Lea-Meadows Industries, said the upholstery line should remain with sales agents.

Lea-Meadows Industries

Lea-Meadows Industries is a small manufacturer of upholstered furniture for use in living and family rooms. The firm is over seventy-five years old. The company has some of the finest fabrics and frame construction in the industry, according to trade sources. Net sales in 1995 were $3 million. Total industry sales of 1,500 upholstered furniture manufacturers in 1995 were $4.4 billion. Company sales had increased 15 percent annually over the last five years, and company executives believed this growth rate would continue for the foreseeable future.

Lea-Meadows Industries employed fifteen sales agents to represent its products. These sales agents also represented several manufacturers of noncompeting furniture and home furnishings. Often a sales agent found it necessary to deal with several buyers in a store in order to represent all lines carried. On a typical sales call, a sales agent would first visit buyers. New lines, in addition to any promotions being offered by manufacturers, would be discussed. New orders were sought where and when it was appropriate. A sales agent would then visit a retailer's selling floor to check displays, inspect furniture, and inform sales people on furniture. Lea-Meadows Industries paid an agent commission of 5 percent of net company sales for these services. Moorman thought sales agents spent 10 to 15 percent of their in-store sales time on Lea-Meadows products.

The company did not attempt to influence the type of retailers that agents contacted. Yet it was implicit in the agency agreement that agents would not sell to discount houses. All agents had established relationships with their retail accounts and worked closely with them. Sales records indicated that agents were calling on furniture and department stores. An estimated 1,000 retail accounts were called on in 1995.

Morgantown Inc.

Morgantown Inc. is a manufacturer of medium- to high-priced living and dining room wood furniture. The firm was formed in 1902. Net sales in 1995 were $50 million. Total estimated industry sales of wood furniture in 1995 were $7.1 billion at manufacturers' prices.

The company employed 10 full-time sales representatives who called on 1,000 retail accounts in 1986. These individuals performed the same function as sales agents, but were paid a salary plus a small commission. In 1995 the average Morgantown sales representative received an annual salary of $65,000 (plus expenses) and a commission of 0.5 percent on net company sales. Total sales administration costs were $112,500.

Source: This case is used with the permission of its author, Roger A. Kerin, Edwin L. Cox School of Business, Southern Methodist University, Dallas, Texas.

The Morgantown salesforce was highly regarded in the industry. The salesmen were known particularly for their knowledge of wood furniture and willingness to work with buyers and retail sales personnel. Despite these points, Bates knew that all retail accounts did not carry the complete Morgantown furniture line. He had therefore instructed John Bott to "push the group a little harder." At present, sales representatives were making ten sales calls per week, with the average sales call running three hours. Remaining time was accounted for by administrative activities and travel. Bates recommended that the call frequency be increased to seven calls per account per year, which was consistent with what he thought was the industry norm.

Merging the Sales Effort

In separate meetings with Bott and Moorman, Bates was able to piece together a variety of data and perspectives on the question. These meetings also made it clear that Bott and Moorman differed dramatically in their views.

John Bott had no doubts about assigning the line to the Morgantown salesforce. Among the reasons he gave for this approach were the following. First, Morgantown had developed one of the most well respected, professional sales groups in the industry. Sales representatives could easily learn the fabric jargon, and they already knew personally many of the buyers who were responsible for upholstered furniture. Second, selling the Lea-Meadows line would require only about 15 percent of present sales call time. Thus he thought the new line would not be a major burden. Third, more control over sales efforts was possible. He noted that Charlton Bates's father-in-law had developed the sales group twenty-five years earlier because of the commitment it engendered and the service "only our own people are able and willing to give." Moreover, our people have the Morgantown "look" and presentation style that is instilled in every person. Fourth, he said it wouldn't look right if we had our representatives and agents calling on the same stores and buyers. He noted that Morgantown and Lea-Meadows Industries overlapped on all their accounts. He said, "We'd be paying a commission on sales to these accounts when we would have gotten them anyway. The difference in commission percentages would not be good for morale."

Martin Moorman advocated keeping sales agents for the Lea-Meadows line. His arguments were as follows. First, all sales agents had established contacts and were highly regarded by store buyers, and most had represented the line in a professional manner for many years. He, too, had a good working relationship with 15 agents. Second, sales agents represented little, if any, cost beyond commissions. Moorman noted, "Agents get paid when we get paid." Third, sales agents were committed to the Lea-Meadows line: "The agents earn a part of their living representing us. They have to service retail accounts to get the repeat business." Fourth, sales agents were calling on buyers not contacted by Morgantown sales representatives. He noted, "If we let Morgantown people handle the line, we might lose these accounts, have to hire more sales personnel, or take away 25 percent of the present selling time given to Morgantown product lines."

As Bates reflected on the meetings, he felt that a broader perspective was necessary beyond the views expressed by Bott and Moorman. One factor was profitability. Existing Morgantown furniture lines typically had gross margins that were 5 percent higher than those for Lea-Meadows upholstered lines. Another factor was the "us and them" references apparent in the meetings with Bott and Moorman. Would merging the sales efforts overcome this, or would it cause more problems? Finally, the idea of increasing the salesforce to incorporate the Lea-Meadows line did not sit well with him. Adding a new salesperson would require restructuring of sales territories, potential loss of commission to existing people, and "a big headache."

Hospital Supply International: Rx for Increased Sales

Hospital Supply International (HSI), an international manufacturer and distributor of hospital supplies, sells a diverse line of high quality patient care products. Over 20 years, HSI built a commanding market share and was known in the industry for its strong salesforce, reliable products, and excellent service.

Profitability, however, had slipped in the last two years as a result of increased competition and new hospital purchasing strategies. For example, many of HSI's largest hospitals had joined buying groups for the purpose of negotiating bulk discounts. HSI's chief competitor, Acme, had developed new products that matched one of HSI's most profitable lines. Reducing price by 40 percent and using a team selling strategy, Acme had taken some of HSI's most profitable hospitals.

The situation was especially challenging for Charles Duffy, 43 years old, who had been recently promoted to sector executive. With direct responsibility for all hospitals on the East Coast, he decided that his first priority was to take a hard look at marketing strategy, and in four weeks he was scheduled to update senior management on his initial thinking. Duffy's predecessor, unable to reverse HSI's decline in market share, was fired.

But while spending time on field visits with some of the salespeople, Duffy observed that they were often unclear about their goals and reasons for making a particular call. During a joint call on New York University Hospital, they met an HSI sales product "specialist" who did not know the sales "generalist" responsible for NYU. Another salesperson got lost while searching for Central Supply in a large suburban hospital. Disturbed by these observations,

---

This case developed by Stephen X. Doyle and Kurt Engemann. Reprinted with permission.

Duffy had hired a respected consultant to conduct an audit and develop recommendations.

The consultant's recommendations were unexpected, and prompted Duffy to circulate the report along with Exhibits I and II, to several key managers.

The managers gave Duffy their own recommendations the following week.

Report From Florence Hoover, VP Marketing/Sales

Dear Chuck:

I've studied the consultant's report, and I agree with his assessment of the situation. We don't have a traditional motivation or training problem; the issue is one of sales strategy and organizational structure.

The sales program he recommends would replace broad territorial coverage with in-depth account management, reassign salespeople from 25 to 30 accounts to only 5 major accounts, and change their title to Account Manager. The individual Account Manager would coordinate and supervise HSI's technical specialists and act as the chief liaison to a particular hospital. A telemarketing and direct mail unit would take over the hundreds of smaller community hospitals in the area.

The program seems to offer several key advantages. The account manager would develop a deeper relationship with individual hospitals. He or she would dedicate more time and resources to a particular customer. And, in order to position HSI as the "preferred supplier," the account manager would develop relationships with administration, finance, engineering, central supply, and other areas that were previously outside our reach.

It was our weak penetration of these decision centers, in part, that made Acme's attack possible. We've had close ties with end users for years, but "buying power" is shifting to finance and administration—especially for high-technology items, long-term contracts and large suppliers. Our contact with key hospitals is too limited, too uncoordinated, and too superficial.

These strengthened relationships could also be our way of addressing the threat posed by buying groups and the preferred supplier arrangements offered by competitors. Just last week, 17 of 32 Connecticut hospitals signed up with a new buying group in Hartford. Two others signed exclusive contracts with Acme, enticed by a discount and special services like custom labeling, a simplified ordering procedure, and floor-specific delivery.

Finally, the program also promises a more focused use of sales resources, particularly time, which should be reserved for high profit products and high revenue hospitals. Sales and service time would be invested where it is likely to reap the

EXHIBIT I

Transactional Selling	*Relationship Selling*
Goal	
Sales and satisfied customer	Position of preferred supplier
Essence	
Probing, handling objections, closing	Building trust and intense service
Length of Relationship	
Short; the sales call itself may only be 30 minutes	Long; months, years
Salesforce Goals	
Closed sale	Manage the relationship
Number of Customers Appropriate for Each Approach	
Many; 30–200 customers/salesperson	Few; 2 to 5 accounts/account manager
Organizational Level and Size of Selling Team	
Low level, one or two sales people involved	Higher level, team selling
Teamwork Required to Support the Selling Effort Low	High, often involves mfg., dist., prod. dev. in the selling process
Examples	
Chicago Commodity Exchange	IBM Main Frame

EXHIBIT II Excerpts from Consultant's Interviews in "City Hospital"

"When you walk into the 'City Hospital,'" according to one of its nurses, "you can tell you're in a small town. We all know each other here; we care about each other. There's a community-mindedness you won't find in large city hospitals."

The hospital itself is three buildings just off the downtown Expressway. Since its founding as a community hospital in 1953, it has served patients primarily from the Central, Southern and Eastern sections of the city and has grown with the community from its original 115 beds to 628 beds and several outpatient clinics in adjoining buildings. Today, it houses more than 2,000 professional staff, 300 affiliated doctors and 1,200 volunteers.

What you notice first, however, is a large volunteer staff—dozens of senior citizens who tend the shops, staff the cafeteria, and offer help and directions—and the seasoned nursing staff, some of whom have been at the hospital for decades.

You also notice the fellowship among the staff. They greet each other with first names. Many seem to know the husbands, wives and children of their co-employees. And just last year, according to one of the nursing directors, the head of physiology lost her husband, a young man in his thirties. "Hundreds of the staff attended the funeral," she recalled, "and the women in the hospital cooked all the food." It was like an old-time gathering, in which a whole town rallied to the side of a family in trouble.

It is this environment—with its emphasis on direct personal contact and responsibility to the local community—that seems to set the tone for "City's" management of suppliers.

Relations with Suppliers

When the staff talks about Martin Troy, president of "City Hospital," they speak in reverential tones, as if they were describing a local minister or elder statesman. "Martin has been with the hospital for 30 years," according to one of the Unit Administrators, "but he's remarkably unpretentious and supportive." As another added, "You can see Martin in the lunchroom and chat with him. He'll ask you how things are going." Speaking with him, one is impressed by the dignity and respect he accords his staff.

"I want the decision making to remain close to the action," he says, "and I think that trust and communication are the basis of our culture. I spend time trying to understand what is going on within the hospital. I make site visits. I meet monthly with senior management. I participate in the committees. I give a presentation at each new employee orientation."

But, despite his involvement, Troy insists on the decentralization of responsibility. "It's not just that I encourage decision making at the lower levels with the organization; I also cannot personally keep track of the technology and the systems. I want those who are closest to patient care to be involved. They know more about how the technology impacts the quality of care." As one of the nursing directors added, "the administration doesn't get involved in the selection of suppliers; they count on materials management and those of us who actually use the products. They don't have the time—and that's also Martin Troy's style."

Consequently, the primary responsibility falls to the materials management department, which is located on the ground floor and handles everything from printing and vending to the purchase of medical and surgical supplies. Medical and surgical supplies alone account for about $12 million in annual expenditures, and are supervised by a director of materials management, a purchasing manager, two purchasing agents, and three assistants.

According to Kathy Smith, the purchasing agent, "about 90 percent of our re-orders are medical/surgical items. On our main line products, we reorder about once a week. The exceptions include emergency items such as those ordered from the surgical suite, like bi-pass materials." Inventory levels are monitored as part of the materials planning process that tracks level for the various departments. When an item is low, it is red-flagged and an order is generated by computer. Manual checks are also used to supplement this system.

Once an order is generated, Kathy designates someone to initiate the purchase. If the item is on contract, price is not discussed. If not, the price must be negotiated, and at least three suppliers are asked to tender bids.

In the tender process, there is a balance of power between the purchasing department and the end users. Typically, end users provide input and recommendations relative to patient care and product technology. They may suggest potential suppliers, share insights on past service or check up on new products by calling other hospitals. Purchasing gets involved to manage the transaction, arrange trials, control costs, and handle the ongoing relationship with the suppliers.

Depending on their particular needs, some end users are more involved in the selection and bidding process than others. Barb Donahue, the director of the surgical unit, explained that in her unit "the purchasing agents protect us. We articulate our needs through them, gather information through them, arrange trials, and set up meetings with suppliers." Others, like Rob Jensen, the Unit Administrator in CH, prefer to leave more of the work to purchasing. "They want us to be involved, to offer input and arrange trials, but I'm really short on time. I usually let purchasing take care of everything, make sure that the product is here, keep the reps out of my hair, and see that we have no stock outs."

continued

EXHIBIT II (continued)

In either case, because it acts as the liaison to suppliers, the purchasing department—and the negotiating and tendering process—is central to the management of supplies at "City Hospital."

When talking about the bidding process, however, it is clear that the staff considers it more than a convenient arrangement. "I believe in the free market," says John Mills, the director of materials management. "I don't like single suppliers; I don't even like oligopoly. For example, I don't hear from an Abbott sales rep anymore and I wonder how that is affecting our pricing." Florence McGuinness, a hospital vice president, described similar feelings: "I believe in competition among suppliers, and I want competitive bids. You have to remember that we get our funding from public sources—90 percent of our budget—and we have a responsibility to these taxpayers in terms of sound fiscal management." Other staffers insist that the bidding process is the only "ethical" and "fair" way to manage suppliers.

Budgeting Concerns

The concern with budgets and pricing seem to be driven by a number of factors. Last year, the hospital ran a $1.4 million deficit and was forced into a period of serious fiscal restraint. It was also the first year that the "City" was forced to reduce staff. "As a taxpayer I feel the crunch," says the head of the OR, "and it motivates me to try and save money here. There's a real crisis today in hospital finances."

Suppliers, at times, have aggravated the hospital by ignoring the seriousness of the budget crunch. The director of Materials Management remarked that "suppliers seem to forget the kind of budget pressures we feel here." For example, he recalled that "last year, some suppliers came in asking for a 15% increase in prices. They just aren't listening, and when that happens, we simply won't deal with them."

Among end users in the labs and on surgical floors, financial imperatives are highlighted by a feedback system that forces accountability and budget-consciousness. On a monthly basis, each of the eight directors receives a report that tracks expenses against the budget established for that fiscal year. "The key," according to the director of the critical care units, "is to make sure that everything balances. If we're over for some reason—maybe because of employee turnover and training time, unexpected patient volume or changes in supply costs—I have to prepare a formal report that explains why my units are over. It makes us all very budget-conscious."

Service Criteria

Despite the attention to budgeting, however, the end users are quick to acknowledge that price is only one of the criteria they consider when evaluating suppliers. The director of the critical care units (who's been at "City" for some 30 years), notes that "only inexperienced people buy just on price—they don't have the track record with suppliers. My experience gives me a more global view, and the realization that factors like quality, longevity and service are crucial. Some people become very short-sighted, narrow in their focus. Fortunately, there are others who balance out this view."

In fact, the "City Hospital" seems to have a two-tiered relationship with its suppliers. At the top is an inner circle of companies and reps who are known and trusted by materials management and the end users. Among these qualified candidated, price competition is encouraged. A purchasing agent commented: "We often prefer to go with a more trusted supplier—we'll even pay a premium for it. Price becomes an issue only with parity products, within a group of known, trusted suppliers who then bid for the contract."

Myra Mills, a director of nursing, recalled a recent choice made by her department. "A few months ago we were buying beds. There are many suppliers for these hospital beds and they all have acceptable quality. But one supplier stood out. They were responsive to our nurses in recognizing that it is not a bed that is being sold, but a concept of care. Frequently, particularly with chronic illnesses, patients will develop bedsores. This company provided inservice, products, follow-up about skin care, and information on how to take care of these patients. They put on training programs. Interestingly enough, though their bed product was just equal to what competitors were offering, they got all our business."

Conversely, poor service has led to the rejection of several suppliers in the past. Rita Diaz, a nursing director, described her dissatisfaction with a potential supplier: "Periodically, one of our suppliers goes through the motions of coming in and doing a sales call. They keep on telling us that they want a presence here. But, bottom line, I don't think they are going to develop the trust and responsiveness we require."

Rita recalled a similar experience: "I don't think that Kendall is much of a contender. What happens is that they sell their product through distributors who carry 500 to 600 products and really don't know the types of in-depth information we require. In fact, I find them next to useless. We need service, follow-up and communication. For example, when I buy morphine, I buy it from one or two pharmaceutical companies that have proven to me that they are responsive. I know their people, I know their names, and I know they are there for me."

greatest return. Telemarketing and direct mail can effectively handle the smaller accounts in hard-to-reach areas; right now these accounts aren't growing at all because no one is selling or servicing them.

I was impressed by the report. Let's seize the opportunity!

REPORT FROM EDWARD SHARP, VP DISTRIBUTION

Chuck:

I took a look at the report, and I can't argue with the fact that the sales effort is in a slump. Even so, his recommendations are a bit too drastic for me.

It worries me, in particular, that we'll take our eye further off the ball—at a time when we need to be playing to our traditional strengths, namely, developing highly profitable, specialized products for the health care system and providing outstanding service. Can we, for example, afford to turn away at this time from investing in our home health care line?

The recommendations are all based on the assumption that we can differentiate ourselves with more coordinated and indepth customer relationships. And he may be right to some extent—hospitals do demand more from their suppliers today—but I don't agree that differentiated, superior products are less important than a relationship. If we accept his advice, broadening and deepening our relationship with a particular hospital, wouldn't we wind up with the same products to offer? Where, ultimately, is the added value? It seems that we run the risk of investing time and money in relationships—only to find ourselves in a price war with other suppliers of commodity products.

The report suggested that we develop value added services like new packaging, special skids and customized information systems that facilitate the hospital's acquisition and ordering cycle. This seems to make sense on paper, but what about the extra costs? And will these services truly differentiate us? Shouldn't we worry about these sorts of innovations—ones that make our products distinct—rather than change the way we sell them?

Also, if we're worried about relationships with customers, we should remember: the new account "quarterback" will create power struggles within HSI, and drastically change the channels of internal communication. This can't help but further destabilize our relationships with hospitals.

The report asks us to budget $250,000 for sales training, and to be prepared to manage salesforce turnover as high as 40 percent. The process will also escalate our selling costs over the next few years, during which we won't likely see any improvement in revenues. As you know, this comes at a particularly bad time, as we're still trying to absorb a major acquisition, and corporate management is pushing all of its divisions for increased R.O.I. I'm not sure we can absorb the added blows right now.

Times may have changed, but that doesn't mean we should abandon our strategy of developing superior products, and selling them aggressively. Let's get back to the basics!

REPORT FROM KEITH ROSE, VP INFORMATION SYSTEMS

Charles:

The consultant may be onto something, but before we proceed let's address the fact that the potential benefits are still soft. His preliminary estimate of a market share increase needs to be solidified. We should work with him to quantify the revenue and cost changes.

I believe the modeling approach he mentions to pinpoint benefits would be a good starting point before we fully commit to organizational changes. I would feel better if we use a model to explore various scenarios to determine if we can pull it off. For example, what happens if more of our products become commodities? A model would help us focus on important issues and clarify our assumptions.

We have much of the data he needs for the model. We can provide the historical data on sales and costs, and Ron Enrico is looking at current costs. It does seem that there will be quite a bit of subjective input needed also. The consultant indicated the need for some workshops to elicit the judgment of knowledgeable participants. This would keep the results consistent with our collective intuition about the future. Hopefully, the results will be robust enough so that changes in our assumptions wouldn't alter our actions drastically.

This model is not a typical MIS project. It will require special talent and a non-traditional approach. Rapid feedback to keep everyone participating is essential. We are ready to work with the consultant to get things going.

If the model works out we should be able to use it as a tool on an ongoing basis, making improvements to it as we learn how it would be useful. There is good linkage to the price discounting project we're working on. Our experience has been that if the development of a model is well managed the return on that investment is outstanding.

REPORT FROM RON ENRICO, VP MANUFACTURING

Dear Charlie:

In light of the consultant's report, let me just bring to the forefront some of our recent observations and efforts. As you know, manufacturing has been working quite earnestly with R&D to keep a competitive edge to HSI's broad product line. However, despite our efforts, we are slipping on several fronts. My initial feeling is that the consultant's recommendations have some validity and should be explored in depth at our next monthly management team meeting. If we implemented his recommendations, we would not only alter our selling approach, but also manufacturing would be impacted. We need to coordinate.

We expect the foreign competitors to increase the pressure. Gusendwerk has been much more adaptive to newer technology than we have been able to because of our budget constraints. As a result, their higher end items contain features which are easily modified to comply with an individual customer's requests. Our traditional strength in the highly specialized products is eroding because of our inability to provide customized changes as casually as they do. We don't recover our fixed costs if we don't have sufficient volume. The proposed Account Managers may be in a unique position to provide valuable feedback about customer requests, but we need to be tooled up to handle them. I'm suggesting that if we want to provide in-depth account management, we'd better be prepared to back it up with custom options for our high-technolgoy items. Otherwise, we're out of the ball game.

There are several maintenance and service issues on the hi-tech products which need to be looked at also.

In addition, from what I can determine, Katsuhora is producing substitute products for our low end items at a much lower cost. Their adherence to high quality standards have decreased their cost by drastically limiting waste. They also have an edge on us with their inventory systems, helping to further keep costs down. We can compete, but to do it right the capital expenditures to manufacturing needs to be shifted up to outfit us properly.

Next week, you'll be receiving the first draft of our productivity study. You won't be surprised that our costs are *escalating because: demand projections are way off, labor turnover costs are high, and inventory is costly. The recent decrease in sales is having a severe impact on our unit cost, when we can least afford it. Discounting to buying groups needs to be looked at very carefully. I'm not a marketing man but I do know it's easier to sell anything if the cost is low.*

We can coordinate with Ed Sharp and Keith Rose to provide the telemarketing customers an automated acquisition process to give them a steady supply of "just in time" goods. We know that hospitals are under a lot of pressure to keep costs down and minimizing their inventory will help. We'll need better coordination to keep our own inventory levels consistent with the new form of selling.

REPORT FROM DICK TRASK, REGIONAL SALES MANAGER

Dear Chuck:

I had just a few thoughts I'd like to add to the consultant's report. In general, I agree: times have changed in the hospital supply business, and we're falling behind. In the old days, we dominated the market with great products. We sold and serviced the hell out of them, and no one tried to attack. If they did attack, the hospitals would let us know, and we'd respond with all types of horsepower and service.

One step above were hard-driving sales managers, and these individuals really built this company—even today, the average length of service is about 17 years. They were taught to cut deals, negotiate price, hire and fire aggressively.

Today, some of them feel like eunuchs. The consultant's report has leaked to the field, and many of them are worried that their days at HSI are numbered. One commented, "What will my job be when they bring in all the new account managers?"

As you know, most of our products are becoming commodities. Acme and others have matched many of our high-end systems, and have attacked us on price. My sales people haven't made any inroads with the new buying groups, and we don't have many relationships outside of end users and purchasing.

Perhaps our problem is that we're not clear on who we are right now. Are we going to become a broad-based distributor that sells thousands of products and makes money doing so? Or are we a company whose profits are driven by a limited number of high-profit products, sold to a limited number of key clients? I'm not sure I have an answer.

Questions:
1. What do you think about the proposed change in selling strategy for HSI?
2. If you were Duffy, what would you do?
3. How would you implement your plan?

Arizonia Company

Gary McGraff, the sales manager for the Arizonia Company, was concerned about developing a successful sales plan for 1992. He and Bob Reece, the General Manager of Arizonia, planned to meet with Stan Dolan, the Senior V.P. of the Lexus Company and President of the Components Group, in two weeks on October 15, 1991. Lexus is the parent company of Arizonia Company, one of the world's largest distributors of electronic components.

Background

Arizonia Company was founded in 1946 by Roger Arizonia. Initially, it was a traditional industrial supply company selling mops, gloves, and brooms for local manufacturers. Over the years the company developed an expertise in hose and fitting and dropped their general lines of mops, gloves and brooms. Under the leadership of Mr. Arizonia, the company became a full line supplier of fluid power products including air and fluid controllers, pneumatic and hydraulic components, actuator cylinders, hydraulic motors, hosing, and fittings. Initially located in Massachusetts, the company expanded to include all of New England. Arizonia was noted in the industry as pneumatic and hydraulic specialists. Their catalogue included products from 30 different manufacturers.

Lexus Company

As a national distributor of electronic components, Lexus was pleased to buy Arizonia in 1968. The purchase extended the Lexus's product line into hydraulic and pneumatic devices, reducing their dependence on electronic components. For a number of years Lexus left the Arizonia Company alone, allowing it to operate as the general manager saw fit. Lexus also owned Signod, a national distributor of electric motors, magnet wire and control devices. Although Signod and Arizonia had some of the same customers, Signod was a national supplier and Arizonia just covered the New England area.

Market

Arizonia's product line served a wide variety of manufacturing industries such as food, electronics, and chemical processing. These types of businesses bought approximately 48MM pneumatic and hydraulic systems and components per year in New England. The market overall was mature. Industry sales were flat from 1986 to 1991 and were expected to remain flat.

The product line included a number of items such as hose, fittings, and hydraulic or pneumatic accessories which were relatively standard and required little or no technical expertise to understand. The product line also included a number of valves, cylinders, compressors, and pumps which required sound technical understanding. In many cases when the customer had a problem, the salesperson could analyze it and recommend an appropriate solution. The technical or application side of the business required salespeople with technical skills and a flair for developing solutions.

Source: This case was made available through the cooperation of a company that prefers to remain anonymous. The names and data were disguised. © H. David Hennessey, 1991 Babson College.

EXHIBIT I — Salesperson Information

Name	Territory	Age	Yrs Service	Base	GP Quota	1990 GP (K)	1990 Commission	1990 Total Salary
Brown	NH, VT Lower Maine	32	6	40	180	316	13,640	53,640
Dover	N. CT	40	10	30	230	350	12,000	42,000
Early	S. RI	52	10	30	230	214	—	30,000
Hughes	Central M	50	New	25	200	—	—	—
Long	Eastern M	60	25	38	250	208	—	38,000
Lynch	N. RI	32	7	25	200	241	4101	29,101
Moore	W. CT	41	New	30	230	—	—	—
Sommer	S. CT	41	15	40	275	465	19,000	59,000

Compensation System

Arizonia salespeople were paid a base salary which provided a draw per month. Along with the draw was an annual quota of gross profit. Every quarter, salespeople were paid 10% on any excess of the monthly gross profit that exceeded the quota (Exhibit I). For example, Dover's yearly gross profit quota was $230,000 or $57,500 per quarter. In the last quarter he sold goods which generated $84,200 of gross profit, therefore, he was to be paid 10% on $26,700 ($84,200-57,500) or $2,670. The quota was carried over from quarter to quarter: if a salesperson did not make quota in one quarter he would have to make up the deficit in the next quarter before earning a commission. The system did not carry over from year-to-year. The salesperson started fresh each year, even if he did not make quota the previous year.

Salespeople

Bob Brown started with the company in 1985, a few years after completing his B.S. in Mechanical Engineering. He developed the New Hampshire territory and the few customers Arizonia had in Vermont. In 1988, the salesperson in Maine was let go and Brown took over that territory. A map of the sales territories is included in Exhibit II. In 1990, Brown, was offered a job by a competitor for $60,000. When he approached the general manager of Arizonia, his base salary was increased and he was given accounts on the North Shore of Massachusetts. The higher base and low quota along with the larger territory of potential accounts was expected to give Brown a total compensation of $60,000 plus.

Roger Dover shared Connecticut with three other salespeople. His territory of northern Connecticut was well served by either the Rhode Island or Hartford warehouse. Dover had good technical skills and could effectively sell new application.

John Emily was one of the oldest Arizonia salespeople. He did a good job selling the nontechnical products, like hose and fittings, as well as the standard off-the-shelf products. He was not comfortable selling new applications as he did not have an engineering background. Also, in 1990, he lost his biggest account. Hawthorn Company, manufacturer of printers, consolidated production of its Rhode Island and New Hampshire plants into its New Hampshire facility. Emily lost over $300,000 of sales revenue to Bob Brown's territory.

Resse Hughes was recently hired by Arizonia to cover central Massachusetts. Having worked for 20 years with a competitor who went bankrupt, Hughes had good technical experience. The recession allowed Arizonia to get an experienced salesperson cheaply. The central Massachusetts territory was previously handled by a combination of the Connecticut salespeople and Steven Long, the eastern Massachusetts salesperson. Long was shifted more toward Boston and the North Shore. Also, Long took over some accounts previously handled by Gary McGraff.

Steven Long, the oldest salesperson, had been with the company 25 years. He had hired Gary McGraff 15 years ago. Long's territory is eastern Massachusetts. His years of experience with the product line resulted in a strong technical orientation. He was excellent discussing potential new applications with customers. To use his applications expertise, Gary McGraff considered having Long work in the office on Mondays and Fridays to help customers with applications over the telephone. This would augment the current telemarketing person, who followed up the medium and smaller accounts the salespeople did not have time to visit.

Brian Lynch covered northern Rhode Island and parts of southeastern Massachusetts. He was good at both selling off-the-shelf products and technical products. The company sent him for a week of technical training in 1991 to enhance his technical skills.

Phil Moore was recently hired to cover the prosperous Fairfield county of Connecticut. Also, his territory extended up Route 7 to cover far western Massachusetts. With Phil's previous sales experience, Arizonia expected him to do well.

EXHIBIT II   Sales Territories

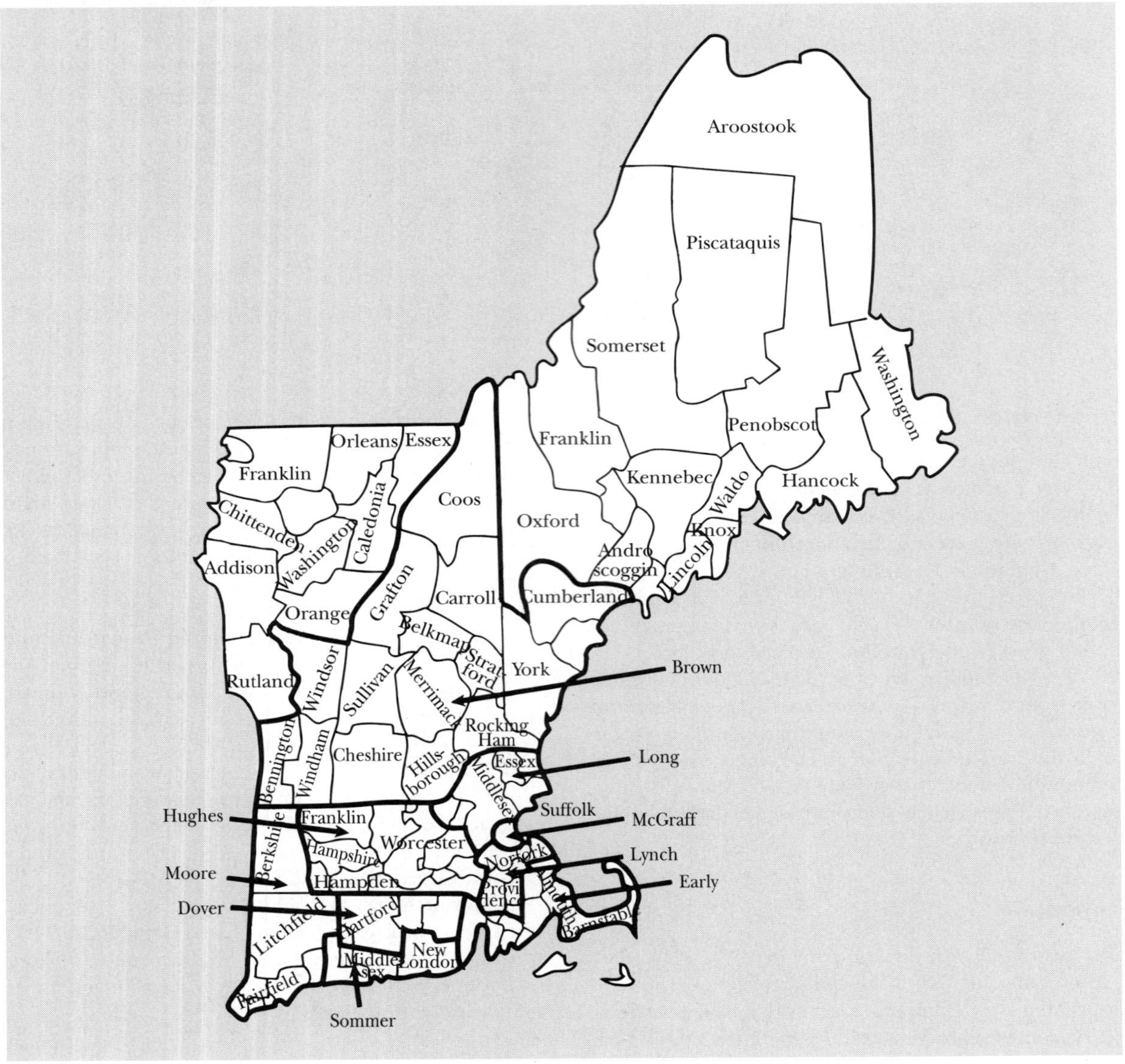

[Map of New England showing counties with sales territory assignments: Hughes, Moore, Dover, Brown, Long, McGraff, Lynch, Early, Sommer]

Stu Sommers served southern Connecticut. He had good skills in both off-the-shelf and technical products. He had developed his territory into one of the most fruitful regions for Arizonia.

Sales Organization

Eight salespeople reported to Gary McGraff. They were expected to meet and exceed their annual gross profit quota. Their territories had evolved over time. The activities of the salespeople and each territory's potential are shown in Exhibit III.

Current Situation

Lexus's performance over the past few years was not outstanding (Exhibit IV). Its shares of the market declined from a peak of 20% in 1984 to 18% in 1990. In 1990 Lexus invested over $10 million to ensure increased productivity and profitability in the future years. The restructuring included combining operations to reduce redundancies, divesting unprofitable businesses, centralizing and automating operations, centralizing customer support into regional hubs, and adding businesses like Arizonia to the IBM 3090 computer system.

EXHIBIT III — Sales Territories

Name	Territory	Population (000)	BPI	IBP	Number of Accounts over 1,000 GP
Brown	NH, VT, Lower ME	1778	.8744	.7921	41
Dover	Northern CT	1084	.5207	.5665	40
Early	Southern RI	980	.4735	.2103	44
Hughes	Central MA	1352	.5867	.6241	28
Long	Eastern MA	1898	.9814	1.1941	35
Lynch	Northern RI	1255	.5911	.7399	54
Moore	W. CT, W. MA	1139	.6264	.7187	32
Sommer	Southern CT	1201	.5705	.8024	40
McGraff	Downtown Boston	656	.2870	.2500	15
Total		11345	5.5127	5.8981	

EXHIBIT IV — Lexus Company Financial Performance

	1984	1985	1986	1987	1988	1989	1990
Sales	1,940	1,320	1,679	1,826	2,155	2,276	2,078
Cost of Interest	1,411	1,332	1,262	1,381	1,636	1,744	1,556
Expense	10	13	12	13	19	19	18
Inc Taxes	93	52	21	28	40	40	50
Earnings	102	58	28	27	62	64	67
Assets	1,079	1,086	1,077	1,260	1,366	1,335	1,373

Since 1989, Lexus had given more attention to the Arizonia Company. Arizonia represented less than 1% of the company's revenue. In 1990, Arizonia was integrated into the Signod Group. The Signod group of electrical and industrial supply companies accounted for 12% of Lexus's revenues. Group sales were down 3% from 1989 and revenue fell from $8.6 million in 1989 to $8.8 million in 1990.

The Signod management was concerned about Arizonia. The company was in a mature market with sales staying relatively flat at $9.0 million over the past 4 years. While gross profit margins were at 30%, the net margins after all expenses and taxes were only 2.5–3%. Arizonia carried an inventory of 1.5 million and had total assets of 1.7 million.

The goal for Arizonia was 5.0% profit after tax. A number of programs at Signod, such as centralized credit and purchasing, would help reduce overhead costs, but most of these benefits were offset by the increased technology costs. The major opportunity for Arizonia seemed to be how to improve the performance of the sales force.

Gary McGraff was considering a number of possibilities, such as reorganizing the sales territories or changing the commission system to increase productivity.

BSI: Manufacturers' Representative Agency—The Dilemma of Expansion

Introduction

With four people and sales of $5.5 million, Barro Stickney Inc. (BSI) had become a successful and profitable manufacturers' representative firm. It enjoyed a reputation for outstanding sales results and friendly, thorough service to both its customers and principals. In addition, BSI was considered a great place to work. The office was comfortable and the atmosphere relaxed but professional. All members of the group had come to value the close, friendly working relationships that had grown with the organization.

Success had brought with it increased profits as well as the inevitable decision regarding further growth. Recent requests from two principals, Franklin Key Electronics and R. D. Ocean, had forced BSI to focus its attention on the question of expansion. It was not to be an easy decision, for expansion offered both risk and opportunity.

Company Background

John Barro and Bill Stickney established their small manufacturers' representative agency, Barro Stickney Inc., ten years ago. Both men were close friends who left different manufacturers' representative firms to join as partners in their own "rep" agency. The two worked very well together, and their talents complemented each other.

John Barro was energetic and gregarious. He enjoyed meeting new people and taking on new challenges. It was mainly through John's efforts that many of BSI's eight principals had signed on with BSI. Even after producing $1.75 million in sales this past year, John still made an effort to contribute much of his free time to community organizations in addition to perfecting his golf score.

Bill Stickney liked to think of himself as someone a person could count on. He was thoughtful and thorough. He liked to figure how things could get done, and how they could be better. Much of the administrative work of the agency, such as resource allocation and territory assignments, was handled by Bill. In addition to his contribution of $1.5 million to total company sales, Bill also had a boy scout troup and was interested in gourmet cooking. In fact, he often prepared specialties to share with his fellow workers.

A few years later, as the business grew, J. Todd Smith (J. T.) joined as an additional salesperson. J. T. had worked for a nationally known corporation, and he brought his experience dealing with large customers with him. He and his family loved the Harrisburg area, and J. T. was very happy when he was asked to join BSI just as his firm was ready to transfer him to Chicago. John and Bill had worked with J. T. in connection with a hospital fund-raising project, and they were impressed with his tenacity and enthusiasm. Because he had produced sales of over $2 million this past year, J. T. was now considered eligible to buy a partnership share of BSI.

Soon after J. T. joined BSI, Elizabeth Lee, a school friend of John's older sister, was hired as office manager. She was cheerful and put as much effort into her work as she did coaching the local swim team. The three salespeople knew they could rely on her to keep track of orders and schedules, and she was very helpful when customers and principals called in with requests or problems.

Most principals in the industry assigned their reps exclusive territories, and BSI's ranged over the Pennsylvania, New Jersey, and Delaware area. The partners purchased a small house and converted it into their present office located in Camp Hill, a suburb of Harrisburg, the state capitol of Pennsylvania. The converted home contributed to the family-like atmosphere and attitude that was promoted and prevalent throughout the agency.

Over the years, in addition to local interests, BSI and its people had made an effort to participate in and support the efforts of the Electronics Representative Association (Ezre solved here, and principals' and members' suggestions were discussed. An established agenda enabled members to prepare. Most meetings took about one to one and one-half hours, with emphasis placed on consensus of the group. It was during this group meeting that BSI would discuss the future of the company.

Opportunities for Expansion

R. D. Ocean was BSI's largest principal, and it accounted for 32% of BSI's revenues. Ocean had just promoted James Innve as new sales manager, and he felt an additional salesperson was needed in order for BSI to achieve the new sales projections. Innve expressed the opinion that BSI's large commission checks justified the additional effort, and he further commented that J. T.'s expensive new car was proof that BSI could afford it.

BSI was not sure an additional salesperson was necessary, but it did not want to lose the goodwill of R. D. Ocean or its business. Also, while it was customary for all principals to meet and tacitly approve new representatives, BSI wanted to be very sure that any new salesperson would fit into the close-knit BSI organization.

Franklin Key Electronics was BSI's initial principal, and it had remained a consistent contributor of approximately 15% of BSI's revenues. BSI felt its customer base was well suited to the Franklin line, and it had worked hard to establish the Franklin Key name with these customers. As a consequence, BSI now considered Franklin Key relatively easy to sell.

Source: This case was originally prepared in 1985 by Tony Langan, B. Jane Stewart, and Lawrence M. Stratton, Jr., under the supervision of Assistant Professor Erin Anderson of the Wharton School, University of Pennsylvania, and updated in 1991 with permission from the author. The writing of the case was sponsored by the Manufacturers' Representatives Educational Research Foundation. The cooperation of the Mid-Atlantic Chapter of the Electronic Representatives Association (ERA) is greatly appreciated.

A few days previously, Mark Heil Franklin's representative from Virginia, perished when his private plane crashed, leaving Franklin Key without representation in its D.C./Virginia territory. Franklin did not want to jeopardize its sales of over $800,000, and was desperate to replace Heil before its customers found other sources. Franklin offered the territory to BSI and was anxious to hear the decision within one week.

BSI was not familiar with the territory, but it did understand that there were a great number of military accounts. This meant there was a potential for sizable orders, although a different and specialized sales approach would be required. Military customers are known to have their own unique approach to purchase decisions.

Because of the distance and the size of the territory, serious consideration was needed as to whether a branch office would be necessary. A branch office would mean less interaction with and a greater independence from the main BSI office. None of the current BSI members seemed anxious to move there, but it might be possible to hire

---

EXHIBIT I **Businessland Computers, Inc.**

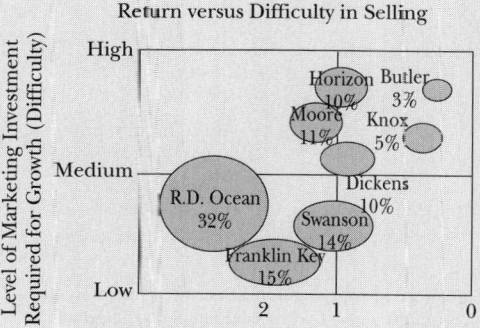

Notes and Explanation

This chart evaluates the amount of sales effort (Difficulty in Selling) necessary in order to achieve a certain percentage of sales in BSI's portfolio (Return). Difficulty in selling is measured by the level of marketing investment required for growth. Stickney's estimate is shown on the vertical axis. Return for this investment is measured by the relative sales commissions as a percent of BSI's portfolio shown on the horizontal axis. If BSI's time were evenly divided among its eight principals, each would receive 12.5 percent of the agency's time. The x-axis shows each principal's time allocation as a proportion of 12.5 percent, the "par" time allocation. The area of each ellipse reflects each principal's share of BSI's commission revenue.

Additional Comments

Swanson's products are being replaced by the competition's computerized electronic equipment, a product category the firm has ignored. As a result, the company is losing its own prominent market position.

Although small amounts of effort are required to promote Ocean's product line to customers in the current sales territory, Ocean is extremely demanding of both BSI and other manufacturers' representative firms.

According to a seminar at the last ERA meeting, the maximum safe proportion of a rep firm's commissions from a single principal should be 25 to 30%. Also, at the meeting, one speaker indicated that if a firm commands 80% of a market, it should focus on another product or expand its territory rather than attempt to obtain the remainder of the market.

The revenue for investment for the manufacturers' representative firm comes from one or more of several sources. These sources include reduced forthcoming commission income, retained previous income, and borrowed money from a financial institution. Most successful firms expand their salesforce or sales territory when they experience income growth and use the investment as a tax write-off.

Before the meeting, Bill Stickney examined the sources of BSI's revenue and the firm's income for the previous year in addition to estimating the future prospects for each of BSI's lines, considering each line's market potential and BSI's level of saturation in each market. Finally, he estimated the costs of hiring a new employee both in the current sales territory, and in the Washington/Virginia area. Immediately before the meeting, Elizabeth finished compiling Bill's data into four charts.

EXHIBIT II — Barro Stickney, Inc.: Estimation of Cost of Additional Sales Representative

Compensation Costs for New Sales Representative

Depending upon the new sales representative's level of experience, BSI would pay a base salary of $15,000 to $25,000 with the following bonus schedule:

- 0% firm's commission revenue up to $500,000 in sales
- 20% firm's commission revenue 1st half-million dollars in sales over $500,000
- 25% firm's commission revenue for the next half-million dollars in sales
- 30% firm's commission for the next half-million dollars in sales
- 40% firm's commission sales above $2 million in sales

Estimate of Support Costs[a] for New Representative[b]

Search applicant pool, psychological testing, hiring, training,[c] flying final choice to principals for approval.[d]	$28,000
Automobile expenses, telephone costs, business cards, entertainment/promotion	$22,000
Insurance, payroll taxes (social security, unemployment compensation)	$16,000
Total expenses	**$66,000**

Incremental expenses for new territory:

Transportation (additional mileage from Camphill to Virginia)	$ 2,000
Office equipment and rent (same regardless of headquarters location)	$ 4,000
Cost of hiring office manager[e]	$18,000
Total incremental expenses	**$24,000**

Notes:
[a] Rounded to the nearest thousand.
[b] In current territory.
[c] Excludes the lost revenue from selling instead of engaging in this activity (opportunity cost).
[d] Although legally rep agencies are not required to show prospective employees to principals, it is generally held to be good business practice.
[e] Discretionary

EXHIBIT III — Barro Stickney, Inc.: Statement of Revenue

Total Sales Revenue 1991 $5.5 million

Principal	Estimated Market Saturation	Product Type	Sales/Commission Rate	Share of BSI's Portfolio	Commission Revenue
R. D. Ocean	High	Components	5%	32%	$96,756
Franklin Key	High	Components	5%	15%	$45,354
Butler	Low	Technical/Computer	12%	3%	$ 9,070
Dickins	Low	Components	5%	10%	$30,236
Horizon	Medium	Components	5.5%	10%	$30,237
Swanson	High	Components	5.25%	14%	$42,331
Moore	Medium	Consumer/Electronics	5.25%	11%	$33,260
Knox	Low	Technical/Communications	8.5%	5%	$15,118

EXHIBIT IV	Barro Stickney, Inc.: Statement of Income for the Year Ending December 31, 1991

Revenue	
Commission income	$302,362.00
Expenses:	
Salaries for Sales and Bonuses (includes Barro & Stickney)	$130,250.00
Office manager's salary	$ 20,000.00
Total non-personnel expenses[a]	$128,279.00
Total expenses	$278,529.00
Net Income.[b]	$ 23,833.00 (7.9% of revenue)

Notes:
[a] Includes travel, advertising, taxes, office supplies, retirement, automobile expenses, communications, office equipment, and miscellaneous expenses.
[b] Currently held in negotiable certificates of deposit in a Harrisburg bank.

someone who was familiar with the territory. There was, of course, always the risk that any successful salesperson might leave and start his or her own rep firm.

In addition to possibilities of expanding its territory and its salesforce, BSI also wanted to consider whether it should increase or maintain its number of principals. BSI's established customer base and its valued reputation put it in a strong position to approach potential principals. If, however, BSI had too many principals, it might not be able to offer them all the attention and service they might require.

Preparation for the Meeting

Each member received an agenda and supporting data for the upcoming meeting asking them to consider the issue of expansion. They would be asked whether BSI should or should not expand its territory, its salesforce, and/or its number of principals. In preparation, they were each asked to take a good hard look at the current BSI portfolio and to consider all possibilities for growth as well as the effect any changes would have on the company's profits, its reputation, and its work environment.

It was an ambitious agenda: one that would determine the future of the company. It would take even more time than usual to discuss everything and reach consensus. Consequently, this week's meeting was set to take place over the weekend at Bill Stickney's vacation lodge in the Poconos starting with a gourmet dinner served at 7:00 p.m. sharp.

Adams Brands

Ken Bannister, Ontario Regional Manager for Adams Brands, was faced with the decision of which of three candidates he should hire as the key account supervisor for the Ontario region. This salesperson would be responsible for working with eight major accounts in the Toronto area. Bannister had narrowed the list to the three applicants and began reviewing their files.

Company

Warner-Lambert, Inc., a large, diversified U.S. multinational, manufactured and marketed a wide range of health care and consumer products. Warner-Lambert Canada Ltd., the largest subsidiary, had annual sales exceeding $200 million. Over one-half of the Canadian sales were generated by Adams Brands, which focused on the confectionery business. The major product lines carried by Adams were:

1. Chewing gum, with brands such as Chiclets, Dentyne, and Trident.
2. Portable breath fresheners including Certs and Clorets.
3. Cough tablets and antacids such as Halls and Rolaids.
4. Several other products, including Blue Diamond Almonds and Sparkies Mini-Fruits.

In these product categories, Adams Brands was usually the market leader or had a substantial market share.

The division was a stable unit for Warner-Lambert Canada, with profits being used for investments throughout the company. Success of the Adams Brands was built on:

1. Quality products.
2. Strong marketing management.
3. Sales force efforts in distribution, display, and merchandising.
4. Excellent customer service.

Adams was organized on a regional basis. The Ontario region, which also included the Atlantic provinces, had 46 sales representatives whose responsibilities were to service individual stores. Five district managers coordinated the activities of the sales representatives. As well, three key account supervisors worked with the large retail chains (e.g., supermarkets) in Ontario and the Atlantic area. The key account supervisor in the Toronto area had recently

---

Source: This case was prepared by Gordon McDougall, Wilfrid Laurier University, and Douglas Snetsinger, Institute of Market Driven Quality.

resigned his position and joined one of Adams' major competitors.

The Market

The confectionery industry comprised six major competitors that manufactured chocolate bars, chewing gum, mints, cough drops, chewy candy, and other products. The 1993 market shares of these six companies are provided in Exhibit I.

In the past few years, total industry sales in the confectionary category had been flat to marginally declining in unit volume. This sales decline was attributed to the changing age distribution of the population (i.e., fewer young people). As consumers grew older, their consumption of confectionery products tended to decline. While unit sales were flat or declining, dollar sales were increasing at a rate of 10 percent per annum as a result of price increases.

In the confectionery business, it was critical to obtain extensive distribution in as many stores as possible and, within each store, to obtain as much prominent shelf space as possible. Most confectionary products were purchased on impulse. In one study it was found that up to 85 percent of chewing gum and 70 percent of chocolate bar purchases were unplanned. While chocolate bars could be viewed as an indirect competitor to gum and mints, they were direct competitors for retail space and were usually merchandised on the same display. Retailers earned similar margins from all confectionary products (25-86 percent of the retail selling price) and often sought the best-selling brands to generate those revenues. Some industry executives felt that catering to the retailers' needs was even more important than understanding the ultimate consumers' needs.

Adams Brands had always provided store display racks for merchandising all confectionary items, including competitive products and chocolate bars. The advantage of supplying the displays was that the manufacturer could influence the number of prelabeled slots that contained brand logos and the proportion of the display devoted to various product groups such as chewing gum versus chocolate bars. The displays were usually customized to the unique requirements of a retailer, such as the height and width of the display.

Recently, a competitor, Effem, had become more competitive in the design and display of merchandising systems. Effem was regarded as an innovator in the industry, in part because of their limited product line and their new approach to the retail trade. The company had only eight fast-turnover products in their line. Effem had developed their own sales force, consisting of over 100 part-time merchandising salespeople and 8 full-time sales personnel, and focused on the head offices of "A" accounts. "A" accounts were large retail chains such as 7-Eleven, Beckers, Loblaws, A&P, Food City, Shopper's Drug Mart, K-Mart, Towers and Zellers. Other than Adams, Effem was one of the few companies that conducted considerable research on racking systems and merchandising.

The Retail Trade

Within Adams Brands, over two-thirds of confectionary volume flowed through wholesalers. The remaining balance was split between direct sales and drop shipments to retailers. Wholesalers were necessary because, with over 66,000 outlets in food, drug, and variety stores alone, the sales force could not adequately cover a large proportion of the retailers. The percentage of Adams sales through the various channels is provided in Exhibit II.

EXHIBIT I Major Competitors in the Confectionery Industry

Company	Market Share (%)	Major Product Lines	Major Brands
Adams	23	Gum, portable breath fresheners, cough drops	Trident, Chiclets, Dentyne, Certs, Halls
Nielsen/Cadbury	22	Chocolate bars	Caramilk, Crunchie, Dairy Milk, Crispy Crunch
Nestlé Canada	15	Chocolate bars	Coffee Crisp, Kit-Kat, Smarties, Turtles
Hershey	14	Gum, chocolate bars, chewy candy	Glossette, Oh Henry, Reese's Pieces, Lifesavers
Effem Foods	11	Chocolate bars, chewy candy	Mars, Snickers, M&M's, Skittles
Wrigley's	9	Gum	Hubba Bubba, Extra, Doublemint
Richardson-Vicks	2	Cough drops	Vicks
Others	4		

Source: Company records and industry data.

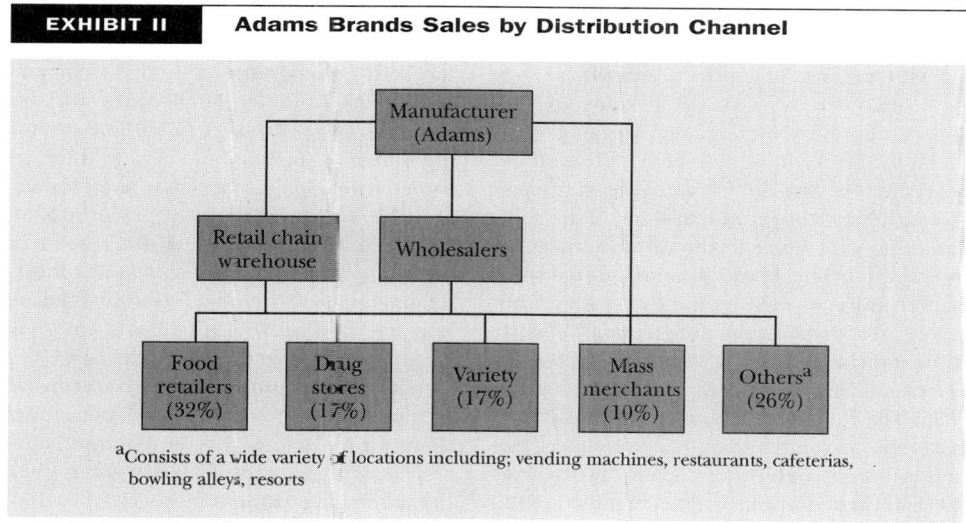

EXHIBIT II Adams Brands Sales by Distribution Channel

Food retailers (32%), Drug stores (17%), Variety (17%), Mass merchants (10%), Others[a] (26%)

[a]Consists of a wide variety of locations including; vending machines, restaurants, cafeterias, bowling alleys, resorts

The volume of all consumer packaged goods sold in Canada was increasingly dominated by fewer and larger retail chains. This increased retail concentration resulted in retailers becoming more influential in trade promotion decisions, including dictating the size, timing, and number of allowance, distribution, and coop advertising events. The new power of the retailers had not yet been fully wielded against the confectionary business. Confectionery lines were some of the most profitable lines for the retailer. Further, the manufacturers were not as reliant on listings from any given retailers as were other food and household product manufacturers.

The increased size of some retail chains also changed the degree of management sophistication at all levels, including that of the retail buyers—those individuals responsible for deciding what products were carried by the retail stores. At one time, the relationship between manufacturers' sales representatives and retail buyers was largely based on long-term, personal associations. Usually the sales representative had strong social skills, and an important task was to get along well with the buyers. Often when the representatives and buyers met to discuss various promotions or listings, part of the conversation dealt with making plans for dinner or going to a hockey game. The sales representative was the host for these social events.

More recently, a new breed of buyer had been emerging in the retail chains. Typically the new retail managers and buyers had been trained in business schools. They often had product management experience, relied on analytical skills, and used state-of-the-art, computer-supported planning systems. In some instances, the buyer was more sophisticated than the sales representative with respect to analytical approaches to display and inventory management. The buyers frequently requested detailed plan-o-grams with strong analytical support for expected sales, profits and inventory turns. The buyer would also at times become the salesperson. After listening to a sales presentation and giving an initial indication of interest the buyer would attempt to sell space, both on the store floor and in the weekly advertising supplements. For example, the buyer for Shopper's Drug Mart offered a dump bin location in every store in the chain for a week. In some instances, both the buyer and the representative had the authority to conclude such a deal at that meeting. At other times, both had to wait for approval from their respective companies.

The interesting aspect of the key account supervisor's position was that the individual had to feel comfortable dealing with both the old and new schools of retail management. The task for Bannister was to select the right candidate for this position. The salary for the position ranged from $31,000 to $54,200, depending on qualifications and experience. Smith expected that the candidate selected would probably be paid somewhere between $38,000 and $46,000. An expense allowance would also be included in the compensation package.

The Key Accounts Supervisor

The main responsibility of the key accounts supervisor was to establish and maintain a close working relationship with the buyers of eight A accounts whose head offices were located in the Toronto area. An important task was to make presentations (15 to 30 minutes in length) to the retail buyers of these key accounts every three to six weeks. At these meetings, promotions or deals for up to five brands would be presented. The supervisor was responsible for all Adams brands. The buyer might have to take the promotions to the buying committee, where the final decision would be made. In addition, the representative used these meetings to hear about and inform the buyer of any merchandising problems occurring at the store level.

Midyear reviews were undertaken with each account. These reviews, lasting for one hour, focused on reviewing sales trends and tying them into merchandising programs, listings, service, and new payment terms. Another important and time-consuming responsibility of the key account supervisor was to devise and present plan-o-grams and be involved with the installation of the displays. The key account representative also conducted store checks and spent time on competitive intelligence. Working with the field staff was a further requirement of the position.

Bannister reflected on what he felt were the attributes of the ideal candidate. First, the individual should have selling and merchandising experience in the retail business in order to understand the language and dynamics of the situation. On the merchandising side, the individual would be required to initiate and coordinate the design of customized display systems for individual stores, a task that involved a certain amount of creativity. Second, strong interpersonal skills were needed. The individual had to establish rapport and make effective sales presentations to the buyers. Because of the wide range of buyer sophistication, these skills were particularly important. Bannister made a mental note to recommend that whoever was hired would be sent on the Professional Selling Skills course, a one-week program designed to enhance listening, selling, and presentation skills. Finally, the candidate should possess analytic skills because many of the sales and performance reports (from both manufacturers and retailers) were or would be computerized. Thus, the individual should feel comfortable working with computers. Bannister hoped that he could find a candidate who would be willing to spend a minimum of three years on the job in order to establish a personal relationship with the buyers.

Ideally, the candidate selected would have a blend of all three skills because of the mix of buyers he or she would contact. Bannister felt it was most likely that these characteristics would be found in a business school graduate. He had advertised the job internally (through the company's newsletter) and externally (in the *Toronto Star*). A total of 20 applications were received. After an initial screening, three possible candidates for the position were identified. None were from Warner-Lambert (Exhibit III).

In early August 1994, Bannister and a member of the personnel department interviewed each of the candidates. After completing the interviews, brief fact sheets were prepared. Bannister began reviewing the sheets prior to making the decision.

EXHIBIT III

Lydia Cohen

Personal:	Born 1963, 168 cm; 64 kg; Single
Education:	B.B.A. (1985), Wilfrid Laurier University, Active in Marketing Club and Intramural sports
Work:	1992–94 Rowntree Macintosh Canada, Inc.—District Manager
	Responsible for sales staff of three in Ottawa and Eastern Ontario region. Establish annual sales plan and ensure that district meets its quota.
	1985–91 Rowntree Macintosh Canada, Inc.—Confectionary Sales Representative
	Responsible for selling a full line of confectionary and grocery products to key accounts in Toronto (1990–91) and Ottawa (1985–89). 1991 Sales Representatives of the Year for highest volume growth.
Interests:	Racquet sports
Candidate's Comments:	I am interested in working in the Toronto area, and I would look forward to concentrating on the sales task. My best years at Rowntree were in sales in the Toronto region.
Interviewer's Comments:	Lydia presents herself very well and has a strong background in confectionary sales. Her record at Rowntree is very good. Rowntree paid for her to take an introductory course in Lotus 1-2-3 in 1991, but she has not had much opportunity to develop her computer skills. She does not seem to be overly ambitious or aggressive. She stated that personal reasons were preeminent in seeking a job in Toronto.

John Fisher

Personal:	Born 1967, 190 cm; 88kg; Single
Education:	B.A. (Phys. Ed.) (1992), University of British Columbia
	While at UBC, played four years of varsity basketball (team captain in 1990–91). Assistant Coach, Senior Basketball, at University Hill High School 1988–92. Developed and ran a two-week summer basketball camp at UBC for three years. Profits from the camp were donated to the Varsity Basketball Fund.
Work:	1987–93 Jacobs Suchard Canada, Inc. (Nabob Foods)
	Six years' experience (full-time 1992–93, and five years part-time, 1987–92, during school terms and full-time during the summers) in coffee and chocolates distribution and sales; two years on the loading docks, one year driving truck, and three years as a sales representative. Sales tasks included calling on regular customers, order taking, rack jobbing and customer relations development.
	1993–94 Scavolini (Professional Basketball)
	One year after completing studies at UBC, traveled to Western Europe and Northern Africa. Travel was financed by playing professional basketball in the Italian First Division.
Candidate's Comments:	I feel the combination of educational preparation, work experience, and my demonstrated ability as a team player and leader make me well suited for this job. I am particularly interested in a job, such as sales, that rewards personal initiative.

John Fisher (continued)

Interviewer's Comments: A very ambitious and engaging individual with a good record of achievements. Strong management potential is evident, but interest in sales as a career is questionable. Minored in computer science at UBC. Has a standing offer to return to a sales management position at Nabob.

Barry Moore

Personal: Born 1954, 180 cm; 84 kg; Married with two children

Education: Business Administration Diploma (1979), Humber College

While at school, was active participant in a number of clubs and political organizations. President of the Young Liberals (1978–79).

Work: 1991–94 Barrigans Food Markets—Merchandising Analyst

Developed merchandising plans for a wide variety of product categories. Negotiated merchandising programs and trade deals with manufacturers and brokers. Managed a staff of four.

1988–91 Dominion Stores Ltd.—Assistant Merchandise Manager

Liaison responsibilities between stores and head office merchandise planning. Responsible for execution of merchandising plans for several food categories.

Barry Moore (continued)

1987 Robin Hood Multifoods, Inc.—Assistant Product Manager

Responsible for the analysis and development of promotion planning for Robin Hood Flour.

1982–87 Nestlé Enterprises Ltd.—Carnation Division Sales Representative.

Major responsibilities were developing and maintaining sales and distribution to wholesale and retail accounts.

1979–82 McCain Foods Ltd.—Inventory Analyst

Worked with sales staff and head office planning to ensure the quality and timing of shipments to brokers and stores.

Activities: Board of Directors, Richview Community Club

Board of Directors, Volunteer Centre of Etobicoke

Past President of Etobicoke Big Brothers

Active in United Way

Yachting—CC 34 Canadian Champion

Candidate's Comments: It would be a great challenge and joy to work with a progressive industry leader such as Adams Brands.

Interviewer's Comments: Very articulate and professionally groomed. Dominated the interview with a variety of anecdotes and humorous stories, some of which were relevant to the job. Likes to read popular books on management, particularly books that champion the bold, gut-feel entrepreneur. He would probably earn more money at Adams if hired.

Westinghouse Electric Corporation

Bob Ray, the marketing manager for the Overhead Distribution Transformer Division (OHDT) of Westinghouse Electric Corporation, was concerned about his field sales engineers. It had been four years since OHDT had initiated any sort of formal training program directed at the field sales force. Company information revealed that the sales force had an annual turnover of 10 percent. His concern for newer sales-persons' depth of training was paralleled by his conviction that the veteran sales engineers would benefit from more exposure to product knowledge, especially in light of recent innovations. Interpretation of direct and indirect feedback revealed that both groups were reaching for more depth in product knowledge.

Westinghouse Electric Corporation

Westinghouse was the world's oldest and second largest manufacturer of electrical apparatus and appliances. Founded by inventor George Westinghouse in 1886, the corporation marketed some 300,000 variations of about 8000 highly diversified basic products ranging from a simple piece of copper wire to a complex commercial nuclear power plant. The firm employed over 145,000 men and women in laboratories, manufacturing plants, sales offices, and distribution centers from coast to coast and around the world. Over 1800 of its scientists and engineers were actively engaged in research and development activities. The corporation had more than 160,000 stockholders.

Because of its size and the diversity required to serve a variety of markets, Westinghouse was organized into four companies operating within the corporation. The companies were Power Systems; Industry and Defense; Consumer Products; and Broadcasting, Learning and Leisure Time.

Each company was headed by a president, who had full responsibility for designing, building, and selling the company's products and services throughout the world. Each company had its own staff of specialists in certain fields. It also could draw on corporate resources for additional specialized support in fields such as marketing, manufacturing, engineering, design, research, personnel and public affairs, finance, and law.

The basic organizational unit of the company was the division, each with its own line of products and services. Each division, in turn, was grouped with a number of other divisions with related products and services, such as major appliances, construction products, or power generation equipment.

Combined sales before taxes were $5.1 billion. The Power Systems Company was the leading contributor to income after taxes, with a 43 percent contribution. The Power Systems Company was divided into two main areas: the Power Generation Group and the Transmission and Distribution Division located in Athens, Georgia.

Overhead Distribution Transformer Division (OHDT)

OHDT considered itself first in facilities, developments, and service; and rightfully so, for it had led the nation in overhead distribution transformer sales since 1971, with a fairly consistent market share of about 23 percent. Industry sales were projected to be nearly $900 million by the early 1980s.

Since 1958, all Westinghouse overhead distribution transformers were designed and manufactured in the Athens plant. The previous manufacturing site was in Sharon, Pennsylvania. OHDT was particularly proud of its engineering leadership. In the past few years, Westinghouse had expanded its staff and facility in a time when others were cutting back. Bob Ray was instrumental making this crucial marketing decision and was later honored with the Corporation's highest award, "The Order of Merit," an award given to three employees each year. In the capacity over demand ratio, the company had been 131 percent, 85 percent, and 88 percent, respectively, for the past three years.

Competition

Westinghouse had been recognized for several decades as the primary innovator in the distribution transformer industry. Four other companies, each of which had active R&D facilities, were considered major innovators: General Electric, RTE, Allis-Chalmers, and McGraw-Edison. Other strong companies among the 29 national competitors were Wagner, Kuhlman, and Colt.

The Westinghouse product was generally ranked tops in its field, representing true value for dollar investment. Some competitors, though, had been successful in promoting a less expensive product.

The Customer and Pricing

The electric utility companies were the consumers for distribution transformers, and they were divided into three major classes: investor-owned utilities, rural electric cooperatives, and municipalities. There were approximately 300 investor-owned utilities, which accounted for about 80 percent of consumption. The coops and municipalities numbered about 920 and 2000, respectively, and together accounted for the remaining 20 percent. With the increasing migration of families and industries to metropolitan outskirts, the coops were expected to represent a considerably larger share of consumption in the years to come. There were about 33 million overhead distribution transformers across the nation. Sales in this market represented about 60 percent changeouts (i.e., replacements in an area where power consumption had increased) and 40 percent new development units.

Source: This case was prepared by Norman A. P. Govoni, Babson College; Richard R. Still, Florida International University; and Kent Mitchell, the University of Georgia. Reproduced by permission.

In pricing, the major utilities negotiated year-long purchasing commitments during November–December of each year. Fierce price competition was prevalent among the investor-owned utilities, and large discounts off list prices were normally expected. Pricing for the coops and municipalities was more stable, with smaller discounts from list being offered. The method of negotiation was small orders throughout the year for the smaller utilities and the sealed bid method for the publicly owned companies.

Promotion

Westinghouse advertised its electrical transmission, generation, and distribution equipment in leading electrical trade journals. Additionally, it was a member of the National Electrical Manufacturers Association (NEMA), which set standards for the industry. NEMA issued monthly reports to its members which included total market volume and member market share information. Distribution was by a field sales force selling direct to customers.

Marketing Management

The marketing department of OHDT consisted of a marketing manager, a marketing services manager, and four area sales managers who were assisted by a staff of their own. The sales areas were divided geographically. Almost all personnel in the marketing department had an engineering background, which was considered a must in this complex field. The department had ultimate responsibility for the success of its product. They were particularly proud that Westinghouse had been number one in market share of transformer sales each year since 1971.

The marketing department had been located in Athens since 1968, when it moved down from Sharon, Pennsylvania. Exhibit I shows where the marketing department fit into the organization of the Athens firm.

The Field Sales Force

Overhead distribution transformers were sold through two of the four Westinghouse companies: the Power Systems company and the Industry and Defense company. Each company had its own sales network, as shown in Exhibit II.

There were over 300 Westinghouse corporate field sales engineers, district managers, and zone managers located throughout the country handling OHDT accounts. In addition to being loaded with OHDT products, the salespeople were responsible for other Westinghouse utility products. For example, they represented the Electrical Relay Division, the Circuit Breaker Division, and the Electric Meter Division, each of which was managed through other corporate channels. The field sales engineers, in serving several product divisions, reported to district managers for product loading.

The area sales managers and their staffs (of OHDT) served the field sales engineers by taking and expediting product orders, answering product questions, and collecting feedback. Additionally, they traveled into the field to hold training seminars and to assist salespeople on important sales. Bob Ray often got involved in following through with especially important customers.

EXHIBIT I Westinghouse Electric Corporation Marketing Department—Athens, Georgia

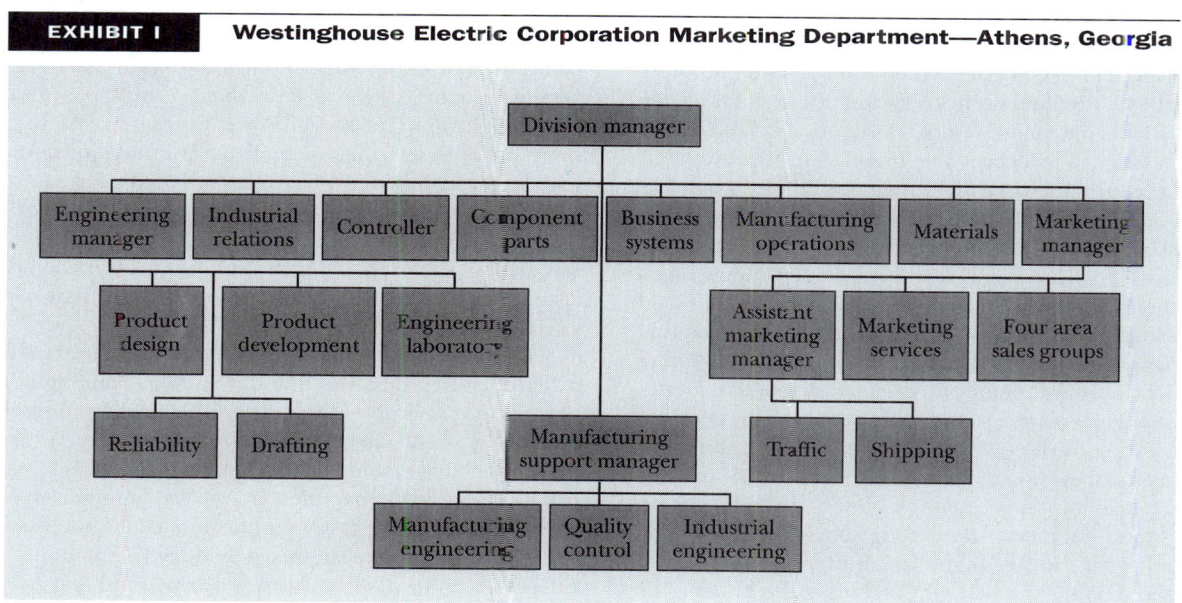

EXHIBIT II — Westinghouse Electric Corporation Sales Organization Chart

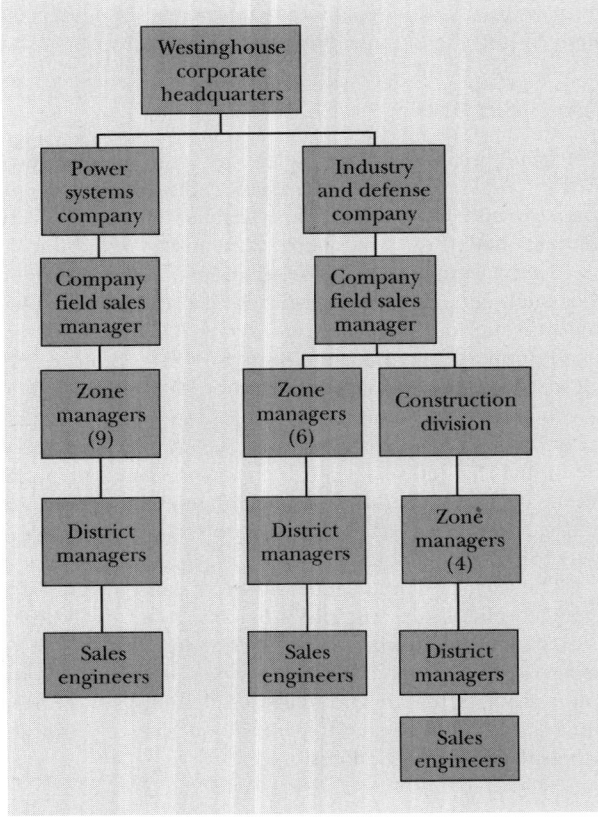

Training a Field Sales Engineer

Westinghouse sales engineers were required to have a Bachelor of Science in Engineering. When brought into the corporation, the new recruit was first sent to Pittsburgh for a basic 3-week orientation to the Westinghouse company. The recruit was then assigned to a corporate "graduate studies program" which lasted from 3 to 12 months, depending on his or her skills. Upon completion, he or she was assigned to the field as an assistant sales engineer to serve a training tenure, which lasted anywhere from 6 to 24 months, again depending on individual requirements. During this period, the person would travel for a 2-week period visiting the various manufacturing plants he or she would later serve. Each plant gave the future salesperson a 2-day training and orientation seminar. Ideally, the sales engineers were supposed to return to these parent manufacturing divisions annually for refresher training. Additionally, they would attend district or zone training seminars held by representatives of the parent divisions.

A sales engineer, depending on experience and length of service to Westinghouse, drew a base salary averaging about $35,000 a year, not including the bonus. The number of calls and the type of customer were established according to ability, experience, and product loading. It took, on the average, about $500,000 worth of sales to support a sales engineer in the field.

Thoughts of an OHDT Area Sales Manager

Marvin Jones was one of the four area sales managers for the OHDT division. Prior to his present assignment, he was a field sales engineer for over 12 years. Reflecting on his days in the field, he remembered quite well the difficulties involved in attending training seminars held by the various divisions. Salespeople recognized that training was essential, that effective selling required sound training, and that a person's potential (not to mention the quota) really could not be realized without training. However, getting a salesperson to a training seminar was a difficult task, because when there was a sale to be made, there wasn't time for training. The training, as important as it was, would have to wait. At least this was the common thing when attendance at refresher training was more or less left to the individual sales engineer.

The Need to Train

Bob Ray was very concerned about the field sales force's depth of knowledge about overhead distribution transformers, especially in light of fairly recent innovations (a trend which would be expected to continue). He knew Westinghouse had become the leading producer of transformers, but he attributed this more to excellent engineering, excessive demand, and the expertise of his department.

As questions were coming in to the area sales managers at a slightly higher than normal rate, he pinpointed the problem to training. He also knew that the economy might be expected to take a slight decline. With the growing threat that demand might slacken in the months to come, he felt that competition would really start getting rough. In addition, he realized that an unprepared salesforce might not fare so well when the time came to give more in-depth and high-quality sales presentations. And it had been a while since Athens had initiated a formal training program. The previous program, which was considered a success, consisted of a campaign to inform the salesforce about the overhead distribution transformer, and, as a gimmick, miniature transformer parts were sent to the salespeople.

Unfortunately, a salesperson's time was an extremely valuable commodity, and Bob Ray knew it. Training in any organization was one of the most difficult tasks to pull off effectively, even when the trainees were geographically close to management; but the Westinghouse field salesforce, scattered across the nation, was another matter. Making the training task even more burdensome was the fact that these sales engineers had more than just the OHDT account to worry about. It was realized that Athens would have to compete for both time and attention.

EXHIBIT III	Westinghouse Overhead Distribution Transformers: "The Problem Solvers" Promotion

General

This document summarizes various elements of the "Problem Solver" promotion. The costs are based on quotations from suppliers who have seen initially prepared layouts.

Puzzles

Five puzzles will be purchased directly from supplier by Westinghouse.

Shipping Boxes for Puzzles

Five puzzles each of the five different size boxes plus one 6"-by-6" envelope (for crossword puzzles and brochure mailing), each to be printed in two colors using the same "Problem Solver" design. (Suggestion: each box to have a different color on the design.)
Delivery time: six weeks from receipt of order.
Cost: including converting boxes, design preparation, color plates and printing: $2500.

Crossword Puzzle

To be completed by salesperson and submitted with photo to get personalized jigsaw puzzle prize.
Timing: Six weeks from receipt of words and clues from Westinghouse. Puzzles to be printed in simple 4-page format and inserted in envelope along with cover letter and brochure.
Cost: $800.

Jigsaw Puzzle

One 11"-by-14" puzzle will be sent to every salesperson submitting photo along with completed crossword puzzle. Photos will be held and sent in bulk to puzzle manufacturer, who will then send completed puzzle directly to each salesperson along with the original photo.
Timing: four weeks delivery from receipt of photographs.
Cost: $1,300.

Cover Letters

Total of five (one for each puzzle mailing), 400 copies of each.
Cost: including artwork for masthead, copy editing, typesetting, and printing: $600.

Brochures

One brochure will accompany each of the five puzzle mailings. Each brochure will focus on one aspect of the overhead transformers. The cover will have a full color cover of the puzzle being sent; inside pages will be black and white and use existing line art.
Cost: including photos, typesetting, tissue layout and key art, copy editing, and production supervision for five 20-page booklets: $12,000.

Total Cost: up to $20,000.

From Ideas to Action

With the facts on the table, Bob Ray called on Larry Deal, who headed Marketing Services, and his assistant, Glynn Hodges, who at that time was involved with marketing communications. Hodges was sent to Pittsburgh a few times to work jointly with Earl Swartz, the corporate contact to the ad agency used by Westinghouse. By June, Hodges had the layout completed for the proposed solution to the training problem—a training campaign to be called "The Problem Solvers." Bob Ray liked it. It was estimated that the campaign would ultimately cost about $20,000 representing a large slice of the OHDT marketing budget. Exhibit III gives an idea of the estimated costs.

About "The Problem Solvers" Campaign

An overview of "The Problem Solvers" appears in Exhibit IV, which contains the following: background, problem objectives, program implementation, elements of the program (Stages 1 and 2), and a summary of elements and timing.

To catch the salesperson's attention, the proposed campaign would consist of expensive, eye-catching adult games which emphasized puzzle problems. The games would cost $4–$5 each; a good example was a three-dimensional tic-tac-toe game made of three clear plastic decks mounted on top of each other. Each player was represented by either clear blue or yellow marbles about an inch in diameter each. The game could be won horizontally, vertically, or diagonally.

Along with the mailing of each game would be a cover letter and an information bulletin emphasizing a particular feature of the overhead distribution transformer. As the salesperson read each information bulletin, he or she would fill in "clues" to a master crossword puzzle. When the mailings were completed, the salesperson would send in the completed crossword puzzle

EXHIBIT IV — **Westinghouse Overhead Distribution Transformers: An Overview of "The Problem Solvers"**

Background

The total market for overhead distribution transformers is very good. For Westinghouse, it is excellent. While Athens is producing at full capacity and the current problem is meeting demand, there still remain several conditions with which Athens must cope if it is to achieve its long-range potential:

1. Many Westinghouse and agent salespeople do not understand the advantages of Westinghouse transformers.
2. There are competitors who manufacture and sell transformers at a cheaper price. These transformers are inferior to those at Westinghouse. The Westinghouse story, which must be communicated through sales personnel to customers, is a *value* story.
3. The present sales boom cannot be expected to continue indefinitely, and the salesforce must be prepared to conduct tougher, more effective sales presentations.

Program Objectives

The object of this program is to make Westinghouse and agent sales personnel more effective representatives for Athens by showing them why Westinghouse is the value leader and by giving them the information and tools needed to make more effective presentations.

By accomplishing these objectives, the sales representatives will become more confident of their abilities—and the Westinghouse line. This growing confidence will, in turn, create even greater success.

Program Implementation

This is a two-stage program. The Stage 1 phase, the more important, is directed to the Westinghouse salesforce and includes an explanation of the program, a summary of the transformer market (and the profit contribution made by Westinghouse transformers), and detailed instructions on transformers (using the theme "The Problem Solvers") along with unique mailings.

The Stage 2 phase is the person-to-person contact between salespeople and customers. Having been effectively indoctrinated into the advantages of Westinghouse transformers, the salespeople are now supplied with effective sales presentation material, which will make contact between sales representatives and customers more productive for the Athens division.

Elements of Program—Stage 1

1. Cover letter No. 1 from Mr. Meierkord (general manager, OHDT) or Mr. Ray spelling out the theme "The Problem Solvers" and that the purpose of the program.
2. Instruction brochure No. 1 on Cover and Bushing Assembly along with puzzle.
3. Cover letter No. 2 from Meierkord or Ray.
4. Instruction brochure No. 2 on Tank Assembly along with puzzle.
5. Cover letter No. 3 from Meierkord or Ray.
6. Instruction brochure on Core Assembly along with puzzle.
7. Cover letter No. 4 from Meierkord or Ray. Letter to state that crosswod puzzle answers are found in instruction booklet. If salesperson returns completed crossword puzzle along with any photograph of his or her choice, Athens will return a custom-made jigsaw puzzle made out of the photo.
8. Instruction brochure No. 4 on CSP (completely self-protected transformer) features along with crossword puzzle. Crossword puzzle will contain such clues as:
   CSP Transformers (OUTLAST) conventional types by 60 percent.
   CSP arresters (LOWER) discharge voltage on high surge currents.
   After overload trips breaker, breaker can be reset to (TEN) percent more capacity.

Elements of Program—Stage 2

After salespeople have studied the four bulletins, they are better prepared to make more effective presentations to their customers. To help them in their calls, they will be furnished with the following:

1. Cover letter (No. 5) again from Meierkord or Ray, reiterating the profitability of transformers, that they are great "Problem Solvers," and that the salespeople (the ultimate "Problem Solvers") are now well prepared to communicate to their customers why Westinghouse transformers are truly tops in the field. Cover letter will dwell on the importance of customer presentations, preparation, and follow-through.
2. Flip chart presentation entitled "Westinghouse Distribution Transformers: 'The Problem Solvers.'" The presentation will summarize the most important "Features/Functions/Benefits" from the four technical bulletins. The presentation will be designed in a horizontal format so that the pages are adaptable for photographic slide or strip film production.
3. Customer booklet to be prepared using same text and artwork from the presentation flip chart. Booklet will be left with the customer as a reminder of what was presented and as a source document for later reference.
4. Capabilities brochure, about to be produced, can be an added ingredient to the presentation. While it emphasizes Athens' manufacturing capability—as opposed to the engineering emphasis of the presentation—the booklet is prestigious and will reflect Westinghouse distribution transformers as being a value line.

If not used as part of the presentation, the capabilities brochure would make an impressive mailing to the customer, along with a "thank you" letter for listening to the presentation.

Summary—Elements and Timing

Stage 1
First Mailing: Cover Letter No. 1 (Program Summary)
                  Bulletin No. 1 Cover and Bushing
                  Puzzle No. 1 (Adult Game)
                  Master Crossword Puzzle
Second Mailing: Cover Letter No. 2
                  Bulletin No. 2 Tank Assembly
(Two months later) Puzzle No. 2
Third Mailing: Cover Letter No. 3
                  Bulletin No. 3 Core and Coil Assembly
(Two months later) Puzzle No. 3
Fourth Mailing: Cover Letter No. 4
                  Bulletin No. 4 CSP Features
(Two months later) Puzzle No. 4
Stage 2
Fifth Mailing: Cover Letter No. 5 (Customer Presentations)
                  Flip Chart Presentation
(Two months later) Presentation Summary for Customer
                  Athens Capability Brochure
                  Puzzle No. 5

and picture of himself or herself (along with the rest of the family if desired) to the marketing department in Athens. Athens would have the picture made into a jigsaw puzzle and return it to the participant a few weeks later.

The Marketing Services Division—A Special Project

Larry Deal's Marketing Services Division had been assigned the responsibility of supporting the ad agency by providing the technical information necessary for turning "The Problem Solvers" idea into a manageable campaign. Brian Kennedy, assigned to marketing communications, and assistant Jody Unsler had been asked to design the instruction brochures and crossword puzzle. Also, coordination with Earl Swartz had resulted in the initial selection of a container for the games. The container was a cardboard box with a design of jigsaw puzzle parts; each part had a letter on it, which when put together spelled out "The Problem Solvers." Kennedy put in long hours working on the instruction brochures. In explaining the various components of the transformer, he had decided to set a conversational sales presentation scene between a Westinghouse salesperson and a purchasing agent. The salesperson, who was "Mr. Problem Solver" or "Ms. Problem Solver," was smoothly answering the questions asked by a purchasing agent, who was appropriately labeled "Mr. A. Gent" or "Ms. A. Lady."

Early November

One morning in early November, Bob Ray was relaxing at his desk sipping a cup of coffee. He was thinking about "The Problem Solvers" campaign. Things were moving along pretty well. At the present rate, he would be able to meet the January 15 target date for the first mailing. He knew $20,000 was a lot of money for OHDT to spend on a training campaign of this type, but he was confident in the overall idea and felt it was the best way to reach such a broad and isolated target. However, a few decisions remained. There was some question about the two-month interval between each of the five mailings. He definitely wanted the salesforce ready for November–December when the big utilities would negotiate year-long contracts for the following year. In a way, he wanted the campaign to last a good while, as it represented a big chunk of the budget, but he wondered whether the field salesforce's attention would be held over such a period. Another thought entered his mind about the effectiveness of the campaign's feedback mechanism. He remembered Glynn Hodges saying he anticipated a 65 percent response. Another point that was undefined in the campaign was what stand OHDT should take on the future newcomers to the field salesforce. Since the previous campaign, the new people learned through OJT (on-the-job training) and sales materials, as well as by picking up what they could from OHDT bulletins. However, this provided only short-range coverage and would break down in the long run or when making sales got tough. This had been one of the factors contributing to the present situation.

With those thoughts in mind, Bob Ray decided to call a division head meeting that afternoon.

Romano Pitesti

Events had come to a head in Tickton-Jones Ltd. and the Marketing Director, Jack Simpson, had called in his Consumer Products Sales Manager, David Courtney, to sort out the problem.

> "To come straight to the point, David," said Jack, "I'm about up to here with this sales rep of yours. Romano Pitesti.... Am I sick of hearing the guy's name! Everywhere I go, someone bends my ear about him. Last week it was the receptionist complaining about his making personal telephone calls during company time. Yesterday it was the security people about his untidy parking habits. And this morning, the accounts department is abuzz with outrage over his expense returns. Quite frankly, David, these are not isolated instances—he's out of control and I want to know what you intend to do about him, before the whole company is in uproar."

Background

Tickton-Jones Ltd. was formed two years previously, when Tickton Flexible Products Ltd. acquired Samuel Jones Ltd., a local family-owned company. At the time, Tickton's annual sales were approaching $12 million and they employed 230 people; compared with Jones' $4.5 million and 110 people, respectively. Tickton was well established as a compounder of polyurethane and rubber materials and had its own molding facility for a wide range of industrial components. Jones, after years of steady business as a manufacturer of shoes, ladies' handbags, and travel goods, had recently moved successfully into sports shoes and for the first time had made an impact in the export field.

Ben Jones was the Chairman and majority owner of Samuel Jones Ltd. He was the grandson of the founder and the last of the Jones family line with an active participation in the business. At age 63, he wanted to sell out and retire to the Channel Islands with his wife, who had a health problem. The remaining two senior Directors were willing to accept early retirement on generous terms.

Ben Jones had been very happy to accept Tickton's offer and was satisfied that the new company would not involve too much upheaval for his employees. He was a paternal Chairman with a strong Protestant work ethic, but in recent years this had softened, and the organization had become somewhat looser in all aspects of its operations.

Not everyone on the Tickton Board had been in favor of the acquisition, largely because it represented a major diversification into consumer products. But the Managing Director had swayed the decision on grounds of too much current dependence on declining customer industries (e.g., motor vehicles, railways, general mechanical engineering). Jones was considered to have good products in growth markets. In the words of Tickton's Managing Director: "An opportunity like this might never pass our way again. Ben Jones assures me that he has a sound labor force and, like our own, they're not strongly unionized. The sports and leisure shoe business looks particularly attractive. Put our expertise in molding technology alongside their distribution network, and it could be one of our main product lines in five years. It's now or never—it would be virtually impossible to find equivalent facilities within a five-mile radius." Within four weeks, the acquisition was agreed upon.

Due to the departure of Jones's senior Directors, integration of managerial staff provided few problems. Jones's production manager, Bill Thompson, was retained and placed in charge of the Jonessite, which was effectively reduced to a manufacturing operation. All nonproduction staff, including the sales manager, David Courtney, were moved to the Tickton site.

However, the absorption of middle/lower-level administrative staff had not been easy, and there were still cliques of former Jones employees who felt aggrieved. For example, certain secretaries had found themselves reporting to managers of lower status; friction in the sales administration office and accounts office caused internal divisions; and there was growing rivalry among the industrial sales engineers and the consumer sales representatives.

The organization of Tickton-Jones's marketing department is shown in Exhibit I. From the marketing point of view, Jack Simpson had merely added another arm to his departmental organization—the Consumer Products Groups under David Courtney.

Prior to the acquisition, David Courtney had been very much a field sales manager. He was responsible for the usual sales management tasks of forecasting and budgeting, and spent most of his time dealing with major existing accounts or on the road developing new accounts. David Courtney, Romano Pitesti, and Jim Wells were all paid a salary plus commission. The commission element accounted for 20–25 percent of their annual pay. On joining Tickton-Jones's salary structure they received salary only, though in money terms this did not constitute a loss of total pay.

On the question of company car policy and day-to-day business expenses, there were major differences. Indeed, since at Samuel Jones Ltd. they applied to so few people, there were no formal procedures and Ben Jones signed off on everything, almost without question. In contrast, Tickton had a written document clearly setting out the type of car applicable to particular grades; spending limits for travel and entertainment, and so on. There was also a handbook covering Tickton's general conditions of service, which automatically became the Tickton-Jones handbook.

Romano Pitesti

To say that Romano Cesare Pitesti was *different* from the industrial sales engineers would be an understatement.

Source: This case was prepared by Tony Millman, University of Buckingham School of Business, United Kingdom. Reproduced by permission.

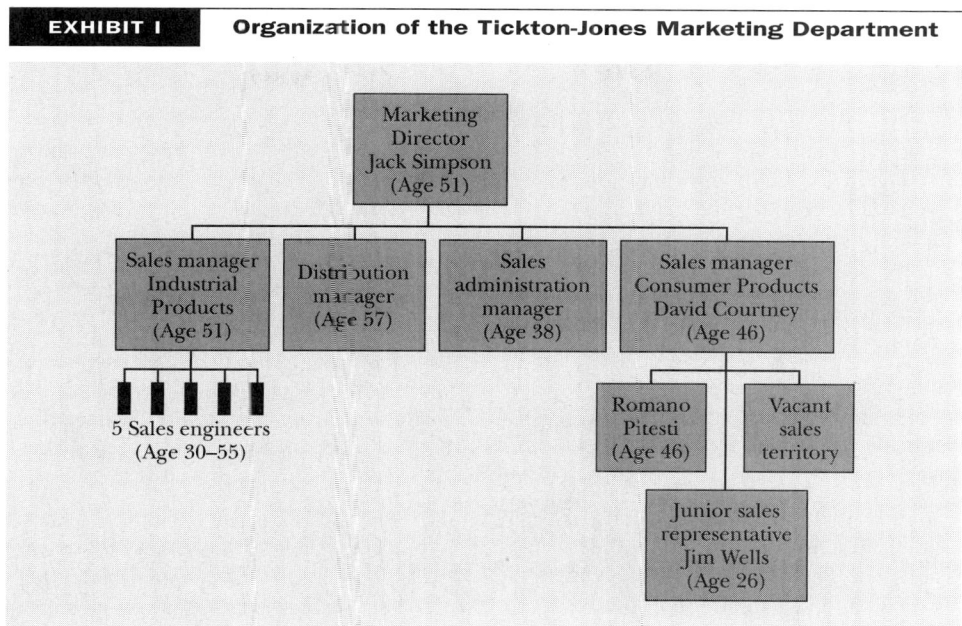

EXHIBIT I   Organization of the Tickton-Jones Marketing Department

While they "toed the line" and had quite similar training and attitudes, Romano "sailed close to the wind."

Romano liked to feel that he was an *individualist* and repeatedly proved disruptive in formal group situations. Though basically conscientious and hardworking, he operated in bursts of enthusiasm that usually came to nothing but sometimes, through sheer tenacity on his part, brought the company an important order.

He was the master of the *instant opinion* and often entered into conversation on a range of issues of which he had only cursory knowledge and experience. This led him into a number of embarrassing situations, reflecting his gullability and boyish naiveté.

There were occasions when he could be charming, understanding, and a good listener, especially in female company. And even more so in the presence of Sheila Jones, his previous Chairman's wife! It was well known that she had a soft spot for Romano and had once saved him from serious trouble following an incident involving a secretary after the office Christmas party.

Romano was flamboyant in all things, yet beneath this facade lay a caring and deeply sensitive person. His colleague, Jim Wells, summed him up as "part hero, part villain, and part clown."

From the day he transferred to Tickton-Jones, Romano was regarded as a curiosity and a "figure of fun." The reasons were not hard to find. He dressed impeccably and in the height of fashion. Some would say that he overdid it for a 46-year-old, and he was soon dubbed "The Great Gatsby," "Peter Pan," and "The Aging Lothario."

In his first year with Tickton-Jones, Romano married Wendy Churchill, a 28-year-old set designer with a regional television company. This brought him in contact with numerous television personalities and turned him into a prolific name dropper. The stories he told provided unlimited ammunition for the industrial sales engineers, who cruelly taunted him at every opportunity. But Romano, unperturbed, shrugged off their remarks, usually with some witty return.

Despite all these oddities and eccentricities, Romano's sales performance was exemplary.

The Meeting with David Courtney

With Jack Simpson's words ringing in his ears, David Courtney summoned Romano to a meeting. Romano insisted that it would upset his call schedule, but after some cajoling agreed to attend the following morning.

David opened the meeting with firm words: Romano, something has to be done about the way you operate in this company. It has been put to me that you are out of control. I'm taking the kicks at the moment and I don't like it! I've got a list of incidents to review with you—and you had better have good answers."

1. **David:** Your time-keeping leaves a lot to be desired, and you've been accused of wasting your own time and other people's. The normal starting time is 8:30 A.M. and not some time after 9:00 A.M. when you can make it!

   Romano: That's all very well, but I'm entitled to a little freedom on time. Only yesterday I left home at 6:00 A.M. to visit a customer and didn't return home until late in the evening. How many of those complaining about my time-keeping would be prepared to join me at such times of the day and night without overtime payments?

David: And what about time wasting? You seem to spend a fair amount of time with secretaries and typists.

Romano: No more than anyone else. It's just that other people spread their time over the week and mine's more concentrated. You know how much importance you attach to letter and report writing. Well, they all have to be typed.

2. **David:** That brings me to the time you claim to spend report writing. Taking Fridays off is a favorite for sniping by the industrial sales engineers.

   Romano: If you want me to write reports, you have got to allow me time to write them—it's as simple as that.

   David: The industrial sales engineers write their reports over their lunch break or between sales calls. Why can't you? There's a rumor circulating the company that you played golf last Friday.

   Romano: Yes, that right. I played golf with Arthur Dixon—you know, Singleton's Purchasing Manager. I'm pretty close to a regular order from them. I'm playing with Arthur again on the 29th—should I cancel it?

   David: No, no—I only wish you to make yourself a little more *visible* on Fridays. Not every Friday, just now and then.

3. **David:** Are you aware that you have higher claims for replacement of damaged clothing than anyone in the company? Why?

   Romano: I can't help it if I wear trendy Italian suits and shoes. That damaged briefcase I claimed last month really was two-tone crocodile skin and cost me $180. I can't visit my customers dressed like those scruffy *Herberts* in the Industrial Group. They wouldn't let me on the premises.

   David: OK, OK, just try to moderate your claims in future. I'm the poor guy who has to sign them off.

4. **David:** The biggest problem, as always, surrounds your company car. It's like a big orange blotch on the company landscape!

   Romano: I can't see what you have against my car, David. It's only a Ford Escort 1.3 and bought within the company rules. We have very little flexibility on choice of model. After all, it's my mobile office—I live in it for 15 hours per week.

   David: Yes, but do you have to choose bright orange and add all those accessories? The industrial sales engineers all have more sober colors such as bottle green and navy blue. Do you really need two large spot lamps with checkered covers, a rear spoiler, and whiplash radio aerial?

   Romano: I paid for the accessories myself. You could do the same if you wish. Incidentally, there's a nice vivid green in the Ford Sierra right now!

   David: I can almost bear the color with my sunglasses on—but not when you park your car on the double yellow lines near the reception area.

   Romano: I knew it! That receptionist has got it in for me. It would be her who complained and not the security people. I only popped in to the switchboard to collect my telephone messages from the overnight answering machine.

   David: I can accept that as an isolated incident. But your car is so obvious—everywhere you go, it's instantly recognizable. Which leads me to a very serious issue—did you or did you not use your company car to ferry voters to the local Council elections?

   Romano: Yes, I did. I had my doubts about it and was on the verge of opting out. Then I realized Bill Thompson, the Production Manager, was using his company car for the Labour Party, so I thought, what's good enough for Labour is good enough for the Liberals.

   David: Perhaps I had better have a word with Bill about the matter. We'll pick this one up later.

5. **Romano:** You've mentioned all these minor irritations, David. Have you ever had cause to question my sales performance? I'm the best salesperson in this company, and you know it! When did I last fail to meet my targets? And have you received any complaints from customers? I was the same at Samuel Jones. Don't forget, we're a rep short at the moment. A few more salespeople like me and we would be a market leader in no time. Who is it who secured the Milan export order?

But at that particular moment there was an interruption. Romano's telephone paging beeper was signaling an incoming call, and he picked up David's telephone. It was Joe Pinkerton. Romano's number two customer, with an urgent query.

Romano sat back in his chair, put his feet on David's wastepaper basket, and entered into a drawn-out conversation. Twenty minutes later he was still engrossed in conversation. David shook his head and decided to abandon the meeting. Romano gave him a wry grin as he left the office.

Windsor Management Company: Are Salespeople Worth It?

Robert M. Dominy, northeast regional manager of Windsor Management Company, was preparing for a meeting on March 6, 1992, with the executive committee to make a final decision on the proposed resident retention bonus program. A decision had to be made by the following week to budget the necessary funds for the renewal bonus. Bob had calculated that this new renewal bonus would cost the entire company $145,000, and would cost his region $60,000. While Bob was aware of the potential economic benefit of the reduced turnover of leases and the support of this program by senior management, he wondered if the bonus program would actually reduce turnover very much. Bob also wondered if he would get more economic benefit by using the $60,000 in some other way in his region.

Company Background

General Investment and Development (GID), together with its affiliated companies, is a privately held real estate investment and development firm specializing in planned, middle- and upper-income, multi-family residential communities; commercial properties; and other related activities. While maintaining an emphasis in development and management of multi-family communities, GID is experienced in a wide variety of real estate activities.

Since its establishment in 1960, GID has built its business on quality. Operating principally under the Windsor trade name, GID began its first building project twelve miles south of Boston in Norwood, Massachusetts. During the next nine years, Windsor Gardens at Norwood grew to include 682 garden apartments, 232 townhouses a child-care center, and a railroad station providing direct service to downtown Boston. During the same period, GID also developed more than 1100 residential apartments and townhouses in Framingham, Beverly, and Waltham, Massachusetts. GID also began to expand geographically, entering other northeastern markets including Long Island, New York, and Pittsburgh, Pennsylvania. In the early 1970s the company completed 300 townhouses in Westborough, Massachusetts and 296 garden apartments near Rochester, New York.

In late 1972, in anticipation of too many apartments being constructed, GID shifted its energies toward the development of condominiums and the acquisition of existing rental apartment communities originally constructed by other developers. This new strategy led to the acquisition of 612 garden apartments in Marlborough, Massachusetts, 818 rental units throughout Wichita, Kansas, and 562 apartments in Peoria, Illinois. By 1974, the apartment portfolio had grown to over 4500 units.

GID's work in condominium development also proved to be lucrative. Beginning in 1970, GID was actively engaged in marketing condominiums and cooperative housing; many of these units were located in resort communities. GID designed, developed, and completed marketing for a 132-unit resort community in Waterville Valley, New Hampshire.

In early 1970, GID also constructed and successfully marketed a 140-unit condominium community near Rochester, New York. Then, in 1976, a major Boston bank approached GID to market and manage a 180-unit resort community on Lake Winnepesaukee in New Hampshire. In 1976, GID purchased this project from the bank. Through physical improvements, expense reductions and innovative marketing, GID was able to sell the entire project by the summer of 1978. In 1979, GID commenced public marketing of its 200-unit condominium development in Framingham, Massachusetts.

From 1979 and throughout the 1980s, GID remained active in both development and acquisitions. In February 1979, GID purchased two additional apartment communities in Wichita, Kansas, bringing the total number of units in that city to 1,277. In December of 1979, GID purchased a 235-unit luxury high-rise apartment building in Syracuse, New York. In the Fall of 1981, GID developed Bower Hill III, a 135-unit high-rise building in Mount Lebanon, Pennsylvania. In that same year, GID also acquired 604 garden apartments in Columbus, Ohio and named them Windsor at Wedgwood Park. Then in 1982, GID added the Benson Apartments to its portfolio. Located north of Philadelphia in Jenkintown, Pennsylvania, the Benson features two high-rise buildings consisting of 440 residential apartments and 175,000 square feet of office and retail space. In 1986, GID expanded into yet another market, acquiring a 900-unit apartment community in Houston, Texas. In 1987, the company expanded into Huntsville, Alabama when it purchased a 514-unit community called Flagstone Apartments. To date, GID's apartment portfolio consists of over 9100 units located in 21 properties in 8 different states. In the fall of 1991, the company acquired four additional properties, three properties totalling 907 units in the Northern Virginia area, and one property in Maryland consisting of 212 units.

During the 1980s GID's expanded into commercial, office and retail acquisition, development, and management. In 1983, GID converted a historic landmark formerly housing a manufacturing facility into 115,000 square feet of modern office and R&D space. Also in 1983, the company, through one of its affiliates, entered into a joint venture to construct, market and manage a 14-story, 375,000 square foot high-rise office building with street level retail space—Market place Center was completed in 1985 and is located in the heart of Boston's world-famous Quincy Market, in the shadow of historic Fanueil Hall. In 1988, GID renovated a historic industrial building in Watertown, Massachusetts, creating 110,000 square feet of office space.

Source: Copyright © 1994 by H. David Hennessey, Babson College. This case was developed with the assistance of Windsor Management Company as a basis for class discussion, rather than to illustrate either effective or ineffective handling of an administrative situation.

Recent years have seen GID continue to grow, expand, and diversify. The portfolio now includes a modular home manufacturing company and a cabinet manufacturer. The company has developed its first hotel and has added two major industrial centers in North Carolina and Massachusetts. Presently, the company is developing its first golf course, surrounded by 484 single-family homes in Pinehurst, North Carolina.

GID was actively considering a number of potential acquisitions for the second half of 1992 and 1993. The reduced cost of capital, due to low interest rates and the depressed real estate markets, made it a particularly good time for GID to acquire new properties. The continued growth of GID depended upon its ability to attract and maintain high quality personnel to manage its facilities and serve the needs of over 9,100 families living in Windsor apartments, townhouses, and condominiums throughout the United States.

Organizational Structure

GID is a private company. The company is broken into two parts. The president oversees the nonproperty management activities which includes finance, accounting, acquisitions, oil and gas, home building, kitchen cabinets, and corporate travel. GID owns a small corporate travel company to handle all its travel needs. The chairman oversees the property management side of the company which is shown in Exhibit I.

Northeast Region

Bob Dominy is the northeast regional manager, overseeing 9 properties with a total of 3800 units. Bob is 40 years old and has an undergraduate degree from Evangel College, and an MBA from Babson College. He began with Windsor Management Company as a marketing representative in 1978 and has risen through the organization. In 1985 he became the northeast regional manager. He receives a salary plus bonus based on the revenues and profit of the northeast region. Each property is managed by the property manager who has complete operational responsibility for the site. Properties range from Norwood with 914 units, 20 employees, and a budget of $8 million to Beverly with 204 units, 9 employees, and a budget of $2 million. The property manager oversees the activities of the marketing representatives and the maintenance staff.

The northeast region generates approximately 65% of the company's operations profit.

Marketing Representatives

The key entry level position at Windsor Management is the marketing representative. These individuals are recruited directly from college to work at one of the Windsor properties. The representatives are responsible for sales, office administration, and marketing. Sales includes showing prospective residents the model apartment and renewing leases for current residents. The marketing includes tracking demand, identifying market trends, shopping competi-

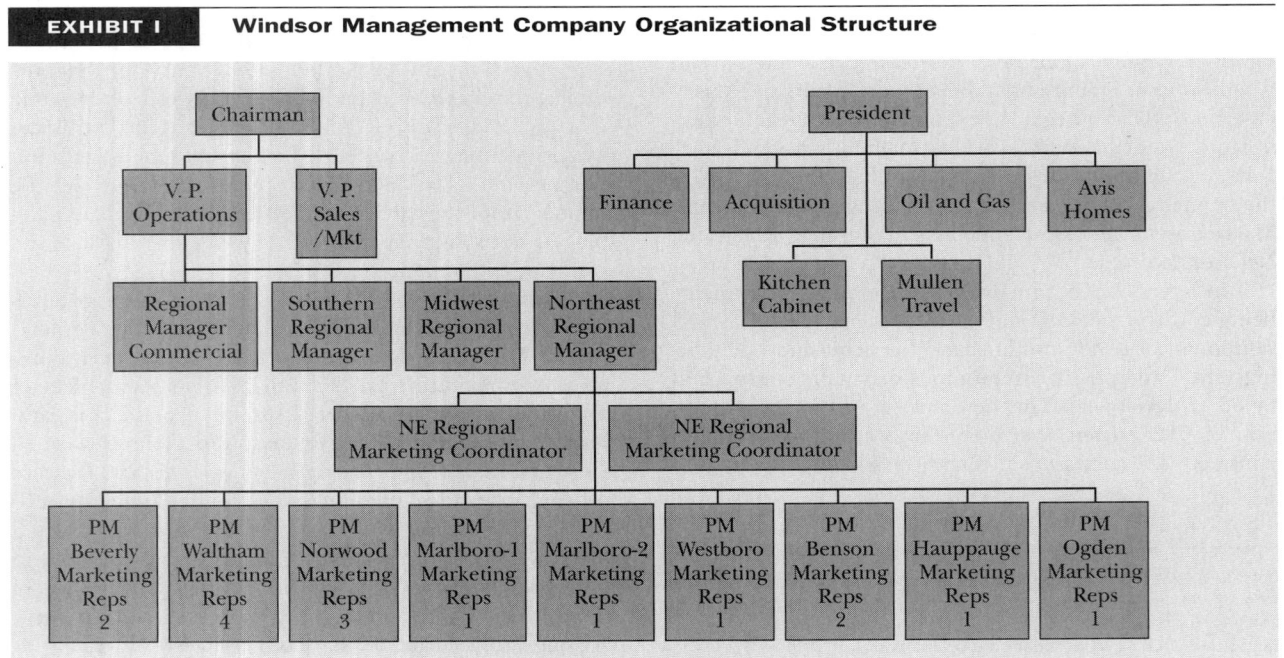

EXHIBIT I Windsor Management Company Organizational Structure

tive properties, and helping the property manager with advertising and special projects. Office administration includes credit checks on potential residents, weekly reports on renewal and visits, executing leases, and solving resident problems. The job description is included in Exhibit II.

The marketing representative position is a very time consuming and challenging position. Most new marketing reps begin work in May or June. The May–September period is the busiest time of the year. No vacations are allowed during the period between Memorial Day and Labor Day. The leasing offices are open all but six days of the year; the marketing reps work most weekends.

Windsor does extensive campus recruiting to hire marketing reps. In the spring, they recruit at Babson College, Bryant College, Bentley College, Boston College, Boston University, Holy Cross and Villanova. Resumes are screened before the interviews, then Windsor managers interview students. For example in 1992, approximately 250 students were interviewed on college campuses; from this group, 30 were asked for a second interview and a personality test. Upon successful completion, 10 received a third interview with Bob Dominy and 5 were offered positions.

The compensation for marketing reps is based upon three components: (1) a base salary of $19,500 per year, (2) a year-end bonus, and (3) a bonus of 0–$800/month depending on the actual versus budgeted vacancy rate. For example, if five percent were budgeted to be vacant in June, but only four percent were vacant, all the marketing reps would receive $600. The concept of the vacancy bonus is to reward marketing reps for outperforming the projected vacancy rate. The average marketing rep earns around $27,500/yr annualized for the first six months and $27,500–$29,000 for the next year depending upon performance.

In addition to the vacancy bonus, marketing reps can receive a $125 gift certificate for dinner or travel if they achieve the highest closing rate per month. The closing rate is calculated by dividing the number of new leases

---

EXHIBIT II Windsor Marketing Representative

Few professional positions provide as much diversity at the outset as that of a Windsor marketing representative. The marketing representative is directly responsible for generating the income necessary to operate a multi-million dollar rental property. To insure profitable operation, skills in marketing and sales as well as administrative technique must be utilized to capacity.

The position provides on-the-job training in the development of marketing strategies, sales skills, office administration, and resident relations. Further, the assignment of a wide range of responsibilities allows the individual to identify and highlight his/her talents in a receptive environment.

Market Research

Accurate data is essential to the success of our marketing program. The marketing representative plays a crucial role in identifying trends in the marketplace. Through research of competitors, tracking demand changes in the rental market, and updating resident demographics, the marketing representative can make informed recommendations on courses of action. Further, the marketing representative develops alliances with chambers of commerce, local government organizations and industry groups in order to keep abreast of activity in the community.

Sales Technique

The Windsor training program includes professional instruction to develop selling skills—our management team is among the finest in the industry and makes every effort to transfer its skills to new personnel.

On a day-to-day basis, the marketing representative will also utilize telemarketing skills to sell the rental product to selected industries. Through developing networking systems, the marketing representative increases visibility in the corporate community and promotes the rental community during presentations to corporate offices.

Office Administration

As an integral member of a property management team, the marketing representative will quickly become versed in operational procedures including weekly reports, computer operations and special projects. In addition, the representative will assist the property manager with the formulation of marketing and advertising strategies. Accordingly, each month, the marketing representative can chart new courses in marketing and watch the profitable results develop!

The Future

The company strongly believes in assigning additional responsibility in recognition of a high level of performance. The on-the-job training program prepares the marketing representative for the position of property manager and provides a vehicle for growth as new opportunities continue to develop within the organization.

As property manager, the individual will draw heavily on the skills developed during the training period. At all times, the company provides extensive support in order to contribute to the development of the individual and to retain high caliber personnel.

(closes) by the number of people who looked at the property. As shown in Exhibit III, the closing rate can vary from 5 percent to 60 percent. Closing rates are discussed at each weekly marketing meeting and are closely monitored by the property managers and the marketing reps. While the gift of $125 is appreciated, the honor comes from being one of the top four to five closers. The closing results are widely circulated to company executives and it is not uncommon for a senior executive to send a personal note to the top performer. In a typical month a marketing rep has 40 showings. Out of these showings it is typical to lease 10 to 15 units. If a marketing rep closed 16–25 units it would be considered above average to excellent.

Windsor Management also offers other awards to recognize good employees. There is an employee of the month for the northeast region. The employee of the month for the northeast region is chosen from the entire management, marketing and maintenance staff. The recipient receives a memo and $125 gift certificate. The memo is also sent to the chairman and vice president of operations who often follow up to congratulate the employee.

At year end, there is an award given to the top three marketing representatives. These awards are given in March at the Marketing Conference Dinner. In addition to a nice plaque the recipients are given travel vouchers as follows: first place—$2,000, second place—$1,500, third place—$1,000. These year-end awards are coveted by all the marketing reps and are a good indication of promotability.

As well as these recognition awards, the management hosts two or three events per year to boost the morale of the marketing reps. For example, Bob Dominy might take the marketing reps to a Red Sox game or Joan Graham, the NE marketing coordinator, might take the reps to Nick's Comedy Club in Boston.

Joan Graham, the northeast regional marketing coordinator, is responsible for training the marketing reps. Usually five or six new reps are hired each year to replace people who had been promoted or left the company. The

EXHIBIT III

Windsor Regional Office
976 Lexington Street • Waltham, Massachusetts 02154
To: N.E. Property Managers
    N.E. Assistant Managers
    N.E. Marketing Managers
    N.E. Marketing Representatives
Fr: Joan Graham
Dt: February 2, 1992
Re: January 1992 Close Ratios

Congratulations to Cana Farr, marketing representative of Windsor Gardens at Ogden! Cana led the region in closing at 62% during the month of January. Second in the region by a very narrow margin was Shannon Murray, marketing representative of Windsor Gardens at Norwood, who closed at 61%. Outstanding job Cana and Shannon!! Other strong performers in January were Heather Jones who closed 43%, Janie Burstein who closed 38% and Tracy Nuttle who closed 36%.

The results for the region are as follows:

Cana Farr	Windsor Gardens at Odgen	62%
Shannon Murray	Windsor Gardens at Norwood	61%
Heather Jones	Windsor Village at Waltham	43%
Janie Burstein	The Benson Apartments	38%
Tracy Nuttle	The Benson Apartments	36%
Kim Haas	Windsor Village at Waltham	35%
Gus Leddy	Windsor Village at Waltham	35%
Maureen Durand	Windsor Gardens at Norwood	33%
Sonia Rochefort	Windsor Courts at Beverly	33%
Doreen Aron	Windsor Village at Waltham	23%
Brad Piver	Windsor Gardens at Norwood	22%
James Libuda	Windsor Ridge at Westboro	21%
Doreen Byron	Windsor Meadows at Marlboro	15%
Scott Peters	Windsor Heights at Marlboro	14%
Dora Damiano	Windsor Village at Hauppauge	9%
Danielle Krinsky	Windsor Ridge/Meadows/Heights	7%

In recognition of her performance, Cana will receive a $125 gift certificate to the restaurant of her choice or to Mullin Travel. Congratulations, again, Cana. Good luck to all in February.

cc: R. M. Dominy

new hires usually begin work in June. Normally, the current marketing reps mentor the new reps. Joan would also visit each rep and provide individual training and guidance. As most people prefer to move during the summer, it is the busiest time of the year for Windsor Management. It is therefore difficult to do much formal training during the summer.

Biweekly marketing meetings are held by Joan Graham to review weekly performance and to discuss a topic in detail. Typical topics would be competitive analysis, prospecting for corporate accounts, handling objections, closing techniques, etc. These biweekly meetings also review the closing ratios and any related problems, and administrative topics such as monthly reports, credit checks, and tenant relations. In addition there is a two-day marketing conference held every March. At this meeting, there is an outside speaker on a major topic, like consumer behavior or closing the sale. This is followed by presentations done by the marketing reps on selected topics. A team competition is used as a team building exercise, followed by the aforementioned dinner and awards to the top three marketing representatives of the year.

The typical career of a marketing rep is two years at the entry level. The first year focuses primarily on sales, the second year focuses more on administration. The representatives who are successful during the first two years are then promoted to either marketing manager of a large property like Waltham or Norwood, or to property manager of a smaller property. The next promotion is usually to property manager of a large property. After 2 to 3 years as a property manager, successful individuals can become regional marketing coordinator, and eventually regional manager. Both Joan Graham and Bob Dominy started their careers at Windsor as marketing reps.

Marketing reps are given performance appraisals twice a year—in June and December. The performance appraisal is prepared by the property manager and reviewed by Bob and Joan to assure that marketing reps are evaluated and treated consistently across all property managers. Joan and the property manager review the performance evaluations with each marketing rep individually. These sessions usually last 15–45 minutes and include setting goals for the next six months. The December review also informs the rep of the increase in his/her base salary beginning in January.

Company Operations

Windsor Management serves 9,100 families in the United States of which 3,800 are in the northeast region. Accord-

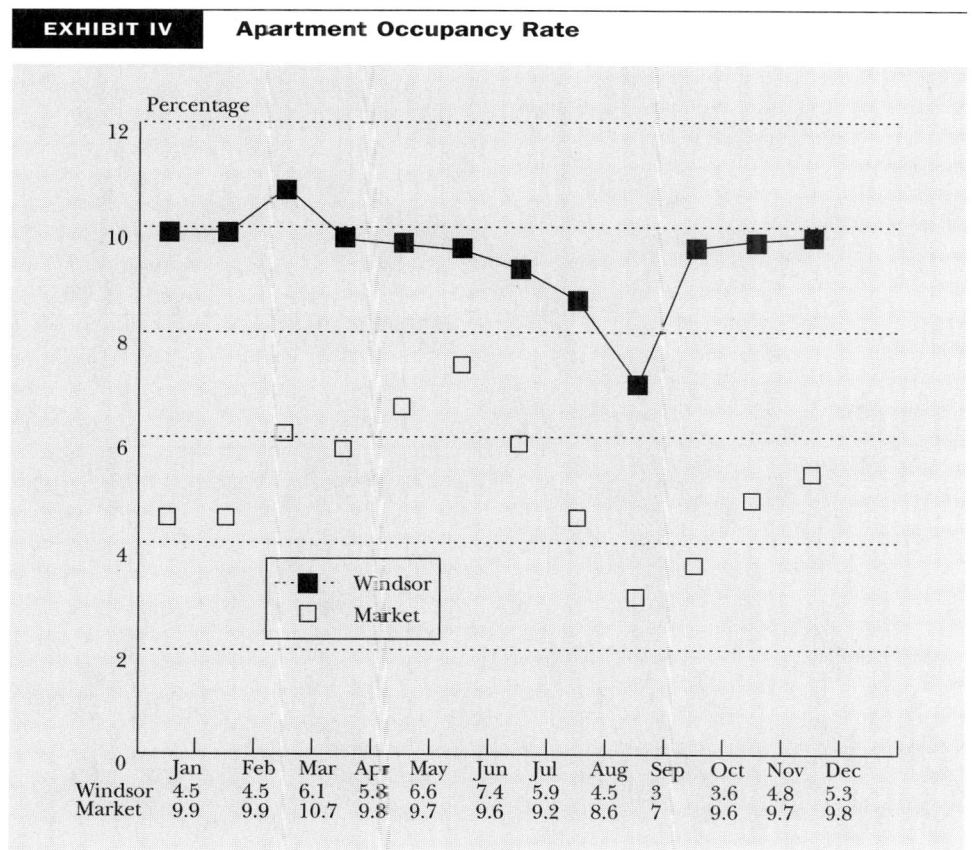

EXHIBIT IV Apartment Occupancy Rate

	Jan	Feb	Mar	Apr	May	Jun	Jul	Aug	Sep	Oct	Nov	Dec
Windsor	4.5	4.5	6.1	5.8	6.6	7.4	5.9	4.5	3	3.6	4.8	5.3
Market	9.9	9.9	10.7	9.8	9.7	9.6	9.2	8.6	7	9.6	9.7	9.8

ing to Bob Dominy, this is a very high fixed-cost business with almost no variable costs. "While they managed their expenses very closely, the emphasis is on having few or no vacancies." in 1991 the apartment occupancy rate averaged 9.5% for the market vs. 5.2% for Windsor, as shown in Exhibit IV. Using these ratios for the northeast region, on average Windsor had approximately 197 units vacant each month spread over 12 properties. The lower vacancy rate of Windsor yielded an increase in rental revenues of approximately $1,568,640 in the northeast region (.043 reduced vacancy rate × 3800 total apartments × $9,600/yr./apt.). As there were almost no variable costs, this additional revenue was almost all profit. The vacancy rate of a property is directly correlated with profitability. For example, in the summer of 1991, the rental market softened and many of Windsor's competitors offered the first month's rent free. When Windsor did not follow suit, their vacancy rate started to climb. Windsor did offer a graduated discount beginning in July which helped reduce the vacancy rate. The graduated rate spread the free month over the life of the lease on a 12-month lease at $900/month (see Exhibit V).

The graduated price scheme appealed to many tenants and was very successful.

Marketing

The marketing effort is directed toward building traffic through the leasing office. Windsor Management advertises in the local papers, especially the Boston Globe.

Other marketing activities include direct mail, promotional campaigns, cold calling local companies, and newsletters to companies and realtors. Each representative must acquire a thorough knowledge of the local market, including a detailed analysis of the immediate competition.

Proposed Bonus for Resident Retention

Lease renewals are very important. Current tenant payment history is established, so there is little or no credit risk. Also, because tenants do not leave the apartments, Windsor does not incur the cost of cleaning and painting apartments for new tenants. Of the approximately 350 leases signed per month in 1992 in the northeast region, 125 were renewals. Therefore, approximately 125 people were leaving the properties. The reasons given for not renewing the leases varied. The reasons people normally give for leaving are shown in Exhibit VI.

To test the concept of a resident retention program which awarded bonuses to marketing reps for lease renewals, Windsor ran a 6 month test for July to December 1993 at Allen House Apartments in Texas. The results comparing 1992 to 1993 are in Exhibit VII.

As Bob prepared for the meeting to discuss the resident retention program he wondered if it were a prudent

EXHIBIT VI

Job transfer	44	27.7%
Too expensive	30	18.9%
Bought house	27	17.0%
Transfer on site	17	10.7%
Location	15	9.4%
Eviction	10	6.3%
Personal situation	4	2.5%
Short term	4	2.5%
Skip	4	2.5%
Maintenance	2	1.3%
Size	1	0.6%
Neighbors	1	0.6%
	159	

EXHIBIT V

	Traditional	1 Free Month	Graduated
	900	0	750
	900	900	750
	900	900	750
	900	900	800
	900	900	800
	900	900	800
	900	900	800
	900	900	850
	900	900	850
	900	900	850
	900	900	900
	900	900	900
	900	900	900
Average	900	825	825

EXHIBIT VII

	July to December	
Reasons for Leaving	1992	1993 (test)
Short-term corporate rental	35	26
Bought home	16	10
Job transfer	10	7
Roommate problem/married	4	0
Price too expensive	4	1
ICY (?)	2	3
Car theft	3	2
Wanted larger apartment	1	1
Health/death	0	0
Location	0	1
Totals	78	52

investment. Do the marketing representatives really influence people to stay at a Windsor property? For example, if someone is transferred, buys a home, gets married, completes his/her corporate short term rental, how could the marketing representatives convince the tenant to stay? Bob wondered if the $145,000 could be used in a better way to reduce the vacancy rate.

Questions

1. What is the role of a marketing representative (MR) at Windsor?
2. What are all the parts of the sales management system to develop, train, and manage marketing representatives?
3. What do you think of the proposed bonus system for resident retention?
4. How else could Windsor invest the $145,000 in the sales management of sales system?

Hongkong Bank of Canada

"We believe that it will be a very stimulating and productive meeting," said David Bond, Vice-President, Marketing and Public Affairs for the Hongkong Bank of Canada. It was mid-August 1991, and he was talking about a branch managers' meeting that would run early the following month. "Senior management decided in May that we would have a two-day branch managers' meeting and that it would be held at Whistler. They asked Steve Tait, our Vice-President, Human Resources, Jim Francis, our Assistant Vice-President, Training & Development, and myself to put together the meeting program. The 100-plus people that will be there include about 35 managers of the former Lloyds branches, the bank that we purchased and took over operations last year. The program that we have put together for them is very different from previous branch managers' meetings in that we're going to use it as the kickoff of a year-long contest."

The Hongkong Bank of Canada

In 1981, the Canadian federal government passed legislation which permitted banks with foreign ownership to operate in Canada. Several dozen banks started up operations in Canada. One of them was the Hongkong and Shanghai Banking Corporation (HSBC), headquartered in Hong Kong, which established a wholly owned subsidiary called the Hongkong Bank of Canada. The head office was established in Vancouver and operations started with one branch in that city in July 1981. The Hongkong Bank was one of the few new foreign-owned banks to open as a full-service bank, i.e. a bank that generated deposits and made loans to individuals as well as to organizations. This was in contrast to the vast majority of the foreign banks, who borrowed their loan funds from other financial organizations and confined their loan activities to commercial organizations. Management of the Hongkong Bank considered their full-service orientation as a natural extension of the operational philosophy of their HSBC parent.

Over the years the bank grew through a combination of additional business in existing branches, the opening of new branches, and an aggressive acquisition strategy. In 1985, they bought the Winnipeg and Halifax sites of the foundering Canadian Commercial Bank. The following year they bought the financially troubled Bank of British Columbia, which had extensive retail operations in 38 branches in British Columbia and two in Alberta.[1] In 1988, the bank bought the Midland Bank of Canada which had operated primarily in the corporate lending market. This was followed in 1990 by the purchase of Lloyds Bank Canada with its 52 branches, most of which were in eastern Canada. Lloyds Bank Canada was the outcome of the Lloyds Bank of England purchase of the Continental Bank of Canada in 1986. There was speculation in the industry at the time of purchase that Lloyds had overpaid to get into the Canadian market. There was later talk that the English parent had never really "bought in" to the Canadian operation after its early discovery that it could make a far better return by investing incremental capital in England than it could in investing comparable funds in its Canadian subsidiary.

The Lloyds Bank Canada that Hongkong purchased was focused on the corporate market. The very limited amount of attention to the retail market was devoted exclusively to high net worth individuals. Small net worth customers were actively discouraged. Low Lloyds earnings in recent years had let to drastic reductions in the bank's renovations budget. As a result, many of the branch physical facilities that the Hongkong Bank acquired were worn and run down. Further, the physical layout in most branches was not appropriate for the Hongkong Bank's emphasis on retail banking. Finally, Lloyds Bank, by Hongkong Bank standards, was overstaffed. This resulted

---

Source: This case was prepared by Professor John R. Kennedy for the sole purpose of providing material for class discussion at the Richard Ivey School of Business. Certain names and other identifying information may have been disguised to protect confidentiality. It is not intended to illustrate either effective or ineffective handling of a managerial situation. This material is not covered under authorization from CanCopy or any reproduction rights organization. Any form of reproduction, storage or transmittal of this material is prohibited without written permission from Richard Ivey School of Business, The University of Western Ontario, London, Canada N6A 3K7. Reprinted with permission, Richard Ivey School of Business. Copyright 1993 © The University of Western Ontario.

---

[1] In 1991, most of the British Columbia branches were still operating with signage that read "Bank of British Columbia" in large letters, followed underneath in smaller letters by the words "A Division of the Hongkong Bank of Canada."

in the departure, in the months following the takeover, of close to 20% of the 1,500 former Lloyds employees.

The acquisition triggered a change in the operating structure of the Hongkong Bank. Four regions were created, Quebec and Atlantic Provinces, Ontario, Western, and B.C., with a senior vice president appointed to head each. One of the major tasks associated with bringing the Lloyds operations into the Hongkong Bank was the integration of computer systems. While substantial work had been accomplished since the merger, it was not expected that the system would be complete until October 1991.

The 1990 Branch Managers' Meeting

The 1990 branch managers' meeting was held in August, just a few months after the acquisition of Lloyds Bank Canada. Thus, it was really the first large meeting of personnel of the two organizations. The day and a half meeting was held in facilities on the University of British Columbia campus, and started with a Thursday evening reception. "The Lloyds folks were understandably a bit wary to begin with," said a Hongkong Bank manager who had been a employee of the Bank of British Columbia at the time it was acquired by the Hongkong Bank. "But the fact that there was even a reception gave a message that most outsiders wouldn't think about. If you are part of a bank organization that is not doing too well financially, one of the first things to go is expenditure on what you might call employee social activities. I can remember back to the dark days of the Bank of BC, where you considered asking employees to pay for their own coffee during a meeting break."

The remainder of the meeting was virtually all one-way communication.

- Here are the Bank's products.
- Here is the way in which they are to be sold.
- Here is the operating system in which you are or will be operating.

"I think it was pretty apparent to everyone at the meeting," recalled another manager originally with the Bank of British Columbia, "that there was going to have to be a lot of work done on systems and organizational integration before we could really get down to the job of focused implementation across the organization."

Planning for the 1991 Branch Managers' Meeting

"When the three of us first got together," said David Bond, "we got talking about our personal experiences with managers' meetings, both here and in other organizations we had worked in. We concluded that they had been, for the most part, one-way communications by head office people designed to provide information and/or motivate the participants, together with some time for leisure and social activities. But when the meeting was over, that was it until the next one. No specific goals. No followup. No nothing! We decided that we wanted to break out of that pattern.

"From there, we spent some time thinking about the objectives we should set for the meeting. After a fair amount of discussion, we concluded that there should be three of them:

> "Stimulate growth of core deposits.
> "Try to build some system to put together the good retailers in our organization with people that don't have those retail skills and abilities.
> "Integrate the Lloyds people into our value system, which is to treat every customer who walks in the door as if they are the most important person on earth.

"It was out of those three objectives that the idea of a contest evolved."

The contest concept and meeting program were fleshed out in a series of meetings which followed.

THE CONTEST. The decision was made that the contest would focus on the growth of core deposits for the one-year period starting September 1, 1991. Core deposits were defined as personal GIC's, RRSP's, demand deposits and time deposits. Extensive discussion went into the development of the contest rules, which are given in Exhibit I. A rule was developed to break a tie should one occur.

THE TEAMS. After some discussion, the decision was reached to have five teams. Steve Tait, together with the bank's marketing department, assumed responsibility for putting the teams together, within the criteria that teams should be the same size, represent all regions, contain a mix of pre-takeover Hongkong branches and Lloyds branches, and be balanced in terms of size of existing personal core deposits, percentage growth over the previous year, and potential for growth over the next year. Steve went through a series of iterations in which he put teams together, shopped them around senior management asking for input as to team equivalence, and then made adjustments. The result of this process was the five teams outlined in Exhibit II.

THE PRIZE. Each branch manager of the winning team, together with a guest, would receive free round trip passage, five nights accommodation and a celebratory dinner in Hawaii in October 1992. Two business meetings would be held during the five-day period. Rules were developed to define manager eligibility.

THE MEETING PROGRAM. "Putting the program together was a lot of fun," said Jim Francis. "We worked hard to get a sequence and mix of activities that would be most effective in development of the team spirit that

EXHIBIT I — Core Deposit Campaign—Contest Rules

(1) The Bank's overall deposit target as defined by the 1992 business plan must be met in order for an overall award to be triggered.

(2) There must be a positive gain in core deposits by a branch on the winning team to be eligible to accompany the winning team to Hawaii.

(3) A Branch Manager on the winning team must be an employee in good standing at the time of the award allocation to be eligible.

(4) In the event a Manager is transferred from one branch to another and that branch is not within the same group but the original branch is among the winning teams, then if the Manager had been at the branch for the majority of the year and had accounted for a majority of the deposit growth, he or she will go on the trip. Otherwise, the new Manager will go.

(5) With the exception of St. Laurent, new branches which open during the campaign will not be included in the contest. Appropriate adjustments will be made to the deposit balances of existing branches which lose core deposits through transfer to a new branch during the first three months of operation.

(6) Points will be awarded as follows:
   (A) Team standing following "initiatives" at Branch Managers' Conference:
      1st — 2.5 Pts
      2nd — 2.0 Pts
      3rd — 1.5 Pts
      4th — 1.0 Pt
      5th — 0.5 Pt
   (B) Greatest absolute dollar increase in core deposits:
      1st — 10 Pts
      2nd — 8 Pts
      3rd — 6 Pts
      4th — 4 Pts
      5th — 2 Pts
   (C) Greatest percentage increase in core deposits:
      1st — 5 Pts
      2nd — 4 Pts
      3rd — 3 Pts
      4th — 2 Pts
      5th — 1 Pt
   (D) Best all-round (i.e., most balanced) results (i.e., smallest percentage difference between largest percentage increase and smallest percentage increase on a team):
      1st — 10 Pts
      2nd — 8 Pts
      3rd — 6 Pts
      4th — 4 Pts
      5th — 2 Pts
   (E) Largest percentage increase in number of new retail deposit accounts:
      1st — 5 Pts
      2nd — 4 Pts
      3rd — 3 Pts
      4th — 2 Pts
      5th — 1 Pt
   (F) Highest absolute increase in net new retail deposit accounts (i.e., new accounts less closed accounts):
      1st — 5 Pts
      2nd — 4 Pts
      3rd — 3 Pts
      4th — 2 Pts
      5th — 1 Pt

   Winning = Highest Points of Sum of A + B + C + D + E + F

(7) In cases of dispute, or extenuating circumstances, the judgement of the C.O.O. will govern.

---

is necessary not only for the contest but for the kind of organization we want to be. We concluded as well that the presentation of the meeting agenda should be a reflection of our operating style. Finally, we decided that we wanted to put a name on the event that described what we were trying to accomplish. We combined the ideas of the Whistler mountain resort where the conference was going to be, Diamond Head in Hawaii where the contest winners will stay, together with the meeting and contest objectives, to get the meeting title and theme, 'Peak Performance'."

Arrangements had already been completed to provide each branch manager at the end of the meeting with a framed custom print of Whistler created by a well-known B.C. artist. The meeting schedule appears as Exhibit III. This schedule had already been distributed to the meeting participants. The titles of the individuals named in the meeting agenda are given in Exhibit IV. While they were not explicitly identified on the schedule, two activities should be highlighted. The first of these would occur early on the morning of September 6th. People were to meet in the hotel lobby as teams for the first time, and take a cable car up the mountain to a restaurant for breakfast. There, if the weather cooperated, everyone would be able to see the sun rise over Whistler mountain. Second, part of the Friday afternoon team activities would be devoted to competition on Whistler streets in a number of races, including

---

[2] See Exhibit V.
[3] Friday, September 6.
[4] See Exhibit VI.

EXHIBIT II — Groups for Core Deposit Campaign

Group 1			Group 2			Group 3		
City/Branch	Prov	Origin	City/Branch	Prov	Origin	City/Branch	Prov	Origin
Brampton	Ont	LBC	Abbotsford	BC	BBC	Vancouver		
Calgary South	Alta	LBC	Calgary			Broadway & Ash	BC	BBC
Cranbrook	BC	BBC	5th Ave.	Alta	LBC	Campbell River	BC	BBC
Edmonton			Vancouver			Chicoutimi	Que	LBC
101st Street	Alta	LBC	Cambie & 42nd	BC	HKBC	Edmonton		
Vancouver			Vancouver			Pacific Rim Mall	Alta	HKBC
Georgia &	BC	LBC	Denman Street	BC	BBC	Halifax	NS	CCB
Thurlow			Vancouver			Vancouver		
Hamilton	Ont	LBC	Dundas Street	BC	HKBC	Kingsway & Senlac	BC	BBC
Vancouver			Edmonton			Markham	Ont	LBC
Hastings &	BC	BBC	Jasper Ave.	Alta	BBC	Mississauga		
Burrard			Fredericton	NB	LBC	Golden Plaza	Ont	HKBC
Lasalle	Que	LBC	Granby	QUE	LBC	Mississauga	Ont	LBC
Vancouver			Vancouver			Montreal		
Lougheed &	BC	BBC	Granville & 12th	BC	BBC	Place Air Canada	Que	LBC
North Road			Vancouver			Oakville	Ont	LBC
Vancouver			Hastings &			Saint John	NB	LBC
Main & Pender	BC	HKBC	Penticton	BC	BBC	Saskatoon	Sask	HKBC
Montreal			Kelowna			Sault Ste.Marie	Ont	LBC
Place Victoria	Que	HKBC	Richter Street	BC	LBC	Scarborough		
Montreal			Vancouver			Dragon Centre	Ont	HKBC
Rene Levesque	Que	HKBC	Kingsway &	BC	BBC	Vancouver		
Nanaimo	BC	BBC	Royal Oak			Sixth & Fifth	BC	BBC
Ottawa	Ont	LBC	Laval	Que	LBC	Vancouver		
Regina	Sask	LBC	Red Deer	Alta	LBC	Main	BC	BBC
Richmond			Richmond			Victoria		
No. 3 & Park	BC	BBC	Parker Place	BC	LBC	731 Fort Street	BC	HKBC
Spadina	Ont	HKBC	St. Catherines	Ont	LBC	Victoria		
St. John's	Nfld	LBC	Vernon	BC	BBC	Douglas &		
Surrey	BC	BBC	Victoria			Hillside	BC	BBC
Vancouver			Fort Street	BC	BBC	Whitby	Ont	LBC
Tenth & Sassamat	BC	BBC	West Vancouver	BC	BBC	White Rock	BC	BBC
Trois-Rivieres	Que	LBC	Windsor	Ont	LBC			

Legend:
HKBC = HongKong Bank of Canada
LBC = Lloyds Bank of Canada
CCB = Canadian Commercial Bank
BBC = Bank of British Columbia

Group 4			Group 5		
City/Branch	Prov	Origin	City/Branch	Prov	Origin
Barrie	Ont	LBC	Calgary		
Chilliwack	BC	BBC	8th Ave.	Alta	BBC
Edmonton			Calgary		
South	Alta	LBC	Good Fortune Plaza	Alta	HKBC
Vancouver			Vancouver		
Fraser & 48th	BC	BBC	Columbia St.	BC	BBC
Haney	BC	BBC	Delta	BC	BBC
Vancouver			Kelowna		
Hasting & Gilmore	BC	BBC	Bernard Ave	BC	BBC
Kamloops	BC	BBC	Kingston	Ont	LBC
Vancouver			Kitchener	Ont	LBC
Kerrisdale	BC	BBC	Lethbridge	Alta	LBC
Langley	BC	BBC	Vancouver		
London	Ont	LBC	Main & Keefer	BC	BBC
Longueuil	Que	LBC	Mississauga		
Medicine Hat	Alta	LBC	Chinese Cultural Centre	Ont	HKBC
Prince George	BC	BBC			
Richmond			Mississauga North	Ont	LBC
Johnson Centre	BC	HKBC	North Vancouver	BC	BBC
Scarborough			Penticton	BC	BBC
Eglinton Ave.	Ont	LBC	Port Coquitlam	BC	BBC
Scarborough			Saint Leonard	Que	LBC
Milliken Square	Ont	HKBC	Sherbrooke	Que	LBC
Ste-Foy	Que	LBC	St. Laurent	Que	HKBC
Thunder Bay	Ont	LBC	Toronto		
Timmins	Ont	LBC	Skyway Park	Ont	LBC
Toronto			Victoria		
70 York Street	Ont	HKBC	Douglas & Johnson	BC	BBC
			Willowdale	Ont	HKBC
			Winnipeg	Man	CCB

EXHIBIT III

Hongkong Bank of Canada
1991 Managers' Conference

September 5th

3:00 PM SHARP	Bus To Whistler Departs Vancouver	Head Office
6:00 - 7:00 PM	Reception	Ballroom
7:00 - 9:00 PM	Dinner	Ballroom
9:00 - 10:00 PM	Regional Meetings	TBA

September 6th

7:00 AM SHARP	1st Group Initiative	Lobby
7:30 - 8:30 AM	Breakfast	TBA
8:30 - 8:45 AM	Official Opening - Chris Crook	"
8:45 - 9:30 AM	The Opportunity - Clyde Ostler	"
9:30 - 9:40 AM	"A Moment With Mould"	"
9:40 - 10:00 AM	The Challenge - Chris Crook	"
10:00 - 11:00 AM	Team Activity - Name That Team	"
11:00 - 11:45 AM	Service Is The Key - Bill Dalton	"
11:45 - 12:15 PM	2nd Group Initiative	"
12:15 - 1:45 PM	Lunch - Hosted by Bob Hemond	Cheakmus
1:45 - 2:00 PM	"Another Moment With Mould"	Ballroom
2:00 - 2:45 PM	Team Activity - Brainstorming	"
2:45 - 3:15 PM	Merchandising Our Way - Chris Crook	"
3:15 - 5:00 PM	Team Activity - Strategy	Breakouts
5:00 - 5:30 PM	Free Time	Optional
5:30 - 6:00 PM	Reception	Ballroom
6:00 - 8:30 PM	BBQ - Hosted by John Ranaldi	"
8:30 - 9:00 PM	Team Activity - Presentations	"

September 7th

Time						Room
7:15 - 8:20 AM	Breakfast - Hosted by Dewar Harper					Cheakmus
8:20 - 8:30 AM	"John Goes On!"					"
	Red	Blue	Yellow	Green	Pink	
	Diamond Head	Black Tusk	Board Room	Sutcliffe A	Sutcliffe B	Meeting Rooms
8:30 - 9:05 AM	CEO & COO	Back At The Branch	H.O. Panel	Local Marketing	Credit Connection	"
9:05 - 9:40 AM	Back At The Branch	H.O. Panel	Local Marketing	Credit Connection	CEO & COO	"
9:40 - 10:15 AM	H.O. Panel	Local Marketing	Credit Connection	CEO & COO	Back at The Branch	"
10:15 - 10:50 AM	Corporate Shuffle					TBA
10:50 - 11:25 AM	Local Marketing	Credit Connection	CEO & COO	Back At The Branch	H.O. Panel	Meeting Rooms
11:25 - 12:00 PM	Credit Connection	CEO & COO	Back At The Branch	H.O. Panel	Local Marketing	"
12:00 - 1:30 PM	Lunch - Hosted by Martin Glynn & Bruna Giacomazzi					Cheakmus
1:30 - 1:40 PM	"The Last Mouldy Moments"					Ballroom
1:40 - 2:30 PM	The Strategic Plan - Jim Cleave					"
2:30 - 3:15 PM	Team Activity - Strategic Plan					"
3:15 - 4:00 PM	Questions to Senior Executive					"
4:00 - 4:30 PM	Wrap-up and Farewell					"

EXHIBIT IV

Titles of Individuals Named in the Meeting Schedule

Name	Title
Chris Cook	Executive Vice President, Banking
Clyde Osler	A senior officer with the Wells Fargo Bank
John Mould	Sr. Vice President & Controller
Bill Dalton	Chief Operating Officer
Bob Hemond	Sr. Vice President, Quebec & Atlantic Provinces Region
John Ranaldi	Sr. Vice President, Western Region
Dewar Harper	Sr. Vice President, Ontario Region
Martin Glynn	Sr. Vice President, B.C. Region
Bruna Giacomazzi	Sr Vice President, Special Credit
Jim Cleave	Chief Executive Officer

Members of the Saturday Morning Panels

Panel Name	Panel Member	Title
CEO & COO	Jim Cleave and Bill Dalton	
H.O. Panel	Steve Tait	VP Human Resources
	Jim Mayhew	AVP Human Resources
	Brian Salvador	AVP Compensation & Benefits
Local Marketing	Al Cummings	AVP Marketing
Credit Connection	Steve Wilson	VP Consumer Credit
	Bert McPhee	Sr. Vice President, Credit
Back at the Branch	Phil Scott	President, Scott Consulting Inc.

EXHIBIT V — Instructions to the Branch Manager Participants

Instructions for Friday Afternoon

You have a number of tasks to accomplish in a relatively limited time period.

You will be expected to present at dinner tonight a logo for your team and to have selected a theme song with appropriate words. The logos and the songs will be judged by the Fabulous Four[5] as to their appropriateness, suitability to the name chosen, ingenuity, originality and presentation. The results of the judging will count towards the trip to Hawaii.

You will need to prepare yourselves to gain maximum benefit from tomorrow morning's activities. To do that you may wish to spend some time understanding the scope of the challenge that you face. What are the characteristics of the group? Just how daunting is the task ahead? What should be your major objectives and how do you plan to accomplish them? What are the strengths within the group and how can you capitalize upon them?

How will you communicate with each other and provide support to each other? The Bank will not pay for conference calls nor travel, so what alternatives are available and how do they get organized and done?

Tomorrow morning between 8:30 and 12 noon you will have the opportunity to meet with five different groups or individuals. Each session is designed to provide you with some "tools" with which you individually and as a team can use to help you get to Diamond Head. Each session has provided an outline of what they plan to discuss with you. You need to make sure that you gain the maximum benefit from these sessions with your group. What are the most important things for you to know with respect to each area? How will you organize to make sure that you accomplish your objectives for each of these consultative sessions?

---

[5]The "Fabulous Four" were the four senior officers of the bank: James H. Cleave, president and chief executive officer; William R. P. Dalton, executive director and chief operating officer; Maurice R. Mourton; executive vice-president, administration; and Chris J. Cook, executive vice-president, banking

EXHIBIT VI — Instructions to the Session Participants on Saturday Morning

The five teams will be meeting with five different groups for 30 minutes at a time. The purpose of these meetings is to give the individual teams information regarding the "tools" that they will be provided with during the year as they strive to win the trip to Diamond Head.

What you are asked to do is to provide, on one page maximum, an outline of the most salient information that you would be willing to provide to the group during your session. For example, the Marketing/Public Affairs group will be providing information on the detailed marketing campaigns planned for the year, and the type of support that will be provided for each branch.

Each group should be given the opportunity to ask you questions, and provide you feedback on what is of concern to them. Thus, any presentation should not be more than 15 minutes. If you wish, *at the conclusion of the session*, you can provide each manager with take-away material.

Thus, the challenge for the individual teams is to make sure that they have organized themselves to gain the maximum benefit from the opportunity of meeting with you. Your challenge is to present material in an interesting, informative and inviting manner. Since the time is limited, you will be forced to concentrate on only the most essential matters. The draft of your material should be sent to Elaine Ranger no later than the 15th of August so that it can be reproduced and included in the Managers' packages.

a Chuckwagon Race in which the wagon would be a child's wagon.

FINAL DETAILS. "To get the most out of the meeting, the branch managers will have to understand that they have to get actively involved in it," said David Bond. "At the same time, the head office participants in the Saturday morning sessions must understand that they have a specific role to play in those sessions. Therefore, we've put together two sets of instructions. The one for the participants[2] will be given out when the contest is introduced on the Friday[3] morning. The one for the head office people[4] has already gone out."

General Electric Appliances

Larry Barr had recently been promoted to the position of district sales manager (B.C.) for G.E. Appliances, a division of Canadian Appliance Manufacturing Co. Ltd. (CAMCO). One of his more important duties in that position was the allocation of his district's sales quota among his five salesmen. Barr received his quota for 1992 in October 1991. His immediate task was to determine an equitable allocation of that quota. This was important because the company's incentive pay plan was based on the salesmen's attainment of quota. A portion of Barr's remuneration was also based on the degree to which his salesforce met their quotas.

Barr graduated from the University of British Columbia in 1983 with the degree of bachelor of commerce. He was immediately hired as a product manager for a mining equipment manufacturing firm because of his summer job experience with that firm. In 1986, he joined Canadian General Electric (C.G.E.) in Montreal as a product manager for refrigerators. There he was responsible for creating and merchandising a product line, as well as developing product and marketing plans. In January 1989, he was transferred to Coburg, Ontario, as a sales manager for industrial plastics. In September 1990, he became administrative manager (Western Region) and when the position of district sales manager became available, Barr was promoted to it. There his duties included development of sales strategies, supervision of salesmen, and budgeting.

Background

Canadian Appliance Manufacturing Co. Ltd. (CAMCO) was created in 1990 under the joint ownership of Canadian General Electric Ltd. and General Steel Wares Ltd. (G.S.W.). CAMCO then purchased the production facilities of Westinghouse Canada Ltd. Under the purchase agreement, the Westinghouse brand name was transferred to White Consolidated Industries Ltd., where it became White-Westinghouse. Appliances manufactured by CAMCO in the former Westinghouse plant were branded Hotpoint. (See Exhibit I.)

The G.E., C.S.W., and Hotpoint major appliance plants became divisions of CAMCO. These divisions operated independently and had their own separate management staff, although they were all ultimately accountable to CAMCO management. The divisions competed for sales, although not directly, because they each produced product lines for different price segments.

Competition

Competition in the appliance industry was vigorous. CAMCO was the largest firm in the industry, with approximately 45 percent market share, split between G.E., G.S.W. (Moffatt & McClary brands), and Hotpoint. The following three firms each had 10 to 15 percent market share: Inglis (washers and dryers only), W.C.I. (makers of White-Westinghouse, Kelvinator, and Gibson), and Admiral.

These firms also produced appliances under department store brand names such as Viking, Baycrest, and Kenmore, which accounted for an additional 15 percent of the market. The remainder of the market was divided among brands such as Maytag, Roper Dishwasher, Gurney, Tappan, and Danby.

G.E. marketed a full major appliance product line, including refrigerators, ranges, washers, dryers, dishwashers, and television sets. G.E. appliances generally had many features and were priced at the upper end of the price range. Their major competition came from Maytag and Westinghouse.

The Budgeting Process

G.E. Appliances was one of the most advanced firms in the consumer goods industry in terms of sales budgeting. Budgeting received careful analysis at all levels of management.

The budgetary process began in June of each year. The management of G.E. Appliances division assessed the economic outlook, growth trends in the industry, competitive activity, population growth, and so forth to determine a reasonable sales target for the next year. The president of CAMCO received this estimate, checked and revised it as necessary, and submitted it to the president of G.E. Canada. Final authorization rested with G.E. Ltd., which had a definite minimum growth target for the G.E. branch of CAMCO. G.E. Appliances was considered an "invest and grow" division, which meant it was expected to produce a healthy sales growth each year, regardless of the state of the economy. As Barr observed, "This is difficult, but meeting challenges is the job of management."

The approved budget was expressed as a desired percentage increase in sales. Once the figure had been decided, it was not subject to change. The quota was communicated back through G.E. Canada Ltd., CAMCO, and

---

Source: Copyright © 1978 by Richard W. Pollay, John D. Claxton, and Rick Jenkner. Adapted with permission.

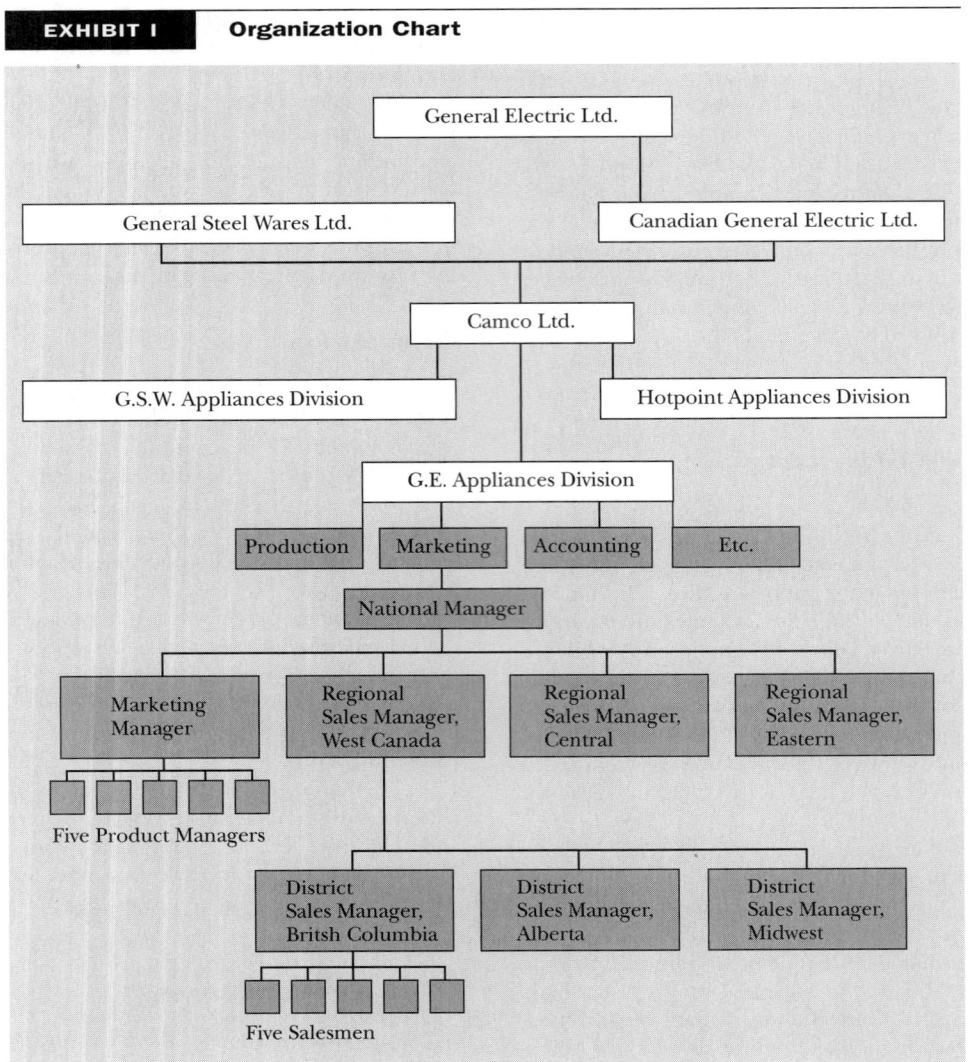

EXHIBIT I Organization Chart

G.E. Appliances, where it was available to the district sales managers in October. Each district was then required to meet an overall growth figure (quota) but each sales territory was not automatically expected to achieve that same growth. Barr was required to assess the situation in each territory, determine where growth potential was highest, and allocate his quota accordingly.

The Sales Incentive Plan

The sales incentive plan was a critical part of General Electric's salesforce plan and an important consideration in the quota allocation of Barr. Each salesman had a portion of his earnings dependent on his performance with respect to quota. Also, Barr was awarded a bonus based on the sales performance of his district, making it advantageous to Barr and good for staff morale for all his salesmen to attain their quotas.

The salesforce incentive plan was relatively simple. A bonus system is fairly typical for salesmen in any field. With G.E., each salesman agreed to a basic salary figure called "planned earnings." The planned salary varied according to experience, education, past performance, and competitive salaries. A salesman was paid 75 percent of his planned earnings on a guaranteed regular basis. The remaining 25 percent of salary was at risk, dependent on the person's sales record. There was also the possibility of earning substantially more money by selling more than quota (see Exhibit II).

The bonus was awarded such that total salary (base plus bonus) equaled planned earnings when the quota was just met. The greatest increase in bonus came between 101 and 110 percent of quota. The bonus was paid quarterly on the cumulative total quota. A holdback system ensured that a salesman was never required to pay back previously earned bonus because of a poor quarter. Because of this

EXHIBIT II Sales Incentive Earnings Schedule: Major Appliances and Home Entertainment Products

Sales Quota Realization (Percent)	Percent of Base Salary Total	Sales Quota Realization (Percent)	Incentive Percent of Base Salary Total
70%	0 %	105	35.00%
71	0.75	106	37.00
72	1.50	107	39.00
73	2.25	108	41.00
74	3.00	109	43.00
75	3.75	110	45.00
76	4.50	111	46.00
77	5.25	112	47.00
78	6.00	113	48.00
79	6.75	114	49.00
80	7.50	115	50.00
81	8.25	116	51.00
82	9.00	117	52.00
83	9.75	118	53.00
84	10.50	119	54.00
85	11.25	120	55.00
86	12.00	121	56.00
87	12.75	122	57.00
88	13.50	123	58.00
89	14.25	124	59.00
90	15.00	125	60.00
91	16.00	126	61.00
92	17.00	127	62.00
93	18.00	128	63.00
94	19.00	129	64.00
95	20.00	130	65.00
96	21.00	131	66.00
97	22.00	132	67.00
98	23.00	133	68.00
99	24.00	134	69.00
100	25.00	135	70.00
101	27.00	136	71.00
102	29.00	137	72.00
103	31.00	138	73.00
104	33.00	139	74.00
		140	75.00

system, it was critical that each salesman's quota be fair in relation to the other salesmen. Nothing was worse for morale than one person earning large bonuses while the others struggled.

Quota attainment was not the sole basis for evaluating the salesmen. They required to fulfil a wide range of duties including service, franchising of new dealers, maintaining good relations with dealers, and maintaining a balance of sales among the different product lines. Because the bonus system was based on sales only Barr had to ensure the salesmen did not neglect their other duties.

A formal salary review was held each year for each salesman. However, Barr preferred to give his salesmen continuous feedback on their performances. Through human relations skills, he hoped to avoid problems that could lead to dismissal of a salesman and loss of sales for the company.

Barr's incentive bonus plan was more complex than the salesmen's. He was awarded a maximum of 75 annual bonus points broken down as follows: market share, 15; total sales performance, 30; sales representative balance, 30. Each point had a specific money value. The system ensured that Barr allocate his quota carefully. For instance, if one quota was so difficult that the salesmen sold only 80 percent of it, while the other salesmen exceeded quota, Barr's bonus would be reduced, even if the overall area sales exceeded the quota. (See Appendix, "Development of a Sales Commission Plan.")

Quota Allocation

The total 1992 sales budget for G.E. Appliances division was about $100 million, a 14 percent sales increase over 1991. Barr's share of the $33 million Western Region

EXHIBIT III G.E. Appliances—Sales Territories

Territory	Designation	Description
9961	Greater Vancouver (Garth Rizzuto)	Hudson's Bay, Firestone, Kmart, McDonald Supply, plus seven independent dealers
9962	Interior (Dan Seguin)	All customers from Quesnel to Nelson, including contract sales (50 customers)
9963	Coastal (Ken Block)	Eatons, Woodwards, plus Vancouver Island north of Duncan and upper Fraser Valley (east of Clearbrook) (20 customers)
9964	Independent and Northern (Fred Speck)	All independents in lower mainland and South Vancouver Island, plus northern B.C. and Yukon (30 customers)
9967	Contract (Jim Wiste)	Contract sales Vancouver, Victoria. All contract sales outside 9962 (50-60 customers)

quota was $13.3 million, also a 14 percent increase over 1991. Barr had two weeks to allocate the quota amongst his five territories. He needed to consider factors such as historical allocation, economic outlook, dealer changes, personnel changes, untapped potential, new franchises or store openings, and buying group activity (volume purchases by associations of independent dealers).

Salesforce

There were five sales territories within B.C. (Exhibit III). Territories were determined on the basis of number of customers, sales volume of customers, geographic size, and experience of the salesman. Territories were altered periodically to deal with changed circumstances.

One territory was comprised entirely of contract customers. Contract sales were sales in bulk lots to builders and developers who used the appliances in housing units. Because the appliances were not resold at retail, G.E. took a lower profit margin on such sales.

G.E. Appliances recruited M.B.A. graduates for their salesforce. They sought bright, educated people who were willing to relocate anywhere in Canada. The company intended that these people would ultimately by promoted to managerial positions. The company also hired experienced career salesmen to get a blend of experience in the salesforce. However, the typical salesman was under 30, aggressive, and upwardly mobile. G.E.'s sales training program covered only product knowledge. It was not felt necessary to train recruits in sales techniques.

Allocation Procedure

At the time Barr assumed the job of district sales manager, he had a meeting with the former sales manager, Ken Philips. Philips described to Barr the method he had used in the past to allocate the quota. As Barr understood it, the procedure was as follows.

The quota was received in October in the form of a desired percentage sales increase. The first step was to project current sales to the end of the year. This gave a base to which the increase was added for an estimation of the next year's quota.

From this quota, the value of contract sales was allocated. Contract sales were allocated first because the market was considered the easiest to forecast. The amount of contract sales in the sales mix was constrained by the lower profit margin on such sales.

The next step was to make a preliminary allocation by simply adding the budgeted percentage increase to the year-end estimates for each territory. Although this allocation seemed fair on the surface, it did not take into account the differing situations in the territories, or the difficulty of attaining such an increase.

The next step was examination of the sales data compiled by G.E. Weekly sales reports from all regions were fed into a central computer, which compiled them and printed out sales totals by product line for each customer, as well as other information. This information enabled the sales manager to check the reasonableness of his initial allocation through a careful analysis of the growth potential for each customer.

The analysis began with the largest accounts, such as Firestone, Hudson's Bay, and Eatons, which each bought over $1 million in appliances annually. Accounts that size were expected to achieve at least the budgeted growth. The main reason for this was that a shortfall of a few percentage points on such a large account would be difficult to make up elsewhere.

Next, the growth potential for medium-sized accounts was estimated. These accounts included McDonald Supply, Kmart, Federated Cooperative, and buying groups such as Volume Independent Purchasers (V.I.P.). Management expected the majority of sales growth to come from such accounts, which had annual sales of between $150,000 and $1 million.

At that point, about 70 percent of the accounts had been analyzed. The small accounts were estimated last. These had generally lower growth potential but were an important part of the company's distribution system.

Once all the accounts had been analyzed, the growth estimates were summed and the total compared to the budget. Usually, the growth estimates were well below the budget.

The next step was to gather more information. The salesmen were usually consulted to ensure that no potential trouble areas or good opportunities had been overlooked. The manager continued to revise and adjust the figures until the total estimated matched the budget. These projections were then summed by territory and compared to the preliminary territorial allocation.

Frequently, there were substantial differences between the two allocations. Historical allocations were then examined and the manager used his judgment in adjusting the figures until he was satisfied that the allocation was both equitable and attainable. Some factors that were considered at this stage included experience of the salesmen, competitive activities, potential store closures or openings, potential labor disputes in areas, and so forth.

The completed allocation was passed on to the regional sales manager for his approval. The process had usually taken one week or longer by this stage. Once the allocations had been approved, the district sales manager then divided them into sales quotas by product line. Often, the resulting average price did not match the expected mix between higher and lower priced units. Therefore, some additional adjusting of figures was necessary. The house account (used for sales to employees of the company) was used as the adjustment factor.

Once this breakdown had been completed the numbers were printed on a budget sheet, and given to the regional sales manager. He forwarded all the sheets for his region to the central computer, which printed out sales numbers for each product line by salesman, by month. These figures were used as the salesmen's quotas for the next year.

Current Situation

Barr recognized that he faced a difficult task. He thought he was too new to the job and the area to confidently undertake an account by account growth analysis. However, due to his previous experience with sales budgets, he did have some sound general ideas. He also had the records of past allocation and quota attainment (Exhibit IV), as well as the assistance of the regional sales manager, Anthony Foyt.

Barr's first step was to project the current sales figures to end-of-year totals. This task was facilitated because the former manager, Philips, had been making successive projections monthly since June. Barr then made a preliminary quota allocation by adding the budgeted sales increase of 14 percent to each territory's total (Exhibit V).

Barr then began to assess circumstances that could cause him to alter that allocation. One major problem was the resignation, effective at the end of the year, of one of the company's top salesmen, Ken Block. His territory had traditionally been one of the most difficult, and Barr believed it would be unwise to replace Block with a novice salesman.

Barr considered shifting one of the more experienced salesmen into that area. However, that would have disrupted

EXHIBIT IV Sales Results

Territory	1989 Budget (× 1,000)	Percent of Total Budget	1989 Actual (× 1,000)	Variance from Quota (V%)
9967 (Contract)	2,440	26.5%	2,267	(7)%
9961 (Greater Vancouver)	1,790	19.4	1,824	2
9962 (Interior)	1,624	17.7	1,433	(11)
9963 (Coastal)	2,111	23.0	2,364	12
9964 (Ind. dealers)	1,131	12.3	1,176	4
House	84	1.1	235	—
Total	9,180	100.0%	9,299	1%

Territory	1990 Budget (× 1,000)	Percent of Total Budget	1990 Actual (× 1,000)	1990 Variance from Quota (V%)
9967 (Contract)	2,587	26.2%	2,845	10%
9961 (Greater Vancouver)	2,005	20.3	2,165	8
9962 (Interior)	1,465	14.8	1,450	(1)
9963 (Coastal)	2,405	24.4	2,358	(2)
9964 (Ind. dealers)	1,334	13.5	1,494	12
House	52	0.8	86	—
Total	9,848	100.0%	10,398	5%

EXHIBIT V Sales Projections and Quotas, 1991–1992

Projected Sales Results 1991

Territory	Oct. 1991 Year to Date	1991 Projected Total	1991 Budget	Percent of Total Budget	Projected Variance from Quota (V%)
9967	$2,447	$ 3,002	$ 2,859	25.0%	5%
9961	2,057	2,545	2,401	21.0	6
9962	1,318	1,623	1,727	15.1	(6)
9963	2,124	2,625	2,734	23.9	(4)
9964	1,394	1,720	1,578	13.8	—
House	132	162	139	1.2	—
Total	$9,474	$11,677	$11,438	100.0	2%

Preliminary Allocation 1992

Territory	1991 Projection	Percent of 1992 Budget*	Total Budget
9967	$ 3,002	$ 3,422	25.7%
9961	2,545	2,901	21.8
9962	1,623	1,854	13.9
9963	2,625	2,992	22.5
9964	1,720	1,961	14.7
House	162	185	1.3
Total	$11,677	$13,315	100.0

*1992 budget = 1991 territory projections + 14% = $13,315.

Tailoring Commission Plan Measurements to Fit Component Objectives

	Objectives	Possible Plan Measurements
1.	Increase sales/orders volume	Net sales billed or orders received against quota.
2.	Increase sales of particular lines	Sales against product line quotas with weighted sales credits on individual lines.
3.	Increase market share	Percent realization (%R) of shares bogey.
4.	Do balanced selling job	%R of product line quotas with commissions increasing in proportion to number of lines up to quota.
5.	Increase profitability	Margin realized from sales. Vary sales credits to emphasize profitable product lines. Vary sales credit in relation to amount of price discount.
6.	Increase dealer sales	Pay distributor *salespeople* or sales manager in relation to realization of sales quotas of assigned dealers.
7.	Increase sales calls	%R of targeted calls per district or region.
8.	Introduce new product	Additional sales credits on new line for limited period.
9.	Control expense	%R of expense to sales or margin ratio. Adjust sales credit in proportion to variance from expense budget.
10.	Sales teamwork	Share of incentive based upon group results.

service in an additional territory, which was undesirable because it took several months for a salesman to build up a good rapport with customers. Barr's decision would affect his quota allocation because a salesman new to a territory could not be expected to immediately sell as well as the incumbent, and a novice salesman would require an even longer period of adaptation.

Barr was also concerned about territory 9951. The territory comprised two large national accounts and seven major independent dealers. The buying decisions for the national accounts were made at their head offices, where G.E.'s regional salesmen had no control over the decisions. Recently, Barr had heard rumors that one of the national accounts was reviewing its purchase of G.E. Appliances. If it were to delist even some product lines, it would be a major blow to the salesman, Rizzuto, whose potential sales would be greatly reduced. Barr was unsure how to deal with that situation.

Another concern for Barr was the wide variance in buying of some accounts. Woodwards, Eatons, and McDonald Supply had large fluctuations from year to year. Also, Eatons, Hudson's Bay, and Woodwards had plans to open new stores in the Vancouver area sometime during the year. The sales increase to be generated by these events was hard to estimate.

The general economic outlook was poor. The Canadian dollar had fallen to 92 cents U.S. and unemployment was at about 8 percent. The government's anti-inflation program, which was scheduled to end in November 1992, had managed to keep inflation to the 3 percent level, but economists expected higher inflation and increased labor unrest during the postcontrol period.

The economic outlook was not the same in all areas. For instance, the Okanagan (9962) was a very depressed area. Tourism was down and fruit farmers were doing poorly despite good weather and record prices. Vancouver Island was still recovering from a 200 percent increase in ferry fares, while the lower mainland appeared to be in a relatively better position.

In the contract segment, construction had shown an increase over 1990. However, labor unrest was common. There had been a crippling eight-week strike in 1990, and there was a strong possibility of another strike in 1992.

With all of this in mind, Barr was very concerned that he allocate the quota properly because of the bonus system implications. How should he proceed? To help him in his decision, he reviewed a note on development of a sales commission plan that he had obtained while attending a seminar on sales management the previous year (see Appendix to follow).

Appendix: Development of a Sales Commission Plan

A series of steps are required to establish the foundation on which a sales commission plan can be built. These steps are as follows:

A. Determine Specific Sales Objectives of Positions to Be Included in Plan

For a sales commission plan to succeed, it must be designed to encourage the attainment of the business objectives of the component division. Before deciding on the specific measures of performance to be used in the plan, the component should review and define its major objectives. Typical objectives might be:

- Increase sales volume.
- Do an effective balanced selling job in a variety of product lines.
- Improve market share.
- Reduce selling expense to sales ratios.
- Develop new accounts or territories.
- Introduce new products.

Although it is probably neither desirable nor necessary to include all such objectives as specific measures of performance in the plan, they should be kept in mind, at least to the extent that the performance measures chosen for the plan are compatible with and do not work against the overall accomplishment of the component's business objectives.

Also, the relative current importance or ranking of these objectives will provide guidance in selecting the number and type of performance measures to be included in the plan.

B. Determine Quantitative Performance Measures to Be Used

Although it may be possible to include a number of measures in a particular plan, there is a drawback to using so many as to overly complicate it and fragment the impact of any one measure on the participants. A plan that is difficult to understand will lose a great deal of its motivation force, as well as be costly to administer properly.

For those who currently have a variable sales compensation plan(s) for their salespeople, a good starting point would be to consider the measures used in those plans. Although the measurements used for sales managers need not be identical, they should at least be compatible with those used to determine their salespeople's commissions.

However, keep in mind that a performance measure that may not be appropriate for individual salespeople may be a good one to apply to their manager. Measurements involving attainment of a share of a defined market, balanced selling for a variety of products, and control of district or region expenses might fall into this category.

Listed in the chart above are a variety of measurements that might be used to emphasize specific sales objectives.

For most components, all or most of these objectives will be desirable to some extent. The point is to select those of greatest importance where it will be possible to establish measures of standard or normal performance for individuals, or at least small groups of individuals working as a team.

If more than one performance measurement is to be used, the relative weighting of each measurement must be determined. If a measure is to be effective, it must carry enough weight to have at least some noticeable effect on the commission earnings of an individual.

As a general guide, it would be unusual for a plan to include more than two or three quantitative measures with a minimum weighting of 15 to 20 percent of planned commissions for any one measurement.

C. Establish Commission Payment Schedule for Each Performance Measure

1. Determine Appropriate Range of Performance for Each Measurement

The performance range for a measurement defines the percent of standard performance (%R) at which commission earnings start to the point where they reach maximum.

The minimum point of the performance range for a given measurement should be set so that a majority of the participants can earn at least some incentive pay and the maximum set at a point that is possible of attainment by some participants. These points will vary with the type of measure used and the degree of predictability of individual budgets or other forms of measurement. In a period where overall performance is close to standard, 90 to 95 percent of the participants should fall within the performance range.

For the commission plan to be effective, most of the participants should be operating within the performance range most of the time. If a participant is either far below the minimum of this range or has reached the maximum, further improvement will not affect his or her commission earnings, and the plan will be largely inoperative as far as he or she is concerned.

Actual past experience of %Rs attained by participants is obviously the best indicator of what this range should be for each measure used. Lacking this, it is better to err on the side of having a wider range than one that proves to be too narrow. If some form of group measure is used, the variation from standard performance is likely to be less for the group in total than for individuals within it. For example, the performance range for total district performance would probably be narrower than the range established for individual salespeople within a district.

2. Determine Appropriate Reward to Risk Ratio for Commission Earnings.

This refers to the relationship of commission earned at standard performance to maximum commission earnings available under the plan. A plan that pays 10 percent of base salary for normal or standard performance and pays 30 percent as a maximum commission would have a 2 to 1 ratio. In other words, the participant can earn twice as much (20 percent) for above standard performance as he or she stands to lose for below standard performance (10 percent).

Reward under a sales commission plan should be related to the effort involved to produce a given result. To adequately encourage above-standard results, the reward to risk ratio should generally be at least 2 to 1. The proper control of incentive plan payments lies in the proper setting of performance standards, not in the setting of a low maximum payment for outstanding results that provides a minimum variation in individual earnings. Generally, a higher percentage of base salary should be paid for each 1%R above 100 percent than has been paid for each 1%R up to 100%R to reflect the relative difficulty involved in producing above standard results.

Once the performance range and reward to risk ratios have been determined, the schedule of payments for each performance measure can then be calculated. This will show the percentage of the participant's base salary earned for various performance results (%R) from the point at which commissions start to maximum performance. For example, for measurement paying 20 percent of salary for standard performance:

Percent Base Salary Earned		Percent of Sales Quota
1% of base salary for each +1%R	0%	80% or below
	20%	100% (standard performance)
1.33% of base salary for each +1%R	60%	130% or above

D. Prepare Draft of Sales Commission Plan

After completing the above steps, a draft of a sales commission plan should be prepared using the outline below as a guide.

Keys to Effective Commission Plans

1. Get the understanding and acceptance of the commission plan by the managers who will be involved in carrying it out. They must be convinced of its effectiveness to properly explain and "sell" the plan to the salespeople.

2. In turn, be sure the plan is presented clearly to the salespeople so that they have a good understanding of how the plan will work. We find that good acceptance of a sales commission plan on the part of salespeople correlates closely with how well they understood the plan and its effect on their commission. Salespeople must be convinced that the measurements used are factors they can control by their selling efforts.

3. Be sure the measurements used in the commission plan encourage the salespeople to achieve the marketing goals of your operation. For example, if sales volume is the only performance measure, salespeople will concentrate on producing as much dollar volume as possible by spending most of their time on products with high volume potential. It will be difficult to get them to spend much time on introducing new products with relatively low volume, handling customer complaints, and so on. Even though a good portion of their compensation may still be in salary, you can be sure they will wind up doing the things they feel will maximize their commission earnings.

4. One good solution to maintaining good sales direction is to put at least a portion of the commission earnings in an "incentive pool" to be distributed by the sales manager according to his or her judgment. This "pool" can vary in size according to some qualitative measure of the sales group's performance, but the manager can set individual measurements for each salesperson and reward each person according to how well he or she fulfills the goals.

5. If at all possible, you should test the plan for a period of time, perhaps in one or two sales areas or districts. To make it a real test, you should actually pay commission earnings to the participants, but the potential risk and rewards can be limited. No matter how well a plan has been conceived, not all the potential pitfalls will be apparent until you've actually operated the plan for a period of time. The test period is a relatively painless way to get some experience.

6. Finally, after the plan is in operation, take time to analyze the results. Is the plan accomplishing what you want it to do, both in terms of business results produced and in realistically compensating salespeople for their efforts?

The Dunn Corporation: What to Do with a Low Performer?

Robert Head, the newly appointed sales manager for the Dunn Corporation, had completed a review of the salesforce that he inherited. He knew that he had an important decision facing him regarding one of his sales representatives, John Little.

COMPANY BACKGROUND. The Dunn Corporation, with headquarters in Tuscaloosa, Alabama, produced and sold asphalt roofing products and other building materials throughout the southeastern United States. The primary market area consisted of the states of Alabama, Tennessee, Georgia, Florida, and Mississippi. There were also selected accounts in Kentucky, Indiana, and South Carolina. Five sales representatives covered the primary marketing area, with each representative having one of the states assigned as a territory. The selected accounts were assigned to the sales representatives at the sales manager's discretion.

Historically, the management of Dunn had pursued a conservative growth strategy with particular emphasis on achieving maximum return on investment. In order to keep costs down, capital expenditures for replacement of worn-out or obsolete equipment were given low priority. This led to a drop in production efficiency at the company's Tuscaloosa plant such that production was unable to keep pace with demand. Thus, from 1983 to 1988 company sales were limited by the availability of the product. However, despite these difficulties, the company had been profitable and had built an excellent reputation in the construction industry for service and quality.

The company had initiated successful capital improvement programs during 1987 and 1988; consequently, the company's production capacity had been greatly increased. No longer would Dunn's sales performance be hindered by lack of product availability. Robert Head recognized that this increase in production capacity would require some revisions in the sales representative's duties. More time would have to be spent seeking new accounts in order to fully realize this new sales potential.

One of the first tasks that Head had undertaken as sales manager was a review of the field operations and performance of each sales representative. Head traveled with the sales representatives for a week in order to obtain as much information on each representative as possible. Head also spent two days with each person compiling a territorial analysis. This analysis broke each representative's district into trade areas that were then analyzed in terms of established accounts, competitive accounts, potential of the trade territory, market position of competitive manufacturers, and selection of target accounts. Head believed that a properly prepared territorial analysis could reveal whether the sales representatives really knew and worked their districts. Some pertinent statistics uncovered by the analysis are reported in Exhibits I and II.

JOHN LITTLE'S PERFORMANCE. Head concluded, after reviewing the results of the territorial analysis, that John Little's sales performance could be improved. Little had been with the company for over 20 years. A tall, handsome individual with a polished, articulate manner, he appeared to be a perfect salesperson, yet his performance never seemed to equal his potential.

While evaluating Little's accounts, call reports, and expense accounts Head uncovered a pattern of infrequent travel throughout Little's district. Little sold only 34 active accounts, well below the company average of approximately 55. With the low number of accounts and a daily call rate of two, it appeared that Little simply was not working very hard. When Little's sales performance was compared to his district's estimated potential, it appeared that Little

---

Source: This case was developed by Professor James L. Taylor, Department of Management and Marketing, University of Alabama. The company name has been changed.

EXHIBIT I — Sales Performance of the Individual Sales Representatives: 1989–90

Sales Representative	Sales Volume 1989	Sales Volume 1990
Peters	$2,732,464	$2,636,832
Little	1,366,232	1,315,916
Homer	1,639,420	1,879,880
Cough	2,368,136	2,443,844
Stiles	1,001,903	1,127,928
Total	$9,108,155	$9,404,400

EXHIBIT II — Results of Territorial Analysis

Sales Representative	Number of Accounts	New Accounts in 1990	Average Daily Calls
Peters	63	3	4
Little	34	0	2
Homer	52	2	5
Cough	78	4	2
Stiles	47	2	3
Average	54.8	2.2	3.2

was realizing only about 60 percent of the potential sales of his area. When compared with the other territories, Little's district ranked last in terms of sales volume per 1,000 housing starts and sales volume per 100,000 population.

Head had questioned Little concerning coverage in his Georgia district. Head recalled part of their conversation:

Head: John, it appears that you simply are not calling on the potential customers in the outer areas of your district. For example, last month you spent 12 out of 20 days working in Atlanta. I know you live in Atlanta, and there is a tendency to work closer to home, but I believe that we are missing a lot of business in your area simply by not calling on people.

Little: Look, I have been selling roofing for a long time, even when the plant couldn't produce and ship it. Why get upset when we have a little extra product to sell?

Head: Look, John, we have increased production by 20 percent. You will have all the product you can sell. This means extra income to you, better services to your accounts, and more profit to the company. I will be happy to assist you in working out a plan for coverage of your district.

Little: Bob, don't you ever look at the volume of our customers? If you did, you would know that the Republic Roofing Supply in Atlanta is the second largest account of Dunn. Upchurch, the owner of Republic, is very demanding concerning my servicing Republic on ordering, delivery, and product promotion. It has taken a long time, but I have gained the trust and respect of Upchurch. That is why he looks to me to take care of the account. The reason that we have not lost the account to our competitors is that I give the type of service demanded by Upchurch.

Head: John, I agree that service to all of our accounts is extremely important. However, service does represent a cost, not only in terms of an outlay of money, but also in the potential loss of business from other accounts. I seriously question the profitability of spending approximately 40 percent of your time with one account.

Little: What do you mean, profitability? My district has always made money. Just because we have new management, why does everything have to change?

Head had continued the conversation by suggesting that he and Little meet at some future date for the purpose of laying out a travel schedule. It was Head's intention to structure the schedule so that Little could make a minimum of four calls per day. Little, however, refused to even consider setting up a schedule or to increase the number of calls per day. His refusal was based on the contention that he needed at least two days a week to service Republic properly. Little further stated that if Dunn would not allow him the two days a week to service Republic, other roofing manufacturers would.

Robert Head pondered his decision regarding John Little and the Georgia territory. He felt that he had three options. First, he could simply fire Little with the possibility of losing the Republic account. Because Republic was Dunn's second largest account, Head realized that this might be a dangerous course of action. Second, Head considered rearranging Little's district by transferring some of the outer counties to other sales representatives. Finally, Head realized that he could simply accept the situation and leave things as they were now. He remembered once being told by a close friend with years of management experience that sometimes a "don't rock the boat" strategy is the best way to handle difficult situations.

Question

What should Robert Head do regarding John Little and his Georgia territory?

Modern Plastics

Institutional sales manager Jim Clayton had spent most of Monday morning planning for the rest of the month. It was early July and Jim knew that an extremely busy time was coming with the preparation of the following year's sales plan.

Since starting his current job less than a month ago, Jim had been involved in learning the requirements of the job and making his initial territory visits. Now that he was getting settled, Jim was trying to plan his activities according to priorities. The need for planning had been instilled in him during his college days. As a result of his three years' field sales experience and development of time management skills, he felt prepared for the challenge of the sales manager's job.

While sitting at his desk, Jim recalled a conversation that he had a week ago with Bill Hanson, the former manager, who had been promoted to another division. Bill told him that the sales forecast (annual and monthly) for plastic trash bags in the Southeast region would be due soon as an initial step toward developing the sales plan for the next year. Bill had laughed as he told Jim, "Boy, you ought to have a ball doing the forecast being a rookie sales manager!"

When Jim had asked what Bill meant, he explained by saying that the forecast was often "winged" because the headquarters in New York already knew what they wanted and would change the forecast to meet their figures, particularly if the forecast was for an increase of less than 10 percent. The experienced sales manager could throw numbers together in a short time that would pass as a serious forecast and ultimately be adjusted to fit the plans of headquarters. However, an inexperienced manager would have a difficult time "winging" a credible forecast.

Bill had also told Jim that the other alternative meant gathering mountains of data and putting together a forecast that could be sold to the various levels of Modern Plastics management. This alternative would prove to be time-consuming and could still be changed anywhere along the chain of command before final approval.

Clayton started reviewing pricing and sales volume history (see Exhibit I). He also looked at the key account performance for the past two and a half years (see Exhibit II). During the past month Clayton had visited many of the key accounts, and on the average they had indicated that their purchases from Modern would probably increase about 15–20 percent in the coming year.

Source: This case was written by Professor Kenneth L. Bernhardt, Georgia State University, Professor Tom Ingram, Colorado State University, and Professor Danny N. Bellenger, Auburn University. Copyright © 1982 the authors.

EXHIBIT I Plastic Trash Bags—Sales and Pricing History, 1994–1996

	Pricing dollars per case			Sales volume in cases			Sales volume in dollars		
	1994	1995	1996	1994	1995	1996	1994	1995	1996
January	$6.88	$ 7.70	$15.40	33,000	46,500	36,500	$ 227,000	$ 358,000	$ 562,000
February	6.82	7.70	14.30	32,500	52,500	23,000	221,500	404,000	329,000
March	6.90	8.39	13.48	32,000	42,000	22,000	221,000	353,000	296,500
April	6.88	10.18	12.24	45,500	42,500	46,500	313,000	432,500	569,000
May	6.85	12.38	11.58	49,000	41,500	45,500	335,500	514,000	527,000
June	6.85	12.65	10.31	47,500	47,000	42,000	325,500	594,500	433,000
July	7.42	13.48	9.90*	40,000	43,500	47,500*	297,000	586,500	470,000*
August	6.90	13.48	10.18	48,500	63,500	43,500	334,500	856,000	443,000
September	7.70	14.30	10.31	43,000	49,000	47,500	331,000	700,500	489,500
October	7.56	15.12	10.31	52,500	50,000	51,000	397,000	756,000	526,000
November	7.15	15.68	10.72	62,000	61,500	47,500	443,500	964,500	509,000
December	7.42	15.43	10.59	49,000	29,000	51,000	363,500	447,500	540,000
Total	$7.13	$12.25	$11.30	534,500	568,500	503,500	$3,810,000	$6,967,000	$5,694,000

*July–December 1996 figures are forecast of sales manager J. A. Clayton and other data comes from historical sales information.

EXHIBIT II — 1996 Key Account Sales History (in cases)

Customer	1994	1995	First Six Months 1996	1994 Monthly Average	1995 Monthly Average	First Half 1996 Monthly Average	First Quarter 1996 Monthly Average
Transco Paper Company	125,774	134,217	44,970	10,481	11,185	7,495	5,823
Callaway Paper	44,509	46,049	12,114	3,709	3,837	2,019	472
Florida Janitorial Supply	34,746	36,609	20,076	2,896	3,051	3,346	2,359
Jefferson	30,698	34,692	25,004	2,558	2,891	4,174	1,919
Cobb Paper	13,259	23,343	6,414	1,105	1,945	1,069	611
Miami Paper	10,779	22,287	10,938	900	1,857	1,823	745
Milne Surgical Company	23,399	21,930	—	1,950	1,828	—	—
Graham	8,792	15,331	1,691	733	1,278	281	267
Crawford Paper	7,776	14,132	6,102	648	1,178	1,017	1,322
John Steele	8,634	13,277	6,663	720	1,106	1,110	1,517
Henderson Paper	9,185	8,850	2,574	765	738	429	275
Durant Surgical	—	7,766	4,356	—	647	726	953
Master Paper	4,221	5,634	600	352	470	100	—
D.T.A.	—	—	2,895	—	—	482	—
Crane Paper	4,520	5,524	3,400	377	460	566	565
Janitorial Service	3,292	5,361	2,722	274	447	453	117
Georgia Paper	5,466	5,053	2,917	456	421	486	297
Paper Supplies, Inc.	5,117	5,119	1,509	426	427	251	97
Southern Supply	1,649	3,932	531	137	328	88	78
Horizon Hospital Supply	4,181	4,101	618	348	342	103	206
Total cases	345,997	413,207	156,094	28,835	34,436	26,018	17,623

Schedule for Preparing the Forecast

Jim had received a memo recently from Robert Baxter, the regional marketing manager, detailing the plans for completing the 1997 forecast. The key dates in the memo began in only three weeks:

August 1	Presentation of forecast to regional marketing manager.
August 10	Joint presentation with marketing manager to regional general manager.
September 1	Regional general manager presents forecast to division vice president.
September 1–September 30	Review of forecast by staff of division vice president.
October 1	Review forecast with corporate staff.
October 1–October 15	Revision as necessary.
October 15	Final forecast forwarded to division vice president from regional general manager.

Company Background

The plastics division of Modern Chemical Company was founded in 1965 when Modern Chemical purchased Cordco, a small plastics manufacturer with national sales of $15 million. At that time the key products of the plastics division were sandwich bags, plastic tablecloths, trash cans, and plastic-coated clothesline.

Since 1965 the plastics division has grown to a sales level exceeding $200 million with five regional profit centers covering the United States. Each regional center has manufacturing facilities and a regional sales force. There are four product groups in each region:

1. Food packaging: Styrofoam meat and produce trays; plastic bags for various food products
2. Egg cartons: Styrofoam egg cartons sold to egg packers and supermarket chains.
3. Institutional: Plastic trash bags and disposable tableware (plates, bowls and so on).
4. Industrial: Plastic packaging for the laundry and dry cleaning market; plastic film for use in pallet overwrap systems.

Each product group is supervised jointly by a product manager and a district sales manager, both of whom report to the regional marketing manager. The sales representatives report directly to the district sales manager but also work closely with the product manager on matters concerning pricing and product specifications.

The five regional general managers report to J. R. Hughes, vice president of the plastics division. Hughes is located in New York. Although Modern Chemical is owned by a multinational oil company, the plastics division has been able to operate in a virtually independent manner since its establishment in 1965. The reasons for this include:

1. Limited knowledge of the plastic industry on the part of the oil company management.
2. Excellent growth by the plastics division has been possible without management supervision from the oil company.
3. Profitability of the plastics division has consistently been higher than that of other divisions of the chemical company.

The Institutional Trash Bag Market

The institutional trash bag is a polyethylene bag used to collect and transfer refuse to its final disposition point. There are different sizes and colors available to fit the various uses of the bag. For example, a small bag for desk wastebaskets is available as well as a heavier bag for large containers such as a 55-gallon drum. There are 25 sizes in the Modern line with 13 of those sizes being available in 3 colors—white, buff, and clear. Customers typically buy several different items on an order to cover all their needs.

The institutional trash bag is a separate product from the consumer grade trash bag, which is typically sold to homeowners through retail outlets. The institutional trash bag is sold primarily through paper wholesalers, hospital supply companies, and janitorial supply companies to a variety of end users. Since trash bags are used on such a wide scale, the list of end users could include almost any business or institution. The segments include hospitals, hotels, schools, office buildings, transportation facilities, and restaurants.

Based on historical data and a current survey of key wholesalers and end users in the Southeast, the annual market of institutional trash bags in the region was estimated to be 55 million pounds. Translated into cases, the market potential was close to 2 million cases. During the past five years, the market for trash bags has grown at an average rate of 8.9 percent per year. Now a mature product, future market growth is expected to parallel overall growth in the economy. The 1997 real growth in GNP is forecast to be 4.5 percent.

General Market Conditions

The current market is characterized by a distressing trend. The market is in a position of oversupply with approximately 20 manufacturers competing for the business in the Southeast. Prices have been on the decline for several months but are expected to level out during the last six months of the year.

This problem arose after a record year in 1995 for Modern Plastics. During 1995, supply was very tight due to raw material shortages. Unlike many of its competitors, Modern had only minor problems securing adequate raw material supplies. As a result the competitors were few in 1995, and all who remained in business were prosperous. By early 1996 raw materials were plentiful, and prices began to drop as new competitors tried to buy their way into the market. During the first quarter of 1996 Modern Plastics learned the hard way that a competitive price was a necessity in the current market. Volume fell off drastically in February and March as customers shifted orders to new suppliers when Modern chose to maintain a slightly higher than market price on trash bags.

With the market becoming extremely price competitive and profits declining, the overall quality has dropped to a point of minimum standard. Most suppliers now make a bag "barely good enough to get the job done." This quality level is acceptable to most buyers who do not demand high quality for this type of product.

Modern Plastics versus Competition

A recent study of Modern versus competition had been conducted by an outside consultant to see how well Modern measured up in several key areas. Each area was weighted according to its importance in the purchase decision, and Modern was compared to its key competitors in each area and on an overall basis. The key factors and their weights are shown below:

		Weight
1.	Pricing	.50
2.	Quality	.15
3.	Breadth of line	.10

EXHIBIT III Competitive Factors Ratings (by competitor*)

Weight	Factor	Modern	National Film	Bonanza	Southeastern	PBI	BAGCO	Southwest Bag	Florida Plastics	East Coast Bag Co.
.50	Price	2	3	2	2	2	2	2	2	3
.15	Quality	3	2	3	4	3	2	3	3	4
.10	Breadth	1	2	2	3	3	3	3	3	3
.10	Sales coverage	1	3	3	3	4	3	3	4	3
.05	Packaging	3	3	2	3	3	1	3	3	3
.10	Service	4	3	3	2	2	2	3	4	3

Overall Weighted Ranking†

1. BAGCO   2.15
2. Modern   2.20
3. Bonanza   2.25
4. Southwest Bag (Tie) 2.50
5. PBI (Tie)   2.50
6. Southeastern   2.55
7. Florida Plastics 2.60
8. National Film   2.65
9. East Coast Bag Co. 3.15

*Ratings on a 1-to-5 scale with 1 being the best rating and 5 the worst.
†The weighted ranking is the sum of each rank times its weight. The lower the number, the better the overall rating.

EXHIBIT IV Market Share by Supplier, 1994 and 1996

Supplier	Percent of Market 1994	Percent of Market 1996	Supplier	Percent of Market 1994	Percent of Market 1996
National Film	11	12	BAGCO	—	6
Bertram	16	0*	Southwest Bag	—	2
Bonanza	11	12	Florida Plastics	—	4
Southeastern	5	6	East Coast Bag Co.	—	4
Bay	9	0*	Miscellaneous and unknown	8	22
Johnson Graham	8	0*			
PBI	2	5	Modern	28	27
Lewis	2	0*		100	100

*Out of business in 1996
Source: This information was developed from a field survey conducted by Modern Plastics.

4.	Sales coverage	.10
5.	Packaging	.05
6.	Service	.10
	Total	1.00

As shown in Exhibit III, Modern compared favorably with its key competitors on an overall basis. None of the other suppliers was as strong as Modern in breadth of line nor did any competitor offer as good sales coverage as that provided by Modern. Clayton knew that sales coverage would be even better next year since the Florida and North Carolina territories had grown enough to add two salespeople to the institutional group by January 1, 1997.

Pricing, quality, and packaging seemed to be neither an advantage nor a disadvantage. However, service was a problem area. The main cause for this, Clayton was told, was temporary out-of-stock situations which occurred occasionally primarily due to the wide variety of trash bags offered by Modern.

During the past two years, Modern Plastics had maintained its market share at approximately 27 percent of the market. Some new competitors had entered the market since 1994 while others had left the market (see Exhibit IV). The previous district sales manager, Bill Hanson, had left Clayton some comments regarding the new competitors. These are reproduced in Exhibit V.

EXHIBIT V	Characteristics of Competitors
National Film	Broadest product line in the industry. Quality a definite advantage. Good service. Sales coverage adequate, but not an advantage. Not as aggressive as most suppliers on price. Strong competitor.
Bonanza	Well-established tough competitor. Very aggressive on pricing. Good packaging, quality okay.
Southeastern	Extremely price competitive in southern Florida. Dominates Miami market. Limited product line. Not a threat outside of Florida.
PBI	Extremely aggressive on price. Have made inroads into Transco Paper Company. Good service but poor sales coverage.
BAGCO	New competitor. Very impressive with a high-quality product, excellent service, and strong sales coverage. A real threat, particularly in Florida.
Southwest Bag	A factor in Louisiana and Mississippi. Their strategy is simple—an acceptable product at a rock bottom price.
Florida Plastics	Active when market is at a profitable level with price cutting. When market declines to a low profit range, Florida manufactures other types of plastic packaging and stays out of the trash bag market. Poor reputation as a reliable supplier, but can still "spot-sell" at low prices.
East Coast Bag Co.	Most of their business is from a state bid which began in January 1989 for a two-year period. Not much of a threat to Modern's business in the Southeast as most of their volume is north of Washington, D.C.

EXHIBIT VI	1997 Real Growth Projections by Segment
Total industry	+5.0%
Commercial	+5.4%
Restaurant	+6.8%
Hotel/motel	+2.0%
Transportation	+1.9%
Office users	+5.0%
Other	+4.2%
Noncommercial	+4.1%
Hospitals	+5.9%
Nursing homes	+4.8%
Colleges/universities	+2.4%
Schools	+7.8%
Employee feeding	+4.3%
Other	+3.9%

Source: Developed from several trade journals.

Developing the Sales Forecast

After a careful study of trade journals, government statistics, and surveys conducted by Modern marketing research personnel, projections for growth potential were formulated by segment and are shown in Exhibit VI. This data was compiled by Bill Hanson just before he had been promoted.

Jim looked back at Baxter's memo giving the time schedule for the forecast and knew he had to get started. As he left the office at 7:15, he wrote himself a large note and pinned it on his wall—"Get Started on the Sales Forecast!"

IDS Financial Services (condensed)

In mid-1987 Reed Saunders, senior vice president of marketing at IDS Financial Services, was reviewing IDS's position. He was pleased by IDS's performance since its acquisition by American Express in January 1984. Revenues and net income had grown by an average of 20% annually. Fees from financial plans had mushroomed at an average annual rate of 174%. In addition, IDS had increased its financial planning team by an average annual rate of 11%.

Source: *Professor John Deighton prepared this case as the basis for class discussion rather than to illustrate either effective or ineffective handling of an administrative situation. Certain data have been disguised. It is a condensed version of the case IDS Financial Services, HBS case #588-044, prepared by Professor Minette E. Drumwright with assistance from Professor Thomas V. Bonoma. Copyright © 1995 by the President and Fellows of Harvard College. To order copies or request permission to reproduce materials, call 1-800-545-7685 or write Harvard Business School Publishing, Boston, MA 02163. No part of this publication may be reproduced, stored in a retrieval system, used in a spreadsheet, or transmitted in any form or by any means—electronic, mechanical, photocopying, recording, or otherwise—without the permission of Harvard Business School.*

IDS's performance had encouraged Harvey Golub, IDS president, to set aggressive goals for the rest of the decade. In January 1987 Golub had called for an average annual growth of 30% in revenues and 24% in earnings between year-end 1986 and year-end 1990, while decreasing the cost of sales. Golub's plan for salesforce expansion would double the IDS field force by year-end 1990, making it the second largest in the industry. Golub declared that his goal was to make IDS the premier financial planning firm in the world. As he explained:

> Our future is not in selling products one at a time, but in selling groups of products and services through the IDS financial planning process. Through this process we hope to help individuals and small businesses achieve their goals in a prudent and ethical manner, better than any other financial firm.

Consumer Financial Services Industry

The consumer financial services industry spanned managing and investing assets, providing credit, and providing financial or tax advice for consumers. At year-end 1986, the 88.5 million U.S. households had financial assets totaling $11.2 trillion and liabilities totaling $2.7 trillion. Transactions involving consumer financial services generated an estimated $200 billion in revenues for financial service providers in 1986.

Financial service providers were a large and diverse group. At one end of the spectrum, the group included commercial banks, savings and loan associations, insurance companies, mutual fund companies, and securities firms. At the other end of the spectrum, the provider group encompassed accountants, lawyers, and financial planners in private practice who primarily were financial advisors.

In the mid-1980s, the traditional boundaries between financial institutions like commercial banks, insurance firms, and securities firms were blurring. Many were becoming financial generalists, offering broad product lines that often included mutual funds, annuities, insurance, and limited partnerships. Nonfinancial firms such as Sears and American Can Company, which was renamed Primerica, entered the market with broad product lines as well. At the same time, households were wrestling with newfound responsibility for the management of their financial lives. The introduction of Individual Retirement Accounts, defined contribution pension plans and so-called 401(k) plans allowed individuals to accumulate tax-deferred savings for retirement, but required the individuals to make the financial planning decisions that before had been made by corporate pension departments. Many individuals turned to mutual funds to invest these savings, so that the value of equity funds grew tenfold from 1982 to mid-1987, reaching $500 billion.

FINANCIAL PLANNING. Many financial services institutions in the mid-1980s claimed to offer some form of *financial planning* or advice. However, the manner in which they used the term varied widely. Some providers used financial planning as a euphemism for a product sales approach, while others used it to refer to informal advice that salespeople offered. Still others used it to refer to a comprehensive process resulting in a professionally prepared plan that would guide clients' overall investment policies.

Financial planning as a comprehensive process began with a financial planner meeting with a client to develop an understanding of his or her financial needs, assist with clarifying financial objectives, and gather financial information. Some companies had financial planners submit the information to the company home office for analysis. After analysis, formal written plans were prepared and sent to the planners, who presented them to their clients. In contrast, other companies merely recommended financial planning software to their planners, who conducted the analyses and prepared the written plans themselves.

Some companies offered the plans free in hopes of earning commissions on product sales made in implementing the plans, while others charged either an hourly or a set fee. Of those charging for financial plans, some offered both the plans and the products to implement them on a fee-plus-commission basis. Others offered only the plans and charged a fee.

COMPETITION. With many of the major financial services industry players offering similar products, distribution was viewed as key. As one industry observer commented, "Anybody can provide the products; the difficulty is in distributing them."

Many financial service firms provided broad product lines on a nationwide basis, distributed through a salesforce. Sixteen of the largest nonbank financial services companies, are listed in **Exhibit I**. Three of these—Merrill Lynch, Integrated Resources, and FSC Securities—were considered particularly strong competitors by IDS management.

Merrill Lynch (ML). A diversified financial services holding company, ML provided securities, mutual funds, insurance, investment management, investment banking, and real estate through its subsidiaries on a nationwide basis. It owned $64 billion in assets and managed $149 billion in assets. Its chief subsidiary Merrill Lynch, Pierce, Fenner & Smith, was the nation's largest stockbroker. ML had the highest consumer-name recognition of any financial firm and was considered a formidable competitor because of its sheer size. Historically, ML had targeted a high-income clientele.

In 1982 ML introduced "Pathfinder," a financial plan with home office analysis.[1] The plan was designed for the

---

[1] In this type of financial planning, brokers gathered data from clients at the beginning of the planning process and interpreted the analyses for clients after the plans were prepared. The actual plan preparation was done by analysts, computer analysis, or both at the home office of the plan vendor.

EXHIBIT 1 Major Nonbank Financial Services Firms (year-end 1986)

Company	Sales Force Size	Sales Status	Historical Businesses	Revenues ($ millions)	Net Income (Loss) ($ millions)	Revenue per Salesperson	Net Income per Salesperson
Merrill Lynch	13,189	E[a]	Securities	$11,616	$ 549	$ 880,734	$ 41,626
Metropolitan[b]	10,052	E	Insurance	91,960	2,196	9,148,428	218,646
Dean Witter Reynolds	10,043	E	Securities	4,132	(45)	411,431	(4,481)
E.F. Hutton	7,623	E	Securities	3,340	(109)	438,148	(14,299)
IDS Financial Services	6,731	IC	Certificates	2,910	129	432,328	19,165
Shearson Lehman	6,655	E	Securities	5,566	382	836,364	57,401
Prudential-Bache	6,292	E	Securities	1,331	NA[c]	211,539	NA
Paine Webber	5,227	E	Securities	2,886	87	552,133	16,644
Integrated Resources	3,630	IC	Limited partnership	100	47	27,548	12,948
A. G. Edwards	3,146	E	Securities	637	65	202,479	20,361
John Hancock[b]	3,093	E	Insurance	4,328	NA	1,399,289	NA
Smith Barney	2,420	E	Securities	957	NA	395,455	NA
FSC Securities	1,513	IC	Securities	110	NA	72,703	NA
Cigna[b]	1,204	E	Insurance	20,647	989	17,148,671	821,429
Edward D. Jones	1,162	E	Securities	217	NA	186,747	NA
Aetna[b]	1,029	E	Insurance	24,784	1,262	24,085,520	1,226,433

[a]E indicates an employee salesforce; IC indicates a salesforce of independent contractors.
[b]Salesforce size for some insurance companies can be deceiving in that in additional to their employee salesforces, they sold through agents, who were neither employees nor independent contractors. As a result, revenue per salesperson and net income per salesperson may be disproportionately high.
[c]The net income for some private companies were not available.

middle market: households with annual income ranging from $36,000 to $85,000. In 1985 ML changed the title of its brokers from *account executive* to *financial consultant* and instituted a training program in consultative selling. By 1987 it provided a second middle-market program, called "Blueprint," which offered reduced investment commissions along with periodic investment advice. Typically, ML Blueprint clients paid up to 55% less in investment commissions on equity transactions, 30% less on mutual fund transactions, and 80% less on precious metal transactions. In 1987 the Pathfinder plan was priced at $300.

ML had never publicly adopted financial planning as its predominant strategy, and its compensation system was not perceived as particularly compatible with financial planning. Typically, financial consultants' income levels at ML depended on the number of brokerage transactions completed and the number of new accounts opened in a day. On average, financial consultants who were ML employees had approximately 600 clients and earned an annual net income (i.e., gross income less business expenses) of approximately $80,000. ML had an excellent training program stressing investments rather than insurance and estate planning, which IDS considered integral components of effective financial planning. It also had strong marketing and sales support.

Integrated Resources (IR). IR owned $6.2 billion in assets and managed $14 billion in assets, provided insurance, investment management, and investment brokerage on a nationwide basis. IR publicly advocated financial planning as its driving corporate strategy. Rather than providing home office analysis, IR recommended financial planning software to its planners, who charged by the plan ($120-$600 per plan) or by the hour ($75-$180 per hour). IR provided investment/asset management for high-net-worth individuals, who typically were the planners' target market.

IR planned to expand its field force aggressively, doubling its size by 1990. Because the company offered little training, it hired experienced financial planners. IDS planners, who were considered among the best trained in the industry, were prime targets for IR recruitment. IR's financial planners were independent contractors, who paid a large part of their own marketing support. On average, IR planners, who served about 300 clients each, earned an annual net income of $31,000.

FSC Securities. Primarily a broker for independent financial planners, FSC provided financial products and financial planning software. Its lines of business were securities brokerage, mutual funds, limited partnerships, and life insurance. FSC offered a plan with home office analysis and recommended planning software for its planners, who determined the prices of all plans. Plan prices ranged from $300 to $4,800, but typically were under $725. FSC's target market varied considerably by planners.

In 1987 FSC was acquired by Mutual of New York (MONY) Financial Services. With $7.7 billion in assets owned and $18 billion in assets managed, MONY was expected to provide FSC with a capital infusion to finance growth. FSC planned to triple its field force by 1990.

FSC financial planners were independent contractors who paid most of their business expenses and received little marketing or field support. Like IR, FSC primarily hired experienced planners and recruited IDS planners. On average, FSC planners served about 300 clients each and earned an annual net income $22,400.

CONSUMER BUYING PATTERNS. According to IDS executives, consumers could be grouped into two broad segments: confident investors and advisor-dependent investors. Confident investors managed their own financial affairs. They were often avid readers of periodicals such as *Money Magazine* or *Sylvia Porter's Personal Financial Planning*. While they might seek counsel of advisors from time to time, they did not delegate the management of their financial affairs to one advisor. One explained, "I just don't trust any single advisor enough." On average confident investors were more affluent and better educated than advisor-dependent investors.

Typically, advisor-dependent investors delegated their financial affairs to trusted advisors. They did not feel versed in financial affairs, often because they lacked the time or the interest to develop financial expertise. As one industry participant observed, "Many people spend the bulk of their time pursuing their careers and the rest trying to keep their marriages intact. They haven't got the time to look after their financial affairs."

Advisor-dependent investors frequently had no clear understanding of financial planning or its benefits. Sometimes they thought that financial planning was only for wealthy people and, thus, inappropriate for them. The different ways in which financial services providers used the term *financial planning*, contributed to consumer confusion.

According to a study conducted by a market research firm in 1987, 16% of the 42 million U.S. households with annual incomes over $25,000 had obtained professionally prepared financial plans by year-end 1986. The factors that motivated consumers to have a plan prepared were the approach of retirement, career advancement, a financial windfall or inheritance, and purchase of a house. The benefits that they received from purchasing a plan were financial security and peace of mind, better investment strategy, and provision for retirement. According to the study, 60% initiated the contact with the planner, and most with a strong referral from a trusted friend or associate. Other factors that motivated consumers were the planner's style (low-key rather than high pressure), objectivity, and the reputation of the planner's firm. Access to information and expertise at the firm was particularly important.

Of those who had no plans (i.e., 84% of households with annual incomes greater than $25,000), 75% had heard of the concept of financial planning, 19% had given serious thought to having a plan prepared, and 7% said they were likely to have a plan prepared in the next 12 months. Factors that deterred consumers from obtaining a financial plan included procrastination, perceptions of financial planners as insurance agents in disguise, beliefs that only wealthy people benefit from financial plans, and a desire to maintain control of personal finances.

The market research firm conducting the study classified nine million heads of households as high-potential customers for financial services because they either already had a plan or said they were likely to obtain one in the next 12 months. Of the high-potential customers, 53% felt that financial planners should be compensated on a fee-only basis; 18% favored a commission-only arrangement; and 16% preferred a fee-plus-commission basis. Approximately half of the high-potential consumers said they would prefer to implement their plans themselves, through stockbrokers, insurance agents, and bankers.

Company History

After witnessing the financial hardships of the 1893-1894 depression, John Tappan, a 25-year-old law student in Minneapolis, wanted to help Americans plan for the future. Tappan recognized that if he could bring together 1,000 people, each investing $5, he would have $5,000 to invest at the higher interest rates available to wealthy individuals. Tappan organized Investors Syndicate to bring together small investors. To take the service directly to the people, he formed a field force. From the beginning, it consisted of independent business people, embodying Tappan's entrepreneurial spirit as well as his desire to help people meet their financial goals and secure their futures.

Through the years, the company grew conservatively, expanding its product lines in response to its clients' changing needs. In the 1940s the company organized three mutual funds, and in 1949 changed its name to Investors' Diversified Services, Inc., to better reflect the growing diversity of its financial products. During the 1950s IDS formed a life insurance company, and in the 1960s it entered the business-to-business market by managing pension funds of small- and medium-sized companies. In the early 1980s IDS introduced financial planning on a fee basis.

As the product lines expanded, the company's mission necessarily blurred. IDS's three major product lines—certificates, mutual funds, and life insurance—were not coordinated or marketed in a synergistic manner. As one IDS manager observed:

> Because nobody said, "This is the business we are in," financial planners were free to define our business

as they wished. While many would have said that we were in business to help people manage their money, others would have said that we were primarily certificate providers, life insurance agents, or mutual funds salespeople. Thus, we missed opportunities for synergy.

In January 1984 the American Express Company acquired IDS and renamed the company IDS Financial Services. The IDS field force, which then comprised approximately 5,000 independent contractors, was among the most valuable assets that IDS brought to the combined company. The field force served approximately 1.2 million clients in the middle market. Although there were IDS representatives from coast to coast, the field force had been most successful in small towns and midsized communities in the Midwest, where the cost of doing business was relatively low and competition was not as strong as in metropolitan areas.

Immediately after the acquisition, Harvey Golub, a partner with McKinsey & Company in New York City and a consultant to American Express, was appointed president and chief executive officer of IDS. Under his direction IDS flourished. (The company's historical performance in terms of revenues, net income, and field force growth is summarized in **Exhibit II**. Income statements for 1984 through 1986, are shown in **Exhibit III** and sales by product line are shown in **Exhibit IV**.) At year-end 1986, IDS owned assets of $12.1 billion, and managed assets of $24.2 billion. Approximately half of the assets were in mutual funds, representing a 3.7% market share. IDS had a 0.5% market share of ordinary life insurance.

In December 1986 IDS served a 1.4 million client base, comprising consumer households and small businesses. (IDS's historical client growth is shown in **Exhibit V**.) In 1986 the average IDS consumer client purchase was approximately $17,000 in investment products, insurance, or annuities. Consumer households accounted for 95% of revenues.

IDS AND FINANCIAL PLANNING. IDS began selling financial plans for a fee in 1979, but it was not until the American Express acquisition in 1984 that plan sales were given strategic priority. From 1983 to 1986 sales of computer-prepared plans doubled each year, from 9,400 to 70,600, and fees from plans grew from $3.1 million to $20 million. Reed Saunders emphasized, however, that plans were less a revenue source than a tool to maintain on-going relationships with clients. He explained:

> We saw a strategic opportunity in the marketplace for someone to provide a value-added approach to managing relationships with clients. Through our concept of financial planning, we offer clients better quality in a financial planning relationship than they could get elsewhere.

IDS's financial planning process began with an in-depth interview to discuss the client's current financial position, short-term financial needs, and long-term goals. On the basis of the interview, the planner submitted detailed forms to the IDS home office for analysis. The simpler, less-expensive plans were computer-analyzed, while the more complicated and more expensive plans were prepared by analysts at IDS's Minneapolis home office, who often conferred with accountants, attorneys, or real estate experts. (An example of each type of plan is shown in **Table A**.) Although the fees ranged from $180 to more than $12,000 depending on the complexity of the plan, the average charge was approximately $360.

The completed plan was sent to the planner, who presented it to the client and recommended IDS products that the client could purchase to implement the plan. Often times, four to six weeks would elapse between the initial meeting with the client about the plan and the sale of any financial products.

Although the financial planning process took longer to generate the first product sale than a product-oriented

EXHIBIT II   IDS Historical Growth

	Revenues ($ millions)	Net Income ($ millions)	Field Force[a]	Revenue/ Field Force Member	Net Income/ Field Force Member
1980	$1,001	$ 67	3,524	$284,052	$19,013
1981	1,249	52	4,127	302,641	12,600
1982	1,422	76	4,773	297,926	15,923
1983	1,543	67	5,036	306,394	13,304
1984	1,907	75	5,337	357,317	14,053
1985	2,666	96	6,075	438,848	15,803
1986	2,910	129	6,731	432,328	19,165

[a] The field force consisted of financial planners and district managers.

EXHIBIT III — IDS Income Statements, 1984–1986 ($ thousands)

	1984	1985	1986
Revenues			
Premiums	$1,062,690	$1,565,692	$1,555,882
Sales loads	102,284	153,940	219,936
Investment management and service fees	103,961	120,155	173,986
Interest and dividends	630,710	822,523	940,604
Other	6,866	4,021	19,538
Total revenues	1,906,511	2,666,331	2,909,946
Expenses			
Provisions for losses and benefits	1,474,280	2,123,883	2,174,376
Compensation and employee benefits	185,829	278,100	395,723
Amortization of intangible assets	66,469	55,096	33,418
Taxes (other than income taxes)	16,035	25,613	24,396
Depreciation and amortization	7,721	11,404	26,777
Rent	19,629	22,041	19,769
Other	21,347	15,279	53,974
Total expenses	1,791,310	2,531,416	2,728,433
Pretax income	115,201	134,915	181,513
Income tax expense	40,165	39,200	52,870
Net income	$ 75,036	$ 95,715	$ 128,643

EXHIBIT IV — IDS Product Lines at Year-End 1986

Product	% of 1986 Sales
Mutual funds	42.0%
Annuities	23.5
Insurance	17.8
Limited partnerships	9.0
Financial plans	4.0
Certificates	3.2
Unit investment trusts	0.5
Securities services	NA[a]
Total	100.0%

[a] Securities services, which included brokerage and portfolio management, were in the start-up phase in 1986 and accounted for a negligible percentage of sales.

TABLE A — Examples of IDS Financial Plan Products

The *Personal Financial Profile* was a computer prepared plan designed for people who wanted to accumulate capital toward one objective, such as retirement income or income needs in the event of premature death. An analysis of objectives for educating children was provided for an additional fee.

    Fee: $180 without education analysis
           $210 with education analysis

The *Retirement Report* was an analyst-prepared plan designed for people who either retired or planning to retire within 12 months. It was appropriate for individuals who had estate-planning concerns regarding income and estate tax reduction, estate settlement and distribution, current resource needs, and survivor-income needs.

    Fee: $880

EXHIBIT V — IDS Client Base Growth, 1984–1986

	1984	1985	1986
Beginning client base	1,197,400	1,264,509	1,317,620
Reactivated clients[a]	4,158	8,266	11,529
New clients	167,086	161,769	177,693
Lost clients	(104,135)	(116,924)	(113,085)
Ending client base	1,264,509	1,317,620	1,393,757
Accounts per client[b]	1.99	2.14	2.34
Accounts per new client	1.71	1.91	2.07

[a] Reactivated clients opened an account with IDS within three years after closing all their previous accounts.
[b] Accounts refer to financial products sold to a client.

---

sales approach, it resulted in more sales per client. An IDS study in 1987 revealed that the average number of products purchased per household was 4.3 for clients who purchased a financial plan, and 1.9 for clients who had not. While 25% of the new clients in 1987 had purchased a financial plan, only 11% of the total client base had done so. Only 4.6% of clients who had been with the company for more than two years had purchased a financial plan.

IDS Field Force

In June 1986 IDS's 6,720 financial planners were grouped into 635 districts, which were supervised by district managers who were both managers and financial planners with active practices. Both the financial planners and the district managers were independent contractors, with the stipulation that they sell only IDS products. The districts were grouped into 215 divisions, each of which was supervised by an officer employee of IDS.

Most financial planners had been attracted to IDS by the opportunity to be in business for themselves, with unlimited income potential and the ability to set their own hours. Many planners had been teachers, small-business owners, or managers with no previous work experience in financial services. The field force had been described as "average people," "the get-rich-slow crowd," and "people who could trust rather than financial gurus."

People aspiring to be IDS financial planners went through an extensive selection process that lasted four to six weeks. Of the 12,328 people who applied for positions as IDS financial planners during the first six months of 1987, only 1,196 were appointed. Those appointed entered a three-month program of orientation to IDS and preparation for licensing examinations. They had to pass examinations to earn the life, accident, and health insurance, fixed annuity and variable annuity licenses required by the state in which they practiced. All planners then entered an 18-month self-study program focusing on financial planning, financial products, and sales skills. Some planners went on to earn the designation of Chartered Life Underwriter, Charter Financial Consultant, and Certified Financial Planner after starting their practices

After the first year, financial planners became independent contractors. Their compensation was based on a complex system of commission schedules, bonuses, awards, and benefits. Because of the wide variety of IDS products, 150 different commission schedules were needed. IDS's compensation system was not perceived as perfectly balanced by the field force; however, planners estimated that it was balanced to the point that it was 80% to 90% objective. Planners perceived that Integrated Resources and FSC Securities gave planners higher and more immediate cash payouts on equivalent production. In contrast, IDS had higher noncash components and more deferred compensation.

While some planners earned more than $350,000 in 1986, planners on average earned $47,200 in monetary compensation (i.e., commissions and bonuses) annually. On average, planners received retirement and insurance benefits valued at $6,650. Planners incurred marketing expenses by participating in home office marketing programs. The median annual marketing expense was $1,752.

Financial planners also paid their own operating expenses, which included rent, office furniture, secretarial support, telephone, postage, and supplies. The median operating expense for planners was $9,100 annually.

Marketing Productivity

IDS President Harvey Golub's challenge to his marketing vice president was to grow sales by 30% per year while decreasing the cost of sales by 5% per year. The cost of sales comprised indirect selling and marketing expenditures but excluded direct compensation. These costs had actually gone up by 4% from midyear 1986 to midyear 1987. (Marketing and sales expenses, along with direct compensation—that is, commissions, overwrites, and fees—are shown in **Exhibit VI**.)

EXHIBIT VI — IDS Marketing/Sales Expenses ($000)

Plan	1984	1985	1986	1987
New-client marketing programs	$ 11,350	$ 18,709	$ 21,388	$ 15,400
Existing-client marketing programs	703	1,627	2,033	2,911
Sales promotion programs	2,061	2,736	7,921	5,859
Sales support programs	2,016	2,236	3,612	5,046
Marketing research	1,249	3,997	7,921	5,859
Education and training	6,171	7,508	10,872	21,072
Recruiting and licensing	1,516	1,572	2,369	3,237
Home office marketing/sales salaries	5,266	7,364	9,189	11,062
Division office expenses	24,349	30,219	36,678	45,162
Infrastructure[a]	12,278	15,820	19,626	22,982
Direct compensation[b]	179,141	209,846	275,158	337,873
Total	$246,100	$301,634	$396,767	$476,463

[a] Infrastructure included a variety of administrative expenses, such as recordkeeping, home office computer support, and legal support.
[b] Direct compensation included commissions, overwrites, and fees paid to the field force.

To increase planner productivity, the IDS home office offered a variety of marketing programs. Saunders explained their purpose:

> Through the marketing program, we provide a core set of systems for acquiring and serving clients that we believe will provide a higher level of success. Our purpose is to help new planners build a professional financial planning practice during their first three years with IDS and to assist veteran planners to expand their practices each year.

Revenues could be increased in two general ways: by increasing productivity (i.e., revenue per planner) and by increasing the salesforce size. Productivity could be leveraged by increasing (1) the number of clients per planner; and (2) the number of sales per client.

Planners participating in home office marketing programs often shared in the program expense individually or through contributing to their division's Marketing Operations Account (MOA). Division managers assessed planners and district managers $30 to $50 each per month for the MOA, which they used to obtain home office marketing programs. The marketing programs were grouped in four categories: new client marketing, existing-client marketing, sales promotions, and sales support.

NEW-CLIENT MARKETING PROGRAMS. The objective of the new-client marketing programs was to optimize contact points between qualified prospects and IDS planners. (Descriptions of the new-client marketing programs and related expenses that IDS and the field force incurred are shown in **Exhibit VII.**) In addition to the program expenses in **Exhibit VII,** IDS spent approximately $11 million on national advertising, in conjunction with new-client marketing programs. Many of the programs generated sales leads, which planners purchased; however, studies indicated that planners pursued only about half of the leads purchased. Some financial planners said that they pursued these leads only as a last resort after exhausting all their referral leads, and complained that the quality of the leads was low. Newer planners tended to use the home office new-client marketing programs most. As a result, some veteran planners felt that they were subsidizing new planners with their MOA contributions.

EXISTING-CLIENT PROGRAMS. Existing-client programs were designed to increase the number of products purchased per client. Although IDS had the capability to manage 80% to 90% of its clients' financial assets, studies indicated that it typically managed about 15%. Research had revealed that it was more efficient for planners to sell to existing clients rather than to new ones. While an average of 24.3 telephone calls were needed to sell a product to prospective new clients, an average of only 5.3 telephone calls would sell a product to existing clients. There were two existing-client marketing programs: client direct marketing and client communications.

Through the client direct marketing program, 16.5 million pieces of promotional literature were mailed to existing clients in transaction statements and monthly consolidated statements as well as through a lead-generation direct mail effort. The program generated 451,000 leads,

EXHIBIT VII 1986 New-Client Program

1. Through the *Right-Number-of-Leads Program*, 18,918,350 pieces of promotional literature generated 539,600 new-client leads. Financial planners paid from $5 to $10 each for the leads, depending on their divisions' conversion rates (i.e., leads converted to clients). Planners in divisions with higher conversion rates were charged less per lead than planners in divisions with lower rates. The leads resulted in 21,100 new clients.

   IDS's expense: $2,523,740
   Planners' expense: $2,470,992

2. Through the *Amex Marketing Program*, 3,945,000 pieces of promotional literature were mailed to American Express cardmembers to generate 108,000 new-client leads, which were sold to planners for $5 to $10 each. The leads resulted in 5,200 new clients.

   IDS's expense: $1,201,530
   Planners' expense: $ 473,100

3. The *Seminar Program* provided field force members with materials such as slides and scripts for conducting consumer seminars from which leads were generated. Division managers purchased seminar materials for $180 from MOA funds. In 1986, 1,806,500 people were mailed invitations to one of 1,378 seminars. Of the 11,606 people attending seminars, 3,190 conferred with planners and 1,913 became clients.

   IDS's expense: $ 370,000
   Planners' expense: $ 78,650

4. Through the *Pre-Retirement-Segment Marketing Program*, sales kits and a direct-mail effort were designed to target 45-64-year-old clients. The direct mail effort generated 31,584 leads, which resulted in 1,232 new clients.

   IDS's expense: $ 182,710
   Planners' expense: $ 187,371

5. Through the *Local Prospecting Program*, the IDS home office and the division offices equally divided the expenses of local marketing efforts, such as sales fairs and local newspaper advertising.

   IDS's expense: $ 752,600
   Planners' expense: $ 556,600

6. Through the *Yellow Pages Program*, IDS paid the entire cost of advertising in the local *Yellow Pages*.

   IDS's expense: $ 521,510

7. Through the *Employee Financial Planning (EFP) Program*, a corporate salesforce approached the companies about providing financial planning through IDS as an employee benefit. In 1986, 33 companies either sponsored seminars led by IDS financial planners or provided lists of prospects. A total of 6,240 people attended 472 seminars, and 3,504 new clients resulted from the seminar leads and the prospect lists. Planners did not participate in the expense in 1986, but in 1987 they received only half the usual commissions on EFP financial plans. Planners received the full commissions on financial products sold in conjunction with EFP financial plans.

   IDS's expense: $4,825,480

Note: The costs given include only the direct expenses associated with each program and exclude the $11 million in national advertising that was included in the New-Client Programs budget.

---

provided to planners at no charge. The leads resulted in sales of 53,240 new accounts. IDS absorbed the entire program expense of $1,651,650 in 1986.

Through the client communications program, 72,600 letters welcoming new clients were mailed, and 1.5 million newsletters, which were mailed along with statements, were printed. Planners were not charged for the letters or the newsletters. The program also enabled planners to have a quarterly magazine, *Financial Directions*, mailed to their clients for an annual charge of $.99 per client. Planners had the option of having response cards enclosed in the magazine for an additional annual charge of 36 cents per client. IDS's expense for the client communication program was $381,000 in 1986; planners paid $375,600.

SALES PROMOTION PROGRAMS. To motivate the field force, IDS spent $7.9 million in 1986 on sales promotions, which included contests, awards, and campaigns. Planners attaining production and financial planning goals could qualify for the IDS national conference held in places like Hawaii, as well as for vacations and prizes. Top financial planners could qualify for the President's Advisory Council, an honorary advisory group.

SALES SUPPORT PROGRAMS. Thirteen product managers, supported entirely by IDS, acted as liaisons between the home office and the field force. They provided product line information personally as well as through literature and videotapes. The product management program cost $916,000 in 1986. Through a second sales support program, toll-free telephone hotlines, were available for planners in need of sales or service information. The telephone hotline program cost $908,000 in 1986. In addition, $1,788,400 of sales literature was printed and provided to planners as sales support.

Growth: Field Force Expansion

By expanding the field force, IDS could increase its revenues substantially. Often, IDS expanded by spinning a new division off of an existing one, and appointing a division manager from the ranks of the district managers in the older division. The division manager then recruited district managers, usually from the ranks of successful financial planners in the older divisions. District managers accepted the assignment of building a district, which required three to four years of arduous work.

Building a district was arduous because district managers had to recruit and train planners. Planner turnover, although low for the industry, made recruiting and training perpetual tasks. For example, 2,321 new planners were appointed to realize a net gain of 633 in 1986 (see **Exhibit VIII**). Field force terminations by length of service for 1986 are presented in **Exhibit IX**. IDS's turnover rate had been negatively impacted by competitors who lured financial planners away (32% of the planners who left IDS in 1986 went to competitors).

EXHIBIT VIII — Historical Field Force Growth

Year	New Financial Planners Appointed	Net Gain	Planners at Year-End
1980	1,223	218	3,161
1981	1,529	560	3,721
1982	1,757	588	4,309
1983	1,980	214	4,523
1984	1,999	231	4,754
1985	2,196	675	5,429
1986	2,321	633	6,062

EXHIBIT IX — IDS Financial Planner Retention, 1986

Length of Service	Active Planners	Terminated Planners	Retention Rate
First year	2,320	327	86%
Second year	1,879	669	64%
Third year	1,116	316	72%
Fourth year	628	154	76%
More than 4 years	1,805	220	88%
Total	7,748	1,686	78%

In addition to achieving numerical expansion, IDS hoped that the field force could achieve strategic geographical expansion. Traditionally, the field force had expanded opportunistically, spinning new divisions and districts off successful ones. Thus, the field of force grew like an amoeba, becoming bigger and stronger in areas where it was already concentrated. For example, at year-end 1986, Minneapolis, St. Paul, and Rochester, Minnesota, each had nine districts. In contrast, Philadelphia had one district; Washington, D.C. had two, and Atlanta had three. In expanding the field force, IDS hoped to build districts to strengthen its position in major metropolitan areas where the company traditionally had not been strong.

CURRENT SITUATION. Saunders had a number of issues to ponder in preparing a plan to dramatically increase production to meet IDS's aggressive growth goals. He had to determine the most effective way or combination of ways to leverage IDS's field force. Among his options were increasing marketing programs, accelerating field force numerical growth, and emphasizing the expansion of the field force in major metropolitan areas. On the other hand, perhaps the most appropriate task would be to counsel restraint in the drive to become America's premier financial services distributor, to ride out the difficult competitive environment in 1987, and be satisfied with a more modest level of growth.

Evaluating the Success of a Salesforce Promotional Program:
Denman Industrial Products (A)

Denman Industrial Products
Serving our Customers Around the World Since 1936

Internal Memorandum

To: A.L. Medina
Sales Manager for South American Operations

From: K.P. DuJong
Vice President of Sales

Date: January 3, 1997

Regarding: Evaluation of 1996 Sales Promotion Efforts

I will be meeting with other senior management officers and the Board of Directors at the upcoming global company meetings in Toronto on February 3rd. In preparation for those meetings I am asking all twelve regional sales managers to assess the outcomes of the two major sales force targeted promotion campaigns held in the last calendar year. More specifically, I need to know which, if either, of the campaigns directed at our sales force was successful in increasing sales to (or beyond) the targeted levels.

Below, and on the accompanying pages, are data from our M.I.S. department concerning sales levels, territory staffing, and related information for each of the territory offices in the South American division. Please analyze the information and provide me a memo of your conclusions by January 17th.

Concerning two related issues, Denman currently employs a single territory office and sales force for the combined Surinam, Trinidad and Tobago, Guyana, and French Guyana areas. The possibility has been advanced of breaking this territory into one or more separate territories, each with its own office and sales force. Additionally, we do not currently service the country of Chile. As regional sales manager, I would like your assessment of the potential benefits and problems connected with (1) breaking up the combined territory and (2) adding Chile as a new territory with our existing personnel.

Worldwide Headquarters
2344 West Zumont Place Toronto, Ontario Canada 1Z3 5CT
Telephone: 1-13-676-8819 Internet: emgr.45.f44@wwh.acme.com.can

Denman Industrial Products
South American Operations Division
Report Alpha/DT - 12 month period ending
12/31/1996
printed 1/2/1997 - 2:05:47 a.m. G.M.T.

Territory Code	Territory Office	Territory in Square Miles	General Population	Number of Salespeople	Local Currency	Exchange Rate to U.S. Dollar
Paraguay	Asuncio'n	157,047	5,026,699	6	Guarani'	1,900.000
Colombia	Bogota'	439,735	37,038,240	17	Peso	894.000
Brazil	Brasilia	3,286,470	160,625,080	128	Real	0.950
Argentina	Buenos Aires	1,072,067	34,787,129	42	Peso	0.999
Venezuela	Caracas	352,143	22,421,998	14	Bolivar	169.790
French Guiana	see Guyana	35,126	150,897	—	Franc	5.390
Guyana	Georgetown	83,000	829,059	7	Guyana Dollar	142.000
Bolivia	La Paz	424,162	8,648,778	17	Boliviano	4.680
Peru	Lima	496,222	23,825,160	19	Nuevo Sol	2.224
Uruguay	Montevideo	68,040	3,251,405	3	Peso	6.410
Surinam	see Guyana	63,251	412,902	—	Surinam Guilder	183.120
Trinidad/Tobago	see Guyana	1,980	1,331,387	—	T & T Dollar	5.560
Ecuador	Quito	106,927	11,327,838	4	Sucre	2,572.000

| | | Annual Hours by Territory | | | | | |
Territory Code	Territory Office	Face-to Face Selling	Phone Selling	Travel	Admin.	Other Non Selling	Vacation	Territory Supervisor
Paraguay	Asuncion	5,025	1,800	2,775	2,250	1,650	540	Carlos Wasmosy
Colombia	Bogota'	14,450	5,100	7,650	6,375	4,675	1,530	Ernesto Menem
Brazil	Brasilia	108,800	38,400	57,600	48,000	35,200	11,520	Marie Caldera
Argentina	Buenos Aires	36,225	12,600	18,375	15,750	11,550	3,780	Luis Lacalle
Venezuela	Caracas	12,075	4,200	6,125	5,250	3,850	1,260	Rafael Lozada
French Guiana	see Guyana	—	—	—	—	—	—	
Guyana	Georgetown	5,863	2,100	3,238	2,625	1,925	630	Edwardo Tagle
Bolivia	La Paz	14,663	5,100	7,438	6,375	4,675	1,530	Gloria Nunez
Peru	Lima	15,913	5,700	8,788	7,125	5,225	1,710	Toma Hernandez
Uruguay	Montevideo	2,700	900	1,200	1,125	825	270	Jill Rodriguez
Surinam	see Guyana	—	—	—	—	—	—	
Trinidad/Tobago	see Guyana	—	—	—	—	—	—	
Ecuador	Quito	3,300	1,200	1,900	1,500	1,100	360	Suzanne Ortega

Denman Industrial Products
South American Operations Division
Report Alpha/DT - 12 month period ending
12/31/1996
printed 1/2/1997 - 2:05:47 a.m. G.M.T.

Territory Code	Territory Office	Large Accounts (5 calls per quarter)		Medium Accounts (3 calls per quarter)		Small Accounts (2 calls per quarter)	
		Number	Avg. Call Duration	Number	Avg. Call Duration	Number	Avg. Call Duration
Paraguay	Asuncion	34	150 min.	114	90 min.	212	45 min.
Colombia	Bogota'	142	150 min.	208	90 min.	601	45 min.
Brazil	Brasilia	1,102	150 min.	1,785	90 min.	3,595	45 min.
Argentina	Buenos Aires	404	150 min.	455	90 min.	1,305	45 min.
Venezuela	Caracas	168	150 min.	145	90 min.	177	45 min.
French Guiana	see Guyana	—	—	—	—	—	—
Guyana	Georgetown	70	150 min.	78	90 min.	159	45 min.
Bolivia	La Paz	195	150 min.	225	90 min.	143	45 min.
Peru	Lima	180	150 min.	352	90 min.	96	45 min.
Uruguay	Montevideo	14	150 min.	22	90 min.	267	45 min.
Surinam	see Guyana	—	—	—	—	—	—
Trinidad/Tobago	see Guyana	—	—	—	—	—	—
Ecuador	Quito	32	150 min.	62	90 min.	97	45 min.

Territory Code	Territory Office	1996 Annual Sales in U.S. $	First Promotional Campaign Period (duration = 5 weeks) Target: 6.50% above non-promotional period amount		
			Large Accounts	Medium Accounts	Small Accounts
Paraguay	Asuncion	$4,688,250	$225,263	$145,321	$110,000
Colombia	Bogota'	$14,082,075	$656,891	$468,597	$398,254
Brazil	Brasilia	$110,085,982	$5,898,214	$3,258,987	$2,145,583
Argentina	Buenos Aires	$35,228,981	$1,453,789	$1,225,698	$1,158,743
Venezuela	Caracas	$10,937,520	$253,974	$479,855	$446,983
French Guiana	see Guyana	—	—	—	—
Guyana	Georgetown	$5,169,875	$185,983	$158,987	$143,352
Bolivia	La Paz	$12,885,250	$789,058	$242,697	$321,542
Peru	Lima	$14,685,791	$648,252	$520,258	$346,853
Uruguay	Montevideo	$2,544,684	$92,018	$72,155	$108,963
Surinam	see Guyana	—	—	—	—
Trinidad/Tobago	see Guyana	—	—	—	—
Ecuador	Quito	$3,325,100	$221,589	$84,644	$35,881

Denman Industrial Products
South American Operations Division
Report Alpha/DT - 12 month period ending
12/31/1996
printed 1/2/1997 - 2:05:47 a.m. G.M.T.
page 5 of 5

			Second Promotional Campaign Period (duration = 4 weeks) Target: 7.25% above non-promotional period amount		
Territory Code	Territory Office	1996 Annual Sales in U.S. $	Large Accounts	Medium Accounts	Small Accounts
Paraguay	Asuncion	$4,688,250	$175,325	$125,869	$88,795
Colombia	Bogota'	$14,082,075	$570,025	$404,255	$331,699
Brazil	Brasilia	$110,085,982	$5,340,185	$2,719,885	$1,422,302
Argentina	Buenos Aires	$35,228,981	$1,089,954	$998,753	$887,452
Venezuela	Caracas	$10,937,520	$221,983	$375,944	$384,933
French Guiana	see Guyana	—	—	—	—
Guyana	Georgetown	$5,169,875	$152,977	$131,558	$163,554
Bolivia	La Paz	$12,885,250	$701,299	$216,379	$296,771
Peru	Lima	$14,685,791	$554,699	$468,008	$226,874
Uruguay	Montevideo	$2,544,684	$82,044	$61,588	$74,611
Surinam	see Guyana	—	—	—	—
Trinidad/Tobago	see Guyana	—	—	—	—
Ecuador	Quito	$3,325,100	$202,446	$73,499	$29,811

Notes to report:

1. Sales representatives work a typical 50 week year of approximately 45 hours per week.

2. For analysis purposes, dollar amounts, time assessments, etc. do not include territory managers. These individual's activities and performance are evaluated under other criteria and with other systems.

3. Sales of Denman products are not subject to seasonal and cyclical variations.

4. Vacation hours taken by sales representatives are sufficiently spread out to have no significant effect on the maintenance of existing accounts.

Source: This case was prepared by Michael R. Luthy, Drake University.

Evaluating the Success of a Salesforce Promotional Program:
Denman Industrial Products (B)

Denman Industrial Products
Serving our Customers Around the World Since 1936

Internal Memorandum

To: A.L. Medina
        Sales Manager for South American Operations

From: K.P. DuJong
        Vice President of Sales

Date: January 21, 1997

Regarding: Further Evaluation of 1996 Sales Promotion Efforts

I have completed reading your analysis of the South American Division's sales performance for 1996 and the effectiveness of the two major annual salesforce promotional programs (memo dated January 17, 1997). Additional information in the form of the accompanying exception report has been generated. I would like your assessment of whether information in that report affects the conclusions you stated in your memo.

Also, the policy concerning the "reward" for each of the promotional programs we have run company-wide over the last three years has been to award one trip for two people, all expenses paid, anywhere in the world for one week for the leading sales representative in each of the twelve regions Denman operates in. It has been suggested that this policy be altered to a "smaller" award for the top sales representative in each sales territory. For the South American Division, this would have the effect of increasing the number of awards substantially. I would like your comments on this issue and how you believe sales representative behavior, motivation, etc. will be affected by January 30th so that I can review them prior to the global company meetings.

Worldwide Headquarters
2344 West Zumont Place Toronto, Ontario Canada 1Z6 5CT
Telephone: 1-13-676-8819 Internet: emgr.45.f44@wwh.acme.com.can

Denman Industrial Products
South American Operations Division
Report Beta/LR - 12 month period ending
12/31/1996
printed 1/20/1997 - 4:14:47 a.m. G.M.T.
page 1 of 3

Sales Exception Report/Large Accounts

Territory Code	Territory Office	First Promotional Campaign 1996			Second Promotional Campaign 1996		
		Pre	Post	Returns	Pre	Post	Returns
Paraguay	Asuncion						
Colombia	Bogota'						
Brazil	Brasilia				(−)	(−)	(+)
Argentina	Buenos Aires						
Venezuela	Caracas						
French Guiana	see Guyana						
Guyana	Georgetown	(+)	(+)	(−)			
Bolivia	La Paz					(−)	(+)
Peru	Lima						
Uruguay	Montevideo						
Surinam	see Guyana						
Trinidad/Tobago	see Guyana						
Ecuador	Quito				(−)	(+)	

Denman Industrial Products
South American Operations Division
Report Beta/LR - 12 month period ending
12/31/1996
printed 1/20/1997 - 4:14:47 a.m. G.M.T.
page 2 of 3

Sales Exception Report/Medium Accounts

Territory Code	Territory Office	First Promotional Campaign 1996			Second Promotional Campaign 1996		
		Pre	Post	Returns	Pre	Post	Returns
Paraguay	Asuncion						
Colombia	Bogota'				(−)	(−)	(+)
Brazil	Brasilia						
Argentina	Buenos Aires	(−)					
Venezuela	Caracas				(−)		(+)
French Guiana	see Guyana						
Guyana	Georgetown	(+)	(+)				
Bolivia	La Paz				(−)	(+)	
Peru	Lima						
Uruguay	Montevideo						
Surinam	see Guyana						
Trinidad/Tobago	see Guyana						
Ecuador	Quito						

Denman Industrial Products
South American Operations Division
Report Beta/LR - 12 month period ending
12/31/1996
printed 1/20/1997 - 4:14:47 a.m. G.M.T.
page 3 of 3

Sales Exception Report/Small Accounts

Territory Code	Territory Office	First Promotional Campaign 1996			Second Promotional Campaign 1996		
		Pre	Post	Returns	Pre	Post	Returns
Paraguay	Asuncion						
Colombia	Bogota'	(−)	(−)	(+)	(−)	(−)	(+)
Brazil	Brasilia						
Argentina	Buenos Aires	(−)					
Venezuela	Caracas						
French Guiana	see Guyana						
Guyana	Georgetown	(−)					
Bolivia	La Paz				(−)	(−)	
Peru	Lima						
Uruguay	Montevideo						
Surinam	see Guyana						
Trinidad/Tobago	see Guyana						
Ecuador	Quito						

Notes to report:

1. Exception reports identify, by account type and territory, sales levels significantly different from forecasts for equal length periods immediately prior to and following promotional periods.

2. Sales return levels and/or contract cancellations for post-promotional periods are also identified where significantly different from forecasts.

Source: This case was prepared by Michael R. Luthy, Drake University.

Dura-plast, Inc. (A): Global Account Management

Tom Parker, CEO of Dura-plast-Americas, Inc (DP-A), directs the U.S. subsidiary of a profitable international equipment manufacturer, Kovner DP International (DP International). He is responsible for directing DP-A's long-term growth and welfare, as well as meeting annual sales and profitability targets. As the head of the manufacturer's largest subsidiary, Parker also has been given the task of developing and implementing sales and marketing strategies that will support the entire Dura-plast group's profitability.

It is now January, 1995, and Mr. Parker is sitting in his office at DP-A's Flint, Michigan headquarters. He is thinking about the efforts his company made and the difficulties it encountered in presenting a successful sales contract to provide Techno Plastics, Inc. with Dura-plast granulator equipment. Techno Plastics, based in France, is a major international plastics producer which had decided to build a plant in the southeastern part of the United States. The sales process was complicated by the need for coordination across DP-A's different country-based subsidiaries and

---

Source: Written by Ryan Oliver under the supervision of Professor Joe Cannon as a basis for classroom discussion. As part of the case development, firm and individual specifics have been disguised. Copyright © 1996 by the Roberto C. Goizueta Business School of Emory University. No part of this publication may be reproduced, stored in a retrieval system, or transmitted in any form or by any means—electronic, mechanical, photocopying, recording, or otherwise—without the permission of the Goizueta Business School. Reproduced March, 1996.

because Techno Plastics was a new customer for DP-A. Parker was pleased to receive reassurance from Techno Plastics that his bid would be successful, but, realizing that more and more plastics manufacturers are setting up global manufacturing operations, Parker wondered if changes were needed to better serve global accounts.

Granulation Equipment

DP-A and its parent company are in the business of designing, manufacturing, assembling, and selling plastics granulators. A plastics granulator is used to chop plastics waste (bad parts and production rejects) into small granules for closed-loop recycling. Granulators are most commonly used in industrial shops, where excess scrap is fed into the granulator hopper for conversion through rotating knives. The small uniform bits of processing scrap and bad parts which emerge from the granulator, called the "regrind," can then be recycled.

Granulators are specified by their infeed or throat size, throughput and weight, and by the composition and chemical makeup of the plastic waste they can process within an hour. Each is fitted with an infeed hopper designed to handle various plastics dimensions. Granulators positioned next to the plastic manufacturing machine to reclaim plastic scraps immediately are known as beside-the-press (B-T-P) granulators. Other types of granulators are placed in a central location (Central) in the plant and scraps are delivered to them manually or by conveyor or sold as smaller, stand alone (Automated) units.

The granulators sold range widely in price, feature, and quality/performance tradeoffs. Because granulators can be tailored to the specific production process of the customer, both the analysis and identification of customer requirements and customization costs are figured into the price of the product.

Thorton Group and Kovner DP International

DP-A is a wholly-owned subsidiary of the Norwegian Thorton Group member, DP International. The group consists of a number of medium-sized engineering companies in the producer-goods industry, each with the developing medium-sized industrial companies in a particular specialty area. The Thorton Group continues to grow through expanded sales and company acquisitions. Its operational structure and tactics support the growth of individual companies operating as important market markers in focused geographic areas. While most subsidiaries hold prominent positions near their customer bases, Thorton Company Headquarters have traditionally been placed close to their representative Norwegian manufacturing plants. Thorton and DP International specifics are provided in Exhibit A (Organizational Structure).

DP International follows a typical Thorton company organizational system: it develops and produces its granulation equipment in Norway and conducts sales through its international subsidiaries, thereby manufacturing globally with local market support. DP International invoiced sales totaling $233 and $326 million in 1992 and 1993 with respective earnings of $11 and $47 million. The parent company had a return on capital of over 35% during this period. In 1994, approximately 2700 units were sold in Europe, 2050 in America, and 500 in Asia. There has been substantial improvement in earnings as a result of the strong volume growth. However, DP International, with its high level of sales abroad, has also benefited from a weaker Norwegian krone rate.[1]

DP International's low-noise granulators have primarily been used for granulating plastic waste in connection with the automated manufacture of plastic products. A proprietary design offers technical superiority which has allowed the company to establish a strong global market presence. Its unique, patented reversible knife design is currently produced only in Norway.

In addition to supplying all the cutting chambers to its international subsidiaries, DP International sells a large number of complete machines because of the complexity of the electrical and drive systems. However, be-

---

[1] The unit of currency is the Norwegian krone, which is abbreviated NOK. NOK 1 = 100 ore. Note that all figures are in US dollars unless otherwise noted. The assumed exchange rate is 7.00 NOK to $1 U.S.

EXHIBIT A   Organizational Structure

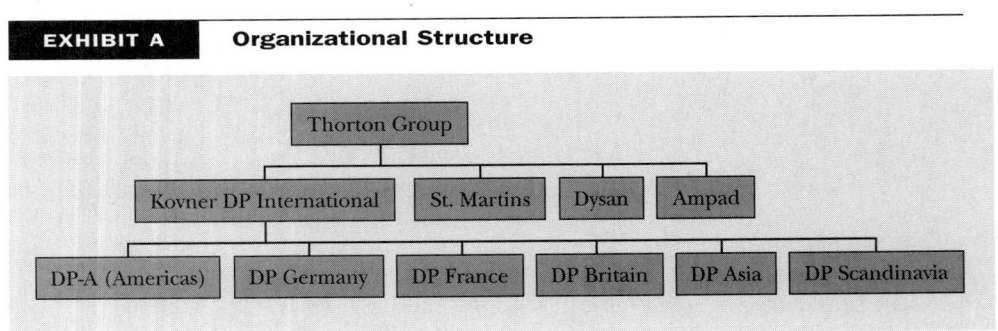

cause products qualifying as locally made have lower costs due to lower import duties, DP International established an assembly and manufacturing plant in the US and an assembly plant in Germany. These run as autonomous P&L locations, typically assembling, customizing and adding local content to the larger granulators that are sourced from Norway for sale throughout the Americas and Europe. The small to medium-sized machines currently do not qualify as US products under NAFTA content requirements, and as such are not free from import duties.

DP International is planning further decentralization of its manufacturing operations with the establishment of a cutting chamber production facility in the US. This move will lower transportation costs, which currently add 6% or more to the final sale price of DP International units. In addition, it would enable the company to meet in-country product requirements, lessen the risk of international currency fluctuations, and lower tax and tariff duties.

DP International has responded to the cost of maintaining large product lines by developing flexibility in the manufacturing cycle. Increasingly, DP International has been able to customize its products to meet customer requirements, an important factor in DP International's low cost, high volume strategy. In fact, during 1992 DP International successfully launched a new product generation based on a modular product system, which brought about a strong volume increase in 1993. In 1994, the US subsidiary, DP-A, developed a US hopper welding cell which allowed for additional, in-house customization of the larger machines.

In order to handle market demand changes and increasing sales, DP International expanded its plant capacity in Norway this past year. When at full capacity the new plant will allow the organization to expand sales from 5,000 to 7,000 with a substantial increase in its large-capacity machine production facilities.

Subsidiary Companies

Torger Erlandsen, the managing director of DP International, directs the integration of the international operations. Under his leadership, each of the subsidiary companies retains significant autonomy in both organizational structure and management. As a result, the operational manager in each of the countries functions in an atmosphere that offers a high degree of entrepreneurial freedom. Country managers make their own decisions with respect to sales strategy, pricing, and promotion. Erlandsen believes that granting this leadership independence is the most effective way to maximize the opportunities within the granulation equipment sales' niche marketplace.

While each of the subsidiary companies reports to the Norwegian headquarters, the subsidiary organizations do not have formal ties with each other. In a growing number of cases, however, an order may be generated from an area outside of a subsidiary's direct responsibility; the individual subsidiaries then have the responsibility to coordinate efforts which take into account specification development and business practice initiatives suitable to that business environment and culture. Final responsibility, however, and authority in decision making is given to the local subsidiary.

However, because of the interrelated nature between international marketing and manufacturing, there have been increasing problems regarding contract specification and pricing issues internationally. Some members of the DP International group, for instance, have begun to wonder if it might be a good idea to set a standard price internationally. With respect to sales strategy, some agree with the DP-A Vice President for Sales, Richard Foster, who argues that confusion in the sales cycle could be limited if the criteria for involvement in the sales relationship were more narrowly defined. His suggestion is for "involvement only when a person can enhance the sales relationship." Others suggest greater or lesser involvement across countries.

Traditionally, most countries have employed Agents[2] to sell and distribute granulators. Agents buy the Dura-plast granulators and then sell them to their own customer base, setting their own price levels. Prices in some cases are higher than DP International has wanted. In this set-up, the agent decides how he wants to sell in the market, and determines his own segmentation, targeting, and positioning, perhaps to the exclusion of some areas of the market. If the market is slumping, the agent argues that the price is too high. However, the manufacturer has limited knowledge of the specific competitors, contract terms, or agent mark-up. In fact, if the agent forgoes the contract, the manufacturer can lose an entire customer base.

One of DP International's new channel strategies is its transition to Manufacturer's Representative (MR)[3] relationships in each of the DP International offices worldwide—thus standardizing part of its selling strategy. This strategy focuses on generating sales through MRs contracts instead of through sales agents. One of the primary benefits of this strategy is to help DP International to protect its current and long-term market position by getting closer to the customer. It is important for DP International to understand where its machines are being sold and to develop brand name loyalty in the market. The global program to

---

[2]Agents are generally businesses that contract with original equipment manufacturers to sell their products for a given period of time. Agents take ownership of the products and usually have protected territories.

[3]Manufacturing Representatives have been employed by many original equipment manufacturers because of their knowledge and ties within a particular industry. Manufacturer's Representatives represent multiple, noncompeting manufacturers, and are generally granted exclusive territories. They represent the supplier, but are not usually involved in distribution or installation. MR's do not take possession or ownership of equipment—they only operate as agents on behalf of (usually) multiple principals (i.e., manufacturers).

take control of the customer has helped to clarify pricing and stabilize production. If the market is slumping, DP International's regional sales managers will be able to intensify the sales efforts or make strategic decisions, such as price reductions.

Each of DP International's subsidiaries handles the MR and other selling issues differently. The following sections provide more detail about DP International's subsidiaries in Germany, France, Britain and North America.

DP GERMANY (DPG). Germany is a large market that is treated as an individual unit in DP International's international planning exercises. Germany's solo status and competitive advantage stems from its market size, homogeneity, and the location of a manufacturing plant which supplies the rest of Europe. The German market is almost as large as the US market with respect to the total number of customers.

German companies typically bid on a packaged basis. Each offer generally includes pricing and terms regarding auxiliary equipment, start-up and installation, plans, and long-term spare part commitments. Each part of the bid package is important to contract acquisition.

Germany recently changed its sales organization structure by shifting from an agent driven salesforce to one which includes both agents and MRs. Under the direction of a DPG sales manager who controls a group of sales reps and one agent, the country has been divided into territories where representatives are given regional exclusivity. In addition to managing the salesforce, the sales manager develops relationships and bids for larger granulation systems, calling on original equipment manufacturers (OEMs) and the largest potential purchasers.

DP FRANCE (DPF). In France, as with the rest of Europe, sales cycles have traditionally been much longer than those in the US. The time from initial inquiry for granulation equipment to delivery averages 12–18 months. As a result, manufacturers and their customers have a longer time to plan and delineate product quote and specifications. Tom Parker suggests that "the introduction of MRs has allowed DP France to manage its customer base more closely." Consequently, DP France has developed sales relationships with several larger firms that have plants throughout France and worldwide. France is currently the smallest DP International European subsidiary. French customers typically expect bids to be presented in the same manner that German customers do—including all details on service, spare parts and support.

DP BRITAIN (DP-UK). The DP International office in Britain still uses an agent system to promote and sell its products. The agent system works because it is a generally accepted practice in the market and because of the limited interaction required in the sales process. Unlike the rest of Europe, distributors in Britain do not have to delineate each of the engineering and sales support requirements in the sales contract. DP-UK is a mid-sized DP International European subsidiary.

DP-AMERICAS (DP-A). DP-A, the biggest company in the DP International Group, faces the challenge of marketing within the quick cycle, volatile US, Canadian, and Mexican marketplaces. Strong in the US and Canada, DP-A has not made significant inroads into the Mexican, Latin American or South American markets as yet, principally because of practically non-existent safety standards, which allow competitors in these developing countries to build machines at a significantly lower cost.

DP-A's operations are led by a board of directors, consisting of Torger Erlandsen, a Norway-based manufacturing expert, and DP-A CEO Tom Parker. While Parker is responsible for day-to-day management of the DP-A activities, major decisions are approved by the board of directors. The board of directors currently meets on a quarterly basis with additional meetings as needed.

DP-A's domestic staff are split into three operational groups. The operations group manages the assembly and small-scale manufacturing operations in Flint, Michigan and a larger manufacturing plant just outside Knoxville, Tennessee, which will come on line in 1998. The Administration and Planning functions, as well as the Sales functions, are centralized in Flint.

The US bidding system is unlike Europe's. In addition to the faster selling cycle (the time from initial inquiry to final sale lasts between 2–8 months), US customers do not require the same amount of specificity and long-term price guarantees as those in Europe. DP-A, for instance, typically bids systems without the inclusion of auxiliary equipment and start-up costs. Start-up tends to be handled in-house and auxiliary equipment purchases are placed as needed. Most equipment installations are designed to be self-service—usually handled easily by in-plant engineers. DP-A does not bid for long-term spare part commitments or with detailed plant location specs either. Primarily because the market does not expect it, but also because the North American market is much more price-driven, bidding is more narrowly focused than in Europe.

DP-A's sales structure primarily relies on a network of Manufacturers Representatives. Each of DP-A's sales managers directs 4–5 MRs, spread out on a regional basis. Sales managers have responsibility for non-contiguous regions, such as a territory covering California, Canada, New England, and Texas. Richard Foster notes that non-contiguous sales areas give DP-A the ability to determine whether sales performance is a result of regional economic downturns or lackluster performance. Rising airline costs may cause DP-A to review this policy.

Currently, DP-A has exclusive, non-compete contracts with 25 MR groups, which in turn employ over 100 sales representatives. The DP-A MRs are located throughout the United States, Canada, and Mexico. MRs are the dominant distribution channel in the granulation industry because of their ability to cross-sell to the customer. A typical MR represents injection molding, blow molding, extrusion molding, vacuum systems for moving plastic, and drying systems equipment to the companies he or she visits. As such, representatives are a one-stop shop for a company's comprehensive plastic production equipment requirements.

The use of MRs allows DP-A to increase coverage while keeping full-time personnel to a minimum. MRs are not always the only contact with the end-user; however, their expertise and relationship with the buyers, built through the cross-sale of different types of plant equipment provides an effective and efficient sales strategy. MRs do not sell to all DP-A accounts. Larger sales are handled by DP-A's own marketing managers on the basis of leads generated from MRs and DP-A's direct advertising. If a lead generated by an MR generates a sale, the MR still receives the standard commission.

The best MRs generally carry the most effective and best known products because of their ability to close deals with a large group of well-established principals. MR groups have between 2-10 salespeople and close total sales in the range of 1 to 15 million dollars annually. Commissions on machines sales are generally 12% for mid-sized machines, 3% for the large-size machines, and 14% for machines under $10,000. If the MR and/or DP-A negotiated price discounts, these are generally split between the MR and DP-A.

MRs do not direct the installation or provide service for DP-A. Installation is not a critical sales factor for the smaller machines, because the machines arrive assembled and ready to run. For the larger central system machines, DP-A typically sends a service technician to the installation sight to check wiring and set-up specifications before the machine is first used. Service is directed from DP-A's central headquarters in Flint, Michigan.

Of DP-A sales, approximately 90% of all machines sold are used for new applications and 10% to replace outdated equipment. DP-A sales managers and MRs sell to a wide variety of individuals and companies on both a transactional and collaborative basis. DP-A classifies its current customers into the following categories

- **Transactional accounts,** where customers purchase with both price and features in mind. In general, there are no long-term relationship or purchase commitments. Machines sold to these customers generally sell for under $10,000.
- **System accounts** are developed when MRs work with customers to define needs and establish fit. Granulators sold to customers in this category generally sell for between $10,000 and $50,000. While the service aspect of the sale provides ground for an ongoing relationship, there are no long-term purchase commitments.
- **Key accounts** represent the top 15% of DP-A sales and include large unit volume and annual dollar sales. The DP-A employee acts as a consultant in this relationship; more technologically proficient DP-A managers discuss the company's long-term plans and project goals. Currently, there are no formal long-term purchase commitments. Machines sold to these customers often cost more than $50,000.

Customers

The plastics industry uses two types of materials—thermoplastics and thermosets—in combination with stabilizers, colorants, flame retardants, and reinforcing agents in the plastic production process. These are then shaped or molded under heat and pressure to a solid state. Thermoplastics can be resoftened to their original condition by heat; however, thermosets cannot. Thermoplastics account for almost 90% of total plastic production and nearly 100% of granulation activity.

In general, thermoplastics output takes the form of pellets, flakes, granules, powders, liquid resins, sheeting, pipe, profile, parts, or film. It can be divided into four production categories:

Type	Examples	% Total Industry
Injection molding	Automobile parts, pudding cups	50
Blow molding	Soda and milk bottles	12
Extrusion	Trash bags, plastic pipes	30
Reclaim	Post consumer recycling	7

DP International sells the largest number of its granulators to injection molding companies. Nonetheless, it generates its highest level of profit from equipment utilizing extrusion processing, because the machines in this production category are significantly larger and more complex.

Large injection molding companies include Ford, Chrysler, and GM, as well as consumer product producers such as Black and Decker. Injection molding is a versatile and quick production process, and companies relying upon it have recently taken advantage of improvements in technology to expand productivity. In 1992 and 1993, this segment's plastic purchases grew by more than 11%.

Blow molding has shown high growth in the last few years because its resulting products are less expensive and easier to design. As new technology makes blow molding more profitable, blow molding firms, which include Coke, Pepsi, Tupperware, and Rubbermaid, have continued to expand their operations.

Extrusion is a popular method of producing large quantities of both uniform and dissimilar material that can be packaged into small units and distributed easily. The demand for plastics used in extrusion grew by over 12% for both 1992 and 1993. Future projections are not so rosy; growth in some segments of the extrusion industry which are expected to drop to less than 1% in 1995, and to contract by 4.4% in 1996, due to excess capacity.

GRANULATOR SALES. DP-A offers approximately 30 different models in four primary product groups and one secondary product group through a strategic alliance with an original equipment manufacturer (OEM). The automation product group focuses on small, automated granulators for the injection molding market segment; the B-T-P product group is geared toward mid-size granulators for the injection molding/blow molding market; the central product group concentrates mostly in central reclamation in the extrusion market, while the parts/auxiliary/service product group is directed toward all customers.

The manufacturing process for DP-A equipment is a flexible multi-step process because of the unique design needs of individual clients. Compact machines generally require less customization. These machines come with DP-A's positive feed and rotating knife systems. Specifically, the design in the cutting chamber ensures positive feed of bulky materials and high throughputs. The reversible rotating knives allow the clearance between the cutting edges of the rotating and bed knives and the screen to remain constant. Both contribute to improved efficiency by reducing energy consumption and averting heat buildup.

The heavy-duty models include the positive feed and reversible rotating knife systems, as well as engineering systems capability and special hopper availability. Specialists in the engineering department are able to design a system to fit particular production requirements. As Tom Parker remarked, "the machines are generic but the applications are specific." Some applications require specially designed hoppers for maximum throughput and increased productivity. Energy efficiency remains a common concern in the design and purchase of both heavy-duty or compact machines.

In recent years, large global purchasers are increasingly seeking suppliers which can provide international turn-key solutions and services as opposed to sourcing from multiple suppliers for products and services. Using a single global supplier enhances negotiating power, standardizes spare parts, and allows the customer to build a closer relationship with one supplier. Global customers are asking granulator manufacturers to solve scrap recycling problems rather than simply sell them machines. This move is partly a result of the reduction in engineers at plastic manufacturer's production facilities. One customer commented that his firm wanted to focus its efforts on manufacturing, not on developing an expertise in recycling systems.

The trend is especially prevalent among European multinational firms, which traditionally have expected a high degree of supplier technical support. Additionally, rather than hiring technical expertise, purchasers are now contracting with companies which provide a centralized rather than local engineering focus.

A recent survey of DP-A customers and MRs found that they most value product performance, features, and the ability to customize the application. When asked to determine the most important attribute in the purchase decision, 41.7% of the customers chose quality/overall performance. In contrast, price was the most frequent response given by the MRs (31.4%). DP-A customers seem to view price as more of an order qualifier rather than an order winner. (Exhibit B provides a price/attribute comparison of DP-A customers and manufacturer representatives).

DP-A's most recent value-added solutions include its efforts within the injection molding, blow molding and film extrusion market segments of the plastic industry. Specialized niche development includes reclaim for scrap plastic, robot-fed injection molding, hot melt resin reclamation, edge trim film/sheet, post consumer waste bottle, vinyl siding and central thermoform scrap market segments. The niche markets are highly customized and provide high gross profits with limited competition. In support of these markets, DP-A engineers have worked with the market managers to further develop product engineered systems to meet their customer's application needs. Identification of these opportunities, however, continues to be a challenge.

DP-A's product portfolio overview provides information on each of the company's three major product groupings, the Automated, B-T-P, and Central. Individual components which are critical to application success and compliance include cutting chamber size, horsepower, rate screen, rotor configuration, RPM, and product features such as the tilt-back hopper and clam-shell screen cradle. Companies also have the choice of specialized features such as low infeed heights, oversized bearings, integral soundproofing, auger in feed, and conveyor infeed.

DP International is one of the largest producers of granulators worldwide and within the United States, DP-A has grown to be the largest supplier in unit volume of granulation equipment. Serving the entire range of companies in the plastic reclamation process, DP-A's installed customer account base includes over 6000 locations across the United States.

Part of this growth comes from the addition of a new OEM client to the DP-A portfolio. DP-A's strategic alliance with Fields (Powerflow) enables it to purchase and distribute up to 500 B-T-P units a year at a percentage discount. These units are sold under Powerflow's nameplate. DP-A is also considering the expansion of its OEM relationships to other major plastics manufacturers. Both partners benefit through these expanded relationships: DP International can increase market share and the OEMs can service their key accounts with a high quality product.

The key factors in DP-A's 1995 $21 million sales effort include the introduction of new machines, expanded service relationships, and enhanced marketing efforts, combined with further expansion of the OEM alliance with Powerflow.

EXHIBIT B — Attribute Weighting

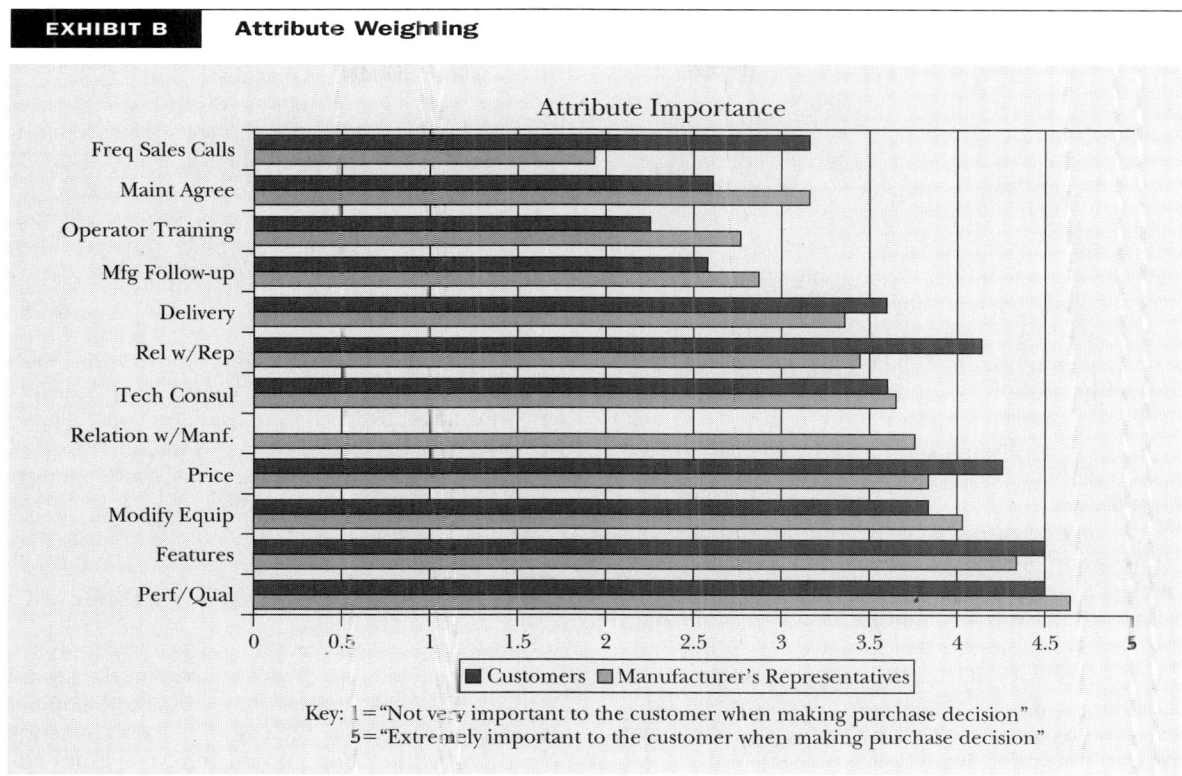

Key: 1 = "Not very important to the customer when making purchase decision"
5 = "Extremely important to the customer when making purchase decision"

For Tom Parker, DP-A volume leadership is "not a reason to be complacent." In addition to the company's drive for customer satisfaction and total quality management in the early 1990's, DP-A must now address issues related to account management and market change. Many of DP-A's larger machine segment clients now conduct business on both a domestic and international basis. Sales efforts have required significant synchronization of efforts between subsidiaries. In addition, under the goal of expanding profitability, management is working to raise the dollar volume on individual sales. Focusing on the mid- to large-size machine sales efforts has resulted in a mixed response from the salesforce. The numbers, however, continue to grow, with DP-A projecting dollar bookings of 45% of the US market in 1995.

In the last year, DP-A has posted record profits, with an average profit margin of 9% per sale. Gross profit, operating income, and net income information for 1993 and 1994 are presented in Table 1.

Competition

DP-A was one of 15 competitors in the US Market which contributed to the 4500 granulators orders received overall in 1989 totaling $32.7 million and 7000 granulators in 1994 totaling $120 million.

Although DP-A is the newest competitor in the US granulator sales marketplace, it is currently the leader in volume sales, primarily through the OEM relationship with Powerflow. Before the linkage, it was number three in the market, driven by a strong sales push.

DP-A's price position in relation to that of its competitors may hamper unit sales in some market segments. Some of its competitors are large conglomerates which often use granulators as loss-leaders in negotiations to close higher dollar, turn-key system orders. DP-A has traditionally had a poor record in acquiring these orders which are generally multi-unit contracts.

DP-A credits its success in the market to outperforming competitors by delivering the highest standard of customer service. While it has created the perception of

TABLE 1

Dura-plast, Inc.*	1993	1994
Gross Profit	$5,067,029	$6,995,259
Operating Income	$294,289	$1,697,332
Net Income	$167,055	$959,810

*Dura-plast, Inc. Income Statement as of December 31, 1994 and 1993.

technical design superiority through marketing proprietary concepts such as the "constant flow methodology," DP-A has traditionally viewed itself as the underdog. The company continues to resist complacency: one corporate motto states "we must provide better service than our competitors; as such, our customers are right 98% of the time."

The market leader in dollars sold is the Northway Corporation, which is owned by the Abrahams Group, a division of the German conglomerate Ludwig-Crow. It averages 35% gross margins on granulators, 60% on parts/knives, and 35% on pelletizers. Its profits last year averaged around 10%–14%.

Northway has a product management organizational structure with a vice president of Marketing and a product manager for its B-T-P/Automation, Central/Systems and Pelletizing product groups. Each product manager has an application engineer and clerical support. The company has a vice president of Sales who manages its regional sales managers, parts department and service department. The marketing group prepares their sales quotes and supports the sales group with marketing intelligence and new products. Northway recently acquired a manufacturer of screen changes and pelletizing which seems, at least in the short run, to have negatively affected the company's ability to support its granulator sales. Northway has, however, been able to use its multi-product sales to continue as a dominant force in the Central and System markets.

Northway distribution efforts have been shifted from a 20-man direct salesforce to 2 regional sales managers and 18 manufacturer representative agencies. Perhaps the two regional sales managers currently cannot provide the level of service necessary to meet customer retention requests; at any rate Northway now has the reputation of being hard to deal with and increasingly non-responsive.

Northway historically has had a wider range of products, as compared to DP-A, because of its ability to offer 20 machines in a market where DP-A has 3–4. Consequently DP-A has had to price aggressively to remain competitive, especially on granulator sales that fall into a DP-A market gap. There are times, for example, when customers want machines specified for power requirements and size that lie in between DP-A's offerings. In order to get the sale, DP-A has to bid its larger machine.

Northway currently is not advertising aggressively. In the past, however, it led the market in advertising dollars spent. The parent company, the Abrahams Group, has a cooperative advertising strategy which promotes a comprehensive turn-key organization. This reputation supplements Northway's exceptional brand awareness and solid reputation. Northway also runs a direct mail program to targeted acquisition and retention customers on a quarterly basis.

DP-A, however, is the leading advertiser in the North American market. It runs full-page color and ¼-page black and white ads in five major publications. It also attends 5–7 trade shows per year in order to exhibit its new products. DP-A has invested heavily in high-tech contemporary literature to complement its quotations.

Techno Plastics Request for Proposals

Techno Plastics, located outside of Paris, is a multinational blow molding company that specializes in the production of hardened plastic fuel tank systems for automobiles. Part of its expansion plan includes the development plan, namely, to be the largest producer of fuel tanks globally. To meet its goals, the company decided to open a new fuel tank plant in the US.

DP International has developed a strong relationship with Techno Plastics over the past 12 years and is currently servicing Techno Plastics manufacturing plants in Germany, UK, and France. Despite this relationship, Techno Plastics submitted a request for proposals (RFP) to each of the major granulator producers as part of a plan to supply the plant it was building in Lawrenceville, Georgia. What follows is a summary and timeline of events related to the RFP, which originated in France. (Exhibit C provides an overview of organization teams within the DP International and Techno Plastics organizations.)

TABLE 2

Competitor	1989				1994			
	Units	Unit %	Dollars	$ %	Units	Unit %	Dollars	$ %
Northway	1200	26%	$18 Million	28%	1400	20%	$33.5 Mill.	28%
Grindall	150	33%	16 Million	25%	1650	23%	27.5 Mill.	23%
DP-A	650	14%	8.5 Million	13%	2050	28%	30 Million	25%
Fields (Powerflow)	450	10%	6 Million	9%	700	10%	12 Million	10%
Smith & Smith	400	8%	5 Million	8%	600	9%	10 Million	8%

AUGUST 1994. DP International's US subsidiary submitted its first quote for Techno Plastics' Georgia granulator services in August of 1994. US executives visiting Europe on a planning trip were introduced to Techno Plastics personnel at a plastics convention. The local French contact for Techno Plastics, Jean Handel, a DP France sales manager, facilitated the introduction. In private, he explained Techno Plastics' strategic importance to DP International, in part due to its annual purchases of $1,000,000 in new equipment, parts and service.

At the plastics convention, the US team members demonstrated several of DP International's latest machines to Techno Plastics and began initial strategy discussions for the upcoming RFP response. Over the next few weeks, Jean Handel followed up with information regarding the US plant's specifications and also provided recommendations with respect to pricing.

With Handel's information, the DP-A bid was developed to mirror the specifications of Techno Plastics' German Plant, currently supplied by DP-G, with slightly higher pricing than the typical US bid. These specifications included a cooling device for regrind and a conveyer system, but did not include self-cleaning capabilities because these were not currently in place at the newest Techno Plastics plant in Germany.

DP-A proposed to provide a "system to meet Techno Plastics specifications," a standard practice for US bidding. Typical of DP-A's bids to its US customers, the bid not provide specifics regarding each piece of individual equipment, formalized engineering drawings, or spare part commitments.

In addition to the bid, the US sales executives traveled to the Lawrenceville plant to meet with Michel Duval, the plant manager. Scott Millar, DP-A Regional Manager, and Richard Foster presented a sales proposal to Duval and other Techno Plastics staff. Both the presentation and bid were well received.

SEPTEMBER 1994. At another plastics convention in Paris in late September, US and European staff met in France for a second time with Stefan Sevan, the Techno Plastics engineer responsible for the Lawrenceville, Georgia plant and Technical Director for Techno Plastics' Blow Molding Division. During this meeting, Sevan and his colleague Bill Dubois were led by Jean Handel in a discussion of the technical specification requirements for the new plant. On the basis of that discussion a new DP International product was offered to the Techno Plastics engineers. At the end of the meeting, Sevan requested that DP-A re-submit its quote for equipment and services, based on the new DP International machine and specification modifications.

The need for outside vendor support for the new offering and associated pricing of additional conveyor and blower equipment in the revised quote forced DP-A to delay its bid resubmittal for six weeks. At the end of this period, Sevan contacted DP International's US office regarding the quote. He requested that it be forwarded as soon as possible. Additional problems surfaced, however, when Sevan contacted DP-A again, telling them he had not received the offer. Evidently it had been misdirected by office staff. Neither side admitted to the error.

During this period, Sevan also contacted Peter Olsen, Technical Director for DP International's Norwegian Headquarters team, in an attempt to gain control over the sale. Following the quote's re-transmission and review, Sevan offered a temporary approval to the sale.

Richard Foster and Scott Millar traveled again to the Lawrenceville plant, following the third quote to meet with Michel Duval. Duval was very pleased with DP-A following rigorous technical discussions.

JANUARY 1995. Notwithstanding the previous multi-quote issues, DP International seemed well positioned to acquire Techno Plastics' granulator business. Then reports from DP International European staff member visiting the Fukuma Plastics's trade show in Germany indicated another problem. The staff member had been informed by Stefan Sevan that the US subsidiary quotation was not adequate. The specifications had been quoted according to proposal requirements (the standard for project conformance), rather than to the current system in use at the Rothenburg, Germany plant. As such, the current bid would not meet all of Techno Plastics' needs.

The bid was re-submitted according to the Rothenburg set-up. However, Sevan contacted the DP International US Headquarters again, claiming that the bid still was not sufficient. Sevan encouraged Tom Parker to cut his price to ensure the order. DP-A responded by lowering its price, because Parker did not want to jeopardize DP-A's global position with Techno Plastics. To support the relationship, Parker and Richard Foster flew to France to find out more about the French specification expectations.

Caucusing with the French DP International subsidiary in Paris, a US, French, and Norwegian corporate management team reviewed the Techno Plastics case, preparing what they hoped would be the final bid. Although Jean Handel offered to negotiate on behalf of the US subsidiary, his offer was rejected, following what DP-A staff considered to be internal coordination errors and technical misinformation.

After lengthy intercompany caucusing, that DP-A and Techno Plastics executives worked through plant specifications and at least half a dozen new issues developed in response to granulation requirements at the German plant. During this meeting, DP International offered its final quotation, following extensive technical discussions with Techno Plastics engineers and management. Both sides were elated with the outcome. Sevan reassured Parker at the meeting saying, "I told you, I've always been a Dura-plast man."

EXHIBIT C — Organizational Structures

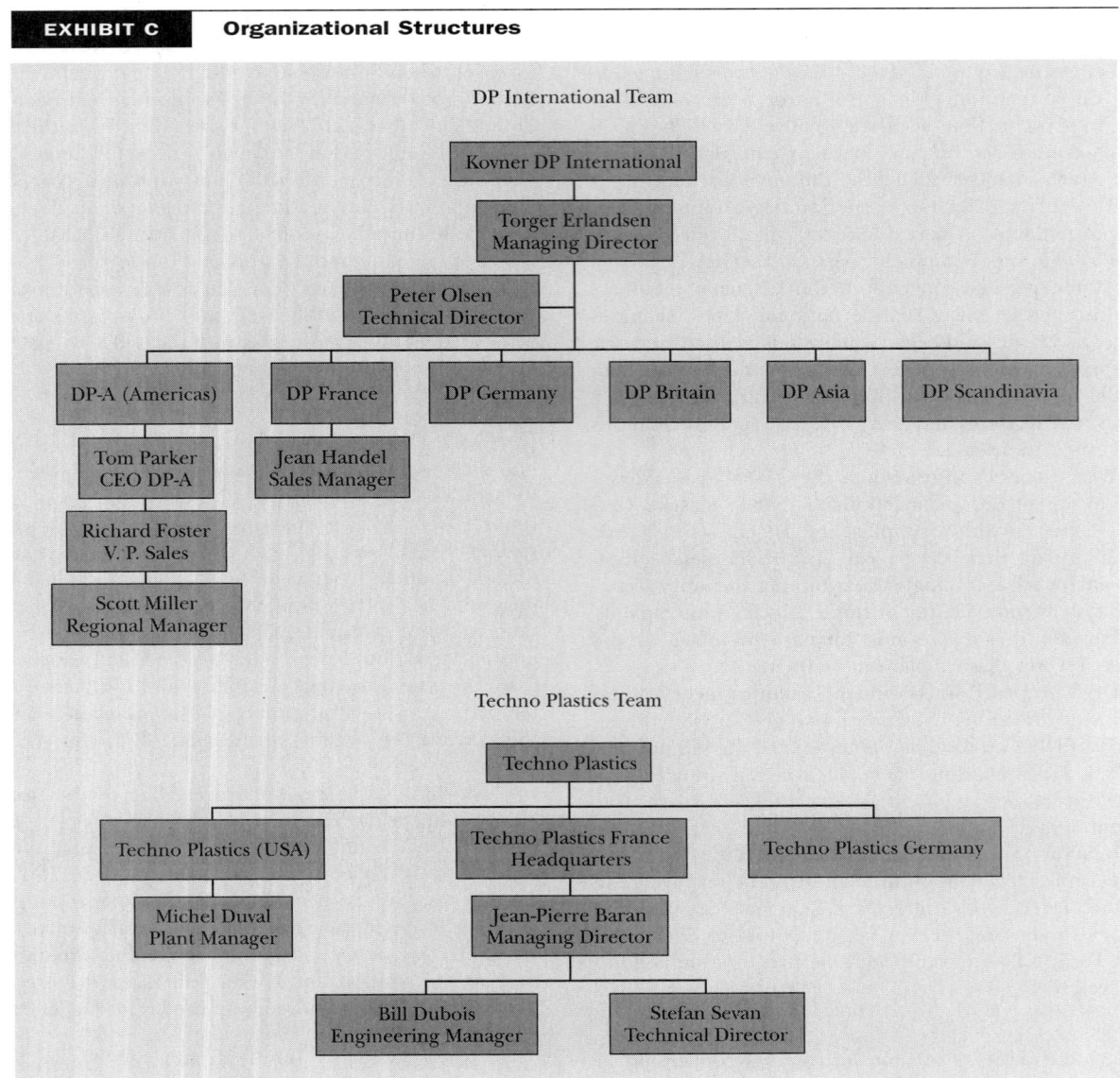

Dura-plast, Inc. (B): Global Account Management

It is June, 1995, and Tom Parker, CEO of Dura-plast, Inc. (DP-A), is reconstructing DP-A's handling of the Techno Plastics granulation equipment order. He was surprised and extremely disappointed to learn that Techno Plastics had not selected DP-A to supply granulators for their new plant.

The considerable expenditure in human and capital resources, along with meetings in both the US and France to clarify issues related to equipment specification, time frame and bid pricing, were not to be justified by first-year earnings alone. DP-A's efforts were targeted at extending the on-going DP International-Techno Plastics relationship in the US through a comprehensive order for both equipment and service for Techno Plastics' new plant in Lawrenceville, Georgia. The talks and the bid had been well received. It had seemed that the only formality left was the paperwork.

However, Torger Erlandsen, managing director of DP International Operations, recently informed Parker that the Lawrenceville plant bid was awarded to Northway, a

Source: *Written by Ryan Oliver under the supervision of Professor Joe Cannon as a basis for classroom discussion. As part of the case development, firm and individual specifics have been disguised.* Copyright © 1996 by the Roberto C. Goizueta Business School of Emory University. No part of this publication may be reproduced, stored in a retrieval system, or transmitted in any form or by any means—electronic, mechanical, photocopying, recording, or otherwise—without the permission of the Goizueta Business School. Reproduced March, 1996.

US-based granulator producer and a major competitor. The news was delivered to Erlandsen by his DP France sales manager, Jean Handel.

To make matters worse, it now seems evident that DP-A sold to the wrong decision maker, and did not offer the right equipment and price package. Technically, there was no problem with the DP International product offering.

It also appears that the final purchase decision was made at the plant level in Lawrenceville by Michel Duval and in France by Stefan Sevan's boss, the Techno Plastics engineer responsible for the Lawrenceville, Georgia plant, Jean-Pierre Baran. DP-A had thought, that the decision would be made by DP-A's main contact, Sevan, and his direct reports. To DP-A's surprise, management in Lawrenceville commented that they were more comfortable with Northway, which "seemed more interested in their business and provided comprehensive information and service specifics in its bid." They also stated that, while price was not the order winner, the Northway offer was lower than the DP-A bid.

Re-examination of the bids, however, showed that Northway's slightly less expensive pricing did not include the same specifications as the DP-A offer. As a result, the Northway package, when complete, will actually be more expensive than the DP-A offer.

For Tom Parker, a significant problem with the Techno Plastics bid failure revolves around the issue of marketing coordination. As a group, Dura-plast did not understand who was the key player in charge and who was the key decision maker. While everyone intended to do the right thing, each member of the DP-A team made mistakes. Parker commented, "When Richard and I went to France and met with Stefan Sevan and his people, he assured us we had the order. We were convinced However, we never really had the order. Sevan may have thought he could give us the order, but he was not the decision maker. It was a nightmare . . . The only solution I see is structured coordination among the DP International groups."

Global accounts are raising new issues for DP International, particularly with respect to pricing, cross-subsidiary coordination, technology and marketing strategy. These issues were brought to a head in the Techno Plastics situation. Currently, Dura-plast is trying to price at the local market, in effect, to maximise the profit potential in each subsidiary. However, there are concerns regarding this practice as a long-term policy.

Up to this point, all of Techno Plastics' granulator purchases had been through a DPI subsidiary—it was very loyal to Dura-plast. Now, however, Northway is also threatening DPG and DP-UK because of disparities between European and US pricing. Northway's inroad is a major concern because it threatens other DP International key accounts.

Known for his critical evaluation and analysis, Mr. Parker is committed to supporting the current DP-A and DP International customer bases. He is currently working on a plan to regain the US Techno Plastics account and is outspoken regarding the importance of avoiding similar situations in the future. He is also committed to supporting business expansion through appropriate corporate change and new, viable projects. Mr. Parker wonders what is the best next step for DP-A.

Toronto-Dominion Bank: Money Monitor

In February 1990, Gary Shore was transferred from Toronto to be the branch manager of the Richmond and King Street branch of the Toronto-Dominion Bank in London. Among other issues, he was considering options for the marketing of Money Monitor, a computer-based product which allowed commercial clients to access their financial data. Although the product had been introduced as a corporate product in 1981 and redeveloped for commercial use in 1986, sales had been below target and were sporadic. The bank executives in Toronto considered this product to be of long term strategic importance. As the largest and most profitable unit in the Ontario Southwest Division, Gary Shore's branch was considered the flagship, and he therefore felt an obligation to increase sales.

The Toronto-Dominion Bank

The face of the Canadian financial industry had changed significantly in the previous decade and was set to experience further adjustment. Deregulation had increased competition both among the "big five" banks and from foreign institutions. Since there was little differentiation among financial products, the institutions were looking for new ways of adding value to their services. The Toronto-Dominion (TD) bank was focusing on computerization as a means of providing added value to its customers.

The TD bank was Canada's fifth largest chartered bank with assets of nearly $60 billion. Although much smaller than the country's largest bank ($130 billion in assets), the TD bank had consistently out performed the other "big five" banks in return on equity and return on assets.

The TD bank had over 1,000 branches across Canada, but was strongest in Ontario. There were two types of branches—those which performed retail banking only (providing mortgages, loans and deposit services to individuals) and those which also provided commercial services (lending funds to businesses). Gary Shore's branch was the commercial banking centre for the London region, with customers as far as 50 kilometres away Other

---

Source: *This case was prepared by Alicia Cestra and Royal Mathews under the supervision of Professor Donald W. Barclay for the sole purpose of providing material for class discussion at the Richard Ivey School of Business. Certain names and other identifying information may have been disguised to protect confidentiality. It is not intended to illustrate either effective or ineffective handling of a managerial situation. This material is not covered under authorization from CanCopy or any reproduction rights organization. Any form of reproduction, storage or transmittal of this material is prohibited without written permission from Richard Ivey School of Business, The University of Western Ontario, London, Canada N6A 3K7. Reprinted with permission, Richard Ivey School of Business.* Copyright 1992 © The University of Western Ontario.

large commercial branches in the Ontario Southwest Division were located in Windsor, Kitchener, and St. Catherines. Smaller commercial branches were located in Cambridge, Chatham, Sarnia and Guelph.

The TD bank's strategy was to be conservative in lending policies, innovative in products and information technology, and competitive on providing customer service. The bank was not only aggressive on pricing commercial loans, and considered relationship building as key to their success.

BRANCH MANAGEMENT. The typical commercial banking centre was divided into three sections: retail banking (personal lending and deposits), commercial banking, and administration. Exhibit I provides an organization chart for the Richmond and King Street branch. This branch was the largest in the Ontario Southwest Division and had a history of low loan losses, excellent customer service and, as a result, good profits.

The branch's commercial client base was diversified among many industries including real estate developers, manufacturers, and service businesses such as moving companies and advertising firms. There was also a substantial group of professional firms—doctors, lawyers and accountants. The scope of the businesses also varied, with small proprietorships on the one hand, and large retail chains and multi-plant manufacturers on the other. Some clients borrowed regularly and some infrequently. There were approximately 500 non-borrowing customers who only utilized deposit, investment and cash management services.

Each branch was operated as a profit centre. As such, the branch manager was responsible for marketing (with some regional advertising and promotion support), cost control, loan losses and human resource deployment. General staff hiring was the branch manager's responsibility, but he/she could not hire management personnel, create a new position, or fire any personnel without divisional approval.

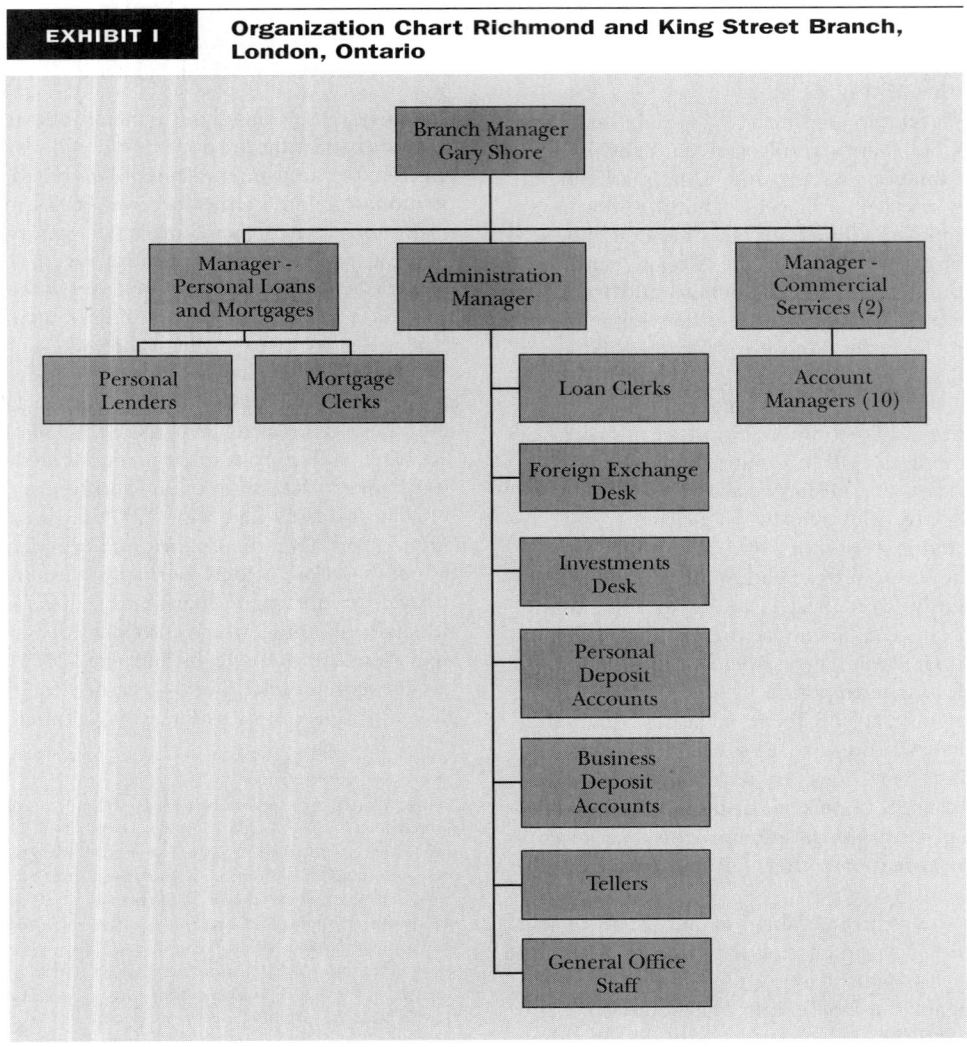

EXHIBIT I **Organization Chart Richmond and King Street Branch, London, Ontario**

THE ACCOUNT MANAGER. An account manager was responsible for a portfolio of business customers to which he/she left funds. He/she was responsible for the bank's profitability on the account, the risk level of the portfolio, and the servicing of each account.

Since the account managers had little control over the timing or complexity of loan requests or client problems, they had to be well organized and efficient, yet flexible. As indicated in Exhibit II, the account managers had a considerable range of responsibilities and answered to the needs of numerous stake-holders both inside and outside the bank. Bottom line responsibility, however, rested on the avoidance of loan losses, which necessitated open, effective communication with clients.

A commerical banking centre utilized three levels of account managers as follows:

> *Independent Business Account Managers:* These individuals managed a portfolio of 140 to 160 small accounts borrowing between $10,000 and $200,000 each. They were given full responsibility for their portfolios and tended to operate independently. The smaller customers had less sophisticated needs and usually required constant, but not detailed, attention. These portfolios were expected to generate higher margins to compensate for the required administration. The Richmond and King street branch had four independent business account managers.
>
> *Account Managers:* These account managers were responsible for approximately 100 clients borrowing from $200,000 to $1,000,000 each. Since this position was an entry level posting for commercial lenders, they were generally assigned less complex accounts. The account managers were expected to cross-sell to existing accounts. (Identify and capitalize on opportunities for selling new products to existing clients rather than attempting to find new clients). There were three account managers at the Richmond and King Street branch.
>
> *Senior Account Managers:* These individuals handled 30 to 60 clients, each of whom generally borrowed in excess of $1 million. Some smaller but complex accounts might also be assigned to these managers. The accounts were much more complicated and therefore the manager of Commercial Services and, in some cases the branch manager, were more often involved. Extensive financial analysis and a greater understanding of the clients' business were required. These clients interacted with the bank on a number of levels since they were more likely to require payroll, foreign exchange and other services. Cross-selling was also done with these clients. There were three senior account managers at this branch.

The account managers were paid a salary ranging in the mid five figures. Each account manager's performance was reviewed on an annual basis by his/her immediate supervisor. Account managers were rated on a four-point scale. The rating reflected the supervisor's view of the account manager's performance in a number of defined areas including loan volumes, account control, product knowledge, cross selling, professionalism, and administration capability. The account manager's evaluation was based on specific targets negotiated at the beginning of the year. Account managers received an annual percentage increase in salary which was computed by the Divisional Human Resource department based on the performance rating, education level and mobility. Promotions, which also resulted in higher salaries, were similarly based on the above criteria.

Money Monitor

Money Monitor was a personal computer software package which allowed clients to access the bank's mainframe via a modem and telephone line. Once the initial link parameters had been established, clients could easily obtain information on their loan balances, account balances, account statements, cheque clearing, plus foreign exchange rates and money market rates. Clients could also transfer funds between their own accounts. Exhibit III outlines the initial features of Money Monitor.

STRATEGIC FIT. The TD bank's executive believed that cash management services would be an important source of future profits. Money Monitor was viewed as a key element of the bank's cash management services. Additional PC based products were being developed which would allow clients to format documentary letters of credit, disburse and collect preauthorized payments, execute wire transactions, process financial Electronic Data Interchange, issue commercial paper and manage investment portfolios. These additional products, along with Money Monitor, would be marketed under a single menu-driven communication software gateway known as 'Business Window." Money Monitor was viewed as a tool to further cement the bank's relationship with the client. In essence, Money Monitor was considered the commercial equivalent of the automatic teller machines used in retail banking.

It was anticipated that significant savings in the bank's personnel costs would eventually result as the number of Money Monitor accounts grew. Nevertheless, there was no exact data on the extent of the savings, if any.

The TD bank's Head Office estimated that 50% of all commercial clients used IBM compatible personal computers, and that 50% of these clients would have use for Money Monitor. In other words, all commercial clients, regardless of size or type of business, were targeted. Individual branch goals were established by division offices and, to date, these goals had not been met. Furthermore, utilization rates were below expectation as some clients were connected to the system but were not accessing data. Exhibit IV shows the divisional targets, branch performance, and utilization rates between 1988 and 1990.

PRICING. The system operated on any IBM compatible personal computer. The client was required to purchase a modem (usually costing $200), but was provided with the software free of charge. The client paid for the information provided by Money Monitor at a flat rate of $40 per month for the first three accounts interfaced and an additional $14 per account thereafter. These fees were highly

EXHIBIT II — An Account Manager's Responsibilities*

1. Direct Loan Products: operating loans, commercial instalment loans, small business loans, commercial mortgages, leases.

2. Direct Non-Loan Products: credit insurance, corporate Visa cards, export receivable insurance, business credit service, Money Monitor, interest bearing business accounts.

3. Referral Products: payroll services, foreign exchange, lock box services, pension fund management, personal mortgages, personal loans, RRSP's, Visa cards, personal accounts.

4. Administration:
   - For each account in a given portfolio, one credit review (usually ten pages) outlining a full analysis of the company's borrowing arrangements, financial performance and future requirements, was completed yearly. For higher risk or more active accounts, reports would be required on a semi-annual, quarterly or even monthly basis. Annual reviews required a visit to the client's premises.
   - Daily administration—required 30 minutes to one hour for checking and initialling reports on overdrafts, loan activity, loan expiries.
   - Credit reviews for new loan requests (volume varies with business/economic cycle).
   - Security documentation was also the responsibility of the account manager. Considerable time was spent following up on security changes, corrections, etc.

5. Marketing:
   - All account managers were expected to grow their portfolios. It was expected that they spend at least one half day per week visiting clients or prospective clients.
   - Account managers were also expected to attend social functions, such as receptions, golf tournaments, chamber of commerce dinners, etc.
   - Much time was spent talking to clients on the telephone. Such communications were of three types: relationship building, client monitoring, and negotiating.
     (A) Relationship building
         Often telephone calls occurred in both directions on a "how are things going" basis. A client might call to ask about the bank's perspective on the economy or to bounce ideas off the manager. An account manager might call to get information on the client's industry sector and to see how the client was doing relative to the competition.
     (B) Monitoring
         Clients usually provided monthly financial information and often had to be reminded to submit the data. A client was called if the company was in an overdraft position and upon the expiry of a credit facility.
     (C) Negotiating
         Whenever the client requested changes to the credit package or the company's performance warranted a change, negotiations were required. Negotiations could include rate changes, security changes, loan limit revisions, loan extensions, company restructuring, and changes in the fee structure.

The breakdown of an account manager's time among the above activities depended on the economic environment. However, every contact with the client would likely involve at least two of the above types of communications and each represented an opportunity to cross sell products.

*Based on discussions with two account managers and the branch manager.

---

competitive, with fees charged by other banks ranging from $80 to $1,000 per month for similar services. Clients typically interfaced their operating loans, general accounts and payroll accounts. Some clients also connected to U.S., trust, and interest bearing accounts.

DISTRIBUTION AND SELLING. The OSW Division had decided to place the marketing of Money Monitor in the hands of the account managers. This was done to accomplish a number of objectives, including:

- utilizing the account managers as a "ready and inexpensive distribution channel";
- promoting a selling orientation among account managers;
- encouraging computer literacy among account managers; and
- ensuring the account manager's understanding of Money Monitor's capabilities.

This distribution method was in contrast to that used for the bank's other cash management products. For example, specialists operating out of Toronto sold payroll systems based on referrals from account managers. A specialist would visit the potential payroll client with the account manager but, once the introduction had been made, would handle the demonstration, price negotiation, installation, user training, and follow up. The payroll specialist responsible for London was professional, enthusiastic, and well-liked by the account managers.

EXHIBIT III — Money Monitor Features

1. Consolidated statement of account and loan balances, providing net cash position.
2. Downloading of account statements—95 days of account information available at any time.
3. Foreign exchange rates.
4. Money market rates.
5. Searches for specific cheques by number or dollar amount.
6. Previous days' account activities, and on-line real-time reporting.
7. Autodial: Daily access to items 1–6 can be pre-programmed into the Money Monitor software. The user enters the password each day and the system then retrieves and prints the specified data. Average user PC time for this procedure is under one minute, as the user does not have to attend to the computer during this process.
8. Customer initiated transfers.
9. Full security system with passwords and system utilization report.

To sell Money Monitor, account managers were expected to identify potential clients, demonstrate the system, sell the product, install the computer link which involved using DOS and complete the registration paperwork. A 1-800 telephone number was provided to the customer and the account manager in case of technical difficulties.

The selling approach varied according to the size of the account. Price was an issue with the smaller accounts who had less need for Money Monitor services due to the lower complexity of their businesses. They often had one business account, an operating loan and one or two term loans. The owners of the businesses often kept their own books and were therefore, the Money Monitor users.

On the other hand, price was not an issue with larger accounts, although they sometimes felt they were being "nickled and dimed." The larger clients had the greatest need for Money Monitor due to the high complexity of their operations. These clients more often utilized payroll services, foreign exchange services and multiple accounts. The larger clients often expected and received good service from bank personnel. The decision to buy Money Monitor was usually made by senior company personnel rather than by the clerk who would use the system.

The buying behaviour of the medium-sized clients was a hybrid of the small and large clients.

REACTIONS OF THE ACCOUNT MANAGERS. When the product was introduced to the account managers, they were immediately enthusiastic about its capabilities. They hoped that the Money Monitor system would reduce their work load, especially with respect to account and loan information. For example, account managers would have to call accounts which were unknowingly in an overdraft position. Money Monitor clients often detected and corrected the overdraft position without account manager involvement. In addition, customers often complained that late arrival of bank statements slowed the completion of their monthly financial statements. Since some clients were required to provide monthly financial statements to the bank, prompt completion would assist the account managers.

While impressed with the above advantages, the account managers were largely unsuccessful in their efforts to sell Money Monitor. Account managers frequently did not have previous selling experience. In addition, they had difficulty setting aside the two to four hours required to install the system and train users. Since some account managers were not computer literate, they were uncomfortable performing the installations. Exhibit V provides an account manager's description of a typical installation.

Finally, the TD bank's strategy of providing good service proved to be a tough competitor. Many clients knew bank staff by name and were used to getting information quickly over the telephone. Some staff would even prepare information in anticipation of certain customer's calls. It was more difficult to sell Money Monitor to such clients.

Gary Shore's Perspective

The issues concerning Money Monitor interconnected with other changes in the banking environment. It was clear that the Canadian economy was heading into a recessionary period and this had implications for branch staff. Client difficulties increased account managers' workloads, while division managers emphasized closer account monitoring and control. Considerable internal changes were occurring as the TD bank introduced new products, systems, and concepts. As a result, the true effectiveness of Money Monitor in personnel savings and improved customer service was nebulous.

As Gary Shore further considered Money Monitor, he questioned the most effective means of motivating the account managers and, indeed, whether the account managers should sell the product at all.

A possible option was to use an outside vendor to install the system once the account manager had sold the concept. Some other commercial branches had designated one account manager as the Money Monitor specialist with a reduced portfolio. Their effectiveness had

EXHIBIT IV Targets, Performance and Utilization of Money Monitor

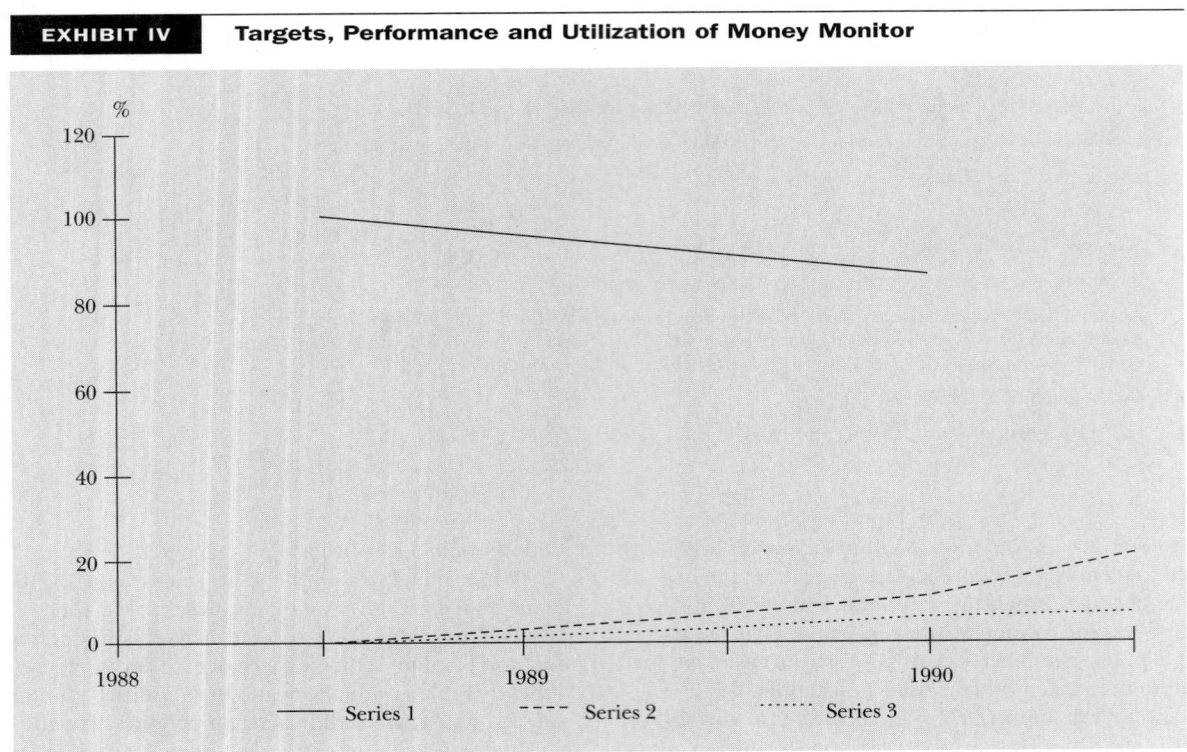

———: Utilization (% of Money Monitor clients using an installed system)
– – – –: Division Target (% of client base*)
······: Branch Performance (% of client base*)
*base includes both borrowing and non-borrowing clients

been debatable. It was evident that an in-branch specialist would be an expensive addition to the branch and Gary Shore would have to influence the division office to have the position created.

Although tangible incentives were typically not used by the bank to encourage the account managers to sell a given product, the possibility of increasing their enthusiasm via incentives was worth considering. Nevertheless, commissions were discouraged by the bank's executive to avoid setting a precedent, as a commission might indicate that selling Money Monitor was in addition to their other responsibilities.

How could customers be convinced that Money Monitor was the future of banking? This challenge was especially difficult given the past success of the Richmond and King Street branch in providing excellent client service.

EXHIBIT V	An Account Manager's Description of a Typical Installation*

"An installation was often time-consuming and cumbersome because the necessary equipment was not always available. I can remember a number of situations where the telephone line was too far from the personal computer and we had to move things around, or they wouldn't be using DOS and we would have to find the DOS disk and boot the computer. More often, we could not set the parameters up correctly or were not able to link up with TD and had to call Toronto who would call us back with an answer. As a result, the customer wasted time and, in one case, the decision maker had to leave the room before the demonstration was completed.

"Money Monitor is user friendly, but there are still enough screens to require at least an hour's training. Even then, it was inevitable that the client would call you later with questions. If the client was convinced that the system was useful, he/she would make an effort to use it, if not, he/she would forget what screen did what and their utilization would drop. Since the security system required a password change every 28 days, clients who used the system less frequently would be irritated when they could not get on the system without making password changes. These customers would inevitably be the ones who didn't have a clear grasp of Money Monitor's full capabilities.

"At one business, we found that two separate people in the same office were obtaining bank information. One used Money Monitor while the other just called the bank. When we found such situations we would have to go back and provide training. Money Monitor is a great product and the concept is easy to sell but the actual implementation is tricky."

*From a discussion with an account manager.

NOTES

MODULE 1

1. These examples are taken from "Here's to the Winners," *Sales and Marketing Management* (July 1999): 46.

2. Michele Marchetti, "Home-Style Selling," *Sales and Marketing Management* (August 1999): 16.

3. Ken Liebeskind, "Guiding Light," *Selling Power* (March 1999): 15.

4. Ken Liebeskind, "Service in Overdrive," *Selling Power* (March 1999): 18.

5. Adapted from Mark A. Moon and Gary M. Armstrong, "Selling Teams: A Conceptual Framework and Research Agenda," *Journal of Personal Selling and Sales Management* (Winter 1994): 17.

6. Tricia Campbell, "Getting Top Executives to Sell," *Sales and Marketing Management* (October 1998): 39.

7. Kate Fitzgerald, "An Automation Breakthrough," *Sales and Field Force Automation* (April 1999): 32.

8. Ken Liebeskind, "An Intranet Culture," *Selling Power* (May 1999): 18.

9. Don Labriola, "Videoconferencing in Action," *Sales and Field Force Automation* (September 1999): 74.

10. Melinda Ligos, "Point, Click, & Sell," *Sales and Marketing Management* (May 1999): 51.

11. David W. Cravens, "The Changing Role of the Sales Force," *Marketing Management* (Fall 1995): 54.

12. "The Right Stuff," *Sales and Marketing Management* (January 1999): 15.

13. "Top Reasons for Voluntary Turnover," *Sales and Marketing Management* (June 1999): 14.

14. Tricia Campbell, "Death of a Salesman's Loyalty," *Sales and Marketing Management* (August 1999): 13.

15. "Sales Execs Need to Lead as Well as Manage," *Selling Power* (May 1999): 103.

16. "The Right Stuff," *Sales and Marketing Management* (January 1999): 15.

17. Michael Adams, "Remote Control," *Sales and Marketing Management* (April 1999): 70.

18. Robert J. Kelly, "Tomorrow's Labor Pool," *Sales and Marketing Management* (March 1994): 34.

19. Chris Sandlund, "There's a New Face to America," *Success* (April 1999): 38.

MODULE 2

1. Marjorie J. Caballero, Roger A. Dickinson, and Dabney Townsend, "Aristotle and Personal Selling," *Journal of Personal Selling and Sales Management* 4 (May 1984): 13.

2. William T. Kelley, "The Development of Early Thought in Marketing," in *Salesmanship: Selected Readings,* ed. John M. Rathmell (Homewood, IL: Irwin, 1969): 3.

3. Thomas L. Powers, Warren S. Martin, Hugh Rushing, and Scott Daniels, "Selling before 1900: A Historical Perspective," *Journal of Personal Selling and Sales Management* 7 (November 1987): 5. For additional review of personal selling from 1600 to the present era, see Robert Desman and Terry E. Powell, "Personal Selling: Chicken or Egg," in *Proceedings,* 13th Annual Conference of the Academy of Marketing Science, ed. Jon M. Hawes (Orlando, FL: 1989).

4. Michael Bell, *The Salesman in the Field* (Geneva: International Labour Office, 1980): 1.

5. Stanley C. Hollander, "Anti-Salesman Ordinances of the Mid-19th Century," in *Salesmanship,* 9.

6. Ibid., 10.

7. Jon M. Hawes, "Leaders in Selling and Sales Management," *Journal of Personal Selling and Sales Management* 5 (November 1985): 60.

8. Charles W. Hoyt, *Scientific Sales Management* (New Haven, CT: George W. Woolson and Co., 1913): 3.

9. Ibid., 4.

10. Edward C. Bursk, "Low-Pressure Selling," *Harvard Business Review* 25 (Winter 1947): 227.

11. "From Push to Pull: Why Market Forces Demand the Conceptual Sell," *Selling* (July–August 1995): 50.

12. Synthesized from Thomas N. Ingram, "Relationship Selling: Moving from Rhetoric to Reality," *Mid-American Journal of Business* 11 (Spring 1996): 5; David W. Cravens, Emin Babakus, Ken Grant, Thomas N. Ingram, and Raymond W. LaForge, "Removing Sales Force Performance Hurdles," *Journal of Business and Industrial Marketing* 9, no. 3 (1994): 19; David W. Cravens, Thomas N. Ingram, and Raymond W. LaForge, "Evaluating Multiple Sales Channel Strategies," *Journal of Business and Industrial Marketing* (Summer/Fall 1991): 37.

13. Michele Marchetti, "The Cost of Doing Business," *Sales and Marketing Management* (September 1999): 56.

[14] "Here's to the Winners," *Sales and Marketing Management* (July 1999): 70.

[15] Kevin J. Corcoran, Laura K. Petersen, Daniel B. Baitch, and Mark F. Barrett, *High Performance Sales Organizations* (Chicago, IL: Irwin, 1995): 152.

[16] "Here's to the Winners," 64.

[17] Michele Marchetti, "A Sales Pro Tries to Energize HP," *Sales and Marketing Management* (September 1999): 15.

[18] Kevin R. Fitzgerald, "What Makes a Superior Supplier?" *Velocity* (Spring 1999): 22.

[19] Thomas N. Ingram and Charles H. Schwepker, Jr., "Perceptions of Salespeople: Implications for Sales Managers and Sales Trainers," *Journal of Marketing Management* 2 (Fall/Winter 1992–93): 1.

[20] Thomas N. Ingram, "Relationship Selling: Moving from Rhetoric to Reality," *Mid-American Journal of Business* 11 (Spring 1996): 5.

[21] "Here's to the Winners," 66.

[22] Michael J. Swenson, William R. Swinyard, Frederick W. Langrehr, and Scott M. Smith, "The Appeal of Personal Selling as a Career: A Decade Later," *Journal of Personal Selling and Sales Management* 13 (Winter 1993): 51

[23] Marchetti, "The Cost of Doing Business," 57.

[24] Steven P. Brown, Thomas W. Leigh, and J. Martin Haygood, "Salesperson Performance and Job Attitudes," in *The Marketing Manager's Handbook*, 3rd ed., ed. Sidney J. Levy, George R. Frerichs, and Howard L. Gordon (Chicago: The Dartnell Corporation, 1994): 107.

[25] *Occupational Outlook Handbook*, 1998–99 ed. (Washington, DC: U.S. Department of Labor, 1998).

[26] Emin Babakus, David W. Cravens, Ken Grant, Thomas N. Ingram, and Raymond W. LaForge, "Removing Salesforce Performance Hurdles," *Journal of Business and Industrial Marketing* 9, no. 3 (1994): 19.

[27] See Herbert M. Greenberg and Jeanne Greenberg, *What It Takes to Succeed in Sales* (Homewood, IL: Dow-Jones Irwin, 1990).

[28] James M. Comer and Alan J. Dubinsky, *Managing the Successful Sales Force* (Lexington, MA: D.C. Heath and Co., 1985): 5; Brown et al., "Salesperson Performance," 107.

[29] Babakus et al., "Removing Salesforce Performance Hurdles," 19.

[30] Rosann L. Spiro and Barton A. Weitz, "Adaptive Selling: Conceptualization, Measurement, and Nomological Validity," *Journal of Marketing Research* 27 (February 1990): 61.

[31] Bruce K. Pilling and Sevo Eroglu, "An Empirical Examination of the Impact of Salesperson Empathy and Professionalism and Merchandise Salability on Retail Buyers' Evaluations," *Journal of Personal Selling and Sales Management* 14 (Winter 1994): 45.

[32] Lyndon E. Dawson, Jr., Barlow Soper, and Charles E. Pettijohn, "The Effects of Empathy on Salesperson Effectiveness," *Psychology and Marketing* (July/August 1992): 297.

[33] Andy Cohen, "Here's to the Winners," 60.

[34] Kevin J. Corcoran, Laura K. Petersen, Daniel B. Baitch, and Mark F. Barrett, *High Performance Sales Organizations* (Chicago: Irwin Professional Publishing, 1995): 77.

[35] Arun Sharma and Rajnandini Pillai, "Customers' Decision-Making Styles and Their Preference for Sales Strategies: Conceptual Examination and an Empirical Study," *Journal of Personal Selling and Sales Management* 16 (Winter 1996): 21.

[36] Victoria Davies Bush and Thomas N. Ingram, "Adapting to Diverse Customers: A Training Matrix for International Marketers," *Industrial Marketing Management* (Spring 1996): 373.

[37] "And the Surveys Say," *Personal Selling Power* (October 1995): 55.

MODULE 3

[1] Robert F. Gwinner, "Base Theory in the Formulation of Sales Strategy," *MSU Business Topics* (Autumn 1968): 37.

[2] Malcolm Fleschner, "How to Sell New Products," *Selling Power* (July/August 1999): 23.

[3] This section on consultative selling is based on Kevin J. Corcoran, Laura K. Petersen, Daniel B. Baitch, and Mark F. Barrett, *High Performance Sales Organizations* (Chicago: Irwin, 1995): 44.

[4] Malcolm Fleschner, "We Want to Be the Biggest Small Company Around," *Selling Power* (April 1999) 48.

[5] Jon M. Hawes, Kenneth E. Mast, and John E. Swan, "Trust Earning Perceptions of Sellers and Buyers," *Journal of Personal Selling and Sales Management* 9 (Spring 1989): 1.

[6] Interview by the authors with Blake Conrad, sales representative with Centurion Specialty Care.

[7] Francy Blackwood, "Out of the Cold," *Selling* (May 1996): 22.

[8] Dana Ray, "Confront Call Reluctance," *Personal Selling Power* (September 1995): 46.

[9] Thomas W. Leigh and Patrick F. McGraw, "Mapping the Procedural Knowledge of Industrial Sales Personnel: A Script-Theoretic Investigation," *Journal of Marketing* 53 (January 1989): 16.

[10] Warren Burger, "Shopping Survival Skills," *Stereo Review* (February 1990): 70.

11. Thomas N. Ingram, Michael D. Hartline, and Charles H. Schwepker Jr., "Gatekeeper Perceptions: Implications for Improving Sales Ethics and Professionalism," *Proceedings of the Academy of Marketing Science* (1992): 328.

12. Theodore Levitt, *Industrial Purchasing Behavior: A Study in Communications* (Boston: Division of Research, Harvard School of Business, 1965).

13. Francy Blackwood, "Building a Record," *Selling* (April 1996): 22.

14. Franco DiCarlo, "An Eye for What Customers Buy," *Selling* (April 1995): 68.

15. Hawes, Mast, and Swan, "Trust Earning Perceptions," 7.

16. For more on the ADAPT questioning model, see Ramon A. Avila, Thomas N. Ingram, Raymond W. LaForge, and Michael R. Williams, *The Professional Selling Skills Workbook* (Fort Worth, TX: The Dryden Press, 1996): 109.

MODULE 4

1. David W. Cravens, *Strategic Marketing* (Homewood, IL: Irwin, 1994): 30.

2. Ibid., 46.

3. Michael E. Porter, *Competitive Strategy* (New York: The Free Press, 1980): 34.

4. Madhubalan Viswanathan and Eric M. Olson, "The Implementation of Business Strategies: Implications for the Sales Function," *Journal of Personal Selling and Sales Management* (Winter 1992): 45.

5. Cyndee Miller, "Marketing Industry Report: Who's Spending What on Biz-to-Biz Marketing," *Marketing News*, January 1, 1996, 1; Cyndee Miller, "Marketing Industry Report: Consumer Marketers Spend Most of Their Money on Communications," *Marketing News*, March 11, 1996, 1.

6. Michael D. Hutt and Thomas W. Speh, *Business Marketing Management* (Fort Worth, TX: The Dryden Press, 1995): 71.

7. Malcolm Campbell, "The New Sales Force," *Selling Power* (July/August 1999): 51.

8. Reported in Chad Kaydo, "You've Got Sales," *Sales and Marketing Management* (October 1999): 29.

9. Ibid., 30.

10. Ibid., 34.

11. Andy Cohen, "Herman Miller," *Sales and Marketing Management* (July 1999): 60.

12. Tricia Campbell, "Who Needs a Sales Force Anyway?," *Sales and Marketing Management* (February 1999): 13.

13. "Team Selling by Industry," *Selling* (January/February 1994): 46.

14. Thomas N. Ingram, "Relationship Selling: Moving from Rhetoric to Reality," *Mid-American Journal of Business* 11, no. 1.

15. "The Team-Selling Edge," *Sales Manager's Bulletin*, August 30, 1995, 1.

16. Tom Dellecave, Jr., "Chipping In," *An Executive's Guide to Sales and Marketing Technology* (June 1996): 37.

17. "Telemarketing Takes the Top Spot," *Direct Marketing* (September 1987): 120.

18. John F. Yarbrough, "Salvaging a Lousy Year," *Sales and Marketing Management* (July 1996): 72.

19. Jeff Tanner, *Curriculum Guide to Trade Show Marketing* (Bethesda, MD: Center for Exhibition Industry Research, 1996).

MODULE 5

1. Reported in "Structuring the Sales Organization," in *Sales Manager's Handbook*, ed. John P. Steinbrink (Chicago: The Dartnell Corporation, 1989): 90.

2. See Robert W. Ruekert, Orville C. Walker, Jr., and Kenneth J. Roering, "The Organization of Marketing Activities: A Contingency Theory of Structure and Performance," *Journal of Marketing* (Winter 1985): 13, for a more complete presentation of structural characteristics and relationships. The discussion in this section borrows heavily from this article.

3. Andy Cohen, "Managing," *Sales and Marketing Management* (April 1996): 77.

4. Charles T. Clark, "Is Your Company Ready for Global Marketing?" *Sales and Marketing Management* (September 1994): 42.

5. Benson P. Shapiro and Rowland T. Moriarity, *National Account Management: Emerging Insights* (Cambridge, MA: Marketing Science Institute, 1982): 19.

6. See Raymond W. LaForge, David W. Cravens, and Clifford E. Young, "Using Contingency Analysis to Select Effort Allocation Methods," *Journal of Personal Selling and Sales Management* (August 1986): 23, for a summary of productivity improvements from decision model applications.

APPENDIX 5

1. For different classification schemes and more detailed discussion of individual forecasting methods, see Harry R. White, *Sales Forecasting: Timesaving and Profit-Making Strategies That Work* (Glenview, IL: Scott, Foresman and Company, 1984): 6; David M. Georgoff and Robert G. Murdick, "Managers's Guide to Forecasting," *Harvard Business Review* (January–Feburary 1986): 113; J. Scott Armstrong, Roderick J. Brodie, and Shelby McIntyre, "Forecasting Methods for Marketing: Review of Empirical Research, *International Journal of Forecasting* 3 (1987): 355.

2. Nada R. Sanders and Karl B. Manrodt, "Forecasting Practices in U.S. Corporations: Survey Results," *Interfaces* 24 (March–April 1994): 92.

[3] See John T. Mentzer, "Forecasting with Adaptive Extended Exponential Smoothing," *Journal of the Academy of Marketing Science* (Fall 1986): 62, for discussion and examples of different exponential smoothing methods.

[4] See "Survey of Buying Power," *Sales and Marketing Management*, August 13, 1990, for a discussion of the Buying Power Index and for the calculated indices throughout the United States.

[5] Conversation with director of marketing at Sherwood Medical in St. Louis, MO.

[6] William Keenan, Jr., "Numbers Racket," *Sales and Marketing Management* (May 1995): 64.

[7] Joel Bryant and Kim Jensen, "Forecasting Inkjet Printers at Hewlett-Packard Company," *Journal of Business Forecasting* (Summer 1994): 27.

[8] Mark Barash, "Eliciting Accurate Sales Forecasts from Market Experts," *Journal of Business Forecasting* (Fall 1994): 24.

[9] Kenneth B. Kahn and John T. Mentzer, "The Impact of Team-based Forecasting," *Journal of Business Forecasting* (Summer 1994): 18.

[10] Norton Paley, "Welcome to the Fast Lane," *Sales and Marketing Management* (August 1994): 65.

[11] Keenan, "Numbers Racket."

[12] "Keeping Sales in the Loop," *Sales and Marketing Management* (June 1995): 34.

[13] These and other recommendations are available in Robin T. Peterson, "Sales Force Composite Forecasting—An Exploratory Analysis," *Journal of Business Forecasting* (Spring 1989): 23; James E. Cox, Jr., "Approaches for Improving Salespersons' Forecasts," *Industrial Marketing Management* 18 (1989): 307.

[14] Essam Mahmoud, Gillian Rice, and Naresh Malhotra, "Emerging Issues in Sales Forecasting and Decision Support Systems," *Journal of the Academy of Marketing Science* (Fall 1988): 53.

[15] See Benito E. Flores and Edna M. White, "A Framework for the Combination of Forecasts," *Journal of the Academy of Marketing Science* (Fall 1988): 95, for an examination of different combination approaches.

[16] Sanders and Manrodt, "Forecasting Practices in U.S. Corporations."

MODULE 6

[1] Michael Munson and W. Austin Spivey, "Salesforce Selection That Meets Federal Regulation and Management Needs," *Industrial Marketing Management* 9 (February 1980): 12.

[2] Judy A. Siguaw and Earl D. Honeycutt, Jr., "An Examination of Gender Differences in Selling Behaviors and Job Attitudes," *Industrial Marketing Management* 24 (January 1995): 45; Robert Kelly, "Tomorrow's Labor Pool," *Sales and Marketing Management* (March 1994): 34; James T. Bond, Ellen Galinsky, and Jennifer E. Swanberg, *The 1997 National Study of the Changing Workforce* (New York: Families and Work Institute, 1998).

[3] Kelly, "Tomorrow's Labor Pool."

[4] Rene Darmon, "Where Do the Best Sales Force Profit Producers Come From?" *Journal of Personal Selling and Sales Management* 3 (Summer 1993): 17.

[5] Julia Lawlor, "Highly Classified," *Sales and Marketing Management* (March 1995): 75; Chad Kaydo, "Overturning Turnover," *Sales and Marketing Management* 149 (November 1997): 50.

[6] Jeanne Greenberg and Herbert Greenberg, *What It Takes to Succeed in Sales: Selecting and Retaining Top Producers* (Homewood, IL: Dow Jones Irwin, 1990).

[7] Georgia Chao, Anne O'Leary-Kelly, Samantha Wolf, Howard Klein, and Philip Gardner, "Organizational Socialization: Its Content and Consequences," *Journal of Applied Psychology* 79 (October 1994): 730.

[8] "RE/MAX's Power Recruiting," *Sales and Marketing Management* 150 (June 1998): 73.

[9] Schein Pharmaceutical, Inc., corporate account manager position description, 1998.

[10] John S. Hill and Meg Birdseye, "Salesperson Selection in Multinational Corporations: A Study," *Journal of Personal Selling and Sales Management* 9 (Summer 1989): 39.

[11] Erika Rasmusson, "Can Your Reps Sell Overseas? How to Make Sure They Have What It Takes," *Sales and Marketing Management* 150 (February 1998): 110.

[12] Lawlor, "Highly Classified."

[13] Michele Marchetti, "The New Gold Rush," *Sales and Marketing Management* 150 (September 1998): 42.

[14] Andy Bargerstock and Hank Engel, "Six Ways to Boost Employee Referral Programs," *HRM Magazine* 39 (December 1994): 72; Kathryn Tyler, "Employees Can Help Recruit New Talent," *HR Magazine* 41 (September 1996): 57.

[15] Darmon, "Where Do the Best Sales Force Profit Producers Come From?"

[16] Mary F. Cook, "Choosing the Right Recruitment Tool," *HR Focus* 74 (October 1997): S7.

[17] Eric R. Chabrow, "Online Employment," *Informationweek*, January 23, 1995, 38.

[18] Robert Carey, "Help Wanted—Now!" *Sales and Marketing Management* 149 (March 1997): 30.

[19] Max Messmer, "Temporary Employees Are Permanent Part of New Europe," *Personnel Journal* 73 (January 1994): 100.

[20] Barb Cole-Gomolski and Tim Ouellette, "Hiring Managers Turn to Video," *Computerworld* 32 (April 1998): 29.

[21] Chad Kaydo, "Northwestern Mutual Life," *Sales and Marketing Management* 150 (July 1998): 40.

[22] Michelle Marchetti, "Sales Reps to Go," *Sales and Marketing Management* 151 (January 1999): 14.

[23] Mike Frost, "Old-Fashioned Career Fairs Gain Favor Online," *HR Magazine* 43 (April 1998): 31.

[24] "PhonApp Delivers Top Quality Applicants," *Wonderlic Newsletter* (1996): www.wonderlic.com/nltop.htm accessed on 1/26/99.

[25] "Probing Sales Recruits' Psyches," *Sales and Marketing Management* (March 1994): 38.

[26] Linda Thornburg, "Computer-Assisted Interviewing Shortens Hiring Cycle," *HR Magazine* 43 (February 1998): 73.

[27] Robert Gatewood and Hubert Feild, Human Resource Selection (Fort Worth, TX: The Dryden Press, 1994).

[28] Wesley J. Johnson and Martha C. Cooper, "Industrial Sales Force Selection: Current Knowledge and Needed Research," *Journal of Personal Selling and Sales Management* 1 (Spring–Summer 1981): 49.

[29] Greg W. Marshall, Miriam B. Stamps, and Jesse N. Moore, "Preinterview Biases: The Impact of Race, Physical Attractiveness, and Sales Job Type on Preinterview Impressions of Sales Job Applicants," *Journal of Personal Selling and Sales Management* 18 (Fall 1998): 21.

[30] Ron Panko, "Getting Testy about Sales Screening Tests," *Best's Review—Life-Health Insurance Edition* 98 (December 1997): 67; Michael Santo, "How to Recruit and Retain Top-Level Talent," *Agency Sales Magazine* 28 (May 1998): 39.

[31] Seymour Adler, "Personality Tests for Salesforce Selection: Worth a Fresh Look," *Review of Business* 16 (Summer/Fall 1994): 27.

[32] "Target Your Hiring Too! Testing Targets Sales Skills before Hiring," *American Salesman* 44 (April 1998): 23.

[33] Based on Samual J. Maurice, "Stalking the High-Scoring Salesperson," *Sales and Marketing Management* (October 7, 1985) 63; George B. Salsbury, "Properly Recruit Salespeople to Reduce Training Cost," *Industrial Marketing Management* 11 (April 1982): 143; Richard Kern, "IQ Tests for Salesmen Make a Comeback," *Sales and Marketing Management* (April 1988): 42.

[34] Susana Schwartz, "NW Mutual Improves Agent Recruitment Process," *Insurance & Technology* 22 (July 1997): 14.

[35] *Wonderlic 1998 Catalog*, Wonderlic Personnel Tests, Inc., Libertyville, IL, 1998.

[36] Weld Royal, "From Socialist to Sales Rep," *Sales and Marketing Management* (August 1994): 63.

[37] E. James Randall, Ernest F. Cooke, and Lois Smith, "A Successful Application of the Assessment Center Concept to the Salesperson Selection Process," *Journal of Personal Selling and Sales Management* 5 (May 1985): 53.

[38] Tom Smith and Binna Kandola, "Dealing Out Work to the Right Staff," *People Management* 2 (January 1996): 28.

[39] Christopher J. Bachler, "Resume Fraud: Lies, Omissions and Exaggerations," *Personnel Journal* 74 (June 1995): 50.

[40] Gatewood and Feild, *Human Resource Selection*.

[41] Ibid.

[42] W. E. Patton III and Ronald King, "The Use of Human Judgement Models in Sales Force Selection Decisions," *Journal of Personal Selling and Sales Management* 12 (Spring 1992): 1.

[43] Michele Marchetti, "The New Gold Rush," *Sales and Marketing Management* 150 (September 1998): 42.

[44] C. David Shepherd and James Heartfield, "Discrimination Issues in the Selection of Salespeople: A Review and Managerial Suggestions." *Journal of Personal Selling and Sales Management* 11 (Fall 1991): 67.

[45] Munson and Spivey, "Salesforce Selection," 15.

[46] For more discussion of what information should not be sought in a job interview, see John P. Steinbrink, ed., *The Dartnell Sales Manager's Handbook*, 14th ed. (Chicago: The Dartnell Press, 1989): 820; Shepherd and Heartfield, "Discrimination Issues in the Selection of Salespeople: A Review and Managerial Suggestions." *Journal of Personal Selling and Sales Management* 11 (Fall 1991): 67.

[47] Jon M. Hawes, "How to Improve Your College Recruiting Program," *Journal of Personal Selling and Sales Management* 9 (Summer 1989): 51.

MODULE 7

[1] Alan J. Dubinsky, Roy D. Howell, Thomas N. Ingram, and Danny N. Bellenger, "Salesforce Socialization," *Journal of Marketing* 50 (October 1986): 195.

[2] Mark W. Johnston, A. Parasuraman, Charles M. Futrell, and William C. Black, "A Longitudinal Assessment of the Impact of Selected Organizational Influences on Salespeople's Organizational Commitment During Early Employment," *Journal of Marketing Research* 27 (August 1990): 341.

[3] Jeffrey K. Sager, "How to Retain Salespeople," *Industrial Marketing Management* 19 (May 1990): 155.

[4] Judy A. Siguaw, Gene Brown, and Robert E. Widing II, "The Influence of the Market Orientation of the Firm on Sales Force Behavior and Attitudes," *Journal of Marketing Research* 31 (February 1994): 106.

[5] Federated Insurance Company brochure. "Your Marketing Opportunity: Anticipations, Expectations, and Realizations" by Federated Mutual Insurance Co. (1995).

[6] Gilbert A. Churchill, Jr., Neil M. Ford, Steven W. Hartley, and Orville C. Walker, Jr., "The Determinants of Salesperson Performance: A Meta-Analysis," *Journal of Marketing Research* 22 (May 1985): 117.

[7] Melanie Berger, "Intel," *Sales and Marketing Management* 149 (October 1997): 56.

[8] Robert Klein, "Nabisco Sales Soar after Sales Training," *Marketing News* 31 (January 1997): 23.

[9] *Sales and Marketing Management* (April 1995): 39.

[10] Christen Heide, *Dartnell's 30th Sales Force Compensation Survey*. (Chicago: The Dartnell Corporation, 1999).

[11] Sarah Lorge, "Getting into Their Heads," *Sales and Marketing Management* 150 (February 1998): 58.

[12] Erika Rasmusson and Melinda Ligos, "Please Tell Me How," *Sales and Marketing Management* 150 (October 1998): 137.

[13] Robert C. Erffmeyer and Dale A. Johnson, "The Future of Sales Training: Making Choices among Six Distance Education Methods," *Journal of Business & Industrial Marketing* 12 (Summer 1997): 185.

[14] For an extensive review of how the sales manager might be involved in the details of sales training, see John P. Steinbrink, ed., *The Dartnell Sales Manager's Handbook*, 14th ed. (Chicago: The Dartnell Corporation, 1989): 850.

[15] See Alan J. Dubinsky and Richard W. Hansen, "The Sales Force Management Audit," *California Management Review* 24 (Winter 1981): 86.

[16] Lorge, "Getting into Their Heads."

[17] William Keenan, Jr., "Getting Customers into the Act," *Sales and Marketing Management* (February 1995): 58; Erika Rasmusson, "20 Questions," *Sales and Marketing Management* 149 (August 1997): 85.

[18] Chad Kaydo, "Training: A Complete Regimen for Making Your Salespeople Smarter," *Sales and Marketing Management* 150 (December 1998): 33.

[19] See "Study Reveals Needs of Business Marketers," *Marketing News* (March 13, 1989) 6; *Success Factors in Selling* (Stamford, CT: Learning International, 1989); "How Do Salespeople Rate Themselves?" *Sales and Marketing Management* (March 1989): 17; *Dartnell's 30th Sales Force Compensation Survey*.

[20] Earl D. Honeycutt, Jr., Vince Howe and Thomas N. Ingram, "Shortcomings of Sales Training Programs," *Industrial Marketing Management* 22 (1993): 117.

[21] *Sales and Marketing Management* (April 1995): 39.

[22] C. David Shepherd, Stephen B. Castleberry, and Rick E. Ridnour, "Linking Effective Listening with Salesperson Performance: An Exploratory Investigation," *Journal of Business & Industrial Marketing* 12 (Fall 1997): 315.

[23] Jaclyn Fierman, "The Death and Rebirth of the Salesman," *Fortune* (July 25, 1994) 80; David Stamps, "Training for a New Sales Game," *Training* 34 (July 1997) 46.

[24] Gillian Flynn, "The Nuts and Bolts of Valuing Training," *Workforce* 77 (November 1998): 80.

[25] Sales-Training Hit List," *Inc.* (November 1994): 126.

[26] Marc Hequet, "Product Knowledge: Knowing What They're Selling May Be the Key to How Well They Sell It," *Training* (February 1988): 18.

[27] Dana Tanyeri, "Sales Cross Training," *ID: The Voice of Foodservice Distribution* 33 (October 1997): 48.

[28] Victoria Davies Bush and Thomas N. Ingram, "Adapting to Diverse Customers: A Training Matrix for International Marketers," *Industrial Marketing Management* 25 (September 1996): 373.

[29] Harish Sujan, Barton A. Weitz, and Mita Sujan, "Increasing Sales Productivity by Getting Salespeople to Work Smarter," *Journal of Personal Selling and Sales Management* 8 (August 1988): 9.

[30] Thayer C. Taylor, "Take Your Time," *Sales and Marketing Management* 146 (July 1994): 45.

[31] Jay Winchester, "Ripe for a Change," *Sales and Marketing Management* 150 (August 1998): 81.

[32] Ned C. Hill and Michael J. Swenson, "The Impact of Electronic Data Interchange on the Sales Function," *Journal of Personal Selling and Sales Management* 14 (Summer 1994): 80.

[33] Jared F. Harrison, ed., *The Sales Manager as a Trainer* (Orlando, FL: National Society of Sales Training Executives, 1983): 7.

[34] Michele Marchetti, "Wealth of Knowledge, Paucity of Funds" *Sales and Marketing Management* 149 (March 1997): 31.

[35] Honeycutt et al., "Who Trains Salespeople?"; Lawrence B. Chonko, John F. Tanner, Jr., and William A. Weeks, "Sales Training: Status and Needs," *Journal of Personal Selling and Sales Management* 13 (Fall 1993): 81.

[36] Joe Mullich, "Copying Xerox's Style," *Advertising Age's Business Marketing* 79 (November 1994): 1.

[37] "RE/MAX's Power Recruiting," *Sales and Marketing Management* 150 (June 1998): 73.

[38] *Dartnell's 30th Sales Force Compensation Survey*.

[39] Erika Rasmusson, "Top of the Charts–GE Capital," *Sales and Marketing Management* (July 1998): 32.

[40] William Keenan, Jr., "Managers Try Checklist Training," *Sales and Marketing Management* (November 1994): 41.

[41] Abby Ellin, "Generation Gap," *Sales and Marketing Management* (October 1998): 115.

[42] Dan E. Hupp, "Selling beyond Quota: Adult Edutainment," *Training & Development* 52 (August 1998): 61.

[43] For guidelines for enhancing role playing, see "Skills," *Personal Selling Power* (January/February 1995): 54. Also see Thomas N. Ingram, "Guidelines for Maximizing Role-Play Activities," in *Proceedings,* National Conference in Sales Management, Dallas, TX, 1990.

[44] Andy Cohen, "Staying in Touch," *Sales and Marketing Management* (April 1994): 35; Barbara Forster, "Let's Go to the Tape," *Boston Business Journal* 17 (March 1997): 20.

[45] Andy Cohen, "Staying in Touch," *Sales and Marketing Management* (April 1994): 35.

[46] Sarah Lorge, "Top of the Charts–Frito-Lay," *Sales and Marketing Management* (July 1998): 38.

[47] Ramon Avila, Stephen Avila, Scott Inks, and Michael Williams, "Advance Technologies for Effective Sales Training," *Mid-American Journal of Business* 11 (Fall 1996): 25.

[48] Robert M. Kahn, "21st Century Training," *Sales and Marketing Management* 149 (June 1997): 80.

[49] Erffimeyer and Johnson, "The Future of Sales Training."

[50] Carl L. Pritchard, "From Classroom to Chat Room," *Training & Development* 52 (June 1998): 76.

[51] Malcom Fleschner, "Training That Lasts," *Personal Selling Power* (March 1995): 32; Kahn, "21st Century Training."

[52] Jon M. Hawes, Stephen P. Huthchens, and William F. Crittenden, "Evaluating Corporate Sales Training Programs," *Training and Development Journal* 36 (November 1982): 44.

[53] Francy Blackwood, "That Rookie Season," *Selling* (September 1996): 26.

[54] Ibid.

[55] Lorge, "Getting into Their Heads."

[56] Alan J. Dubinsky, Marvin A. Jolson, Ronald E. Michaels, Masaaki Kotabe, and Chae Un Lim, "Ethical Perceptions of Field Sales Personnel: An Empirical Assessment," *Journal of Personal Selling and Sales Management* 12 (Fall 1992): 9; Karl A. Boedecker, Fred W. Morgan, and Jeffrey J. Stoltman, "Legal Dimensions of Salespersons' Statements: A Review and Managerial Suggestions," *Journal of Marketing* 55 (January 1991): 70.

[57] Boedecker et al., "Legal Dimensions of Salespersons' Statements."

MODULE 8

[1] E. Stephen Grant and Alan J. Bush, "Salesforce Socialization Tactics: Building Organizational Value Congruence," *Journal of Personal Selling and Sales Management* 16 (Summer 1996): 17.

[2] Alan J. Dubinsky, Roy D. Howell, Thomas N. Ingram, and Danny N. Bellenger, "Salesforce Socialization," *Journal of Marketing* 50 (October 1986): 192; Richard P. Bagozzi, "Performance and Satisfaction in an Industrial Sales Force: An Examination of Their Antecedents and Simultaneity," *Journal of Marketing* 44 (Spring 1978): 65.

[3] Emin Babakus, David W. Cravens, Mark Johnston, and William C. Moncrief, "Examining the Role of Organizational Variables in the Salesperson Job Satisfaction Model," *Journal of Personal Selling and Sales Management* 16 (Summer 1996): 33.

[4] Ronald E. Michaels, William L. Cron, Alan J. Dubinsky, and Erich A. Joachimsthaler, "Influence of Formalization on the Organizational Commitment and Work Alienation of Salespeople and Industrial Buyers," *Journal of Marketing Research* 25 (November 1988): 376.

[5] Ronald E. Michaels, Alan J. Dubinsky, Masaaki Kotabe, and Chae Un Lim, "The Effects of Organizational Formalization on Organizational Commitment and Work Alienation in U.S., Japanese and Korean Industrial Salesforces," *European Journal of Marketing* 30 (July 1996): 8.

[6] Rosemary R. Lagace, "An Exploratory Study of Trust between Sales Managers and Salespersons," *Journal of Personal Selling and Sales Management* 11 (Spring 1991): 49; David Strutton, Lou E. Pelton, and James R. Lumpkin, "The Relationship between Psychological Climate and Salesperson–Sales Manager Trust in Sales Organizations," *Journal of Personal Selling and Sales Management* 13 (Fall 1993): 1.

[7] Howard J. Klein and Jay S. Kim, "A Field Study of the Influence of Situational Constraints, Leader–Member Exchange, and Goal Commitment on Performance," *Academy of Management Journal* 41 (February 1998): 88.

[8] Alan J. Dubinsky, Francis J. Yammarino, Marvin A. Jolson, and William D. Spangler, "Transformational Leadership: An Initial Investigation in Sales Management," *Journal of Personal Selling and Sales Management* 15 (Spring 1995): 17.

[9] Frederick A. Russ, Kevin M. McNeilly, and James M. Comer, "Leadership, Decision Making and Performance of Sales Managers: A Multi-Level Approach," *Journal of Personal Selling and Sales Management* 16 (Summer 1996): 1.

[10] Daniel A. Sauers, James B. Hunt, and Ken Bass, "Behavioral Self-Management as a Supplement to External Sales Force Controls," *Journal of Personal Selling and Sales Management* 10 (Summer 1990): 81.

[11] Based on John French, Jr., and Bertram Raven, "The Bases of Social Power," in *Studies in Social Power,* ed. D. Cartwright (Ann Arbor, MI: The University of Michigan Press, 1959).

[12] Paul Busch, "The Sales Manager's Bases of Social Power and Influence upon the Sales Force," *Journal of Marketing* 44 (Summer 1980): 95.

[13] Ibid., 98.

¹⁴Prescott Tolk, "Supplying Success," *Sales and Marketing Management* 150 (April 1998): 22.

¹⁵Janet E. Keith, Donald W. Jackson, Jr., and Lawerence A. Crosby, "Effects of Alternative Types of Influence Strategies under Different Channel Dependence Structures," *Journal of Marketing* 54 (July 1990): 30.

¹⁶Donald W. Jackson, Jr., Stephen S. Tax, and John W. Barnes, "Examining the Salesforce Culture: Managerial Applications and Research Propositions," *Journal of Personal Selling and Sales Management* 14 (Fall 1994): 1.

¹⁷Francis J. Yammarino and Alan J. Dubinsky, "Salesperson Performance and Managerially Controllable Factors: An Investigation of Individual and Work Group Effects," *Journal of Management* 16 (1990): 87.

¹⁸Michele Marchetti, "Master Motivators," *Sales and Marketing Management* 150 (April 1998): 38.

¹⁹Tolk, "Supplying Success."

²⁰William L. Cron and John W. Slocum, Jr., "Career Stages Approach to Managing the Sales Force," *Journal of Consumer Marketing* 3 (Fall 1986): 11.

²¹This discussion of influence strategies is largely based on Madeline E. Heilman and Harvey Hornstein, *Managing Human Forces in Organization* (Homewood, IL: Irwin, 1982): 116.

²²Ajay K. Kohli, "Some Unexplored Supervisory Behaviors and Their Influence on Salespeople's Role Clarity, Specific Self-esteem, Job Satisfaction, and Motivation," *Journal of Marketing Research* 22 (November 1985): 424.

²³Ibid., 118.

²⁴L. B. Gschwandter, "How to Influence with Integrity," *Personal Selling Power* (January–February 1990): 40.

²⁵Mary J. Cronin, "Bye-Bye, Wild Web," *Fortune* 136 (October 1997): 264.

²⁶Gregory A. Rich, "The Constructs of Sales Coaching: Supervisory Feedback, Role Modeling and Trust," *Journal of Personal Selling and Sales Management* 18 (Winter 1998): 53.

²⁷Saul W. Gellerman. "The Tests of a Good Salesperson," *Harvard Business Review* 68 (May–June 1990): 68

²⁸Barton A. Weitz, Harish Sujan, and Mita Sujan, "Knowledge, Motivation, and Adaptive Behavior: A Framework for Improving Sales Effectiveness," *Journal of Marketing* 50 (October 1986): 183.

²⁹Ibid.

³⁰Rich, "The Constructs of Sales Coaching."

³¹Gregory A. Rich, "The Sales Manager as a Role Model: Effects on Trust, Job Satisfaction, and Performance of Salespeople," *Journal of the Academy of Marketing Science* 25 (Fall 1997): 319.

³²Rich, "The Constructs of Sales Coaching."

³³Elaine Evans, "How to Create Sales Meeting Magic," *Personal Selling Power* (September 1990): 34.

³⁴Chad Kaydo, "Unforgettable Meetings," *Sales and Marketing Management* 150 (February 1998): 71.

³⁵Sir Adrian Cadbury, "Ethical Managers Make Their Own Rules," *Harvard Business Review* 65 (September–October 1987): 70.

³⁶Archie B. Carroll, "In Search of the Moral Manager," *Business Horizons* 30 (March–April 1987): 7.

³⁷Michele Marchetti, "Whatever It Takes," *Sales and Marketing Management* 149 (December 1997): 28.

³⁸Ibid.

³⁹Michael R. Hyman, Robert Skipper, and Richard Tansey, "Ethical Codes Are Not Enough," *Business Horizons* (March–April 1990): 15.

⁴⁰Joseph A. Bellizzi and Robert E. Hite. "Supervising Unethical Salesforce Behavior." *Journal of Marketing* 53 (April 1989): 36.

⁴¹James A. Waters and Frederick Bird. "Attending to Ethics in Management," *Journal of Business Ethics* 8 (June 1989): 493.

⁴²Thomas R. Wotruba, "A Comprehensive Framework for the Analysis of Ethical Behavior, with a Focus on Sales Organizations," *Journal of Personal Selling and Sales Management* 10 (Spring 1990): 30.

⁴³Melinda Ligos, "Are Your Reps High?" *Sales and Marketing Management* 149 (October 1997): 80.

⁴⁴Ibid.; Andy Cohen, "Getting Personal," *Sales and Marketing Management* (May 1996): 45.

⁴⁵Thomas N. Ingram, Keun S. Lee, and George H. Lucas, Jr., "Commitment and Involvement: Assessing a Salesforce Typology," *Journal of Academy of Marketing Science* 19 (Summer 1991): 187.

⁴⁶Leslie M. Fine, C. David Shepherd, and Susan L. Josephs, "Sexual Harassment in the Sales Force: The Customer Is Not Always Right," *Journal of Personal Selling and Sales Management* 16 (Fall 1994): 15.

⁴⁷Michael Barrier, "Sexual Harassment," *Nation's Business* (December 1998): 14.

⁴⁸Julia Lawlor, "Stepping Over the Line," *Sales and Marketing Management* (October 1995): 91.

⁴⁹Barrier, "Sexual Harassment."

⁵⁰Barrier, "Sexual Harassment."

MODULE 9

¹Orville C. Walker, Jr., Gilbert A. Churchill, Jr., and Neil M. Ford, "Where Do We Go from Here? Selected Conceptual and Empirical Issues Concerning the Motivation and Performance of the Industrial Salesforce," in *Critical Issues in*

Sales Management: State-of-the-Art and Future Research Needs, ed. Gerald Albaum and Gilbert A. Churchill, Jr. (Eugene, OR: Division of Research, College of Business Administration, University of Oregon, 1979): 25.

[2]Barton A. Weitz, Harish Sujan, and Mita Sujan, "Knowledge, Motivation, and Adaptive Behavior: A Framework for Improving Selling Effectiveness," *Journal of Marketing* 50 (October 1986): 180.

[3]See Thomas R. Wotruba, "The Effect of Goal-Setting on Performance of Independent Sales Agents in Direct Selling," *Journal of Personal Selling and Sales Management* 9 (Spring 1989): 22; Jeffrey K. Sager and Mark W. Johnston, "Antecedents and Outcomes of Organizational Commitment: A Study of Salespeople," *Journal of Personal Selling and Sales Management* 9 (Spring 1989): 30.

[4]A study of salespeople that illustrates the interrelationship, yet distinctiveness, of intrinsic and extrinsic dimensions of motivation is Thomas N. Ingram, Keu S. Lee, and Steven J. Skinner, "Empirical Assessment of Salesperson Motivation, Commitment, and Job Outcomes," *Journal of Personal Selling and Sales Management* 9 (Fall 1989): 25.

[5]Jeanne Greenberg and Herbert Greenberg, *What It Takes to Succeed in Sales: Selecting and Retaining Top Producers* (Homewood, IL: Dow-Jones Irwin, 1990): 112.

[6]Judith A. Ross, "Japan: Does Money Motivate?" *Harvard Business Review* 75 (September–October 1997): 9.

[7]*Trilogy, Selling Chain Commission* brochure by the Trilogy Development Group, Austin, TX: 1997.

[8]Andy Cohen, "Off to a Quick Start," *Sales and Marketing Management* 150 (January 1998): 14.

[9]Ram C. Rao, "Compensating Heterogeneous Salesforces: Some Explicit Solutions," *Marketing Science* 9 (Fall 1990): 319.

[10]See William L. Cron, Alan J. Dubinsky, and Ronald E. Michaels. "The Influence of Career Stages on Components of Salesperson Motivation," *Journal of Marketing* 52 (January 1988): 78; Gilbert A. Churchill, Jr., Neil M. Ford, and Orville C. Walker, Jr., "Personal Characteristics of Salespeople and the Attractiveness of Alternative Rewards," *Journal of Business Research* 7 (June 1979): 25; Neil M. Ford, Gilbert A. Churchill, Jr., and Orville C. Walker, Jr., "Differences in the Attractiveness of Alternative Rewards among Salespeople: Additional Evidence," *Journal of Business Research* 13 (April 1985): 123; Thomas N. Ingram and Danny N. Bellenger, "Personal and Organizational Variables: Their Relative Effect on Reward Valences of Industrial Salespeople," *Journal of Marketing Research* 20 (May 1983): 198.

[11]Christen P. Heide, *Dartnell's 30th Sales Force Compensation Survey* (Chicago: The Dartnell Press, 1999).

[12]Aileen Crowley, "Getting a Grip on Filing T&E Paperwork: Enterprise Software Helps Streamline the Tasks of Processing Expense Reports," *PC Week* 15 (March 30, 1998): 89.

[13]Andy Cohen, "Why Some Contests Are Losers," *Sales and Marketing Management* (August 1996): 39; Thayer C. Taylor, "Selling with Sales Contests," *Sales and Marketing Management* (June 1995): 35; Andy Cohen "Motivating the Masses," *Sales and Marketing Management* (January 1996): 30; William H. Murphy and Peter A. Dacin, "Sales Contests: A Research Agenda," *Journal of Personal Selling and Sales Management* 18 (Winter 1998): 1; Melanie Berger, "When Their Ship Comes In: How to Create an Incentive Program That Motivates All of Your Salespeople and Sends More Happy Winners on That Coveted Trip," *Sales and Marketing Management* 149 (April 1997): 60.

[14]From a presentation by Ron Burke, Towers Perrin Consulting, at the New Horizons in Personal Selling and Sales Conference, July 14, 1996, Orlando, Florida.

[15]Michele Marchetti, "Regarding Team Players," *Sales and Marketing Management* (April 1996): 35.

[16]Burke, op. cit.

[17]C.K., "Joe Forster Won't Tolerate a Dry Spell," *Sales and Marketing Management* 150 (November 1998): 78.

[18]Sonke Albers, Manfred Krafft, and Wilhelm Bielert, "Global Salesforce Management: A Comparison of German and U.S. Practices," in *Emerging Trends in Sales Thought and Practice*, ed. Gerald J. Bauer, Mark S. Bauchalk, Thomas N. Ingram, and Raymond W. LaForge (Westport, CT: Quorum Books, 1998).

[19]Earl D. Honeycutt, Jr., and John B. Ford, "Guidelines for Managing an International Sales Force," *Industrial Marketing Management* (March 1995): 135.

[20]Michele Marchetti, "Paring Expatriate Pay," *Sales and Marketing Management* (January 1996): 28.

[21]Charlene Marmer Solomon, "Global Compensation: Learn the ABCs," *Personnel Journal* (July 1995): 70.

[22]Michelle Marchetti, "Basking in Their Glory," *Sales and Marketing Management* 149 (September 1997): 103.

MODULE 10

[1]For a more complete discussion of this issue, see Orville C. Walker, Jr., Gilbert A. Churchill, Jr., and Neil M. Ford, "Where Do We Go from Here? Selected Conceptual and Empirical Issues Concerning the Motivation and Performance of the Industrial Salesforce," in *Critical Issues in Sales Management: State-of-the-Art and Future Research Needs*, ed. Gerald Albaum and Gilbert A. Churchill, Jr. (Eugene, OR: University of Oregon, 1979). Also see David Cravens, Thomas Ingram, Raymond LaForge, and Clifford Young, "Behavior-Based and Outcome-Based Salesforce Control Systems." *Journal of Marketing* 57 (October 1993): 47.

[2]David W. Cravens, Thomas N. Ingram, Raymond W. LaForge, and Clifford E. Young, "Hallmarks of Effective Sales Organizations" *Marketing Management* 1 (March 1992): 56.

³Much of the discussion in this section comes from Alan J. Dubinsky and Richard W. Hansen, "The Sales Force Management Audit," *California Management Review* (Winter 1981): 86.

⁴Harold J. Novick, "The Rep Audit—Planning for the New Millennium Sales Force," *Agency Sales Magazine* 28 (April 1998): 13.

⁵George Smith, Dorris Ritter, and William Tuggle, "Benchmarking: The Fundamental Questions," *Marketing Management* 2 (1993): 43.

⁶Stanley Brown, "Measures of Perfection," *Sales and Marketing Management* 147 (May 1995): 104.

⁷C. Jackson Grayson and Carla O'Dell, "Horse and Carriage: Benchmarking and Knowledge Management," *Across the Board* 35 (April 1998): 25.

⁸Stanley Brown, "Don't Innovate—Imitate!" *Sales and Marketing Management* 147 (January 1995): 24.

⁹C. Jackson Grayson, "Benchmarking," in *Marketing Encyclopedia*, ed. Jeffrey Heilbrunn (Chicago: American Marketing Association, 1995): 324.

¹⁰Paulette Kitchen, "Sales Quality," *Sales Manager's Bulletin* 1351 (April 1995): 3.

¹¹"Benchmarking Made Easy: Benchmarking Websites," *The Public Manager: The New Bureaucrat* 27 (Summer 1998): 62.

¹²Grayson, "Benchmarking."

¹³Michael Morris, Duane Davis, Jeffrey Allen, Ramon Avila, and Joseph Chapman, "Assessing the Relationships among Performance Measures, Managerial Practices, and Satisfaction When Evaluating the Salesforce A Replication and Extension," *Journal of Personal Selling and Sales Management* 11 (Summer 1991): 25.

¹⁴Nigel F. Piercy, "The Marketing Budgeting Process: Marketing Management Implications," *Journal of Marketing* (October 1987): 45.

¹⁵For a more complete presentation of this concept, see J. S. Schiff, "Evaluate the Sales Force as a Business," *Industrial Marketing Management* 12 (1983): 131.

¹⁶Thomas Stevenson, Frank Barnes, and Sharon Stevenson, "Activity-Based Costing: An Emerging Tool for Industrial Marketing Decision Makers," *Journal of Business and Industrial Marketing* 8 (1993): 40; William M. Baker, "Understanding Activity-Based Costing," *Industrial Management* 36 (March/April 1994): 28.

¹⁷Kip R. Krumwiede, "ABC: Why It's Tried and How It Succeeds," *Management Accounting* (USA) 79 (April 1998): 32.

¹⁸Jagdish Sheth and Rajendra Sisodia, "Improving Marketing Productivity," in *Marketing Encyclopedia*, ed. Jeffrey Heilbrunn (Chicago: American Marketing Association, 1995): 217.

MODULE 11

¹Adapted from Jan P. Muczyk and Myron Gable, "Managing Sales Performance through a Comprehensive Performance Appraisal System," *Journal of Personal Selling and Sales Management* (May 1987): 41; Steven Thomas and Robert Bretz, "Research and Practice in Performance Appraisal: Evaluating Employee Performance in America's Largest Companies," *SAM Advanced Management Journal* (Spring 1994): 28.

²For more complete results, see Donald Jackson Jr., John Schlacter, and William Wolfe, "Examining the Bases Utilized for Evaluating Salespeople's Performance," *Journal of Personal Selling and Sales Management* 15 (Fall 1995): 57; William Wolfe, John Schlacter, and Donald Jackson, Jr., "Examining How Sales Managers Evaluate Their Salespeople's Performance," *National Conference in Sales Management Proceedings*, Timothy Longfellow, ed. (Normal, IL, Illinois State University, 1995): 75; Michael H. Morris and Sean R. Aten, "Sales Force Performance Appraisal: Contemporary Issues and Practices," in *Progress in Marketing Thought*, eds. L. M. Capella, H. W. Nash, J. M. Starling, and R. D. Taylor (MS: Southern Marketing Association, 1990): 413; Michael H. Morris, Duane L. Davis, Jeffrey W. Allen, Ramon A. Avila, and Joseph Chapman, "Assessing the Relationships between Performance Measures, Managerial Practices, and Satisfaction when Evaluating the Salesforce," *Journal of Personal Selling and Sales Management* (Summer 1991).

³Dana Ray, "See the Big Picture," *Personal Selling Power* (October 1995): 32.

⁴Stephen B. Knouse and David Strutton, "Molding a Total Quality Saleforce through Managing Empowerment, Evaluation, and Reward and Recognition Processes," *Journal of Marketing Theory & Practice* 4 (Summer 1996): 24; Andy Cohen, "General Electric," *Sales and Marketing Management* 149 (October 1997): 57.

⁵John Mentzer, Carol Bienstock, and Kenneth Kahn, "Benchmarking Satisfaction," *Marketing Management* 4 (Summer 1995): 41.

⁶Robert Hoffman, "Ten Reasons You Should Be Using 360-Degree Feedback," *HR Magazine* 40 (April 1995): 82; Ray, "See the Big Picture."

⁷Clive Fletcher, "Circular Argument," *People Management* 4 (October 1998): 46.

⁸David W. Bracken, Lynn Summers, and John Fleenor, "High-Tech 360," *Training & Development*, 52 (August 1998): 42.

⁹Helen Rheem, "Performance Management: A Progress Report," *Harvard Business Review* (March–April 1995): 11.

¹⁰William Fitzgerald, "Forget the Form in Performance Appraisals," *HR Magazine* 40 (December 1995): 134.

¹¹Rheem, "Performance Management."

[12] David Cravens, Raymond LaForge, Gregory Pickett, and Clifford Young, "Incorporating a Quality Improvement Perspective into Measures of Salesperson Performance," *Journal of Personal Selling and Sales Management* 13 (Winter 1993): 1.

[13] Thomas R. Wotruba, "The Transformation of Industrial Selling: Causes and Consequences," *Industrial Marketing Management* 25 (September 1996): 327.

[14] Knouse and Strutton, "Molding a Total Quality Salesforce."

[15] Lynn Metcalf, "Sales Management Practices for a New Age: Deming's Principles Applied," *National Conference in Sales Management Proceedings* (1995): 61.

[16] Paulette Kitchen, "Sales Quality," *Sales Manager's Bulletin* 1351 (April 1995): 3.

[17] For a more complete discussion and theoretical rationale for these perspectives, see Erin Anderson and Richard L. Oliver, "Perspectives on Behavior-Based versus Outcome-Based Salesforce Control Systems," *Journal of Marketing* 51 (October 1987): 76.

[18] Richard Oliver and Erin Anderson, "Behavior- and Outcome-Based Sales Control Systems: Evidence and Consequences of Pure-Form and Hybrid Governance," *Journal of Personal Selling and Sales Management* 15 (Fall 1995): 1.

[19] Douglas M. Lambert, Arun Sharma, and Michael Levy, "What Information Can Relationship Marketers Obtain from Customer Evaluation of Salespeople?" *Industrial Marketing Management* 26 (March 1997): 177.

[20] Arun Sharma and Dan Sarel, "The Impact of Customer Satisfaction–Based Incentive Systems on Salespeople's Customer Service Response: An Empirical Study," *Journal of Personal Selling and Sales Management* 15 (Summer 1995): 17.

[21] John Hill and Arthur Allaway, "How U.S.-Based Companies Manage Sales in Foreign Countries," *Industrial Marketing Management* 22 (1993): 7.

[22] Melissa Campanelli, "Rising to the Top," *Sales and Marketing Management* (April 1994): 83.

[23] Goutam Challagalla and Tasaduq Shervani, "Dimensions and Types of Supervisory Control: Effects of Salesperson Performance and Satisfaction," *Journal of Marketing* 60 (January 1996): 89.

[24] For a review and more complete discussion of this approach, see Adrian B. Ryans and Charles B. Weinberg, "Territory Sales Response," *Journal of Marketing Research* (November 1979): 453; Adrian B. Ryans and Charles B. Weinberg, "Territory Sales Response Models: Stability Over Time," *Journal of Marketing Research* (May 1987): 229.

[25] David J. Good and Robert W. Stone, "Selling and Sales Management in Action: Attitudes and Applications of Quotas by Sales Executives and Sales Managers," *Journal of Personal Selling and Sales Management* 11 (Summer 1991): 57.

[26] For specific examples of regression analysis used to establish territory sales quotas, see David W. Cravens, Robert B. Woodruff, and James C. Stamper, "An Analytical Approach for Evaluating Sales Territory Performance," *Journal of Marketing* (January 1972): 31; David W. Cravens and Robert B. Woodruff, "An Approach for Determining Criteria of Sales Performance," *Journal of Applied Psychology* (June 1973): 240.

[27] Jhinuk Chowdhury, "The Motivational Impact of Sales Quotas on Effort," *Journal of Marketing Research* 30 (February 1993): 28.

[28] Geoffrey Brewer, "Top of the Charts–Tosco," *Sales and Marketing Management* (July 1998): 32.

[29] See Mark R. Edwards, W. Theodore Cummings, and John L. Schlacter, "The Paris-Peoria Solution: Innovations in Appraising Regional and International Sales Personnel," *Journal of Personal Selling and Sales Management* (November 1984): 27.

[30] For a comprehensive scale for evaluating salesperson performance, see Douglas N. Behrman and William D. Perreault, Jr., "Measuring the Performance of Industrial Salespersons," *Journal of Business Research* 10 (1982): 355.

[31] Jim Meade, "Automated Performance Appraisal," *HR Magazine* 43 (October 1998): 42.

[32] Edwards, Cummings, and Schlacter, "The Paris-Peoria Solution," 30.

[33] For a more complete discussion of this process, see A. Benton Cocanougher and John M. Ivancevich, "BARS' Performance Rating for Sales Force Personnel," *Journal of Marketing* (July 1978): 87.

[34] Bernard Jaworski and Ajay Kohli, "Supervisory Feedback: Alternative Types and Their Impact on Salespeople's Performance and Satisfaction," *Journal of Marketing Research* 28 (May 1991): 190.

[35] Cathy Owens Swift and Constance Campbell, "The Effect of Vertical Exchange Relationships on the Performance Attributions and Subsequent Actions of Sales Managers," *Journal of Personal Selling and Sales Management* 15 (Fall 1995): 45.

[36] Thomas E. DeCarlo and Thomas W. Leigh, "Impact of Salesperson Attraction on Sales Managers' Attributions and Feedback," *Journal of Marketing* 60 (April 1996): 47.

[37] Greg Marshall, John Mowen, and Keith Fabes, "The Impact of Territory Difficulty and Self versus Other Ratings on Managerial Evaluations of Sales Personnel," *Journal of Personal Selling and Sales Management* 12 (Fall 1992): 35.

[38] Greg Marshall and John Mowen, "An Experimental Investigation of the Outcome Bias in Salesperson Performance Evaluations," *Journal of Personal Selling and Sales Management* 13 (Summer 1993): 31.

[39] Peter Allan, "Designing and Implementing an Effective Employee Appraisal System," *Review of Business* 16 (Winter 1994): 3.

[40] Robert Trent and Robert Monczka, "Guidelines for Developing Team Performance Appraisal Systems," *NAPM Insights* (July 1994): 30.

[41] Michael Campion and A. Catherine Higgs, "Design Work Teams to Increase Productivity and Satisfaction," *HR Magazine* 40 (October 1995): 101.

[42] Trent and Monczka, "Guidelines for Developing Team Performance Appraisal Systems."

[43] Profile Booklet, *Teamwork Effectiveness/Attitude Measurement (TEAM)* (New York: Education Research, 1994).

[44] Betsy Wiesendanger, "Making (and Staying on) the Team," *Selling* (April 1996): 46.

[45] For examples of these studies, see A. Parasuraman and Charles M. Futrell, "Demographics, Job Satisfaction, and Propensity to Leave of Industrial Salesmen," *Journal of Business Research* 11 (1983): 33; Charles M. Futrell and A. Parasuraman, "The Relationship of Satisfaction and Performance to Salesforce Turnover," *Journal of Marketing* (Fall 1984): 33; Steven Brown and Robert Peterson, "Antecedents and Consequences of Salesperson Job Satisfaction: Meta-Analysis and Assessment of Causal Effects," *Journal of Marketing Research* 30 (February 1993): 63; Emin Babakus, David W. Cravens, Mark Johnston, and William C. Moncrief, "Examining the Role of Organizational Variables in the Salesperson Job Satisfaction Model," *Journal of Personal Selling and Sales Management* 16 (Summer 1996): 33.

[46] For examples of this research, see Richard P. Bagozzi, "Performance and Satisfaction in an Industrial Sales Force: An Examination of Their Antecedents and Simultaneity" *Journal of Marketing* (Spring 1980): 65; Douglas N. Behrman and William D. Perreault, Jr., "A Role Stress Model of the Performance and Satisfaction of Industrial Salespersons," *Journal of Marketing* (Fall 1984): 9; Steven Brown and Robert Peterson, "The Effect of Effort on Sales Performance and Job Satisfaction," *Journal of Marketing* 58 (April 1994): 70.

[47] For a complete discussion of the scale, see Gilbert A. Churchill, Jr., Neil M. Ford, and Orville C. Walker, Jr., "Measuring the Job Satisfaction of Industrial Salesmen," *Journal of Marketing Research* (August 1974): 254. For validation support, see Charles M. Futrell. "Measurement of Salespeople's Job Satisfaction: Convergent and Discriminant Validity of Corresponding INDSALES and Job Descriptive Index Scales," *Journal of Marketing Research* (November 1979): 594; Rosemary Lagace, Jerry Goolsby, and Jule Gassenheimer, "Scaling and Measurement: A Quasi-Replicative Assessment of a Revised Version of INDSALES," *Journal of Personal Selling and Sales Management* 13 (Winter 1993): 65. See also Sarath A. Nonis and S. Altan Erdem, "A Refinement of INDSALES to Measure Job Satisfaction of Sales Personnel in General Marketing Settings," *Journal of Marketing Management* 7 (Spring/Summer 1997): 34.

[48] Futrell and Parasuraman, "Relationship of Satisfaction and Performance to Salesforce Turnover."

[49] Jaworski and Kohli, "Supervisory Feedback."

[50] Jeffrey K. Sager, Junsuab Yi, and Charles M. Futrell, "A Model Depicting Salespeople's Perceptions," *Journal of Personal Selling and Sales Management* 18 (Summer 1998): 1; Gregory A. Rich, "The Sales Manager as a Role Model: Effects on Trust, Job Satisfaction, and Performance of Salespeople," *Journal of the Academy of Marketing Science* 25 (Fall 1997): 319; Melissa Campanelli, "What Price Sales Force Satisfaction," *Sales and Marketing Management* (July 1994): 37.

[51] Melissa Campanelli, "What Price Sales Force Satisfaction."

CREDITS

MODULE 1

Exhibit 1.1: Adapted from Mark A. Moon and Gary M. Armstrong, "Selling Teams: A Conceptual Framework and Research Agenda," *Journal of Personal Selling and Sales Management,* Winter 1994, 23.

Exhibit 1.2: Adapted from William Keenan, Jr., "The Man in the Mirror," *Sales and Marketing Management,* May 1995, 95.

MODULE 2

Exhibit 2.2: Excerpted from Sales and Marketing Executives International Certified Professional Salesperson Code of Ethics (Cleveland: Sales and Marketing Executives International, 1994). Reprinted by permission of SME International at 800-999-1414.

Exhibit 2.3: *Occupational Outlook Handbook, 1998–99 ed.* (Washington, DC: U.S. Department of Labor, 1998).

MODULE 3

Exhibit 3.1: Ramon A. Avila, Thomas N. Ingram, Raymond W. LaForge, and Michael R. Williams, *The Professional Selling Skills Workbook* (Fort Worth, TX: The Dryden Press, 1996), 20.

Exhibit 3.2: Adapted from D. Forbes Ley, *The Best Seller* (Newport Beach, CA: Sales Success Press, 1986).

Exhibit 3.3: Adapted from A. J. Dubinsky, "A Factor Analytic Study of the Personal Selling Process," *Journal of Personal Selling and Sales Management* 1, no. 1 (Fall–Winter, 1980–81): 28. Used with permission.

Exhibit 3.4: Tri-State Advertising Co. Inc., Warsaw, Indiana, as printed in Tweed Robinson and Mark L. Boos, "Get 'Em while They're Hot," *Marketing Tools* (June 1996): 67.

Exhibit 3.6: John I. Coppett and William A. Staples, *Professional Selling: A Relationship Approach,* 2 ed. (Cincinnati, OH: South-Western Publishing Co., 1994): 220.

MODULE 4

Exhibit 4.2: Adapted from William Strahle and Rosann L. Spiro, "Linking Market Share Strategies to Salesforce Objectives, Activities, and Compensation Policies," *Journal of Personal Selling and Sales Management* (August 1986): 14, 15. Used with permission.

Exhibit 4.3: Adapted from William L. Cron and Michael Levy, "Sales Management Performance Evaluation: A Residual Income Perspective," *Journal of Personal Selling and Sales Management* (August 1987): 58. Used with permission.

Exhibit 4.4: David W. Cravens, Gerald E. Hills, and Robert B. Woodruff, *Marketing Management* (Homewood, IL: Irwin, 1987), 546.

Exhibit 4.5: Cyndee Miller, "Marketing Industry Report: Who's Spending What on Biz-to-Biz Marketing," *Marketing News,* January 1, 1996, 1, 7; Cyndee Miller, "Marketing Industry Report: Consumer Marketers Spend Most of Their Money on Communications," *Marketing News* (March 11): 1996, 1, 5.

Exhibit 4.6: Adapted from Michael D. Hutt and Thomas W. Speh, *Business Marketing Management* (Fort Worth, TX: The Dryden Press, 1995), 18–21.

Exhibit 4.7: David W. Cravens, Gerald E. Hills, and Robert B. Woodruff, *Marketing Management* (Homewood, IL: Irwin, 1987), 161.

Exhibit 4.10: Adapted from Harold J. Novick, "The Case for Reps vs. Direct Selling: Can Reps Do It Better?" *Industrial Marketing,* March 1982, 90–98; and "The Use of Sales Reps," *Small Business Report* (December 1986): 72–78.

Figure 4.7: Adapted from Michael D. Hutt, Wesley J. Johnston, and John R. Rouchelto, "Selling Centers and Buying Centers: Formulating Strategic Exchange Patterns," *Journal of Personal Selling and Sales Management* (May 1985): 34. Used with permission.

MODULE 5

Exhibit 5.1: Robert W. Ruekert, Orville C. Walker, Jr., and Kenneth J. Roering, "The Organization of Marketing Activities: A Contingency Theory of Structure and Performance," *Journal of Marketing* (Winter 1985): 20–21.

Figure 5.4: David W. Cravens, *Strategic Marketing* (Homewood, IL: Irwin, 1991), 541.

Figure 5.9: Adapted from Benson P. Shapiro and Rowland T. Moriarity, *National Account Management: Emerging Insights* (Cambridge, MS: Marketing Science Institute, March 1982), 6.

Figure 5.10: Adapted from Benson P. Shapiro and Rowland T. Moriarity, *Organizing the National Account Force* (Cambridge, MS: Marketing Science Institute, April 1984), 1–37.

Figure 5.13: David W. Cravens and Raymond W. LaForge, "Salesforce Deployment," in *Advances in Business Marketing*, ed. Arch G. Woodside (Greenwich, CN: JAI Press, 1986), 76.

Figure 5.14: Raymond W. LaForge, David W. Cravens, and Clifford E. Young, "Improving Salesforce Productivity," *Business Horizons*, September–October 1985, 54. Copyright 1985 by the Foundation for the School of Business at Indiana University. Reprinted by permission.

Exhibit 5.5: Raymond W. LaForge, David W. Cravens, and Clifford E. Young, "Improving Salesforce Productivity," *Business Horizons* (September/October 1985): 57.

MODULE 6

Exhibit 6.1: Excerpted from Hershey's "A Career in Sales" brochure.

Exhibit 6.2: Michael Bruce, "How to Get Better Sales Talent Through State-of-the-Art Advertising," *Personal Selling Power* 13 (March 1993): 46–47.

Exhibit 6.3: Adapted from Earl Honeycutt and John Ford, "Guidelines for Managing an International Sales Force," *Industrial Marketing Management*, 24 (March 1995): 135–144.

Exhibit 6.4: Michael Bruce, "How to Get Better Sales Talent Through State-of-the-Art Advertising," *Personal Selling Power* 13 (March 1993): 46–47; "What's Wrong with Your Recruitment Ads?" *Sales and Marketing Management* (November 1994): 50; and William H. Krause, "Advertising for Agents?" *Agency Sales Magazine* 28 (May 1998): 4–7.

Exhibit 6.5: "Interviewing the Candidate," Sales Consultants International, Inc., Cleveland, Ohio.

Exhibit 6.6: Alan J. Dubinsky, Roy D. Howell, Thomas N. Ingram, and Danny N. Bellenger, "Salesforce Socialization." Reprinted from *Journal of Marketing* 50 (October 1986): 203, published by the American Marketing Association; and Mike Delaney, "Background Checks: Five Steps Toward Compliance," *HR Focus* 74 (December 1997): S6.

MODULE 7

Exhibit 7.1: Christen P. Heide, *Dartnell's 30th Sales Force Compensation Survey* (Chicago: The Dartnell Corporation, 1999).

Exhibit 7.2: Alan J. Dubinsky and Thomas N. Ingram, "A Classification of Industrial Buyers: Implications for Sales Training," *Journal of Personal Selling and Sales Management* 2 (Fall–Winter 1981–1982): 49.

Exhibit 7.3: Andy Cohen, "Global Do's and Don'ts," *Sales and Marketing Management*, 148 (June 1996): 72.

Exhibit 7.4: Adapted from Linda Cecere, "Picking the Perfect Training Program," *Sales and Marketing Management* (July 1994): 38.

Exhibit 7.5: Robert C. Erffmeyer, K. Randall Russ, and Joseph F. Hair, Jr., "Needs Assessment and Evaluation in Sales-Training Programs," *Journal of Personal Selling and Sales Management* 11 (Winter 1991): 17–30.

Exhibit 7.6: Adapted from Alan J. Dubinsky, Marvin A. Jolson, Ronald E. Michaels, Masaaki Kotabe, and Chae Un Lim, "Ethical Perceptions of Field Sales Personnel: An Empirical Assessment," *Journal of Personal Selling and Sales Management* 12 (Fall 1992): 9–21.

MODULE 8

Exhibit 8.1: Adapted from L.B. Gschwandtner, "Personal PR Strategies for Creating Power and Influence," *Personal Selling Power* (October 1990): 20.

Figure 8.2: ExecuCall Incorporated, Cincinnati, Ohio. Used with permission.

Exhibit 8.2: Compiled from Barry J. Farber, "Sales Managers: Do Yourself a Favor," *Personal Selling Power* April 1990, 33; "First Train Them, Then Coach Them," *Sales and Marketing Management* (August 1987): 54–65; Stuart R. Levine, "Performance Coaching," *Selling Power* (July/August 1996): 46; and Bill Cates, "A Coach for all Reasons," *Selling Power* (June 1996): 64–65.

Exhibit 8.3: Compiled from Rayna Skolnik, "Salespeople Sound Off on Meetings," *Sales and Marketing Management*, November 1987, 108; and Hank Trisler, "Million Dollar Meetings," *Selling Power* (March 1996): 66–67.

Exhibit 8.4: "Six Secrets to Holding a Good Meeting," furnished by 3M Visual Systems Division. Reproduced by permission of and copyrighted by Minnesota Mining and Mfg. Co.

Exhibit 8.5: Archie B. Carroll, "In Search of the Moral Manager," *Business Horizons* 30 (March–April 1987): 12. Copyright 1987 by the Foundation for the School of Business at Indiana University. Reprinted by permission.

Exhibit 8.6: Adapted from James A. Waters and Frederick Bird, "Attending to Ethics in Management," *Journal of Business Ethics* 8 (June 1989): 494.

Exhibit 8.7: Donald J. Moine and Gerhard Gschwandter, "How to Manage the 7 Most Difficult (but Promising) Sales Personalities," *Personal Selling Power*, 15th Anniversary Issue (1995), 71.

MODULE 9

Exhibit 9.1: Compiled from two studies: Thomas N. Ingram and Danny N. Bellenger, "Personal and Organizational Variables: Their Relative Effect on Reward Valences of Industrial Salespeople," *Journal of Marketing Research* 20 May 1983): 198–205; and Neil M. Ford,

Gilbert A. Churchill, Jr., and Orville C. Walker, Jr., "Differences in the Attractiveness of Alternative Rewards Among Industrial Salespeople: Additional Evidence," *Journal of Business Research* 13 (April 1985): 123–138. Another study confirmed pay as salespeople's most preferred reward, but did not provide rankings of alternative rewards. This study is: Lawrence B. Chonko, John F. Tanner, and William A. Weeks, "Selling and Sales Management in Action: Reward Preferences of Salespeople," *Journal of Personal Selling and Sales Management* 12 (Summer 1992): 67–75.

Exhibit 9.2: Christen P. Heide, *Dartnell's 30th Sales Force Compensation Survey* (Chicago: The Dartnell Corporation, 1999), 43.

Exhibit 9.4: Amiya K. Basu, Rajiv Lal, V. Srinivasan, and Richard Staelin, "Salesforce Compensation Plans: An Agency Theoretic Perspective," *Marketing Science* 4 (Fall 1985): 270. Reprinted by permission. Copyright 1985, The Institute of Management Sciences and the Operations Research Society of America.

Exhibit 9.6: Christen P. Heide, *Dartnell's 30th Sales Force Compensation Survey* (Chicago: The Dartnell Corporation, 1999), 121.

Exhibit 9.7: Gene Garofalo, *Sales Manager's Desk Book* (Englewood Cliffs, NJ: Prentice-Hall, 1989), 128.

MODULE 10

Figure 10.1: Adapted from David Cravens, Thomas Ingram, Raymond LaForge, and Clifford Young, "Behavior-based and Outcome-based Salesforce Control Systems," *Journal of Marketing* 57 (October 1993): 47–59.

Figure 10.2: © 1981 by the Regents of the University of California. Adapted from Alan J. Dubinsky and Richard W. Hansen, "The Sales Force Management Audit," *California Management Review* (Winter 1981): 87, by permission of The Regents.

Exhibit 10.1: © 1981 by the Regents of the University of California. Reprinted from Alan J. Dubinsky and Richard W. Hansen, "The Sales Force Management Audit," *California Management Review* (Winter 1981): 90, by permission of The Regents.

Exhibit 10.2: Gary Beasley and Joseph Cook, "The 'What,' 'Why,' and 'How' of Benchmarking," *Agency Sales Magazine* 25 (June 1995): 52–56.

Figure 10.3: Adapted from George Smith, Dorris Ritter, and William Tuggle, "Benchmarking: The Fundamental Question," *Marketing Management* 2 (1993); 43–48.

Exhibit 10.3: Adapted from Michael Morris, Duane Davis, Jeffrey Allen, Ramon Avila, and Joseph Chapman, "Assessing the Relationships among Performance Measures, Managerial Practices, and Satisfaction When Evaluating the Salesforce: A Replication and Extension," *Journal of Personal Selling and Sales Management* 11 (Summer 1991): 25–36.

Exhibit 10.7: Christen P. Heide, *Dartnell's 30th Sales Force Compensation Survey* (Chicago: The Dartnell Corporation, 1999).

Exhibit 10.11: Robin Cooper and Robert S. Kaplan, "Measure Costs Right: Make the Right Decisions," *Harvard Business Review* 66 (September/October 1988): 96–103.

MODULE 11

Exhibit 11.1: Adapted from Allan Church, "First-Rate Multirater Feedback," *Training and Development* 49 (August 1995): 42–43; and Scott Wimer and Kenneth M. Nowack, "13 Common Mistakes Using 360-Degree Feedback," *Training & Development* 52 (May 1998): 69–78.

Exhibit 11.2: Adapted from Erin Anderson and Richard L. Oliver, "Perspectives on Behavior-based versus Outcome-based Salesforce Control Systems," *Journal of Marketing* 51 (October 1987): 86, published by the American Marketing Association.

Exhibit 11.3: David Cravens, Thomas Ingram, Raymond LaForge, and Clifford Young, "Behavior-based and Outcome-based Salesforce Control Systems," *Journal of Marketing* 57 (October 1993): 47–59; and Richard Oliver and Erin Anderson, "An Empirical Test of the Consequences of Behavior- and Outcome-based Sales Control Systems," *Journal of Marketing* 58 (October 1994): 53–67.

Exhibit 11.4: Donald Jackson, Jr., John Schlacter, and William Wolfe, "Examining the Bases Utilized for Evaluating Salespeople's Performance," *Journal of Personal Selling and Sales Management* 15 (Fall 1995): 57–65.

Exhibit 11.5: Donald Jackson, Jr., John Schlacter, and William Wolfe, "Examining the Bases Utilized for Evaluating Salespeople's Performance," *Journal of Personal Selling and Sales Management* 15 (Fall 1995): 57–65.

Exhibit 11.6: Donald Jackson, Jr., John Schlacter, and William Wolfe, "Examining the Bases Utilized for Evaluating Salespeople's Performance," *Journal of Personal Selling and Sales Management* 15 (Fall 1995): 57–65.

Figure 11.2: Raymond W. LaForge and David W. Cravens, "A Market Response Model for Sales Management Decision Making," *Journal of Personal Selling and Sales Management* (Fall/Winter 1981–1982): 14. Used with permission.

Exhibit 11.7: Adapted from Adrian B. Ryans and Charles B. Weinberg, "Territory Sales Response Models: Stability Over Time," *Journal of Marketing Research* (May 1987): 231, published by the American Marketing Association.

Exhibit 11.8: David J. Good and Robert W. Stone, "Selling and Sales Management in Action: Attitudes and Applications of Quotas by Sales Executives and Sales Managers," *Journal of Personal Selling and Sales Management* 11 (Summer 1991): 57–60.

Exhibit 11.9: Donald Jackson, Jr., John Schlacter, and William Wolfe, "Examining the Bases Utilized for Evaluating Salespeople's Performance," *Journal of Personal Selling and Sales Management* 15 (Fall 1995): 57–65.

Exhibit 11.10: Adapted from Mark R. Edwards, W. Theodore Cummings, and John L. Schlacter, "The Paris-Peoria Solution: Innovations in Appraising Regional and International Sales Personnel," *Journal of Personal Selling and Sales Management* (November 1984): 29. Used with permission.

Exhibit 11.12: Jan P. Muczyk and Myron Gable, "Managing Sales Performance Through a Comprehensive Performance Appraisal System," *Journal of Personal Selling and Sales Management* (May 1987): 46. Used with permission.

Exhibit 11.13: Eastman Chemical Company, "checking customer value through continual improvement" survey.

Exhibit 11.14: Adapted from Mark R. Edwards, W. Theodore Cummings, and John L. Schlacter, "The Paris-Peoria Solution: Innovations in Appraising Regional and International Sales Personnel," *Journal of Personal Selling and Sales Management* (November 1984): 31. Used with permission.

Figure 11.15: A. Benton Cocanougher and John M. Ivancevich, "BARS' Performance Rating for Sales Force Personnel." Reprinted from *Journal of Marketing* 42 (July 1978): 91, published by the American Marketing Association.

Exhibit 11.16: Adapted from Peter Allan, "Designing and Implementing an Effective Employee Appraisal System," *Review of Business* 16 (Winter 1994): 3–8; Minda Zetlin, "How to Avoid Lawsuits," *Sales and Marketing Management* (December 1994): 86.

Exhibit 11.17: *Profile Booklet, Teamwork Effectiveness/Attitude Measurement (TEAM)* (New York, NY: Education Research, 1994). Reprinted with permission from Education Research, N.Y. Tel.: 212-661-9280. FAX: 212-953-5899.

Exhibit 11.18: James M. Comer, Karen A. Machleit, and Rosemary R. Lagace, "Psychometric Assessment of a Reduced Version of INDSALES," *Journal of Business Research* 18 (1989): 295–296.

COMPANY INDEX

A&P, 350
ABC Enterprises, 71
Abrahams Group, 414
ACCO World Corporation, 178
AchieveGlobal, 185
Acme Computers, 309
Adams Brands, 349–353
ADP, 178
ALC Communications Corporation, 213
American Airlines, 32
American Express Company, 223, 224, 395
American Express Financial Advisors (Amex), 48–49
American Ford, 17
American Productivity and Quality Center, 254
America Online (AOL), 67–68, 70, 72
Apple, 96
Applied Materials, 184–185
Armstrong World Industries, 183
Arthur Andersen LLP, 254
AT&T, 27, 205, 254, 282, 327, 332
AT&T's Middle Markets Division, 9
Atlantic Packaging Products Ltd., 88
Avon, 229

Barneys, 57
Barro Stickney Inc. (BSI), 346–349
Beauty Glow Cosmetics Company, 273
Beckers, 350
Beecham Products, U.S.A., 26
BellSouth, 186
The Benchmarking Network, 254
Best Practices, 254
Bickford Publishing, 311
Biomod, Inc., 62–63
BI Performance Services, 279
Boise Cascade Office Products, 1
Brennan Communications, 55, 56
Bryan Associates, Inc. (BAI), 275
Burlington Industries, 218
Businessland Computers, Inc., 307, 308

Caliper, 161
Calvin Klein, 57
Canadian Appliance Manufacturing Co. Ltd. (CAMCO), 377
Canadian General Electric (C.G.E.), 377
Catalyst, Inc., 27
Centurion Specialty Care, 45
Century 21 People Services Reality, 12
Century Maintenance Supply, 202, 205
Chemical Bank, 162
Chrysler, 411

Cisco Systems, 84
Coca-Cola, 211, 411
Combustion Engineering, 204
Compusystems, Inc., 192–193
Courtyard, 6

Dartnell Corporation, 234
Dealer Truck Accessory Warehouse (DTAW) 249–251
Denman Industrial Products, 401–407
Diamant Boart, 265
Dictaphone, Inc., 148
Digital River, 27
Dow Chemical, 139
DP-Americas (DP-A), 410–411
DP Britain (DP-UK), 410
DP France (DPF), 410
DP Germany (DPG), 410
DP International, 408–410, 412, 414–415
Dunn Corporation, 385–386
Du Pont, 69, 77, 211, 254
Dura-plast, Inc., 407–417
DXI, 7

Eastman Chemical Company, 254, 291, 439
Eastman Kodak, 226, 254
Eatons, 380, 383
EDS, 96
Edward Jones, 145–146, 150
EFAX, 23
Effem, 350
Entergy Utility, 275–276
EPR, 252
Ernst & Young, 5

Fairfield Inns, 5
Federated Cooperative, 380
FedEx, 279
Firestone, 380
FirstEnergy, 204, 234
Fisher Scientific International, 10
Floor-Shine Cleaning Products, 245–246
Food City, 350
Ford, 7, 254, 411
The Forum Corporation, 32, 183
Franklin Key Electronics, 346–347
Frito-Lay, 25, 185
Frontier Corporation, 205
FSC Securities, 392, 393–394
Fuji, 32

Gallup, Inc., 158
GE Capital Services, 5, 184
General Electric, 7, 183, 254, 278

General Electric Appliances, 377–385
General Foods, 211
General Investment and Development (GID), 363–364
General Mills, 28
General Motors, 411
General Motors Service Parts Operation (GMSPO), 7–8
General Steel Wares Ltd. (G.S.W.), 377
GEONAV, 57
George F. Cram Company, 39
Global Enterprise, 221–222

Harcourt College Publishing, 106, 118
Herman Miller, 31, 85
Hershey Chocolate U.S.A., 148, 150
Hewlett-Packard Company, 27, 139, 208, 254
Hill and Knowlton, 202
Holophane Corporation, 9
Hongkong and Shanghai Banking Corporation (HSBC), 369–377
Hormel Foods Corporation, 255, 265
Hospital Supply International (HSI), 337–342
Hudson's Bay, 380

IBM, 81–82, 163, 183, 186, 226, 254, 282
IDS Financial Services, 391–400
Induplicate Copiers, Inc., 273–274
Integrated Resources (IR), 392, 393
Intel, 173
Intel's Business Conferencing Group, 9–10
International Data Corporation (IDC), 239–240
International Enterprises, 269

JBL Transport, 57
Johnson Control's Automotive Systems Group (ASG), 6

Kmart, 350, 380
K/P Corporation, 279
KXKT-FM, 223, 237

Labels Express, 304
Landnet, 23
Lands' End, 173
Lea-Meadows Industries, 336
Learning International, 183
Lexus Company, 342, 344–345
LLC, 254
Lloyds Bank Canada, 369–370
Loblaws, 350

Lotus Notes, 211
Lucent Technologies, 27, 45, 49
Lunsford Electronics, 123

McDonald Supply, 380, 383
McKinsey & Company, 395
Marley Cooling Tower, 86
Marriott, 6
Mary Kay Cosmetics, 229
Massachusetts Mutual Life Insurance, 186
MCI, 205
MCI Vision, 322–336
MCI WorldCom Advanced Networks, 11
Merrell Dow Pharmaceutical, 88
Merrill Lynch (ML), 392–393
Mervyn's, 55–56
Midland Bank of Canada, 369
Milliken, 254
Milwaukee Zoo, 211
Mine Safety Appliances, 238–239
Minnesota Mining and Mfg. Co., 437
Modern Plastics, 387–391
Morgantown Inc., 336–337
Motorola, 186, 254
Mutual of New York (MONY), 394

Nabisco, 173, 187
Nalco, 8–9
National Communications Manufacturing, 94
National Semiconductor, 84
Nation's Carriers, 308
NBC, 177
Netserve, 23
NIBCO, Inc., 185–186
Nike, 158
Northway Corporation, 414, 417
Northwestern Mutual Life, 156, 211
Norwegian Thorton Group, 408
Noxell Corporation, 183

Oakmaster Furniture Inc., 304–305
Opti-Tax Consulting (OTC), 128–129
Oscar Mayer, 203
Overhead Distribution Transformer Division (OHDT) [Westinghouse], 354–359

Pepsi, 411
Performax Inc., 186
Pfizer Animal Health Care, 140
Pfizer Pharmaceuticals, 5
Pinacor, 95–96, 100
Pitney Bowes Office Systems, 238, 281
Plastico Inc., 63–64
Polyethylene Division of Atlantic Packaging Products Ltd., 88
Pronto Retail Center, 93
Protek Packaging, Inc., 127–128
Prudential HMO, 155
Prudential Insurance Company of America, 212

Raleigh USA Bicycle Company, 171–172
RE/MAX International, Inc., 148, 183–184
Reynolds & Reynolds Automotive Products Group, 17
Ricoh Corporation, 139, 184
Ritz-Carlton, 6
Royal Corporation, 309–318
Royal Reproduction Center (RRC), 311
Rubbermaid, 411

Saks Fifth Avenue, 57
Sales Consultants, 155
Sales Staffers International, 155
SALESworld, 155
Samuel Jones Ltd., 360
SAS Institute, 197–198
SC Commission, 230
Schein Pharmaceutical, Inc., 149, 152, 210, 289
Scott, 32
Scottsdale Plaza Resort, 239
Scottsker Inc., 231
7-Eleven, 350
Shachihata Inc., 88
Shopper's Drug Mart, 350, 351
SkillSearch, 157
Solutions Software, Inc., 192
Sony, 32
The Southwestern Company, 22
Specialty Chemicals, 87
Sprint, 205, 327

Stalwart Industrial Products, 245
STI International, 171
Sun Microsystems Computer Company, 186
Sweet-Treats, Inc., 168–169

Tasti-Fresh Bakery Products, 221
Techno Plastics, Inc., 407–408, 414–417
Texas Nameplate Company (TNC), 7
Thompson & Associates, 87
3M, 177, 437
Tickton Flexible Products Ltd., 360
Tickton-Jones Ltd., 360–362
Titan Industries, 169–170
Topnotch Investment Company (TICO), 319–321
Toronto-Dominion Bank, 417–423
Towers and Zellers, 350
Trilogy Development Group, 230
Tri-State Advertising Co. Inc., 436
Tupperware, 229, 411

Ultimo, 57
Universal Internet Services, 98
U.S. Learning Inc., 183

Visual AccountMate SQL, 249
Volume Independent Purchasers (V.I.P.), 380

Warner-Lambert, Inc., 349
Westinghouse Electric Corporation, 354–359
Whirlpool, 7
White Consolidated Industries Ltd., 377
White-Westinghouse, 377
Wilson Learning Corporation, 186
Windsor Management Company, 363–369
Wonderlic Personnel Test, Inc., 156–157
Woodwards, 383
Worderlic Personnel Test, Inc., 161

Xerox, 7, 32, 183, 226, 254, 278

YourWay, 29

NAME INDEX

Adams, Michael, 424
Albaum, Gerald, 432
Albers, Sonke, 432
Allan, Peter, 435, 439
Allaway, Arthur, 434
Allen, Jeffrey W., 433, 438
Allison, Peggy, 250
Anderson, Erin, 434, 438
Apple, Sandy, 14, 175, 178
Arizonia, Roger, 342
Armstrong, Gary M., 424, 436
Armstrong, J. Scott, 426
Aten, Sean R., 433
Avila, Ramon A., 426, 430, 433, 436, 438
Avila, Stephen, 430

Babakus, Emin, 424, 425, 430, 435
Bannister, Ken, 349
Bachler, Christopher J., 428
Bagozzi, Richard P., 430, 435
Baitch, Daniel B., 425
Baker, William M., 433
Baran, Jean-Pierre, 417
Barash, Mark, 427
Barclay, Donald W., 417
Bargerstock, Andy, 427
Barnes, John W., 431
Barrett, Mark F., 425
Barrier, Michael, 431
Barr, Larry, 377–380, 381, 383
Barro, John, 346
Barnes, Frank, 433
Bass, Ken, 430
Basu, Amiya K., 438
Bates, Charlton, 337
Bauchalk, Mark S., 432
Bauer, Gerald J., 432
Baxter, Robert, 388
Bearden, Terry, 123
Beasley, Gary, 438
Beccia, Toni-Marie, 223
Behrman, Douglas N., 434, 435
Bellenger, Danny N., 387, 428, 430, 432, 437
Bellizzi, Joseph A., 431
Bell, Michael, 424
Bemis, Carol, 17
Benassi, Gene, 31
Berger, Melanie, 429, 432
Bernhardt, Kenneth L., 387
Bielert, Wilhelm, 432
Bird, Frederick, 431, 437
Birdseye, Meg, 427
Black, William C., 428
Blackwood, Francy, 425, 426, 430

Blake, Paul, 315
Block, Ken, 381
Boedecker, Karl A., 430
Bond, David, 369, 370, 377
Bond, James T., 427
Bonoma, Thomas V., 391
Boos, Mark L., 436
Bott, John, 336, 337
Bracken, David W., 433
Brennan, Gregory, 55–56
Bretz, Robert, 433
Brewer, Geoffrey, 434
Brodie, Roderick J., 426
Brown, Bob, 343
Brown, Gene, 428
Brown, John, 165, 315
Brown, Stanley, 433
Brown, Steven P., 425, 435
Bruce, Michael, 437
Bryant, Joel, 427
Burger, Warren, 425
Burke, Ron, 432
Bursk, Edward C., 424
Busch, Paul, 430
Bush, Alan J., 430
Bush, Victoria Davies, 425, 429

Caballero, Marjorie J., 424
Cadbury, Sir Adrian, 431
Campanelli, Melissa, 434, 435
Campbell, Constance, 434
Campbell, Malcolm, 68, 426
Campbell, Tricia, 424, 426
Campion, Michael, 435
Canham, David, 95
Cannon, Joe, 416
Capella, L. M., 433
Carey, John, 14, 106, 118
Carey, Robert, 427
Carroll, Archie B., 431, 437
Castleberry, Stephen B., 429
Cates, Bill, 437
Cecere, Linda, 437
Cespedes, Frank V., 322
Cestra, Alicia, 417
Chabrow, Eric R., 427
Challagalla, Goutam, 434
Chambers, Martha, 315
Chao, Georgia, 427
Chapman, Joseph, 433, 438
Chonko, Lawrence B., 429, 438
Chowdhury, Jhinuk, 434
Churchill, Gilbert A., Jr., 429, 431, 432, 435, 438
Churchill, Wendy, 361

Church, Allan, 438
Clampitt, Jane Hrehocik, 14, 69, 77
Clark, Charles T., 426
Claxton, John D., 377
Clayton, Jim, 387, 388, 391
Cleave, James H., 376
Clopton, Douglas, 14, 49, 148, 150
Cocanougher, A. Benton, 434, 439
Cohen, Andy, 180, 425, 426, 430, 431, 432, 433, 437
Cohen, Lydia, 352
Cohn, Joel, 275
Cole-Gomolski, Barb, 427
Comer, James M., 31, 430, 439
Conrad, Blake, 45
Cook, Chris J., 376
Cook, Joseph, 438
Cook, Mary F., 427
Cooke, Ernest F., 428
Cooper, Martha C., 428
Cooper, Robin, 438
Coppett, John I., 436
Corcoran, Kevin J., 425
Corvino, Paul, 67
Courtney, David, 360, 361–362
Cox, James E., Jr., 427
Crane, Jonathan, 327
Cravens, David W., 424, 425, 426, 430, 432, 434, 435, 436, 437, 438
Crittenden, William F., 430
Cronin, Mary J., 431
Cron, William L., 430, 431, 432, 436
Crosby, Lawerence A., 431
Crowley, Aileen, 432
Crum, 319
Cullens, Theresa, 202
Cummings, W. Theodore, 434, 439

Dacin, Peter A., 432
Dalrymple, 319
Dalton, William R. P., 376
Daniels, Scott, 424
Darmon, Rene, 427
Davis, Duane L., 433, 438
Dawson, Lyndon E., Jr., 425
Deal, Larry, 357, 359
DeCarlo, Thomas E., 434
Deighton, John, 391
Delaney, Mike, 164
Dellecave, Tom, Jr., 426
Desman, Robert, 424
DiCarlo, Franco, 57–58, 426
Dickinson, Roger A., 424
Dilenschneider, Robert, 202
DiMonti, Jerry, 12

443

Name Index

Dix, Ian, 329
Dolan, Stan, 342
Dominy, Robert M., 363, 364, 365, 366–368
Dover, Roger, 343
Doyle, Stephen X., 337
Drucker, Peter, 22
Drumwright, Minette E., 391
Dubinsky, Alan J., 31, 428, 429, 430, 431, 432, 433, 436, 437, 438
Dubois, Bill, 415
Duffy, Charles, 337–338
Duke, Rachel, 42
Duval, Michel, 417

Edwards, Mark R., 434, 439
Ellin, Abby, 429
Elnes, Conrad, 171
Emily, John, 343
Engel, Hank, 427
Engemann, Kurt, 337
Enrico, Ron, 341–342
Erdem, S. Altan, 435
Erffimeyer, Robert C., 429, 430, 437
Erlandsen, Torger, 409, 416
Eroglu, Sevo, 31, 425
Evans, Elaine, 431

Fabes, Keith, 434
Farber, Barry J., 437
Farr, Cana, 366
Faulds, Mary, 71
Favre, Brett, 211
Feild, Hubert, 428
Fine, Leslie M., 431
Fiorina, Carly, 27
Fisher, John, 352–353
Fitzgerald, Kate, 424
Fitzgerald, Kevin R., 315, 318–319, 425
Fitzgerald, William, 433
Fleenor, John, 433
Fleschner, Malcolm, 17, 425, 430
Fletcher, Clive, 433
Flores, Benito E., 427
Flynn, Gillian, 429
Ford, John B., 432, 437
Ford, Neil M., 429, 431, 432, 435, 437
Ford, Terri, 332, 336
Foster, Richard, 415
Francis, Jim, 370–371
French, John, Jr., 430
Frerichs, George R., 425
Frost, Mike, 428
Futrell, Charles M., 428, 435

Gable, Myron, 433, 439
Galinsky, Ellen, 427
Gardner, Philip, 427
Garofalo, Gene, 438
Gassenheimer, Jule, 435
Gatewood, Robert, 428
Gellerman, Saul W., 431
Georgoff, David M., 426

Gilkison, Chris, 145
Glass, Chris, 198
Goldstein, Bob, 314
Golub, Harvey, 392, 395, 397
Good, David J., 434, 438
Goode, Laura, 322
Goodrich, Jonathan N., 319
Goolsby, Jerry, 435
Gordon, Howard L., 425
Graham, Joan, 366–367
Grant, E. Stephen, 430
Grant, Ken, 424, 425
Grayson, C. Jackson, 433
Greenberg, Herbert M., 31, 32, 226, 425, 427, 432
Greenberg, Jeanne, 31, 32, 226, 425, 427, 432
Gschwandter, Gerhard, 437
Gschwandter, L. B., 431, 437
Gwinner, Robert F., 425

Hair, Joseph F., Jr., 437
Handel, Jean, 415, 417
Hansen, Richard W., 429, 433, 438
Hanson, Bill, 387, 391
Harrison, Jared F., 429
Hart, Herb, 171
Hartley, Steven W., 429
Hartline, Michael D., 426
Hawes, Jon M., 424, 425, 428, 430
Hawkins, Ron, 23
Haygood, J. Martin, 425
Head, Robert, 385–386
Heartfield, James, 428
Heffel, Jerry, 14, 22
Heide, Christen P., 429, 432, 437, 438
Heilbrunn, Jeffrey, 433
Heilman, Madeline E., 431
Heil, Mark, 347
Heiman, Stephen E., 20
Hennessey, H. David, 309, 363
Hequet, Marc, 429
Higgs, A. Catherine, 435
Hill, John S., 427, 434
Hill, Ned C., 429
Hills, Gerald E., 436
Hite, Robert E., 431
Hitz, Colleen McCoy, 223–224
Hodges, Glynn, 357
Hoffman, Robert, 433
Hollander, Stanley C., 424
Hollingworth, Bryan, 39–40
Honeycutt, Earl D., Jr., 427, 429, 432, 437
Hoover, Florence, 338, 341
Horner, Jill, 185
Hornstein, Harvey, 431
House, David, 223
Howell, Roy D., 428, 430, 437
Howe, Vince, 429
Hoyt, Charles W., 19, 424
Hughes, J. R., 389
Hughes, Resse, 343

Hunt, James B., 430
Hupp, Dan E., 430
Husner, Steve, 308
Huthchens, Stephen P., 430
Hutt, Michael D., 426, 436
Hyman, Michael R., 431

Ingram, Thomas N., 387, 424, 425, 426, 428, 429, 430, 431, 432, 436, 437, 438
Inks, Scott, 430
Ivancevich, John M., 434, 439

Jackson, Donald W., Jr., 431, 433, 438, 439
Jackson, Ron, 57
Jaworski, Bernard, 434, 435
Jenkner, Rick, 377
Jensen, Kim, 427
Joachimsthaler, Erich A., 430
Johnson, Barbara, 87
Johnson, Dale A., 429, 430
Johnston, Mark W., 428, 430, 432, 435
Johnston, Wesley J., 428, 436
Jolson, Marvin A., 430, 437
Jones, Ben, 360
Jones, Marvin, 356
Jones, Mary, 309–315, 318–319
Josephs, Susan L., 431
Joyner, Barrett, 197–198

Kahn, Kenneth B., 427
Kahn, Robert M., 430
Kalunian, Barbara, 309
Kandola, Binna, 428
Kaplan, Robert S., 438
Kaydo, Chad, 426, 427, 428, 429, 431
Keenan, William, Jr., 427, 429, 436
Keith, Janet E., 431
Kelley, William T., 424
Kelly, Robert J., 424, 427
Kelly, Terry, 23
Kennedy, John R., 369
Kerin, Roger A., 336
Kern, Richard, 428
Kim, Jay S., 430
King, Ronald, 428
Kitchen, Paulette, 433, 434
Klein, Howard J., 427, 430
Klein, Robert, 429
Knouse, Stephen B., 433, 434
Kohli, Ajay K., 431, 434, 435
Kotabe, Masaaki, 430, 437
Kowalczyk, Charlie, 14, 238, 281
Krafft, Manfred, 432
Krause, William H., 437
Krumwiede, Kip R., 433

Labriola, Don, 424
LaForge, Raymond W., 424, 425, 426, 432, 434, 436, 437, 438
Lagace, Rosemary R., 430, 435, 439
Lal, Rajiv, 438
Lambert, Charles, 29, 30

Lambert, Douglas M., 434
Langan, Tony, 346
Langrehr, Frederick W., 425
Lawlor, Julia, 427, 431
Lee, Keun S., 431, 432
Leigh, Thomas W., 425, 434
Levine, Stuart R., 437
Levitt, Theodore, 55, 426
Levy, Michael, 434, 436
Levy, Sidney J., 425
Ley, D. Forbes, 436
Liebeskind, Ken, 424
Ligos, Melinda, 424, 429, 431
Lim, Chae Un, 430, 437
Little, John, 385–386
Lockhart, Anthony, 14, 204, 234
Loewe, Doug, 11–12
Loman, Willy (fictional character), 28
Longfellow, Timothy, 433
Lorge, Sarah, 429, 430
Lucas, George H., Jr., 431
Lumpkin, James R., 430
Luthy, Michael R., 404, 407
Lynch, Brian, 343

Machleit, Karen A., 439
Mackenzie, John, 211
Mahmoud, Essam, 427
Malhotra, Naresh, 427
Mangold, Fred, 123
Manrodt, Karl B., 426
Marchetti, Michele, 145, 224, 424, 425, 427, 428, 429, 431, 432
Marshall, Greg W., 428, 434
Martin, Warren S., 424
Maschuzik, John, 28
Mast, Kenneth E., 425
Mathews, Royal, 417
Maurice, Samuel J., 428
McDougall, Gordon, 349
McGowan, William, 323, 325, 327
McGraff, Gary, 342, 344
McGraw, Patrick F., 425
McIntyre, Shelby, 426
McKenzie, Frank, 57
McNeilly, Kevin M., 430
Meade, Jim, 434
Mentzer, John T., 427
Messmer, Max, 427
Metcalf, Lynn, 434
Michaels, Ronald E., 430, 432, 437
Millar, Scott, 415
Miller, Arthur, 28
Miller, Cyndee, 426, 436
Millman, Tony, 360
Mitchell, L. A., 14, 45, 49
Moine, Donald J., 437
Moncrief, William C., 430, 435
Monczka, Robert, 435
Moon, Mark A., 424, 436
Moore, Barry, 353
Moore, Jesse N., 428
Moore, Phil, 343

Moorman, Martin, 336, 337
Morgan, Fred W., 430
Moriarity, Rowland T., 426, 436
Morris, Michael H., 433, 438
Mourton, Maurice R., 376
Mowen, John, 434
Muczyk, Jan P., 433, 439
Mulich, Joe, 429
Munson, Michael, 146, 427, 428
Murdick, Robert G., 426
Murphy, William H., 432

Nash, H. W., 433
Nonis, Sarath A., 435
Novick, Harold J., 433, 436
Nowack, Kenneth M., 438

O'Dell, Carla, 433
O'Leary-Kelly, Anne, 427
Oliver, Richard L., 434, 438
Oliver, Ryan, 407, 416
Oliver, Von, 1, 2, 14
Olsen, Peter, 415
Olson, Eric M., 426
O'Meara, Charles, 53
O'Neil, Tim, 17
Ouellette, Tim, 427

Paley, Norton, 427
Panko, Ron, 428
Parasuraman, A., 428, 435
Parker, Tom, 407–408, 413, 416–417
Patterson, John H., 19
Patton, W. E., III, 428
Pelton, Lou E., 430
Perreault, William D., Jr., 434, 435
Perry, Tony, 311, 312
Petersen, Laura K., 425
Peterson, Robert, 435
Peterson, Robin T., 427
Pettijohn, Charles E., 425
Pfaff, Bill, 307
Philips, Ken, 380
Pickett, Gregory, 434
Piercy, Nigel F., 433
Pillai, Rajnandini, 425
Pilling, Bruce K., 31, 425
Pitesti, Romano, 360–362
Plato, 18
Pollay, Richard W., 377
Porter, Michael E., 426
Powell, Terry E., 424
Powers, Thomas L., 424
Pritchard, Carl L., 430

Query, Jerry, 318, 319

Randall, E. James, 428
Randazzo, Steve, 14, 210, 289
Rao, Ram C., 432
Rasmusson, Erika, 172, 427, 429
Rathmell, John M., 424
Raven, Bertram, 430

Ray, Bob, 354, 356–357, 359
Ray, Dana, 40, 425, 433
Rheem, Helen, 433
Rice, Gillian, 427
Rich, Gregory A., 431, 435
Ridnour, Rick E., 429
Ritter, Dorris, 433, 438
Robinson, Tweed, 436
Roering, Kenneth J., 426, 436
Ronning, Joel, 27
Rose, Keith, 341
Ross, Judith A., 432
Rouchelto, John R., 436
Royal, Weld, 428
Ruekert, Robert W., 426, 436
Rushing, Hugh, 424
Russ, Frederick A., 430
Russ, K. Randall, 437
Ryans, Adrian B., 434, 438

Sager, Jeffrey K., 428, 432, 435
Salsbury, George B., 428
Sanders, Nada R., 426
Sandlund, Chris, 424
Santoro, Richard, 329
Sarel, Dan, 434
Sauers, Daniel A., 430
Saunders, Reed, 391, 398
Schiff, J. S., 433
Schlacter, John L., 433, 434, 438, 439
Schwartz, Susana, 428
Schwepker, Charles H., Jr., 425, 426
Scott, Jim, 9
Scott, Randy, 44
Sevan, Stefan, 415
Shannon, Joe, 171, 172
Shapiro, Benson P., 426, 436
Sharma, Arun, 425, 434
Sharp, Edward, 341
Shepherd, C. David, 428, 429, 431
Sherman, Bob, 17
Shervani, Tasaduq, 434
Sheth, Jagdish, 433
Shore, Gary, 417, 421–422
Siguaw, Judy A., 427
Simpson, Jack, 360, 361
Sisodia, Rajendra, 433
Skinner, Steven J., 432
Skipper, Robert, 431
Skolnik, Rayna, 437
Slocum, John W., Jr., 431
Smith, Bob, 218
Smith, Debbie, 11
Smith, George, 433, 438
Smith, Herb, 71
Smith, Joe, 185, 311
Smith, Lois, 428
Smith, Scott M., 425
Smith, Sherry, 240
Smith, Tom, 428
Snetsinger, Douglas, 349
Solomon, Charlene Marmer, 432
Soper, Barlow, 425

Spangler, William D., 430
Speh, Thomas W., 426, 436
Spiro, Rosann L., 31, 425, 428, 436
Spivey, W. Austin, 146, 427
Srinivasan, V., 438
Staelin, Richard, 438
Stamper, James C., 434
Stamps, Miriam B., 428
Staples, William A., 436
Starling, J. M., 433
Steinbrink, John P., 426, 428, 429
Stevenson, Sharon, 433
Stevenson, Thomas, 433
Stewart, B. Jane, 346
Stickney, Bill, 346, 347, 349
Stoltman, Jeffrey J., 430
Stone, Robert W., 434, 438
Strahle, William, 436
Stratton, Lawrence M., Jr., 346
Strutton, David, 430, 433, 434
Sujan, Harish, 429, 431, 432
Sujan, Mita, 429, 431, 432
Summers, Lynn, 433
Summers, Stu, 344
Swanberg, Jennifer E., 427
Swan, John E., 425
Swenson, Mary, 98
Swenson, Michael J., 425, 429
Swift, Cathy Owens, 123, 434

Swinyard, William R., 425

Tait, Steve, 369
Talk, Prescott, 431
Tanner, Jeff, 426
Tanner, John F., Jr., 429, 438
Tansey, Richard, 431
Tanyeri, Dana, 429
Tappan, John, 394
Tax, Stephen S., 431
Taylor, James L., 385
Taylor, R. D., 433
Taylor, Thayer C., 429, 432
Thomas, Steven, 433
Thornburg, Linda, 428
Townsend, Dabney, 424
Trask, Dick, 342
Trent, Robert, 435
Trisler, Hank, 437
Tuggle, William, 433, 438
Tyler, Kathryn, 427

Visintainer, Pat, 45

Walker, Orville C., Jr., 426, 429, 431, 432, 435, 436, 438
Waters, James A., 431, 437
Wedell, Allen J., 307
Weeks, William A., 429, 438

Weinberg, Charles B., 434, 438
Weiss, Jo, 27
Weitz, Barton A., 31, 425, 429, 431, 432
White, Betty, 309, 310
White, Edna M., 427
White, Harry R., 426
Wickham, Andre, 14, 265
Widing, Robert E., II, 428
Wiesendanger, Betsy, 435
Wigger, Tim, 86
Williams, Fred, 98
Williams, Michael R., 426, 430, 436
Wiltgen, Chuck, 17
Wimer, Scott, 438
Winchester, Jay, 429
Wolf, Samantha, 427
Wolfe, William, 433, 438, 439
Woodruff, Robert B., 434, 436
Wotruba, Thomas R., 431, 432, 434

Yammarino, Francis J., 430, 431
Yarbrough, John F., 426
Yi, Junsuab, 435
Young, Clifford E., 426, 432, 434, 437, 438

Zecola, Steven, 322, 328, 332
Zetlin, Minda, 439

SUBJECT INDEX

Bold indicates key terms

absorption training, 185–186
account managers (TD bank), 419, 420–421, 423
account opportunity, 112
account targeting strategy, 81–82
achieving clarity, 56
achieving congruence, 147–148
achieving realism, 147–148
activity-based costing (ABC), 265, 266
Adams Brands case study, 349–353
adaptive selling, 40
advertising-driven marketing communications strategies
    personal selling-driven vs., 75
    recruitment using, 153, 154–155
    targeting, 75
AIDA (attention, interest, desire, and action), 42
amoral management, 212
anticipation, 205
apathetics, 217
appointments, 53–54
approaching the customer, 53–54
assessment center, 161–162
Automatic Data Processing (ADP), 175

background investigation, 162
Ball State University, 186
Barro Stickney Inc. (BSI) case study, 346–349
Beauty Glow Cosmetics Company case study, 273
behavioral criteria, 281–282
behaviorally anchored rating scales (BARS), 294–295
behavioral self-management (BSM), 200
behavioral simulations, 185
behavior approach, 203
behavior-based perspective, 279–281
benchmarking, 253–255
Biomod, Inc. case study, 62–63
bottom-up forecasting approach, 134, 139–140, 141
boundary-role performers, 29
breakdown approach, 115–116
building credibility, 55–56
Building Sales Management Skills, 13
building trust, 58
business consultant role, 44
business marketing, 74
business strategy
    defining, **68**
    sales function and, 71–72
    summary of, 72

    types of, 72
business unit portfolio, 70
buyer types, 179
    See also customers
buying centers
    described, 79–80
    team selling and, 87
buying needs, 80–81
Buying Power Index (BPI), 137–139
buying process, 80

campus placement centers, 155–156
canned sales presentation, 19, 51
Career Mosaic Web site, 154
Career Resource Center Web site, 154
centralization, 97
chemical abuse/dependency, 215–216
City Hospital interviews, 339–340
classroom/conference sales training, 184
coaching leadership role, 209–210
code of ethics, 23, 214
coercive power, 202
cognitive consistency principles, 57
cognitive feedback, 209
cold-call reluctance, 48–49
combination sales job, 26
commission base, 229
commission payout event, 229
commission plans
    determining reward to risk ratio for, 384
    keys to effective, 384–385
    for performance payments, 384
    preparing draft of sales, 484
    quantitative performance measures used in, 383–384
    sales objectives included in, 383
    variations in, 229–232
    See also financial compensation; salesforce compensation
commission rate, 229
commission splits, 229
communication
    influence strategies and, 206–207
    mechanisms of, 207–209
    ranking of tools for marketing, 77
    two-way, 53
communication mechanisms, 207–208
compensation rewards, 225
competency model, 275–276
competitive knowledge, 180–181
competitive position, 112
Comprehensive Personality Profile (Wonderlic Personnel Test, Inc.), 161

Compusystems, Inc. case study, 192–193
computerized matchmaking services, 156–157
confectionery industry competitors, 350
conflicts of interest, 215
conservative claims, 55
constant rate, 229
consultative selling, 44–45
contingency approach, 203
continued affirmation approach, 40–41
contribution approach, 264
Core Deposit Campaign (HongKong Bank of Canada case study), 371–372
corporate citizens, 217
corporate strategy
    defining, **68**
    sales function and, 69–71
    summary of, 71
corporations
    mission statement of, 69–70
    organizational strategy levels of, 68–69
cost analysis, 260–263
cost per sales call index, 21
costs
    comparing salesforce/independent reps, 86
    estimated SMA, 309
    relationship between sales and, 114
    relationship strategy selling, 83
    of sales by industry, 262
    of sales training, 174
credibility, 55–56
current spendable income, 227
customer knowledge, 179–180
customers
    addressing concerns of, 56
    approaching the, 53–54
    developing relationships with, 54–56
    DP International, 411–413
    enhancing relationships with, 57–58
    gaining commitment of, 56–57
    initiating relationships with, 47–49
    salesforce specialization and, 101
    salespeople and, 22–23
    survey of MCI Vision, 334–335
    types of, 179
    understanding foreign, 180
customer survey, 177

Death of a Salesman (Miller), 28
decision model, 113
decomposition methods, 135–136, 142
Delphi method, 139, 142

Denman Industrial Products case study (A), 401–404
Denman Industrial Products case study (B), 404–407
Depression era, 19
depth of inquiry, 53
detailer, 24
Developing Sales Management Knowledge, 13
diagnostic skills, 205
DIALOG, 49
differentiation business strategy, 72
diffusion of innovation, 21
direction, 224
direct-to-consumer salespeople, 25–26
discriminatory appraisal lawsuits, 296
Double D, Double M process, 197
Dow Jones News/Retrieval, 49
Dunn Corporation case study, 385–386
Dura-plast, Inc. case study (A), 407–415
Dura-plast, Inc. case study (B), 416–417

Eastman Chemical Company Customer Satisfaction Survey, 291
economic stimuli, 21
effectiveness index, 260
ego drive, 31
ego strength, 31
empathy, 31
employee referral programs, 154
employment termination, 217
enthusiasm, 32
Equal Employment Opportunity Commission (EEOC), 164, 217–218
Equal Pay Act of 1963, 238
equal pay issue, 238
Ethical Dilemma boxes, 12
expatriate salesforce, 153, 239
expense account padding, 236
expense budgets, 235
Expense Reports (Extensity Inc.), 235
expenses. *See* costs
expert power, 201
exponential smoothing, 135, 136, 141
extensive problem solving, 79
extrinsically motivated, 225

FAB Job-Search Matrix example, 35
farmers, 122
feedback
 anticipation and seeking of, 205
 cognitive, 209
 outcome, 209
 reception of immediate, 27–28
field marketing specialist (FMS), 330
financial compensation
 current spendable income, 227
 equal pay issue of, 238
 global considerations in, 239
 performance bonus, 230
 salary plus incentive, 231
 straight commission, 228–230
 straight salary, 228
 summary of plans for, 227
 team, 238–239
 types of, 227
 See also commission plans; salesforce compensation
financial compensation mix, 231
Financial Directions magazine, 399
financial planning services, 392–400
Floor-Shine Cleaning Products case study, 245–246
forecasting
 bottom-up approach to, 134, 139–140, 141
 described, **131**
 top-down approach to, 133–139, 141
 types of, 131–133
 usage of different approaches, 140–142
 uses of, 133
 See also sales forecast
foreign customers, 180
formalization, 199
formula approach, 41–42
full cost approach, 264
functional specialization, 105, 108

General Electric Appliances case study, 377–385
General Electric sales incentive plan, 378–379
generic business strategies, 72
geographic specialization, 102, 103, 108
global account management (GAM), 106
Global Enterprise case study, 221–222
government organizations, 78
graphic rating/checklist methods, 290, 292
guarantees and warranties, 55–56

halo effect, 292
Harvard Business Review, 19, 211–212
hierarchical sales analysis, 257–259
Hongkong Bank of Canada (1991 Managers' Conference), 374–376
Hongkong Bank of Canada case study, 369–377
Hospital Supply International (HSI) case study, 337–342
host-country nationals salesforce, 153
hub concept, 207–208
hunters, 122
hybrid sales organization, 108–109

IDS Financial Services (condensed) case study, 391–400
Illinois State University, 186
immoral management, 212
income statement analysis, 264
incremental approach, 116–117
independence of sales career, 28
independent representatives, 85–86
INDSALES scale, 300–301

Induplicate Copiers, Inc. case study, 273–274
industrial distributors, 85
Industrial Revolution era, 18
influence strategies, 206–207
information
 importance of, 241
 using performance, 296–299
 See also Internet
initial interviews, 158
initiation to task, 172
inside sales, 25
institutional stars, 217
institutional trash bag industry, 387–391
institutional trash bag market, 389
institutions, 78
integrated marketing communications (IMC), 76
integrative meeting, 210–211
intensity, 224
intensive interviews, 158, 160
Internet
 precall planning using, 49
 recruitment advertisements on the, 154–155
 sales strategy channeling using, 84–85
interpersonal communication skills, 31–32
interviewer bias, 158, 160
Interview Guide, 159–160
interviews (job), 157–160
intrinsically motivated, 225

job analysis, 149, 177
job application form, 157
job candidates
 background investigation of, 162
 physical examination of, 162
 recruitment of, 145–157
 selection of, 148–163
job description, 150–151
job design, 241–242
job fairs, 156
job involvement, 199
job preview, 147–148
job qualifications, 149–150
job rotation, 184–185
job satisfaction, 299–301
job security, 26–27, **234**
job variety, 29
jury of executive opinion method, 139, 142

Labels Express case study, 304
Leader-Member Exchange (LMX) model, 199, 200
leadership
 described, **198**
 power and, 200–202
 skills of, 204–205
 See also sales leadership
legitimate power, 201
LEXIS-NEXIS, 49

"Life Themes" series (Gallup, Inc.), 158
limited problem solving, 79
line sales management, 98–100
lone wolf, 217
long-term ally, 44
low cost business strategy, 72
"Low-Pressure Selling" (*Harvard Business Review*), 19

major account organization, 105–108
major account selling, 88
Making Sales Management Decisions, 13
Malcolm Baldrige National Quality Award, 254
management by objectives (MBO), 292–294
management levels, 98
manipulation, 207
manufacturers' representatives, 85
market bonus, 163
market factor methods, 136–139
market forecast, 133
marketing communications tools ranking, 77
marketing mix, 73–74, 75
marketing strategy
  defining, 69
  sales function and, 72–76
  summary of, 76
market potential, 133
market response framework, 285
market sales organization, 104
market specialization, 104, 108
maverick salespeople, 216–217
MCI Eastern Division Marketing Organization, 328
MCI Eastern Division Sales Organization, 329–330
MCI organization (November 1990), 326
MCI Vision, 331–336
MCI Vision (A) [Condensed] case study, 322–336
mental states selling, 41–42, 43
mentor, 184
Million Dollar Roundtable, 233
misrepresentation, 165
missionary salespeople, 24
MIT, 204
Modern Plastics case study, 387–391
modified rebuy buying situation, 79
Money Magazine, 394
Money Monitor software (TD bank), 419–423
Monster Board Web site, 156
moral management, 212
Morgantown Inc. case study, 336–337
motivation
  described, 224–225
  guidelines for, 240–242
  See also salesforce reward system
moving averages, 135, 141
multilevel selling, 88

national account management (NAM), 106
National Cash Register Company (NCR), 19
National Communications Manufacturing case study, 94
needs assessment, 175–181
need satisfaction selling, 43
new task buying situation, 79
New York Times, 154
niche business strategy, 72
noncompensation rewards, 225
nonfinancial compensation, 232–236
nonrole act, 214

Oakmaster Furniture Inc. case study, 304–305
objective and task method, 262
observation, 176
  See also sales training
Occupational Outlook Handbook (U.S. Department of Labor), 30
"$100 million in 1,000 days" program, 197–198
Online Career Center Web site, 156
on-the-job training (OJT), 184
opportunities for personal growth, 233
opportunity for promotion, 232
Opti-Tax Consulting (OTC) case study, 128–129
order-getters, 25
order-takers, 25
organizational commitment, 199
organizational strategy levels, 68–69
organizations
  buyer behavior of, 78–81
  personal vs. needs of, 81
  selling situation factors and structure of, 101
  types of, 79
  See also sales organizations
organized sales presentation, 51
original equipment manufacturers (OEM), 78
outcome-based perspective, 279–281
outcome bias, 295
outcome feedback, 209

Pathfinder financial plan (Merrill Lynch), 392–393
percentage of sales method, 262
performance bonus, 230
Performance Learning System (Fisher Scientific International), 10
performance management, 279
performance testing, 176
persistence, 224
personal behavior, 55
Personal Financial Profile (IDS), 396
personal selling
  auto dealer's profits through, 17
  contributions of, 20–23
  defining, 2
  defining strategic role of, 3
  evolution of, 18–20
  function of, 3
  marketing strategy and, 73
  See also selling
personal selling approaches
  advantages/disadvantages of, 74
  advertising-driven vs., 75
  classification of, 40–45
  importance of trust in, 39–40
  marketing mix elements and, 74, 76
  sales process of, 45–58
  transaction-focused vs. trust-based, 41
persuasion, 207
  physical examination, 162
  See also job candidates
pioneers, 24
planned earnings, 228
planning activities, 148
planning and control unit, 120
plastic trash bag industry, 387–391
Plastico Inc. case study, 63–64
portfolio models, 111–113
post-Industrial Revolution era, 18–19
power/leadership link, 200–202
preapproach, 49–51
presentation format, 51
presentation pace, 53
presentation scope, 53
President's Club, 233
prestige/image of salespeople, 27–28
Priority One video (Frito-Lay), 186
private employment agency, 155
"The Problem Solvers" promotion (Westinghouse), 357–359
problem-solving selling, 43–44
productivity analysis, 267–268
product knowledge, 178–179
product specialization, 102–104, 108
professional development criteria, 282–284
"Professional Selling Program" (Nabisco), 173
professional societies, 156
profitability analysis, 264–267
profitability criteria, 287–288
profit contribution, 264, 265
progressive rate, 229
promises, 206
Pronto Retail Center case study, 95
prospecting, 47–49
prospect screening, 50
Protek Packaging, Inc. case study, 127–128

quota evaluation examples, 293

ranking methods, 292
recognition programs, 233–234
recruitment, 148
  See also salesforce recruitment
recruitment and selection strategy, 151–154

referent power, 201
regression model example, 286
regressive rate, 229
relationship enhancement, 58
relationships, 207
relationship selling, 338
relationship strategy, 82
relationship strategy selling costs, 83
resellers, 78
results criteria, 284–287
resume screening, 157
return on assets managed (ROAM), 265–267
revenue producers, 21–22
reward power, 201
reward system management, 225, 237–240
See also salesforce reward system
role conflict, 29
role definition, 172
role distortion act, 214
role failure act, 214
role playing, 185
role stress, 30
Romano Pitesti case study, 360–362
routinized response behavior, 79
Royal 750 color copier case study, 312–315, 318–319
Royal Corporate Copy Center (CCC), 309–311, 312, 314, 316–318

salary compression, 228
salary plus incentive, 231
sales
 defining, 256
 types of, 258–259
 See also sales function; spelling
sales analysis, 256–260
sales call, 54
sales career characteristics, 26–30
sales channel strategy, 84–89
sales contests, 237–238
sales dollars, 256, 257
Sales Executive Panel, 12
sales expenses, 234–236
salesforce
 Businessland automation of, 307
 determining effectiveness/ performance of, 4–5
 developing the, 4
 directing the, 4
 independent representative costs vs., 86
 international development of, 153
 See also salespeople
salesforce audit, 176
salesforce compensation
 of Arizona Company salespeople, 343
 nonfinancial, 232–236
 overview of, 28–29
 types of financial, 227–231
 See also commission plans; salesforce reward system

salesforce composite method, 139–140, 142
salesforce deployment
 analytical tools used in, 115–117
 described, **109**–110
 designing territories for, 117–122
 models of, 110–113
 people considerations in, 122–123
 salesforce size and, 113–117
salesforce promotional program (Denman Industrial Products), 401–407
salesforce recruitment
 advertisements used for, 153, 154–155
 at Edward Jones, 145–146
 ethical issues regarding, 165–166
 guidelines for sales managers, 164–165
 importance of, 146–147
 key legislation regarding, 163–164
 motivating/rewarding systems and, 241
 objectives of, 151
 planning for, 148–151
 sources of, 154–157
 strategy for, 151–154
salesforce reward system
 changing the, 239–240
 equal pay issues of, 238
 global considerations of, 239
 guidelines for, 240–242
 management of, 225
 optimal, 225–226
 sales contests and, 237–238
 team compensation and, 238–239
 types of compensation as, 226–232
 See also salesforce compensation
salesforce selection
 job offer following, 162–163
 key legislation on, 163–164
 motivating/rewarding systems and, 241
 objectives of, 151
 planning for, 148–151
 process of, 157–163
 strategy for, 151–154
 testing during, 160–161
salesforce socialization
 described, **147**–148
 elements of, 198–199
 information and, 241
 role of sales training in, 172–173
salesforce specialization continuum, 97
salesforce survey, 176–177
salesforce turnover, 114
sales forecast, 133, 259
 See also forecasting
sales function
 business strategy and, 71–77
 corporate strategy and, 69–71
 marketing strategy and, 72–76
 See also sales
sales incentive plan (General Electric), 378–379

sales leadership
 behavioral self-management (BSM) model of, 200
 coaching function of, 209–210
 communication and, 206–209
 defining, 198
 ethical and moral responsibilities of, 211–215
 LMX model of, 199–200
 problems within, 215–218
 situational factors of, 202–203
 skills of, 204–206
 transformational, 199–200
 See also leadership
Sales Management in the 21st Century, 12
sales management
 approaches to ethics of, 213
 defining, 2
 morally questionable acts by, 214
 process of, 2–5
 trends in, 5–12
 typical day description in, 1–2
sales management model, 2
sales management trends
 from individuals to teams, 8–9
 from local to global, 11–12
 from management to leadership, 10–11
 from sales volume to productivity, 9–10
 from transactions to relationships, 7–8
sales managers
 avoidance of outcome bias by, 295
 guidelines for motivating/rewarding, 240–242
 halo effect and, 292
 meeting review list for, 212
 performance evaluation methods by, 289
 performance information used by, 296–299
 recruitment/selection guidelines for, 164–165
 stress interview used by, 165–166
 See also sales leadership
Sales and Marketing Automation (SMA), 308–309
Sales and Marketing Executives International, 156
Sales and Marketing Management magazine, 21
Sales and Marketing Management's (1999 Best Sales Forces), 5
sales meetings
 sales manager's review list for, 212
 tips for conducting, 211
sales mix model, 52
sales organization audit, 5, **251**–252, 253
sales organization effectiveness
 benchmarking and, 253–255
 cost analysis of, 260–267

ethical issues of, 268–269
framework for, 255
productivity analysis of, 267–268
sales analysis for, 256–260
sales analysis of, 256–260
sales organizations
concepts relating to, 96–100
effectiveness evaluations for, 255–268
recognition programs of, 233–234
salesforce deployment and, 109–122
salesperson performance vs.
effectiveness of, 250
selling situation contingencies and, 100–102
span of control by, 98, 99, 286
See also organizations
sales organization structures
comparing types of, 108–109
listed, 102–108
salespeople
attributes required by, 46
BARS scale on, 294–295
code of ethics for, 23
dealing with problem, 216–217
direct-to-consumer, 25–26
employing firm and, 21–22
farmer and hunter assignments of, 122
as future managers, 22
goals and objectives of, 204
leadership skills of, 204–206
market research role by, 22
needs and wants of, 203–204
occupational outlook for, 27
personal behavior of, 55
qualifications/skills required by, 30–33
reimbursement of expenses to, 234–235
reward system for, 225–232
society and, 21
termination of, 217
tips for conducting meetings by, 211
trustworthy, 39–40, 58
types of jobs for, 24–27
See also customers; salesforce
salespeople job satisfaction, 299–301
salespeople's self-esteem, 242
salesperson classifications, 24–26
salesperson performance evaluation
approaches to, 277–279
behavioral criteria for, 281–282
behaviorally anchored rating scales (BARS) and, 294–295
bias during, 295
changes in, 275–276
comparison of methods for, 290
discriminatory appraisal lawsuits and, 296
graphic rating/checklist methods for, 290, 292
management by objectives (MBO) and, 292–294

outcome-based vs. behavior-based, 279–281
professional development criteria for, 282–284
profitability criteria for, 287–288
purposes of, 276–277
ranking methods for, 292
results criteria for, 284–287
sales managers' methods for, 289
for sales teams, 296
using information from, 296–299
sales potential, 133
sales presentation delivery, 54–55
sales presentation planning, 51
sales process
defining, 45–46
initiating customer relationships, 47–49
sales productivity, 113–114
sales professionalism, 19–20
sales proposal, 52
sales quota, 284–285, 287
sales strategy
account targeting strategy and, 81–82
channeling, 84–89
framework of, 77–78
relationship strategy and, 82
sales support personnel, 24
sales techniques
credibility building and, 55–56
needs assessment of, 177–178
sales trainer, 182–183
sales training
for buyer types, 179
choosing outside, 183
designing program for, 186–187
ethical and legal issues of, 188–189
evaluating alternative, 182
follow-up and evaluation of, 187–188
as investment, 173–174
locations for, 183–184
needs assessment during, 175–181
performing, 187
selecting media for, 186
selecting method of, 184–186
socialization and, 172–173
for specific buyer types, 179
time/financial costs of, 174
sales training media, 186
sales training objectives, 181–182
sales units, 256, 257
screening criteria, 47–48
seek feedback, 205
See also feedback
selection, 148
See also salesforce selection
self-efficacy, 31
selling
adaptive, 40
consultative, 44–45
costs of relationship strategy, 83
major account, 88
mental states, 41–42, 43

multilevel, 88
need satisfaction, 43
organization structure and, 101
problem-solving, 43–44
relationship, 338
stimulus response, 40–41, 42
transactional, 338
See also personal selling
"Selling beyond Quota" CD-ROM (AchieveGlobal), 185
selling budget, 260–263
Selling magazine, 20
selling strategy, 82–84
See also personal selling; sales
sense of accomplishment, 232–233
service motivation, 32
sexual harassment, 217–218
Simulation System Trainer (Performax Inc.), 186
single factor models, 110–111
Solutions Software Inc. case study, 192
source credibility, 55
span of control, 98, 99, 286
specialization, 97
staff sales management, 98–99
Stalwart Industrial Products case study, 245
stimulus response selling, 40–41, 42
straight commission, 228–229
straight rebuy buying situation, 79
straight salary, 228
strategic business unit (SBU), 68, 70, 71, 73–74
strategic orchestrator, 44
stress interview technique, 165–166
supervision, 198
survey of buyer intentions method, 139, 142
Sweet-Treats, Inc. case study, 168–169
Sylvia Porter's Personal Financial Planning, 394

target market, 73
task-specific self-esteem, 198
Tasti-Fresh Bakery Products case study, 221
teams
approaches to selling by, 87–88
compensation for, 238–239
evaluating performance of, 296
team selling, 87–88
teamwork effectiveness/attitude measurement (TEAM), 297
technical support salespeople, 24
telemarketing, 88–89
termination, 217
territories
assigning salespeople to, 122
described, **117–118**
design data for, 120
designing, 118–122
of G.E. Appliances, 380
Lexus's sales, 344, 345

territories—cont'd
    training for management of, 181
    workload evaluations of, 121
testimonials, 55
testing, 160–161
    See also salesforce selection
Third-Country nationals salesforce, 153
third-party evidence, 55
threats, 206
360–degree feedback, 277–278
time and territory management (TTM), 181
Titan Industries case study, 169–170
top-down forecasting approach, 133–139, 141
Topnotch Investment Company (TICO) case study, 319–321
Toronto-Dominion Bank case study, 417–423
total quality management (TQM), 279
tracking system, 50
trade shows, 89
trait approach, 202–203

transactional selling, 338
transformational leadership, 199–200
trash bag industry, 387–391
trustworthy sales professional, 39–40, 58
two-way communication, 53
type-of-sales analysis, 259

Understanding Sales Management Terms, 13
University of Memphis, 186
U.S. Department of Health and Human Services, 215
U.S. Department of Labor, 30
U.S. long-distance industry, 324

Vision Customer Satisfaction Survey, 334–335
Vision (MCI), 331–336
visual aids, 53

Wall Street Journal, 154

Westinghouse Electric Corporation case study, 354–359
Westinghouse Electric Corporation Marketing Department, 355
Westinghouse Electric Corporation Sales Organization Chart, 356
Westinghouse Overhead Distribution "Problem Solvers" Promotion, 357–359
Windsor Management Company case study, 363–369
Windsor Management Company Organizational Structure, 364
Windsor Marketing Representative, 365
Winner's Circle, 233
work alienation, 199
workload approach, 116
World War era, 19

Xerox Document University, 183
Xpense Management Solution (Portable Software), 235